Instructor Preview

The Modern Language Association has announced it will release updated style guidelines in April 2021. *The Writer's Mindset* will be updated in Spring 2021 to reflect these changes.

Available for Fall 2021 Courses!

The Writer's Mindset will include updated MLA style guidelines in the print text, ebook, and Connect resources.

Available to preview now:

- This instructor's edition
- Ebook for *The Writer's Mindset*
- Connect Composition for *The Writer's Mindset* including the following assessments and resources:
  - SmartBook adaptive reading experience for *The Writer's Mindset*
  - Adaptive Learning Assignment for Composition
  - Writing Assignment Premium
  - Power of Process for Composition
  - Instructor's Resources

COMING FOR FALL 2021 COURSES
The Writer's Mindset with MLA Update!

The Writer's Mindset

A Rhetorical Guide to Reading, Writing, and Arguing

LISA WRIGHT HOEFFNER

McLennan Community College

TITLE: THE WRITER'S MINDSET: A Rhetorical Guide to Reading, Writing, and Arguing

Published by McGraw Hill LLC, 1325 Avenue of the Americas, New York, NY 10121. Copyright ©2022 by McGraw Hill LLC. All rights reserved. Printed in the United States of America. No part of this publication may be reproduced or distributed in any form or by any means, or stored in a database or retrieval system, without the prior written consent of McGraw Hill LLC, including, but not limited to, in any network or other electronic storage or transmission, or broadcast for distance learning.

Some ancillaries, including electronic and print components, may not be available to customers outside the United States.

This book is printed on acid-free paper.

2 3 4 5 6 7 8 9 LKV 24 23 22 21

ISBN 978-1-266-60261-0 (instructor's edition)
MHID 1-266-60261-5 (instructor's edition)

Portfolio Manager: *Erin Cosyn*
Product Developers: *Cara Labell, Marion Castellucci, Victoria DeRosa*
Product Development Manager: *Dawn Groundwater*
Marketing Manager: *Byron Kanoti*
Content Project Managers: *Lisa Bruflodt, George Theofanopoulos*
Buyer: *Susan K. Culbertson*
Designer: *Beth Blech*
Content Licensing Specialist: *Brianna Kirschbaum*
Cover Image: *John Lund/Blend Images LLC*
Compositor: *Aptara, Inc.*

All credits appearing on page or at the end of the book are considered to be an extension of the copyright page.

Library of Congress Cataloging-in-Publication Data

Names: Hoeffner, Lisa, author.
Title: The writer's mindset : a rhetorical guide to reading, writing, and
  arguing / Lisa Wright Hoeffner, McLennan Community College.
Description: Dubuque : McGraw Hill Education, [2022] | Includes index.
Identifiers: LCCN 2020024276 (print) | LCCN 2020024277 (ebook) | ISBN
  9781260526349 (hardcover) | ISBN 9781260526356 (spiral bound) | ISBN
  9781264251254 (hardcover) | ISBN 9781260526387 (ebook) | ISBN
  9781260526394 (ebook other)
Subjects: LCSH: English language–Rhetoric–Study and teaching (Secondary)
  | English language–Composition and exercises–Study and teaching
  (Secondary) | English language–Rhetoric–Problems, exercises, etc. |
  Critical thinking. | Persuasion (Rhetoric)
Classification: LCC LB1631 .H554 2022 (print) | LCC LB1631 (ebook) | DDC
  808/.0420712–dc23
LC record available at https://lccn.loc.gov/2020024276
LC ebook record available at https://lccn.loc.gov/2020024277

The Internet addresses listed in the text were accurate at the time of publication. The inclusion of a website does not indicate an endorsement by the authors or McGraw Hill LLC, and McGraw Hill LLC does not guarantee the accuracy of the information presented at these sites.

mheducation.com/highered

Brief Contents

PART 1 DEVELOPING A WRITER'S MINDSET *1*

1 **What Is a Writer's Mindset?** *1*
2 **Reading with a Writer's Mindset** *14*
3 **Composing with a Writer's Mindset** *34*
4 **Using Rhetorical Patterns as Tools** *59*

The four chapters in Part 1 explain how to think rhetorically and why such thinking matters in academic, professional, public, and personal life.

In these chapters, you will learn how to read rhetorically and how to write from a rhetorical point of view. You'll begin to use specific strategies to develop a writer's mindset.

PART 2 WRITING PURPOSES *84*

5 **Writing to Reflect** *84*
6 **Writing to Inform** *114*
7 **Writing to Analyze** *143*
8 **Writing to Evaluate** *174*
9 **Writing to Persuade** *200*

The five chapters in Part 2 present writing purposes that are used in academic, professional, public, and personal writing. In this part, you will think rhetorically and use rhetorical strategies to accomplish your writing purposes.

PART 3 RESEARCH STRATEGIES *222*

10 **Conducting Research** *222*
11 **Using Sources Accurately and Ethically** *245*
12 **Documenting Sources in MLA and APA Style** *261*

In Part 3, you will learn how to find relevant sources and evaluate their credibility. You will also learn how to use sources ethically and accurately and how to cite them in MLA and APA style.

PART 4 ARGUMENTS IN DEPTH 305

13 **Recognizing Arguments** 305
14 **Analyzing an Argument's Elements** 327
15 **Understanding an Argument's Appeals** 349
16 **Recognizing Fallacies** 365
17 **Writing a Rhetorical Analysis** 383
18 **Classical, Rogerian, and Visual Arguments** 405

In Part 4, you will further develop your writer's mindset by analyzing the persuasive strategies used in arguments, a skill you can use in all areas of life.

You will learn how to recognize an argument and how to analyze its logical structure, its appeals to credibility, emotion, and reasoning, and its fallacies, if any. You will then write a rhetorical analysis of an argument. You will also examine specific argument types—classical, Rogerian, and visual—and their uses.

PART 5 WRITING A RESEARCHED ARGUMENT 423

19 **Planning an Argument** 423
20 **Selecting Evidence and Drafting Reasons** 440
21 **Drafting Counterarguments, Introductions, and Conclusions** 453
22 **Revising and Finishing Your Argument** 467

In Part 5, you will write a researched argument. Each chapter presents guidance and several mini argument assignments that build on each other and enable you to write a well-developed argument.

PART 6 AN ANTHOLOGY OF READINGS 489

Part 6 provides additional readings arranged in thematic groups. Each reading is followed by questions and additional writing prompts to help develop your writer's mindset.

PART 7 HANDBOOK OF READING AND WRITING SKILLS 603

1 **Improving Your Reading Skills** 603
2 **Improving Your Writing Skills** 634

Reading difficult material can be challenging, and writing grammatically correct and stylistically appropriate prose can be equally challenging. The two chapters in Part 7 provide concrete suggestions for improving your reading comprehension and writing skills.

GLOSSARY 672

The Glossary provides a handy reference of rhetoric and composition terms useful in the development of a writer's mindset.

Contents

PART 1
DEVELOPING A WRITER'S MINDSET *1*

Chapter 1
What Is a Writer's Mindset? *1*

What Is Rhetorical Thinking? *2*
Analyzing the Rhetorical Situation *4*
   RHETORICAL TOOLBOX 1.1
   Analyzing the Rhetorical Situation *6*
Recognizing Three Rhetorical Domains *7*
   Public Rhetoric *7*
   Rhetoric in the Academic and Professional World *7*
   Personal Rhetoric *8*
Thinking Rhetorically to Develop a Writer's Mindset *9*
CHAPTER PROJECT Thinking Rhetorically *11*
FAQ DOING INFORMAL RESEARCH *12*

Chapter 2
Reading with a Writer's Mindset *14*

Three Ways to Read a Text *15*
Reading to Understand, Summarize, and Respond *16*
   Writing a Summary *17*
   A Model Summary *21*
   Writing a Response *22*
   RHETORICAL TOOLBOX 2.1
   Responding to a Text *23*
   A Model Response *23*
Reading to Analyze *24*
   Analyzing the Rhetorical Situation *25*
   Analyzing Rhetorical Strategies *25*
   RHETORICAL TOOLBOX 2.2
   Reading to Analyze Rhetorical Strategies *27*
Reading to Critique *28*
Using Rhetorical Reading to Become a Better Writer *29*
CHAPTER PROJECT Reading to Understand, Analyze, and Critique *30*
FAQ OUTLINING A TEXT *30*

Chapter 3
Composing with a Writer's Mindset *34*

Using a Recursive Writing Process *35*
Thinking Rhetorically to Write Well *36*
Basic Stages in the Writing Process *38*
   Stage 1: Planning *38*
   RHETORICAL TOOLBOX 3.1
   Analyzing a Writing Assignment Rhetorically *39*
   Stage 2: Drafting *43*
   Stage 3: Revising *43*
   PEER REVIEW TOOLBOX *44*
   Stage 4: Editing *49*
   Stage 5: Formatting *50*
Alexis Williams (Student), Social Media in the Classroom *50*
Personalizing Your Writing Process *53*
   Personality *53*
   Time Management *54*
   Writing Strengths and Weaknesses *54*
CHAPTER PROJECT A Personal Writing Process *55*
FAQ WRITING WITH CLARITY *57*

Chapter 4
Using Rhetorical Patterns as Tools *59*

Using Rhetorical Patterns as Tools *60*
Description *61*

A Sample of Descriptive Writing 62
Thinking Rhetorically about Description 62
RHETORICAL TOOLBOX 4.1
Using Description as a Writing Tool 63

Narration 63
A Sample of Narrative Writing 64
Thinking Rhetorically about Narration 64
RHETORICAL TOOLBOX 4.2
Using Narration as a Writing Tool 65

Illustration 65
A Sample of Illustration 65
Thinking Rhetorically about Illustration 67
RHETORICAL TOOLBOX 4.3
Using Illustration as a Writing Tool 67

Definition 67
A Sample of Definition 67
Thinking Rhetorically about Definition 69
RHETORICAL TOOLBOX 4.4
Using Definition as a Writing Tool 69

Classification 69
A Sample of Classification 70
Thinking Rhetorically about Classification 71
RHETORICAL TOOLBOX 4.5
Using Classification as a Writing Tool 71

Comparison and Contrast 72
A Sample of Comparison/Contrast Writing 72
Thinking Rhetorically about Comparing and Contrasting 73
RHETORICAL TOOLBOX 4.6
Using Comparison and Contrast as a Writing Tool 74

Cause and Effect 75
A Sample of Cause and Effect 75
Thinking Rhetorically about Cause and Effect 77
RHETORICAL TOOLBOX 4.7
Using Cause and Effect as a Writing Tool 77

Process Analysis 78
A Sample of Process Analysis 78
Thinking Rhetorically about Process Analysis 79

RHETORICAL TOOLBOX 4.8
Using Process Analysis as a Writing Tool 80

CHAPTER PROJECT Using Rhetorical Patterns 80

FAQ KEY WORDS AND PHRASES FOR THE RHETORICAL PATTERNS 81

PART 2
WRITING PURPOSES 84

Chapter 5
Writing to Reflect 84

Reflective Writing from a Writer's Mindset 84
RHETORICAL TOOLBOX 5.1
The Rhetorical Concerns of Reflective Writing 85

Models of Reflective Writing 86
Rigoberto González, Easter Rock 1983 86
Leath Tonino, Thoughts after an Owl 92

CHAPTER PROJECT Writing to Reflect 95

DRAFTING TOOLBOX
Terms and Phrases for Reflective Essays 100

PEER REVIEW TOOLBOX: REFLECTIVE WRITING 102

Janilyn Lee (Student), Stay Wild 104
FAQ WORKING WITH DIALOGUE 111

Chapter 6
Writing to Inform 114

Informative Writing from a Writer's Mindset 115
RHETORICAL TOOLBOX 6.1
The Rhetorical Concerns of Informative Writing 115

Models of Informative Writing 116
Lauren Migliore, The Violent Brain: Ingredients of a Mass Murderer 116
Rachel Ehrenberg, What We Do and Don't Know about How to Prevent Gun Violence 120

CHAPTER PROJECT Writing to Inform *126*

> **DRAFTING TOOLBOX**
> Terms and Phrases for Informative Texts *131*
>
> **PEER REVIEW TOOLBOX: INFORMATIVE WRITING** *133*

Liam Wilson (Student), The Power of Crowds *136*

FAQ CREATING INTRODUCTIONS AND CONCLUSIONS *141*

Chapter 7
Writing to Analyze *143*

Analytical Writing from a Writer's Mindset *144*
   The Process of Analyzing *144*
   Types of Analysis *146*
   Creating an Analytical Text *146*
   RHETORICAL TOOLBOX 7.1
   The Rhetorical Concerns of Analytical Writing *147*

Models of Analytical Writing *148*

> Michael Greenstone and Adam Looney, Is Starting College and Not Finishing Really That Bad? *148*
>
> Nathanael Johnson, Reducing Food Waste Takes More than Finishing Your Plate *153*

CHAPTER PROJECT Writing to Analyze *157*

> **DRAFTING TOOLBOX**
> Terms and Phrases for Analytical Texts *163*
>
> **PEER REVIEW TOOLBOX: ANALYTIC WRITING** *164*

Reese Abrams (Student), Should College Students Adopt Dogs? A Cost/Benefit Analysis *165*

FAQ WRITING IN THIRD PERSON *171*

Chapter 8
Writing to Evaluate *174*

Evaluative Writing from a Writer's Mindset *175*
   Purposes of Evaluations *176*
   Analyzing and Judging *176*
   Selecting Criteria *176*
   RHETORICAL TOOLBOX 8.1
   The Rhetorical Concerns of Evaluative Writing *177*

Models of Evaluative Writing *178*

> Maddy Folstein, "Hostiles" Tries to Revise History and Western Film Traditions *178*
>
> Stanford History Education Group, Evaluating Information: The Cornerstone of Civic Online Reasoning *180*

CHAPTER PROJECT Writing to Evaluate *186*

> **DRAFTING TOOLBOX**
> Terms and Phrases for Evaluative Texts *191*
>
> **PEER REVIEW TOOLBOX: EVALUATIVE WRITING** *192*

Tierra Delgado (Student), A Food Pantry Worth Admiring *194*

FAQ ORGANIZING AN EVALUATIVE COMPARISON *198*

Chapter 9
Writing to Persuade *200*

Persuasive Writing from a Writer's Mindset *200*
   Key Elements of Persuasive Texts *201*
   Three Appeals: Logos, Ethos, and Pathos *203*
   Audience Analysis *204*
   RHETORICAL TOOLBOX 9.1
   The Rhetorical Concerns of Persuasive Writing *204*

Models of Persuasive Writing *205*

> David Rosen, It's Time to Decriminalize Sex Work *205*
>
> Kyle Sheehy, Standardized Test Requirement Should Be Removed from College Admissions *207*

CHAPTER PROJECT Writing to Persuade *210*

> **DRAFTING TOOLBOX**
> Terms and Phrases for Texts that Persuade *214*

PEER REVIEW TOOLBOX: PERSUASIVE WRITING *215*

Jesse Martinez (Student), Should College Athletes Be Paid? *216*

FAQ IDENTIFYING ARGUABLE ISSUES *220*

PART 3
RESEARCH STRATEGIES *222*

Chapter 10
Conducting Research *222*

Developing an Effective Research Process *222*
    Recording Citations in a Working Bibliography *223*
    Bookmarking Sources *224*
    Downloading and Saving Sources *225*
    Copying Quotations and Creating Attributions *226*
Selecting Source Types *227*
    Primary Sources *227*
    Secondary Sources *228*
    Field Research *229*
    RHETORICAL TOOLBOX 10.1
    Selecting Source Types by Analyzing the Rhetorical Situation *230*
Using Effective Search Strategies *230*
    Conducting Library Database Searches *231*
    Searching for Statistics and Factual Information *233*
    Finding Reliable Sources on the Internet *233*
Evaluating Sources *235*
    Examining Authors *235*
    Examining Audiences *236*
    Examining Date and Historical Context *236*
    Examining Bias and Credibility *236*
    RHETORICAL TOOLBOX 10.2
    Questions for Evaluating Sources *240*
Creating an Annotated Bibliography *241*
    Descriptive Annotated Bibliography *241*
    Critical Annotated Bibliography *241*

CHAPTER PROJECT Creating an Annotated Bibliography *242*

FAQ TIME MANAGEMENT FOR RESEARCH PROJECTS *243*

Chapter 11
Using Sources Accurately and Ethically *245*

Using Sources from a Writer's Mindset *245*
    When to Use a Source *246*
    How to Use Sources *247*
    RHETORICAL TOOLBOX 11.1
    When and How to Use Sources *248*
Practical Strategies for Working with Sources *249*
    Annotating Effectively *249*
    Creating a Source Chart *249*
    Incorporating Sources into Your Paper's Outline *250*
Integrating Sources Accurately and Correctly *251*
    Representing the Source Fairly and Accurately *251*
    Using Attributive Tags *251*
    Integrating Direct Quotations *252*
    Creating and Integrating Indirect Quotations *256*
    Creating and Integrating Summaries *256*
    Creating and Integrating Paraphrases *257*
    Referring to Repeated Sources *257*
Avoiding Plagiarism *258*

CHAPTER PROJECT Creating a Source Chart *259*

FAQ RECOGNIZING COMMON KNOWLEDGE *259*

Chapter 12
Documenting Sources in MLA and APA Style *261*

The Importance of Style Guides *261*
Locating Bibliographic Information *263*
    Finding Bibliographic Information in an Online Database *263*
    Finding Bibliographic Information for Websites *264*
    Finding Bibliographic Information for Books *264*
    Finding Bibliographic Information for Journal Articles in Print *267*

Using MLA Style 267
   Creating In-Text Citations 267
   Creating the List of Works Cited 271
   Formatting a Paper in MLA Style 278

Tori Manning (Student), Finding a Treatment for Anorexia (Sample Paper in MLA Style) 279
   Checking MLA Style 285
   RHETORICAL TOOLBOX 12.1
   Checking for MLA Style 285

Using APA Style 286
   Creating In-Text Citations 286
   Creating the References List 289
   Formatting a Paper in APA Style 296

Tori Manning (Student), Finding a Treatment for Anorexia (Sample Paper in APA Style) 296

FAQ TWO DOCUMENTATION SHORTCUTS 303

PART 4
ARGUMENTS IN DEPTH 305

Chapter 13
Recognizing Arguments 305

What Is an Argument? 306
Identifying an Argument by Its Claim and Reasons 308
   Claims 308
   Reasons 310
Identifying Arguments by Examining the Rhetorical Situation 311
   Analyzing the Writer or Speaker's Credentials and Bias 311
   Analyzing the Writer or Speaker's Tone and Voice 312
   Analyzing the Writer or Speaker's Purpose 312
   Analyzing the Genre and Publication 313
   RHETORICAL TOOLBOX 13.1
   Identifying Arguments 315
Model Argument and Introduction to Rhetorical Analysis 315
   Mark Greene, Why Manning Up Is the Worst Thing to Do 316

Model of an Introductory Paragraph for a Rhetorical Analysis 320
CHAPTER PROJECT Writing the Introductory Paragraph of a Rhetorical Analysis 320
   Alex Epstein, The Moral Case for the Fossil Fuel Industry 321
FAQ MAKING ACCURATE INFERENCES 324

Chapter 14
Analyzing an Argument's Elements 327

An Overview of Toulmin Analysis 327
   Claims and Qualifiers 328
   Reasons and Grounds 329
   Warrants 329
   Backing 331
   Counterarguments and Rebuttals 332
Conducting a Toulmin Analysis of an Argument 334
   Problem Spot 1: Identifying Implied Elements 334
   Problem Spot 2: Identifying "Out of Order" Elements 335
   Problem Spot 3: Distinguishing between Similar Elements 335
   Using Questions to Identify Toulmin Elements 337
   RHETORICAL TOOLBOX 14.1
   Identifying the Toulmin Elements of an Argument 337

Model of a Toulmin Analysis of an Argument 338
   Joel Michael Reynolds, Why Parents Should Think Twice about Tracking Apps for Their Kids 338
   Sarit Fisher (Student), A Toulmin Analysis of an Argument 340
CHAPTER PROJECT Writing a Toulmin Analysis 343
   Robert Zaretsky, How Football Can Wreck a University 343
FAQ BECOMING FAMILIAR WITH TOULMIN ANALYSIS 346

Chapter 15
Understanding an Argument's Appeals *349*

An Overview of the Three Appeals *350*
Appeals to Ethos *351*
   Appealing to Ethos by Demonstrating Knowledge *352*
   Appealing to Ethos by Demonstrating Fairness and Respect *352*
   Appealing to Ethos by Demonstrating Good Character *353*
Appeals to Pathos *353*
Appeals to Logos *355*
Analyzing Rhetorical Appeals *356*
   RHETORICAL TOOLBOX 15.1
   Analyzing Rhetorical Appeals *356*

   Jody Kent Lavy, "Juvenile Lifers" Deserve Second Chance *357*

   CHAPTER PROJECT Analyzing Rhetorical Appeals *359*

   Ernest Owens, Equal When Separate *360*

   FAQ MISIDENTIFYING AND OVERLOOKING APPEALS *362*

Chapter 16
Recognizing Fallacies *365*

Identifying Fallacies *365*
   Presenting Causes or Effects *366*
   Referring to Others *368*
   Summarizing the Position of Others *370*
   Presenting Options or Choices *370*
   Using Language in Tricky Ways *370*
   Theorizing About a Group of Things, People, and So On *371*
   Pointing Out a Lack of Evidence *372*
   Diverting Attention or Changing the Subject *372*
   Presenting Irrelevant Reasons *373*
   Making a Comparison *374*
   Using Emotional Appeals *374*
   Using Faulty Data or Statistics *375*
Analyzing Fallacies in an Argument *376*
   RHETORICAL TOOLBOX 16.1
   Identifying and Analyzing Fallacies *376*

   Martina Velez, Thinking of Getting a Tattoo? Think Again *377*

   CHAPTER PROJECT Analyzing Fallacies in an Argument *379*

   FAQ AVOIDING COMMON ERRORS IN IDENTIFYING AND ANALYZING FALLACIES *380*

Chapter 17
Writing a Rhetorical Analysis *383*

Analyzing Arguments *383*
Analyzing an Argument Rhetorically *384*
   Guy Bentley, The CDC Botched Its Vaping Investigation and Helped Spark a National Panic *384*

   Analyzing the Rhetorical Situation *387*
   RHETORICAL TOOLBOX 17.1
   Rhetorical Situation Questions *387*

   Analyzing Claim, Reasons, and Other Elements *388*
   RHETORICAL TOOLBOX 17.2
   Identifying the Toulmin Elements of an Argument *388*

   Analyzing Appeals *389*
   RHETORICAL TOOLBOX 17.3
   Analyzing Rhetorical Appeals *389*

   Analyzing for Fallacies *390*
   RHETORICAL TOOLBOX 17.4
   Identifying and Analyzing Fallacies *390*

   Organizing and Drafting a Rhetorical Analysis *391*

Jacob Trinh (Student), A Rhetorical Analysis: The CDC Botched Its Vaping Investigation and Helped Spark a National Panic *395*

CHAPTER PROJECT Writing a Rhetorical Analysis *399*

   Robert Reich, Public Health First *399*

FAQ SELECTING CONTENT AND DRAFTING A THESIS STATEMENT FOR A RHETORICAL ANALYSIS *402*

Chapter 18
Classical, Rogerian, and Visual Arguments *405*

Argument Styles *405*

RHETORICAL TOOLBOX 18.1
Selecting an Argument Style *406*

Classical Argument *406*
   The Introduction *407*
   The Narration *408*
   The Confirmation *409*
   The Refutation *409*
   The Conclusion *410*
   Model of a Classical Argument *411*
Rogerian Argument *412*
   Model of a Rogerian Argument *414*
Visual Argument *416*
   Images without Words *416*
   Images with a Few Words *417*
   Images That Support Text *417*
   Analyzing and Creating Visual Arguments *418*

FAQ USING TECHNOLOGY TO CREATE VISUAL ARGUMENTS *421*

PART 5
WRITING A RESEARCHED ARGUMENT *423*

Chapter 19
Planning an Argument *423*

PART 5 PROJECT Writing a Researched Argument *424*

Selecting a Topic and Writing an Issue Question *425*
Creating a Guidance Rubric *427*
Identifying Your Research Needs and Finding Sources *428*

RHETORICAL TOOLBOX 19.1
Identifying Your Research Needs *428*

Analyzing Your Research and Creating a Viewpoints Chart *429*
Drafting a Claim *432*
   Using Qualifiers in Claims *432*
   Identifying Claim Types *433*
Selecting and Evaluating Reasons *434*
   Selecting Reasons by Claim Type *434*
   Selecting Reasons that Appeal to Readers *434*
   Evaluating Reasons *436*

RHETORICAL TOOLBOX 19.2
Evaluating Your Argument's Reasons *436*

FAQ FINDING RESEARCH FROM MULTIPLE VIEWPOINTS *437*

Chapter 20
Selecting Evidence and Drafting Reasons *440*

Creating an Outline *440*
Selecting Evidence to Support Reasons *441*
Organizing Reasons and Drafting Content *444*
   Organizing Reasons *444*
   Drafting Content *445*
   Organizing Support for Reasons *446*
   Introducing Evidence *448*

RHETORICAL TOOLBOX 20.1
Organizing Reasons and Drafting Content *449*

DRAFTING TOOLBOX
Templates for Introducing Evidence *449*

Avoiding Fallacies *450*

RHETORICAL TOOLBOX 20.2
Identifying and Analyzing Fallacies *451*

FAQ USING A TEMPLATE TO PLAN THE BODY OF AN ARGUMENT *452*

Chapter 21
Drafting Counterarguments, Introductions, and Conclusions *453*

Addressing Counterarguments *453*
   Basic Approaches for Dealing with Counterarguments *454*
   Developing Rhetorically Effective Rebuttals *455*

RHETORICAL TOOLBOX 21.1
Addressing Counterarguments *459*

Drafting Introductions and Conclusions 460
   Creating Introductions 461
   Creating Conclusions 463
FAQ CONCEDING A POINT WITHOUT CONFUSING READERS 465

Chapter 22
Revising and Finishing Your Argument 467

Using a Rubric for Revision 467
Revising for a General Audience 469
   Revising for Development 469
   Revising for Unity and Organization 470
   Revising for Clarity 471
   RHETORICAL TOOLBOX 22.1
   Revising Your Argument for a General Audience 473
Revising for a Critical Audience 476
   RHETORICAL TOOLBOX 22.2
   Revising Your Argument for a Critical Audience 476
Finishing Your Argument 478
   Editing 478
   Formatting 479
   Checking for Plagiarism 479
Jada Spalding (Student), Why Employers Should Adopt Telecommuting Policies 479
FAQ TOO SHORT? TOO LONG? SOLVING LENGTH PROBLEMS 486

PART 6
AN ANTHOLOGY OF READINGS 489

1. Environmental Issues 489

   Sandra Steingraber, The Fracking of Rachel Carson: Silent Spring's Lost Legacy, Told in Fifty Parts 489
   Justine Calma, Big Oil Touts Offshore Drilling Jobs to Communities Most Harmed by Oil 499
   Basav Sen, Want to Create More Jobs? Reduce Fossil Fuel Use 502
   Lauren DeCicca, Thais Rally in Bangkok for Global Climate Strike (Photograph) 505

2. Animal Welfare 506

   April Pedersen, The Dog Delusion 506
   Sabine Heinlein, The Cruelty of Kindness 512
   Liz Sanchez, How Zoos Help Preserve the World's Species for the Future 523
   South Africans Protest against Rhino Poaching (Photograph) 525

3. Diversity 526

   Darnell L. Moore, Urban Spaces and the Mattering of Black Lives 526
   Andrew Ham, I Am an Asian-American Who Benefits from Affirmative Action 532
   Laura Collins, Pervasive Myths about Immigrants 535
   Linda Hogan, Black Walnut: A Sweet Blood History 540

4. Crime and Punishment 546

   Reginald Dwayne Betts, Only Once I Thought about Suicide 546
   Nikole Hannah-Jones, Yes, Black America Fears the Police. Here's Why. 553
   Wendy Sawyer and Peter Wagner, Mass Incarceration: The Whole Pie 561

5. Media and Culture 571

   Rachel Alter and Tonay Flattum-Riemers, Breaking Down the Anti-Vaccine Echo Chamber 571
   Gloria Steinem, Erotica and Pornography 574
   George H. Pike, Love It or Hate It: Native Advertising on the Internet 579
   Government of Alberta, Canada, It Shouldn't Be This Dangerous (Public Service Advertisement) 583
   U.S. Department of Transportation and the Ad Council, Save a Life: Don't Drive Home Buzzed (Public Service Advertisement) 584

6. Personal Growth 586

   Justin Huang, How I Overcame My Stuttering 586
   U.S. Marine Corps, Find Your Fight (Advertisement) 590

Bishnu Maya Pariyar, Peace Corps' Influence Changed My Fate *591*

Timothy J. Hillegonds, Men Explain Toxic Masculinity to Me, a Man Writing About Toxic Masculinity *594*

PART 7
HANDBOOK OF READING AND WRITING SKILLS *603*

Handbook 1
Improving Your Reading Skills *603*

1A. Using an Effective Reading Process *603*
   1A1. Before Reading *603*
   1A2. During Reading *606*
   1A3. After Reading *612*
1B. Identifying Main Ideas *616*
   1B1. Finding the Main Idea of a Paragraph *616*
   1B2. Finding the Implied Main Idea of a Paragraph *618*
   1B3. Finding the Thesis Statement of an Essay *619*
   1B4. Using Topic Sentences to Identify the Thesis Statement *620*
   1B5. Figuring Out an Implied Thesis Statement in an Essay *624*
1C. Making Accurate Inferences *625*
   1C1. Avoiding Inaccurate Inferences *626*
   1C2. Using Common Knowledge *627*
   1C3. Avoiding Unsupported Inferences *629*
   1C4. Analyzing Tone *629*

CHAPTER PROJECT Reading Skills *633*

Handbook 2
Improving Your Writing Skills *634*

2A. Sentence Basics *634*
   2A1. Subjects *634*
   2A2. Predicates *636*
2B. Sentence Types *638*
   2B1. Simple Sentences *638*
   2B2. Compound Sentences *638*
   2B3. Complex Sentences *641*
   2B4. Complex Sentences with More than One Dependent Clause *642*
   2B5. Compound-Complex Sentences *642*
2C. Avoiding Sentence Fragments *643*
   2C1. Missing Subject or Verb Fragments *643*
   2C2. Phrase Fragments *644*
   2C3. Dependent-Clause Fragments *645*
   2C4. Extra Information Fragments *646*
2D. Avoiding Run-Ons and Comma Splices *647*
   2D1. Joining the Clauses of a Run-on or Comma Splice *647*
   2D2. Separating the Clauses of a Run-on or Comma Splice *648*
2E. Writing Clear Sentences *649*
2F. Writing Sentences with Parallel Structure *650*
2G. Writing Good Paragraphs *652*
   2G1. Topic Sentences *652*
   2G2. Paragraph Support *652*
2H. Avoiding Pronoun Reference and Verb Tense Errors *655*
   2H1. Pronoun Reference Errors *655*
   2H2. Verb Tense Consistency *657*
2I. Avoiding Common Punctuation Errors *660*
   2I1. Commas *660*
   2I2. Apostrophes *663*
2J. Using Appropriate Capitalization *665*
   2J1. Using Capital Letters to Begin Sentences *665*
   2J2. Using Capital Letters for Proper Nouns *665*
2K. Mastering Commonly Confused Words *667*

Glossary *672*
Index *675*

Preface

To become good writers, students must learn more than a writing process: they must develop a writer's mindset—the rhetorical skills to read critically, analyze and synthesize sources, and write with their audiences in mind. How can we help students with the challenges involved in thinking like a writer? By using incremental steps that move from literal thinking to analytical and critical understanding, *The Writer's Mindset* makes the development of college-level writing capabilities possible for all students, whatever their level of preparedness. Students are guided to use rhetorical thinking, and in so doing, their ability to emulate the strategies of successful writers develops, and their capacity to use intentional, audience-based strategies in their own writing increases. *The Writer's Mindset* provides students with tools to transform the way they approach reading, writing, and arguing through five key pillars.

RHETORICAL FOCUS
All successful writing—from an informative report to an argument—depends on the writer's audience awareness and rhetorical skill. *The Writer's Mindset* helps students understand and develop the rhetorical thinking needed for any writing purpose.

INCREMENTAL APPROACH
The Writer's Mindset breaks down the thinking required to be an effective writer and offers students methods to develop a writer's mindset in incremental steps.

EMBEDDED SUPPORT
The Writer's Mindset helps even struggling students develop high-level reading, writing, and arguing skills by offering extra help for the more difficult topics and tasks.

STUDENT APPEAL
The Writer's Mindset meets students' needs for relevancy and value. The approachable tone, high-interest readings, and reflective writing prompts help students make personal connections with the content. The breadth of coverage allows the text to be used in both semesters of composition, making it a great value.

INSTRUCTOR SUPPORT
The Writer's Mindset offers extensive instructor support created by the author, a writing professor with over thirty years' experience, including an annotated instructor's edition; topical PowerPoints; teaching plans for face-to-face courses, online courses, and co-requisite courses; chapter tests; and much more.

The five pillars are supported by McGraw Hill Connect for Composition. McGraw Hill Education Connect is a digital assignment and learning platform that strengthens the link between faculty, students, and coursework. With a suite of comprehensive and flexible resources designed to help students meet outcomes in first-year composition while reducing instructor workload, Connect Composition includes SmartBook 2.0, Writing Assignment Premium, Power of Process, Adaptive Learning Assignments, and instructor resources.

RHETORICAL FOCUS

***The Writer's Mindset* presents rhetoric in an easy-to-understand way and provides students with effective steps for applying rhetorical thinking to any reading or writing assignment.** Clear explanations and practical exercises help students understand what rhetorical thinking is and how to practice it. The rhetorical focus of *The Writer's Mindset* prompts students to recognize writers' strategies whenever they read a text and to intentionally select strategies that fit the rhetorical situation of any composition they craft.

▶ **Annotated readings** point out writing strategies and purposes to move students beyond comprehension to greater rhetorical awareness.

▶ **Your Turn questions** guide students to analyze readings rhetorically, helping them learn effective strategies for their own writing.

▶ **Models of student thinking and writing-in-progress** demonstrate the kind of rhetorical awareness needed to plan, draft, and revise with an audience in mind.

> **Jada, on using her guidance rubric:** "I actually used the guidance rubric several times when I was researching and drafting my paper. Adding the two rhetorical goals at the end was important because I figured out that my argument might not be convincing if I can't show that I'm thoroughly knowledgeable about the topic and if I can't overcome the objections of my worst critics. I ended up using the rubric a lot during revision. It helped me remember my goals and make changes that made my paper more effective."

▶ **Rhetorical Toolboxes** help students develop a writer's mindset by providing questions students can use for reading and writing tasks.

> **RHETORICAL TOOLBOX 7.1**
> **The Rhetorical Concerns of Analytical Writing**
>
> 1. **Purpose.** What is the purpose of your analysis? Is the purpose of the analysis to aid understanding? To draw conclusions to make decisions? Figure out the purpose so that you can present the analysis in such a way that readers follow the logic and understand any conclusions you

▶ **Drafting Toolboxes** help students find the words and organization strategies that they need to write well.

> **DRAFTING TOOLBOX**
> **Templates for Introducing Evidence**
>
> **Templates for Summaries**
> To provide an overview of research that shows similarities:
> - Many of the researchers have shown that . . .
> - A survey of the research suggests that . . .

▶ **Peer Review Toolboxes** help students develop the habit of thinking rhetorically to critique their own and others' writing.

> **PEER REVIEW TOOLBOX: REFLECTIVE WRITING**
>
> 1. Does the writer clearly communicate a main idea in the composition? If so, what is the main idea?
> 2. Look at the areas in the paper where the writer describes an event or memory. Are there any details missing that would help you better understand the event or memory?

INCREMENTAL APPROACH

***The Writer's Mindset* helps students develop their thinking and writing skills in small steps.** By explaining, offering relevant examples, and providing students with opportunities to practice, the text provides a scaffold for students to achieve high-level goals.

▶ **Warm-Ups** at the start of each chapter help students connect what they already know to new information and skills.

> **WARM-UP**
> Imagine you are reading the texts in the list that follows. Would you use the same process to read each text? If not, in what ways would your reading process change for each one?
> 1. A letter from your mobile phone provider about how they take privacy seriously
> 2. A long text from someone you are dating expressing how he or she feels

▶ **Scaffolded instruction** makes difficult concepts easier to understand. New information is tied to information students already know, and ample examples and exercises help students learn new skills and content.

TABLE 16.1 Recognizing Fallacies

Argument Strategies When a writer . . .	Potential Fallacies . . . these fallacies may result:
Presents causes or effect	Slippery slope Post hoc Correlation error
Refers to or characterizes others	Ad hominem False authority Guilt by association

▶ **Activities** provide brief incremental tasks that help students learn not only by reading but also by doing. For example, in one activity students are asked to set up folders for a research project, and in the next activity, they must decide what types of sources might be useful.

▶ **Chapter Projects** build on the chapter content and provide more substantial writing assignments. In Part 2, three project options are provided for each writing purpose and are followed by writing guidelines illustrated with a student's writing process, rhetorical thinking, and model paper.

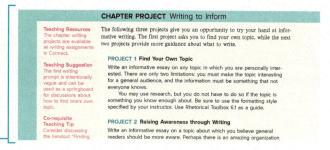

▶ **A major Researched Argument Project divided into 17 mini-assignments** makes the creation of a well-developed argument more achievable.

- Select a topic and issue question for an argument.
- Create a guidance rubric for an argument.
- Identify research needs and find sources.
- Explain diverse viewpoints on an issue.
- Write a claim for an argument.
- Evaluate and select reasons to support a claim.

▶ **Writing Assignment Premium in Connect** supports each chapter by providing students with low stakes writing opportunities, including automated feedback, to help develop their writing abilities. In Writing Assignment Premium, students draft responses to writing prompts and receive feedback from instructors. Grammar checkers and originality detection alert students to issues before they submit their work. A customizable rubric provides assessment transparency and allows students to see why they got their grade and how to improve. Connect includes pre-loaded writing assignments and assignments with automated feedback. Additionally, instructors can add their own writing assignments.

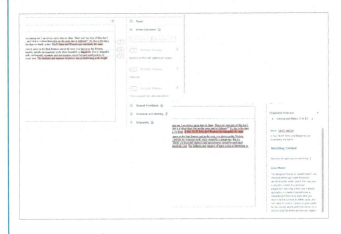

▶ **Power of Process Assignments in Connect** provide the practice students need to read real-world texts analytically and critically by guiding them through the thinking required for deep understanding. Power of Process leads students through performance-based assessment activities using the pedagogy of strategies instruction. Students use strategies to read and respond to the text. Instructors can assess students' depth of engagement with the text. Instructors can choose from pre-built templates for guiding students through literal and critical reading, as well as research and writing. A bank of carefully chosen readings is available with Power of Process. In addition, readings from *The Writer's Mindset* can be assigned. Finally, instructors can upload their own readings.

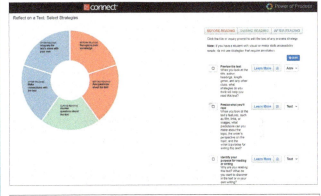

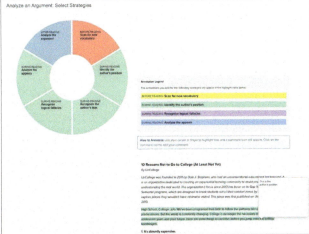

EMBEDDED SUPPORT

The Writer's Mindset **helps even struggling students develop college-level reading, writing, and arguing skills.** Students enter the first-year composition classroom with a range of preparatory experiences and skills, and English faculty are challenged to meet the diverse range of needs. Thus *The Writer's Mindset* embeds a variety of materials for students at various levels. For the instructor, the Annotated Instructor's Edition presents tips for helping struggling students to achieve college-level thinking and writing goals.

▶ **End-of-chapter FAQ sections** offer a deeper dive into one of the chapter's most difficult topics so that students have additional help with learning the content.

> **FAQ WRITING IN THIRD PERSON**
>
> Many academic and professional assignments will require papers to be written in third person. Writing in third person means avoiding the pronouns associated with first and second person. See the chart that follows for a quick review.

▶ **Try It activities** accompany FAQ sections and give students low-stakes opportunities to try new skills before using those skills for higher-stakes assignments.

> **TRY IT!**
>
> Reword the following paragraph to avoid second person:
>
> Your body language is often more powerful than the actual words that come out of your mouth. For example, certain postures—such as crossing your arms—suggest defensiveness, and if you stand and talk to a colleague with crossed arms, regardless of what you say, that colleague may think you are standoffish or guarded.

▶ **Part 7, Handbook of Reading and Writing Skills** anticipates the areas in which students have the most difficulty and provides practical strategies for improvement.

▶ **SmartBook 2.0 in Connect** helps students study more efficiently by highlighting what to focus on in the chapter and asking review questions. SmartBook creates a personalized study path customized to individual student needs, continually adapting to pinpoint knowledge gaps and focus learning on concepts requiring additional study. By taking the guesswork out of what to study, SmartBook fosters more productive learning and helps students better prepare for class.

> **ANALYTICAL WRITING FROM A WRITER'S MINDSET**
>
> A successful writer of analysis must keep the audience in mind throughout the process of thinking and writing. Thinking rhetorically will guide the process you use, and it will help you to convey the results of your analysis to an audience so that readers can follow your logic and conclusions.
>
> **THE PROCESS OF ANALYZING**
>
> The process of analyzing always precedes the writing process. In the Warm-Up exercise, you were asked to think about the processes you would use for three scenarios requiring analysis. If you are like most people, the processes you thought of included verbs such as *examine, try, experiment, survey, research, check, compare, find,* and so on. You probably found that the process you would use for analyzing potential colleges is different from the process you would use to analyze 3D printing or identify demographic patterns in a city. Conducting a successful analysis depends on using an analytical process that works for your purpose.
>
> Additionally, as you plan the process you will use for analysis, it is important to think about audience expectations. For example, if you are analyzing the costs of two colleges to help readers decide which one is the best value, readers will expect particular information, such as the cost of living at the university, the cost of fees, the cost of tuition, the availability of part-time jobs in the city to offset tuition costs, and so on. The process you use for the analysis should take into consideration what readers will expect the analysis to cover. To figure out the best process for an analysis, use these questions:
>
> **Analytical Process Questions**
>
> 1. What is the purpose of the analysis? In other words, what do I want to learn by conducting the analysis?
> 2. Who is the audience? What expectations will the audience have, and how will these expectations influence the process of your analysis?
> 3. What information must I find to conduct the analysis?
> 4. What will I need to do with the information to analyze it properly?
>
> In the Warm-Up, you thought about the process steps used for particular analyses. You probably realized that you would not use the same process for each of the tasks. But what, exactly, should the process be for the three scenarios in the Warm-Up? Using the Analytical Process

▶ **Adaptive Learning in Connect** provides students with adaptive, individualized support to help them with trouble spots in the reading and writing processes, grammar, and mechanics. Learning Resources provide instruction and remediation for topics as needed by the individual student.

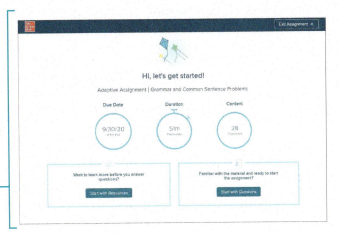

▶ **Practice and Homework Activities in Connect** offer a range of quizzes and activities that can be used as low-stakes practice and assessment.

STUDENT APPEAL

The Writer's Mindset meets students' expectations for value and relevancy. Students are focused on value. *The Writer's Mindset* helps students see how the reading, thinking, and writing skills they are learning are relevant to their academic, professional, public, and personal lives.

▸ **Reflecting to Develop a Writer's Mindset** activities prompt students to make connections between the chapter's content and their own writing experiences.

> **Reflecting to Develop a Writer's Mindset**
>
> Reflect on this chapter. What is a mindset? What is rhetoric? How might understanding rhetoric change your mindset as a writer? Write a paragraph or two in response.

▸ **Contemporary readings** were chosen with today's students in mind and present a wide variety of voices. Issues are diverse and include attitudes about pets, vaccination policies, policing, solving racial injustice problems, immigration, masculinity, and more.

▸ **Student models** present rhetorical thinking and writing tasks from a student's point of view and provide relevant solutions to common writing problems.

> **Jada, on selecting reasons by claim type:** "I am arguing a claim of policy, so the types of reasons that applied most were that an effective work-from-home policy will save money, produce the results a company desires, increase happiness, and has shown itself to work in similar situations."

▸ The **flexible content of *The Writer's Mindset*** makes it a text that can be used for both semesters of first-year composition, offering students value and continuity.

INSTRUCTOR SUPPORT

***The Writer's Mindset* offers extensive instructor support created by the author, a writing professor with over thirty years' experience.** Author Lisa Wright Hoeffner provides a wealth of materials to help both new and experienced faculty develop their own courses.

- ▶ An **Annotated Instructor's Edition** written by the author provides teaching suggestions and a guide to resources in the Instructor's Manual and Connect. It also provides ideas for teaching the content to co-requisite students and to students with varying levels of competency in reading and writing.
- ▶ An **Instructor's Manual** written by the author presents practical strategies, as well as exercises and activities, that are useful in the classroom. Included in the Instructor's Manual are:
  - **Syllabi/Calendars.** Ideas and week by week plans for using *The Writer's Mindset* to teach Composition 1 and 2 in various formats: 6-unit, 8-unit, and 15-unit courses; co-requisite courses; and online courses.
  - **Best Practices for Teaching Composition Online**
  - **Best Practices for Teaching Co-requisite or Struggling Students**
- ▶ **Accessible PowerPoints** in an editable format that present important topics, such as "How to Participate in Peer Review," "Avoiding Plagiarism," "Presenting a Causal Analysis—Without Fallacies," and "Analyzing Ethos."
- ▶ **Google drive.** Access to the author's personal Google drive where she shares her teaching materials and additional resources.
- ▶ **Support at every step** is provided by McGraw Hill Education. McGraw Hill Education's Connect offers comprehensive service, support, and training throughout every phase of your implementation. If you're looking for some guidance on how to use Connect or want to learn tips and tricks from super users, you can find tutorials as you work. Our Digital Faculty Consultants and Student Ambassadors offer insight into how to achieve the results you want in Connect. Additionally, McGraw Hill integrates your digital products from McGraw Hill with your school LMS for quick and easy access to best-in-class content and learning tools.

Acknowledgments

Writing a book is always a team effort, and I have been lucky to have worked with an amazing team at McGraw Hill in the creation of *The Writer's Mindset*. In particular, I would like to thank Kelly Villella, senior director of innovation strategy, for making the entire project possible. Her steadfast belief that we can create products that truly improve student learning makes her a real asset both for McGraw Hill and for instructors as we attempt to turn our ideas into meaningful learning experiences. I would also like to thank Erin Cosyn, portfolio manager, for her project leadership and guidance. Erin's creativity and analytical skills have helped our team think beyond the confines of the text's margins. Also crucial to the development of *The Writer's Mindset* were McGraw Hill product developers Beth Tripmacher and Mary Ellen Curley. Beth's personable, positive, can-do creativity was a hallmark of our weekly meetings, and Mary Ellen's gentle guidance and well-honed expertise were invaluable. And I could not have asked for a more experienced, witty, and hands-on product developer than Marion Castellucci. Her ideas and sharp insights mark each page of *The Writer's Mindset*. Additionally, I would like to thank Cara Labell, lead product developer; Victoria DeRosa, product developer; Brianna Kirschbaum, content licensing specialist; Lisa Bruflodt, lead content project manager; Linda Landis-Clark, copy editor; and Byron Kanoti, marketing manager, for their contributions to this first edition.

Words cannot express how important faculty reviewers are to the process of creating a text. I would like to thank each of the following faculty members who provided formative feedback throughout the writing process:

Alamance Community College
Susan Dalton, Anne Helms

Alamo Colleges, Northwest Vista College
Britt Benshetler, Britt Posey

Amarillo College
Judith Carter

Bevill State Community College
Stephen Rizzo

Bismarck State College
Erin Price

Blinn College
Lisa Wall

Bluegrass Community & Technical College
Jim Fenton

Bowie State University
Nicole Wilson

California State University–Fresno
Ginny Crisco

Cape Fear Community College
Blythe Bennett, Lynn Criswell, Anitra Louis, Kerry A. McShane-Moley, Cheryl Saba

Catawba Valley Community College
Robert Canipe

Cecil College
Kathleen Weiss

Clark State Community College–Springfield
Paige Huskey

College of Southern Nevada
Megan Padilla, John Ziebell

College of the Desert
Vida Rossi Dean

Crowder College
Stephanie Witcher

Cuyahoga Community College
Neeta Chandra

Dallas College–Brookhaven
Nimmy Nair

Delaware Technical and Community College
Carl Becker, Nicholas David

Delgado Community College
Emily Cosper, Lilian Gamble, Erin Vonsteuben

Des Moines Area Community College
Will Zhang

East Central College
Leigh Kolb

Eastern Florida State College
Maureen Groome

El Centro College
Rachel Key

Fayetteville Technical Community College
Bea Peterson

Florence-Darlington Technical College
Mark Rooze

Garden City Community College
Sheena Hernandez

Genesee Community College
Shawn Adamson

Grayson College
Karen Campbell, Jean Sorensen

Henderson Community College
Lilia Joy

Holmes Community College
Arnetra Pleas

Holyoke Community College
Sarah Gilleman

Houston Community College
Cecilia Bonnor

Illinois Eastern Community Colleges
Kelly Payne

Indian River State College–Fort Pierce
Camila Alvarez

Iowa Western Community College
Coreen Wees

Johnson County Community College
Theodore Rollins

Johnston Community College
Susan Austin

Joliet Junior College
Tamara Ponzo Brattoli

Lake Land College
Casey Reynolds

Lee College
Jill Gos

Lone Star College
Leslie Jewkes, Rhonda Jackson Joseph, Anna Schmidt, Laura Taggett, Brooke Thrift

Macomb Community College
Linda Brender, Ludger Brinker

Maysville Community and Technical College
Christina McCleanhan

McHenry County College
Starr Nordgren, Cynthia VanSickle, Cynthia Wolf

Mississippi Delta Community College
Jenni Hargett

Moberly Area Community College
Beth Marchbanks

Montgomery College
Joseph Couch

Motlow State Community College
Wesley T. Spratlin

Murray State College
Jeana West

Nashville State Community College
Dawn M. Adkerson, Agnetta Mendoza, Bridgette Weir

National American University
Brigit McGuire

North Central State College
Patricia Herb

North Idaho College
Lucas J. Brown

North Lake College
Sonia Bush

Northern Oklahoma College
Stephanie Scott

Northern Virginia Community College
Cheri Lemieux Spiegel

Ocean County College
Kristyn Stout

Oklahoma State University–Oklahoma City
Joe Myers

Ozarks Technical Community College
Kelly Anthony

Pellissippi State Community College
Kelly Rivers, Marilyn Sue Yamin

Pensacola State College
Debra A. Ryals

Pitt Community College
Daniel Stanford

Prince George's Community College
Mary Dutterer, Francois Guidry

Raritan Valley Community College
Justin Felix

Ridgewater College
Peggy Karsten

Robert Morris University–Moon Township
Julianne M. Michalenko

Robeson Community College
Daniela Newland

Schoolcraft College
Anna Maheshwari

Seminole State College of Florida
Karen Feldman, Frankie Huff, Chrishawn Speller, Rochelle Swiren

Somerset Community College
Michael Bloomingburg, Erin Stephens

Southeastern Louisiana University
Natasha Whitton

St. Johns River State College–Orange Park
Melody Hargraves

St. Petersburg College
Amber Estlund

Tarantino County College
Sara Edgell

Texas State University
Chad Hammett, Nancy Wilson

Three Rivers College
Tiechera Samuell

Tyler Junior College
Jim Richey

University of North Alabama–Florence
Tammy Winner

University of South Carolina
Esther Godfrey, Celena E. Kusch

Vance-Granville Community College
Frankie Frink, Maureen Walters

Virginia Commonwealth
 University–Monroe Park
Joan Kalyan

Volunteer State Community College
Shellie Michael

Waubonsee Community College
Dan Portincaso

Waukesha County Technical College
Lisa Baker

West Kentucky Community and
 Technical College
Tyra Henderson

Western Technical College
Pam Solberg

Wright State University
Cynthia Marshall Burns

Additionally, I am grateful to my colleagues and administrators at McLennan Community College: Bill Matta, Nick Webb, Linda Crawford, Chad Eggleston, Fred Hills, and Johnette McKown. Their support has been invaluable and has made possible the writing of a text along with teaching a full-time load.

Finally, I appreciate my family: Tim, Gail, Richard, Hannah, and Abby. They have always been there to help when they could and to provide encouragement and cheer.

LISA WRIGHT HOEFFNER

About the Author

Lisa Wright Hoeffner earned a Ph.D. in English with a specialization in rhetoric from the University of Houston. She has taught a wide range of courses over the past thirty years, including English composition and rhetoric, integrated reading and writing, critical thinking, American and British literature, world literature, humanities, and business writing. She began teaching college composition in 1989 and is currently a professor of English at McLennan Community College in Waco, Texas.

In addition to her teaching role, Dr. Hoeffner speaks nationally on topics relevant to teaching first-year writing, including writing assessment strategies that facilitate student growth as writers, deep learning in the online composition classroom, the role of emotional intelligence in student growth and persistence, and strategies supporting students who struggle in first-year composition.

She is the author of *Common Places: Integrated Reading and Writing* and *Common Ground: Integrated Reading and Writing–Basic* (both McGraw Hill, 2019) and has written and published scholarly articles and poetry. A native Texan, Dr. Hoeffner enjoys exploring the flora and fauna of regional ecosystems, traveling, hiking, and dreaming about living off the grid.

PART 1 Developing a Writer's Mindset

1 What Is a Writer's Mindset?

CHAPTER OBJECTIVES

You will learn to:

- Explain the terms *rhetoric* and *writer's mindset*.
- Analyze the rhetorical situation of a communication.
- Describe three rhetorical domains: public, professional/academic, and personal.
- Develop rhetorical thinking.

In this text, you are going to be prompted to think about how language works. You will be prompted to examine the language choices of others to see how those choices create meanings and help shape reality. In turn, you will be challenged to think about how your own language choices influence those around you, help shape your identity, and affect the opportunities you have in life.

Let's take a simple example. Imagine you are a manager who tries to use language to create a better workplace. You frequently remind employees that they work for a top-notch company that values them as employees as much as it values its customers, and you back up your words with good deeds. Your words can be powerful: they can influence employees' attitudes about their jobs and the company. If employees have positive attitudes and feel valued, your language helped to create something real: an effective and friendly workplace.

How might your life change if you were always aware of the power of your words? What would happen if, in addition to this constant awareness, you had a set of strategies you could use to craft language carefully and purposefully—strategies to help you communicate exactly what you mean to communicate? In part, developing your mastery of language is what this text is about. But it's about more than that. The way you communicate reflects the way you think. People who are excellent communicators have a highly developed set of thinking skills that help them analyze situations so that they can know both *what* they should say and *how* they should say it.

Furthermore, good communicators can also read the messages around them accurately. In our technology-focused world, we are barraged with messages from social media, websites, news channels, and the like. Which messages are

Connect Adaptive Learning Assignment
Consider assigning Connect's Adaptive Learning Assignments to support this chapter.

Teaching Resources
See the Instructor's Manual (IM) for suggestions about how to teach this chapter, and consider assigning this chapter's test-bank quiz.

important? Which are true? If you can think critically about the language others use, you can sift through information—and misinformation—to find ideas worth believing and taking action on.

As you work through this text, you will be challenged to think about language in ways you may not have considered before. Ideally, you will learn strategies to help you harness the power of language so that you can grow personally, academically, and professionally.

> **WARM-UP**
>
> Read each description. What do Veronica, Darla, and Mark have in common?
>
> - Veronica recently became single, and she has decided to start dating again. Before she sets up an online dating profile, she checks her other social media pages. She wants to make sure that the information there—including the items in which she is tagged—reflects the image she wants to project.
> - Darla has been asked to chair a committee that will negotiate pay raises for employees. At the first meeting, Nolan, one of the committee members, talks nonstop and dominates the conversation. Darla skillfully and tactfully intervenes: "Nolan, you have so many ideas that you're making it too easy on everyone else. We need to put the other committee members to work!" He says, "You're right. What do the rest of you think?"
> - A high-ranking legislator, Mark, has been accused of tax evasion. When asked about the issue by a news reporter, Mark simply changes the subject.

WHAT IS RHETORICAL THINKING?

You may have already figured out what Veronica, Darla, and Mark have in common: they have well developed communication skills. Another way to describe them is to say that they think *rhetorically*. We define **rhetoric** as the use of tools and strategies to convey a message or persuade. Successful communicators are often masters of rhetoric. They are aware of a variety of rhetorical tools and strategies, and they use them effectively in personal, academic, and professional communications.

rhetoric: The use of tools and strategies to convey a message or persuade.

- Veronica demonstrates rhetorical thinking when she decides to analyze her social media pages. She knows that social media will influence the impressions she makes, and since she is going to start dating again, she wants to control the messages her profiles send.
- Darla, too, demonstrates rhetorical thinking by finding a way to rein in a domineering committee member without offending him. She reads the situation, realizes that other people are getting frustrated, and finds the right words to persuade Nolan to give others a chance to talk.
- Mark, the legislator who is asked about tax evasion, also thinks rhetorically. He avoids answering the question by changing the subject. This

rhetorical strategy is designed to take the attention off the legislator's potential wrongdoing and refocus it.

Veronica, Darla, and Mark make communication decisions by thinking rhetorically. Developing your writing skills requires more than using a sound writing process or mastering grammar and mechanics. It requires thinking in a different way by developing a different kind of mindset. A *mindset* is a way of thinking that consists of the mental patterns you regularly use. It is a collection of thinking habits that help you process the information you encounter. If you are an artist, for instance, your mindset may include constant awareness of the patterns or shading you see. You may notice the play of shadows and light on a bridge, whereas a person who is not an artist would not notice such a thing. You have an artist's mindset. A person who is always upbeat and hopeful has an optimistic mindset. They tend to think positively, grant the benefit of the doubt when unsure, and believe that problems are solvable.

In this text, you will learn how to develop a **writer's mindset**, an awareness of the rhetorical means by which language can be used to communicate, influence, and persuade. Thinking from a writer's mindset means being aware of the rhetoric around you and the rhetoric that you yourself use. We make rhetorical choices for almost all of the communication in which we engage. For instance, if you have a car accident and write a summary of what happened for your insurance company, you will think rhetorically to compose a summary that makes sense and clarifies who was to blame. Reflective writing, such as a blog post, is also rhetorical. The post is crafted to convey a particular message to a particular audience—those who read the blog. Of course, when we hope to persuade, using a writer's mindset is especially important: doing so helps us anticipate how to tap into readers' beliefs and values so that they will see the significance of our ideas.

The ability to think the way readers think and to anticipate their needs, objections, and motivations helps you to write more effectively. Once you have well-developed rhetorical thinking skills, you will not need to be reminded to think about how an audience will perceive your words when you write. Thinking with a writer's mindset about your readers' needs and reactions will become automatic.

Imagine analyzing the language you use *before* you use it, and imagine being able to reasonably predict the effect your language will have on others. Now, imagine having goals—such as getting a job promotion, or convincing your teenage daughter to dress appropriately, or writing a college paper that will impress your professor—and knowing you are more likely to reach those goals because your writer's mindset is well developed. Similarly, when you are the reader or listener, using a writer's mindset to think rhetorically will help you sift through information, analyze it, and critique it. As you work through the chapters in this text, you will acquire the rhetorical thinking skills you need to think differently—and more effectively—about the communications in which you engage.

> **Teaching Suggestion**
> Consider having students write their own vignettes. On note cards, students describe a situation that requires rhetorical awareness. Take up the cards and group students, giving each group a few cards. Groups answer this question: How does the character in the vignette show rhetorical awareness?

> **writer's mindset:** An awareness of the rhetorical means by which language can be used to communicate, influence, and persuade.

▶ **ACTIVITY 1 Thinking Rhetorically About Social Media**

Examine a few of your most recent posts on social media from the perspective of a stranger. Based only on what you see in these posts, how might a stranger describe you? What kind of impressions might your posts create? How might thinking rhetorically about your social media postings affect what you write?

ANALYZING THE RHETORICAL SITUATION

One way to start developing your writer's mindset is to become aware of the factors that affect communication. These factors are summarized in what we call the *rhetorical situation*. At its simplest, the **rhetorical situation** consists of three essential elements: the writer or speaker, the message, and the audience (see Figure 1.1). These three elements work together when we communicate.

> **rhetorical situation:** A situation consisting of the writer or speaker, the message, and the audience.
>
> **Teaching Resources**
> The PowerPoint "What Is Rhetoric?" presents an overview of the rhetorical situation.

1. **The writer or speaker.** The person communicating the message is the writer or speaker. For example, Senator Johnson is a speaker when she delivers a message to Congress, but she is a writer when she sends a letter to her constituents.

2. **The message.** The main idea the writer or speaker hopes to convey is the message. The message may be conveyed in a variety of ways: through speeches, written communications, advertisements, ordinary dialogue, and so on. Senator Johnson, for example, may deliver a speech urging increased funding for opioid abuse prevention programs. She may also write a guest column in a newspaper to communicate the same message.

3. **The audience.** Any time a writer or speaker attempts to communicate a message, there is an intended audience. The audience may be general, such as the readers of a public newspaper, or it may be very specific, such as members of the U.S. Senate or a group of health-care professionals. An understanding of the audience's knowledge and values helps the writer or speaker craft the message so that the particular audience will understand and accept it. For example, when speaking to Congress, Senator Johnson uses different language to convey her message about opioid abuse prevention programs than she uses when speaking to health-care professionals. Likewise, she changes her language when crafting her message for a high school assembly or the general readers of a newspaper.

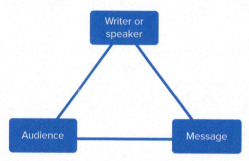

FIGURE 1.1 The basic rhetorical situation: Three essential elements.

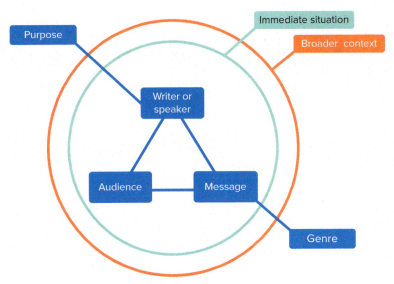

FIGURE 1.2 The expanded rhetorical situation.

While these three elements are the primary components of the rhetorical situation, we can add a few more: immediate situation, broader context, purpose, and genre (see Figure 1.2). Let's look at each of these additional elements in more depth:

- **Immediate situation.** Any time a writer produces a text, they do so in response to a particular situation. For example, Andre is taking Introduction to Nursing, a class required for his nursing major. His professor assigned a paper asking students to select a social or interpersonal issue that affects nurses and to write a brief paper to help classmates understand how to deal with the issue should they ever encounter it. The rhetorical choices Andre makes will depend on the immediate situation: he is writing for student nurses, so he will need to use language that works for them, and he must select an issue that new nurses are likely to encounter in order to make the paper relevant to his classmates.
- **Broader context.** Andre is motivated to write the paper because it is a required assignment for a particular class. But he knows there is a broader context: the world of nursing, a world that he will be entering. He realizes that a current event—the COVID-19 pandemic—is affecting the lives of nurses. This broader context helps him decide on an important and timeless topic: how to handle the personal risk of contracting life-threatening diseases.
- **Purpose.** The writer's purpose—what the writer wants to accomplish—is another part of the rhetorical situation. Andre's immediate purpose is to complete an assignment, but he realizes there are other purposes for the assignment. By thinking about an issue nurses may encounter, he is preparing himself for the world of nursing; and by sharing his insights with

genre: A type or form of writing, for example, an email, a short story, or a research paper.

classmates, he is helping to prepare them. When considered from a writing purpose perspective, Andre's goal is to inform.

- **Genre.** Another part of the rhetorical situation is the **genre**, the type of writing that will be the most appropriate or effective to communicate the message. A writer or speaker selects a genre that is appropriate for her purpose and audience. As Andre researches his topic, he finds a variety of genres used to present issues in nursing: blog posts, short articles, articles in academic journals, and so on. Andre does not have to choose a genre because his instructor has already selected the genre—a brief essay—but if he were a nurse manager and wanted to provide this information to his employees, he could choose to write a memo, produce a video, create a podcast, or use one of the written genres noted above.

By thinking critically about the rhetorical situation of a writing assignment, you can make sound decisions that will help you write more effectively. You can also gain a deeper understanding of the written and oral communications you receive by analyzing their rhetorical situations. Rhetorical Toolbox 1.1 is the first of many Rhetorical Toolboxes that you will find in this text. These toolboxes equip you with thinking strategies for developing a writer's mindset, strategies that will help you think rhetorically and write effectively.

Teaching Resources
Consider using the assignment "Analyzing a Rhetorical Situation."

RHETORICAL TOOLBOX 1.1
Analyzing the Rhetorical Situation

Use these questions to gain deeper insight into the rhetorical situation of any communication.

1. **Speaker or writer.** Who is the speaker or writer? What values, beliefs, or personal interests of the speaker or writer can help you understand the message?
2. **Message.** What is the message? What is the purpose of the message? In other words, what does the speaker or writer hope to accomplish with this message? What is the immediate situation of the message? What is the broader context?
3. **Audience.** Who is the intended audience? How does the speaker or writer attempt to meet the audience's needs or craft the message for this specific audience? What genre does the speaker or writer select for a message to this audience? Why is the genre appropriate?

Teaching Suggestion
Consider having students work in groups to do a quick search for Veterans of Foreign Wars and to use the information they find to complete Activity 2.

▶ **ACTIVITY 2** Analyzing a Rhetorical Situation

Imagine that you are applying for a scholarship awarded by the local Veterans of Foreign Wars organization. The application requires you to write a letter explaining why you are a good candidate for the scholarship. Explain how analyzing the audience of this rhetorical situation might help you write a convincing letter.

RECOGNIZING THREE RHETORICAL DOMAINS

We use rhetoric to communicate messages and to persuade; as such, rhetorical situations are all around us. As you develop a writer's mindset, you will begin to recognize these situations. One way to understand how rhetoric is used is to consider three rhetorical domains: public, professional or academic, and personal.

Public Rhetoric

Public discourse consists of the dialogues, deliberations, and interactions about issues that are important to society. In a democracy, public discourse is vital. By discussing viewpoints on issues such as health care, immigration, social justice, crime, and the like, democratic societies decide on the laws that will govern them. Any person in a democracy may influence these decisions, and the people who are the most influential usually have a firm grasp of rhetoric. Articles in newspapers and magazines are examples of public discourse, but so are media productions such as newscasts and talk shows. Face-to-face dialogues, such as town hall meetings, the deliberations of legislators, political speeches, and debates, are also used for public rhetoric. And these days, social media also play an important role in public rhetoric. Twitter and Facebook, for instance, are highly influential platforms for public discourse.

You don't have to be a politician or journalist to engage in public discourse. For example, students used rhetorical thinking to bring about social change in response to the mass shooting at Marjory Stoneman Douglas High School in Parkland, Florida. After the horrific shooting that killed seventeen and injured another seventeen, a large group of students formed a political action committee, Never Again MSD. Determined to change gun laws, the students organized marches, created petitions, and wrote and spoke publicly. Their persuasive rhetorical tactics resulted in new laws in Florida that ban bump stocks, remove firearms from people who pose a threat to society, raise the age limit to purchase firearms to 21, and strengthen the requirements for background checks. Far from being powerless, these students realized that they have a place in public discourse and can use their rhetorical power to create the changes they believe need to happen.

Further, rhetorical thinking is just as useful to the listener (audience) of public discourse as it is to a speaker. Think of the paid programming (long advertisements for products) you have seen on television or of the personal "testimonial" videos or short advertisements that are posted on social media. These ads are often so well done that it is difficult even to see that they are ads instead of objective, informative content! Thinking from a rhetorical point of view equips us to view these ads more skeptically, to detect the rhetorical strategies the ad makers use, and to think more critically—and thus exercise more personal power—before falling victim to the advertisements that surround us.

Rhetoric in the Academic and Professional World

In both college and the workplace, rhetorical thinking helps us to communicate ideas clearly and persuasively. In college, students are challenged to

Teaching Suggestion
Students do not always see the ways in which social media function as public rhetoric. Consider having students analyze a social media app or site and find examples of public rhetoric.

Teaching Suggestion
To discuss this topic in more depth, consider assigning the reading "Love It or Hate It: Native Advertising on the Internet" by George H. Pike, available in Part 6, An Anthology of Readings.

think critically about the ideas they encounter and to write papers that summarize, analyze, evaluate, and argue about those ideas. Thinking rhetorically helps students both to identify the messages in the texts they encounter and to craft intentional and effective responses to those messages. Students who write high-quality papers keep rhetorical concerns, such as these, in mind:

- What qualities would this instructor expect in an excellent paper?
- What qualities are found in professional papers written in this subject area? Which of these qualities should I try to use in my own writing?
- What content fits this rhetorical situation?
- What strategies can I use in my paper to go beyond my instructor's expectations and show her that I really know what I'm talking about?

Students who keep these rhetorical concerns in mind while writing papers think about far more than the assignment requirements. By imagining what their instructor or audience may value and by using intentional strategies to imitate writing in the field, student writers can use their rhetorical skills to their personal advantage.

While rhetoric is very important in college, it is a crucial skill in the workplace. Earlier, you read about Darla's experience as a committee chair. By thinking rhetorically, Darla was able to rein in her colleague and avoid offending him. She considered the viewpoint of the other committee members: she realized that if she didn't control the situation, the talkative committee member would make dialogue impossible. Darla's realization was the first part of her rhetorical thinking; the second part was crafting the right kind of response so that she could control the situation without sounding like a tyrant or embarrassing her talkative colleague.

Thinking rhetorically is also crucial for written communications in the workplace. Gilbert, a middle-level manager, wrote frequent emails to his employees, but he was frustrated because it seemed like no one read them. One day Gilbert had lunch with another manager, Jill, and asked her if she had the same problem. Jill said, "No, because I used to have a boss who sent awful emails that no one read. I was determined I wouldn't ever do that. So I send emails that are short, to the point, and that tell my employees exactly what I would like them to do." Jill's words changed the way Gilbert thought about emails. He read over some of the emails he had just sent, and he realized they were too long, too detailed, and too vague in terms of directions. Employees probably did not know what to do with the information he sent them. His conversation with Jill changed the way Gilbert composed emails, and his employees began to read what Gilbert sent and do what he asked them to do.

Personal Rhetoric

One way to begin to develop a writer's mindset is to realize the many ways you use rhetoric in your day-to-day personal interactions. Let's revisit the definition

---

Teaching Suggestion
Help students to see that even following instructions is a rhetorical choice in that attention to the reader's (instructor's) directions and expectations involves thinking about the reader, a rhetorical act.

Teaching Suggestion
Have students critique the efficacy of an email. You might pull up an email you received from a student (removing personal information, of course) or have students find emails they have sent to their instructors or supervisors. For background reading, this article is helpful: https://www.danpink.com/pinkcast/pinkcast-2-20-this-is-how-to-write-a-cold-email-to-a-big-kahuna/

of rhetoric: *rhetoric* is the use of tools and strategies to convey a message or persuade. Think about the many messages you actively convey in interpersonal communications. Here are some examples:

- You like your new friend, but she texts you too often. You need to politely let her know that you prefer not to text so much.
- You need to return a jacket to a department store but do not have a receipt. You think about what you will say to the store clerk to convince him to accept the return.
- Your neighbor's dog barks at night and keeps you awake. You like your neighbor and want to have a good relationship with him, but you need to ask him to quiet his dog. You mull over the way you will bring up the subject and how you will ask him to keep his dog from barking.

In all three scenarios, thinking rhetorically will help you convey the right message and get the right results. What happens, though, when we fail to think rhetorically? Almost everyone has had moments when they've said the wrong thing or when they've spoken in a moment of anger and later regretted their words. We have all experienced times when we have not used language clearly enough to communicate what we need or want. The resulting miscommunications can have serious and lasting effects on our lives and relationships. Obviously, thinking rhetorically can help us on a personal level.

The kind of rhetorical thinking required for a well-developed writer's mindset offers advantages to us as citizens, students, professionals, and individuals. If you cultivate the habit of thinking rhetorically about what you want to say and write and then intentionally craft your messages, you will be on the path to developing the communication and writing skills that are necessary to open doors and reach your life goals.

> ▶ **ACTIVITY 3** **Reflecting on Rhetorical Domains**
>
> Think of a time when you were intentional about the words you used to communicate with another person. Perhaps you made an appointment with your boss to ask for a raise and, beforehand, thought about the words you would use. Or maybe you needed to break up with a romantic partner and planned what you would say. Write a few sentences explaining why you thought rhetorically in that situation and explain what happened.

THINKING RHETORICALLY TO DEVELOP A WRITER'S MINDSET

As you read the chapters in this text, you will learn some very specific skills that help you identify, analyze, and respond to rhetorical situations. These skills will help to improve your writer's mindset. Here are some ways to start thinking rhetorically.

Teaching Suggestion
Consider having students carefully word responses for each of the situations in bullet points. Discuss the potential reactions of the audience based on the words and phrases students use in their responses.

Co-requisite Teaching Tip
Use the teaching suggestion above, and have students examine the grammar and mechanics of their responses.

Teaching Suggestion
Consider using the PowerPoint "Examples of Rhetoric from Everyday Life."

- **Identify rhetorical situations and analyze them using rhetorical situation questions in Rhetorical Toolbox 1.1.** If you expand the concept of rhetoric to include any communication that conveys a message, you will begin to see rhetoric everywhere. For example, examine billboards. What messages are they trying to convey? What methods do the ad writers use to get people to understand and believe the message?
- **Notice the subtle messages conveyed by the décor and atmosphere of shops and restaurants.** Business owners know that to attract business, they must make intentional choices about the physical environment. For example, think about shopping malls. Modern malls include play areas for children and food courts and are often built to be bright, sunny, and attractive. The message is simple: *You'll enjoy shopping here!* What rhetorical choices are evident in the environments around you?

Co-requisite Teaching Tip
Have students analyze the course syllabus rhetorically.

- **Look at everyday communications rhetorically.** Look at a syllabus for one of your classes. What messages does the professor hope to convey in the syllabus? Most instructors use the syllabus as a place to state policies, grading information, and the like. But you may find that instructors are sending additional messages. A syllabus with repeated warnings about not submitting work late or missing class may be sending the message that the instructor is strict. What might a syllabus that includes links to all the various types of help on campus (counseling, tutoring, etc.) say about the instructor?
- **Read your own writing rhetorically.** Take out an assignment you have submitted. What rhetorical choices did you make when you wrote the assignment? How aware of your audience were you as you composed? Could you have done a better job by planning your writing according to the rhetorical situation? Which parts of the rhetorical situation should you have spent more time working on?
- **Look and listen for persuasive texts and speech, and think about how they work.** For example, your best friend may urge you to get a tattoo with her. She wants to persuade you, so she comes up with reasons to support her request. What are those reasons? How do they work? Does she try to make you feel a certain way about getting (or not getting) a tattoo? How is she trying to get you to join her?

▶ **ACTIVITY 4** Share a Rhetorical Insight

We all make personal choices that have rhetorical implications. For example, we might dress up to go to a job interview. The formal clothes we choose to wear are intended to send a message about us to an employer. People who wear cowboy hats, boots, and big belt buckles send the message that they are cowboys or ranchers and have all the attributes we imagine them having: toughness, strength, and so on. Find an example of personal rhetoric, either your own or someone else's, and write a brief paragraph in which you present the speaker or writer, the intended audience, the message, and the rhetorical choices made by the speaker or writer to convey the message.

CHAPTER PROJECT Thinking Rhetorically

PROJECT 1 Public Issues on Social Media

Use rhetorical thinking to analyze social media messages on public issues. In this chapter, we discussed how social media is a very influential platform for public discourse. Using your own social media accounts, find evidence to prove this statement is true. One way to do this is to take screenshots that show examples of people using social media to speak their minds on an issue or to encourage friends and family to believe a certain way. Write a paragraph for each screenshot, explaining each and showing how it supports the idea that social media is an influential platform for public discourse. Alternatively, you can quote from social media sites and explain how those quotes demonstrate the importance of social media for public discussions.

PROJECT 2 Communication with a Professor

Imagine that you and your classmates are confused about an upcoming writing assignment. Your instructor, Professor Greene, said he would provide an example of what the written product should look like, but he has not done so yet, and the assignment is due in two days. To make matters worse, one of the links he has provided in the assignment does not work. No one wants to say anything to him, but you are determined to do the assignment well, and you need some answers. You decide to ask Professor Greene yourself.

- **A.** How might thinking rhetorically help you to write to him? Explain your answer.
- **B.** Analyze the rhetorical situation by using the questions in Rhetorical Toolbox 1.1.
- **C.** Choose a genre and write to Professor Greene to get the help you need.

Co-requisite Teaching Tip
Consider having students complete Project 2C. See the IM for rationale and more information.

PROJECT 3 The Rhetorical Situation of a Text, Advertisement, or Event

Select one of the following items, and then analyze its rhetorical situation. You may need to do some informal research to learn more about the event or text you choose. For help doing informal research, see "FAQ: Doing Informal Research" at the end of this chapter.

Speech: The testimony of Facebook CEO Mark Zuckerberg to the U.S. House of Representatives: "Facebook: Transparency and Use of Consumer Data" (available online at https://docs.house.gov/meetings/IF/IF00/20180411/108090/HHRG-115-IF00-Transcript-20180411.pdf).

Event: The Me Too movement as it appears on Twitter (#MeToo).

Advertisement: Any television or YouTube commercial or print ad.

- **A.** After you have made your selection and done some research, answer the rhetorical situation questions in Rhetorical Toolbox 1.1.

B. Answer these two questions by writing a paragraph: How does thinking rhetorically about the event, speech, or advertisement differ from the way you might ordinarily think about it? How does thinking rhetorically affect what you write? What effects might developing a writer's mindset have on your life?

Reflecting to Develop a Writer's Mindset

Reflect on this chapter. What is a mindset? What is rhetoric? How might understanding rhetoric change your mindset as a writer? Write a paragraph or two in response.

FAQ DOING INFORMAL RESEARCH

Sometimes doing a bit of quick online research can help you understand a word, a text, or a rhetorical situation. This kind of quick research differs from the more extensive formal research tasks you will complete when you are writing a research paper. To do quick, informal research effectively, use these do's and don'ts:

1. **What should you do when conducting informal research?**
   - DO use Wikipedia for a quick overview of a topic, but also use additional websites for information. If the information in Wikipedia is the same as you find in these additional websites, the information is probably trustworthy.
   - DO find a site from an educational institution (often denoted by .edu) on the topic. While such sites are not always credible, they are more likely to contain solid information than .com sites.
   - DO run a search of the writer's name and the word *biography*.
   - DO use your library's resources. You may have a "master search bar" on your library's home page. Enter keywords and see what kind of information appears. Narrow the information by type. For example, for basic information, avoid peer-reviewed articles, but look at the encyclopedia entries and book reviews.

2. **What should you NOT do when conducting informal research?**
   - DON'T go to sites such as Quora or Yahoo Answers where random people post answers to questions. The quality of these responses is often poor.
   - DON'T use papers posted by students or essay-writing service companies as sources of information. The information may or may not be credible.
   - DON'T use sites where students post their own notes, create flashcards, or post quizzes. These types of sites offer tools you can use to

study, but relying on the information students post can sometimes be a problem.
- DON'T get sidetracked by extensively researched peer-reviewed articles that narrow the topic significantly. While these articles are highly credible and useful for other purposes, they will probably not give you the basic information you're seeking.

TRY IT!

Imagine you have received an assignment to write an evaluative essay, but you aren't sure what an evaluative essay is or what it should contain. Conduct informal research and find two online resources that are high quality and can help you to write such an essay. Write a few sentences explaining why you believe the sites you have chosen are quality resources.

2 Reading with a Writer's Mindset

CHAPTER OBJECTIVES

You will learn to:
- Identify three purposes for reading.
- Read to understand, summarize, and respond to the ideas of a text.
- Read to analyze a text rhetorically.
- Read to critique a text.
- Use insights from reading rhetorically to become a better writer.

Connect Adaptive Learning Assignment
Consider using Connect's Adaptive Learning Assignments to support this chapter.

Teaching Suggestion
Consider opening the discussion by analyzing a Super Bowl commercial. Many are available on YouTube.

reading rhetorically: A type of reading that reveals the *how* (the strategies) of a text and not merely the *what* (the message).

According to *Sports Illustrated,* running a thirty-second ad during the Super Bowl costs at least five million dollars. With a price tag in the millions, ads are produced with great care. Ad executives spend significant time analyzing the rhetorical situation and creating the perfect ad to sell their products. It may be tempting to think that the study of rhetoric applies only to texts that sell, or attempt to persuade, but that is not the case. Rhetorical thinking applies to all writing. Any time a writer hopes to convey ideas to an audience, he or she can use rhetorical strategies to communicate effectively.

When you read from a writer's mindset, you read rhetorically. **Reading rhetorically** enables you to see the strategies writers use to communicate their ideas and achieve their writing purposes. Reading rhetorically goes beyond finding the idea that is presented. It is a type of reading that reveals the *how* (the strategies) of a text and not merely the *what* (the message). In this chapter, you will learn to read a text from a writer's mindset. While you may think of a text as a textbook or a text message, any communication can be considered a text, and any text can be analyzed. As you develop your ability to analyze texts, you will continue to develop your writer's mindset, and doing so will make you a more critical thinker and writer.

WARM-UP

Imagine you are reading the texts in the list that follows. Would you use the same process to read each text? If not, in what ways would your reading process change for each one?

1. A letter from your mobile phone provider about how they take privacy seriously
2. A long text from someone you are dating expressing how they feel
3. A complicated assignment page for an essay assignment

THREE WAYS TO READ A TEXT

We read texts in different ways, depending on our goals (see Figure 2.1):

1. **To understand.** Sometimes our goal is simply to understand the text. For example, you might do a quick internet search to learn how to brine a turkey or to get an understanding of a medical condition. In such cases, your goal is simple understanding.
2. **To analyze.** We read to analyze when we want to move beyond a simple understanding. Analysis can involve reading for a variety of purposes. For instance, you may analyze an article to figure out the writer's biases, or you may analyze the ideas in a textbook by comparing them to ideas in other textbooks you have read. You may notice the strategies a writer uses in the text, such as the writer's use of quotations from particular sources, when you read to analyze.
3. **To critique.** Critical reading involves critiquing, or evaluating, a text. You might critique the message, the way the message was constructed, and so on. Evaluating or critiquing requires determining how effectively the writer presents the message, conveys it, and in the case of argument, succeeds in persuading. When you read critically, you notice not only the rhetorical components in the text, but also the strength of those components.

Teaching Resources
See the Instructor's Manual (IM) for suggestions about how to teach this chapter, and consider assigning this chapter's test-bank quiz.

Co-requisite Teaching Tip
Students who struggle with reading will have an especially difficult time reading rhetorically. Consider working on literal comprehension in the co-requisite section while students work on rhetorical and critical reading in the composition section.

Additionally, assign the appropriate sections of Handbook 1 to help students who struggle with literal comprehension.

The IM includes additional suggestions.

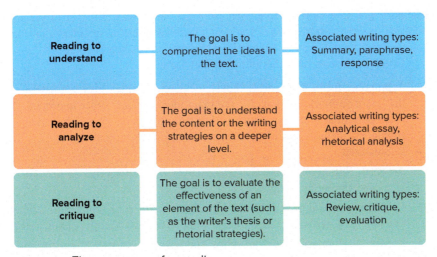

FIGURE 2.1 Three purposes for reading.

Co-requisite Teaching Tip

If summary writing is not covered in the composition section, consider teaching this skill in the co-requisite section. See the IM for the rationale and more explanation.

All three types of reading—to understand, analyze, and critique—are part of a rhetorical reading process. In this chapter, we will briefly examine each purpose, and in later chapters you will practice reading for all three purposes.

READING TO UNDERSTAND, SUMMARIZE, AND RESPOND

The most fundamental goal of reading is reading to understand. Some texts are easily read and understood. For example, a well-written recipe should be easily understood. Other texts, however, are more difficult and require more effort. Reading for understanding means reading in such a way that you can articulate the writer's main point and the support provided for that point. To really understand a text, you need to understand the words the writer uses and the ideas the writer presents.

One way to make sure you understand what you read is to summarize the text. The goal of a **summary** is to find and articulate the main ideas in a text; thus, to write a summary, you have to read a text with an eye toward identifying the main ideas and putting them into your own words. You may find that as you write a summary, you engage in a recursive process, that is, a process that is circular. For example, you may attempt to write the main idea only to find that you need to return to the text to understand more fully how certain details fit in. You may then decide to reword the main idea so that it more accurately articulates the text's **thesis**, the main idea the writer hopes to convey.

summary: A shortened version of a text that presents basic source information, the writer's thesis, and the major lines of support for the thesis.

thesis: The main idea of a text. When stated directly in a sentence, it is called a *thesis statement*.

Summary writing is a skill that is transferable to many writing situations. In the workplace, reports often begin with an *executive summary,* a condensed version of the entire report. Employment cover letters include a summary of a candidate's skills and abilities, and minutes of a meeting summarize what was said during the meeting. In academic writing, summaries are used in the research process. For example, as you read articles for a research project, creating a short summary of each article will help you remember the writer's ideas. You may even use a short summary you have written (or a portion of one) in a research paper to provide information from a source. When you read a textbook, creating summaries of what you read can provide handy reminders of the main ideas you encounter.

Good summaries have the following four features:

1. **Appropriate focus.** Summaries should focus on the main idea (or thesis), the major supporting points for the main idea, and any other important ideas presented after, or in conjunction with, the main idea. Summaries should *not* include any information not found in the text being summarized.

2. **Accuracy.** Summaries must correctly identify the writer's message (main idea) and the writer's support for that message.

3. **Objectivity.** A summary does not express the opinion of the person writing the summary. It simply recounts the ideas in the text that are summarized.

4. **Brevity.** A summary should be short. The goal is to express the main point and major supporting points in a concise way.

Writing a Summary

What follows are six steps for writing a summary, as well as the work that student Jose Baracos completes to write a summary. (For help figuring out a text's main idea and major supporting details, see "Improving Your Reading Skills" in the Handbook section.) Jose's assignment was to read and summarize one to two pages from one of his college textbooks. He chose a passage from a textbook he is reading for his mass communications class. The passage, reprinted in this section, comes from Stanley Baran's *Introduction to Mass Communication.* When Jose did some research about the rhetorical situation, he learned that Baran is a professor of communications at Bryant University. He has a Ph.D. in communication research and has widely published on topics ranging from television violence to online journalism.

As you read the six steps for writing a summary, notice how Jose responds to each one, and then read Jose's complete summary, which you can use as a model for your own summary writing assignments.

Step 1: Read and annotate the source. Read the source carefully, making sure you understand how the ideas in it relate to each other. Make a note of the topic, and annotate the thesis statement (if it is stated explicitly) and major supporting details. If these elements are not stated explicitly, put them into your own words in marginal annotations. Notice how Jose annotated the passage from Baran's text.

> **Co-requisite Teaching Tip**
> In the co-requisite section, assign the appropriate parts of Handbook 1, Improving Your Reading Skills, that cover annotation strategies.
>
> **Teaching Resources**
> The PowerPoint "Effective Annotation Strategies" can also help students master this skill.
> A homework exercise "Annotating Effectively" is also available.

Interpreting Intentional Imprecision
Stanley Baran

Passage	Annotations
Advertisers often **use intentional imprecision in words and phrases to say something other than the precise truth,** and they do so in all forms of advertising—profit and nonprofit, scrupulously honest and less so. **There are three categories of intentional imprecision: unfinished statements, qualifiers, and connotatively loaded words and expressions.** **We are all familiar with unfinished statements,** such as the one for the battery that "lasts twice as long." Others include "You can be sure if it's Westinghouse," "Magnavox gives you more," and "Easy-Off makes oven cleaning easier." A literate advertising consumer should ask, "Twice as long as what?" "Of what can I be sure?" "Gives me more of what?" "Easier than what?" Better, more, stronger, whiter,	Topic: Intentional Imprecision Definition of intentional imprecision Thesis statement First type—unfinished statements Examples

faster—all are comparative adjectives whose true purpose is to create a comparison between two or more things. When the other half of the comparison is not identified, intentional imprecision is being used to create the illusion of comparison.

Qualifiers are words that limit a claim. A product helps relieve stress, for instance. It may not relieve stress as well as rest and better planning and organization. But once the qualifier "helps" appears, an advertiser is free to make just about any claim for the product because all the ad really says is that it helps, not that it does anything in and of itself. It's the consumer's fault for misreading. A product may fight grime, but there is no promise that it will win. In the statement "Texaco's coal gasification process could mean you won't have to worry about how it affects the environment," "could" relieves the advertiser of all responsibility. "Could" does not mean "will." Moreover, the fact that you could stop worrying about the environment does not mean the product does not harm the environment—only that you could stop worrying about it.

Some qualifiers are more apparent. "Taxes not included," "limited time only," "only at participating locations," "prices may vary," "some assembly required," "additional charges may apply," and "batteries not included" are qualifiers presented after the primary claims have been made. Often these words are spoken quickly at the end of radio and television commercials, or they appear in small print on the screen or at the bottom of a newspaper or magazine ad.

Other qualifiers are part of the product's advertising slogan. Boodles gin is "the ultra-refined British gin that only the world's costliest methods could produce. Boodles. The world's costliest British gin." After intimating that the costliest methods are somehow necessary to make the best gin, this advertiser qualifies its product as the costliest "British" gin. There may be costlier, and possibly better, Irish, U.S., Russian, and Canadian gins. Many sugared children's cereals employ the tactic of displaying the cereal on a table with fruit, milk, and toast. The announcer says or the copy reads, "Coco Yummies are a part of this complete breakfast"—so is the tablecloth. But the cereal, in and of itself, adds little to the nutritional completeness of the meal. It is "a part of" it.

How unfinished statements work

Second type—qualifiers

Example of "helps"

More examples

More apparent qualifiers

Presented after primary claims

Qualifiers that are part of slogans

Examples

| Advertising is full of words that are connotatively loaded. | Third type—connotatively loaded words |
Best-selling may say more about a product's advertising and distribution system than its quality. More of the pain-relieving medicine doctors prescribe most means aspirin. Cherry-flavored products have no cherries in them. On the ecolabeling front, no additives is meaningless; the manufacturer decides what is and is not an additive. Cruelty free—again, the company decides. Other connotatively loaded ecolabels are hypoallergenic (advertiser-created, scientific-sounding, and meaningless), fragrance free (you can't smell the scent because of the chemicals used to hide it), nontoxic (won't kill you, but could cause other health problems), and earth smart, green, and nature's friend—all meaningless. Advertisers want consumers to focus on the connotation, not the actual meaning of these words.

Examples

Words have certain connotations but are actually meaningless

Intentional imprecision is puffery. It is not illegal; neither is it sufficiently troubling to the advertising industry to warrant self-regulatory limits. But puffery is neither true nor accurate, and its purpose is to deceive. This means that the responsibility for correctly and accurately reading advertising that is intentionally imprecise rests with the media-literate consumer.

Conclusion—puffery (exaggerated language to help sell a product or idea)

Consumer has a responsibility

Step 2: Create an outline. By outlining the source, you will have most of the information you need to write a summary. Jose has created an outline that includes the main idea of the passage (thesis statement), the major supporting points, and the details that support each major supporting point. (For help writing an outline, see "FAQ: How to Outline a Text" later in this chapter.)

Jose's Outline

Thesis statement: There are three categories of intentional imprecision: unfinished statements, qualifiers, and connotatively loaded words and expressions.

Major Supporting Point 1: Unfinished statements are statements that sound meaningful but really do not contain enough information to mean anything.

- Provides examples of unfinished statements
- Some unfinished statements are comparative in nature but don't really compare

(Continued on next page)

> **Major Supporting Point 2:** The use of qualifiers can also lead to intentional imprecision.
> - Defines "qualifier"
> - Qualifiers are often vague
> - Some appear after the claim
> - Some are part of the slogan
>
> **Major Supporting Point 3:** Another way advertisers create intentional imprecision is to use connotatively loaded words.
> - Provides examples
> - Use of words with positive connotations

Step 3: Start with source information. Your summary should present source information, including

- Author's name and credentials, if available
- Title of the source (use quotation marks for an article title; italics for a book title)
- Type of publication (specify book or journal; use italics for journal titles)

Jose begins his summary with one sentence that offers source information.

> In his textbook *Introduction to Mass Communication*, Stanley Baran, professor of communications at Bryant University, wrote a short section called "Interpreting Intentional Imprecision."

Co-requisite Teaching Tip
Consider reviewing how to quote accurately and grammatically. More information on this topic is available in Chapter 11.

Step 4: Present the main idea. If you find a thesis statement, you can quote it, or you can write the main idea in your own words. Jose has found a sentence in Baran's first paragraph that Jose considers as the main idea, so he quotes it.

> Baran suggests that "There are three categories of intentional imprecision: unfinished statements, qualifiers, and connotatively loaded words and expressions."

Step 5: Present the major supporting points. A writer supports the main idea with major supporting points. Include each major supporting point in your summary. Sometimes a point is not clear unless additional information is provided. In the sentences that follow, Jose added an example to help clarify the concept of "unfinished statements." He put the ideas into his own words.

> Unfinished statements are statements that sound meaningful but really do not contain enough information to mean anything. Baran provides an example: "You can be sure if it's Westinghouse." Baran points out that critical readers will ask, "Of what can I be sure?"

Step 6: Tell how the source ends. End your summary by briefly noting how the writer ends his or her article. Jose provides this information in a single sentence that ends his summary.

> Baran ends his article by reminding readers that consumers must be responsible and media-literate to be able to identify puffery in the form of intentional imprecision.

Teaching Suggestion Consider assigning the Power of Process activity "Writing a Summary," available in Connect. The exercise presents a reading and leads students through each step in the summary writing process so that they finish with a complete summary.

A Model Summary

Here is a Jose's complete summary of the passage from Baran's textbook composed for a freshman composition class.

Baracos 1

Jose Baracos
Prof. Walsh
ENGL 1301
15 October 2020

A Summary of "Interpreting Intentional Imprecision"

In his textbook *Introduction to Mass Communication*, Stanley Baran, Professor of Communications at Bryant University, wrote a short section called "Interpreting Intentional Imprecision." Baran suggests that three types of advertisements are intentionally imprecise and that consumers need to be aware of how these advertisements work. The first type of ad Baran addresses is the "unfinished statement." Unfinished statements are statements that sound meaningful but really do not contain enough information to mean anything. Baran provides an example: "You can be sure if it's Westinghouse." Baran points out that critical readers will ask, "Of

— Source information
— Main idea
— First major supporting point

[Annotation — Second and third major supporting points]: what can I be sure?" A second type of intentional imprecision is the use of qualifiers such as *could* and *helps*. Finally, Baran addresses words that have power because of their connotations.

Baran points out that advertisers hope consumers will focus on the connotations rather than the actual meanings of the words being used in ads.

[Annotation — How the passage concludes]: Baran ends by reminding readers that consumers must be responsible and media-literate to be able to identify puffery in the form of intentional imprecision.

Baracos 2

Work Cited

Baran, Stanley. *Introduction to Mass Communication.* McGraw-Hill, 2018.

Teaching Resources
To support the development of summary writing, consider using the assignment "Kim's Summary: What Went Wrong?"

▶ **ACTIVITY 1 Summarizing in Real Life**

How might being able to write an accurate and concise summary help you in each of these scenarios? Explain your answer.

1. You are a supervisor and one of your employees has repeatedly violated company policies.
2. You are seeing a new doctor who will be taking over the care of a chronic condition you have.
3. You are going to court to contest a traffic ticket.

Teaching Suggestion
Consider assigning one of the summary and response writing prompts that follow some of the readings in Part 6. A detailed list of writing prompts is available in the IM.

Writing a Response

A common academic assignment is to compose a summary and response paper. Such a paper includes (1) a summary of a text and (2) a response to the ideas in the text. While summaries should *not* include the writer's opinion, summary and response papers *do* require the writer to comment on what he or she has read and summarized.

Responses may be personal or they may focus on a particular aspect of the text that was summarized. For instance, a computer science instructor may ask students to read and summarize an article about a new technology and to then respond to the article by reflecting on how the technology could change the way people use computers. To write a response to a text, consider the questions in Rhetorical Toolbox 2.1.

RHETORICAL TOOLBOX 2.1
Responding to a Text

1. **Message.** How do you feel about the writer's main idea? Is it an idea with which you agree or disagree? Why?
2. **Significance.** What is something new that you learned from the text you summarized? How relevant or important is this knowledge?
3. **Related issues.** What related issues did you think of as you read the text? What are the relationships between the issues, and how does the main idea of the text affect these related issues?
4. **Point of view and level of formality.** Should you write in first person? Third person? Should the response focus on your personal reactions? Should it be more targeted?

A Model Response

As we saw, Jose wrote a summary of "Interpreting Intentional Precision" for a mass communications class. If Jose had been required to write a summary and response paper, he could have written a response like the one that follows. This response would be placed immediately after the conclusion paragraph of the summary.

> Baran's explanations of intentional imprecision are fascinating and have the power to change the way people think when they read advertisements and see marketing. I know that I have not always been a critical thinker when it comes to advertising. I have never thought about intentional imprecision, but after reading Baran's article, I have seen this marketing technique everywhere. For example, this morning on my commute to college I saw a billboard advertising a local beer. It says "more flavor, more character." I immediately thought, "More flavor than what?" And then I analyzed the word "character." What does that word even mean when applied to a beer? The meaning is really imprecise, and I think that's how the writers wanted it. The idea of character is that something local has more character (whatever that means) than something that is mass produced. I guess I'm supposed to feel like something with character will taste better, but that really doesn't make sense. Baran's explanation helped me to see the billboard in a different way.
>
> I think that the way Baran encourages people to read ads goes deeper than advertisements, though. I think he wants people to think critically about

> everything, or maybe that's just how I am feeling because I am taking college classes that constantly challenge the way I think. I used to take most ads at face value, but Baran's ideas helped me to see that there is more to an advertisement than meets the eye.

Jose's response is informal; he uses first person, talks about his experiences on his commute to college, and relates his personal college experiences to the reading. When you are assigned a summary and response paper, determine the level of formality required in the response. Analyzing the assignment and the rhetorical situation will help you formulate a response that is appropriate.

READING TO ANALYZE

Analysis is used for a wide variety of purposes. We might analyze a text by examining each of the writer's points or by comparing the text to others that are similar. Because this text is about developing a writer's mindset, we will focus here on **rhetorical analysis**, an examination of the strategies a writer uses to accomplish a writing purpose. In Part 4 of this text, you will learn how to write a complete rhetorical analysis. For now, it is important to start analyzing the texts you read from a writer's mindset.

rhetorical analysis: An examination of the strategies a writer uses to create an effective message.

Analyzing a text rhetorically starts with a consideration of the writer's purpose. A writer's purpose in creating a text may be to explain a concept. Alternatively, a writer may want to critique an idea, a product, or a movie. Often, writers compose texts that reflect on the world or on their lives, and creative writers present their thoughts in fiction and poetry, which are types of writing that engage and entertain readers. Student writers often are asked to compose texts for the purpose of expressing, supporting, and defending their positions on issues.

Regardless of their purposes for writing, writers use rhetorical strategies to convey their ideas to particular audiences. Any writing decision—a writing move, we might say—designed to help the writer communicate effectively with a reader is a rhetorical strategy. For example:

- A writer may select words with emotional connotations to help readers feel a certain way about a topic; this is a rhetorical strategy.
- A writer presenting complex information may use bulleted lists to help readers process the information more easily: this, too, is a rhetorical strategy.
- A writer may use quotations to sound more authoritative or to aid the reader's understanding of a concept. The choice to use quotations is also a rhetorical strategy.

Teaching Suggestion
Students may need help understanding the purpose of rhetorical analysis versus the purpose of more traditional analysis assignments (the kind covered in Chapter 7). Consider having students compare and contrast a rhetorical analysis with an analysis of a subject, such as the analysis of types of student financial aid.

Reading a text rhetorically involves analyzing the text to find rhetorical strategies such as these. Once you find rhetorical strategies, you will be able to analyze how they work.

Analyzing the Rhetorical Situation

To read a text rhetorically, start by analyzing its rhetorical situation. Let's return to "Intentional Imprecision," the textbook passage Jose summarized. Using the questions from Rhetorical Toolbox 1.1 in Chapter 1 is a helpful way to start reading for rhetorical analysis.

1. **Speaker or writer.** Who is the speaker or writer? What values, beliefs, or personal interests of the speaker or writer can help you understand the message?

   The speaker is a professor of communications at Bryant University. We can assume that he knows a lot about the topic. Although we can't figure out much about his beliefs or personal interests, it's clear that by trying to educate students about advertising techniques that are deceptive, he values critical thinking.

2. **Message.** What is the message? What is the purpose of the message? In other words, what does the speaker or writer hope to accomplish with this message? What is its immediate situation? What is the broader context?

   The message conveys that intentional imprecision is used to deceive consumers and to sell products. The purpose of the message is probably to educate students, but it may also be to help them become better consumers and more critical thinkers. The immediate situation is the need to educate students. The broader context is the world in which we live, a world where we are bombarded by advertisements that can be confusing and deceptive.

3. **Audience.** Who is the intended audience? How does the writer attempt to meet the audience's needs or craft the message for this specific audience? What genre does the speaker or writer select for a message to this audience? Why is the genre appropriate?

   The speaker is a textbook writer, so we can assume he is writing for students. The selection comes from a textbook, and students are likely to read textbooks. Because readers are students, Baran provides examples and definitions to aid understanding.

After you have considered the Rhetorical Situation Questions, you can do a more in-depth analysis focusing on the rhetorical strategies the writer uses.

Analyzing Rhetorical Strategies

By answering the Rhetorical Situation Questions, we figured out that the writer hopes to educate students and help them think critically about advertisements. Any analysis should start with a clear statement of the writer's thesis. Jose articulated the thesis: "Baran suggests that three types of advertisements are intentionally imprecise and that consumers need to be aware of how these advertisements work." Now we can analyze the text to figure out *how* Baran tried to get that message across to readers.

Let's examine two of Baran's body paragraphs. The annotations point out some of the rhetorical choices Baran makes. As you read, think about how these choices help Baran educate students about how qualifiers work to create intentional imprecision.

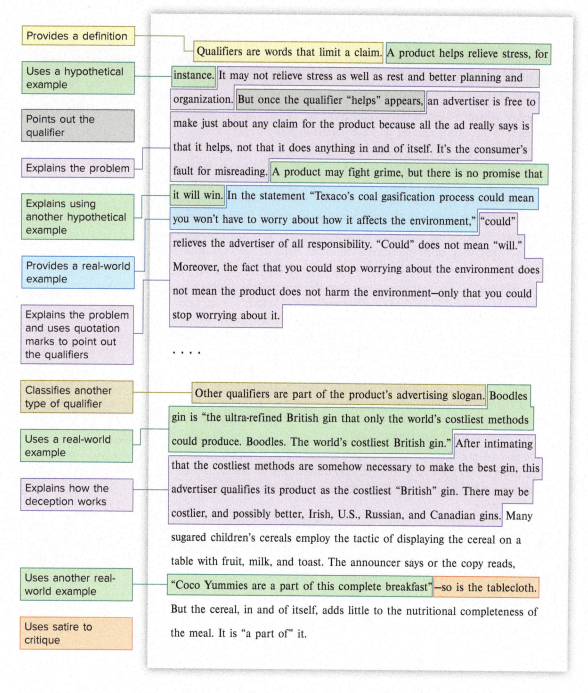

Analyzing Baran's text to figure out the rhetorical strategies he uses leads us to several insights:

- The primary way Baran presents the information is by providing hypothetical and real-world examples.

- He often follows up the examples with explanations.
- On one occasion, he uses satire.

Once you have identified these kinds of writing moves, you can more fully analyze each one by asking, *Why does the writer use this strategy?* Rhetorical Toolbox 2.2 presents two questions you can use to begin a rhetorical analysis. We will answer both questions for the four strategies we have identified from Baran's text.

> **RHETORICAL TOOLBOX 2.2**
> ## Reading to Analyze Rhetorical Strategies
>
> 1. **Strategies.** What strategies does the writer use to make sure the audience understands and/or accepts the message?
> 2. **Purposes.** For each strategy you have identified, answer these questions: Why does the writer use the strategy? In other words, how does the writer hope the strategy will work to help convey the message to the audience?

When we answer the questions in Rhetorical Toolbox 2.2 for Baran's text, we engage in rhetorical analysis. Here are some possible answers for the questions:

Strategy	Purpose
1. The primary way Baran presents the information is by providing hypothetical and real-world examples.	Since this is a textbook and Baran is writing to help students understand, he probably uses examples that will aid understanding. He uses hypothetical examples because they are easy to understand, and then by following up with real-world examples, Baran shows that these deceptive claims do exist. By bringing real-life claims that students may have heard of before, Baran subtly makes the point that learning to critique these claims is a skill that can affect students' real lives and decision-making processes. This makes the reading and topic relevant.
2. He often follows up the examples with explanations.	Baran uses explanations because he does not assume readers will necessarily understand what he's pointing out in the examples. These explanations are used primarily to aid understanding.
3. On one occasion, he uses satire.	Satire creates a gently mocking tone in the passage where Baran uses it. The use of satire is a subtle attempt to make fun of the faulty thinking involved in the advertisement's logic. The satire may also be an attempt to nudge the reader into thinking that he or she should think more critically.

When you read a text rhetorically, you begin to see strategies and writing moves. You can then analyze these moves to try to figure out the purpose for writer's methods. In Part 4 of this text, you will use this kind of analysis to write a rhetorical analysis essay. For now, work on developing your writer's mindset by reading to analyze in addition to reading to understand. As you read texts, mark a few of the strategies the writer uses to accomplish his or her purpose. You will eventually begin to use those strategies when you write your own texts.

▶ **ACTIVITY 2** Thinking Rhetorically

A student is taking a mid-term exam in political science. One essay question asks her to explain criticism of the Electoral College. She provides an explanation, but she also uses this strategy: she adds names of the scholars who have been most influential in the criticism. How might using this strategy help the writer achieve her writing purpose?

READING TO CRITIQUE

A critique is an evidence-based evaluation of something: a text, a performance, a movie, a song, a restaurant, and so on. You have probably looked at product reviews online or read movie reviews before selecting a movie to watch. And you have probably read reviews that you have disagreed with. A critique or review presents the writer's point of view on the quality of the subject being reviewed. To write a convincing critique, a writer must explain how he or she evaluated the subject and must provide evidence for the judgment he or she presents. In later chapters, you will learn how to write an evaluative essay, a type of critique.

As you work to develop your writer's mindset, you will start critiquing the texts you encounter. A critique of a text might focus on the ideas, or on the organization, the examples, and even the individual words the writer chooses. Once you understand a text and identify the rhetorical strategies a writer is using, you can begin to critically evaluate the effectiveness of those strategies.

For instance, you know that Baran's piece, "Interpreting Intentional Imprecision," is written for the purpose of teaching students about how deceptive advertising works. If you were to write a critique of Baran's piece, you might ask the question, *How effectively does Baran's piece accomplish its purpose?* To answer that question, you might examine some of the rhetorical strategies you found when you analyzed the text. For instance, we saw that Baran uses examples and explanations to explain concepts that could be difficult to understand. Is Baran's use of examples and explanation sufficient? Or would students likely need more explanation? Is his use of satire effective at helping students understand the concept, or might the use of satire confuse students? These are the kinds of questions you focus on as you critique a text. In the chapters that follow, you will be prompted to find the rhetorical strategies that make texts effective and to use some of those same strategies in your own writing.

USING RHETORICAL READING TO BECOME A BETTER WRITER

Good writers are almost always people who read a lot. Why? When you read something, you are influenced not only by the content but also by the strategies the writer uses to convey his or her thoughts. When you write, your unconscious mind pulls up what you have read or heard, and you intuitively imitate those texts. You have already seen how Stanley Baran uses a pattern of providing examples followed by explanations to help readers understand ideas that may be new or foreign. You may find that the next time you are writing to inform, you use the same method Baran used. The more exposure you have to writing strategies, the more likely you are to use them yourself. While these strategies are influential on an unconscious level, you can also use them intentionally. By intentionally analyzing the writing moves in the texts you read, you will become more aware of moves that are available to you as a writer.

As you work through the chapters in this text, you will learn more about how to analyze and critique texts from a writer's mindset. To begin this process, use the steps shown in Figure 2.2 when you read texts.

As you become better at reading texts rhetorically, you will become more aware of the methods writers use for communication and persuasion. The remaining chapters in this text discuss many more rhetorical strategies. Take the initiative to try some of these strategies in your own writing.

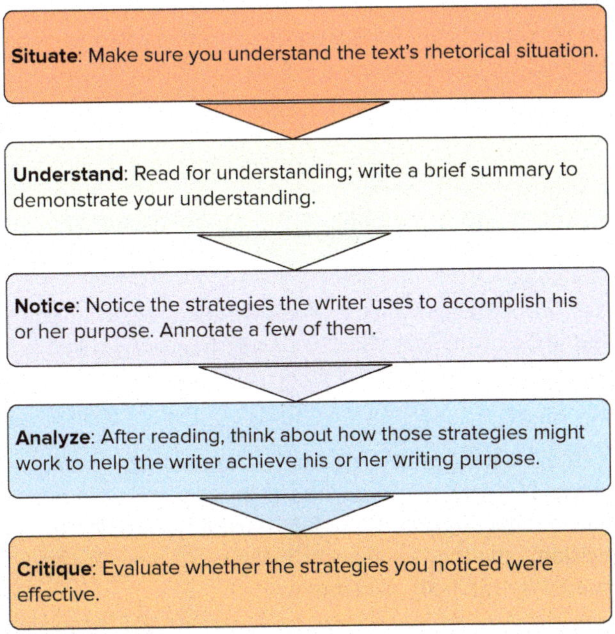

Situate: Make sure you understand the text's rhetorical situation.

Understand: Read for understanding; write a brief summary to demonstrate your understanding.

Notice: Notice the strategies the writer uses to accomplish his or her purpose. Annotate a few of them.

Analyze: After reading, think about how those strategies might work to help the writer achieve his or her writing purpose.

Critique: Evaluate whether the strategies you noticed were effective.

FIGURE 2.2 Reading rhetorically.

CHAPTER PROJECT Reading to Understand, Analyze, and Critique

PROJECT 1 Reading for Understanding

Complete the same assignment Jose completed: Select one to two pages from one of your texts and summarize and respond to it.

PROJECT 2 Reading for Analysis

Read the article, "The Fracking of Rachel Carson: *Silent Spring's* Lost Legacy, Told in Fifty Parts," by Sandra Steingraber, found in Part 6 of this text. What is Steingraber's purpose for writing? Identify two writing strategies Steingraber uses to help achieve her purpose. Explain her purpose and the two strategies you identified in a paragraph or two.

PROJECT 3 Reading for Critiquing

Read the article, "The Fracking of Rachel Carson: *Silent Spring's* Lost Legacy, Told in Fifty Parts," by Sandra Steingraber, found in Part 6 of this text. The writer uses a unique format: she creates fifty parts—small paragraphs—to support her point. Do you think this is an effective method to present her thesis? Why or why not? Respond in one paragraph.

Reflecting to Develop a Writer's Mindset

In Chapter 1, you learned that rhetoric is the use of tools and strategies to convey a message or to persuade. What did you learn in this chapter that helps you to understand the concept of rhetoric more fully? How does reading a text contribute to rhetorical awareness and the development of a writer's mindset?

FAQ OUTLINING A TEXT

Co-requisite Teaching Tip
Some co-requisite students will struggle with outlining. Consider having students practice this skill. Use the "Try It" exercise that follows this FAQ.

The most important skill in outlining someone else's writing is figuring out the relationships among the ideas in the text. Here are some frequently asked questions about outlining.

1. **What is the main idea?**

   The main idea or thesis statement of a reading is the point the writer makes about the topic. As such, the main idea is broader than the points that support it. For example, in the textbook passage for "Interpreting Intentional Imprecision," the thesis statement includes *all three* of the topics that are covered by the body paragraphs:

   > There are three categories of intentional imprecision: unfinished statements, qualifiers, and connotatively loaded words and expressions.

Because the thesis statement mentions "three categories," it is considered a broader statement than a sentence that mentions only one category. Start your outline by clearly noting the thesis statement.

2. **What are the main lines of support?**

As you read the body paragraphs, find the main lines of support for the thesis statement. These lines of support may be reasons, but they may alternatively be factors, principles, considerations, and so on. Sometimes writers do not tell you the type of support they are providing. In such cases, you must read the body paragraphs, find the major supporting points, and figure out the type of support the writer is using. In "Interpreting Intentional Imprecision," we know that the writer presents three categories, and we might expect to find a topic sentence that clearly presents each category.

First line of support. As we look for a topic sentence for Baran's first point—his point about unfinished statements—the *last* sentence of the second paragraph is the topic sentence: *When the other half of the comparison is not identified, intentional imprecision is being used to create the illusion of comparison.*

Second line of support. However, finding a topic sentence for Baran's next point is not accomplished so easily. This point is about qualifiers. He devotes three paragraphs to explaining qualifiers and how they work, so we can treat all three paragraphs as pertaining to the same topic. However, there is no single sentence that sums up what Baran is saying in these paragraphs. The only sentence in the paragraph that provides a partial overview of the content of the three paragraphs is the first one:

> Qualifiers are words that limit a claim. A product helps relieve stress, for instance. It may not relieve stress as well as rest and better planning and organization. But once the qualifier "helps" appears, an advertiser is free to make just about any claim for the product because all the ad really says is that it helps, not that it does anything in and of itself. It's the consumer's fault for misreading. A product may fight grime, but there is no promise that it will win. In the statement "Texaco's coal gasification process could mean you won't have to worry about how it affects the environment," "could" relieves the advertiser of all responsibility. "Could" does not mean "will." Moreover, the fact that you could stop worrying about the environment does not mean the product does not harm the environment—only that you could stop worrying about it.

The problem is, the first sentence doesn't tell us how qualifiers are problematic. The first sentence, "Qualifiers are words that limit a claim," is simply a definition. In this case, we will write a topic sentence that states Baran's point about qualifiers:

> The use of qualifiers can also lead to intentional imprecision.

Third line of support. The final major supporting point should be about connotations because a single, long paragraph presents connotations and how they function as intentional imprecision. In the paragraph, the first and the last sentences are general enough to tell readers the major supporting point. Notice that the sentences in between are very specific:

> Advertising is full of words that are connotatively loaded. Best-selling may say more about a product's advertising and distribution system than its quality. More of the pain-relieving medicine doctors prescribe most means aspirin. Cherry-flavored products have no cherries in them. On the ecolabeling front, no additives is meaningless; the manufacturer decides what is and is not an additive. Cruelty free—again, the company decides. Other connotatively loaded ecolabels are hypoallergenic (advertiser-created, scientific-sounding, and meaningless), fragrance free (you can't smell the scent because of the chemicals used to hide it), nontoxic (won't kill you, but could cause other health problems), and earth smart, green, and nature's friend—all meaningless. Advertisers want consumers to focus on the connotation, not the actual meaning of these words.

To create the third major supporting point for your outline, you can take the two general sentences (highlighted in the passage here) and combine them in your own words into a single sentence that sums up the paragraph:

> Another way advertisers create intentional imprecision is to use connotatively loaded words.

3. What details should be added to an outline?

Once you have identified the writer's main idea and the major supporting points, you can add to your outline. For example, there were three paragraphs about the use of qualifiers. On your outline, underneath Major Supporting Point 2, you can make a list of the details presented in these paragraphs, like this:

- Defines "qualifier"
- Qualifiers are often vague
- Some appear after the claim
- Some are part of the slogan

4. How do you check an outline for accuracy?

Once you have added details to each of the major supporting points, you will have a finished outline. To check the accuracy of your outline, reread the text and stop after each paragraph. Determine whether the ideas in the paragraph fit into one of the major supporting points in your outline. If they do not, you may have skipped a major supporting point. Add it if necessary. Also, make sure you have not confused minor details, such as statistics, examples, and so on, for major supporting points. Major supporting points are broader, more general statements than details. Finally, if any of the sentences in your outline are taken directly from the text, put the sentences in quotation marks to avoid plagiarism.

CHAPTER 2 Reading with a Writer's Mindset

TRY IT!

In Part 6 of this text, find the article, "How Zoos Help Preserve the World's Species for the Future" by Liz Sanchez. Read and annotate the article, and then outline it.

Teaching Suggestion
An outline for this article has been provided in the Instructor Resources. Consider handing out the outline to have students check their work against it.

CREDIT

Page 17. Baran, Stanley J. (2011). *Introduction to Mass Communication: Media Literacy and Culture*. New York: McGraw Hill. Used with permission.

3 Composing with a Writer's Mindset

Connect Adaptive Learning Assignment
Consider using Connect's Adaptive Learning Assignments to support this chapter.

CHAPTER OBJECTIVES

You will learn to:
- Use a recursive writing process.
- Use rhetorical thinking and questioning during all stages of the writing process.
- Describe a writing process that includes planning, drafting, revising, editing, and formatting.
- Develop a personalized writing process.

Teaching Resources
See the Instructor's Manual (IM) for suggestions about how to teach this chapter, and consider assigning this chapter's test-bank quiz.

Creating an amazing product—whether a clay pot, a dog house, a music video, or an essay—requires using an effective process. You may be familiar with the most basic writing process: plan your paper, draft it, and then revise and edit it. But you may not know that *how* you go through that process can have a major effect on your paper's quality—and grade. Many students are tempted to use a "one and done" approach to writing papers: they create a draft and turn it in. This strategy is almost certain to result in writing that is less powerful than it could be and a grade that is less than remarkable.

In addition to using a sound writing process, thinking rhetorically as you plan, draft, and finish your writing projects will make a great difference in the quality of your work. You have seen that part of a writer's mindset consists of being aware of the methods—the rhetorical strategies—that writers use to convey their messages. As a writer, thinking rhetorically means using some of those rhetorical strategies yourself. How can you best communicate your particular message to your audience? Should you include a hypothetical example? Should you present a personal anecdote? Is one word more effective than another word as you try to communicate a certain idea? In this chapter, you will analyze effective writing processes and create a personalized process that puts your writer's mindset to work.

WARM-UP

A recursive process is one that involves multiple steps *and* that requires you to go back and repeat steps occasionally to ensure that the final product will be high quality. Based on this definition, how might painting a room be a recursive process? What would be the steps one would take to paint a room? Which steps would occasionally need to be repeated?

USING A RECURSIVE WRITING PROCESS

Few universal truths about good writing exist, but there is one principle upon which almost all writers agree: to write something that is amazing, you have to use a recursive writing process. A recursive process is one that involves going back to an earlier stage and making changes. If you have ever had to go back and do more research, change your thesis statement, or add or delete sections of your paper, you have used a recursive writing process. While most writers understand this kind of process, few writers use recursive strategies effectively.

One reason for this is that using a recursive writing process requires a lot of engagement. It takes a great deal of mental energy and commitment to write a draft. Going back and deleting or rethinking or redrafting takes even more energy, and frankly, writers are sometimes wary about committing themselves to the task.

So why should you, as a student, engage in a recursive writing process, a process that takes time, commitment, and energy? The most important reason is that doing so changes the way you think: it engages, challenges, and helps to develop your writer's mindset. What makes a person educated? The answer is complex, but in part, education means learning new ways to solve problems, thinking creatively about complex issues, developing rhetorical awareness, and learning to work through difficult tasks to find solutions. The struggle involved in thinking and learning is what causes your brain to develop and change. In the same way that weight lifters push their muscles to the point of fatigue, the work you do in college should at times be uncomfortable. By embracing the difficulty of college work, you are saying *yes* to true brain development.

What does all this have to do with writing? Writing is a complex process that starts with thinking. Thinking your way clear to writing an amazing essay is much like painting a room. You do some prep work and put down a first coat (or a first draft), only to stand back and see flaws and problems. You may have to go back and patch the wall in places. You may decide the paint color is wrong and have to return to the store for a new color. You'll probably get paint on surfaces that require some clean up, and you'll definitely need more than one pass at getting the paint on perfectly. If you have ever seen a room that was painted in a hurry, you know why using a recursive process for painting is important. The same is true for writing. Your instructor is able to tell whether your essay is the result of a rushed effort or whether you truly engaged in a recursive writing process. As you work through the steps of the writing process in this chapter, keep in mind that good writers often return to previous steps. Engaging in the process means accepting the fact that good writing takes time, energy, and investment.

▶ **ACTIVITY 1** **What Went Wrong?**

Think of a project you completed quickly just to finish it, a project that, in the end, did not turn out well. Perhaps you tried to make a pie, build a deck, create a website, or study for a test. In what ways did the process you used affect the final product? Would using a recursive process have helped the project turn out better? Explain your answer.

THINKING RHETORICALLY TO WRITE WELL

When you compose a text with a writer's mindset, you are constantly aware of how your words, organization, and other writing choices affect your readers. The novelist who wants the reader to keep turning the pages has to predict when readers will get bored, the college student must predict the content his instructor will find valuable, and the website manager has to imagine what users might click on. A rhetorical thinking process puts the readers—or clients or web page visitors—at the forefront of the creative process.

One practical way to start any college writing project is to analyze the writing prompt so that you can figure out your instructor's expectations. Analyzing in this way is a rhetorical act: you are thinking about your audience—your instructor—and predicting what he or she will expect in a good paper. Let's look at a writing assignment from the perspective of Alexis Williams, a college student, to examine how she thinks rhetorically about her assignment. Alexis's first-year composition instructor has given the following assignment:

Teaching Suggestion Consider using the "Analyzing a Writing Assignment" exercise to have students think rhetorically about an assignment.

Essay #1 Assignment: Student Perspectives on Social Media

Professors are always investigating teaching methods that work for their students, including using social media. As a student, you have a unique perspective on social media, both for personal and classroom use. A national education journal is going to publish a special issue on student perspectives on social media. This journal is read primarily by college instructors, and your viewpoint as a student will influence their educational practices.

Your first assignment is to write an essay on this topic, using the journal's writing guidelines, which are printed below. This essay will count for a grade in this class, and you are also encouraged to submit it for possible publication in the journal. Here are the guidelines:

> Social media is changing the way we think and the way we teach. For a special issue of our journal, we are soliciting student essays on the topic of social media in the classroom. How can your instructors use social media—such as blogs, social websites, phone apps, YouTube, and the like—effectively for teaching? Specifically, we want to know what works and what doesn't. We value students' opinions and experiences. Submissions must meet these criteria:
>
> - Length: 1000-1500 words
> - The article should be written in first person and should rely primarily on the student's personal experiences with social media used for education.
> - The paper should be formatted according to MLA style.

Here are Alexis's thoughts as she examines the assignment:

> "At first, I felt intimidated by this assignment because it's going to be read by college professors all over the country. But the fact that I could use first person and that the real goal was just to listen to my experiences made me feel more confident. I am going to have to make sure that the way I'm defining 'social media' is right. I didn't think of blogs as social media, but this journal does. Since the description says, 'students' opinions and experiences,' I think the focus of this paper will be persuasive, but the only evidence will be my experiences. To get it published, the paper will need to sound professional, offer some good observations, be grammatically correct, and be written in MLA format."

By thinking rhetorically about the assignment, Alexis has some important insights:

- She will be writing to persuade and will be using her experiences as support for her opinions.
- She will need to be clear about the definition of "social media."
- She will need to write from a student's point of view using first person, but she will need to write for an audience of professors.
- The audience will expect a well-written paper, free of errors and formatted correctly.

With these rhetorical considerations in mind, Alexis can start working through the writing process to craft the best essay possible.

BASIC STAGES IN THE WRITING PROCESS

An effective writing process includes five basic stages: planning, drafting, revising, editing, and formatting (Figure 3.1). Since writing is a recursive process, you can expect to go back and forth between the steps involved in each stage. You may even return to an earlier stage, such as going back to planning while you are drafting. Let's look at each stage in more depth to see how Alexis uses a sound writing process to engage with her assignment.

Stage 1: Planning

Planning involves everything you do before drafting. Read on to see how to think rhetorically as you complete the steps involved in planning your project.

Planning Step 1: Read and annotate the assignment. You have already seen how Alexis completed the first step in the planning process by analyzing the assignment. Notice that Alexis did not merely look at the requirements: she also thought about her message and her audience. Considering these elements of the rhetorical situation helped her to gain some insights into what she needs to do to write an effective essay. As you analyze an assignment, use the questions in Rhetorical Toolbox 3.1.

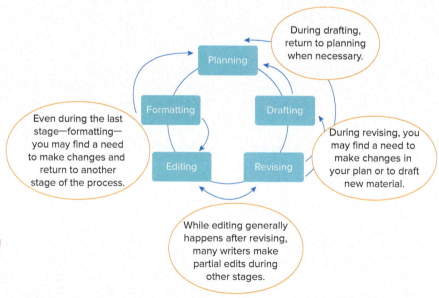

FIGURE 3.1 A recursive writing process.

RHETORICAL TOOLBOX 3.1
Analyzing a Writing Assignment Rhetorically

1. **Purpose.** Why did the instructor create the assignment? What might she be wanting students to demonstrate by completing the assignment?
2. **Genre.** What kind of text will the instructor expect you to submit? How can you tell?
3. **Audience.** Who is the audience?
   A. What is their education level?
   B. What do they already know about the topic?
   C. What expectations will the audience have about genre?
   D. What special considerations will you have to keep in mind to communicate effectively with this audience?
4. **Voice.** Given your purpose, genre, and audience, what kind of voice or persona would be most effective? First person? Third person? (If your instructor has not specified, write in third person, the standard point of view used in academic papers.) Will your presence, as the writer, be apparent, or will you write with an objective tone?
5. **Other rhetorical issues.** What other rhetorical issues should you consider for this assignment?

▶ **ACTIVITY 2** Using the Questions for Analyzing a Writing Assignment

What additional insights might Alexis have had by using the questions in Rhetorical Toolbox 3.1 to analyze her writing assignment?

Planning Step 2: Analyze your instructor's grading rubric or create a guidance rubric. If your instructor has provided a **rubric**, read it carefully. Figure out how you will address each item on the rubric. If you do not have a rubric, you can create a *guidance rubric*. A guidance rubric lists the qualities and features you believe are important for the assignment. This rubric is just for your use, not your instructor's, but it will help you make sure your paper has everything in it. Because it is a personalized rubric, you can add your own personal notes to it. The last item on the rubric is one that Alexis added because she struggles with that grammatical issue.

rubric: A set of criteria used to evaluate an assignment.

Alexis's Guidance Rubric					
	How Well You Met the Requirement (5 best, 1 worst)				
Requirement	5	4	3	2	1
Write a thesis statement that offers my opinion on the value of using social media in teaching.					
Present my own experiences in first person to support my thesis statement.					

(Continued on next page)

(Continued from previous page)

Requirement	How Well You Met the Requirement (5 best, 1 worst)				
	5	4	3	2	1
Make it relevant to professors by showing how tech use affects students and by offering suggestions professors would find useful.					
Put everything in MLA style.					
Check spelling and grammar.					
Read each sentence to find the fragments!!					

Planning Step 3: Do on-the-page and off-the-page prewriting.
On-the-page prewriting activities include making lists, creating idea maps, freewriting (writing down everything you can think of about the topic in a short period of time), and asking journalistic questions (who, what, where, when, why, how).

Off-the-page prewriting consists of conversations and other nonwritten activities. You might talk about your topic with friends, make an appointment to talk with your instructor, or visit a writing lab if your campus has one. Other off-the-page methods of prewriting are researching, recording your thoughts on a voice recorder (freetalking), and letting ideas incubate. Giving ideas time to settle, especially when you are writing about complex topics, can help you achieve clarity before you construct an outline.

Alexis's written prewriting demonstrates that she is not only thinking about content: she is also thinking about how her audience might view that content. This is the kind of rhetorical thinking that will help her write a successful paper.

Alexis's On-the-Page Prewriting
- Social media/tech as a teaching tool—not good
- Not effective—Facebook, Twitter, discussion boards, blogs
- What's the other side of the argument?
- Talk about ways my instructors have used social media in the classroom
- Are there effective methods?
- Professors might disagree. Don't we all learn differently?
- Some instructors may be defensive . . . word it all carefully. Don't want to step on toes.

You can find evidence of Alexis's recursive thinking in her notes. Originally, she had planned to say that social media does not help students learn, but after talking with her friends and doing more prewriting, she realized that she had positive experiences she could include in her paper.

Alexis's Notes

Social media teaching/learning techniques that can be effective:

- Using Twitter to make us write summaries.
- Facebook, when the prof included her recorded lectures and links to helpful YouTube videos.
- Using videoconferencing to go over papers.
- Using online polling to enable us to ask questions or see if we got a question right.

Social media teaching/learning techniques that didn't help:

- Live tweeting in the classroom.
- Having a Facebook class page. Maybe helped with keeping up with work, but it didn't help me learn.
- Discussion board—making me respond to my classmates' ideas just didn't help me.
- Writing a blog that no one ever read.

Planning Step 4: Draft a thesis statement. Your thesis statement is the main idea you hope to convey to readers in your essay. Write your thesis statement in a number of ways. Figure out which version is the most effective in helping readers understand your main idea.

Here are Alexis's attempts to word her thesis statement. She decides to evaluate each thesis statement from a writer's mindset by asking this question: *Which one most accurately conveys to readers the idea I'm trying to communicate?* Examine Alexis's draft thesis statements and her comments on each one.

Alexis's Draft Thesis Statements

- Some social media and technological activities can really contribute to learning, but others do not.
  Alexis's comment: "This is not specific enough. The words 'some' and 'others' may lead the reader to wonder, *which ones?* I'll be telling them in the paper, but this sentence may just leave them hanging too much."
- Facebook, online polling, Twitter, and videoconferencing are social media tools that contribute to learning.
  "This is okay."
- Certain types of social media are more effective learning tools than other types.
  "Reader might ask, *which types?* I'm not being specific enough."
- While social media and technology can be a distraction in the classroom, it can also enhance learning if instructors carefully select the social media and technological tools to use.

(Continued on next page)

Teaching Suggestion
A simple way to present the task of writing a thesis statement is to tell students the thesis consists of the topic and the point they wish to make about the topic. Some students will include every supporting point, which often leads to problems in parallelism. Consider presenting parallelism (in Handbook 2 on writing).

Teaching Resources
Consider using the PowerPoint "What You Need to Know About Thesis Statements."

For students who struggle to write thesis statements, consider assigning the worksheet "Practice Writing Thesis Statements."

(Continued from previous page)

> "Good because this sentence acknowledges that *some* social media/tech can be a problem, and by acknowledging that, I may help win over readers who don't see a place for social media/tech in education. They will know that I see their point but that I have other ideas for them to consider."

Teaching Resources
See the IM for a formal outline of Alexis's essay.

Planning Step 5: Use your prewriting and thesis statement to create an outline. Your outline does not have to be formal in structure. Alexis's outline includes her thesis statement and the support she thinks will work to convince her audience. The column on the right presents some of the rhetorical thinking that helped Alexis decide what to include in her paper.

Alexis's Outline	Alexis's Thinking
Intro Paragraph: Talk about how students are often distracted by social media while they are in class. Explain why instructors may want to use social media as a teaching tool. Lead to thesis statement.	Professors will probably relate to the info in this introduction.
Thesis statement: While social media can be a distraction in the classroom, it can also enhance learning if instructors carefully select the social media tools to use.	Acknowledges that some uses are not effective. Instructors may be interested to keep reading to figure out which tools are effective.
Body Par. 1: Not all social media tools are effective. To be effective, social media has to be social. Some of the social media tools instructors have used are not effective because students don't truly participate. (Talk about my experiences with blogs and discussion boards where students just write something to be done with the assignment.)	Starting with this paragraph makes it clear that I'm not saying ALL tools work. This may make readers find my thesis more believable. Use my personal stories here as support and as a way to add interest.
Body Par. 2: Some social media tools seem to be more of a fun distraction than real learning tools. (Talk about how live tweeting in the classroom ended up being useless to students. Talk about how the classroom Facebook page in one of my classes was pretty useless except for keeping track of assignments.)	Use stories from my own educational experiences but focus on how these social media experiments failed.
Body Par. 3: While not all social media and technology uses are effective in the classroom, one use that truly helped me learn was videoconferencing. (Explain how it was used and how other teachers have used it.)	Instructors may be interested in the details here. I'll include enough details so that they will know how they could use this in their teaching.
Body Par. 4: Finally, texting is a simple tool, but it can be a very helpful way for students to learn. (Explain how we used texting in my English class and how I loved it.)	This is one of the most effective social media tools, so I want to end with it.
Conclusion Paragraph: Maybe offer advice to instructors? (Is that arrogant?) Maybe summarize my ideas?	

Stage 2: Drafting

The goal of drafting is to put your ideas into words, using your outline as a guide and keeping your audience in mind. Use these three steps to draft your paper.

Drafting Step 1: Using your outline, draft paragraphs for the introduction, body, and conclusion. The goal is to simply get your ideas onto the page. While you should not worry about grammar, *do* think about finding the right words to express your thoughts clearly and accurately.

Drafting Step 2: As you draft, reread your paper aloud, thinking of yourself as a reader, not a writer. One goal to keep in mind is *cohesion*. A paper is cohesive when each sentence seems to fit naturally and stay on topic. One way to keep your ideas cohesive is to frequently go back to the beginning of the paragraph you are writing and read what you've composed. This recursive habit will help you see if you have left out content or need to make changes to wording. Further, if you can imagine how a reader would experience what you are reading, you will be able to make rhetorical choices that improve your draft, such as adding explanations, examples, or other types of support readers may need. You can also return to the beginning of your paper and reread it every time you finish writing a paragraph.

Drafting Step 3: When you finish, use peer review to get helpful suggestions. Ideally, have your rough draft finished a week before the final draft is due. During this week, ask someone such as a classmate, relative, or tutor to read your paper and offer suggestions for improvement. Most students have had the experience of reading a paper their instructor graded and thinking, *I didn't mean to say that!* or *I thought I had included an example!* Plan your time wisely so that you have opportunities to improve your draft.

The purpose of **peer review** is to receive feedback from an objective reader so that you can make changes to the content and organization of your draft. Don't focus on grammatical issues: at this stage, the focus should be on ideas. Use the suggestions in Peer Review Toolbox to make peer review a useful activity.

Stage 3: Revising

The key to effective **revising** is *engagement with your draft and your reader*: you have to be willing to make your paper excellent, whether that means starting over, removing whole paragraphs, or adding significant amounts of text. Using the six steps that follow will help you revise effectively.

Revising Step 1: Reread the assignment. Start the revision process by rereading the assignment to make sure your paper meets the requirements.

Revising Step 2: Use a rubric to revise. Using your instructor's rubric, if you have one, or the guidance rubric you have created, revise your paper to meet each objective.

Teaching Suggestion
For peer review, an alternative method is to have students draft a single (but complete) body paragraph. By requiring only one paragraph instead of a complete essay, more students may participate, and the process may not be as overwhelming (and ineffective) as it can be when students are required to bring entire drafts.

Co-requisite Teaching Tip
The co-requisite section is an ideal place to have students learn how to participate in peer review and self-assessment. Consider making these activities a routine part of the co-requisite experience.

peer review: A process for receiving suggestions for revision by exchanging papers with classmates or others and answering a set of specific review questions.

revising: Improving the content, organization, and language of a draft by adding, deleting, moving, and replacing copy.

Teaching Suggestion
See the IM for suggestions about how to ease student anxiety regarding peer review.

PEER REVIEW TOOLBOX

If you are the writer:

- Draft three to four specific questions about the content of your paper you would like answered.
- Ask the peer reviewer to answer the questions and make suggestions for improvement.

If you are the peer reviewer:

- Realize that your comments about content can make a great difference. You do not have to be an English major to offer helpful suggestions about a classmate's paper.
- Do not worry about finding errors in grammar, spelling, formatting, and the like. Focus on the questions you have been given by the writer.
- Read the paper to critique it. That is, read it with an eye toward finding any problems in it. While it may be tempting to write only kind comments, those comments are not helpful to the writer. Peer review is powerful only when reviewers offer honest commentary and constructive criticism.
- Offer suggestions for improving the issues you find. If you think an example would help explain a concept, make that suggestion. If the wording of a section makes it hard to understand, point out the issue and suggest a rewording if one comes to mind.

Helpful Questions for Peer Review

- Is the thesis statement clear? If not, what seems to be the main idea? How could the writer articulate the main idea as a thesis statement?
- Does the paper remain focused on the main idea throughout? If not, where does the paper lose or change focus?
- Does the writer offer enough support for the main idea? If not, what could the writer add to offer additional support?
- Are there any sections that are written unclearly? Or are there any sections that, while written in clear sentences, do not make sense to you? How could the writer improve these areas?
- What is the writer's purpose? (To reflect? Inform? Analyze? Evaluate? Persuade?) How can you tell? Does the writer need to make revisions so that the purpose is realized?
- Is the paper engaging? How could the writer make it more engaging?
- Do the introduction and conclusion paragraphs function effectively? How could the writer improve them?

Using the Peer Reviewer's Suggestions

- When you receive comments from a peer, read each one carefully and figure out whether or not to make revisions. An important part of peer review is evaluating your peers' comments. For example, a peer may suggest that you remove an example, but you may believe the

Teaching Suggestion
Since peer review can be used for many purposes, the questions students use for review are crucial. Consider having students think about the specific purposes of a specific peer review session and create the questions themselves—in class, collaboratively. Doing so may result in greater engagement in the peer review process.

Teaching Suggestion
The importance of formative feedback in the teaching of writing cannot be overstated. For an overview of how to use formative feedback in the assessment process, see "How to Grade Writing Effectively: An Overview of the Research," in the IM.

> example is critical and should stay. Try to figure out why your peer suggested you remove the example. Perhaps you need to tie the example to the point you are making in the paragraph. Analyze and make decisions about each suggestion for revision.

Revising Step 3: Revise to help readers understand your thesis and support. Keeping your audience in mind, use these questions as a guide to make revisions that enhance your thesis statement and support.

- **Would a reader be able to identify my main idea?** If not, reword your thesis statement or change its location so that readers will be able to find it.
- **Would a reader be able to find the support for my main idea?** If not, revise topic sentences so that your supporting points are clear and identifiable.
- **Where might a reader need more explanation to understand fully my ideas?** If needed, add details, examples, or explanations.
- **Would a reader need additional support to agree with my thesis statement?** If so, add additional support paragraphs. Consider using a rhetorical pattern, such as a brief story, a definition, a comparison, and so on, as additional support for a point. See Chapter 4 for more details about the rhetorical patterns you can use as support.

Revising Step 4: Revise to help readers follow your ideas. Use these questions to revise for organization:

- **Are there parts of my essay that do not fit—that do not relate to my main idea?** If so, remove them.
- **Would placing my thesis statement earlier in the essay help readers understand my points?** If so, make this change.
- **Have I used transitions effectively to help readers follow my organization?** Add transitions if necessary.

Revising Step 5: Revise to enhance clarity. Clarity begins at the level of sentences. Someone once said that being a good writer requires using the perfect word in the perfect spot all the time. While you do not have to aim for perfection, do aim to make each sentence clear. One good habit is to find the three sentences in your composition that you feel are the weakest in terms of clarity and to rewrite each one. For tips on how to write clearer sentences, see "FAQ: Writing with Clarity" at the end of this chapter.

Revising Step 6: Revise to meet readers' needs and desires. Readers expect an introduction that is appropriate for the topic. They expect a conclusion that brings a sense of closure, a sense that the essay is finished and can come to an end. (For help in writing effective introductions and conclusions, see the

FAQ section in Chapter 6.) In addition, readers want an essay that is pleasing to read. Use these questions to guide your revision:

- **Can I improve the introduction by using a different method?** If so, review the methods for writing introductions provided in the Handbook and revise.
- **Does the conclusion leave readers with a sense of closure, the idea that the essay has finished and should end?** If not, review the methods for writing conclusions in Chapter 6, and revise your conclusion paragraph.
- **Have I used language in pleasing ways?** For example, when you read your essay aloud, does it sound smoothly written or choppy, monotonous, or varied? If appropriate, have you used metaphors and other figurative language to enhance meaning? If humor is appropriate to your subject matter, have you used it? Which parts of your writing are you particularly proud of? Revise until you have at least a few sentences or paragraphs you believe are particularly pleasing.

Revising Step 7: Revise using suggestions from peers or your instructor. Having another person read your paper and provide suggestions for revision can be invaluable. Instead of imagining what a reader will think, you will have comments from a genuine reader. Use the Peer Review Toolbox to participate in the peer review process.

Alexis's Revision Choices. By using a thorough revising process as well as peer review, Alexis revised her rough draft. What follows are some of the revisions Alexis made and her reasons for doing so.

> **Alexis, on revising her introduction:** "I felt like the intro in the rough draft was flat and boring. The lemonade saying is a cliché. So I decided to describe a scene and then ask a question. The rest of the intro answers that question and leads to my thesis statement. I also made the decision to break the intro into two paragraphs. It just seemed too long, and since the second paragraph answers the question in the first part, it made sense to divide the two paragraphs where I did."

Rough Draft of Introduction Paragraph	Revision
Social media and smartphone technology have enriched our lives in many ways but these new tools have also caused a few problems. One of these problems is distraction. So some professors have decided that when life gives you lemons, you have to make lemonade. They have embraced	As I sit in my college history class and look around the room, I do not see students furiously taking notes. I see very few students who are even looking at the instructor or their notepads. I see, instead, fingers flying on smartphones, as students silently text their friends. I see the distracted

social media as a learning tool, allowing students to keep their phones out and to use them. These instructors realize that while social media can be a distraction in the classroom, it can also enhance learning if they carefully select the social media tools to use.

half-smile of a classmate watching a video and listening on her Bluetooth headphones. I would estimate that eighty percent of my classmates are not paying attention to the professor. Can instructors do anything to curb this wild enthusiasm for social media?

Professors are well aware of the problems social media have caused in the classroom. Students often seem glued to their phones, unable to concentrate on classroom activities, and unwilling to put away their technology. The solution to this addiction to social media may seem to be banning cell phones, but not many instructors have success when they try this. One response to the social media problem is to stop fighting its power. Instead, many instructors have embraced social media as a learning tool, allowing students to keep their phones out and to use them. These instructors realize that while social media can be a distraction in the classroom, it can also enhance learning if they carefully select the social media tools to use.

Alexis, on revising two body paragraphs: "I realized I was making a lot of accusations but not backing them up. For example, I said blogs were ineffective, but I didn't explain why. I needed a whole new paragraph to add that explanation! I also saw the word 'lame' in my first draft and thought it might be offensive to professors, so I reworded. This section is much better now because I included examples and explanations that back up my opinion. And I think the tone is more appropriate because it's more respectful."

Rough Draft of Two Body Paragraphs	Revision
Not all social media tools are effective. To be effective, social media has to be social. Some of the social media tools instructors have used are not effective because students don't participate. I have been in many classes that required me to post on discussion boards knowing that the idea behind discussion boards is great, students post	Carefully selecting tools is important, because not all social media tools are effective. To be effective in the classroom, social media has to be social. Some of the social media tools instructors have used are not effective because students do not truly participate. I have been in many classes that required me to post on discussion boards. The idea

(Continued on next page)

(Continued from previous page)

Rough Draft of Two Body Paragraphs	Revision
thought-provoking ideas and respond to each other's thoughts. In fact, in real life, people use social media to do this all the time. Using twitter or facebook or commenting on online pages or articles can generate some fascinating conversation and make you think. However, in the classes where I had to use discussion boards, students did not really want to talk to classmates. Discussion boards were simply not effective, and blogs were just the same. Some social media tools seem to be more of a fun distraction than real learning tools. One of my instructors decided to use twitter but only a few students responded. Another lame attempt to use social media for teaching is to create a facebook class page. I've had several professors who have done this, and in only one case was the facebook page useful. Most of the time, it was just a place where the instructor stored documents. Again, very few students would post comments, no meaningful dialogue enhanced my learning experience.	behind discussion boards is great. In theory, students post thought-provoking ideas and respond to each other's thoughts. In real life, people use social media to do this all the time. Using Twitter or Facebook or commenting on online pages or articles can generate some fascinating conversation and thinking. However, in the classes where I had to use discussion boards, students did not really want to talk to classmates. They just wanted to get the assignment done. They would post some general comment and everyone would say, "Great idea." Nobody really cared what classmates said, so the discussion board, honestly, was not an effective teaching tool. Blogs were equally ineffective at promoting learning. In one class, we had to write a blog entry every week about what we read, and we were then supposed to read each other's blogs and comment on them. Most of the comments could have been written without even reading the student's blog, and honestly, no one really read anyone else's blogs. For one thing, the blogs were boring. Most students just summarized what they read, so there was not much to comment on. While the idea of getting students to talk to each other in meaningful ways is a good one, blogs and discussion boards did not work in my experiences. Often, social media tools seem to be more of a fun distraction than real learning tools. One of my instructors decided to use Twitter to throw out some interesting ideas that students could respond to. Responding was not required, so only a few students took the time to respond. As for learning, I cannot imagine how those students (or those of us who read the tweets) learned anything they could not have learned from reading the book. Another common way instructors use social media for teaching is to create a Facebook class page. I have had several professors who have done this, and in only one case was the Facebook page useful. Most of the time, it was just a place where the instructor stored documents. Again, very few students would post comments, no meaningful dialogue enhanced my learning experience.

Stage 4: Editing

Once you have revised your paper, you can look closely at grammar and **mechanics** to fine-tune your work. **Editing** works, however, only when you know what to look for! Many students turn in work they have edited but the work still contains errors. The best way to edit is to know your weaknesses and search for errors in those areas. Follow these steps to edit your work effectively.

Editing Step 1: Identify the grammatical and mechanical errors you tend to make. You may already know some of the errors you tend to make, but if you are unsure, look over previous papers or take a grammar, punctuation, and mechanics test to identify areas of weakness. Visit your campus's learning resources to learn about resources they may have that can help you identify and work on these errors.

Editing Step 2: Make an editing checklist and use it to edit your papers. The first items on your checklist should be the errors you tend to make the most often. You may already know the errors you tend to make, but if you don't, you can look back at papers you have submitted and identify them. Alternatively, you can provide a writing sample to your campus writing center so that a tutor can tell you errors you need to work on. You might even take a diagnostic writing exam to figure out where your strengths and weaknesses lie. The following checklist presents the most common grammatical and mechanical errors. For a more complete discussion of writing errors, see Handbook 2, "Improving Your Writing Skills."

- Check for sentence fragments, comma splices, and run-on sentences.
- Check for subject/verb agreement errors.
- Check for pronoun reference and pronoun agreement errors.
- Check for verb tense shifts.
- Check for commonly confused words.
- Check mechanics and punctuation.

Editing Step 3: Use spelling and grammar checkers. If you use Microsoft Word, the program can check your spelling and grammar. While spelling and grammar checkers are not perfect, they can help you find errors that you may not otherwise see. Of course, you will need to review each of the suggested changes and make sure the changes are actually necessary.

Editing Step 4: Use a unique reading strategy to find errors. Try reading your paper from the end to the beginning. In other words, start editing by reading the last sentence of your paper. Work at the sentence level. If the sentence is correct, go on to the previous sentence. Another strategy is to read each sentence aloud or have a classmate read your paper aloud while you listen for errors.

Editing Step 5: After you edit your paper, reread it or ask a writing center tutor to read it with you. This final check will enable to you to make sure you have addressed all grammatical and mechanical errors.

---

mechanics: Rules about written language, including capitalization, punctuation, use of numerals, and spelling.

editing: Correcting errors in grammar and mechanics.

Teaching Suggestion
Consider having students keep an error log, noting each type of grammatical or mechanical error in their writing assignments. Students will then have a better idea of the specific errors to work on.
    Research suggests students become better writers when they use intentional mapping to transfer the lessons they learn from one writing assignment to the next. See "How to Grade Writing Effectively: An Overview of the Research," in the IM.

Teaching Suggestion
Composing good sentences sounds like an elementary skill, but it is really the foundation for good writing, and even students who have been in AP classes sometimes struggle with issues such as clarity and sentence structure. To help students compose better sentences, consider assigning the exercise "Seven Ways to Improve Your Sentences."

Stage 5: Formatting

Once your paper's content, grammar, and mechanics are the way you want them, put your paper in the proper format. Your instructor will probably tell you how to format your paper using a style guide, such as MLA (Modern Language Association) or APA (American Psychological Association). Style guides such as these tell you how to format everything, including headings, page numbers, in-text citations, and works-cited pages. Use these steps to make sure you have formatted your paper properly. Chapter 12 provides information about how to use MLA and APA styles for formatting. In this text, you will see models of student writing in both MLA and APA formats.

Formatting Step 1: Put a proper heading on your paper. The heading includes information such as your name, the course, and date. The heading required for an MLA-style paper is different than the one required for an APA paper.

> **Teaching Suggestion**
> Consider sharing with students the MLA and APA templates that are available in Microsoft Word.

Formatting Step 2: Adjust margins, line spacing, and indentions. Become familiar with your word-processing program so that you can make sure margins, line spacing, indented quotes, and the like are formatted according to your style guide.

Formatting Step 3: Put a proper header in the top margin. A paper's header usually includes page numbers. (Note: A header and a heading are different, so do not confuse them.) Check your style guide to see what your paper's headers should include. Note that sometimes the second page of a paper contains a different type of header than the first. Your style guide will explain the requirements.

Formatting Step 4: Make sure in-text citations are formatted correctly. Each time you use a source, you must give credit to it. Check that you have done that, making sure that you have used the proper method for giving credit to sources. Be aware that there are rules about punctuating and spacing the in-text citations; make sure you format citations correctly.

> **Teaching Resources**
> Consider using the handout "Tips and Tricks for Formatting Works Cited/References Entries." Additional resources are noted in the annotations in Chapter 12.

Formatting Step 5: Make sure each source mentioned in the text is included in a correctly formatted works-cited page. Check to make sure you have entries on your works-cited page for each source used. Use your style guide to format the entries. Pay attention to the details, such as abbreviating, spacing, italicizing, and punctuating.

Alexis Williams, Social Media in the Classroom (Final Draft)

Alexis has revised and edited her paper, and she has put it in MLA format. Notice that there is no works-cited page for her paper because Alexis did not use any sources other than her own experiences. Here is Alexis's final draft.

Williams 1

Alexis Williams
Dr. Jones
ENGL 1301.15
15 February 2020

Social Media in the Classroom

  As I sit in my college history class and look around the room, I do not see students furiously taking notes. I see very few students who are even looking at the instructor or their notepads. I see, instead, fingers flying on smartphones, as students silently text their friends. I see the distracted half-smile of a classmate watching a video and listening on her Bluetooth headphones. I would estimate that eighty percent of my classmates are not paying attention to the professor. Can instructors do anything to curb this wild enthusiasm for social media?

  Professors are well aware of the problems social media have caused in the classroom. Students often seem glued to their phones, unable to concentrate on classroom activities, and unwilling to put away their technology. The solution to this addiction to social media may seem to be banning cell phones, but not many instructors have success when they try this. One response to the social media problem is to stop fighting its power. Instead, many instructors have embraced social media as a learning tool, allowing students to keep their phones out and to use them. These instructors realize that while social media can be a distraction in the classroom, it can also enhance learning if they carefully select the social media tools to use.

  Carefully selecting tools is important, because not all social media tools are effective. To be effective in the classroom, social media has to be social. Some of the social media tools instructors have used are not effective because students do not truly participate. I have been in many classes that required me to post on discussion boards. The idea behind discussion boards is great. In theory, students post thought-provoking ideas and respond to each other's thoughts. In real life, people use social media to do this all the time. Using Twitter or Facebook or commenting on online pages or articles can generate some fascinating conversation and thinking. However, in the classes where I had to use discussion boards, students did not really want to talk to classmates. They just wanted to get the assignment done. They would post some general comment and everyone would say, "Great idea." Nobody really cared what classmates said, so the discussion board, honestly, was not an effective teaching tool.

Blogs were equally ineffective at promoting learning. In one class, we had to write a blog entry every week about what we read, and we were then supposed to read each other's blogs and comment on them. Most of the comments could have been written without even reading the student's blog, and honestly, no one really read anyone else's blogs. For one thing, the blogs were boring. Most students just summarized what they read, so there was not much to comment on. While the idea of getting students to talk to each other in meaningful ways is a good one, blogs and discussion boards did not work in my experience.

Often, social media tools seem to be more of a fun distraction than real learning tools. One of my instructors decided to use Twitter to throw out some interesting ideas that students could respond to. Responding was not required, so only a few students took the time to respond. As for learning, I cannot imagine how those students (or those of us who read the tweets) learned anything they could not have learned from reading the book. Another common way instructors use social media for teaching is to create a Facebook class page. I have had several professors who have done this, and in only one case was the Facebook page useful. Most of the time, it was just a place where the instructor stored documents. Again, very few students would post comments, so no meaningful dialogue enhanced my learning experience.

While not all social media uses are effective in the classroom, one technology that truly helped me learn was videoconferencing. In two of my classes, my instructors used videoconferencing to teach. Videoconferencing is simply using a computer to talk to another person and share screens. In algebra, we were required to participate in at least one videoconference where our instructor met with us, one on one, online, and showed us how to do a problem we had difficulty with. After that first videoconference session, she encouraged us to request additional sessions if we needed help. I met with her through videoconferencing three times and she helped me learn some things that I simply was unable to understand on my own. In addition to my math experience, my anthropology instructor required us to write a real long research paper, and she required four drafts. After each draft, we "met" with her online in a videoconference and she explained what we needed to do to improve that draft. I learned so much about writing in that class, and it was not even an

English class! These were both effective learning experiences because they enabled me to have a personal meeting with my instructor and get explanations I really needed.

Finally, texting is a simple technology tool, but it can be a very helpful way for students to learn. My English instructor in high school actually required us to text her with our ideas as we were developing papers and any time we had a question. At first, I was hesitant to text her, but over time, I got used to sending her quick questions and talking with her through texting. The best thing about using texting as a teaching tool was that when I was at home writing papers, I could get help in a timely way, not next week in class. Sometimes my teacher would respond instantly, but even if she did not respond immediately, I knew that she would answer my question eventually. I probably also asked more questions than I would have in class. I am shy by nature, and I do not like to speak up in class. Being able to text probably helped me make a higher grade in that class.

Social media is fun, and obviously, students are addicted to it. Congratulations to those professors who find creative ways to use social media to really enhance learning.

▶ **ACTIVITY 3** Creating a Personalized Writing Checklist

You have now studied the entire writing process. Based on the advice in this chapter, create a basic checklist that you will use for your writing assignments.

PERSONALIZING YOUR WRITING PROCESS

Every successful writer uses a process that works, but not all writers use the same process. You have read about steps in the writing process in this chapter. Now it is time to think about your individual preferences and the way you work best to create a personalized writing process.

Personality

First, consider your personality. Introverts, people who gain energy by being left alone, often need time by themselves to think and to do their best work. Extroverts, on the other hand, are energized by talking with others. What energizes

Teaching Suggestion
Students are sometimes resistant to changing their writing processes. Consider using an assignment that asks students to create a video blog in which they reflect on the writing processes they are using. Such an assignment fosters metacognition about the effectiveness of their processes. See the IM for more information and for the assignment "Video-Blogging Your Writing Process."

your thinking? Can you find a method of prewriting that works well with your personality type? Based on your personal preferences, decide on which you prefer: peer review, reading your paper aloud, or recording your paper and listening to the recording to make changes.

Time Management

Next, think about your time management skills—honestly. If you struggle to meet deadlines, determine whether you need help with organization or whether you procrastinate. If you need help with organization, ask your instructor for help, or visit a learning lab on your campus. Make an appointment as soon as you get your assignment; that way, you will be more likely to follow through.

If you struggle with procrastination, consider using one of these tips:

- If you procrastinate because you dread doing the work, ask yourself why you dread it so much. Does dread come from not understanding the assignment? If so, reread the assignment. Take it to your college's writing center or to a tutor and ask for help. Be proactive. Don't avoid the task because of dread or fear.

- If you procrastinate because you worry about making a bad grade, figure out the tasks you fear the most. For example, do you fear getting a bad grade for grammatical errors? If so, create a writing process that will give you time to work on the grammar for a few days before your essay is due.

- If you feel like you just cannot get started, try this: set a timer on your phone for ten minutes. During that time, reread the assignment. On a sheet of paper or on your computer, start prewriting about the assignment. When the timer goes off, take a break if you wish and then return. Set the timer for another ten minutes and repeat the process. You may find that eventually you are so involved in the writing process that you no longer need the timer.

Teaching Suggestion
Procrastination is a problem for many students. Consider addressing the problem directly by having students read "Why You Procrastinate," by Charlotte Lieberman (https://www.nytimes.com/2019/03/25/smarter-living/why-you-procrastinate-it-has-nothing-to-do-with-self-control.html). Have students discuss the topic so that they can be more intentional about their choices.

Writing Strengths and Weaknesses

Next, review all the writing process steps in this chapter, and figure out the best way you can engage in those processes. Focus on the parts of the writing process that you have not fully mastered. For example, you may be great at drafting but not very patient with revising and editing. How will you become better at revising and editing? You know these steps are important; what can you do to pay more attention to them? What real-life revising and editing activities would you be willing to do? Would you be willing to meet with a tutor to work on revising and editing? To ask your instructor for comments?

Using a personalized writing process that gives you enough time to pay attention to the rhetorical situation and to plan, draft, revise, and edit helps you do your very best work.

CHAPTER PROJECT A Personal Writing Process

You have learned about a general writing process that encourages you to use planning, rhetorical thinking, and recursiveness. The questions that follow prompt you to review each step and think about how you can customize the step to fit your personality, your time needs, your workspace, and so on. Write about your customized writing plan by creating a paragraph for each stage: planning, drafting, revising, and editing. In each paragraph, explain how you will use the steps. When you finish, put your paragraphs together, and you will have a summary of your personalized writing process.

Here are some questions to help you create a personalized writing process.

Thinking Rhetorically
- How will you make your personalized writing process a rhetorical process?
- When will you analyze the rhetorical situation of your assignment?
- In what ways will you prompt yourself to think about your message and how best to communicate it to readers?
- What revision strategies will you use? How will you revise with an audience in mind?

Planning
- How will you make time for planning?
- What prewriting methods work best for you?
- Will you work with others, or will you work alone?
- When will you do the planning for an essay? (Will you do the planning a week before the essay is due, for instance?)
- What is the best way for you to outline your paper? (For example, do you like to create a formal outline? Will you handwrite an informal outline?)
- Will you schedule time to work with a tutor or lab instructor on assignments?
- If procrastination has been a problem in the past, how will you make sure you start your writing project in a timely way?
- Which of the steps of the planning process might present an obstacle to you? How will you deal with that obstacle?

Drafting
- When will you need to get a draft finished so that you have time to revise it and edit it before the paper is due?
- Will you use a computer to draft, or will you draft by hand?
- What will you do if you get stuck and cannot come up with enough content?
- Which of the steps of the drafting process might present an obstacle to you? How will you deal with that obstacle?

Revising

- Which of the revising steps do you believe will help you the most?
- What is the most effective revising method you have used in the past? How can you use that step in the future?
- Will you work with another person when revising? If so, who will you work with? What do you hope this person will be able to help you with?
- What writing weaknesses will you focus on when revising? Are you aware of areas that you tend to need to work on when revising? What are these areas? For example, some people need to work on organization when revising, while others need to work on revising individual sentences to make sure they are clearly written.
- Which of the steps of the revising process might present an obstacle to you? How will you deal with that obstacle?

Editing

- What are the errors in grammar and mechanics you tend to make?
- How will you look for these errors in your writing?
- How much time do you need to edit your paper carefully?
- Will you work with another person during the editing process? If so, who? What do you hope this person will help you accomplish?
- Which of the steps of the editing process might present an obstacle for you? How will you deal with that obstacle?

Formatting

- What is the best way for you to format your paper? Working with someone else? Using the style manual? Using websites that provide tools and information about formatting?
- Do you need help using your word processor to format your paper? If so, how will you get that help?
- How will you make sure your paper is correctly formatted?
- Which of the steps of the formatting process might present an obstacle to you? How will you deal with that obstacle?

Reflecting to Develop a Writer's Mindset

This chapter discussed you as a writer. The goal of the chapter was to help you develop both a rhetorical way of thinking about writing assignments and a personalized writing process. Write a few paragraphs in which you reflect on your experiences as a writer. When have you been the most successful? What processes helped you write successfully? When have your writing attempts been the least successful? In what ways do you believe you are capable of developing into a better writer? How will what you have learned in this chapter affect your future writing?

FAQ WRITING WITH CLARITY

To improve the clarity of a sentence, ask these questions.

1. **Does each sentence include only one idea?**

   A common error is to try to cram too many ideas into one sentence. Even if the resulting sentence is not a comma splice or run-on, a sentence that contains too many ideas can be confusing for the reader. Create new sentences for each idea to improve the clarity of a sentence that is too long.

   Original: One of the most famous French painters, Pierre-Auguste Renoir, was actually better at singing than he was at drawing, at least initially, but one can argue that because Renoir lived close to the Louvre gallery in Paris, where he frequently visited to ponder the paintings as a refuge from his boring job at a porcelain factory, Renoir developed an artist's eye.

   Revision: One of the most famous French painters, Pierre-Auguste Renoir, was actually better at singing than he was at drawing, at least initially. Renoir had a job at a porcelain factory that he found quite boring. To relieve his boredom, he frequently visited the Louvre gallery in Paris, which was near his home. One can argue that these frequent visits helped Renoir develop an artist's eye.

2. **Can vague words and expressions be replaced with concrete words?**

   Concrete words are easy to visualize and, thus, to understand. It's easy to imagine what a *chair* is, but it is not easy to visualize an *object* because the word can refer to many things. You can improve the clarity of your sentences by using words that are more concrete in place of words that are abstract or vague.

   Original: The politician's speech covered certain noble ideals that she valued.

   Revision: The politician's speech was about her commitment to prison reform and universal health care.

3. **Is the antecedent of each pronoun clear?**

   Another common error that contributes to unclear sentences is the use of a pronoun without a clear antecedent (the word to which the pronoun refers). Make sure a pronoun has a clear antecedent nearby that can be easily identified.

   Original: The people who live in the town say they still use an old-fashioned cash register in the drugstore, and they prefer to do it that way.

   Revision: The people who live in the town say that the drugstore clerks still use an old-fashioned cash register. The townspeople prefer doing their transactions in this old-fashioned way.

4. Can a thought be expressed in a simpler way?

Some of the best writing expresses ideas simply.

Original: In due time, one can predict addiction to the habit of vaping due to the problem of nicotine addiction.

Revision: Because nicotine is addictive, vaping can become addictive.

TRY IT!

Revise each of the following sentences to make them clearer.

1. There is a littering problem on our campus, so when people come to tour our school, they get a portraying outlook that is not positive.
2. Possible blames would be lack of trash cans within the school premises and dumpsters, and the school can obviously afford trash cans if it can build big parking garages so why are there so few of them around the campus?
3. In this day and age, students know that it is not morally right or ethically okay to throw their trash down, but they do it anyway.

4 Using Rhetorical Patterns as Tools

CHAPTER OBJECTIVES

You will learn to:
- Explain how rhetorical patterns are used as tools in purpose-based writing.
- Analyze and write descriptive texts.
- Analyze and write narrative texts.
- Analyze and write illustrative texts.
- Analyze and write texts that define.
- Analyze and write classification texts.
- Analyze and write comparison and contrast texts.
- Analyze and write cause and effect texts.
- Analyze and write process texts.

Connect Adaptive Learning Assignment
Consider using Connect's Adaptive Learning Assignments to support this chapter.

Although you may not use the term *rhetorical patterns*, you use rhetorical patterns every day. **Rhetorical patterns**, sometimes called *rhetorical modes*, are actually thinking patterns. For example, our brains are wired to analyze causes and effects. Anticipating what would probably happen if we were to cross a six-lane highway is natural: inferring causes and effects is a thinking skill that is necessary for survival.

It is no wonder, then, that we use rhetorical patterns, such as explanations of cause and effect, to communicate. If you are late for a meeting at work, for instance, you will probably explain why. You do this because explaining the cause may help your colleagues understand your situation. You may offer additional details by describing what you saw or narrating what happened. Describing and narrating are also rhetorical patterns that structure the way we think about our experiences and the way we communicate them.

In ordinary communication, we rarely take time to analyze the rhetorical patterns we use. When we write, however, we can choose the rhetorical patterns that will be most effective for a writing purpose. Whether you are writing to reflect, inform, analyze, evaluate, or persuade, the rhetorical patterns discussed in this chapter are transferable: you can use them for a wide variety of writing

rhetorical patterns: Thinking patterns, sometimes called rhetorical modes, including description, narration, definition, illustration, classification, comparison and contrast, cause and effect, and process analysis that are used as ways to support main ideas.

Teaching Resources
See the Instructor's Manual (IM) for suggestions about how to teach this chapter, and consider assigning this chapter's test-bank quiz.

59

> **Teaching Suggestion**
> Rhetorical patterns are introduced as tools to be used to fulfill writing purposes rather than as ends in themselves. See the IM for more about this approach.

tasks. The key to using them effectively is thinking rhetorically to determine the right pattern to use, given your purpose, audience, message, and genre.

WARM-UP

DeShawn is creating a GoFundMe page to raise money for a family who lost their home to a flood. He knows that the page will be read by people who do not know any of the details about this family. DeShawn also knows that few people will read long passages online, so he has to be selective about what he includes. He has made a list of ideas about what to put on the site. Which three types of content do you think would be most effective at persuading people to donate? Why?

- the story of what happened
- a description of the flood, the house, and town after the flood
- examples of why the family needs money
- a discussion of the effects of the flood on the family
- a discussion of the types of assistance the family needs the most
- an explanation of how GoFundMe works
- a before and after comparison showing the house before the flood and the house after the flood

> **Teaching Suggestion**
> One of the Chapter Projects guides students to create a GoFundMe site. Consider tying in the Warm-up to this assignment.

> **Teaching Resource**
> Consider using the PowerPoint "Mixing Rhetorical Patterns" and the accompanying analysis assignment "Analyzing Rhetorical Pattern Choices."

> **Co-requisite Teaching Tip**
> Consider having students practice writing using individual rhetorical modes in the co-requisite section. Students can combine those modes in the credit section.

USING RHETORICAL PATTERNS AS TOOLS

Rhetorical patterns are transferable tools you can use for a wide variety of writing purposes. For instance, if you can master descriptive writing for academic assignments, you can also use it for a personal project, such as a GoFundMe page or a restaurant review. Your power to describe may also transfer to workplace writing, such as an incident report or a proposal.

The most common rhetorical patterns—sometimes called rhetorical modes—are description, narration, definition, illustration, classification, compare and contrast, cause and effect, and process. In the past you may have written essays that required you to use a single text pattern almost exclusively. For instance, you may have written a comparative essay about two works of literature or a history paper exploring the causes or effects of an important event. Some writing purposes can be accomplished by using just one rhetorical pattern, but often writers use several patterns in a single text. In the Warm-Up activity, DeShawn's writing purpose—to persuade people to contribute to a worthy cause—could be supported by using a number of rhetorical patterns. He could narrate what happened, describe what he saw or what the family experienced, explain the effects of the flood, provide examples of the family's needs, and so on. Obviously, some rhetorical patterns would be more effective than others. While a discussion of how GoFundMe works (which involves using the *process* rhetorical pattern) might be interesting, it would not likely move readers to make a contribution. Similarly, classifying the types of assistance the family needs might be informative, but it may not be the best way to solicit contributions. On the other hand, describing the house and comparing it in a "before and after" way may help readers understand just how much damage occurred. Additionally, explaining the effects of the flood on the family may help readers see that their contributions are genuinely needed. DeShawn can create a convincing GoFundMe page by selecting the most appropriate rhetorical patterns for his purpose: persuasion.

In this chapter, we examine each text pattern to understand how to use it rhetorically. In the chapters that follow, you will select the best rhetorical patterns to use for your writing purpose.

DESCRIPTION

Being able to describe something accurately is crucial for a variety of work-related writing tasks, such as report writing. But **description** also serves the rhetorical function of creating a mood or a dominant impression. One rhetorical use of description is to help readers experience a situation the way the writer has. Used this way, description transports readers and helps them feel like they have encountered or experienced the object being described. Some basic purposes for using description are shown in Table 4.1.

> **Teaching Resources**
> For writing assignments that emphasize description, see the Additional Writing Prompts in the IM.

> **description:** A rhetorical pattern in which language is used to help readers understand the physical attributes of something or to understand what something is like.

TABLE 4.1 Purposes for Using Description

Writing purpose	How description can be used	Example
To support a variety of writing purposes	To set a mood, create a dominant impression, or to evoke feelings	A descriptive passage in an argument essay may help readers to experience an emotion and be swayed to agree with the writer's point.
To reflect	To help readers experience something the way the writer has experienced it	A writer who reflects on what it was like to win the lottery may use description to help readers understand their experiences.
To inform	To help readers understand the physical attributes of a subject	An essay about preserving the Everglades might include description so that readers can understand the uniqueness of the habitat.
To analyze	To give readers a deeper understanding of a subject by describing each of its parts	An article that analyzes the aurora borealis (the Northern Lights) might describe it in depth.
To evaluate	To support a judgment in an evaluation	A restaurant review will include descriptions of the food, service, and surroundings.
To persuade	To set a mood, to evoke feelings, or to provide descriptive details that logically support a claim	A city that wants to host an Olympics may include descriptions of its exemplary features in its proposal.

A Sample of Descriptive Writing

What follows is a selection from "Black Walnut: A Sweet Blood History," a reflective essay by Linda Hogan. Hogan's goal is to help readers experience a memory from her childhood as a young Chickasaw girl growing up in Oklahoma. You can find the entire essay in Part 6 of this text. As you read, notice the concrete language Hogan uses. Annotate at least three descriptive words or phrases you think are effective in creating an impression.

> From one seed of childhood memories, I recall a stormy night and seeing my grandfather ride his horse toward home through a thunderstorm. I watched through the leaves of a large tree. In each flash of lightning as he came closer, the world was also a bright display of daylight green grass and trees.
>
> Even through the strong odor of rain, from the open window I smelled the powerful soul of the black walnut tree near the window. It had an odor that was unique, a medicinal scent of herb and something fragrant I couldn't name.
>
> I had an affinity for that tree, a love that eventually grew to contain other trees. By day, I liked to put my small fingers in the dark, furrowed bark and let them travel. I considered this particular tree my own in some way, its long leaves that held other leaves and shaped something like a fern, the green cluster of nuts together in young groups until ready to fall. It even had its own unique sound as the warm winds passed through its leaves.
>
> But it was the odor of this tree that really distinguished it from others. It had a beautiful smell I believed. It was strong enough that broken layers of shells or even the leaves kept insects from entering the house.

▶ ACTIVITY 1 Analyzing Description

Select one descriptive detail from Hogan's passage that you found effective. What impression did this detail make? What is one lesson or takeaway you can learn as a writer about descriptive writing from Hogan's example?

Thinking Rhetorically about Description

To determine when you should include description in your writing and what that description should entail, start by analyzing the rhetorical situation. What message are you trying to convey? How might description help readers understand or believe that message? Use the questions in Rhetorical Toolbox 4.1 as a guide.

▶ ACTIVITY 2 Using Description

In a marketing class, you are assigned to write a description of an effective advertisement. Describe the advertisement so as to demonstrate how it works and why it is effective. Think rhetorically about the elements you should include in your description, and write a paragraph to present the advertisement you have chosen.

RHETORICAL TOOLBOX 4.1
Using Description as a Writing Tool

1. **Audience.** What descriptive details might be meaningful to readers? Be highly selective about the details you choose.
2. **Purpose.** What is the purpose for the details you provide? Make sure the details you choose meet the purpose. For instance, for technical, work-related, or scientific writing, make sure the details in the description are accurate.
3. **Sensory details.** Can you use concrete, sensory details to help readers gain a more accurate understanding or to set a tone? If so, include details that evoke the senses, such as the way something feels, smells, looks, sounds, or tastes.

NARRATION

Narration is storytelling. In a narrative essay, the story itself is the focus of the entire composition. However, you can use a brief story—often called an anecdote—or a set of brief anecdotes to support a variety of writing purposes (see Table 4.2). Research suggests that the human mind has a particular affinity for narration: we tend to structure our experiences as stories. By tapping into this

Teaching Resources
For writing assignments that emphasize narration, see the Additional Writing Prompts in the IM.

narration: A rhetorical pattern that tells a story, whether fiction or nonfiction.

TABLE 4.2 Purposes for Using Narration

Writing purpose	How narration can be used	Example
To support a variety of writing purposes	• To structure an essay • To introduce and/or conclude	• An essay about overcoming math anxiety might feature several short anecdotes that tell the stories of people who have succeeded. • Writers sometimes begin an essay with the first part of a story and end the essay by telling how the story concludes.
To reflect	To provide a subject on which writers comment and reflect	A single, long narrative or a set of personal stories can be the focus of a reflective or narrative essay.
To inform	To illustrate a point	An informative essay about how DNA testing is used in cancer treatment might include the story of how a person survived cancer through the use of DNA.
To evaluate	To provide anecdotal evidence	An evaluation of a restaurant may include anecdotes about patrons' experiences as a type of evidence for a judgment.
To persuade	To appeal to the emotions of readers	An essay about the value of a college education may include a student's story to help readers see education from a personal point of view.

tendency to think in narrative terms, you can create support that readers can understand, relate to, and enjoy. Who doesn't like a good story?

A Sample of Narrative Writing

Justin Huang was a high school student when he wrote "How I Overcame My Stuttering." His article was published on the International Stuttering Association's website, and you can find it in Part 6 of this text. What follows is a narrative used in the first three paragraphs of his article. As you read the passage, think about its effectiveness as an introduction. Does the story make you want to keep reading? Think also about how Huang structured the story. Is there an introduction? Is there a crisis in the story (the climax)? Is there a resolution to the crisis?

> Beads of sweat began to collect on my forehead, as snickers of laughter echoed throughout the classroom. I opened my mouth to speak and a staccato of 'buh's' shot out. 'Buh-buh, buh-buh, b-bonjour'. Any confidence I had, disintegrated. And I trudged through my three-minute French presentation, facing for countless times my worst enemy—my stutter.
>
> As I spoke, I could feel the eyes of my classmates cutting to pieces any remains of my confidence. Even those who usually dozed off during presentations looked in my direction, as if waiting to see when I would stutter next. Midway through, I hazarded a glance toward my French teacher. Usually kind and supportive, his face was draped with the initial stages of a frown. *This is going terribly*, I thought. My thoughts turned into anguish, and helplessly, I stumbled onward.
>
> When the presentation was over, my mind tried to block out what had just happened, but the damage to my confidence had been done. I wondered why this experience felt so awful. After all, stuttering was nothing new to me. Any time I was forced to speak in front of others, I would have to do battle with it. In French class, my worst class, I almost always lost. But even then, this was a new low. After talking to my parents about it, I realized I was disturbed by the fact that this was the worst my stuttering had ever been, and the worse it became, the more non-existent my confidence became. I was caught in a relentless downward spiral.

▶ **ACTIVITY 3** Analyzing Narration

There is no resolution to the conflict in the brief story Huang uses to introduce his article. Thinking rhetorically, why might Huang intentionally omit a resolution to the story? Explain your answer.

Thinking Rhetorically about Narration

Sometimes using a story or brief anecdote can be a powerful writing strategy. Think rhetorically about using narration by answering the questions in Rhetorical Toolbox 4.2.

> **RHETORICAL TOOLBOX 4.2**
> ## Using Narration as a Writing Tool
>
> 1. **Context**. Does the rhetorical situation of your assignment make story-telling appropriate? For instance, a letter to the editor of a newspaper might include a story, but a scientific report might not.
> 2. **Audience.** How would the use of a story affect the reader's understanding or acceptance of your thesis statement? What would be the purpose of including a story? Will the story you are considering interest readers?
> 3. **Purpose.** How long should the story be to accomplish your purpose? Are you attempting to use stories as evidence? If so, do so with care. Use a variety of types of evidence in persuasively oriented texts.
> 4. **Other rhetorical patterns**. Will your story benefit from coupling it with description? If the story needs descriptive elements, plan to add them.
> 5. **Rhetorical strategies**. Where will the story be most effective? Might it be effective to introduce and/or conclude your writing? Will the story appeal to emotions? Would such an appeal be appropriate for the rhetorical situation?

▶ **ACTIVITY 4 Using Narration**

Imagine that you are writing to urge readers to regularly donate blood. Write a narrative paragraph, either a true story or a hypothetical one, that would help you support the idea that regularly donating blood is important.

ILLUSTRATION

The word **illustration** literally means a graphic that helps readers understand something. Any kind of graphic—such as artwork, charts, graphs, photos, and the like—can be used for a rhetorical purpose. These kinds of graphics help readers visualize the information being conveyed. Another type of illustration is the example. Like visual work, written examples help to make concepts easier to grasp. Examples are one of the most common—and most helpful—rhetorical tools available to writers, as you can see in Table 4.3.

illustration: A rhetorical pattern in which an example or a graphic helps readers understand a concept.

Teaching Resources
For writing assignments that emphasize illustration, see the Additional Writing Prompts in the IM.

A Sample of Illustration

In "Mass Incarceration: The Whole Pie," authors Wendy Sawyer and Peter Wagner discuss why so many people are incarcerated in the United States. In the passage that follows, the writers argue that too many youth are incarcerated for offenses that are not criminal. To support their point, they provide examples and statistics. Identify the specific examples the writers use. If the writers had not provided the examples, would their point still be clear?

TABLE 4.3 Purposes for Using Illustration

Writing purpose	How illustration can be used	Example
To support a variety of writing purposes	To present information visually	Actual illustrations—such as graphics, artwork, charts, and photos—might be used in an informative report about poisonous snakes of the Southwest.
To reflect	To support an insight	In a reflective paper, a writer might provide examples of behaviors that led him to realize he has a talent for organization.
To inform	To make abstract information more concrete and understandable	A writer discussing egocentrism might use an example to help readers understand the concept: *Brianna is in an egocentric stage of development. When people are talking, Brianna assumes they are talking about her.*
To analyze	To present how something works	An analysis of a proposed tax on fast food might present hypothetical scenarios to help readers understand how such a tax would work.
To evaluate	To present hypothetical situations and their likely outcomes	An evaluation of a plan to decrease funding available for student loans might include examples to demonstrate how the plan would affect specific students.
To persuade	To present a real person's experience as a form of proof for an idea.	Some types of persuasive writing, such as advertisements, cite testimonials to support the idea being conveyed. In essays about social issues, citing the testimonials of real people can have a dramatic impact on readers.

Looking more closely at incarceration by offense type also exposes some disturbing facts about the 63,000 youth in confinement in the United States: Too many are there for a "most serious offense" that is not even a crime. For example, there are over 8,100 youth behind bars for technical violations of their probation, rather than for a new offense. An additional 2,200 youth are locked up for "status" offenses, which are "behaviors that are not law violations for adults, such as running away, truancy, and incorrigibility." Nearly 1 in 10 youth held for a criminal or delinquent offense is locked in an adult jail or prison, and most of the others are held in juvenile facilities that look and operate a lot like prisons and jails.

▶ **ACTIVITY 5 Analyzing Illustration**

What purpose is served by the examples Sawyer and Wagner provide? To consider this question, imagine what the passage would be like if the examples were removed. Without examples, what impression would the paragraph leave? How do the examples function? Explain your answer.

Thinking Rhetorically about Illustration

We use illustrations for a wide variety of purposes. As a writer, you must determine when readers need an illustration; you must also identify the best kind of illustration to use for your purpose. Use the questions in Rhetorical Toolbox 4.3 as a guide.

> **RHETORICAL TOOLBOX 4.3**
> ### Using Illustration as a Writing Tool
>
> 1. **Rhetorical situation.** Does the rhetorical situation suggest that illustrations would be appropriate tools for supporting your thesis statement or supporting other ideas in your text?
> 2. **Clarification.** Are there concepts that readers are likely to find confusing? If so, would examples help to clarify these ideas? Using illustrations and examples can help a reader understand an idea or concept that cannot be visualized, such as self-esteem. If you have significant data to present, consider using graphics such as photos, charts, or diagrams.
> 3. **Audience.** What kind of illustration will readers find acceptable or most helpful?
>   a. If you choose to use a hypothetical example, be sure that it is believable. If it is not, readers will probably be skeptical about the point you are trying to make.
>   b. If you use a testimonial, make sure it comes from a source that readers would find credible. Also, be careful to include more objective types of support, such as data, the statements of experts, and so on.

▶ **ACTIVITY 6** Using Illustration

Write a paragraph in which you use an example—either hypothetical or from real life—to help readers believe this idea: *Sometimes we must fail repeatedly before we experience success.* Make sure the example you use meets the conditions in Rhetorical Toolbox 4.3.

DEFINITION

Effective communication requires us to share the same vocabulary, and **definition** is one strategy that helps writers make sure readers accurately understand a word or concept. Sometimes a definition is paired with an example to provide one more level of explanation for readers. Definition is a useful pattern in all types of writing, as Table 4.4 shows.

definition: A rhetorical pattern in which the meaning of a word or phrase is discussed.

Teaching Resources
For writing assignments that emphasize definition, see the Additional Writing Prompts in the IM.

A Sample of Definition

In textbooks, writers commonly use definition to help readers understand terms and concepts. The excerpt that follows is from *Communication Matters,* a textbook

TABLE 4.4 Purposes for Using Definition

Writing purpose	How definition can be used	Example
To support a variety of writing purposes	To define unfamiliar, important words and concepts	In an essay about governmental power for general readers, the phrase *eminent domain* should be defined.
To reflect	To provide one's personal definition of a word or concept	A writer may reflect about their struggles with the world's definition of beauty and how they have come to define the word differently as a result of their life experiences.
To inform	To aid in understanding	In an essay written for the general public, a writer may define words that an audience is not likely to understand, such as a technical term like *Python*, a computer programming language.
To analyze	To show a word's different meanings	A writer may analyze the use of the word "brother" and discuss how the uses have changed over time.
To evaluate	To determine whether something meets the definition of a word or phrase	An essay in which a writer evaluates whether social media can truly be an addiction uses the definition of *addiction* as a standard by which to judge social media behaviors.
To persuade	To argue that a certain meaning is correct	An extended definition can be the foundation for an entire essay. For example, a writer may argue that a certain interpretation of the Second Amendment's "right to bear arms" is the correct definition of that phrase.

by Kory Floyd. As you read it, think about why Floyd felt compelled to define the two terms he defines.

WHAT IS CULTURE?

We use the term *culture* to mean all sorts of things. Sometimes we connect it to a place, as in "Norwegian culture" and "New England culture." Other times we use it to refer to an ethnic or a religious group, as in "Asian American culture" and "Jewish culture." We also speak of "hip-hop culture" and the "culture of the rich." What makes a culture?

Although the word *culture* can have different meanings, we define *culture* as the totality of learned, shared symbols, language, values, and norms that distinguish one group of people from another. That definition tells us that culture is not necessarily tied to countries or ethnicities or economic classes. Rather, it's a characteristic of people. Groups of people who share a culture with one another are called *societies*.

Each of us identifies with one or more societies, and we are usually keenly aware which ones. It is fundamental to our human nature, in fact, to notice people's similarities and differences with respect to ourselves, so that we know which groups of people we belong to and which ones we are separate from. That distinction comprises the difference between in-groups and out-groups.

▶ **ACTIVITY 7** **Analyzing Definition**

Most students use the words *culture* and *societies*, so why does Floyd define them? Also, Floyd creates definitions in his own words, and he uses examples. Why do you think he makes these choices for his audience of student readers?

Thinking Rhetorically about Definition

The questions in Rhetorical Toolbox 4.4 will guide you to think rhetorically about when and how to use definition in your writing.

RHETORICAL TOOLBOX 4.4

Using Definition as a Writing Tool

1. **Audience.** Is a definition necessary for the reader? Include a definition, if so. Do not provide a definition unless you have a good reason for doing so.
2. **Extended and brief definitions.** Will your writing focus on presenting an extended definition, or will you need to present only a brief definition?
   - **Use extended definitions** for papers that are exclusively about defining. An extended definition is a writer's complete explanation of a word or phrase. This kind of definition is created in multiple paragraphs and sometimes is phrased as an argument.
   - **Use brief definitions** to define words that will be new to most readers or that are considered jargon for a discipline or field of study. Rather than quoting a dictionary definition, put the meaning of a term in your own words.
3. **Other rhetorical patterns: examples.** Will a definition be sufficient for readers to gain an accurate understanding of the term or concept? If not, pair definition with an example. A textbook might define *homeostasis* as "the body's attempt to regulate itself." While this definition is correct, readers may need an example, such as body temperature, to understand the concept.

▶ **ACTIVITY 8** **Using Definition**

Imagine that a parent or grandparent asked you what a slang word means. How would you define it so that if your relative chose to use it, he or she would use it correctly? Write a paragraph in which you provide this definition. Choose a slang word or use one of these: *salty, ghost, hangry*.

Teaching Resources
For writing assignments that emphasize classification, see the Additional Writing Prompts in the IM.

CLASSIFICATION

Classification occurs when we analyze a set of information and put that information into groups, based on shared characteristics (see Table 4.5). For instance, an article about the kinds of financial support available to students might classify the support into these types: scholarships, grants, and loans.

classification: A rhetorical pattern in which things are separated into types, classes, or kinds according to their characteristics.

TABLE 4.5 Purposes for Using Classification

Writing purpose	How classification can be used	Example
To support a variety of writing purposes	To demonstrate precise thinking	A writer discussing financial literacy may need to classify the types of credit that affect consumer credit scores. The writer might classify credit products into types, such as installment credit, revolving credit, consumer loans, personal lines of credit, and so on. This kind of classification will help the writer educate consumers about credit.
To reflect	To entertain in a reflective paper	A reflection on the types of bosses a writer endured might use classification to entertain.
To inform	To aid understanding by dividing into types and characterizing these types	An article about macronutrients (protein, carbohydrates, and fats) may classify foods into these categories. Each category can then be discussed separately, and the attributes or characteristics of items in that category can be explained.
To analyze	To explain types, groups, or parts	An analysis of the effects of social media on teens may begin with a classification of social media types: videos, collective sites (such as Facebook), instant messaging apps, and so on.
To evaluate	To create a fair evaluation	To evaluate a horror film, a writer must judge the film against other films in the same category. Classifying correctly is important in such an evaluation.
To persuade	To argue about the characteristics of types or groups, or to argue that a certain item or action belongs in a certain type or group	A writer might classify censorship into two types, acceptable and unacceptable, and then the writer may go on to argue that the local library is practicing unacceptable censorship.

A Sample of Classification

People often talk about depression as if all depression were the same, but an article on the National Institute of Mental Health website helps to correct this mistaken assumption. As you read the passage, notice that the writer uses a similar structure and similar types of content to discuss each type.

> Persistent depressive disorder (also called dysthymia) is a depressed mood that lasts for at least two years. A person diagnosed with persistent depressive disorder may have episodes of major depression along with periods of less severe symptoms, but symptoms must last for two years to be considered persistent depressive disorder.
>
> Postpartum depression is much more serious than the "baby blues" (relatively mild depressive and anxiety symptoms that typically clear within two weeks after delivery) that many women experience after giving birth. Women with postpartum depression experience full-blown major

depression during pregnancy or after delivery (postpartum depression). The feelings of extreme sadness, anxiety, and exhaustion that accompany postpartum depression may make it difficult for these new mothers to complete daily care activities for themselves and/or for their babies.

Psychotic depression occurs when a person has severe depression plus some form of psychosis, such as having disturbing false fixed beliefs (delusions) or hearing or seeing upsetting things that others cannot hear or see (hallucinations). The psychotic symptoms typically have a depressive "theme," such as delusions of guilt, poverty, or illness.

Seasonal affective disorder is characterized by the onset of depression during the winter months, when there is less natural sunlight. This depression generally lifts during spring and summer. Winter depression, typically accompanied by social withdrawal, increased sleep, and weight gain, predictably returns every year in seasonal affective disorder.

Bipolar disorder is different from depression, but it is included in this list because someone with bipolar disorder experiences episodes of extremely low moods that meet the criteria for major depression (called "bipolar depression"). But a person with bipolar disorder also experiences extreme high—euphoric or irritable—moods called "mania" or a less severe form called "hypomania."

▶ **ACTIVITY 9 Analyzing Classification**

The writer provides the same types of information for each type of depression. For example, the symptoms of each type are provided. What other information is provided for each type of depression?

Thinking Rhetorically about Classification

Use the questions in Rhetorical Toolbox 4.5 to determine when—and how—to use classification in your writing.

RHETORICAL TOOLBOX 4.5
Using Classification as a Writing Tool

1. **Rhetorical situation.** Does the rhetorical situation call for classification? How will classification help you to communicate your message?
2. **Audience need for definitions.** If you include classification in your writing, will you need to provide definitions? The groups or categories may need to be defined, depending on the audience's knowledge.
3. **Audience need for comparison and contrast.** Should you include comparison and contrast? The way to classify is to analyze things (items, ideas, people, actions, and so on) by their similarities. Consider readers' needs to determine whether or not to compare and contrast the classified items.
4. **Accuracy and stereotypes.** Will readers see your classifications as accurate? Make sure you use sound thinking to classify. Avoid stereotyping. Sorting people or actions into types can be tricky.

> ▶ **ACTIVITY 10** Using Classification
>
> Imagine you are a journalist for a newspaper. You have been asked to write a humorous article on "types of spenders." If you had to classify people into types according to their spending habits, what categories would you create? We all know someone who spends money recklessly, so one type of spender might be called the reckless spender. Think of at least two other types and give them names. Next, write a paragraph for at least two of the types in which you describe their spending habits.

COMPARISON AND CONTRAST

If we did not have the mental ability to recognize similarities and differences, we would not be able to process any knowledge. We recognize a lamp, in part, because it is not a table! The human mind is wired for **comparison and contrast**. When we say *compare*, we are technically referring to finding similarities among things, whereas the term *contrast* technically means to find the differences. However, it is common to use the term *compare* to mean the act of identifying both similarities and differences. Comparing and contrasting is a rhetorical tool that is effective for a variety of writing tasks (see Table 4.6).

> **comparison and contrast:** A rhetorical pattern in which the similarities (comparing) and differences (contrasting) of two or more things are discussed.
>
> **Teaching Resources**
> For comparison and contrast writing assignments, see the Additional Writing Prompts in the IM.

A Sample of Comparison/Contrast Writing

In "The Dog Delusion," April Pedersen writes, "Within the past decade, however, pets—primarily dogs—have soared in importance." Pedersen questions whether this trend is healthy. One of her paragraphs, excerpted below, presents an extended comparison. As you read the paragraph, see if you can figure out the comparison and the criteria used to make it. To read the entire article, see Part 6.

> In a Pew Research Center study, 85 percent of dog owners said they consider their pet to be a member of their family. However the latest trend is to take that a step further in seeing the animal as a child. A company that sells pet health insurance policies has dubbed the last Sunday in April as "Pet Parents Day." Glance through magazines like *Bark*, *Cesar's Way* (courtesy of "Dog Whisperer" Cesar Millan), and other mainstream publications, and the term "pet parent" crops up regularly. The "my-dogs-are-my-kids" crowd isn't being tongue-in-cheek, either. They act on their beliefs, buying Christmas presents, photos with Santa, cosmetic surgery, and whatever-it-takes medical care for their animal. In fact having a puppy, claimed one "mother," is "exactly the same in all ways as having a baby." And while pushing a dog around in a stroller would have gotten you directions to a mental health facility twenty years ago, today it's de rigeur to see a canine in a stroller (or a papoose), and some passersby are downright disappointed to discover a human infant inside.

TABLE 4.6 Purposes for Using Comparison and Contrast

Writing purpose	How comparison and contrast can be used	Example
To support a variety of writing purposes	To provide a comparison in figurative language	A writer may use an analogy to help readers see a subject in a negative (or positive) way. For instance, comparing the legalization of recreational marijuana to a tsunami suggests that legalization is a negative thing. Analogies, similes, and metaphors can create suggestive language.
To reflect	To contrast the past and present	In reflective writing, a writer might compare attitudes about relationships they had as a teen with attitudes they have as a mature adult.
To inform	To explain similarities and differences	A writer's purpose may be to show how two things are similar or different. For instance, a writer may wish to help readers understand the differences in two fields, geography and geology.
To analyze	To understand something by recognizing its similarities or differences to other things	To explain what a blog is, a writer might compare it to a journal; since readers will be familiar with journals, they can begin to understand what blogs are.
To evaluate	To weigh the benefits of two or more courses of action.	An evaluation of two choices—for example, whether to lease or purchase a car—can help a writer evaluate which of those choices is best.
To persuade	To show that because *x* is like *y*, *x* should be treated the way *y* is treated	A writer may use an analogy between drunk driving and texting while driving to argue that because both are similar, texting while driving should be illegal, just as driving under the influence is illegal.

▶ **ACTIVITY 11 Analyzing Comparison and Contrast**

What effect does Pedersen intend to produce on readers by using this comparison? What is your personal response to the comparison?

Thinking Rhetorically about Comparing and Contrasting

To determine when you should include comparison and contrast in your writing and what that comparison and contrast should entail, start by analyzing the rhetorical situation. What message are you trying to convey? How might comparison and contrast help readers understand or believe that message? Use the questions in Rhetorical Toolbox 4.6 as a guide.

RHETORICAL TOOLBOX 4.6
Using Comparison and Contrast as a Writing Tool

1. **Rhetorical situation.** Does the rhetorical situation call for a comparison? Should there also be discussion of contrasts? How might readers benefit from such content?
2. **Purpose.** How much of your writing will be comprised of comparing or contrasting? For example, you might write an essay-length comparison and contrast if the purpose of the comparison and contrast is to inform readers about the differences or similarities between two or more things.
3. **Criteria for comparing and contrasting.** What criteria will readers find meaningful in your comparison and contrast? If you are analyzing plans to overhaul health care in the United States, for example, readers would probably want to read about criteria such as cost, quality of care, prescription drug costs, availability of care, and so on.
4. **Organization.** How will you make your comparison or contrast clear to the reader? In lengthy comparisons, you can organize your material using a block structure or a point-by-point structure as shown here.

Block arrangement	Point-by-point arrangement
Subject 1: Buying a car • Monthly payments • Mileage limits • Warranty • Ownership *Subject 2: Leasing a car* • Monthly payments • Mileage limits • Warranty • Ownership	*Point 1: Monthly payments* • Buying a car • Leasing a car *Point 2: Mileage limits* • Buying a car • Leasing a car *Point 3: Warranty* • Buying a car • Leasing a car *Point 4: Ownership* • Buying a car • Leasing a car

5. **Brief comparisons.** Is a brief comparison and contrast appropriate or effective for your purpose? If the purpose is to establish tone through figurative language, for example, use a brief comparison or analogy.
6. **Fairness.** Will readers judge your comparison and contrast to be fair? If a comparison is used as the basis for an evaluation, the comparison should be fair. A fair comparison analyzes two things in the same category. For instance, while it would be fair to compare two professionally produced romantic comedies, it would not be fair to compare a student's amateur video to a professionally produced film.

▶ **ACTIVITY 12** **Using Comparison and Contrast**

Imagine that you are filling out a job application for your first professional job in a field that interests you. One question asks why you chose this career over another one you had considered. For example, if you chose to be a nurse but had considered being a teacher, in this paragraph, you would show—via comparing and contrasting—why you chose nursing. What points would you focus on in your comparison? For instance, you might compare and contrast the two jobs by looking at job satisfaction, annual salary, working hours, travel requirements, and so on. Select the criteria that matter the most to you, and write a single-paragraph comparison of the two careers. Keep in mind that the audience is the hiring director for the job that interests you.

CAUSE AND EFFECT

Discussions about **cause and effect** center on the questions beginning with *why* and *how*. In almost all persuasive writing, writers spend significant time explaining why their positions are reasonable. These explanations often take the form of cause and effect analysis. You can use cause and effect explanations for a number of writing tasks, from explaining phenomena, to proposing solutions, to arguing why something happened or predicting what might happen in the future (see Table 4.7).

cause and effect: A rhetorical pattern in which the factors that contributed to an event or resulted from an event are presented.

Teaching Resources
For writing assignments that emphasize cause and effect, see the Additional Writing Prompts in the IM.

A Sample of Cause and Effect

What makes a person commit a murder? This is the question Laura Migliore asks and seeks to answer in her article, "The Violent Brain: Ingredients of a Mass Murderer." In the excerpt that follows, notice that Migliore is careful to use qualifiers in her brief presentation of what causes a person to become homicidal. Migliore's article is almost solely about causes and effects, and it appears in its entirety in Chapter 6.

> Here's the thing: On paper, James Holmes measured up seemingly well. Intelligent, disciplined, and raised by successful parents—his father, a senior scientist; mother, a nurse. Holmes graduated from UC San Diego at the top of his class and was working towards a Ph.D. in neuroscience. It's hard to imagine that this would be a person to carry out one of the nation's deadliest recent massacres. But upon taking a closer look into the details of his behavior and characteristics leading up the massacre, experts agree that he does indeed fit the profile of a typical mass murderer.
>
> Holmes has been put behind bars, but the question still lingers: What drives someone to go on such a violent rampage, indiscriminately killing innocent people? Are there clear motives behind these violent acts? Insanity, or a psychotic break? An absent conscience? Or are some people just born natural killers?
>
> Researchers have posed the same questions and, with recent scientific advancements, have been able to note personality-based, neurological, and

TABLE 4.7 Purposes for Using Cause and Effect

Writing purpose	How cause and effect can be used	Example
To support a variety of writing purposes	To answer "why," "how," and "what if"	In an article about a violent incident, a writer tries to figure out why the incident occurred. Equally important is speculation about what might have happened if certain other conditions had been in place.
To reflect	To examine a personal event from the past and ponder its causes or effects	A personal narrative that explores the writer's love for nature might involve narrating formative experiences that helped him develop his feelings about the physical world.
To inform	To clarify and instruct	A biology textbook might explore the causes of genetic mutations; a history textbook might explore the effects of colonization on native peoples; an economics textbook might present the causes and effects of trade policies and tariffs.
To analyze	To understand an event or phenomenon	A journalist may write an article on the effects of social distancing measures taken during the coronavirus epidemic.
To evaluate	To compare and judge options	To evaluate three plans for reducing carbon emissions, a writer may discuss the effects the three plans might have on the environment.
To persuade	To propose an action	A writer may support a proposal to create a new law, for instance, by claiming the law will result in positive effects and presenting those effects. Alternatively, if a writer can show that an action or policy causes harm, the writer may be more likely to persuade the reader that the action or policy should be changed.

even genetic-based commonalities in these violent individuals. Most experts will agree that there isn't a single determining factor that creates a mass murderer, but when multiple triggers are combined, a killer is born. Furthermore, through various studies looking at brain images and scans of murderers, psychopaths, and violent individuals, researchers are gaining leverage in mapping out the neural activity behind impulsive violence.

▶ **ACTIVITY 13** Analyzing Cause and Effect

How is Migliore careful to not overgeneralize about the characteristics of a murderer? Explain your answer.

Thinking Rhetorically about Cause and Effect

Using cause and effect discussions in your writing can be tricky. Readers will rightfully question whether you have accurately identified the causes and effects you present. To determine when you should include discussions of cause and effect, start by analyzing the rhetorical situation. Use the questions in Rhetorical Toolbox 4.7 as a guide.

RHETORICAL TOOLBOX 4.7

Using Cause and Effect as a Writing Tool

1. **Purpose.** Is a discussion of causes and effects necessary? Will readers expect you to address causes and effects? For instance, when lawmakers propose a new law, a discussion of how the law will affect citizens is expected.
2. **Accuracy.** Do you have enough information to accurately discuss causes or effects? Writers must think critically to avoid making fallacious assumptions about causes. The science of *causality* consists of figuring out the actual causes of an event or phenomenon. It is easy to make mistakes in determining causes. Likewise, predicting effects is challenging. Be sure that any discussion of cause and effect is not fallacious. For more information about identifying faulty thinking in cause and effect discussions, see Chapter 16, Logical Fallacies.
3. **Causal chains.** Will readers criticize your understanding of the domino effect? Sometimes causes are complex. A causes B, and then B causes C, and so on. This chain of effects is often called the *domino effect*. When discussing causes and effects, be aware that the phenomenon you are presenting may be a part of a chain of causes and effects.
4. **Organization.** Will you need to use chronological arrangement to clarify your cause and effect discussion? Sometimes a discussion of cause and effect is similar to writing about a process. Consider using a chronological arrangement to organize cause and effect writing.
5. **Qualifiers.** How and when should you use qualifiers? According to the greatest philosophers, no one can ever know with complete certainty that *x* caused *y*. Use qualifiers such as *may* and *probably* to signify to readers the degree of certainty you have about causality.

▶ **ACTIVITY 14 Using Cause and Effect**

Think of a policy on your college campus that you would create or change if you could do so. For example, would you change the drop policy? Your professor's late policy? The parking policies on campus? Write a paragraph in which you explain what policy you would change, and support and defend the change using cause and effect.

TABLE 4.8 Purposes for Using Process Analysis

Writing purpose	How process analysis can be used	Example
To reflect	To understand personal development	A writer may seek to understand how they triumphed over addiction by examining their personal process of recovery.
To inform	To train or instruct about procedures	Training instructions for new employees, for example, will probably include process analysis. A textbook on nutrition will present the processes involved in metabolizing food.
To analyze	To understand something by seeing how it works	An analytical writing task, such as the analysis of how internet privacy works, might benefit from a discussion of a process. In this case, readers may need to know the process of how the internet works before they can understand privacy issues.
To evaluate	To judge effectiveness	A paper examining methods for losing weight might examine weight loss processes to determine which one is most effective.
To persuade	To propose a new process	For instance, a proposal to make higher education free would need to include proof that there is a process—a funding mechanism—that could make the proposal feasible.

PROCESS ANALYSIS

process analysis: A rhetorical pattern in which the stages, phases, or steps that are used to accomplish a purpose are identified.

Process analysis is a rhetorical tool that can be used as support. It can also be used to structure a product manual or to inform readers about a scientific, business, or social process. Some processes are concrete, such as how to set up a home network. Other processes—such as how people fall in love—are psychological and will require explanations of the mental steps that explain human behavior. More uses for process analysis are discussed in Table 4.8.

Teaching Resources
For writing assignments that emphasize process analysis, see the Additional Writing Prompts in the IM.

A Sample of Process Analysis

A graphic from a U.S. government website presents the process of becoming a U.S. citizen (Figure 4.1). As you study it, think about its appropriateness for a particular rhetorical situation.

FIGURE 4.1 An infographic that shows a process.

▶ **ACTIVITY 15 Analyzing Process**

For what purposes will this graphic be most helpful? For what purposes might a more lengthy text-based explanation of the process of becoming a U.S. citizen be appropriate? Explain your answer.

Thinking Rhetorically about Process Analysis

Use the questions in Rhetorical Toolbox 4.8 as a guide to help you determine when and how to include process analysis in your writing.

> **RHETORICAL TOOLBOX 4.8**
> ## Using Process Analysis as a Writing Tool
>
> 1. **Purpose.** Will readers benefit from the discussion of a process?
> 2. **Audience.** How extensively will you need to explain the process? Analyze the audience to figure out which steps must be discussed. Consider whether you should explain the process in brief or whether readers will need a lengthy explanation. For instance, in an essay for general readers about voter fraud in the United States, a brief explanation of how the Electoral College works would be sufficient to help refresh the memories of readers. There would be no need, however, to provide an extensive review of the process unless the Electoral College was the focus of the essay.
> 3. **Illustration.** Will process analysis alone be sufficient for readers, or should you couple it with illustration? Many processes can be presented visually. Infographics, flowcharts, and other types of visual information are commonly used to present each step of a process in a brief format.
> 4. **Transitions.** Will the use of transitions help readers to understand the process more clearly? Transitions such as *first, next, simultaneously, finally,* and so on aid comprehension, especially when the process is complex.

▶ **ACTIVITY 16** Using Process

Create a "how to" guide for a process with which you are familiar for readers who have never analyzed the process before. For example, if you are a proficient guitar player, what is the process one should take to master guitar? If you are familiar with a work process, such as checking in patients at a clinic, what are the steps of that process? Use Rhetorical Toolbox 4.8 as a guide.

CHAPTER PROJECT Using Rhetorical Patterns

PROJECT 1 Analyzing Rhetorical Patterns of an Essay

Most texts consist of a mixture of rhetorical patterns used for support. Select any article or essay in this text, including those with excerpts presented in this chapter. Read the full piece and annotate each rhetorical pattern the writer uses. Then write an analytical essay in which you present the writer's thesis statement, and discuss each of the rhetorical patterns he or she uses as support. In your essay, explain why using the rhetorical pattern is (or is not) appropriate.

PROJECT 2 Using a Rhetorical Pattern for Different Purposes

The ability to use rhetorical patterns is a transferrable skill because the patterns can be used for a variety of writing purposes. Select one rhetorical pattern, and demonstrate how you could use it for these three writing types: personal writing (e.g., blogs, reflections, social media postings); professional writing (e.g., a business report, employee evaluation); and academic writing (e.g., an essay, report).

PROJECT 3 **Writing the Story for a GoFundMe Page**

In the Warm-Up activity for this chapter, you read about DeShawn's attempt to create a GoFundMe page. Find a cause that you believe is worthwhile, and draft a GoFundMe page. If you have never seen the GoFundMe website, examine it. You will see a section called "Story" that presents the reason the cause should be funded. For this assignment, write the "Story" part of your GoFundMe page. Use at least three rhetorical patterns to develop the content on the page.

Reflecting to Develop a Writer's Mindset

What does this chapter mean when it asserts that rhetorical patterns are tools? In what ways are patterns tools? Provide an example of how you have used a rhetorical pattern as a tool in everyday communication.

FAQ KEY WORDS AND PHRASES FOR THE RHETORICAL PATTERNS

The words and phrases that follow can help you as a reader to identify rhetorical patterns. As a writer, you can use these words and phrases in your own compositions.

1. **What are key words and phrases for description?**

adjectives:	adverbs:	sensory words:	similes and metaphors:	spatial descriptors:
dusty, clammy, yellow, stony-faced, self-absorbed, gnarly, smooth, slithering, and so on	hoarsely, slowly, energetically, half-heartedly, and so on	pungent smell, scent of lilacs, peppery, spicy, silky, rough, noisily, and so on	the little car looked like a coffin on wheels; she lives in a shoebox	to the left, behind, on top, and so on

2. **What are key words and phrases for narration?**

after	finally	initially	not long after	then
as soon as	first, second . . .	later	now	today
before	following	meanwhile	once	until
during	immediately	next	soon	when

3. **What are key words and phrases for definition?**

consists of	idea	is known as	redefine
define	involves	meaning of	refers to
entails	is characterized by	means	term

4. **What are key words and phrases for illustration?**

consider	imagine	such as	to clarify
for example	like	support	to explain
for instance			

5. **What are key words and phrases for classification?**

characteristic	feature	quality	subtype
classify	group	section	trait
cohort	identify	sort	type
distinguish	kind	species	variety

6. **What are key words and phrases for comparison and contrast?**

although	different	in comparison	on the other
but	dissimilar	likewise	hand
by the same	equal	nonetheless	otherwise
token	however	on the contrary	point
criteria			similar

7. **What are key words and phrases for cause and effect?**

as a result	cause	for that reason	so
at last	consequently	if . . . then	therefore
because of	effect	since	thus

8. **What are key words and phrases for process analysis?**

after	first, second,	next	stage	to begin
before	third . . .	now	step	to continue
finally	later	phase	then	to end
	meanwhile			

TRY IT!

Read the following paragraph, determine its rhetorical pattern(s), and rewrite it, adding transitions.

> While COVID-19 affects people differently, some patients, such as James Woods, are at a higher risk of dying from it. James is a 52-year-old man who has several chronic diseases but no primary care doctor. Like many other Americans, James does not have health insurance. He smokes two packs of cigarettes a day. He has developed emphysema. He also has a poor diet. He has developed Type II diabetes. He makes frequent visits to the emergency department but never follows up with a doctor or gets his prescriptions filled. These behaviors take a toll on James' health and increase his chance of dying from the virus if he contracts it.

CREDITS

Page 62. Hogan, Linda. "Black Walnut: A Sweet Blood History." Cold Mountain Review, 2016. Accessed March 05, 2019. https://www.coldmountainreview.org/issues/fall-2016-special-issue-on-forests/black-walnut-a-sweet-blood-history-by-linda-hogan. Used with permission.

Page 64. Huang, Justin, "How I Overcame My Stuttering," International Stuttering Association, 2015. http://isad.isastutter.org/isad-2015/papers-presented-by-2015/stories-and-experiences-with-stuttering-by-pws/how-i-overcame-my-stuttering-and-why-thats-made-all-the-difference/. Copyright ©2015 by Justin Huang. All rights reserved. Used with permission.

Page 72. Pedersen, April. "The Dog Delusion." TheHumanist.com. March 17, 2014. Accessed March 05, 2019. https://thehumanist.com/magazine/november-december-2009/features/the-dog-delusion. Used with permission.

Page 75. Migliore, Lauren. (2017, Oct. 7). "The Violent Brain: Ingredients of a Mass Murderer," Brain World. All rights reserved. Used with permission.

Page 79. U.S. Citizenship and Immigration Services, Pathway to U.S. Citizenship, March 2019.

PART 2 Writing Purposes

5 Writing to Reflect

CHAPTER OBJECTIVES

You will learn to:
- Identify key rhetorical concerns of reflective writing.
- Analyze reflective texts.
- Compose a reflective text.

Connect Adaptive Learning Assignment
Consider assigning Connect's Adaptive Learning Assignments to support this chapter.

"The unexamined life is not worth living." These famous words, spoken by the ancient Greek philosopher Socrates, capture the value of personal reflection. Reflection requires us to pause. It invites us to spend time in our thoughts, examining our experiences so that we can understand more about ourselves and the world. Our reflections are sometimes life changing, and they are often worth sharing with others.

Some types of reflective writing, such as writing in a journal, record the *process* of reflecting. Journal writing is a reflective activity designed to help the writer discover insights. The act of writing itself brings clarity to situations we may have difficulty understanding or processing. Other reflective writing genres, such as narrative essays and memoirs, present the *insights* gleaned from reflection. The readings in this chapter, as well as the writing assignment and student work in progress, help you understand how reflective writing works and how you as a writer can use this genre for your own purposes.

WARM-UP

Shamaya is determined to make a name for herself on social media. Hundreds of people already follow her on Twitter and watch her funny videos on YouTube. She recently began a daily blog, posting an hour-by-hour recap of the day's events with her reflections. Even though her blog posts are humorous, they do not seem to attract her Twitter and YouTube followers; she is getting very few clicks. What could be the problem?

Teaching Resources
See the Instructor's Manual (IM) for suggestions about how to teach this chapter, and consider assigning this chapter's test-bank quiz.

REFLECTIVE WRITING FROM A WRITER'S MINDSET

Unlike journal writing, reflective writing that is written for others to read requires the writer to be aware of their audience. Many of the events we reflect on and find personally interesting, such as having a child, graduating from college, or buying a house, may not be interesting to readers. The key to finding a good subject for reflective writing is thinking rhetorically by analyzing the audience who will read your work. You can do that by putting yourself in the reader's shoes. Would you be interested in reading about another person's graduation? Unless something extraordinary happened at the ceremony, such a topic would probably be a bit boring.

On the other hand, you might be interested in reading about something you have not experienced. For example, an essay about a young woman's night spent in jail for drunk driving might be interesting. The experiences do not have to be extraordinary to be interesting. A college student who reflects on his dad's racism and its effects on his family might attract readers because most of us have experienced awkward family relationships, and the issue of racism is of interest to many people. In the Warm-Up exercise, you read about Shamaya's problem attracting readers to her blog. If you surmised that readers simply do not care to know what happened every hour of every day, you are correct. Shamaya was writing a chronicle: a list of things that happened to her. Even if the chronicle included humor, reading a chronological account of a person's day is tedious. To attract more readers, Shamaya could be more selective about her topics. Instead of writing her blog every day, she could write only when she has insights to share that a general audience might find interesting or thoughtful.

Thinking rhetorically as you write a reflective paper involves several specific concerns. As you embark on a reflective project, use the questions in Rhetorical Toolbox 5.1 to stimulate your thinking on how to engage readers.

Teaching Suggestion See the IM for examples of blogs that students can analyze in terms of reader interest.

RHETORICAL TOOLBOX 5.1
The Rhetorical Concerns of Reflective Writing

1. **Topic and audience.** On what topic would you most like to reflect? Will this topic be meaningful to readers? Selecting a topic requires thinking about both your own interests and whether readers can gain insight from the topic you choose.
2. **Purpose.** What is your purpose in writing the reflection? That purpose is usually to communicate unique or poignant insights gained after reflecting on an event or situation.
3. **Details.** What details, description, and background information does the audience need? A reflective essay includes a description of the event, memory, or situation upon which you are reflecting. How much description or narration is necessary? How much background information should you provide?
4. **Message.** What message do you want your reflective writing to convey? The goal of reflection is to arrive at insights worth sharing. These insights constitute the message of a reflective essay. Readers should not have to wonder why you are sharing a memory or a story.

▶ **ACTIVITY 1** Analyzing Topics to Predict Interest and Relevance

Shamaya is rethinking the content she posts on her blog. Instead of blogging about her day, she has jotted down three topics she thinks would be interesting. If you stumbled upon Shamaya's blog and didn't know anything about her, would any of these entries be interesting to you? Why or why not? Which one would you find most interesting? Why? Which would be least interesting? Why?

1. In this blog entry, I'll talk about the concept of "rage cleaning," cleaning one's place to deal with anger. It's an amazing experience!
2. In this blog entry, I'll talk about how the recent wildfires in my area have changed my views about the environment.
3. In this blog entry, I'll talk about the eccentric people in my family.

Teaching Resources
Consider using the PowerPoint "Choosing Topics: Predicting Readers' Interest and Creating Relevancy."

MODELS OF REFLECTIVE WRITING

Easter Rock 1983
Rigoberto González

Teaching Suggestion
For additional models of reflective writing, see Part 6, An Anthology of Readings.

The first text, "Easter Rock 1983," is a chapter from Rigoberto González's book, Red-Inked Retablos. *González has written five books of poetry and twelve books of prose, and he has won numerous awards for his writing. He is a professor of English and director of the MFA Program in Creative Writing at Rutgers-Newark.* Red-Inked Retablos, *as the University of Arizona Press notes, "offers an in-depth meditation on the development of gay Chicano literature." In the annotations, we note the rhetorical strategies González uses to create a reflective essay that readers can enjoy.*

The details González chooses to describe his family are very specific; they help readers experience his world.

Concrete details—things the reader can visualize—help readers see what the writer saw.

My family took to Easter much like it took to Halloween because even though we were a non-church-going Day-of-the-Dead–celebrating immigrant family from Michoacán, we wanted to fit in. We nailed down the basics—plastic Easter eggs filled with candy, marshmallow Peeps, and chocolates shaped like bunnies—and then, once we renamed the religious holiday "el día de la coneja" (Day of the Rabbit), we filled in the rest of the blanks the González way. That meant buying braids of intestines, cured sirloin, and beer, oiling the shotguns, and heading out to the middle of the southern California desert, where the men in our family got drunk and lit the grill with gasoline siphoned from one of their cars.

Because this was what my family did I learned to enjoy it, though I knew Americans celebrated Easter much differently—I had seen them do so many times on television with their delicately decorated eggs and baskets brimming with curly seaweed grass. Still, I liked the freedom of the desert, the way the adults clustered around the food and laughed while the kids were allowed to explore unsupervised. We'd climb trees and boulders, fall and skin our knees, pick wildflowers, and above all else we'd keep our eyes open for snakes.

"And don't scare it away if you find one," Abuelo* called out. "That's lunch!"

I remember these outings as the only times we actually looked like a happy family and I always regretted that we were so far off the main roads that not a single car passed by to take note of our harmony. How unfortunate that our neighbors had such a one-sided view of us: nineteen people squeezed into a tiny apartment in which ten kids ran out of the house fleeing the belt and nine adults argued on the porch until someone threw a half-consumed beer at someone else and the can would stay on the ground growing warm for hours until someone had sense enough to pick it up.

But at the Easter Sunday outing no one got a beer thrown at them, not even in jest. Instead, the radio played and we'd laugh at Abuelo dancing with a piece of meat dangling from the tongs. And then, once the men got a few drinks in them, they walked over to the car and popped open the trunk.

On one such Easter celebration, from the corner of my eye I saw my uncle pull out the burlap sack containing the shotguns and that's when my anxiety began. All week my uncle kept promising my older cousins that this year was their turn to shoot and each time he mentioned it my cousins would beam. I wasn't too keen on the idea so I didn't react. My father must have misunderstood my apathy for wistfulness because on one occasion he walked up behind me and said, "Don't worry, I'll make sure you get your turn too."

I was too stunned to correct him so when the sack came out of the trunk, I hoped they would forget it was our turn to shoot, but my cousins hadn't forgotten. As soon as they noticed the guns being pulled out they ran over, hollering, and left me sitting alone on a rock.

---
* Grandfather.

Sidenotes:

He describes the actions of the day but does not tell a chronological story.

He uses dialogue and humor.

González presents reflective thoughts on these activities.

Continued use of concrete details helps the reader see and imagine the scenes.

González narrates the event that is the center of his reflection.

He reflects on the men in his family and their interest in guns.	What was it about guns that intrigued the men in my family? I didn't understand it. I had grown up around them—rifles for hunting deer, BB guns for pigeons and doves. I was more interested in the shells, big plastic ones with a copper base, round like a penny, and metal ones that I could use to whistle. One time I pocketed so many my shorts kept sliding down my hips and my father made me throw them out before I climbed back into the car.
González reveals that he doesn't have the same interests and attitudes as his male relatives.	The truth was: guns frightened me. Their weight, their bang, their boom, the ricochet that left my ears ringing, the harm they did to the birds whose eyes looked so human with the lids closed. That was my job on those hunting trips. I had to pick them off the ground, dig for them in the brush, the red wound disrupting the smooth surface of feathers and down. Sometimes my uncle would pluck them on the spot and their naked little bodies of pimpled skin looked violated, not edible at all.
	I had never killed a living thing, except for an injured hummingbird once, and by accident, because I thought I was saving its life by pulling out that funny-looking twig sticking out of its beak. As soon as I figured out it was its tongue I burst into tears and prayed for forgiveness over its tiny grave for a month.
González moves from reflection back to the central event. He shows, through details, the disconnect between him and his father.	But neither did I want to shoot a gun. Guns were not pretty or graceful or pleasant, they were vulgar things without much imagination: they caused damage or death and nothing else. Because the younger kids were not allowed to shoot (they would have to wait to be at least twelve years old like me) they were enlisted to collect the empty cans and line them up at the clearing. I made the mistake of picking a can up. My father quickly corrected me by grabbing it out of my hands and throwing it back.
For this limited part of the essay, González uses a narrative strategy: he introduces the story, works up to the moment when he has to shoot, and then provides a resolution. Using these plot elements helps the reader experience the anxiety about what is about to happen.	I don't know what I was hoping would happen, but as soon as the action started I made no effort to fight to be the first to shoot or to even stand close to my uncle as he demonstrated the safe way to load, hold, and shoot. I wanted to say something clever like, Wouldn't it be safest not to even touch the gun? but I pictured my uncle giving me the knuckle on the head. Instead, I just kept quiet, wishing that somehow I would become invisible.
My fifteen-year-old cousin went first. He stepped up to the firing range like he had been born for this and made a big show of taking

aim, deliberately drawing out the moment to the point that even his mother called out, "Shoot the damn thing before I fall asleep already!" He shot his two rounds. Everyone clapped and he bowed. And then another cousin stepped up, but he was a big lug with a man's body at thirteen, so no one expected anything less than a seasoned performance.

When my turn came, I sensed the enthusiasm plummet. The rifle was heavier than I thought and when I almost dropped it my uncle said, "That was my fault," and I knew no one had believed him, especially not my father who looked like he was wishing for the miracle of instantaneous testosterone.

The dialogue consists only of the most important things that were said.

When my uncle stood close behind me, positioning my stance, he whispered into my ear, "Don't fuck this up. Your father's watching." And I knew then that I would indeed fuck this up. I fucked it up so badly because when I shot once then twice, the rounds didn't even make the same noise they made when my cousins pulled the trigger. Or at least it didn't sound like it to me. I couldn't even tell if they had hit the ground or if the shots had raised dust or anything because I didn't see very clearly, even with my eyes wide open. The whole thing was anti-climactic: our audience had seen it done twice before and done better. To add insult to injury, no one clapped and my father simply turned around and reached into the cooler for another beer.

My oldest cousin broke the spell by shouting out that it was his turn again, but by now everyone had lost interest and had moved onto other activities. I relinquished the rifle and it felt like I had just handed over whatever it was that my father had wanted me to be. And so I slipped away, watching the fun taking place without me. I sat back on my rock and recalled every other time I had disappointed my father. One moment stood out, though that Easter Sunday had already risen to the top three. Once we were visiting family across the border and I bowed out of a game of hide-and-seek because there were too many creepy places to hide in that badly lit street. I was called a chicken but didn't think much of it, until I got bored watching television inside the house all by myself so I decided to go back out. I saw my father sitting on the sidewalk with a few of the boys, and I thought it would be funny to sneak up and

The writer moves from the event to more reflection. This reflection brings up the central conflict: González felt he was a disappointment to his father.

| | scare them with a nicely timed scream. But as I approached them I caught a snippet of their conversation.
Significant dialogue is included. | "Why is your son so afraid of everything?" one of the boys asked.

"Like what?" my father said.

"Of everything. Like, of the dark."

"Well, he was raised differently. In the North. There are plenty of lights up there."

González returns to describing the scene. | I wasn't sure what hurt me more: my father's shame or my own at having to witness my father making up an excuse that no one really believed. At that moment I changed my mind about sneaking up on them. I slunk back into the house and tried to sit in the living room with the television off. Eventually, predictably, I got scared of the dark and turned the light on.

González tells a final story, one that leads him to a central insight. | Just as easily as I slipped away I slipped back into the Easter Sunday party. We had our meal, drank orange soda, and set off to look for the Easter eggs. This year we didn't have enough of the plastic ones, so my aunt fashioned a bunch out of aluminum foil. So many other activities took place that no one mentioned the disaster with the rifle, and I would have forgotten it myself except that it all flushed back into my face each time I saw my father. Once we had found enough eggs, we sat around wherever we could find shade to eat the candy. I sat next to a boulder and picked the nettles off the cuffs of my pants. When my father came up to me I didn't even look up. Whatever reprimand I was going to get I would take with my head down.

"I found something too," he said.

The gentleness in his voice disarmed me. I looked up. He held something out in his hand. "What is it?"

"Take it," he said.

It was a rock. A smooth rock, egg-like but not quite. On one small part of its surface it had been engraved with a perfect circle, a white ring. "Is it an Indian symbol?"

"Maybe," he said. "But keep it to yourself. There's only one."

The reflection's significance is summed up in the paragraph "At that moment...": as a child, he realized he wanted a closer relationship with his father. Readers should know, from this section, why this day was important to González. | At that moment I wanted more, that's how much I realized what an important gesture it was. I wanted him to say that it was fine that I didn't know how to shoot a gun or that I was afraid of the dark, I wanted him to bend down and touch my shoulder or even tap the side of my leg with his foot. Or maybe it should be me who makes the first move. Maybe I should stretch my arms and ask him to pull me up, and then we could hug and begin all over again, no hard feelings for all the disappointments that came before. Maybe I should dare to say, Next time you show me how to shoot the rifle. Yes, maybe that was the way to go.

But before I could get the first word out my father walked away, breaking the small space that opened this level of intimacy between a father and his son.

He ends the essay by showing how the event ended.

I didn't call him back because these moments have brief lives, that much I knew. It was like that tiny hummingbird, which might have lived had I let it be. At that moment all that was left to do was to stuff the rock in my pocket and jump to my feet. It was Easter Sunday. The González family packed up its guns and leftovers and put away their found treasures and surprise gifts, leaving no evidence (although no one had seen us arrive) that anything special had transpired in the southern California desert.

Analyzing González's Rhetorical Strategies

1. **What is the writer or speaker's purpose?** González wants to share with readers a moment that was significant in his childhood. To help readers understand why this moment was so important, he must recreate the kind of tension he felt as a sensitive boy in a family that seemed to value machismo over sensitivity. He must also help readers see how his father's simple act communicated a message of acceptance. To achieve these purposes, González both *shows* and *tells*. He shows what his family is like by having readers visualize concrete details, and he tells readers how he felt in the situations he describes.

2. **What is a good topic for reflection?** González chose an event that might seem mundane, but because of the rhetorical choices he made, he was able to convey the significance of his father's actions on that typical Easter Sunday. The conflict in the event comes from the feeling that he is a disappointment to his father. Because most readers understand (and have experienced) the need for parental acceptance, readers can relate to González's feelings and needs.

3. **What details, description, and background information does the audience need?** González knows that he must help readers understand the kind

of family he came from because it is the family dynamic that produces the tension in the story. But González does not provide the typical information (names, ages, occupations) one might use to describe a family. Instead, he includes concrete details such as the foods they ate and the apartment they lived in. These details help readers visualize the scene. González must also decide how explicit to be about the insight he gained on that Easter day.

4. **What kinds of messages are presented in reflective writing?** If we were to write a thesis statement for the piece, it might sound something like this: "In one simple act, my father expressed to me that he loved me in spite of the fact that I was not like the other boys and men in the family." Notice, however, that González does not write such a sentence. He presents all the details readers need to infer that central insight. Rigoberto González's skillful mix of memory, insight, and detail contributes to the success of his memoir.

Thoughts after an Owl
Leath Tonino

Now that you read the selection by Rigoberto González and examined some of his rhetorical strategies, you are more prepared to identify the rhetorical moves of another writer, Leath Tonino. Tonino is the author of The Animal One Thousand Miles Long, *a book of reflections on his experiences in Vermont. The following essay, originally printed in* Camas: The Nature of the West, *presents his experiences, especially his perceptions, on spending time in nature. As you read, make notes about the rhetorical strategies Tonino uses and anything else you think is important.*

Yesterday, wandering at dusk in the brown hills that rise from this condo-sprawl called Palm Springs, California, I spent half an hour with a long-eared owl. I tell you most sincerely that there are few creatures as stirringly strange and spookily awesome and mystically mystical as birds from the order *Strigiformes*. Very much the griffin of legend, these birds—that is if the griffin of legend upped its weirdness by a factor of, say, eleven.

Dinosaur feet. Shaggy sheep legs. A body of feathers and fur and leaves and twigs and shattered bits of light and shadow. Of course, the face is part human, part cat, part seal, and affixed to a head that twists 360 degrees. If that's not enough, this vision, this being, this power, my how it launches into the air and glides silently on—no, can't be possible—on 40 inches of wing!

I hate to make a bold statement (hyperbole, my nemesis) but it feels more and more that every single time I go outdoors I am buckling up for some kind of borderline hallucinatory experience. The natural world just does not fail to provoke in me awe, wonder, vibes of fear, tingles of trepidation, and a kind of meditative drift-state wherein all the senses knit all their sense-data together at once into a kind of synesthetic carpet, a magic rug upon which I sail off to who knows where. Did I tell you about the desert blister beetles I ran into recently, *Lytta magister* in nasty gooey sexed-up swarms? As Harvey, my old redneck neighbor from childhood would say, *Sheeeit*. To spend ten minutes with these beetles, damn, you better be buckled, maybe even helmeted.

A week ago, hiking solo in that very same parched, rugged, so-brown labyrinth of hills, that topographic maze flanking the commercial shitstrip of mega churches, payday loan pawnshops, car dealerships, windborne litter, bearded men masticated by a brutal economic system and subsequently regurgitated back onto the street with only junk-filled shopping carts to call home—hiking solo in them thar wacky hills, I couldn't even put my hand down to touch things, like interesting rock-things or plant-things or stick-things.

The reason I couldn't touch, say, a strange stick that drew my attention, and that a considerable part of me did badly want to touch, was that my hands, my flesh, my integument, was almost scared to do so. It was like these hands, which are so freakin' sensitive, would just gather too, too, too much information, too, too, too much vital presence and place-specific truth. My feet were sheltered by leather, soled with rubber. My body *needed* that mediation. The hands, though, were and are naked, literally naked, naked nonstop.

It's interesting, don't you agree? We all recognize that if you show up at work buckass, birthday-suit nude you will feel very awkward, the entire experience intensified, altered. Pause here. Consider. That's what your hands do every day! They live *outside*, with nothing to hide behind. Bushwhacking around last week, as mentioned, was very odd indeed: I was nervous to even lay a wee digit on this sweet dry earth.

Granted, there was probably one more thing at play, which is the prickliness and poisonousness of the desert, the possibility of camouflaged snakes and spiders and scorpions and whatnot (the equivalent in the mossy green Vermont of my youth would be putting your hand down on a huge slug or something, maybe a rotting possum, a sodden deer carcass). And that loops back to my initial point regarding the nearly hallucinatory quality of a simple, routine, back-of-the-shitstrip-at-dusk walk: Any moment it can feel like some griffin or mystical face is about to pop out and look at you with huge yellow eyes. It can feel like a stick beneath your hand might not be a stick but the body of a serpent, or a mass of writhing ants, or some small something that has a soul and a voice and will speak across the self-other boundary. It can feel like you might be encountering—the divine?

Once, camping on and with a big Coloradan mountain, heart of the heart of winter, blue moonlight washing over snow, me sitting in that snow, no tent, no plan, just sitting there in the middle of a clear-cold night's vast crystalline silence, a fox pawed up within five feet, looked me in the eye, hung out, swung its tail, then walked away. I will repeat that: A blue moony fox faced my face, eyed my eye, hung *out*, came rushing in (the sparking electric current of unadulterated perception!), then walked away.

YOUR TURN Analyzing Tonino's Rhetorical Strategies

Explain your answer for each question in two or three sentences. Use examples from the text to support your points.

1. Why is Tonino's essay considered reflective writing?
2. What insights did the writer have upon reflecting on his experiences in nature?
3. In what ways does Tonino's essay differ from a journal entry? In other words, how is this essay written to appeal to readers?
4. How does Tonino make his personal experience in nature relevant to a general reader?
5. Which of Tonino's writing strategies would you use if you were to write a reflective essay? Explain where or how or why you would use the strategies.

CHAPTER PROJECT Writing to Reflect

Here are three reflective writing projects. The first project asks you to find your own topic, while the next two projects provide more guidance about what to write.

PROJECT 1 Find Your Own Topic

Write a reflective essay in which you discuss the significance of a particular event in your life. Make sure your essay meets these criteria:

1. A general audience would be able to relate to the topic. A general audience would find the topic interesting.
2. The essay includes both an account of the significant moment and your reflective insights about that moment.

Use the formatting style specified by your instructor.

PROJECT 2 Tracing Personal Evolution in a Reflective Essay

Changing, evolving, developing, becoming: we all experience changes over time in the ways that we think and behave. Stories about how we evolved or changed for the better can be interesting to readers. For instance, overcoming an addiction, becoming confident about a subject or skill, or taking charge of one's physical health are changes that happen over time and have a positive effect on one's life. Think of who you are today. What challenges did you have to overcome to develop into the person you are? Write a reflective essay in which you use a series of brief stories and reflections on those stories to show how you have changed and developed over time.

PROJECT 3 A Reflective Blogging Project

Blogs are ideal for reflective writing. A blog, after all, is a personal space. Readers expect the writer to present their thoughts, reactions, feelings, and experiences. In this project, you will find a personal blog that demonstrates reflective writing that you admire, and you will create a blog posting of your own. Here are the steps to follow:

1. Find a blog posting that you believe is an excellent model of reflective writing *and* that you find interesting. One way to find blogs is to look for blogs associated with well-known newspapers or magazines. Search "New York Times" + blogs, for example, and you will be taken to a list of the blogs sponsored by *The New York Times*.
2. Once you find a blog posting you admire, write a brief analysis of the blog. (You will post this analysis in the next step.) In your analysis, answer these questions:
   A. How can you tell the purpose of the writing is to reflect?
   B. How does the writer make the topic relevant for readers?
   C. What choices did the writer make about detail, description, and background information? In other words, what content did

---

Teaching Resources
The chapter writing projects are available as writing assignments in Connect.

Teaching Suggestion
Another reflective assignment is to have students reflect on something they have read or have learned for a college class. Students are not always aware of the power of reflection in the learning process. For information you can share with students, see "The Power of Reflection for Deep Learning" by Todd Kettler, https://www.researchgate.net/publication/321169028_The_Power_of_Reflection_for_Deep_Learning.

Teaching Resources
A more detailed assignment page in the IM includes a link to an actual blog model that shows how one student finished the assignment. Screenshots of the student's blog are also included on the detailed assignment sheet, and additional suggestions for finding professional blog models are provided.

the writer include? What kind of content did the writer *not* include?

   D. What is the message or insight?

   E. What made you select this blog? Why is it a good model of reflective writing?

3. Create your own blog on a free blogging site such as blogger.com, wordpress.com, or the blogging program in your school's learning management system (ask your instructor about this). Create three postings. In the first posting, provide a link to the reflective blog you found and analyzed, and include your analysis (the information you composed in step B above). In your second posting, present your own reflective writing. In your third posting, analyze *your own reflective blog post.* Use these questions to analyze your blog posting:

   A. Discuss at least three rhetorical choices you made as you composed this blog posting.

   B. Why do you think a reader might find the topic interesting? Explain.

   C. How might you use reflective writing, such as this blog posting, in other areas of your life? In other words, how might reflective writing be a transferable skill?

Co-requisite Teaching Tip
Consider using the co-requisite section as a writing workshop where students work through the planning, drafting, and revising of one of the writing projects. See the IM for information on how to use formative assessment to grade students' workshop progress.

In the remaining pages of this chapter we see how another student, Janilyn Lee, wrote an essay in which she reflects on a difficult period in her life. As you observe Janilyn's writing process and revision choices, you will be prompted to make rhetorical choices of your own so that you can craft an essay that allows you to reflect on something that matters to you in a way that is interesting for readers. Regardless of the assignment you choose, you can use the steps that follow to craft your reflective writing.

Selecting a Topic

Consider aspects of the rhetorical situation to help you choose a topic.

Speaker or Writer: What experiences or particular moments in your life have led you to insights worth sharing?

Audience: Which of these moments or insights might a reader find interesting? Could the reader apply your experiences and insights to their life? As you consider ideas for reflective papers, realize that some topics may be too intimate to share or may, in fact, be troubling to remember. You may be sharing your paper with classmates for peer review, so be sure to write about a topic you are comfortable discussing.

Message: What is the main idea you hope to convey by sharing your reflection? Finding a significant experience or moment in your life is important, but to make this moment in your life relevant to readers, it is important to convey the insight you gained from your experiences. This insight is the main idea you will be sharing; it is the message of your reflection.

> **Janilyn, on choosing a topic:** "I knew—immediately—that I wanted, even *needed*, to write about my trip to the Amazon and how it helped me overcome my grief. I worried, though, that I wouldn't be able to find the words to show how magical that trip was. And since I was writing about miscarriage, I also worried that male readers might not be able to relate. That's why I tried to make the more general point that even in dark moments, we can find hope."

Planning

You can use the following three stages of planning to start working on your reflective project:

1. **Use a method of prewriting to generate ideas.** Select an on-the-page method of prewriting to jot down your thoughts, your memories, your reflections, your insights, and anything else that comes to mind as you consider your topic. Next, consider talking with someone who is familiar with your background, such as a sibling or other family member. Discussing your memories or reflective topics with a trusted family member or even a close friend can help you realize why the events were so significant. Eventually you can make a list of all the details you remember, and later, you can select which details to include in your paper.

2. **Draft a working thesis statement.** In reflective writing, the thesis statement tells readers the central insight you have gained from the experience on which you have reflected. Not all reflective writing includes an explicitly stated thesis statement. Whether you choose to state the main idea directly or not, you should have a working thesis in mind as you write your paper. To figure out a thesis statement, consider what you learned when you reflected. Write a sentence that answers this question: *What insights did I gain upon reflecting on X?* Remember, you can always change the wording of your thesis statement later.

> **Janilyn's Working Thesis Statement**
>
> I left the Amazon a changed person. My pain was not gone, and it will never be gone, but it has taken a new form, a shape that is more tolerable perhaps.
>
> **Janilyn, on writing a thesis statement:** "This was hard. I couldn't figure out whether I should just say that the Amazon changed me or that I knew I'd visit the Amazon again. What I wanted to get across was that my visit somehow helped me to deal with the pain. It didn't take away the pain, but it made it tolerable. After about fifteen tries, I think I finally wrote a two-sentence thesis statement that I liked."

3. **Create an outline.** You have decided on a topic and written a thesis statement. Now you can plan the body paragraphs of your reflective composition. You may have noticed that the reflective texts in this chapter read more like stories, with occasional commentary, rather than academic essays. As such, there may be moments when you want to use the elements of narrative storytelling—rising action, climax, falling action—to present the event upon which you are reflecting. At other times, you may want to offer rich descriptions that help readers gain an insight into the world you are talking about. A variety of rhetorical tools, including narration and description, are available to you as a writer. Consider using some of these strategies to develop your essay:

- **Alternate between narrating or describing and reflecting.** The two professional essays in this chapter demonstrate how the writers talk about things that happened and then discuss the significance of those events. Moving back and forth between events and reflections may be a natural way to structure your thoughts.

- **Avoid the temptation to use a strict chronological narrative.** Doing so can make an otherwise interesting topic tedious to read about.

- **Provide description.** Create descriptive details when needed for readers to understand something or to experience a situation the way you experienced it. Be selective about when to describe; too much description will bore readers.

- **Anticipate points of confusion, and provide enough information to provide clarity for readers.** For example, González describes the males in his family so that the reader can understand why shooting a gun poorly causes so much conflict.

- **Use concrete language.** Words that can be visualized are more concrete than those that cannot. Help readers see what you saw.

- **Use dialogue sparingly.** Both professional essays include some dialogue, but it is used only occasionally and only when the dialogue between the characters illustrates a point or seems particularly important. For information on how to punctuate dialogue, see "FAQ: Working with Dialogue" at the end of this chapter.

- **Consider starting your essay with the story (event or memory) upon which you are reflecting.** Because reflective essays do not take the same shape that traditional academic essays do, you have more freedom to craft an introduction that entices the reader.

- **Place your thesis statement in a natural location.** While you might put your thesis statement in the introduction of a traditional academic essay, doing so in a reflective essay may not seem natural. As you write, you will be able to determine the best place for your thesis statement. It may even work to make the thesis statement the first sentence or the last sentence of your essay. Alternatively, if the insight you gained is obvious, adding an overt thesis statement may be unnecessary. If you are considering *not* including a thesis statement, be sure to ask your instructor about this choice.

Co-requisite Teaching Tip
Consider having students intentionally practice these writing strategies in class, reading their paragraphs aloud in a writer's workshop or analyzing their paragraphs with classmates.

Teaching Resources
Consider reinforcing these strategies by having students use them. You can do so by assigning the exercise "Revising Reflective Writing."

Once you have done some initial planning, you are ready to create an outline. You will notice that Janilyn's outline includes specific information. She has tried to make a complete list of the content she will be putting into her essay. Notice how the paragraphs include narration, description, and reflection.

Janilyn's Outline

Preliminary Thesis Statement: I left the Amazon a changed person. My pain was not gone, and it will never be gone, but it has taken a new form, a shape that is more tolerable perhaps.

Section 1: Introduction
- Memory of swimming in the Amazon amid the children's peals of laughter.
- "Why was I here?"

Section 2: Planning the Trip and My Loss
- Planning the trip
- My loss: considering backing out

Section 3: Getting There
- The plane ride
- Driving through town
- "Life here is always precarious."

Section 4: The First Night and Next Morning
- Going to sleep
- Traveling on the Amazon

Section 5: The Village
- Arriving at Z
- Encountering the children
- Jungle hike
- Eating cherimoya
- Eating sugar cane

Section 6: Main Reflection
- Dangers and hope in the jungle
- "I began to feel a glimmer of hope."

Section 7:
- The little girl
- Thoughts on leaving

Janilyn, on creating an outline: "Honestly, I had a hard time creating an outline. The ideas just didn't seem to flow. I had to go back through my notes and move the ideas around. For example, I had started the introduction in chronological order, but it just didn't feel right. Starting with that magical moment swimming in the Amazon seemed like a better way to get readers interested."

Drafting

Having an outline like Janilyn's to guide you as you draft makes writing easier. However, do not feel that you *must* follow your outline. In the same way that Janilyn decided to make changes, feel free to cut sections, add details, and make any changes that you believe will help you convey the significance of your reflection to readers.

To think rhetorically as you write a rough draft, keep these tips in mind:

- **Write a paragraph and then read it from a reader's perspective.** Is there any background information a reader would need to make sense of the ideas? If so, provide that information.
- **Develop your descriptions.** While you have experienced the events upon which you are reflecting, readers have only your words to understand the significance of those events. Have you included enough description to help readers experience the event the way you experienced it?
- **Use dialogue for effect.** Are there places where dialogue would help to reveal the character of a person or where the specific words of an individual are important to repeat? If so, use dialogue in those places.
- **Use the right tenses and transitions.** Does your paper move back and forth between the past and the present? If it does, make sure readers will not be confused.
- **Make changes if your outline isn't working.** If you find that an idea in your outline just isn't working out, go back to the planning stage. Should you replace the idea? Move it? Cut it entirely? Make changes during the drafting process.
- **Occasionally stop and read your paper from the beginning.** Rereading and rethinking is part of the recursive nature of writing. Doing this will help you detect missing information, make sentence-level revisions, and add transition words to facilitate the flow of your ideas.

Consider using terms and phrases that guide readers through the information you are presenting (see the Drafting Toolbox).

DRAFTING TOOLBOX

Terms and Phrases for Reflective Essays

- Some memories trigger . . .
- Some events stand out . . .
- Over time, I have realized that . . .
- While I didn't understand it at the time, now I know that . . .
- An insight I have gained . . .
- Time transitions: *When I was five; two years ago; today*

Thinking Recursively in the Writing Process

Good writers constantly go back and forth between writing, reading what they have written, and rewriting. This recursive back and forth process helps writers to test out their words and ideas without feeling like everything they write must stay on the page.

> **Janilyn, on recursive writing:** "Originally, my essay was over twenty pages, and that was way too long for the assignment. I started to cut parts out, but it made more sense to reorganize it first. I went back to the planning stage—even after I had drafted the whole essay! I guess I needed the content first and then I could see it and reorganize it. I probably moved sections around about five or six times before I got it right."

Revising

Think rhetorically about your message as you revise. You have presented memories or events that you have found significant. Have you communicated their significance to a general reader? It is challenging to try to read your paper objectively, the way a reader would, but good writers use this technique all the time. The following suggestions will help you make revision decisions.

1. **Read your paper objectively, from a reader's point of view.** What would a general reader's first impression be? Would the reader understand why you are writing about the topic? Would a reader be able to relate to the thesis statement? Do you need to more clearly show why the events or memories are so meaningful?

2. **Highlight the sections in which you talk about an event or memory.** For each of these sections, determine whether you should add (or delete) descriptive details so that readers can experience the event or memory the way you do.

3. **In the sections you have highlighted, underline all the dialogue.** Is the dialogue necessary? Are there sections where adding dialogue would give readers a clearer understanding? Revise if necessary.

4. **Make sure you have communicated the insights you gained upon reflecting.** Highlight the insights you are sharing with readers. If you do not find sections where you shared these insights, then you will need to add content. This content will consist of the thoughts you have as you reflect on the events or memories.

5. **Use storytelling techniques to craft the narrative sections of your paper.** Often, reflective writers tell stories from the past. Use the elements of plot to make sure readers experience the tension in the story, as well as the

Teaching Suggestion
One of the most difficult parts of writing reflections is figuring out how many details to include. To help students with this skill, consider using the exercise "Selecting Details for Reflective Writing."

resolution, that you are telling. If need be, revise the stories to improve the way you tell them.

6. **Make sure the paper is organized logically.** You can organize a reflective essay in many ways. Whichever way you choose, make sure readers will not be confused.

7. **Start the paper with an interesting beginning, and create an ending that gives readers a sense of closure.** Reread your introduction and conclusion, and revise them if necessary.

8. **Use peer review to help you make revision decisions.** The following questions will help a peer read your paper and give you constructive suggestions.

PEER REVIEW TOOLBOX: REFLECTIVE WRITING

1. Does the writer clearly communicate a main idea in the composition? If so, what is the main idea?
2. Look at the areas in the paper where the writer describes an event or memory. Are there any details missing that would help you better understand the event or memory?
3. Are there any confusing parts in the text? If so, where, and why do you find them confusing?
4. Would reorganizing the essay help in any way? Explain.
5. How does the writer make clear why the events or memories in the paper are significant or meaningful? Could the writer improve in this regard?

Teaching Suggestion
Consider having students bring only a portion of their essay for peer review, such as the first two paragraphs. Doing so often means more students will be prepared for peer review and makes the process less overwhelming.

Janilyn, on her revision decisions: "In this section, I thought I focused too much on my own thoughts (telling what I was thinking) without explaining the moment enough (by showing what happened). Adding the experience with the little girl, I think, helps readers get a better vision of what happened."

Draft: Nightfall descended upon the jungle and moonlight rippled across the water. I snapped out of my reverie and realized it was time to head back to the village to sleep. As I emerged from the river, I took one final look around and smiled. I could feel that I was already a different person than the one who stepped off that plane. I thanked

Revision: Nightfall descended upon the jungle and moonlight rippled across the water. I snapped out of my reverie and realized it was time to head back to the village to sleep. As I emerged from the river, the same little girl that had greeted me in the morning found me. She grabbed my hand and walked with me to the canoe. She was shy and didn't say much but I felt a bond had developed between us. I couldn't believe I had almost avoided her because of my own pain. It was in that moment

God for allowing me to see such beauty and promised to come back again and again.

that I realized that even though I had lost a baby, there were still so many babies and kids out there who needed love and I had so much to give.

Janilyn on the introduction: "I didn't like the introduction. I felt like it was too chronological, so instead of starting at the 'beginning' so to speak, I decided to start with a magical moment in the Amazon River and then transition into what happened."

Draft: Nothing quite prepares you for a trip to the Amazon Rainforest. I had known for months that I was going as part of a mission team for a week to feed the poor, build a septic tank for a family in Brazil and visit an orphanage. I spent countless hours poring over documentaries, travel blogs and images on the internet trying to get an idea of what I was going to encounter. Of course, none of these things really helped me. It wasn't until I glimpsed the immense Amazon River from my plane window, high above the clouds that I started to realize that just like Dorothy, I wasn't in Kansas anymore, or, Texas, as it were. As we made our very bumpy descent, I cleverly made sure Guns 'n' Roses's hit song "Welcome to the Jungle" was playing in my headphones. There was never a more appropriate time to play that song than then.

Revision: I tossed my rubber boots onto the *playa* as our jungle guide grabbed my hand and pulled me into the Amazon River. Wiggling my feet nervously in the gritty riverbed, I let out a sigh of relief that nothing snatched me from the bottom and pulled me under. For a moment I seriously worried that an anaconda or black caiman might swim over and swallow me whole. My fears were soon allayed by tribal children who splashed me with water and giggled. Peals of happy laughter filled the air as we played a game of splashing each other while tossing a ball back and forth while shouting "Bomba!"

Every bone, muscle, and tendon in my body ached after our jungle hike, so I leaned back to float into the cool water and sighed as if my body was thanking me for the much-needed relief. The sun looked like a melting butterscotch as it sank in the horizon. It would be dark soon. The nearly full moon was already in view but the sun stubbornly clung onto the horizon.

I wanted to cling to this moment forever.

Janilyn on her thesis statement: "I couldn't figure out where to put the thesis statement. At first I put it in the third paragraph, but having the thesis come so early seemed to give away what happened. I wanted readers to experience the trip the way I did. I didn't know the Amazon would help me heal until after I had experienced it. So I ended up putting my thesis statement in the last paragraph, and I think it works much better there."

Draft (introduction): Every bone, muscle and tendon in my body ached after our jungle hike, so I leaned back to float into the cool water and sighed as if my body was thanking me for the much-needed relief. The sun looked like a melting butterscotch as it sank in the horizon. It would be dark soon. The nearly full moon was already in view but the sun stubbornly clung onto the horizon.

Revision (conclusion): I left the Amazon a changed person. My pain was not gone, and it will never be gone, but it has taken a new form, a shape that is more tolerable perhaps. Before getting on the plane, I took one last, long look at the exotic beauty around me, beauty that had become part of my mental landscape. I knew that this would not be the last jungle I visited and that, in spite of the potential

(Continued on next page)

(Continued from previous page)

I wanted to cling to this moment forever. I left the Amazon a changed person. My pain was not gone, and it will never be gone, but it has taken a new form, a shape that is more tolerable perhaps. dangers, I would be back, ready to experience again, to learn, to grow.

Finishing

Finishing your paper involves editing and formatting. Thinking rhetorically during this stage of the writing process is crucial because it will enable you to imagine how a reader will experience your paper. Use these guidelines to finish your reflective essay.

Editing. Edit your paper to find the errors in grammar and mechanics. Use one or more of these methods to find and correct errors:

- Use the grammar and spell-checking tools in your word processor.
- Keep a running list of errors that you tend to make, and check for those. Examine your previous papers to figure out your weaknesses.
- Read each sentence aloud, starting with the last sentence in the paper and proceeding to the first. Make sure each sentence is complete and carefully worded.

Formatting. Before preparing a final draft, review your instructor's guidelines for formatting and submitting your paper. If you used sources, make sure you use the proper citation and documentation method for your purposes.

Janilyn Lee, Stay Wild (Final Draft)

What follows is Janilyn's finished paper. Her instructor required her to use MLA style, so her paper is formatted accordingly. Read Janilyn's reflective essay and then answer the questions that follow.

Teaching Suggestion
Consider having students maintain a Writing Progress Log in which they record their strengths and weaknesses for each writing assignment. Doing so helps students intentionally learn from past mistakes and make progress as writers over the semester. See the IM for more information.

Lee 1

Janilyn Lee
Professor Klein
ENGL 1301
24 October 2020

Stay Wild

I tossed my rubber boots onto the *playa* as our jungle guide grabbed my hand and pulled me into the Amazon River. Wiggling my feet nervously in the gritty riverbed, I let out a sigh of relief that nothing snatched me from the bottom and pulled me under. For a moment I seriously worried that an anaconda or black caiman might swim over and swallow me whole. My fears were soon allayed by tribal children who splashed me with water and giggled. Peals of happy laughter filled the air as we played a game of splashing each other while tossing a ball back and forth while shouting "Bomba!"

Every bone, muscle, and tendon in my body ached after our jungle hike, so I leaned back to float into the cool water and sighed as if my body was thanking me for the much-needed relief. The sun looked like a melting butterscotch as it sank in the horizon. It would be dark soon. The nearly full moon was already in view but the sun stubbornly clung onto the horizon.

I wanted to cling to this moment forever.

As the muddy brown water rippled placidly around me, I stared into cloudless twilit sky. *Why was I here?* Nothing quite prepares you for a trip to the Amazon Rainforest. I had known for months that I was going as part of a mission team for a week to feed the poor, build a septic tank for a family in Brazil, and visit an orphanage. I had spent countless hours poring over documentaries and travel blogs, trying to get an idea of what I was going to encounter. It wasn't until I glimpsed the immense Amazon River from my plane window, high above the clouds, that I started to realize that just like Dorothy, I wasn't in Kansas anymore, or Texas, as it were. I'd seen the Amazon River on television lots of times in my life, but no one can experience the Amazon without being on the Amazon in person. Still, I wondered if this trip—even with all its wonder and magic—would do anything to help erase the pain.

As we began our bumpy descent so many thoughts raced through my mind as I looked around. All of us on that plane had our own reasons for making this trip. A few weeks prior I had decided to back out entirely. I wasn't sure I could be around children, not after the pain I had experienced. But I found myself saying *yes,* hoping against hope for healing.

Exactly one month before the trip I suffered my fourth miscarriage. No one can explain what it's like to go through that experience—four times. In fact, I cannot find words even now to express the loss, the devastation, and the fear that this loss is to be my burden in life. What would a trip to the Amazon do? I certainly had nothing to lose.

....

When the plane door opened, the air was unlike anything I had ever experienced. I had expected humidity, but this was something different. Somehow from the steps of the plane to the uneven pavement my hair transformed into a frizzy, tangled mess that looked better suited for a dog than a human. The air felt as heavy as a thick fog and draped my body like a wet blanket. Beads of sweat trickled down my skin as I made my way through the unairconditioned airport to retrieve my luggage. I was beginning to doubt that thrusting myself into misery would do anything to relieve my mental state.

Outside the airport, three of us were crammed into a subcompact car and my luggage was tossed, unrestrained, atop the roof. As we plowed through bumps and potholes, I hoped my luggage wouldn't topple off into the road, spilling all my belongings. If there was a speed limit sign, our taxi driver didn't seem to care as he zoomed along weaving in and out of traffic, honking and muttering swear words to himself in Spanish while blaring *Vallenato* music from his radio. Time is money, even in the slower paced, relaxed atmosphere of Leticia, Colombia. Leticia is a quaint little city, literally in the middle of nowhere. Nestled on the bank of the Amazon River, it is completely inaccessible by road. The only way in or out is by plane. Though technically in Colombia, one can easily walk a few blocks and be in Brazil or take a five-minute boat ride and be in Peru. It's an area called *Tres Fronteras*, or Three Borders.

It was immediately apparent to me: life here is always precarious. Whole families rode on single motorbikes—of course, helmet-free. Mothers clutched babies or balanced toddlers on their knees, clearly just a bump away from death. Most tourists were transported in a tuk-tuk, a sort of motorized rickshaw with three wheels. These generally have no doors. Seat belts? Not a chance. The drivers honk and wave their hands at anything and anyone that gets in their way. During my first ride, I was white-knuckling it, expecting to crash any second as we jostled back and forth, but somehow, we made it through the streets where vendors hawked their beaded jewelry, hand-woven hammocks, and fresh squeezed *limonada*.

    Falling to sleep that night proved to be more difficult than I had anticipated. A bar next door played loud Vallenato music into the early morning hours. I had not been asleep long before I awoke to the sunlight creeping through my curtain and the sounds of parrots chattering in trees outside my room. The sun rises early in Colombia, and once the birds are up and being noisy, there's not much use in trying to get a few more minutes of sleep. Today would begin the real adventure. We would travel down the Amazon by boat to the little village of Zaragosa, the place where we hoped that we could do some good. Besides, on day two, a new adventure awaited! Our group was going to an indigenous village about a two-hour boat ride down the Amazon River. After packing for our night's stay in the jungle, we headed down to the boardwalk, or the *malecon* as it's called in Spanish, to wait for our boats to arrive. The Amazon River cuts through the heart of Leticia. It's not very wide but is littered with colorful shanties bustling with commerce and dug-out canoes filled with bright green and yellow bananas threatening to spill over on every side.

    We dressed and prepped to the best of our ability, not really knowing what we would need, and made it to the Amazon's edge to await our boat. No one had prepared me for the beauty I would encounter, the colors that would permeate the landscape. The Amazon River cuts through the heart of Leticia. It's not very wide but is littered with brightly painted shanties bustling with commerce and dug-out canoes filled with bright green and yellow bananas threatening to spill over on every side. Soon, our wooden motorboat chugged up to take us on the first leg of our journey down river. It was little more than a canoe that had the engine of a weed eater rigged up to be a motor, a vessel that was impressive and terrifying all at once. Twelve of us piled in as it swayed and sputtered along before gaining an impressive speed after we hit the open water. Pink dolphins jumped in and out of the water as we headed deeper into the jungle. Indigenous villages dotted the riverbanks and I was reminded of a shop's sign I had seen in town on the way from the airport that read "Stay Wild." This was indeed the wildest place I had ever seen. I wasn't sure I was wholly prepared, but I was thrilled beyond measure.

    A couple of hours and a few hundred pictures later, we arrived at Zaragosa. The villagers greeted us with friendly smiles and called us *hermanos* and *hermanas*, welcoming us as brothers and sisters. They led us to the cabanas where we would spend the night in our hammocks. After we had set up camp, we headed outside. I could already see what was about to unfold. The curious children were eager to play, and my colleagues—content, as they were, with their own families and lives—were eager to engage. It was the bittersweet moment that I dreaded. My mind raced. Could I handle this moment? I swept the landscape to find a way out, and fortunately, I saw a group of adults that I could join. I began to quickly walk toward them, but something touched my hand.

    I looked down and saw a sweet-faced girl with long black hair and a dimpled smile. She looked at me expectedly. What did she want from me? Why me? Of all these happy, well-adjusted, adults, why did she choose me?

    I couldn't engage in those thoughts long because she grabbed my hand and pulled me to the field where the other children were gathering and playing with the adults. A friend of mine had opened a package of balloons and was making animals. *I can do that*, I thought to myself. *Maybe she'll take the balloon animal and be happy, and then I can retreat from this sadness.* But after I gave her the balloon animal, other children made their way to me. They, too, wanted animals. I had made a cat, a dog, and several monkeys before I could stop to wipe the tears that had collected and spilled from behind my sunglasses. And then they wanted swords. My mission became to create as many balloon swords as I could for the lines of children who waited. Once equipped with a "sword," they would run off, yelling *espada* or something similar and chasing one another. Their joy was so pure, their happiness so simple, that I couldn't help but relish the moment. *This is good. This is good for me,* I began to realize.

    After a lunch of peanut butter sandwiches, we began our hike through the jungle, clad in loose fitting clothing and rubber boots and led by our tribal guides. "Hydrate or die-drate" became the motto we repeated half seriously, half-jokingly as we sipped on our water, ever conscious of how much we were sweating. Above us in a canopy of trees as tall as cathedrals, cat-sized monkeys swung from branch to branch. Parrots and toucans chattered happily nearby. As we ventured deeper into the jungle, the muddy path became less visible and more difficult to traverse as it was covered in fronds, moss, downed trees, and at least a dozen or so other plants I didn't recognize. Vines slithered down from trees like snakes. Dense undergrowth concealed much of the jungle floor. Stepping off the path might have meant a fall down a steep cliff. Wings flapping in nearby trees and a series of grunts off to the side reminded us that the jungle was very much alive and that we were not alone. The air was wet and warm and smelled like dirt, wild boar, and vegetation. It hung in the air so strongly that my mouth began to taste salty, pungent, and earthy. Before long we were so deep in the jungle it was hard to see any sky and our path scarcely looked like any kind of path at all. It struck me that it was a good thing we trusted our jungle guides because I had no idea how to get back to the village.

 I finally understood how easily people get disoriented and lost in the jungle. I finally understood that I had been lost myself—in my own jungle. I had been trapped, unable to imagine life without a child, unable to move forward after suffering yet another loss.

 We paused to take a break before making our trek back. One of the little village girls that tagged along scaled a tree in mere seconds, completely barefoot. I was thoroughly impressed. Up top, she started shaking limbs and fruit began to fall around us. It felt like a moment out of National Geographic. I had never seen anything like this fruit before. The skin was a light green with a golden hue and looked like the love child of a pine cone and an artichoke. It looked more like something I would expect to see in a cartoon than in real life. The flesh was a soft, creamy white that resembled sherbet in texture. It was undeniably exotic. The guides called it cherimoya. Trepidation long cast aside in favor of adventure, I boldly took a bite, careful to avoid the toxic black seeds and I was not disappointed. It tasted like bubblegum with hints of strawberry, banana, and pineapple. I understand now why Mark Twain called the cherimoya the "most delicious fruit known to man."

As we neared the village, our guide decided to surprise us with another treat. As monkeys swung above us, he chopped down raw sugar cane with his machete and explained how to eat it. First, we had to sink our teeth into it and then suck the juice out. Eating it was out of the question because it is so tough and filled with sharp fibers that would easily cut our mouths. The taste was as sweet as I had imagined but in a much different way than the sugar I'm more familiar with. It had a much warmer flavor, more reminiscent of molasses or rum.

I used this luxurious moment to let my mind wander about the vast depths of the jungle. Were jaguars lounging lazily nearby waiting for nightfall? What dangers were here, dangers I would only know by taking risks like the one I chose to take when I decided to say yes to this adventure? What undiscovered cures to diseases were growing at my feet? What does this jungle hold for us as humans? What does it hold for me, as a woman making my way through life, figuring out my meaning, my potential? I began to feel a glimmer of hope. Yes, there are jaguars here, but there are also riches and meanings beyond my imagination.

After our sore, achy bodies reached the village, the kids suggested a trip across the river to the playa. Soaking our feet in the river sounded like a nice idea so we piled into a wooden dug-out canoe, with legs and arms dangling off the sides while our guide rowed us across the river.

Nightfall descended upon the jungle and moonlight rippled across the water. I snapped out of my reverie and realized it was time to head back to the village to sleep. As I emerged from the river, the same little girl that had greeted me in the morning found me. She grabbed my hand and walked with me to the canoe. She was shy and didn't say much but I felt a bond had developed between us. I couldn't believe I had almost avoided her because of my own pain. It was in that moment that I realized that even though I had lost a baby, there were still so many babies and kids out there who needed love and I had so much to give.

I left the Amazon a changed person. My pain was not gone, and it will never be gone, but it has taken a new form, a shape that is more tolerable perhaps.

Lee 8

Before getting on the plane, I took one last, long look at the exotic beauty around me, beauty that had become part of my mental landscape. I knew that this would not be the last jungle I visited and that, in spite of the potential dangers, I would be back, ready to experience again, to learn, to grow.

YOUR TURN Analyzing Lee's Rhetorical Strategies

1. Review the strategies in this chapter under "Thinking Rhetorically to Develop Your Paper." Which of these strategies did Janilyn use in her essay?
2. How successful do you think Janilyn was at making her reflective essay relevant to readers?
3. Do you think most readers would find her essay interesting? Why or why not?
4. Was Janilyn's placement of the thesis statement in the last paragraph an effective writing strategy? Why or why not?
5. Find one strategy Janilyn used that you would like to use in your own writing. What is that strategy? How could you use it in your own reflective essay?

Reflecting to Develop a Writer's Mindset

You have just finished reading a chapter on reflective writing. You may have noticed that at the end of each chapter in this text, you are asked to reflect on the contents of the chapter. How might such reflections help you as a learner? Why do you think instructors require them?

FAQ WORKING WITH DIALOGUE

When you want to tell readers what someone said, you have two choices. You can create indirect quotations and direct quotations.

1. **What is the difference between indirect and direct quotations?**

   Indirect quotations are formed when the writer tells readers what the person said. Such quotes do not necessarily use the exact words the person used. Do not use quotation marks with indirect quotations.

Diane said she was tired and wanted to go to bed.

When I asked Mark about his injury, he said it was no big deal. He told me that he hadn't even needed to see a doctor.

Trinity confirmed that she skipped class that day.

Direct quotations allow the character to do the talking. Such quotations do require quotation marks.

Diane said, "I'm tired. I really just want to go to bed."

When I asked Mark about his injury, he said, "It's no big deal. I didn't even go to the doctor about it."

Trinity said, "Yes, I skipped class that day."

2. **What are the rules for writing dialogue?**

   A. Use attributive tags. An attributive tag, such as *he said* or *she replied,* tells the reader who is doing the speaking.

   B. Use a comma after an attributive tag that starts a sentence or after the quoted passage if the attributive tag is at the end of the sentence.

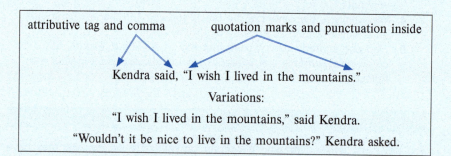

   C. Use quotation marks around the words that are spoken.

   D. Put the punctuation at the end of the sentence *inside* the quotation marks.

   E. If you interrupt a sentence with an attributive tag, do not capitalize the remaining part of the sentence.
   "I must admit that I would miss the conveniences of the city," continued Kendra, "but I would be willing to make that sacrifice."

   F. When the speaker changes, use a new paragraph.

   "Wouldn't it be nice to live in the mountains?" Kendra asked.

   "It truly would," said Veronica. "I've always wanted to get out of the city and live in a place where there aren't so many people."

   "Me too, but of all the natural landscapes in the world, I love mountains the best," said Kendra.

TRY IT!

Imagine you are writing a reflective essay in which you present an important conversation you had with a friend or relative. Create at least ten sentences of dialogue. Demonstrate both direct and indirect dialogue in your text.

CREDITS

Page 86. From *Red-Inked Retablos* by Rigoberto Gonzalez ©2013 The Arizona Board of Regents. Reprinted by permission of the University of Arizona Press.

Page 92. Tonino, Leath, "Thoughts After an Owl," *The West Will Swallow You: Essays* (Trinity University Press, 2019). Copyright 2019, All Rights Reserved.

Page 104. Lee, Janilyn. "Stay Wild." Used by permission.

6 Writing to Inform

CHAPTER OBJECTIVES

You will learn to:
- Identify key rhetorical concerns of informative texts.
- Analyze informative texts.
- Compose an informative text.

Connect Adaptive Learning Assignment
Consider assigning Connect's Adaptive Learning Assignments to support this chapter.

Teaching Resources
See the Instructor's Manual (IM) for suggestions about how to teach this chapter, and consider assigning this chapter's test-bank quiz.

Many of the texts you encounter every day are written to inform. Textbooks, for example, are written to inform about the subjects they cover. News and magazine articles are often written to provide information and facts about events, discoveries, and ideas. We live in an era when information is so readily available on any topic that a typical internet search leads to thousands of results. However, not all information is helpful. Some of it is poorly written, and some of it is downright inaccurate. As a college student, you will often need to find high-quality information, and as a writer, regardless of the academic or career path you choose, you at some point will have to write a text that presents information.

It may be tempting to think informative texts lack rhetorical strategies, but that is far from the case. In this chapter, you will see that thinking rhetorically can help you to communicate information in ways that are effective for your particular audience. You will observe how the rhetorical thinking process of Liam, a student in a college English course, results in an excellent informative essay.

WARM-UP

Imagine that you are an emergency dispatcher who answers 9-1-1 calls. In such a position, you must provide information and instructions to those who call. How important would audience analysis be as you communicate with callers? In other words, what would you need to know about the caller to be able to provide the most helpful information?

INFORMATIVE WRITING FROM A WRITER'S MINDSET

While all writing should be composed with an audience in mind, effective informative writing absolutely depends on a writer's awareness of the audience. This awareness is important because we communicate information differently to different audiences. Both *what* we say and *how* we say it is affected by the audience's needs. For example, we might explain divorce to a young child by using very simple terms and by touching on the aspects of divorce that will affect the child. A discussion of divorce written for an audience of people who are considering divorcing might involve the emotional, legal, and financial aspects of divorce, and it would certainly involve a more diverse vocabulary than would the explanation given to the child.

In the Warm-Up exercise, you were asked to think about how important audience analysis would be if you were an emergency dispatcher. Obviously, to give instructions the caller understands, you need to know something about the caller. For instance, if a child calls 9-1-1, the dispatcher must provide different instructions than those provided for an adult. Language needs to be adjusted, and additional explanations may have to be provided. As a writer, you are in a situation that is similar to the dispatcher's. Because you cannot be in the mind of the reader, you must try to predict accurately where readers will need more details, where they might misunderstand the ideas you are presenting, and where they might be confused. Since the focus of informative writing is to convey information that is new to readers, thinking about how the reader will experience the text is crucial. One way to think rhetorically about an informative writing task is to analyze the rhetorical situation. In Rhetorical Toolbox 6.1 we take a look at the specific rhetorical concerns involved in communicating information.

Teaching Suggestion
Consider having students think of informative texts they've encountered that are confusing, such as the manuals that come with unassembled furniture or information on the IRS's website. Have students explain why the instructions didn't work well.

Teaching Resource
Consider using the PowerPoint "Informative Writing: Avoiding the Pitfalls."

▶ **ACTIVITY 1** The Rhetorical Concerns of Informative Writing

Return to the Warm-Up exercise in which you imagined you were an emergency dispatcher. Which of the rhetorical concerns in Rhetorical Toolbox 6.1 would be the most important to focus on? Explain your answer.

RHETORICAL TOOLBOX 6.1

The Rhetorical Concerns of Informative Writing

1. **Writer.** What do you, as the writer, need to know about the subject? Obviously, if you are providing information, you need to be knowledgeable about the subject, or the audience may not trust the information. To become knowledgeable, you may have to do research and cite sources in the text.
2. **Purpose.** What is the your writing purpose? Is it to inform or to instruct? Keeping this purpose in mind help you avoid the temptation to offer your opinion on the topic.

(Continued on next page)

(Continued from page 115)

3. **Audience.** Who is the intended audience, and what knowledge does this audience have about the topic? Analyzing the audience will help you figure out how to present the information in effective ways.
4. **Message.** What specific message do you wish to convey? So much information is available on any given topic you must be very clear about the specific message—the thesis statement—that you want to convey to an audience. These three rhetorical concerns must also be addressed:
   A. **Into how much depth should your writing go?** The answer to this question depends on the message you are conveying as well as the preexisting knowledge of the audience.
   B. **How should you handle new vocabulary?** Which words should be defined? Should some words be avoided? Are some words absolutely necessary for an understanding of the subject? You will need to make critical decisions about the language to use based on how the audience will understand that language.
   C. **How will you help readers understand the information?** Which rhetorical strategies—providing examples, creating analogies, telling brief stories, using visuals, and so on—will be the most effective at helping the audience understand your ideas?

MODELS OF INFORMATIVE WRITING

The Violent Brain: Ingredients of a Mass Murderer
Lauren Migliore

A self-described "neuroscience junkie," Lauren Migliore is a regular contributor to Brain World *magazine in addition to being a freelance copywriter and author. This article appeared in the March 2019 edition of* Brain World, *a magazine that describes its readers as "educators, political and business leaders, health professionals, and individuals everywhere who are interested in the daily revelations granted by neuroscience and the ways in which they can be applied to our lives and the world in which we live." As you read the article, notice the annotations that point out the rhetorical features Migliore uses to explain the insights gained by applying neuroscience to the study of criminology.*

> Starts with a concrete example

On July 20, 2012, a heavily armed young man walked into a movie theater in Aurora, Colorado, and opened fire on the audience, killing 12 people and injuring nearly 60.

Teaching Suggestion
For additional models of informative writing, see Part 6, An Anthology of Readings.

Here's the thing: On paper, James Holmes measured up seemingly well. Intelligent, disciplined, and raised by successful parents—his father, a senior scientist; mother, a nurse. Holmes graduated from UC San Diego at the top of his class and was working towards a Ph.D. in neuroscience. It's hard to imagine that this would be a person to carry out one of the nation's deadliest recent massacres. But upon taking a closer look into the details of his behavior and characteristics leading up the massacre, experts agree that he does indeed fit the profile of a typical mass murderer. *[Details of the example]*

Holmes has been put behind bars, but the question still lingers: What drives someone to go on such a violent rampage, indiscriminately killing innocent people? Are there clear motives behind these violent acts? Insanity, or a psychotic break? An absent conscience? Or are some people just born natural killers? *[Transition from example to the question brain scientists are answering]*

Researchers have posed the same questions and, with recent scientific advancements, have been able to note personality-based, neurological, and even genetic-based commonalities in these violent individuals. Most experts will agree that there isn't a single determining factor that creates a mass murderer, but when multiple triggers are combined, a killer is born. Furthermore, through various studies looking at brain images and scans of murderers, psychopaths, and violent individuals, researchers are gaining leverage in mapping out the neural activity behind impulsive violence. *[Thesis statement / Causes are not easily determined]*

The human brain was designed with natural checks and balances that control our impulses and behavior and regulate our emotions. So it's no surprise that the brain of a mass murderer has a glitch in its regulatory system which may increase the risk of impulsive violent acts. *[Explanation of how the brain works]*

Psychologist Richard Davidson and his colleagues at the University of Wisconsin analyzed brain-imaging data from a large, diverse group of studies done on violent individuals, including those with aggressive personality disorder, those with childhood brain injuries, and convicted murderers. Davidson's findings showed similarities in brain activity among these more than 500 subjects. *[Citation of an expert's studies to show that violent individuals share similarities in brain activity]*

One of the core discoveries involved abnormalities in three distinct brain regions involved in regulating emotions: the anterior

Explanation of brain's physiology	cingulate cortex, the orbital frontal cortex, and the amygdala. The anterior cingulate cortex works to communicate with and recruit other brain regions in response to conflict, while the orbital frontal cortex is involved with ethical behavior, moral decision-making, and impulse control; it works to moderate and constrain our impulsive outbursts. The amygdala is involved with aggression, fear, and other emotional processing.
How brain regions work	
Explanation of differences in brains of violent individuals	In many of the subjects, Davidson noted diminished or entirely absent brain activity in the orbital cortex region while the amygdala showed normal and sometimes heightened activity. This imbalance, and the inability of the two brain regions to effectively counteract each other, may help explain how threatening situations can become explosive in some people.
Quotation from expert Fallon for an explanation of orbital cortex activity	Neuroscientist James Fallon of the University of California, Irvine, elaborates on this same concept, saying, "When there's an imbalance of brain activity to which the orbital cortex isn't doing its job, the area of the brain that drives your impulsive behaviors will take over. People with low activity in the orbital frontal cortex are either freewheeling types or sociopaths." Additionally, brain injury to the frontal region of the brain in an otherwise healthy person can also lead to similar violent results.
Establishment of Fallon's authority in the field	
Fallon's personal experience shows causality is not automatic	Fallon has spent over 20 years of his career studying the brains of psychopaths, trying to decipher what makes their brains different from ours. Fallon observed findings parallel to those of Davidson. But along the way, Fallon ran into his own personal findings: that he comes from a lineage of violent ancestors—eight alleged murderers, in fact. What's more, he scanned his own brain and found that he had the underpinnings of a murderer. Yet, to this day, Fallon has yet to commit a violent crime, or, for that matter, any sort of violence.
Implications of the research	Just as we know that the brain of a killer reflects abnormalities, genetic makeup has also raised curiosity. If genes determine everything from our eye color and hair color to our height and body structure, could they also define our behavioral fate?
	In recent years, scientists have been able to pin down the genetic makeup—one gene, in particular—that predisposes certain people to aggression and impulsive violent behavior. The gene is

the monoamine oxidase A, or MAO-A. Individuals with a certain variation of the MAO-A gene, which has earned the name "warrior gene," have been shown to display higher levels of aggression in response to provocation, according to recent research published in the Proceedings of the National Academy of Sciences.

To confirm this, researchers conducted an experiment in which subjects played a computer game that offered the option to seek revenge by causing simulated physical pain on an opponent they believed had taken money from them. Researchers also tested the genetic makeup of each participant. The results of the study showed that MAO-A carriers were more likely than noncarriers to respond with "behavioral aggression" toward someone they thought had cheated them out of the hypothetical money.

Why such an effect because of one gene? The warrior gene is an enzyme that breaks down and regulates important mood-altering neurotransmitters in the brain, including dopamine, norepinephrine, and serotonin. We have various forms of the gene, which yield different levels of activity. Approximately one in three people carry the low-activity variation, which is associated with higher levels of aggression. Many researchers suggest that with the low-activity variation of MAO-A, the brain doesn't respond to the calming effects of serotonin as it normally would.

Margin annotations:
- Explanation of correlation between genes, aggression, and impulsive violent behavior
- How researchers confirmed MAO-A link to violence and aggression
- Explanation of why the gene affects behaviors

Analyzing Migliore's Rhetorical Strategies

Migliore uses rhetorical strategies to present a complex topic to a general audience. Each of the rhetorical concerns identified earlier is addressed in Migliore's article.

1. **What does the writer need to know about the subject?** Migliore needs to understand what brain scientists have learned by studying the brains and genetic makeup of violent individuals. As a journalist, Migliore has not done original research; however, she has read the research of experts in the field.
2. **What is the writer's purpose?** Her purpose is to inform readers about the correlations between brain activity, genes, and violent tendencies.
3. **Who is the intended audience, and what knowledge does this audience have about the topic?** The article appears in a specialty magazine written for general readers. Readers may be interested in neuroscience, but Migliore

Co-requisite Teaching Tip
Students sometimes struggle with predicting the kind of information they need to become knowledgeable enough to write with authority. Consider helping students think critically about the preparation they need for informative writing. See the IM for more information.

cannot assume readers have any in-depth knowledge of brain physiology or function.

4. **What specific message will the writer convey?** Migliore wants readers to understand what neuroscientists are learning about violent behavior by studying the brain and genetics.

5. **Into how much depth should the writer go?** Migliore has to use care in her presentation because too much biological information about neuroscience or genetics may alienate readers; on the other hand, she has to explain enough so that readers can understand how the brain's regions may contribute to violent behavior and how a gene may contribute to aggression and impulsivity.

6. **How should the writer handle new vocabulary?** Migliore uses terminology to present the regions of the brain and the gene associated with violence and aggression, but she explains each of the terms she presents so that readers unfamiliar with the terms can understand the points she makes.

7. **How will the writer help readers understand the information?** Migliore anticipates some of the questions readers might have and answers them. She also anticipates that some readers might incorrectly think that brain chemistry is the sole cause of violence, so she is careful to explain that the connections scientists are discovering show correlations, not causes.

What We Do and Don't Know about How to Prevent Gun Violence

Rachel Ehrenberg

Co-requisite Teaching Tip
Developing writers often struggle to balance their writing voice with information from sources. Consider discussing this topic as you analyze Ehrenberg's article.

Teaching Resources
This reading is available as a Power of Process assignment in Connect.

Rachel Ehrenberg has degrees in botany and political science from the University of Vermont and a master's degree in evolutionary biology from the University of Michigan. She graduated from the science writing program at the University of California, Santa Cruz. The following article was published on ScienceNews.org, a website that presents scientific research for general readers.

You saw how Lauren Migliore presented a complex topic to a general audience by thinking rhetorically. Read and annotate the following article to demonstrate how writer Rachel Ehrenberg addresses the rhetorical concerns involved in informative writing for a general audience.

> In the fraught days following a mass shooting, people often ask if an assault weapons ban or allowing concealed carry permits would reduce the likelihood of further violence. But reliable evidence on the effects of those policies can be hard to find.

Now the largest comprehensive analysis of research on U.S. gun policy in years offers some answers, but also troublingly little guidance. A glaring finding of the study, published by the RAND Corporation March 2, is how little work has been done to know which policies work.

"The research literature on gun policies is really very thin," says Andrew Morral, a behavioral scientist at RAND, a nonpartisan institute based in Santa Monica, Calif.

Ideally, solid research leads to effective public health policies, which then reduce deaths, be it from guns, car accidents or fires. But when it comes to gun research, good science is lacking, says Morral, who led the study. So legislators typically turn to experts and advocates who can disagree vehemently about the effects of laws.

The goal of the report is to help people understand "what is reasonably well-known and what isn't," says Morral. "Hopefully we can work from there and identify where research can be most helpful."

Gun shy

Compared with other leading causes of death, research into gun violence is among the least funded, an analysis of U.S. mortality data and federal funding from 2004 to 2015 reveals. Funding for research

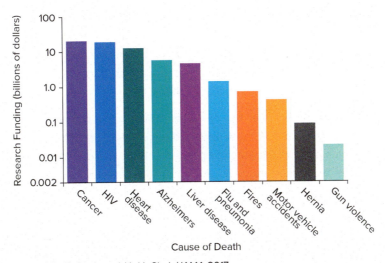

Source: D. E. Stark and N. H. Shah/*JAMA* 2017.

on gun violence is 1.6 percent of what would be expected, given the number of gun deaths.

Morral and his colleagues reviewed existing research on 13 types of gun policies, including concealed carry laws and waiting periods, and their impact on health, and safety, including mass shootings, suicides and accidental deaths. Next the researchers looked to see if those studies were any good. Out of thousands of studies considered for the analysis, a mere 63 met the research team's strict criteria: Studies had to use rigorous methods and establish cause and effect.

The team ranked the strength of the evidence of a given policy's effectiveness as limited (at least one study showed an effect, which wasn't contradicted by other studies), moderate (two or more studies showed the same effect, no contradictory studies) or supported (three or more studies with at least two independent datasets found an effect with no contradictory studies). Here are the biggest takeaways:

1. **There's not enough data to show what would prevent mass shootings.** There is no universal definition of a mass shooting, which, along with their relative rarity, makes it hard to spot trends, such as whether mass shootings are on the rise. Studies looking at seven of the investigated policies, including concealed carry laws and background checks, were inconclusive about whether those policies lowered the likelihood of a mass shooting. For nearly half the gun policies, including gun-free zones, prohibitions associated with mental illness and stand-your-ground laws, no studies met the researchers' criteria.

2. **Keeping guns out of the hands of kids is good policy.** There's solid evidence that these laws reduce unintentional firearm injuries and deaths among children. There's some evidence these laws also reduce adult unintentional firearm injuries and deaths.

3. **Gun policies can decrease the number of suicides.** This is no small thing: Of the more than 36,000 U.S. gun deaths each year, two-thirds are suicides. Laws that prevent kids from

getting access to guns reduce the number of suicides by young people. And there's some limited evidence that keeping guns away from people with certain mental illnesses, minimum-age requirements and background checks all prevent suicides.

4. **Background checks can work.** Designed to prevent certain people, such as convicted felons or those subject to a restraining order, from buying guns, background checks do reduce some gun violence. There's moderate evidence that these laws can reduce the number of firearm homicides and suicides and limited evidence that background checks reduce violent crime and homicides in general.

5. **Keeping guns out of the hands of the mentally ill has mixed effects.** While there's limited evidence that these laws can reduce the number of suicides, there's slightly stronger proof that these laws reduce the amount of violent crime in general.

6. **Allowing people to carry concealed guns ups gun violence.** There's limited evidence that laws that guarantee a right to carry increase unintentional firearm injuries among adults and increase violent crime.

7. **Saying it's OK to "stand your ground" can also lead to gun violence.** Rather than curtailing gun deaths, there's moderate evidence that laws that let people claim self-defense even if they don't try to retreat from a perceived threat lead to an uptick in homicide rates. There were no studies that met the researchers' strict criteria demonstrating that stand-your-ground laws lower the likelihood of any gun-related violence.

Few smoking guns

Some gun policies, such as background checks, do curtail gun violence, while others, like concealed carry laws, lead to an uptick. But for most policies, the data are inconclusive or lacking entirely.

Outcomes of Selected Gun Policies

Policy	Increase in gun violence	Decrease in gun violence	No reliable data
Concealed carry	X		
Stand-your-ground	X		
Background checks		X	
Child-access prevention		X	
Mental illness-access prevention		X	
Minimum age requirements		X	
Ban on sales of assault weapons and high-capacity magazines			X
Licensing and permitting requirements			X
Waiting periods			X

Source: A. R. Morral et al./RAND Corporation 2018.

Effects of gun laws

The analysts found little or no research on the impact of other policies, including gun-free zones, firearm sales reporting requirements and bans on assault weapons.

Many scientists, including the authors of the RAND report, blame federal directives that, for the past two decades, have forbidden the Centers for Disease Control and Prevention from "advocating or promoting gun control" and slashed its funding.

"That sent a very loud signal that firearms research was dangerous to your budget," Morral says.

Similar language was added to the funding bill for the National Institutes of Health in 2012 and the end result is today the U.S. government invests very little in research on firearms and public health (*SN: 5/14/16, p. 16*). A recent *JAMA* study comparing spending on leading causes of mortality, such as cancer, malnutrition and hypertension, found that gun violence research funding was only 1.6 percent of what would be expected, given the number of people that die from guns each year. The same analysis looked at the volume of scientific papers published for each cause of death and, relative to mortality rates, guns were the least researched.

Good data are needed for good policy, says David Hemenway, an expert on injury and violence prevention at Harvard T.H. Chan School of Public Health. To understand, for example, whether collapsible steering columns in cars prevent driver deaths, it takes data on head-on collisions, says Hemenway, not just motor vehicle deaths in general. Such fine-grained data are lacking for much of gun-related violence.

Those data likely will reveal that there's no one-size-fits-all policy to reduce gun-related violence, says Hemenway. Interventions that reduce gun violence in at-risk communities might be very different than, say, policies for reducing mass shootings. But without the research, it's hard to know. Hemenway is confident that over time, data and science will win out. "Every success in public health meets with opposition," he says. "You have to fight and fight and it takes much longer than you hope."

Citations

A. R. Morral *et al*. The science of gun policy: A critical synthesis of research evidence on the effects of gun policies in the United States. The RAND Corporation, published online March 2, 2018.

D. E. Stark and N. H. Shah. Funding and publication of research on gun violence and other leading causes of death. *JAMA*. Vol. 317, January 3, 2017, p. 84. doi:10.1001/jama.2016.16215

YOUR TURN **Analyzing Ehrenberg's Rhetorical Strategies**

Explain your answer for each question in two or three sentences. Use examples from the text to support your points.

1. What is the writer or speaker's purpose?
2. What does Ehrenberg need to know about the subject?
3. Who is the intended audience, and what knowledge does this audience have about the topic?
4. What specific message will Ehrenberg convey?
5. Into how much depth does Ehrenberg go?
6. How does Ehrenberg handle new vocabulary?
7. How does Ehrenberg help readers understand the information?

CHAPTER PROJECT Writing to Inform

Teaching Resources
The chapter writing projects are available as writing assignments in Connect.

Teaching Suggestion
The first writing prompt is intentionally vague and can be used as a springboard for discussions about how to find one's own topic.

Co-requisite Teaching Tip
Consider discussing the handout "Finding an Informative Topic."

The following three projects give you an opportunity to try your hand at informative writing. The first project asks you to find your own topic, while the next two projects provide more guidance about what to write.

PROJECT 1 Find Your Own Topic

Write an informative essay on any topic in which you are personally interested. There are only two limitations: you must make the topic interesting for a general audience, and the information must be something that not everyone knows.

You may use research, but you do not have to do so if the topic is something you know enough about. Be sure to use the formatting style specified by your instructor. Use Rhetorical Toolbox 6.1 as a guide.

PROJECT 2 Raising Awareness through Writing

Write an informative essay on a topic about which you believe general readers should be more aware. Perhaps there is an amazing organization in your city that is doing great work, and you believe people should know about it. Or maybe there is help available for a condition—such as depression or suicidality—and you believe people need to know about such help. Another idea is to find a problem that needs more publicity. For example, not everyone knows that many college students deal with food scarcity and homelessness. Select a topic that you believe deserves more public awareness, and write an informative essay. Select a specific audience for your essay. For example, if your essay would be suitable for publication in your city's newspaper, write your essay for a general audience.

You may use research, but you do not have to do so if the topic is something you know enough about. Be sure to use the formatting style specified by your instructor. Use the Rhetorical Toolbox 6.1 as a guide.

Teaching Resources
A more detailed assignment page—including screenshots of a student's webpage—is available in the IM. Also included is a list of currently available free website creation resources.

PROJECT 3 An Informative Web Page

Think about all the times you have "Googled" to find a solution to a problem. From the simplest problems to the most complex, we often look to informative writing when we have problems that we need to solve. Think of a problem that you have learned how to solve, and write an informative website page that instructs others about how to solve the problem. Here are the steps to follow.

1. **Select a topic.** Here are some examples of problems you may have solved:

    A. Problems affecting college success (examples: finances, time management)

    B. Problems affecting relationships (examples: a specific parenting problem, a difficult boss)

    C. Bad habits (examples: procrastination, poor eating habits)

    D. Practical problems (examples: finding a good used car, finding pest control solutions)

- E. Personal problems (examples: overcoming loneliness, overcoming shyness)
- F. Hobby/leisure problems (examples: building furniture, vacationing on a shoestring budget)

2. **Find a model web page.** Find a website that presents the solution to a problem in a way that you believe is an excellent model of informative writing. After you find the website, write a brief analysis by answering the three questions that follow. (You will post this analysis in the next step.)
   - A. How can you tell the purpose of the writing is to inform?
   - B. In what ways was this web page written with an audience in mind? Explain.
   - C. What made you select this website? Why is it a good model of informative writing?

3. **Create your informative project.** If you wish, create an actual web page using a free website creation tool; alternatively, create a document that shows the text you would use, any images or illustrations you would use, and how you would organize the page.

4. **Reflect on your work.** After you create your informative project, reflect on your work by answering this question: What rhetorical choices did you make so that readers would find your web page useful? Refer to Rhetorical Toolbox 6.1 for questions you can use to analyze your work.

5. **Submit your work.** Submit these three items: (a) the analysis of an informative web page you used as a model; (b) your informative project; (c) your reflection on your work.

In the remaining pages of this chapter, you will see how Liam Wilson wrote about a topic that he found interesting and that will be new to many readers: crowdsourcing. In addition, you will find steps for writing informative texts that you can use as you craft your own informative project. You will see how Wilson's rhetorical thinking helped him to make sound writing decisions.

Selecting a Topic

If you choose the Assignment Option A, you need to select a topic for an informative project. Selecting a topic in which you are interested is important, but it is also important to think about your audience. If you are writing for a general audience, make sure to select a topic about which that audience needs to know. Otherwise, it will be difficult to make your topic relevant to readers.

> **Liam, on choosing a topic:** "As a computer science major and social media addict, I really wanted to write about three-dimensional integrated circuits. LOL. I knew that most readers would not care about this topic, so then I thought I'd write about crowdsourcing. I figured that most people were familiar with some types of crowdsourcing, but they probably didn't know how prevalent it is as a social media tool. I was pretty sure I could make this topic relevant and interesting."

Planning

Planning an informative paper from a writer's mindset means thinking critically about the rhetorical situation. Here are some questions to guide you through planning, followed by Liam's thoughts.

1. **Speaker or Writer.** How knowledgeable on the topic will audiences expect you to be? Do you need additional information to know enough about the topic? If so, how do you plan to get that information?

2. **Audience.** How can you make the topic relevant to readers? What can you reasonably expect a general audience to already know about the topic? What information is be new? Are there terms or concepts you should define? What rhetorical strategies—such as providing analogies, examples, illustrations, and so on—can you use to help readers understand the information you are presenting?

3. **Message.** Is the thesis statement—the central message—informative in nature? Is the message about the topic narrow enough to communicate in an essay?

Planning an informative project involves figuring out exactly what you hope to communicate and organizing your thoughts. You can do this in three stages.

1. **Use a method of prewriting to generate ideas.** Once you have chosen a topic, figure out what you plan to include in your text. If you are writing an essay, readers expect certain conventions, such as an introduction, a thesis statement, body paragraphs, and a conclusion paragraph. What will these contain? Does the genre you have chosen affect the types of content you include? Will you use bulleted points? Illustrations? Prewrite by using listing, brainstorming, mapping, or any other on-the-page method to come up with ideas. After you have a page of ideas, use an off-the-page planning method, such as talking about your ideas with a classmate, family member, or your instructor, to further refine your thoughts.

2. **Draft a working thesis statement.** Start planning by focusing on the main idea. You can do this by drafting a preliminary thesis statement. You may find that you need to do some research before you know exactly what you want to say in the thesis statement.

> **Liam's Working Thesis Statement**
>
> Crowdsourcing is the intentional use of a crowd of people to accomplish a task.
>
> **Liam, on writing a thesis statement**: "I thought the main thing I should do in my thesis statement is to define the term *crowdsourcing*. The entire essay will focus on helping readers understand the term by providing examples."

3. **Create an outline.** Once you have your preliminary thesis statement, you can outline the way you plan to communicate its message to a general

audience. Asking rhetorically focused questions such as the ones that follow helps you plan with an audience in mind:

- Read your thesis statement. What might the audience already know about the topic? Make a list.

- What information must you provide to help the audience understand the topic? Make a list.

- Of the information the audience needs, which information is important to present first? Are there ideas that need to be understood before other ideas make sense? Put the ideas you have listed in order.

- Which words or concepts will readers need to have defined?

- Imagine knowing nothing about this topic. What kinds of support—examples, explanations, stories, statistics, visual aids, and so on—help you to understand the topic better? Which of these support types can you use, and where can you use them?

Based on your answers to these questions, create an outline. If you are using research, make a note on your outline where the research is to go. Notice that Liam's outline includes his research and the kinds of support he thinks are helpful for readers to understand his message.

Co-requisite Teaching Tip Writing an informative text may require research. Consider discussing how to select and integrate research into informative texts.

Liam's Outline

Working Thesis Statement: Crowdsourcing is the intentional use of a crowd of people to accomplish a task.

Ideas for Introduction: Tell the story of finding the Boston Marathon bombers. Define the term.

Section 1: How crowdsourcing is used in fundraising. How crowdsourcing is used for project development.
- wikis
- collaborative writing platforms
- IdeaStorm (use source)

Section 2: How crowdsourcing is used to do collaborative projects. How crowdsourcing is used to raise funds.
- crowdsourcing for fundraisers
- crowdsourcing for causes (use source: Causes.com)
- crowdsourcing for personal fundraising (use source: Gofundme)

Section 3: How crowdsourcing is used to support small businesses.
- getting investors (use source: Kiva.com)
- getting ideas (contests, crowdsourcing for concepts, names, logos, etc.)
- getting publicity (rent-a-crowd)

> **Section 4:** How crowdsourcing is used for consumer research in computer science.
> - app development
> - software development
> - open source software
>
> **Ideas for conclusion:** Maybe go back to story of Boston Marathon?

> **Liam, on writing an outline:** "Using bullets for each of the details in the major supporting points really helped me figure out whether I had a balanced amount of information for each point."

Drafting

Thinking from a writer's mindset is important at every stage of the writing process, and it is crucial during drafting. Successful writers are constantly trying to anticipate what readers will think when they read the words on the page. Thinking rhetorically while drafting includes anticipating questions readers will have and providing answers to those questions. It includes figuring out where ideas might be confusing to readers and offering additional explanations, examples, or other types of support to help readers understand. Drafting from a writer's mindset means thinking about seemingly minor issues, such as whether one word would be more effective at conveying an idea than another or whether having two long sentences in a row will make the reader frustrated.

To think rhetorically as you write a rough draft, keep these tips in mind:

- **Imagine an ordinary reader as you write.** Perhaps this is one of your classmates whom you do not know very well. As you present information, constantly think about whether this reader will be able to understand what you are writing.
- **Imagine an expert reader.** Perhaps this is your instructor who is an expert on the topic. Present the information so accurately that an expert would not disagree with your writing.
- **Revise sentences as you draft.** After you write a sentence or two, reread them as if you were a classmate, an instructor, or an expert on the topic. Revise as necessary.
- **Keep clarity in mind.** Don't cram too many ideas into one sentence. It will be easier for readers to understand new information in chunks, and these chunks can be complete sentences. Take the time to explain carefully and methodically.
- **Use examples.** Examples can be both real and hypothetical if they will help readers understand your point.
- **Reread your writing during drafting.** Ask whether there is preliminary information that readers need to know. Should some points come earlier than others? Rearrange your outline if you find that, when you are

Teaching Suggestion
Informative writing requires an objective tone, and that is most often achieved by using third person. See "FAQ: Writing in Third Person" in Chapter 7.

Co-requisite Teaching Tip
Consider helping students learn how to write compelling hypothetical examples in the co-requisite section.

writing, ideas seem to make more sense in another arrangement. Should you include background information, definitions, or other explanations to help readers follow your ideas? If so, add that information.

- **If an idea in your outline just isn't working out, go back to the planning stage.** Can you replace the idea? Do you need to do more prewriting to figure out additional content to include?

- **Periodically, stop writing and read your paper from the beginning.** Going back and rethinking is part of the recursive nature of writing. Doing this will help you detect missing information, make sentence-level revisions, and add transition words to facilitate the flow of your ideas.

Consider using terms and phrases that guide readers through the information you are presenting.

DRAFTING TOOLBOX

Terms and Phrases for Informative Texts

- The concept of _____ may seem difficult to understand, but . . .
- An (event/phenomenon/machine, etc.) few people understand is . . .
- One way to understand _____ is to compare it to a/an . . .
- A good example of _____ is . . .
- To understand _____, it is first necessary to understand . . .
- One questions readers often have about _____ is . . .
- _____ can be defined as . . .
- One confusing part of _____ is . . .
- _____ works in a fashion similar to . . .
- For example . . .
- For instance . . .
- To illustrate . . .

Thinking Recursively in the Writing Process

Writing is a recursive process. That means you occasionally need to return to earlier parts of the process. As you write your outline, for example, you may decide you don't like the topic at all, or perhaps you need to go back to planning to tweak some of the details. As you create your project, you will be prompted occasionally to think recursively.

Liam, on recursive writing. "At first I thought I would write a paragraph about how crowdsourcing is used to do consumer product research in computer science. When I started drafting that paragraph, it was clear to me that I didn't know enough about it. Even after researching it, I realized that to explain it to a general audience, I'd have to go into way too much depth. I decided to change that paragraph to the topic of using crowdsourcing for

> creative projects because I already knew about that and could explain it much more easily.
>
> "Also, I had planned to end the essay by returning to the story of the Boston Marathon to introduce the topic of crowdsourcing, but during drafting it just seemed like referring to the story again did not make sense, so I changed the ending."

Revising

Finishing your informative project consists of using a thorough revising process, editing your paper, and formatting your work in the appropriate style.

1. **Skim your paper to see it the way a reader would.** What would a general reader's first impression be? Is the paper lengthy? Brief? Do the paragraphs seem well developed? Do the first few sentences engage you as a reader? Keep these impressions in mind as you do a substantive analysis of your paper.

2. **Read your first paragraph as if you have never read it before and as if you know nothing about the topic.** Is the introduction engaging? Would a general reader want to keep reading? How could you make the introduction more interesting? Are there areas where the reader could already be confused? How can you make these areas clearer? For help with an introduction, see the FAQ: "Creating Introductions and Conclusions" at the end of this chapter.

3. **Read your paper in its entirety as if you know nothing about the topic.** Can you figure out the writer's message (the thesis statement)? As a reader, what would you need explained to fully understand the message? Has the writer provided those explanations? Are there places where examples might help? Might visual aids or other types of support help you understand the message?

4. **Analyze the organization of your paper.** Can readers easily understand why you put things in the order they are in? Would adding transitions such as *next*, *as a result*, or *however* help readers to logically progress through your paper? Is there any background information that is needed early in the paper for readers?

5. **Read the conclusion.** As a reader, do you have a sense that the message has been delivered and that the paper can successfully end? Or are there ideas that need more development? Does the conclusion paragraph deliver a sense of closure? For help with a conclusion, see the FAQ: "Creating Introductions and Conclusions" at the end of this chapter.

6. **Read your paper again, this time focusing on each sentence individually.** Read each sentence for clarity. Are there sentences in your paper that need revision so that they are clear? Are there sentences that contain many different ideas? Consider creating multiple sentences so that each idea is clearly articulated.

7. **Reread the assignment.** Does your paper meet all of the requirements of the assignment? If not, revise.
8. **Use peer review to help you make revision decisions.** The Peer Review Toolbox will help a classmate read your paper and give you constructive suggestions.

> **PEER REVIEW TOOLBOX: INFORMATIVE WRITING**
>
> 1. Does the writer clearly communicate a main idea in the composition? If so, what is the main idea?
> 2. Mark two to three sections that are confusing. In a sentence for each one, explain what you find confusing.
> 3. Are there any places where adding an example, definition, analogy, graphic, or other feature might improve the text? If so, where?
> 4. Would readers understand how this text is relevant to them? If not, how could the writer make the content relevant?

Liam, on his revision decisions: "When I reread the introduction, I realized that I didn't know enough about the Reddit situation, so I did some more research. I also felt like I needed to take out the stuff about positives and negatives because that might make readers think I was going to discuss both sides, but I didn't discuss both sides. I also removed 'you' to stay in third person."

Draft: A thread on Reddit, r/findbostonbombers, invited users to post information that might lead to finding the perpetrators. What happened, however, is that two innocent men were falsely accused, and if police had not found the real criminals quickly, who knows what might have happened to those falsely accused men. Reddit's ability to use the power of a crowd is only one example of a powerful, new tool: crowdsourcing. You will find examples of using crowdsourcing to bully or bring out the worst in the crowd, but for the most part, crowdsourcing is used for good purposes. Crowdsourcing is the intentional use of a crowd of people to accomplish a task, and it is becoming a powerful tool that can be leveraged in a wide variety of situations.

Revision: *Reddit* is a social media website that combines the best and the worst of social media. At its best, *Reddit* is a site where users contribute amazing information, information that can lead to solving crimes, lending a helping hand to those in need, and finding the best egg rolls in San Francisco. At its worst, though, *Reddit* can incite a mob to violence, as was almost the case after the Boston Marathon bombings. A thread on *Reddit*, r/findbostonbombers, invited users to post information that might lead to finding the perpetrators. What happened, however, as Kate Pickert and Adam Sorensen report in *Time* magazine online, is that two innocent men were falsely accused, and if police had not found the real criminals quickly, who knows what might have happened to those falsely accused men. *Reddit*'s ability to harness the power of a crowd is only one example of a powerful, new tool: crowdsourcing. For the most part, crowdsourcing is used for good purposes. Crowdsourcing is the intentional use of a crowd of people to accomplish a task, and it is becoming a powerful tool that can be used in a wide variety of situations.

Liam: "I didn't think I had given enough info on what happened in Iceland. And honestly, I didn't remember all the details. So I went back, did some research, and wrote another paragraph to add this information. I also added more info to the explanation of how Wikipedia works."

Draft: Wikipedia is one of the most well-known projects, offering an encyclopedia-like collection of topics that users contribute and revise. And it is a great example of how crowdsourcing is used for collaboration. The value of wiki-style information is that users can revise, edit, and correct the information. Of course, users can also add faulty content and poor writing, but some of the larger wikis such as Wikipedia have ways to manage the crowd-sourced content without interfering in the open process. A fascinating example of how crowdsourcing can be used in project development comes from Iceland. In 2013, Iceland decided to rewrite its constitution, and they used a crowdsourcing method to let the people do the writing.

Revision: One way crowdsourcing is used is in project development. Contributing to a *wiki*, an open resource on the web where anyone can add, edit, or delete the content, is an example of using a crowd to create a project. *Wikipedia* is one of the most well-known projects, offering an encyclopedia-like collection of topics that users contribute and revise. The value of wiki-style information is that users can revise, edit, and correct the information. Of course, users can also add erroneous content and poor writing, but some of the larger wikis such as *Wikipedia* have found methods for managing the crowd-sourced content without interfering in the open process. *Wikipedia* uses "a few hundred administrators with special powers to enforce good behavior, and a judicial style arbitration committee that considers the few situations remaining unresolved" but implies that the self-governing of users makes little intervention necessary ("Editorial").

A fascinating example of how crowdsourcing can be used in project development comes from Iceland. In 2013, Iceland decided to rewrite its constitution, and they used a crowdsourcing method to let the people do the writing as Hélène Landemore notes, the procedure was complicated, but the final part of writing the constitution was to use social media such as *Facebook* and *Twitter* to crowdsource the content and the wording of the constitution. As suggestions, revisions, and edits came in over social media, the constitution was changed. And as Landemore writes, "While the crowd did not ultimately 'write' the constitution, it contributed valuable input. Among them was the *Facebook* proposal to entrench a constitutional right to the Internet, which resulted in Article 14 of the final proposal." Although two-thirds of voters in Iceland approved the crowdsourced constitution, the bill that would make the constitution legal failed in Parliament (Landemore). Regardless, this innovative experiment in crowdsourcing shows that mass collaboration has exciting potential to transform the way projects are completed.

Liam: "I realized that this new paragraph about creativity might not make sense to readers who don't get what Amazon is doing. I went to Amazon's website and found a quote to help me explain it better. I also needed to be more specific about what the app was that helped in disasters, so I added that info here. I ended up with so much information that I made two paragraphs instead of one."

Draft: By thinking creatively about the potential of crowdsourcing, some people have come up with some interesting uses. "Microtasking" refers to assigning really tiny tasks to a huge number of people so that a large project can be accomplished. For example, Amazon has an app that employs the general public for tasks that are finite in nature but require human intelligence. The tasks these workers perform vary greatly, such as verifying data and classifying photos to taking surveys, all of which are minor tasks but tasks that can be completed by thousands of workers and save companies money. Another creative use of crowdsourcing is emergency management. Twitter, Facebook, and specialized apps such as FEMA's Disaster Reporter enable real-world users to post messages that provide important data during emergencies. As Jennifer Johnson says "During the Boulder, Colorado, flooding in 2013, people used Disaster Reporter to capture geo-tagged photos of the disaster area. The Disaster Reporter data is publicly available and can be of significant use to cities' first responders." The apps created by FEMA provide constantly updated information about shelters and their capacities, real-time weather reports, and photos uploaded by users. When crowdsourced information is mapped by geographic information systems, responders know exactly where they are needed and can decrease response time.

Revision: By thinking creatively about the potential of crowdsourcing, some people have come up with some interesting uses. "Micro tasking" refers to assigning really tiny tasks to a huge number of people so that a large project can be accomplished. For example, Amazon's *Mechanical Turk* site employs the general public for tasks that are finite in nature but require human intelligence. Amazon explains it like this: "Businesses or developers needing tasks done (called Human Intelligence Tasks or "HITs") can use the robust MTurk API to access thousands of high quality, global, on-demand Workers—and then programmatically integrate the results of that work directly into their business processes and systems" ("Human"). The tasks these workers perform vary greatly, from verifying data on the Internet to classifying photos to taking surveys. By paying thousands of people to do these minor tasks, companies can accomplish large projects, and people can earn money.

Another creative use of crowdsourcing is emergency management. *Twitter, Facebook*, and specialized apps such as FEMA's *Disaster Reporter* enable real-world users to post messages that provide important data during emergencies. As Jennifer Johnson reports, "During the Boulder, Colorado, flooding in 2013, people used Disaster Reporter to capture geo-tagged photos of the disaster area. The Disaster Reporter data is publicly available and can be of significant use to cities' first responders." The apps created by FEMA provide constantly updated information about shelters and their capacities, real-time weather reports, and photos uploaded by users. When crowdsourced information is mapped by geographic information systems, responders know exactly where they are needed and can decrease response time.

Finishing

Finishing your informative project consists of editing your paper and formatting your work in the appropriate style.

Editing. Editing means looking for and correcting any errors in grammar, spelling, and mechanics. Always use spell-checkers, but realize that the ultimate responsibility for making sure words are spelled correctly rests on you, the writer. To find errors in grammar and mechanics, be aware of the errors you tend to make and look for those specifically. For example, if you know that you tend to use apostrophes incorrectly, do a search through the document for all of the apostrophes, and check to see that you have used them correctly.

Formatting. Before preparing a final draft, review your instructor's guidelines for formatting and submitting your paper. If you used sources, make sure you use the proper citation and documentation method for your purposes. In Liam's case, he was required to use APA style, so his paper is formatted and documented accordingly.

Liam Wilson, The Power of Crowds (Final Draft)

Liam's finished paper is printed here in its entirety. His instructor required the use of APA style, so his paper is formatted accordingly. Read Liam's essay and then answer the questions that follow.

1

The Power of Crowds

Liam Wilson

Department of English, McLennan Community College

ENG1101

Professor Remy Janssen

January 27, 2020

2

The Power of Crowds

Reddit is a social media website that combines the best and the worst of social media. At its best, Reddit is a site where users contribute amazing information, information that can lead to solving crimes, lending a helping hand to those in need, and finding the best egg rolls in San Francisco. At its worst, though, Reddit can incite a mob to violence, as was almost the case after the Boston Marathon bombings. A thread on Reddit, r/findbostonbombers, invited users to post information that might lead to finding the perpetrators. What happened, however, as Kate Pickert and Adam Sorensen (2013) report in *Time* magazine online, is that two innocent men were falsely accused, and if police had not found the real criminals quickly, who knows what might have happened to those falsely accused men. Reddit's ability to harness the power of a crowd is only one example of a powerful, new tool: crowdsourcing. For the most part, crowdsourcing is used for good purposes. Crowdsourcing is the intentional use of a crowd of people to accomplish a task.

One way crowdsourcing is used is in project development. Contributing to a wiki, an open resource on the web where anyone can add, edit, or delete the content, is an example of using a crowd to create a project. Wikipedia is one of the most well-known projects, offering an encyclopedia-like collection of topics that users contribute and revise. The value of wiki-style information is that users can revise, edit, and correct the information. Of course, users can also add erroneous content and poor writing, but some of the larger wikis such as Wikipedia have found methods for managing the crowd-sourced content without interfering in the open process. Wikipedia uses "a few hundred administrators with special powers to enforce good behavior, and a judicial style arbitration committee that considers the few situations remaining unresolved" but implies that the self-governing of users makes little intervention necessary ("Editorial," 2018).

A fascinating example of how crowdsourcing can be used in project development comes from Iceland. In 2013, Iceland decided to rewrite its constitution, and they used a crowdsourcing method to let the people do the writing as Hélène Landemore (2014) notes. The procedure was complicated, but the final part of writing the

3

constitution was to use social media such as Facebook and Twitter to crowdsource the content and the wording of the constitution. As suggestions, revisions, and edits came in over social media, the constitution was changed. And as Landemore writes, "While the crowd did not ultimately 'write' the constitution, it contributed valuable input. Among them was the Facebook proposal to entrench a constitutional right to the Internet, which resulted in Article 14 of the final proposal." Although two-thirds of voters in Iceland approved the crowdsourced constitution, the bill that would make the constitution legal failed in Parliament (Landemore, 2014). Regardless, this innovative experiment in crowdsourcing shows that mass collaboration has exciting potential.

Another popular use of crowdsourcing is in funding and fundraising. Funding means providing the funds for a project to take place. Kiva is an excellent example of how crowdsourcing can be used for funding projects. People from all over the world who need funds to start a small business can apply to Kiva, and Kiva puts their profiles on the site. These people are often asking for small sums of money to fund home-grown businesses, such as $500 to buy a vending cart to sell produce. Investors read about the people asking for loans and then invest money to help these small start-ups. Kiva is actually a non-profit organization designed "to create economic and social good" (Kiva, 2020). Related to investing is fundraising, another venture crowdsourcing supports. For example, a softball team hoping to go to a national competition might create a site on GoFundMe, another crowdsourcing website, to raise money. Contributors can go to sites such as GoFundMe and Causes.com, a site that crowdsources to fundraise for worthy causes, to read about them and contribute money. Projects that may have never been funded in the past now have access to millions of potential contributors through crowdsourcing.

While crowdsourcing can provide funding for projects, it can also be a great source for small businesses. Facebook is an application that is widely used for eliciting responses from large crowds. For example, a company trying to find a new logo may advertise a logo contest on Facebook to solicit ideas from viewers. The responses sent in will not only help the company find a logo but will also generate publicity. And the responses will help the company see what is important to the public. Companies may use crowdsourcing to float new ideas or to conduct surveys before launching new products or marketing campaigns. By listening to the

4

suggestions of ordinary people, a company can spend its time developing products that are in demand. And crowdsourcing is not limited to online applications. Real, physical crowds can help fledgling businesses take off. Sites such as Rent-a-Crowd, CrowdsOnDemand, and CrowdsforRent offer "swarms" of people to support any project, including grand openings and special events.

By thinking creatively about the potential of crowdsourcing, some people have come up with some interesting uses. "Microtasking" refers to assigning really tiny tasks to a huge number of people so that a large project can be accomplished. For example, Amazon's Mechanical Turk site employs the general public for tasks that are finite in nature but require human intelligence. Amazon explains it like this: "Businesses or developers needing tasks done (called Human Intelligence Tasks or "HITs") can use the robust MTurk API to access thousands of high quality, global, on-demand Workers—and then programmatically integrate the results of that work directly into their business processes and systems" ("Human," 2020). The tasks these workers perform vary greatly, from verifying data to classifying photos. By paying thousands of people to do these minor tasks, companies can accomplish large projects, and people can earn money.

Another creative use of crowdsourcing is emergency management. Twitter, Facebook, and specialized apps such as FEMA's Disaster Reporter enable real-world users to post messages that provide important data during emergencies. As Jennifer Johnson (2016) reports, "During the Boulder, Colorado, flooding in 2013, people used Disaster Reporter to capture geo-tagged photos of the disaster area. The Disaster Reporter data is publicly available and can be of significant use to cities' first responders." The apps created by FEMA provide constantly updated information about shelters and their capacities, real-time weather reports, and photos uploaded by users. When crowdsourced information is mapped by geographic information systems, responders know exactly where they are needed and can decrease response time.

Crowds, once thought of as only a nuisance, have great power to do good. By using the power of crowds, projects that seem daunting to one person are easily managed. Dreams that seemed impossible—such as finding the funds to start a business—are suddenly within the realm of possibility. With a bit of creativity, crowdsourcing is sure to be used to change the way humans live and work.

References

Editorial oversight and control. (n.d.). Wikipedia. Retrieved January 21, 2020, from https://en.wikipedia.org/wiki/Wikipedia:Editorial oversight and control

How FEMA delivers anytime, anywhere information during disasters. (2016, January 28). Digital.gov. https://digital.gov/2016/01/28/how-femadeliversanytimeanywhere-information-during-disasters/

Human intelligence through an API access a global, on-demand, 24 × 7 workforce. (n.d.). Retrieved January 20, 2020, from http://www.mturl.com/

Kiva. (n.d.) *About us.* Retrieved January 20, 2020, from https://www.kiva.org/about

Landemore, H. (2014, July 31). *Iceland tried to crowdsource a new constitution. It didn't work.* Slate. https://slate.com/technology/2014/07/five-lessons-from-icelands-failed-crowdsourced-constitution-experiment.html

Pickert, K. (2013, April 23). *Inside Reddit's hunt for the Boston bombers.* Time. http://nation.time.com/2013/04/23/inside-reddits-hunt-for-the-boston-bombers/

YOUR TURN Analyzing Wilson's Rhetorical Strategies

1. Review the strategies in this chapter under "Thinking Rhetorically to Develop Your Paper." Which of these strategies did Wilson use in his essay?
2. Do you think most readers would find his essay relevant to their lives? Why or why not?
3. Where did Wilson place his thesis statement? Was this placement effective in your opinion? Why or why not?
4. Find one strategy Wilson used that you would like to use in your own writing. What is that strategy? How could you use it in your own informative writing project?

Reflecting to Develop a Writer's Mindset

In college and at work, you will need to use informative writing strategies to convey information. What are some of the tips you have learned in this chapter that you can transfer and use in any situation that requires you to inform? Explain how you might use these tips in a particular writing situation.

FAQ CREATING INTRODUCTIONS AND CONCLUSIONS

If you struggle to write introductions and conclusion, you are not alone. It is challenging to craft an introduction that engages readers, and finding the right words to bring closure to an essay can be equally daunting. Use the strategies that follow to come up with creative ideas for introducing and concluding your compositions.

1. How can you write an introduction?

- **Remember your purpose.** If your purpose is to inform, you can start doing that in the introduction itself by providing background information. If you are writing for another purpose (such as to persuade or to analyze), think about how the introduction can help you accomplish that purpose.

- **Provide background information, if appropriate.** If the topic is new to readers or if the audience might benefit from an overview, the introduction is a good place to provide such information.

- **Work backward from your thesis statement.** Read your thesis statement as if you have never seen it before. Imagine a reader asking, "What? Why are you telling me this?" Think about how you would answer those questions and write sentences that gradually lead up to the thesis statement.

- **Start with a question.** This common method for introducing is often effective because the question you begin with is the focus of your essay. The remaining sentences in the introduction lead readers to your answer to that question: your thesis statement.

- **Start with a story, a fact, a statistic, a quotation, or a saying.** Using an "item" such as a story, a statistic, or the like, can be an effective way of introducing the topic and leading readers to your thesis statement. Make sure the item you use is not so specific that it requires its own introduction! Additionally, make sure the item you use supports your writing purpose. For instance, if you are writing an informative essay on COVID-19 (the pandemic virus), using a statistic might be effective because statistics help to inform. Telling a sad story might be an effective way to begin a persuasive essay but may not be appropriate for an informative purpose.

2. How can you write a conclusion?

- **Remember your purpose, again!** If your purpose was to inform, what did you want readers to know? Would readers benefit from a brief summary of what you have said in your essay? If your purpose was to persuade, the final paragraph is a great place to make one last, strong effort at persuasion, perhaps by ending a story you began in the introduction or by repeating your most compelling reason for your claim.

- **Draw implications.** One way to write a conclusion is to remind readers of the importance of the topic. For instance, the informative essay on COVID-19 might end by reminding readers that understanding how the virus spreads is important because such understanding can save lives.
- **Repeat the question you asked in the introduction, but this time, emphasize the answer to the question.** You will have already provided ample information and support to develop your thesis statement. You can repeat the question and briefly summarize how you have answered it.
- **Give readers a way forward.** Essays on some topics lend themselves to a conclusion that provides suggestions to readers, such as how readers can find more information on the topic, how they can solve the problems addressed in the essay, or what kind of additional research needs to be done. Providing this information is a good way to conclude such essays.

TRY IT!

Imagine that you are writing an essay to help readers understand how viruses work. Your goal is to provide this general information so that readers can more clearly understand why and how the coronavirus poses threats to unprepared populations. Your thesis statement is, "To understand why the newest coronavirus (COVID-19) poses such a threat to humans, it is important to understand how viruses work." Write an introduction paragraph and a conclusion paragraph for the essay.

CREDITS

Page 116. Migliore, Lauren. (2017, Oct. 7). "The Violent Brain: Ingredients of a Mass Murderer," *Brain World*. All rights reserved. Used with permission.

Page 120. Ehrenberg, Rachel, "What We Do and Don't Know About How to Prevent Gun Violence," *Science News*, March 9, 2018. https://www.sciencenews.org/article/evidence-preventing-gun-violence-deaths-research. © Society for Science & the Public 2000–2019. All rights reserved.

7 Writing to Analyze

CHAPTER OBJECTIVES

You will learn to:
- Identify key rhetorical concerns of analytical texts.
- Examine analytical texts.
- Compose an analysis.

You finished your degree and just landed a great job. In a team meeting, your boss is discussing a new project and assigning tasks. "We'll have to do a needs study—I'll get started on that, and Jeff, if you'd do a technical analysis, that would be great. Marietta, you can get started on a cost/benefit analysis to help us narrow our options, and Amir, please take a look at the bids we have gotten so far to figure out how they differ." Whether you are Jeff, Marietta, or Amir, you need to know how to think analytically because all four tasks the supervisor presented require analysis.

Analysis is both a process and a product. As a process, analysis requires careful, detailed thinking about a subject—the kind of thinking we examine in this chapter. As a product, a written analysis can take many forms, from comparative charts to reports to academic papers to family budgets. Because analysis is used for so many different purposes, written analyses vary greatly in how they are composed. For instance, an analytical paper in a nursing journal is structured differently than a rhetorical analysis or a literary analysis.

As a written product, analysis requires thinking from a writer's mindset. Writers must compose a text that will guide readers through the analysis so that readers understand the conclusions the writer has made. As you work through this chapter, you will learn how to think analytically and how to use rhetorical thinking to compose an analysis that readers will find effective and compelling.

Connect Adaptive Learning Assignment
Consider assigning Connect's Adaptive Learning Assignments to support this chapter.

Teaching Resources
See the Instructor's Manual (IM) for suggestions about how to teach this chapter, and consider assigning this chapter's test-bank quiz.

WARM-UP

What steps are involved in analyzing a subject? Are the steps the same, regardless of subject? To answer these questions, consider the three projects that follow. Jot down the steps you would take to accomplish each one. Are the steps the same?

Project 1: For a marketing class, analyze the most recent U.S. Census population data to write a report about demographic patterns in a city. You will use the report later in the semester to develop a marketing plan.

Project 2: For personal planning, analyze two colleges to determine which one is better for you.

Project 3: For an employer, explain how 3D printing works to determine whether the company should consider replacing traditional manufacturing with 3D printing.

ANALYTICAL WRITING FROM A WRITER'S MINDSET

A successful writer of analysis must keep the audience in mind throughout the process of thinking and writing. Thinking rhetorically will guide the process you use, and it will help you to convey the results of your analysis to an audience so that readers can follow your logic and conclusions.

The Process of Analyzing

The process of analyzing always precedes the writing process. In the Warm-Up exercise, you were asked to think about the processes you would use for three scenarios requiring analysis. If you are like most people, the processes you thought of included verbs such as *examine, try, experiment, survey, research, check, compare, find,* and so on. You probably found that the process you would use for analyzing potential colleges is different from the process you would use to analyze 3D printing or identify demographic patterns in a city. Conducting a successful analysis depends on using an analytical process that works for your purpose.

Additionally, as you plan the process you will use for analysis, it is important to think about audience expectations. For example, if you are analyzing the costs of two colleges to help readers decide which one is the best value, readers will expect particular information, such as the cost of living at the university, the cost of fees, the cost of tuition, the availability of part-time jobs in the city to offset tuition costs, and so on. The process you use for the analysis should take into consideration what readers will expect the analysis to cover. To figure out the best process for an analysis, use these questions:

Analytical Process Questions

1. What is the purpose of the analysis? In other words, what do you want to learn by conducting the analysis?
2. Who is the audience? What expectations will the audience have, and how will these expectations influence the process of your analysis?
3. What information must you find to conduct the analysis?
4. What will you need to do with the information to analyze it properly?

In the Warm-Up, you thought about the process steps used for particular analyses. You probably realized that you would not use the same process for each of the tasks. But what, exactly, should the process be for the three scenarios in the Warm-Up? Using the Analytical Process Questions can help you determine a process that will produce the kind of analysis the assignment calls for. Notice how these questions result in differing processes for each task:

Project 1: For a marketing class, analyze the most recent U.S. Census population data to write a report about demographic patterns in a city. You will use the report later in the semester to develop a marketing plan.

1. What is the purpose of the analysis? In other words, what do you want to learn by conducting the analysis? *The purpose is to provide useful information—population patterns based on the most recent demographic information—that will be helpful in a marketing plan.*
2. Who is the audience? What expectations does the audience have, and how will these expectations influence the process of your analysis? *The marketing professor is the primary audience, but she instructed students to write the marketing plan as if they were employed at a marketing firm. The instructor will expect students to use a process for analyzing demographic data that is sound.*
3. What information must you find to conduct the analysis? *You will need to select a city and find current census data.*

Project 2: For personal planning, analyze two colleges to determine which one is better for you.

1. What is the purpose of the analysis? In other words, what do you want to learn by conducting the analysis? *The purpose is to figure out the best college to attend.*
2. Who is the audience? What expectations does the audience have, and how will these expectations influence the process of your analysis? *In this case, there is no external audience. You are conducting this analysis for your own information.*
3. What information must you find to conduct the analysis? *You will need information from each college that helps me do my analysis.*
4. What will you need to do with the information to analyze it properly?
   - *Identify the factors that are important to me (majors, costs, location, job placement assistance, and so on)*
   - *Find information from each college about the factors that are important*
   - *Compare the data found for each factor*
   - *Determine the relative importance of each factor and then weigh them*
   - *Examine all of the information found and make a decision*

Project 3: For an employer, explain how 3D printing works to determine whether the company should consider replacing traditional manufacturing with 3D printing.

1. What is the purpose of the analysis? In other words, what do you want to learn by conducting the analysis? *The purpose is to explain how a technology works and to make a recommendation about whether or not to use it.*

2. Who is the audience? What expectations does the audience have, and how will these expectations influence the process of your analysis? *A supervisor will be the audience, and he may send the explanation along to others. You will need to include in the analysis the points that matter to an administrator: how 3D printing works, its costs, its advantages and disadvantages.*

3. What information must you find to conduct the analysis? *You will need to find information that helps you to understand how 3D printing works, what it costs, and how it compares to traditional manufacturing.*

4. What will you need to do with the information to analyze it properly? *You will need to read enough to understand and explain how 3D printing works and then to compare 3D printing with traditional manufacturing by looking at criteria, such as the costs involved, the space required, and so on.*

For each of the tasks, the steps involved in analysis differ. You can figure out a productive process by keeping in mind the purpose of your analysis.

Types of Analysis

Since analysis as a process is a mental task used for a wide variety of purposes, analytical skills are involved in many writing projects. Table 7.1 lists a few of the more common types of analysis. As a reader, you can use the table to understand the type of analysis a text is presenting; as a writer, it can help you classify the analytical process you need to use to accomplish a purpose.

> ▶ **ACTIVITY 1 Identifying the Audience for Analytical Writing**
>
> Table 7.1 cites a report that compares the public education systems of Germany and the United States. If you were authoring such a report, how would the report differ for differing audiences? Specifically, if you were writing for an audience of middle school students, what are some rhetorical choices you would make? If you were writing for a national newspaper, what are some rhetorical choices you would make? How would the two reports differ, and how might they be similar?

Creating an Analytical Text

Once you complete your analysis, you are ready to create a product, such as an essay, a report, a chart, or another genre that works for your purpose. Thinking rhetorically throughout the writing process helps you craft a text that accurately and clearly conveys to readers the results of your analysis (Rhetorical Toolbox 7.1).

One choice writers must make is whether to create an objective or subjective analysis. An objective analysis is one that is based on facts and is written in third person. For example, an analysis of the newest iPhone might be written from an objective point of view, presenting characteristics and features of the phone and perhaps comparing it to the previous iPhone's characteristics and features. A writer who wishes to review the phone, however, presents his or her opinion within the analysis. When the writer's opinions are included, the analysis is subjective. In a subjective analysis, a writer presents the analytical details as objectively as possible, using third person. Somewhere in the analysis, often the beginning or the end, the writer offers his or her thoughts about the subject that is analyzed.

Teaching Resources
Consider using the PowerPoint "Analysis: Process and Product."

TABLE 7.1 Types of Analysis and Their Purposes

Type of analysis	Purpose	Example
Causal analysis	To identify the causes of an event or phenomenon	An article that examines the anti-vaccination movement to try to figure out its origin
Comparative analysis	To understand by comparing two or more things	A report that compares the public education systems of Germany and the United States
Cost/benefit analysis	To determine whether a course of action or purchase is a wise choice	An essay that presents what it would cost to make higher education free and compares that cost to the benefits society would gain from such an action
Descriptive analysis	To understand the attributes of something	A report that describes the demographic makeup of a city
Predictive analysis	To use data to predict what might happen under certain conditions	A report that uses data to predict what might result in a certain area if a tsunami were to occur
Process analysis	To understand a process	An article about the process of (and stages in) grieving
Product analysis	To understand and work with a product or to select the right product for a particular purpose	A web page that analyzes high fructose corn syrup: its makeup, production process, uses, and so on
Literary analysis	To understand a literary work on a deeper level by examining its parts, its context, the writer's choices, and so on	An essay that examines the dialect used by characters in a novel
Rhetorical analysis	To understand a text by examining the message it conveys and the means for conveying that message	An essay that examines the rhetorical strategies of an editorial arguing for open borders

RHETORICAL TOOLBOX 7.1
The Rhetorical Concerns of Analytical Writing

1. **Purpose.** What is the purpose of your analysis? Is the purpose of the analysis to aid understanding? To draw conclusions to make decisions? Figure out the purpose so that you can present the analysis in such a way that readers follow the logic and understand any conclusions you make.
2. **Knowledge.** Do you know enough about the subject or have enough research to analyze the subject? Analysis requires information; as a writer, you must have accurate and sufficient knowledge about the

(Continued on next page)

(Continued from page 147)

subject for readers to find the analysis credible. What additional information might you need? How will you find it?

3. **Audience.** Who is the intended audience, and what knowledge does this audience have about the subject or the process used for the analysis? As a writer, you must determine how much of the analysis to explain to readers; this determination depends on what readers already know about the topic or about the method of analysis.

4. **Rhetorical strategies.** What rhetorical strategies will help you convey the message to the readers? Analyzing the audience's needs will help you figure out when to provide explanations, examples, illustrations, comparisons, graphics, definitions, and so on.

MODELS OF ANALYTICAL WRITING

Is Starting College and Not Finishing Really That Bad?

Michael Greenstone and Adam Looney

The first analytical article seeks to answer the question, "Is Starting College and Not Finishing Really That Bad?" The writers, Michael Greenstone and Adam Looney, respond to that question by analyzing economic data. Greenstone is a professor of economics at the University of Chicago, and Looney is a senior fellow at the Brookings Institution, a nonprofit public policy organization. Both Greenstone and Looney also work with The Hamilton Project, a nonprofit group that produces evidence-based economic analyses and proposals. As you read the article, notice the annotations, which point out the analytical features of the text.

Teaching Suggestion
For additional models of analytical writing, see Part 6, An Anthology of Readings.

Co-requisite Teaching Tip
Consider discussing some of the verbs in the annotations. The verbs that identify writing moves (such as *explain, present, provide, illustrate, acknowledge, refocus*) can point students to strategies they can use in their own writing.

The latest jobs and unemployment statistics do not tell the full story of how all Americans are faring in today's economic climate, as workers with more education continue to be employed at higher rates and earn more than their less-educated counterparts. Indeed, as previous Hamilton Project work has shown, the rates of return to a two- or four-year college degree are high. In recent years, however, there has been increasing concern about students who begin two- and four-year colleges but fail to complete a degree—particularly in light of the large increase in student debt and growing talk about the high costs of college.

In this month's employment analysis, The Hamilton Project examines whether starting college is worth it for students who fail to complete a degree. Our startling finding is that it is: these students' lifetime earnings are roughly $100,000 higher (in present value) than that of their peers who ended their education after high school. Measured by the rate of return, getting some college is an investment with a return that exceeds the historical return on practically any conventional investment, including stocks, bonds, and real estate. (Of course, the return to some college is considerably smaller than the return to finishing either an associate's or bachelor's degree.) We also continue to explore the nation's "jobs gap," or the number of jobs needed to return to pre-recession employment levels.

THE COLLEGE EARNINGS PREMIUM

More education corresponds to better employment opportunities, even in the current, tepid job market. In April 2013, according to BLS* data, the unemployment rate for individuals age twenty-five and older without a high school diploma was 11.4 percent; for high school graduates, 7.2 percent; for individuals with an associate's degree, 5.0 percent; and for graduates with a bachelor's degree or higher, unemployment was only 3.6 percent. Based on a more expansive measure of employment—the employment-to-population ratio—these disparities are even larger. Of all individuals without a high school diploma, age twenty-five and older, only 39.9 percent had a job; for high school graduates with no additional education, the employment rate was 54.5 percent; for individuals with an associate's degree it was 68.6 percent; and for graduates with a bachelor's or higher it was 73.2 percent. Interestingly, the unemployment rate for individuals that reported some college but no degree was below the national average at 6.6 percent and the employment-to-population ratio was 60.9 percent. These numbers, and all the calculations presented in this report, are described in detail in the report's technical appendix.

---

* Bureau of Labor Statistics, a federal agency that collects data on employment and related issues.

> The subject of the analysis: effects of starting but not finishing a degree.

> A startling finding—the results of the analysis.

> Explanation of how the analysis led the writers to their conclusion.

> They present data for readers.

> The writers provide a technical appendix in which they present the sources of all the data they use.

They illustrate the data by creating a chart. This visual aid helps readers understand the analysis.

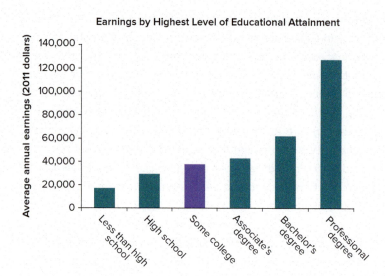

In addition to increasing the chances of employment, education also has a substantial effect on one's earnings potential. The graph [above] shows the average annual earnings of individuals with varying levels of educational attainment. Those with a bachelor's degree earn a premium of roughly $30,000 each year relative to those with just a high school diploma. Over a lifetime of work, a college graduate with a bachelor's degree would earn over $500,000 more than an individual with just a high school diploma.

A second conclusion drawn from the analysis is that one's earnings potential increases with higher education.

What has not been previously appreciated is that even those who enroll in a two- or four-year program but do not attain a degree also experience substantial increases in earnings. On average, these individuals made about $8,000 per year more than those with just a high school diploma. Over a lifetime, this results in over $100,000 more in earnings.

They present the data used for their analysis.

The writers explain the finding that even those who do not graduate from college benefit from it. Discussing lifetime earnings helps readers understand the significance of the data.

ARE THE INCREASED EARNINGS WORTH THE INVESTMENT?

In today's job market, where even some college graduates are struggling to find work, many wonder whether the high cost of college is worth the eventual earnings payoff. First, students face the out-of-pocket costs of tuition. On average, annual tuition and fees are about $3,000 at two-year colleges, $13,000 at four-year colleges, and $27,000 at professional-degree programs.

This part of the analysis addresses the cost of college and its benefits.

The writers present the data.

But the true cost of college is more than just tuition; it also includes the opportunity cost of being in school and not working, as college students forgo income that they could have earned by being in the classroom. (The cost of college does not, however, include the price of room and board; all individuals must pay for food and shelter regardless of if they are in college.) Between the ages of eighteen and twenty-one, the earnings of individuals with only a high school degree (and not in school) rise substantially, from $8,000 to $15,000—and that's among individuals that actually have a job. Thus, the forgone earnings associated with going to college are about $49,000 for a four-year program and $20,000 for a two-year program.

> They acknowledge that an analysis must include more than tuition costs.

> They explain the way they calculated the cost of college.

Despite these daunting costs, as we showed in earlier work, the annual rates of return of investing in an associate's or bachelor's degree are two to three times higher than those from alternative investments including stocks, bonds, gold, treasury bills, and the housing market. But what about students who start college but find that they are unable to complete their degree? Do the costs they incur for achieving some college outweigh any benefits they receive for their years in school?

> A finding from earlier work is that the investment in college is a fiscally wise investment.

> They refocus the question to determine if *some college* is fiscally wise.

In the graph below, we extend our earlier analysis to include the returns to investing in a professional degree and investing in some college. The graph shows that, on average, attending some college

Returns to Education Compared to Other Investments

Category	Percent return
Associate's degree	~20
Professional degree	~16
Bachelor's degree	~15
Some college	~9
Stocks	~6
Gold	~2.5
10-Year Treasury bonds	~2.5
T-Bills	~1
Housing	~1

> They visually demonstrate the data.

but not receiving a degree also has a higher return than all other conventional investments. The annual rate of return of an investment in some college was 9.1 percent. This rate of return is more than 3 percentage points higher than the average stock market returns and 7 percentage points higher than the returns from investing in Treasury bonds.

They present their finding: even having some college without a degree is a wise investment.

Of course, the high rate of return associated with attending a few years of college does not imply that dropping out of college is a better option compared to completing a bachelor's or associate's degree. Graduates with a bachelor's degree annually make about $32,000 more than individuals with only some college. Instead, what this analysis suggests is that the downside risk of trying for a college degree but not making it all the way to a degree is not that bad, and could still be worth the investment of time and tuition.

They anticipate that readers might be confused about an issue and clarify it.

Our method of analysis does not reveal whether college education causes the increased earnings. It is likely that college graduates have different aptitudes and ambitions that might affect earnings. However, a large body of academic research suggests that there is a causal relationship between education and later earnings, and that the investment in education causes the later increased earnings. Our analysis also only looks at the average returns for those who have attended some college; these returns may not apply to potential students considering attending but who have lower levels of preparation or determination than this group. And, naturally, the outcomes for any one person may be higher or lower than these averages.

They acknowledge the limits of their method of analysis.

CONCLUSION

As the unemployment rate continues to decline, it is important to remember that Americans without a college or high school education are still experiencing above-average rates of unemployment. Addressing this problem requires not only creating new jobs but also ensuring that the workforce has the skills necessary to fill these jobs. Although some people currently question whether the cost of college is worth the investment, the evidence suggests that rate of return is much higher than many alternative investments, even for students that don't ultimately finish a degree.

The writers summarize the conclusions they have drawn from their analysis.

Analyzing Greenstone and Looney's Rhetorical Strategies

1. **Do the writers know enough about the subject or have enough research to analyze the subject?** The writers demonstrate their credibility and knowledge by providing ample data from reliable sources. They provide their sources in the technical appendix (not included here).
2. **What is the purpose of the analysis?** The purpose is to determine whether people who have some college hours but do not have a college degree fare better economically than those who have no college.
3. **Who is the intended audience, and what knowledge does this audience have about the topic?** The audience is the general public and policy makers.
4. **What rhetorical strategies do the writers use to help readers follow the logic of their analysis or understand the points they are making?** When the data is complex, the writers create charts that help readers visualize the data. They also use the data in examples that readers can relate to their own lives. For example, in this sentence, they help readers see the extent to which a bachelor's degree matters in terms of annual salary: "Graduates with a bachelor's degree annually make about $32,000 more than individuals with only some college."

Teaching Suggestion
The writers do not address racial disparities in college attendance and completion. Consider discussing with students whether or not the writers should have done so.

Reducing Food Waste Takes More than Finishing Your Plate

Nathanael Johnson

The author of two full-length books, Unseen City: The Majesty of Pigeons, the Discreet Charm of Snails, and Other Wonders of the Urban Wilderness *and* All Natural: A Skeptic's Quest to Discover if the Natural Approach to Diet, Childbirth, Healing, and the Environment Really Keeps Us Healthier and Happier, *as well as articles for a number of publications, Nathanael Johnson is a senior writer for the website Grist. His article "Reducing Food Waste Takes More Than Finishing Your Plate" first appeared on Grist in 2014. As you read Johnson's article, think about why it is classified as an analysis. What does Johnson analyze? How does he conduct his analysis?*

Co-requisite Teaching Tip
Identifying the strategies the writer uses to analyze and to present his analysis can be challenging. Consider working together on this task. Another way is to dissect product reviews, such as those on Wirecutter.com; doing so can pave the way for looking at more complex texts such as this one.

Teaching Resources
This reading is available as a Power of Process assignment in Connect.

> In southeast Costa Rica near the Panamanian border, there's a group of farmers growing bananas and cocoa without pesticides. Two indigenous groups work communally owned land in the buffer zone surrounding La Amistad National Park. Their cooperative is called the Talamanca Small Farmers Association.

But Talamanca's growers face the same discouraging problem year after year: They work in a rural area. Some farmers transport their bananas for an hour by boat, and then another three hours by truck, to a processing plant owned by a Chiquita subsidiary. Often, the bananas have to wait for the truck, and they rot. It rains a lot there—the roads frequently flood in the wet season—and sometimes the farmers lose whole truckloads of bananas waiting for the waters to recede. The estimated losses are 40 percent of the crop, said Stephanie Daniels of the Sustainable Food Lab, which has been working with Talamanca to solve the problem of spoilage.

Between 30 and 40 percent of the food grown around the world is lost: spoiled, wasted, or eaten by vermin. Saving even a portion of that could make a huge difference for poor farmers and the environment. Combine a reduction in food waste with increases in farm yields and better livelihoods for the poorest, and we'd have a realistic scenario in which we could improve overall human health and happiness without expanding our agricultural footprint.

As the example of Talamanca illustrates, solving the waste problem can make more food available to eaters while enriching the farmers. (Feeding the world is really a problem of enriching the poor, as I've written about [in other places]).

As Daniels explained it, solving the waste problem is an important step forward to the larger goal of plugging small farmers into the world market. There are people all around the world who want what these Costa Rican farmers grow and are willing to pay a premium for it. Stonyfield Farms buys their bananas to mix with yogurt. People in Switzerland eat their unusual fruits. Basically, there's a lot of wealth that wants to go to rural Costa Rica in exchange for the stuff that's already growing there—but instead, a lot of that stuff is rotting on the ground.

And so Talamanca is working on a solution. With money from the government, from Stonyfield, and from the Danone Ecosystem Fund, it's investigating building a small-scale processor: A machine to peel the bananas, squish them, and aseptically seal them into shelf-stable bags. Today, the farmers depend on Chiquita's machinery; if they had the food processing technology, they would make a lot more money—and have a lot more control over their destiny.

Around the world

The farmers of Costa Rica aren't alone. This year the Rockefeller Foundation and the Global Knowledge Initiative produced an in-depth report on food waste in Africa, which showcased dozens of Talamanca-like stories. When farmers simply have airtight bags for their beans, cowpeas, and corn, the lack of oxygen kills insects inside, resulting in millions of dollars in savings. Farmers are using cassava graters and solar driers to process crops that rot easily. They are tapping into the world market with cellphones.

This is a systems-based report, looking at the entire network of farmers, buyers, agricultural educators, and technological capacity. As I read it, it became clear that reducing food waste is not necessarily an end unto itself, but something that comes naturally if you are trying to help poor farmers sell their food and earn a living wage.

North America

Food waste, however, looks very different depending where on Earth you stand. In poorer countries, the bulk of food waste is due

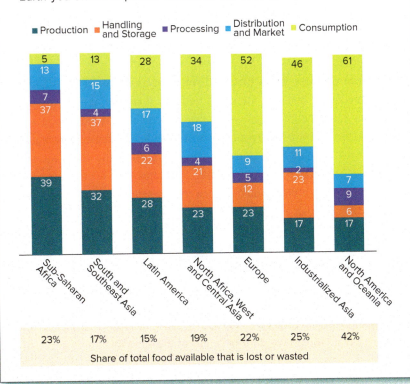

to lack of technology and the inability of farmers to sell their goods. In the richer countries, food waste is all about culture.

"It truly is wasted in this country," said Dana Gunders of the NRDC, the author of this landmark report. "If we took someone out of Cambodia—or their consumer expectations for food—and combined that with the U.S. technology for preserving food, realistically we could cut a lot of our food waste."

People often come to Gunders to ask if they should go ahead and eat moldy bread. But she said that sort of thing is a tiny part of the problem.

"It is about eating carrot tops, in a way—but it's really about having 4,000 sandwiches left over at a conference. It's about plowing under an entire field because the market shifted." And it's about throwing away tons of produce because it doesn't fit the exacting standards of size and aesthetics that we've come to expect and enshrined in our regulations.

Cutting post-harvest waste can be a huge boon to small farmers. But in this country, where a large share of the waste occurs at the consumer level, the impact is a little less clear. Perhaps having more food around would mean fewer farms; that could be good for the environment or bad, depending on what replaced them.

But Gunders thinks that food waste won't decrease so fast that it dramatically outstrips the rising demand. If we are able to cut waste in this country, that would probably mean that more food produced in the U.S. might be exported as animal feed, as rising affluence increases the demand for meat. Or the land might increase biofuel production. Neither of these outcomes gets environmentalists too excited, but both would reduce the pressure to expand farmland in more sensitive areas.

The takeaway

If we continue business as usual, we're going to need a lot more food by 2050. This is what food futurists have been calling "the food gap." The World Resources Institute has suggested that a reasonable goal might be cutting our current food waste in half. Just doing that would take care of a fifth of the food gap.

> When we talk about food waste in richer countries, we are mostly talking about consumer waste—reducing that is important for cutting the food gap. But when we talk about food waste in poorer countries we are talking about losses (the yellow and red bars on the graph above) that take money out of farmers' pockets. And there, the potential in reducing waste is even greater: By enriching small farmers, it would reduce poverty—which is the ultimate goal, and the root cause of hunger.

YOUR TURN Analyzing Johnson's Rhetorical Strategies

Explain your answer for each question in two or three sentences. Use examples from the text to support your points.

1. What is the purpose of this analysis?
2. What subject is analyzed and in what ways is the subject examined?
4. Who is the intended audience, and what knowledge might this audience have about the topic?
5. What rhetorical strategies help readers follow the logic of the analysis or understand the points the writer makes?

CHAPTER PROJECT Writing to Analyze

The three projects that follow require you to analyze a subject and write about your analysis. The first project asks you to find your own topic, while the next two projects provide more guidance about what to write.

PROJECT 1 Find Your Own Topic

Write an analysis on any topic in which you are personally interested. Write your analysis for a general audience. Here are some ideas:

- If you are needing to decide something (such as a major purchase, a career choice, and so on), create a cost/benefit analysis.
- Find a topic within your field of interest and analyze it. For example, if you are interested in computers, analyze how artificial intelligence or machine learning are going to affect health care in the future.
- Find an event or political or social phenomenon and analyze its causes or effects. For example, what caused the Black Lives Matter movement? What effects has the movement had?

Use research if you need to know more about the subject or if you need to find data, and cite your research according to the citation style specified by your instructor. Use Rhetorical Toolbox 7.1, as well as the Analytical Process Questions, as you plan and compose your analysis.

Teaching Suggestion
See the IM for additional analytical writing projects.

Teaching Resources
The chapter writing projects are available as writing assignments in Connect.

Teaching Resources
If you assign a cost/benefit analysis, consider using the handout, "Creating a Cost/Benefit Analysis."

PROJECT 2 Analyzing Career Choices

Write a subjective, comparative analysis of three careers in which you are interested. Identify the criteria that you will use to compare the careers, such as working hours, annual salary, training or educational requirements, job satisfaction, and so on. Find information about each career by conducting research. Consider using the Occupational Outlook Handbook on the Bureau of Labor Statistics website for information, and consider interviewing people who have worked in the careers you are analyzing. Your analysis will consist of factual data, subjective experiences, and finally, your conclusion about which of the three jobs best fits your life goals. Cite any research you use in the style your instructor specifies. Use Rhetorical Toolbox 7.1, as well as the Analytical Process Questions, to plan and write your analytical essay.

PROJECT 3 A Product Analysis

Consumers often use the internet to learn more about new products and to judge whether they are worth purchasing. A product analysis helps consumers make informed choices by providing the research and by making recommendations. This kind of analysis often starts with the objective facts about a product—how it works, how it compares to the competition, how it is priced—and ends with a subjective recommendation to consumers regarding whether or not the product is worth buying. Other product analyses compare brands of the same product to recommend which one is superior. Your assignment is to select a product and write the kind of product analysis that you might find on Wirecutter.com. Here are the steps to follow:

1. **Read some product analyses.** To get an idea about what a product analysis includes, find some models on the internet to examine. Visit these websites for examples: Wirecutter.com (compares products and offers recommendations); ewg.org (reviews consumer products for environmental safety), reviewed.com (some articles are comparisons and some address individual products); online magazines such as *MIT Technology Review* and websites such as cnet.com. Select a particular product analysis to use as a model.

2. **Analyze the features of the product analysis you have chosen.** For the model you have selected, answer these questions:
   - Is the analysis objective, subjective, or both?
   - Does the analysis use comparison? If not, what method does the writer use to analyze the product?
   - List at least three strategies the writer uses to help readers understand the analysis.

3. **Select a product (or set of products if you are comparing) for your product review.** You will need to find information about any product you review. Manufacturers' websites are helpful, but so is having the product in your hands and examining it. Make sure you can find research for the product(s) you choose.

4. **Analyze the product(s).** Make a list of questions you plan to answer such as these: *What are its parts? How does it work? How effective is the product?* If you are conducting a comparison, identify the points of

comparison you will use. For example, if you are analyzing robotic vacuums, you may want to compare how they work, the types of vacuuming they do, how easy to clean they are, their prices, and so on.

5. **Draw conclusions based on your analysis.** When you finish analyzing the product, you should be able to draw conclusions that are helpful to readers. Should they purchase the product or not? What considerations should readers keep in mind?

6. **Write your analysis.** Use the steps of the writing process to plan, draft, revise, and edit your analysis. Keep in mind the questions in Rhetorical Toolbox 7.1 so that you write with an audience—and a clear message—in mind.

7. **Submit your work.** Submit these two items: (a) your answers to the questions about the product analysis web page you used as a model, and (b) your product analysis, including a works cited or references page if you used research.

The rest of this chapter leads you through the process of conducting and writing an analysis essay. We follow the work of Reese Abrams as she writes a cost/benefit analysis on the topic of pet ownership during the college years. Reese struggled with the question of whether or not to adopt a dog, and her cost/benefit analysis presents the method she used to answer that question and the conclusion she came to.

Selecting a Topic

While an analysis may be personally meaningful, it must also be meaningful to readers. As you consider topics, find one that will help answer a question that you and your readers are likely to have. For instance, the first article in this chapter analyzed whether merely having some college resulted in economic benefits. This is a question many people would find relevant, since most people must work and are probably concerned with the salaries they earn.

Notice how Reese thought about audience interest as she considered topics:

> **Reese, on choosing a topic:** "I knew I wanted to do a cost/benefit analysis, but the first topics I thought of were things I want to buy, such as a Louis Vuitton handbag. I knew that probably half of the readers (the males) and even several of the females wouldn't care about this topic, so I made a list of other topics. The one that I thought was most interesting personally *and* that most readers could relate to is whether having a dog while in college is worth the trouble and cost. I knew my classmates would be interested in that topic, and it's a decision that I needed to make."

Planning

Keep these rhetorical considerations in mind as you plan your analysis:

1. **Speaker or Writer.** How will you become knowledgeable about the subject? Will you need to find research? What type of research will you need, and where will you find it?

2. **Audience.** You will be using a process to analyze the subject. How will you explain this process to readers? What will readers need to know to understand the method you used to analyze the subject?

3. **Message.** Will your analysis be objective or subjective? What message will guide your analysis?

The three stages that follow can help you plan your analytical project.

1. **Use a method of prewriting to generate ideas.** You may find it helpful to first conduct research, read that research, and then use an on-the-page method of generating ideas. Another approach is to write down ideas as you read the research. You can then use these ideas to sharpen and focus your analysis. Among the ideas you generate, make sure you think about the process you will use for analysis. Consider using an off-the-page planning method, such as talking to classmates or others, once you have figured out the subject and the process you will use for analysis. If you need help figuring out the process to use for analysis, return to the Analytical Process Questions earlier in this chapter.

2. **Draft a working thesis statement.** Readers will want to know the message you are conveying to them by sharing your analysis. What is this message? Your thesis statement should articulate the conclusion you draw or the focus of your analysis.

> **Reese's Thesis Statement**
>
> For many college students, adopting a dog is a temptation, but as a cost/benefit analysis shows, it is not a wise decision in the long run.

3. **Create an outline.** Thinking about your audience, create an outline that reveals to them the process you are using to analyze the subject. The questions that follow can help you think rhetorically as you plan your paper:

    - **Thesis statement.** Read your thesis statement. What parts of your analysis will help readers follow, believe, or understand your thesis statement? These are the elements you need to put into your paper (and outline).
    - **Information.** What objective information about the subject will you include in your analysis? For example, if you are analyzing data, what data should you include? If you are analyzing a product, what facts or descriptions of the product should you include? What objective information do readers need to believe your thesis statement?
    - **Sources.** Have you obtained information about the subject from sources your readers will find trustworthy? For example, if you are writing about a career, you need more than just a worker's subjective experience; what kind of data sources could you use to help readers to trust your analysis?

- **Organization.** How will you organize the analysis? What information must go first for the analysis to be clear?
- **Support**. Imagine knowing nothing about this topic. What kinds of support—graphics, descriptions, anecdotes, and so on—would help readers follow your analysis? Which of these support types will you use, and where will you use them?

Create an outline based on your answers to these questions, noting where you plan to use research. Here is Reese's outline:

Reese's Outline

Working Thesis Statement: For many college students, adopting a dog is a temptation, but as a cost/benefit analysis shows, it is not a wise decision in the long run.

Ideas for Introduction: Why so many students want to own dogs. Could include my roommate's story.

Section 1: Analyzing the benefits

- companionship
- stress reduction
- safety
- exercise partner
- joy

Section 2: Analyzing the costs

- financial costs (adoption fees, veterinarian fees, food, increased rental fees and deposits, kennel fees)
- time commitments
- constraints on life decisions
- potential relationships

Section 3: Making a decision

- when the benefits outweigh the costs
- when the costs outweigh the benefits

Ideas for conclusion: My decision and how I get my "dog fix" when I need one

---

Drafting

What do readers need to know? That is one of the most important questions you can use to guide your writing and to think rhetorically. Other thinking strategies also help you draft from a writer's mindset. Keep these tips in mind:

- **Imagine your readers arguing with your analysis.** A reader might object to your analysis with comments like these: *Where did you get that information?*

I don't see how you calculated that. Why aren't you considering X or Y or Z? Write in such a way that readers' potential objections are anticipated and addressed.

- **Make sure your analysis includes the evidence to support any conclusions you draw.** Readers might object to the conclusions a writer draws if the writer does not use careful, logical thinking.

- **Use a drafting process that includes microrevisions.** Microrevising simply means rewording sentences or paragraphs to make them fit your purpose. Don't wait until the end of the writing process to tweak wording.

- **Write clearly.** An analysis depends on clarity. Make sure the method you use to analyze the information is apparent. For example, if the analysis compares costs and benefits, use the terms *cost* and *benefit* to help readers clearly follow your reasoning.

- **Arrange your analysis in a logical way.** One way to arrange an analysis is to start by focusing on the purpose for the analysis. You can then present details about the subject being analyzed (the data, the physical description of the subject, or whatever it is you are analyzing). End your analysis by presenting the conclusions you have drawn.

- **Make changes if your outline isn't working.** An outline is meant to help you write in a logical, organized way. During drafting, you may end up changing the ideas that you include in your paper. An outline is a tool that should not prevent you from making changes during the drafting stage. If you find that your outline is not working at all, go back to the planning stage and regroup.

- **Be aware of point of view as you write.** Write objective analyses in third person. If your analysis is subjective, you may still be able to write in third person. Make point-of-view choices that are consistent with your writing purpose. If you need help avoiding the pronouns associated with first person (I, my) and second person (you, your, yours), see "FAQ: Writing in Third Person" at the end of this chapter.

- **Occasionally, read your paper from the beginning and make changes.** Doing this will greatly improve the quality of your sentences if you take the time to make improvements.

Consider using terms and phrases that guide readers through the information you are presenting.

Thinking Recursively in the Writing Process

Writing recursively means returning to an earlier stage of the writing process to make choices and changes. For instance, as you draft a body paragraph, you may decide that you simply do not have enough information to write a good paragraph. By returning to the planning process and revisiting your outline, you can decide whether to conduct additional research and revise the paragraph or eliminate it entirely.

DRAFTING TOOLBOX
Terms and Phrases for Analytical Texts

- An analysis will show that . . .
- First, it is important to examine . . .
- A close look at _____ reveals . . .
- The three most important factors to consider when comparing X and Y are . . .
- Based on this analysis, it is clear that . . .
- The costs of X are . . .
- The benefits of X are . . .
- A close reading of X will show that . . .
- Based on the data, one can predict that . . .
- The parts of X include . . .
- Several causes involved in X are . . .
- The most important features of the product are . . .
- Several steps are involved in the process of . . .

> **Reese, on recursive writing:** "As I started drafting my introduction, I found a more natural way to state my thesis statement, so I changed it. It's funny how I get better ideas during drafting sometimes than I do during planning or outlining. I also decided to NOT tell readers whether college students should own a dog. During writing, it became clear to me that the purpose of my analysis was to give students the facts and let them make their own decisions."

Revising

To revise an analysis, imagine your most critical reader. Keeping this reader in mind, follow these steps:

1. **Take a look at the entire paper.** Don't read it word for word. Just look at the whole thing, taking in its length, its features, its formatting, the words that jump out. What is your impression? Does the paper seem complete? Does it look like the writer did significant research or analytical work to produce the paper? Do the first few sentences engage you as a reader? Make notes about how you should revise your paper based on this first look.

2. **Read your analysis to check its logic.** An analysis is a logical product. It takes apart a subject to reveal its parts and help readers gain an understanding. Is the analysis in your paper adequate for readers to understand the point you are making? Have you left out any information—descriptions, explanations of how you reached a conclusion, data—that readers need to follow the logic you used? If so, revise.

3. **Check your conclusions.** If you draw conclusions based on your analysis, are those conclusions justified? Can readers find the evidence you are using to draw the conclusions? Revise if necessary.

4. **Check organization.** Because analyzing is a logical act, organization is important. Make sure your analysis starts with information that readers need to understand the process you are using, and lead readers through the analysis in an ordered, systematic way. Consider using transitions such as *first*, *next*, or key words from the Drafting Toolbox in this chapter.

5. **Check for relevancy and purpose.** Can readers figure out the point you are making by presenting this analysis? One thing you do not want to do is present an analysis with no relevancy or explanation of why the analysis is important. Make sure readers can figure out the point you are making by presenting the analysis in a way that is relevant to their lives.

6. **Read the introduction and conclusion.** Does the introduction engage the reader? Does the conclusion provide a sense of closure? Revise to improve, if necessary.

7. **Revise at the sentence level.** Good writing starts with clearly written sentences. Read each sentence for clarity. Are there sentences in your paper that need revision so that they are clear? Are there sentences that contain many different ideas? Consider creating multiple sentences so that each idea is clearly articulated.

8. **Reread the assignment.** Does your paper meet all the requirements of the assignment? If not, revise.

9. **Use peer review to help you make revision decisions.** The following questions will help a peer read your paper and give you constructive suggestions.

PEER REVIEW TOOLBOX: ANALYTIC WRITING

1. What is the purpose of the writer's analysis? Does the writer make this purpose clear?
2. Are there any places in the analysis where you cannot figure out the writer's logic or follow the writer's thinking? Mark these spots.
3. Underline any conclusions the writer draws based on the analysis. Has the writer provided enough support for these conclusions? Explain.
4. Is anything missing from the analysis? For example, should the writer include more research? Should the writer add explanations? Does the writer need to add transitions to help you follow the thinking?

Reese, on her revision decisions: "I revised my thesis statement so that it fit my introduction and worked more naturally. I liked leading into the thesis statement with a question."

Draft: For many college students, adopting a dog is a temptation, but as a cost/benefit analysis shows, it is not a wise decision in the long run.	**Revision:** Are the costs of ownership really worth the benefits of that furry canine's company? A cost/benefit analysis can help college students make that decision from an informed point of view.

Reese: "I started out saying that the costs outweigh the benefits for college students, but then I used the suggestion to revise with a reader in mind who disagrees. I imagined that the reader would say that some college students don't have limited finances and that some clearly know what they will be doing or have predictable schedules. So I changed my approach to say that for *many* (not all) college students, owning a dog is not a reasonable decision."

Draft: There is no doubt that for many people, owning a dog makes life better. But for college students, the costs of pet ownership outweigh the benefits. The investments of money and time can be tremendous, but even more importantly, because college students do not know their futures, having a dog can limit their choices. Fortunately, plenty of pet adoption agencies welcome volunteers, so perhaps instead of owning a dog, volunteering at a local pet shelter is the way to go. Not only will volunteering give students a "dose" of the companionship they long for, but they will also have another volunteer activity to add to their resumes!

Revision: There is no doubt that for many people, owning a dog makes life better. But for many college students, the costs of pet ownership will outweigh the benefits. There are some exceptions, of course. Students who are independently wealthy may be able to afford pet sitters, dog walkers, and any other kind of support they need. Most students, however, struggle to stay afloat financially. For these students, dog ownership during the college years may simply be impractical. And having a dog may also be more feasible for students who know their major, have a clear-cut academic schedule, and have some predictability in their lives. For many students, this is not the case. Fortunately, plenty of pet adoption agencies welcome volunteers, so perhaps instead of owning a dog, volunteering at a local pet shelter is the way to go. Not only will volunteering give students a "dose" of the companionship they long for, but they will also have another volunteer activity to add to their resumes!

Finishing

To finish your paper, edit it for errors, and put it in the format readers will expect or the format required by your instructor.

Editing. Editing requires the writer to focus on errors in grammar, spelling, and mechanics. Use the tools readily available to you, such as spell-checkers and grammar checkers, but also look at previous papers to see the errors you are likely to make. Check for those errors in your paper and make corrections.

Formatting. Review your instructor's guidelines for formatting and submitting your paper. Reese has formatted her paper in MLA style.

Reese Abrams, Should College Students Adopt Dogs? A Cost/Benefit Analysis (Final Draft)

What follows is Reese's final draft. Her paper is presented in MLA form.

Reese Abrams
Dr. Saenz
ENGL 1301.15
14 February 2020

Should College Students Adopt Dogs? A Cost/Benefit Analysis

What's a college student without a laptop? What's a college student without a bicycle? What's a college student without a smartphone? And what's a college student without a dog? In modern America, pet ownership is a given. Most people have a pet of one sort or another. For many, the pet of choice is a dog, especially college students. Look around any apartment complex near a university or college to see just how much college students love their dogs! Some pets are low maintenance. Fish, for example, need only food, and a properly regulated water tank. Cats are more needy than fish, but most cats can live on their own for a few days if their owner needs to leave town. Dogs are a different story. They need care and companionship, and they are higher maintenance than any other inside pet. Still, college students insist on owning dogs. Why? Are the costs of ownership really worth the benefits of that furry canine's company? A cost/benefit analysis can help college students make that decision from an informed point of view.

The benefits of having a dog are abundant. For one, many college students want a dog for companionship. They are living on their own for the first time in their lives, and while they may have roommates, there is no guarantee that they will like their roommates (and vice versa). A dog, on the other hand, will always like its owner. A dog can be the companion that helps the first-year or second-year college student decide that living away from home is okay. When she was at the University of Pennsylvania, Haleigh Wright adopted a dog. "Living on your own can be challenging, but when you have a dog it's a wonderful feeling to know that you're never alone," Wright says. The companionship a dog offers is clearly one of the benefits.

Dogs not only help with companionship, they also help with stress reduction. The growing number of service animals in our society demonstrates that pets can help reduce stress, anxiety, and depression. According to Christine Junge and Anne MacDonald,

> [s]tudies going back to the early 1980s support the idea that dogs—and other pets—have enormous health benefits for people. Pets have been shown to lower

blood pressure, improve recovery from heart disease, and even reduce rates of asthma and allergy in children who grow up with a Fido or a Frisky in the house. Pets also improve people's psychological well-being and self-esteem. College students are in some of the most difficult years of life. They are making decisions that will affect their lives forever, and these decisions are often about stressful things like moving away from home, deciding on a major, entering into and breaking off relationships, trying to pass classes, and affording to go to college. A dog can provide the kind of stress relief that college students need.

Another reason some people, especially women, want a dog is for safety. People believe that dogs are instinctively protective, but whether a dog will actually protect an owner is debatable. Some studies have shown that unless a dog has been trained to protect, it may not go to its owner's aid in the case of a break-in (Fullbright). Even if the dog has not been trained, having a big dog nearby may be enough to ward off a potential intruder because of the general perception of dogs as protective.

Owning a dog can also promote a healthier lifestyle. Most dogs require some kind of daily exercise, and Americans are notorious for not getting enough exercise. Having a dog to walk helps owners to get out and exercise themselves. Exercising itself also helps with stress reduction, so the benefits of walking a dog are multiplied. According to HelpGuide, a website published in collaboration with Harvard University, "studies have shown that dog owners are far more likely to meet their daily exercise requirements" ("Mood-boosting").

If these benefits were the end of the story, the answer would be simple and everyone would have a dog. But analyzing whether dog ownership is the right choice for a college student is more complicated. To properly analyze, one must also examine the costs of dog ownership. The first cost that comes to mind is the financial cost. Owning a dog can be costly. The American Society for the Prevention of Cruelty to Animals (ASPCA) provides statistics that help put these costs into perspective (Table 1). A large dog, the kind that might make its owner feel more safe and secure, will cost a whopping $2000 the first year and $1040 a year after that. Even a small dog will require $1400 from its owner the first year, and these costs do not include emergency vet visits, chronic disease care, and other expenses that come up.

TABLE 1 Costs of Owning a Dog			
Costs	Small dog	Medium dog	Large dog
Initial costs			
Spay or neuter	$190	$200	$220
Other vet costs	$70	$70	$70
Collar, leash	$25	$30	$35
Carrier bag	$40	$60	n/a
Crate	$35	$95	$125
Training class	$110	$110	$110
Initial total	$470	$565	$560
Annual costs			
Food	$212	$319	$400
Regular vet costs	$210	$235	$260
Toys and treats	$40	$55	$75
License	$15	$15	$15
Health insurance	$225	$225	$225
Long hair grooming	$264	$320	$408
Other	$35	$45	$65
Annual total	$737	$894	$1040
First year total	$1471	$1779	$2008

    The costs of feeding and care are important, but students must also consider the added costs of housing. Most apartments charge higher rates for pets, some as much as $100 extra per month. In addition, pet deposits can be expensive. "On a one-year lease, 71 percent of the pet owners Rent.com surveyed said they would expect to spend $200 or less on a pet deposit, while nearly a third (29 percent) said they would typically spend more than $200" according to Niccole Schreck. These costs also do not include any fees for kenneling, replacing torn up furniture or goods, and other unforeseen expenses. For most college students, having the money for college and an apartment is a challenge, so adding the costs of caring for a dog may be too much of a strain on their budget.

Abrams 4

    The need for exercising one's dog can be seen as a benefit because it encourages good health for its owner, but there is a negative to this benefit: time requirements. Unlike many other types of pets, dogs require attention. They need to be let out to use the bathroom. They need to be walked. They need to have time with their owners for emotional well-being. College students think that they will have time, but for the student who is juggling a part-time job, a full-time course load, and a social life, having the time to care for a dog may be a challenge. Veterinarian Marty Becker writes, "The least amount of time you can 'get away with' is probably an average of an hour a day, all told, for feeding and cleaning up after your dog, and for that all-important exercise. For dogs with high levels of energy (what many people call 'hyper'), double that." Not all college students will have one to two hours a day to devote to a dog.

    Finally, and maybe most importantly, having a dog limits the options available to college students. Many students enter college having a major in mind but, midway through, change their major to something that requires a full-time internship, or they are given the option to study overseas, or they find that they need to spend countless hours in a lab. All of these scenarios would be much more difficult if one has a dog to take care of. Predicting the future is impossible, so while it may seem wise to adopt a dog during one's freshman year, having that dog may not be such a good idea when a prospective internship comes up during junior year. Relationships can complicate matters, too. Falling in love with a person who is allergic to dogs is only one potential problem! The decision to adopt a pet is one that cannot be taken lightly; it is a decision that will probably make future decisions more complicated. For college students, this is especially a problem since their futures are so uncertain.

    There is no doubt that for many people, owning a dog makes life better. But for many college students, the costs of pet ownership will outweigh the benefits. There are some exceptions, of course. Students who are independently wealthy may be able to afford pet sitters, dog walkers, and any other kind of support they need. Most students, however, struggle to stay afloat financially. For these students, dog ownership during the college years may simply be impractical. And having a dog may also be more feasible for students who know their major, have a clear-cut academic schedule, and have some predictability in their lives. For many students, this is not the case. Fortunately, plenty of pet adoption agencies welcome volunteers, so perhaps instead of owning a dog, volunteering at a local pet shelter is the way to go. Not only will volunteering give students a "dose" of the companionship they long for, but they will also have another volunteer activity to add to their resumes!

Works Cited

Becker, Marty. "How Much Time Does It Really Take to Care for a Dog?" *Vetstreet*, 21 Dec. 2011, www.vetstreet.com/dr-marty-becker/how-much-time-does-it-really-take-to-care-for-a-dog.

Fullbright, Lori. "Would Your Dog Protect You from An Intruder?" *News On 6*, 8 Nov. 2012, www.newson6.com/story/20049010/would-your-dog-protect-you-from-an-intruder.

Junge, Christine, and Anne MacDonald. "Therapy Dog Offers Stress Relief at Work." *Harvard Health Blog*, 30 Oct. 2015, www.health.harvard.edu/blog/therapy-dog-offers-stress-relief-at-work-201107223111.

"Mood-Boosting Power of Pets." *HelpGuide.org*, 26 Mar. 2019, www.helpguide.org/articles/mental-health/mood-boosting-power-of-dogs.htm/.

"Pet Care Costs." *American Society for the Prevention of Cruelty to Animals*, www.aspca.org.

Schreck, Niccole. "How Much Should You Pay for a Pet Deposit?" *U.S. News & World Report*, 17 July 2017, money.usnews.com/money/blogs/my-money/2013/07/17/how-much-should-you-pay-for-a-pet-deposit.

Wright, Haleigh. "Why Adopting a Dog as a College Student Was the Best Decision I've Ever Made." *The Odyssey Online*, 13 Nov. 2017, www.theodysseyonline.com/adopting-dog-as-college-student-was-the-best-decision-ive-ever-made.

YOUR TURN Analyzing Abrams' Rhetorical Strategies

1. Does the writer know enough about the subject or have enough research to analyze the subject?
2. What is the purpose of the analysis?
3. Who is the intended audience, and what knowledge does this audience have about the topic?
4. What rhetorical strategies help readers follow the logic of this analysis and understand the points the writer makes?

Reflecting to Develop a Writer's Mindset

As you reflect on this chapter, think about analysis as a process and analysis as a product. What is the relationship between these activities? How does one activity affect the other?

FAQ WRITING IN THIRD PERSON

Many academic and professional assignments will require papers to be written in third person. Writing in third person means avoiding the pronouns associated with first and second person. See the chart for a quick review.

First-Person Pronouns	Second-Person Pronouns	Third-Person Pronouns
I, we, me, us, my/mine, our/ours	you, your, yours	he, she, it, they, him, her, them, his, her, its, their, hers, theirs

1. How can first person be converted to third person?

Use these tips to avoid first-person pronouns.

First Person: In my opinion, gambling should never be legal.	Third Person: Gambling should never be legal.

The problem: Phrases such as *in my opinion* and *I think* are in first person.

The solution: Simply avoid these phrases. Readers do not need them to know that the information represents the writer's opinion.

First Person: In the first article I read, the writer points out that finding a long-term solution to the problem of immigration will be challenging.	Third Person: The writer points out that finding a long-term solution to the problem of immigration will be challenging (Mahoney). **or** Chris Mahoney points out that finding a long-term solution to the problem of immigration will be challenging.

The problem: "I read" is a third person phrase, and it is unnecessary.

The solution: Omit such phrases. Simply start the sentence without them.

Teaching Suggestion
Consider discussing with students the growing use of non-gender specific third person pronouns such as *they* and *their*.

First Person: Having experienced homelessness, I can tell you that not only did the condition make me feel like a second-class citizen, but it made me feel hopeless that I would ever find a home again.	Third Person: Those who experience homelessness often feel like second-class citizens, and many are hopeless about ever finding a home again.

The problem: The writer wants to use a personal experience, but doing so would result in a first-person passage.

The solution: Convey the same ideas in third person by wording the ideas as if others have expressed them.

2. **How can second person be converted to third person?**

Converting a thought from second person can be tricky. The examples that follow show how to convert second person writing to third person.

Second Person: Managing your finances, monitoring your credit score, and maintaining a savings account will contribute to your financial health.	Third Person: Managing finances, monitoring one's credit score, and maintaining a savings account will contribute to financial health.

The problem: The use of *your* is second-person point of view.

The solution: Simply remove the second-person pronouns (*your*). If the sentence needs a noun in place of the second-person pronoun, use a noun such as *one* or *one's*." Here are a few more examples:

Second Person: If you are worried about heart disease, ask your doctor about preventive measures.	Third Person: Patients who are worried about heart disease can ask their doctors about preventive measures.

The problem: *You* in the sentence cannot simply be replaced with *one*. The sentence would sound odd if *one* were used: "If one who is worried about. . . ."

The solution: In such cases, find a noun that fits better, such as *patients* or *people*.

Second Person: When you get off the bus, cross the street in front of the bus, not behind it.	Third Person: After getting off the bus, riders should cross the street in front of the bus, not behind it.

The problem: The instructions are in second person.

The solution: Since the sentence is talking about bus riders, the word *riders* can be used in place of *you*.

| Second Person: Limit social media use, which can lead to social media addiction for some people. | Third Person: Limiting social media use is advisable because it can lead to social media addiction for some people. |

The problem: The first sentence implies second person because the sentence is a demand to the reader. Even though *you* is not in the sentence, it is implied: "[You should] limit social media use. . . ."

The solution: Reword so that *you* is not implied.

TRY IT!

Reword the following paragraph to avoid second person:

> Your body language is often more powerful than the actual words that come out of your mouth. For example, certain postures—such as crossing your arms—suggest defensiveness, and if you stand and talk to a colleague with crossed arms, regardless of what you say, that colleague may think you are standoffish or guarded. On the other hand, when you lean in to listen to what someone else is saying, your body language suggests you are open and that you are interested in the person. Some body language even suggests romantic interest. Understanding how to read body language can help you understand human communications.

CREDITS

Page 148. Greenstone, Michael and Looney, Adam, "Is Starting College and Not Finishing Really That Bad?," The Hamilton Project, June 7, 2013. https://www.brookings.edu/wp-content/uploads/2016/06/May-Jobs-Blog-20130607-FINAL.pdf. Reprinted by permission of Brookings Institution Press.

Page 150, graph. Greenstone, Michael and Looney, Adam, "Is Starting College and Not Finishing Really That Bad?," The Hamilton Project, June 7, 2013. https://www.brookings.edu/wp-content/uploads/2016/06/May-Jobs-Blog-20130607-FINAL.pdf. Reprinted by permission of Brookings Institution Press.

Page 151, graph. Greenstone, Michael and Looney, Adam, "Is Starting College and Not Finishing Really That Bad?," The Hamilton Project, June 7, 2013. https://www.brookings.edu/wp-content/uploads/2016/06/May-Jobs-Blog-20130607-FINAL.pdf. Reprinted by permission of Brookings Institution Press.

Page 153. Johnson, Nathanael. "Reducing Food Waste Takes More Than Finishing Your Plate." *Grist*. Used with permission.

Page 155, graph. Searchinger, Tim, "World Resources Institute, Creating a Sustainable Food Future: World Resources Report 2013-14: Interim Findings" https://www.wri.org/sites/default/files/wri13_report_4c_wrr_online.pdf. Copyright 2013 World Resources Institute. All rights reserved. Used with permission.

8 Writing to Evaluate

CHAPTER OBJECTIVES

You will learn to:

- Identify key rhetorical concerns of evaluative writing.
- Analyze evaluative texts.
- Compose an evaluative text.

Connect Adaptive Learning Assignment Consider assigning Connect's Adaptive Learning Assignments to support this chapter.

Teaching Resources See the Instructor's Manual (IM) for suggestions about how to teach this chapter, and consider assigning this chapter's test-bank quiz.

From reviews of services to reviews of college professors, evaluations are readily accessible online. However, reviews are only one type of evaluative writing. As you will learn in this chapter, evaluation is used for a wide variety of purposes. We use it to judge the value of something in the past, such a college course; we use it to plan future actions, such as promoting high-achieving employees. We also use evaluation to judge ideas, to analyze the effectiveness of processes, and to make decisions based on comparisons.

Like analysis, evaluation is both a process and a product. As a process, evaluation often involves using criteria to make a judgment. For example, if you are evaluating the gyms in your town, the criteria you might use are monthly costs, convenience of the location, machines available, and so on. As a product, evaluation presents the reasoning on which the evaluation is based and the judgment of the writer. As you know from reading reviews of restaurants, albums, and films, some evaluations are more trustworthy than others. What rhetorical concerns must a writer consider to convince an audience that his or her evaluation is sound and trustworthy? How can a writer know that the criteria he or she used for an evaluation are those the audience will value? How much support should a writer provide for an evaluation? In this chapter, we will examine how to conduct an evaluation and write an effective evaluative essay.

WARM-UP

Luis must write a film review for one of his college classes. Jackson must evaluate investment strategies to determine which are best for senior citizens, a topic requested by the many seniors who read his newsletter. Colleen must produce annual evaluation reports for the three employees she supervises. How will these writers' evaluative processes be similar? How will they be different? How will the products they create differ?

EVALUATIVE WRITING FROM A WRITER'S MINDSET

Evaluative texts come to a conclusion about the value or effectiveness of a particular thing, idea, or course of action. Evaluation always starts with analysis, but the kind of analysis differs depending on the rhetorical situation of the project. For instance, to evaluate the quality of a film, Luis's objective, he must first analyze the film. The method he uses to analyze the film can vary, but it will depend on his audience and his purpose. If his instructor wants a comparative evaluation, Luis could compare the film to other films in the same genre. If Luis's instructor wants a movie review appropriate for publication in a newspaper, Luis's analysis and evaluation would need to focus more strictly on the film and a handful of criteria that are commonly analyzed in newspaper film reviews, such as character development, cinematography, directing, and so on.

Jackson's evaluation project also requires thinking about the rhetorical situation. He already knows that his audience has many senior citizens, and he can carefully craft his evaluation to address their concerns. Out of dozens of investment strategies, Jackson must first select a handful to compare. He probably will not include high-risk investment strategies because many seniors depend on income from investments; thus, they value strategies that are relatively safe. After Jackson chooses strategies to compare, he will select and use criteria to evaluate the investment strategies. The criteria will need to be those that are valuable to his audience.

Colleen's rhetorical situation is not as complex as Luis's or Jackson's because she is writing for a narrow audience (her supervisors and the employees she supervises) and must use an existing evaluative procedure. Most companies have an evaluation plan consisting of criteria that are measured for every worker, such as job performance, professionalism, interpersonal communication skills, and so on. These are the criteria Colleen will analyze for her evaluation. However, Colleen's evaluative project requires rhetorical thinking. She must carefully word her evaluation so that her criticism is constructive, and she must also pay attention to the legal implications of her writing. Employee evaluations are legal documents that can be used in court, so Colleen must use care as she composes her evaluations.

The evaluative processes used by Luis, Jackson, and Colleen differ because the elements of each rhetorical situation differ. For instance, Colleen does not have the liberty to choose the evaluative criteria she will use because her company has already chosen them. Jackson will limit the kinds of investments he analyzes because of his audience's specific needs. By analyzing the rhetorical situation and the purpose of the evaluation, you will be able to choose the most appropriate items to analyze and the best criteria for your evaluation.

▶ **ACTIVITY 1 Planning an Evaluation**

Jenny is in a biology class. Her instructor has assigned students to select a personal health-care choice and write an evaluation that includes a recommendation. Jenny has chosen the question of whether or not to get a flu shot. She will evaluate the risks and benefits and then offer a recommendation. Jenny attends a community college, and the average age of her classmates is twenty-one. How might the rhetorical situation of Jenny's project affect the criteria she uses for her evaluation? If Jenny were writing for an audience of senior citizens, how might her evaluation change?

Purposes of Evaluations

As Luis's, Jackson's, and Colleen's evaluation projects demonstrate, different types of evaluation can be used for a wide variety of purposes. Table 8.1 summarizes some of the more common types of evaluations.

Analyzing and Judging

No matter its purpose, all evaluative writing consists of at least two parts: analysis and judgment.

- The analysis section of an evaluative text tells readers how the subject was analyzed. In the analysis section, a writer generally presents the criteria on which the evaluation is based.
- The judgment part of an evaluation presents the writer's evaluation, and this opinion is supported by the analysis.

In addition to presenting an analysis and a judgment, most evaluative texts are written using an objective tone. When making a judgment about the value of something, a writer must show that the judgment is not based merely on his or her preferences or biases.

Co-requisite Teaching Tip
Consider discussing how to identify the tone of a reading and how to develop tone as a writer. See the handout "Identifying and Establishing Tone."

Selecting Criteria

The most common method for evaluating is to select pertinent criteria to use as a means for making a judgment. The criteria you select must be based on

TABLE 8.1   Types of Evaluations

Type	Purpose	Example
Product evaluation	To identify the best product or service	A review of treadmills
Process evaluation	To identify the best process for meeting objectives	Comparison and evaluation of hiring processes
Predictive evaluation	To identify the best course of action by evaluating potential outcomes	Comparison and evaluation of college majors or careers
Effectiveness evaluation	To analyze the effectiveness of a procedure, employee, product, etc.	Employee evaluation
Literary/artistic/rhetorical evaluation	To evaluate the quality of an artistic or literary work	A movie review
Source evaluation	To identify accurate and credible sources	A website review A critical annotated bibliography

the purpose of the evaluation and the values of your readers. For example, an employee evaluation measures how well a worker performs in areas that are important to the company, such as productivity, communication, leadership, and so on. An evaluation of a website uses criteria to help determine whether the website is credible and can serve as a good source of information. As you will learn in Chapter 10, evaluating potential sources for a research paper requires examining criteria such as author, reputation of the publishing organization, currency (whether the source is new enough to be relevant), and so on.

Writers select criteria to use for evaluative projects by analyzing their writing purposes and their readers' needs. For instance, a writer who is reviewing a movie for a parenting magazine will probably be writing to recommend whether the movie is appropriate for children. This writing purpose will result in the selection of criteria that help the writer to make that judgment. Keeping readers in mind, the writer may decide to evaluate the movie's message and whether that message is appropriate for children. Other concerns parents have are language, violence, and sexually explicit scenes, so the writer may evaluate these three factors when analyzing the movie. If the review is written for a different purpose and audience, some of the criteria may change. For instance, a review of the same movie for a magazine read by animation professionals would measure different criteria—criteria the audience is familiar with and uses to judge the quality of films, such as lens choices, backgrounds, and visual effects.

By keeping in mind your writing purpose and your readers' expectations, you will be able to choose criteria that are effective for your evaluation. Use the questions in Rhetorical Toolbox 8.1 to plan an effective evaluation.

> **Teaching Resources**
> Consider using the PowerPoint "Planning an Evaluative Project" to introduce the rhetorical concerns of evaluative writing and to help students plan evaluative projects.

RHETORICAL TOOLBOX 8.1
The Rhetorical Concerns of Evaluative Writing

1. **Purpose.** What is your purpose for the evaluation? Refer to the chart in this chapter to determine the purpose of the evaluation, and put the purpose in your own words.
2. **Audience.** What can readers expect to learn from reading the evaluation? Readers may expect to be given advice, or they may expect to be provided with a recommendation or some other type of conclusion based on the evaluation.
3. **Evaluative criteria.** Which criteria should you use to support the purpose of your evaluation? Which criteria will readers expect to be included in your discussion?
4. **Support.** How can you support the judgment? What would be the best types of support to provide for the particular audience? Will readers expect the evaluation to be based on research, sources, or some other type of information?

MODELS OF EVALUATIVE WRITING

"Hostiles" Tries to Revise History and Western Film Traditions

Maddy Folstein

A literary review—an evaluation of a book, movie, or other artistic work—is a common genre of evaluative writing. The following article is a movie review by Maddy Folstein, a writer at the **Minnesota Daily**, *a newspaper for the University of Minnesota and the surrounding community. She has written about arts and entertainment and has served as resident reviewer, as well as assistant arts and entertainment editor. Folstein's review of the film* **Hostiles** *depends on criteria usually used in film reviews, but it is also comparative in nature. As you read it, notice the annotations that point out the features of evaluative writing.*

> *[Teaching Suggestion: Students can study popular movie review sites, such as Rotten Tomatoes or IMDB, and make a list of the criteria used to evaluate films. Students will find that the criteria change depending on the genre.]*
>
> *[Teaching Suggestion: For additional models of evaluative writing, see Part 6, An Anthology of Readings.]*

[Folstein sets up the comparison between traditional Westerns and a new style of Western.]

"Hostiles" opens with a symbol of Western movies—a prairie home nestled between rocky ridges, horses milling about in a corral and a picturesque American family.

Within minutes, the house burns to the ground. **In this moment, "Hostiles" begins its attempt to do the same to the tired conventions of the Western genre, but the match never quite strikes.**

[Folstein's judgment (thesis statement)]

Directed by Scott Cooper, "Hostiles" follows Army Captain Joseph Blocker (Christian Bale), as he leads Cheyenne chief and U.S. prisoner Yellow Hawk (Wes Studi) and his family back to Montana. Along the way, Blocker encounters Rosalie Quaid (Rosamund Pike), stranded in her burnt house and mourning the murder of her entire family. During this journey to Montana, the dwindling group of travelers faces their individual biases and gruesome personal histories.

[A brief summary is included.]

"Hostiles" delivers sweeping landscape montages like any good Western should; we see the expansive, endless sky, jagged cliffs and rolling plains. The desolation of this natural world plays well in the background, highlighting the messiness of the drama on screen.

[Folstein describes one of the movie's features: visual beauty.]

Despite the beauty of the natural landscape, "Hostiles" is unflinchingly violent. There are brawls and shootings and stabbings and scalpings, and these painful moments remind us of the violence of the West, or at least the movies that pay tribute to it.

[She describes another of the movie's features: violence.]

The performances in "Hostiles" are fine. Rosamund Pike of "Gone Girl" encapsulates the isolation of the desolate Western life

[Folstein discusses performances (criterion).]

the movie portrays. Timothée Chalamet ("Call Me by Your Name" and "Lady Bird") and Jesse Plemons ("Breaking Bad" and "Black Mirror") play members of Blocker's party, though their roles are relatively small and forgettable. Bale's portrayal of an army captain with a violent past is both shallow and heavy handed; in one montage, he shouts at the sky in anguish, a sequence that drags on just a little too long. In other words, it would be easier and more enjoyable to seek out these actors in better movies.

But "Hostiles" doesn't suffer at the hands of its actors; it instead falters in its pace and politics. The cinematography is beautiful, but the film's use of endless landscape montages causes the film to drag.

She discusses cinematography and pace (criteria).

Blocker's personal development and atonement intermingle with the film's desire to revise the messy politics of a traditional Western film. In an attempt to rewrite the stereotypes and whitewashing of earlier Westerns, "Hostiles" centers its narrative arc around Blocker's hatred of Native Americans and his ability to move toward acceptance.

She discusses political subtext (criterion).

The resolution to this conflict? Yellow Hawk and his family are rarely placed at the forefront of the screen. The history of American settlement in the West is rarely mentioned in the film, and this forgotten detail is only heightened by the film's focus on violence as a unifying element.

She describes the resolution of the plot.

Because Blocker, his crew and Yellow Hawk have all seen gruesome, unspeakable violence during their time, they can't be that different, "Hostiles" claims. This form of equality, however, does little to address the history of the American West.

Rooting its conflicts in personal redemptions could have grounded the larger history of the Western genre, giving the film's politics a specific, individual angle. Instead, Blocker is hollow and unlikeable, and his unyielding hatred of Native Americans, though historically accurate, is difficult to hear in 2018.

Revisionist Westerns aren't unheard of, but most are better than this one, with its minimal character development and sluggish pace. This hero's journey is not one that redeems, but instead, one that frustrates. Blocker's atonement happens at the cost of the unexplored indigenous stories onscreen, and the result is an empty jab at the Western genre.

Folstein restates her judgment.

She concludes her comparison of the film with its genre.

Analyzing Folstein's Rhetorical Strategies

By examining Folstein's article in light of Rhetorical Toolbox 8.1, we can see how she crafts a review that meets audience expectations.

1. **What is the writer's purpose for the evaluation?** The purpose is to provide an informed opinion on the value of *Hostiles* for readers of the newspaper in which the review was published, members of the university community.

2. **What can readers expect to learn from reading the evaluation?** People usually read reviews to help determine whether a movie is worth viewing. Readers will expect the writer to pronounce a judgment on the movie's quality and to explain and support that judgment with specific examples.

3. **Which criteria can the writer use to meet his or her purpose and to meet the expectations of readers?** Folstein chooses to address how well the movie transforms the traditional Western movie. She also addresses the performances, cinematography, pace, and political subtexts of the movie.

4. **How can the writer support the judgment? What would be the best types of support to provide for the particular audience? Will readers expect the evaluation to be based on research, sources, or some other type of information?** In a movie review, readers expect the information to be based on the writer's experience of the movie itself. Folstein provides examples from the movie as support when she discusses the criteria she is using for her evaluation and when she presents her judgment.

Evaluating Information: The Cornerstone of Civic Online Reasoning

Stanford History Education Group

The following is an executive summary (a presentation of the main ideas in a text) of a report on digital literacy—the ability to evaluate online information. The report demonstrates evaluation on two levels: the writers are evaluating how well students are equipped to evaluate the sources they find online. As you read the report, identify the evaluative criteria the writers use to evaluate students' competencies.

Teaching Resources
This reading is available as a Power of Process assignment in Connect.

Teaching Suggestion
Consider teaching this chapter in tandem with the parts of Chapter 10 that address evaluating sources, and consider assigning Project 2.

> **EXECUTIVE SUMMARY**
>
> Evaluating Information: The Cornerstone of Civic Online Reasoning
> November 22, 2016
>
> **The Big Picture**
>
> When thousands of students respond to dozens of tasks there are endless variations. That was certainly the case in our

experience. However, at each level—middle school, high school, and college—these variations paled in comparison to a stunning and dismaying consistency. Overall, young people's ability to reason about the information on the internet can be summed up in one word: *bleak*.

Our "digital natives" maybe able to flit between Facebook and Twitter while simultaneously uploading a selfie to Instagram and texting a friend. But when it comes to evaluating information that flows through social media channels, they are easily duped. We did not design our exercises to shake out a grade or make hairsplitting distinctions between a "good" and a "better" answer. Rather, we sought to establish a reasonable bar, a level of performance we hoped was within reach of most middle school, high school, and college students. For example, we would hope that middle school students could distinguish an ad from a news story. By high school, we would hope that students reading about gun laws would notice that a chart came from a gun owners' political action committee. And, in 2016, we would hope college students, who spend hours each day online, would look beyond a .org URL and ask who's behind a site that presents only one side of a contentious issue. But in every case and at every level, we were taken aback by students' lack of preparation.

For every challenge facing this nation, there are scores of websites pretending to be something they are not. Ordinary people once relied on publishers, editors, and subject matter experts to vet the information they consumed. But on the unregulated internet, all bets are off. Michael lynch, a philosopher who studies technological change, observed that the internet is "both the world's best fact-checker and the world's best bias confirmer—often at the same time."[1] Never have we had so much information at our fingertips. Whether this bounty will make us smarter and better informed or more ignorant and narrow-minded will depend on our awareness of this problem and our educational response to

---

[1] Michael P. Lynch, "Googling Is Believing: Trumping the Informed Citizen," *New York Times*, March 9, 2016. Retrieved from http://opinionator.blogs.nytimes.com/2016/03/09/googling-is-believing-trumping-the-informed-citizen/

Co-requisite Teaching Tip
Consider having co-requisite students work in groups to read and analyze this article. Have students collaboratively answer the post-reading questions. This article is complex in that it evaluates the evaluative skills of students. See if students can figure out that purpose as they work collaboratively.

it. At present, we worry that democracy is threatened by the ease at which disinformation about civic issues is allowed to spread and flourish.

Sequence of Activities

Our work went through three phases during the 18 months of this project.

Prototyping assessments. Our development process borrows elements of "design thinking" from the world of product design, in which a new idea follows a sequence of prototyping, user testing, and revision in a cycle of continuous improvement.[2] For assessment development, this process is crucial, as it is impossible to know whether an exercise designed by adults will be interpreted similarly by a group of 13-year-olds.

In designing our assessments, we directly measured what students could and could not do. For example, one of our tasks sent high school and college students to *MinimumWage.com*, ostensibly a fair broker for information on the relationship between minimum wage policy and employment rates. The site links to reputable sources like the *New York Times* and calls itself a project of the Employment Policies Institute, a non-profit organization that describes itself as sponsoring nonpartisan research. In open web searches, only nine percent of high school students in an Advanced Placement history course were able to see through *MinimumWage.com*'s language to determine that it was a front group for a D.C. lobbyist, or as *Salon*'s headline put it, "Industry PR Firm Poses as Think Tank."[3] Among college students the results were actually worse: Ninety-three percent of students were snared. The simple act of Googling "Employment Policies Institute" and the word "funding" turns up the *Salon* article along with a host of other exposés. Most students never moved beyond the site itself.[4]

---

[2] Tim Brown, "Design Thinking," *Harvard Business Review* 86, no. 6 (2008): 84–95.
[3] Lisa Graves, "Corporate America's New Scam: Industry P.R. Firm Poses as Think Tank!" *Salon*, November 2013. Retrieved from http://www.salon.com/2013/11/13/corporate_americas_new_scam_industry_p_r_firm_poses_as_think_tank/
[4] We recommended that students spend about ten minutes on this task, but there was nothing that prevented them from spending more, as the exercise was self-administered. We can say with some assurance that the issue here was not one of running out of time.

Validation. To ensure that our exercises tapped what they were supposed to (rather than measuring reading level or test taking ability), we engaged in extensive piloting, sometimes tweaking and revising our exercises up to a half-dozen times. Furthermore, we asked groups of students to verbalize their thinking as they completed our tasks. This allowed us to consider what is known as *cognitive validity*, the relationship between what an assessment seeks to measure and what it actually does.[5]

Field Testing. We drew on our extensive teacher networks for field testing. The Stanford History Education Group's online *Reading Like a Historian* curriculum[6] is used all over the country and has been adopted by Los Angeles Unified School District,[7] the second largest school district in the U.S. With help from teachers in L.A. and elsewhere, we collected thousands of responses and consulted with teachers about the appropriateness of the exercises. Together with the findings from the cognitive validity interviews, we are confident that our assessments reflect key competencies that students should possess.

Overview of the Exercises

We designed, piloted, and validated fifteen assessments, five each at middle school, high school, and college levels. At the middle school level, where online assessment is in its infancy, we designed paper-and-pencil measures using digital content. We used screen shots of *Slate*'s landing page to assess students' ability to distinguish between a news item and an ad. Similarly, we used screenshots of tweets, Facebook posts, and a reproduction of CNN's website in crafting other exercises. We are mindful of the criticism of using paper-and-pencil measures to assess students' ability to judge online sources. At the same time, there is evidence from the OECD that important abilities for evaluating online sources can be measured

---

[5] James W. Pellegrino, Naomi Chudowsky, and Robert Glaser, eds., *Knowing What Students Know: The Science and Design of Educational Assessment*. (Washington: National Academies Press, 2001).
[6] http://sheg.stanford.edu
[7] achieve.lausd.net/page/5965

offline.[8] Even more crucial in our decision, however, was the hope that our assessments would be used in under-resourced schools where online assessment often remains a remote possibility. Our middle school assessments provide easy-to-use measures that teachers and others can use to gauge students' basic skills. At the high school level, we designed more complex tasks that asked students to reason about multiple sources; at the college level, the exercises were administered online. When students are working at advanced levels, there is nothing to prevent the high school exercises from being used with middle school students, or the college exercises from being used with high school students.

Summaries of each of our exercises are below. The exercises in bold appear in the following pages.

Middle School

1) *News on Twitter:* Students consider tweets and determine which is the most trustworthy.
2) *Article Analysis:* Students read a sponsored post and explain why it might not be reliable.
3) *Comment Section:* Students examine a post from a newspaper comment section and explain whether they would use it in a research report.
4) *News Search:* Students distinguish between a news article and an opinion column.
5) *Home Page Analysis:* **Students identify advertisements on a news website.**

High School

1) *Argument Analysis:* Students compare and evaluate two posts from a newspaper's comment section.
2) *News on Facebook:* Students identify the blue checkmark that distinguish a verified Facebook account from a fake one.
3) *Facebook Argument:* Students consider the relative strength of evidence that two users present in a Facebook exchange.

---

[8] Organisation for Economic Cooperation and Development, *Students, Computers and Learning: Making the Connection* (Paris: OECD Publishing, 2015).

4) *Evaluating Evidence:* **Students decide whether to trust a photograph posted on a photo-sharing website.**
5) *Comparing Articles:* **Students determine whether a news story or a sponsored post is more reliable.**

College

1) *Article Evaluation:* In an open web search, students decide if a website can be trusted.
2) *Research a Claim:* Students search online to verify a claim about a controversial topic.
3) *Website Reliability:* Students determine whether a partisan site is trustworthy.
4) *Social Media Video:* Students watch an online video and identify its strength and weaknesses.
5) *Claims on Social Media:* Students read a tweet and explain why it might or might not be a useful source of information.

Next Steps

We envision several next steps that build on what we have accomplished. These include:

Assessment for Learning. Although our tasks could be used in a variety of ways, we think they are powerful tools for classroom instruction. Rather than simply serving as assessment of learning, they can also be assessments for learning, or what are known as "formative assessments." Teachers can use our tasks to track students understanding and to adjust instruction accordingly. Similarly, teachers can use these exercises as the basis for broader lessons about the skills these tasks measure. We also hope to create accompanying materials that help teachers incorporate these tasks into the flow of classroom instruction.

Curriculum development. Teachers also need curriculum focused on developing students' civic online reasoning. Drawing on our experiences in developing the *Reading Like a Historian* curriculum, we have begun to pilot lesson plans that can be used in conjunction with our assessments. In the coming months, we will be working closely with teachers to refine these materials and to implement them in classrooms.

Awareness of the Problem. When we begin our work we had little sense of the depth of the problem. We even found ourselves rejecting ideas for tasks because we thought they would be too easy. Our first round of piloting shocked us into reality. Many assume that because young people are fluent in social media they are equally savvy about what they find there. Our work shows the opposite. We hope to produce a series of high-quality web videos to showcase the depth of the problem revealed by students' performance on our tasks and demonstrate the link between digital literacy and citizenship. By drawing attention to this connection, a series of videos could help to mobilize educators, policymakers, and others to address this threat to democracy.

YOUR TURN: Analyzing Stanford History Education Group's Rhetorical Strategies

Explain your answer for each question in two or three sentences. Use examples from the text to support your points.

1. What is the purpose of this evaluative report?
2. What can readers expect to learn from reading the summary of the report?
3. Which criteria are used to assess students' evaluative abilities?
4. What was the evaluative method the writers used to judge the students' abilities?
5. For whom do you believe this report was written? Why? Explain your answer.

CHAPTER PROJECT Writing to Evaluate

Teaching Suggestion
See the IM for additional evaluative writing projects.

The three projects that follow require that you create an evaluative paper. The first project asks you to find your own topic, while the next two projects provide more guidance about what to write.

PROJECT 1 Find Your Own Topic

Write an evaluation on any subject in which you are personally interested. Identify a target audience for your evaluation, such as your community, your peer group, or your college. Here are some ideas:

- Evaluate the dangers of vaping to recommend whether or not it is a safe practice. Write this paper for your peer group.

- Write a comparative evaluation of a product and offer a judgment. Write this article for readers who would be likely to research the product before purchasing it.
- Evaluate the quality of a movie, book, or local restaurant. Write this article for your local newspaper.

Use research if you need to know more about the subject or if you need to find data, and cite your research according to the documentation style specified by your instructor. Use Rhetorical Toolbox 8.1 as you plan and compose your evaluation.

Teaching Resources
The chapter writing projects are available as writing assignments in Connect.

PROJECT 2 Comparative Evaluation of Websites and Sources

Write a comparative evaluation of two sources found on websites. First, select a topic that is controversial, such as raising the minimum wage, gun control, or making college free. Next, find two articles on the topic, both from websites, and use the criteria below to evaluate the credibility of the articles and websites. In your evaluation, compare the credibility of your sources and make a judgment about which of the sources is most credible. For more guidance on evaluating sources, see Rhetorical Toolbox 10.1 in Chapter 10, "Finding Good Sources."

Write an essay to present your evaluation.

PROJECT 3 Evaluating a GoFundMe Campaign

The fundraising website, GoFundMe, offers people a chance to raise money for worthy causes. On the website, you will find information about the factors that make GoFundMe campaigns successful. Start this evaluative project by studying the information provided on the website, and identify the criteria that you believe are most important for an effective GoFundMe campaign.

Next, select two GoFundMe sites, one you believe is not constructed effectively and one you believe is destined to succeed. Using the criteria you have identified, explain your evaluation and judgment of these two campaigns.

In the next sections, you will see how student Tierra Delgado evaluates the food pantry options in her community. As a person who frequently volunteers, Tierra understands the differences in the local food pantries and wants to write a paper that can help community members understand that not all charities are equal. Tierra hopes her evaluation will be published in her local newspaper. We follow Tierra's process as she creates her evaluative article.

Selecting a Topic

If you are not using one of the topics provided in this chapter, find a topic that is personally interesting or useful. For example, Tierra has a passion for ending hunger, and in addition to her volunteer work, she has read many articles on the topic. Evaluating food pantries in her town is a natural topic for Tierra. Are there issues about which you are passionate? Can you evaluate an aspect of one of those issues to help a general audience make more informed decisions or gain a deeper understanding of the issue?

> **Tierra, on choosing a topic:** "I kind of live for social issues and social justice, so when I got the assignment to evaluate something, the idea of evaluating the food pantries here in Lexham Valley popped into mind quickly."

Planning

As you plan your evaluation, keep these concerns in mind.

1. **Speaker or Writer.** How will you become knowledgeable about the subject? Will you need to do research to learn background information? Will you need to have first-hand experience to evaluate the subject?
2. **Audience.** An evaluation starts with an analysis based on criteria. What criteria will the audience expect you to use in the evaluation? Are there additional criteria that you believe are important?
3. **Message.** The message of your evaluation is the judgment you will make. How likely is it that the audience will agree with the judgment? What kind of support will make your judgment more believable?

Use these strategies to plan your evaluation.

Co-requisite Teaching Tip
Consider working with co-requisite students in class to create criteria charts for their projects.

Creating a Criteria Chart. A criteria chart can help you organize your thoughts and cover your topic systematically. Tierra's chart lists the three food pantries in her town along the top and the criteria on the left. She will use the chart to record notes about each criterion. To plan her evaluation, Tierra identifies the factors that affect the quality of a food pantry and uses these as her criteria.

Criteria	Everyone Eats	Haven Outreach	Hope Shelter
Location/accessibility/hours			
Volunteer training/ professionalism			
Food safety/cleanliness			
Eligibility policies			
Client experience			
Availability of fresh food			
Educational programs			

Drafting a working thesis statement. Once you have completed the analysis portion of your evaluation, draw an evaluative conclusion, a judgment about the value or worth of the item(s) you have evaluated.

> **Tierra's Working Thesis Statement**
> Each of the three food pantries in Lexham Valley does quality work, but Haven Outreach is an exemplary charity that deserves support.

Outlining Your Essay. Once you have used criteria to evaluate the subject and have articulated your working thesis statement, you can create an outline. Use these tips.

- **Judgment.** Your evaluation presents a judgment, and this judgment is your thesis statement. Reread your thesis statement. Which parts of your analysis will help readers follow, believe, or understand your thesis statement? These are the elements you need to put into your paper (and outline).
- **Criteria.** Will you need to justify why you selected the criteria you are using (and why other criteria were not included)? To answer this question, think about the readers. Will readers accept that the criteria you have chosen are the best ones to use for this evaluation?
- **Background.** Will readers need background information to fully understand the evaluation? For example, in a movie review, the background information that readers need is the plot. Without knowing the plot, readers may not be able to follow the evaluative thinking the reviewer presents. In Tierra's case, she plans to describe the three food pantries she is evaluating before she presents the criteria used to evaluate them.
- **Support.** Will you need to use sources in the evaluation? Tierra, for example, plans to interview food pantry directors and use the interviews as sources. What will readers expect?
- **First-hand experience.** Will you need to experience the subject first-hand to evaluate it? By visiting the food pantries and talking with their directors, Tierra plans to gain first-hand experience.
- **Organization.** How will you organize the evaluation? Will you start with your judgment and follow it with a discussion of the criteria you used to form that judgment? Would it be better to start with the criteria? What information must go first for the evaluation to be clear?

Using these questions, create an outline. What follows is Tierra's outline for her evaluation.

Tierra's Outline

Working Thesis Statement: Each of the three food pantries in Lexham Valley does quality work, but Haven Outreach is an exemplary charity that deserves support.

Ideas for Introduction: Explanation of the criteria commonly used to evaluate food pantries.

Section 1: Description of the three food pantries.
- Everyone Eats
- Haven Outreach
- Hope Shelter

> **Section 2:** Evaluation of Everyone Eats
> - Location/accessibility/hours
> - Volunteer training/professionalism
> - Food safety/cleanliness
> - Eligibility policies
> - Client experience
> - Availability of fresh food
> - Educational programs
>
> **Section 3:** Evaluation of Haven Outreach
> - Location/accessibility/hours
> - Volunteer training/professionalism
> - Food safety/cleanliness
> - Eligibility policies
> - Client experience
> - Availability of fresh food
> - Educational programs
>
> **Section 4:** Evaluation of Hope Shelter
> - Location/accessibility/hours
> - Volunteer training/professionalism
> - Food safety/cleanliness
> - Eligibility policies
> - Client experience
> - Availability of fresh food
> - Educational programs
>
> **Ideas for conclusion:** All three are providing important services, but Everyone Eats and Hope Shelter can learn from Haven Outreach and make improvements.

Drafting

As you draft your evaluation, keep readers in mind by following these tips:

- **The critical reader.** Write your evaluation with a critical reader in mind. Imagine a reader asking questions such as these: *Why is this criterion important? How do you know? Why didn't you discuss this other criterion?* Write in such a way that readers' potential objections are anticipated and addressed.
- **Weighting the criteria.** To reach an evaluative judgment, you may need to weight the criteria. Which criteria are the *most* important to you and to the readers? Write in such a way that readers can understand why you weight some criteria more heavily than others.
- **Background.** If you are writing for a general audience, determine how much background information readers need to know about the subject before they can understand your evaluation. Provide this information.

- **Organization**. Arrange your evaluation in a way that readers can easily follow your logic. If your evaluation is comparative, use a subject-by-subject organization style (such as Tierra's), or organize your paper by discussing each criterion separately (point by point). If you find that your outline is not working, go back to the planning stage and regroup. For an example of how to organize an evaluative text that involves comparisons, see "FAQ: Organizing Evaluative Comparisons" at the end of this chapter.
- **Reread**. After composing a few paragraphs, reread your paper from the beginning and make changes. This task greatly improves the cohesiveness of ideas in your paper.

Consider using wording that guides readers through the information you are presenting, as suggested by the Drafting Toolbox.

> **DRAFTING TOOLBOX**
> ### Terms and Phrases for Evaluative Texts
> - The evaluation will show that . . .
> - A good [topic] should meet several criteria, including . . .
> - An important criterion is . . .
> - The most important criterion is . . .
> - Examining these criteria leads to the conclusion that . . .
> - Based on this evaluation, it is clear that . . .
> - The evaluation suggests that . . .
> - Based on these criteria, one can predict that . . .

Thinking Recursively in the Writing Process

Writing is not a linear activity: it is circular. Good writers often stop in the middle of creating a draft and go back to conduct more research, to reorganize material, and so on. Allow yourself the freedom to change your outline and content by using a recursive writing process.

> **Tierra, on recursive writing:** "When I created the outline, I thought I would be able to cover seven criteria for each food pantry. I figured out, though, that I really didn't have enough material to analyze the client experiences, so I decided to cut that section out."

Revising

Start the revision process by thinking about the audience. What does the audience need your paper to accomplish? What will they expect to find in a paper such as yours? Use the steps that follow to revise in depth.

1. **Reverse outline your paper to check for completeness.** A reverse outline is an outline you extract from a paper, rather than an outline you use. By

creating an outline of your draft, you will be able to see if you have left out any criteria, analysis of criteria, or other content important to your evaluation. Make sure you have applied the same criteria to every element you are analyzing (if you are analyzing more than one element.)

2. **Check background information.** To evaluate an element, you must have thorough knowledge of that element. As the writer, you probably have this knowledge, but does the reader? Have you supplied all the background information readers may need?

3. **Check your judgment and its wording.** You used your evaluative analysis to form a judgment. Is your judgment accurate? Is it worded precisely?

4. **Check for support.** Will readers believe you provided enough support to reach the evaluative judgment you reached? Add more support in the form of examples, explanations, or data, if necessary.

5. **Check for relevancy.** Do readers understand why the evaluation is important? If its importance is not obvious, add content that helps readers see how the evaluation is relevant to their lives.

6. **Read the introduction and conclusion.** How does the introduction encourage the reader to keep reading? Can you improve the level of engagement the introduction creates? Does the conclusion provide a sense of closure? Revise to improve, if necessary.

7. **Examine and revise sentences and paragraphs.** Make sure sentences are clearly written and that the ideas in your paper are separated into logical paragraphs.

8. **Check assignment requirements.** Does your paper meet all of the requirements of the assignment? If not, revise.

9. **Use peer review to help you make revision decisions.** The following questions will help a peer read your paper and give you constructive suggestions.

PEER REVIEW TOOLBOX: EVALUATIVE WRITING

1. What is the purpose of the writer's evaluation? Does the writer make this purpose clear?

2. What criteria does the writer use to evaluate? Are these criteria easy to identify?

3. What is the writer's judgment? Underline it.

4. Has the writer provided enough support for the judgment in the paper? Explain.

5. Is anything missing from the evaluation? For example, should the writer include more research? Should the writer add explanations? Does the writer need to add transitions to help you follow the thinking?

Tierra, on her revision decisions: "When I reread this paragraph, I realized that readers may not know what I meant by 'selective,' so I added some information."

Draft: While Hope Shelter is more convenient than Everyone Eats, it is also more selective. In spite of being the oldest food pantry in town, Hope Shelter ironically serves a smaller percentage of Lexham's hungry than the other two food pantries. The citizenship requirement is partly to blame for this, as is the fact that no transportation between the nearest bus stop and the Hope Shelter exists. Age has not helped Hope Shelter in terms of its cleanliness. In April, 2020, Hope Shelter received a Health Department warning for failing to maintain proper temperatures for refrigerated items. No other food pantry in town has received a citation. Managing Director Tom Haynes explains, "We were understaffed and overwhelmed; someone just dropped the ball."

Revision: While Hope Shelter is more convenient than Everyone Eats, it is also more selective. To be eligible for food pantry items, patrons are screened using the income guidelines set by the U.S. Department of Agriculture. In addition, patrons must be U.S. citizens living within the city limits of Lexham. In spite of being the oldest food pantry in town, Hope Shelter ironically serves a smaller percentage of Lexham's hungry than the other two food pantries. The citizenship requirement is partly to blame for this, as is the fact that no transportation between the nearest bus stop and the Hope Shelter exists. Age has not helped Hope Shelter in terms of its cleanliness. In April, 2020, Hope Shelter received a Health Department warning for failing to maintain proper temperatures for refrigerated items. No other food pantry in town has received a citation. Managing Director Tom Haynes explains, "We were understaffed and overwhelmed; someone just dropped the ball."

Tierra: "In one of my paragraphs, I said that Haven Outreach was a popular food pantry, but I didn't know how to prove that. I imagined that a reader might say, 'How do you know it's popular?' So I asked a volunteer, and I revised my paper to include a part of what he said in my paper as support."

Draft: Haven Outreach provides fresh fruit, produce, meat, and dairy products to its patrons, and each fresh item comes with instructions for storing and preparing. There are even online videos produced by students and volunteers to help patrons learn more about preparing healthy meals with the produce and fresh foods they take home. The quality of food, availability of products, and policies of Haven Outreach make it a popular food pantry.

Revision: Haven Outreach provides fresh produce, meat, and dairy products to its patrons, and each fresh item comes with instructions for storing and preparing. There are even online videos produced by students and volunteers to help patrons learn more about preparing healthy meals with the produce and fresh foods they take home. The quality of food, availability of products, and policies of Haven Outreach make it a popular food pantry. James Linney, a volunteer, said, "I have volunteered at all three food pantries, and I've never seen people line up the way they do at Haven Outreach. It's just a great place."

Tierra: "I had written a very brief introduction that started with the city's population. When I reread the introduction, the population statistic seemed irrelevant, so I deleted it and provided a more general introduction."

Draft: Lexham Valley, a town of 80,000, has its share of hunger. Fortunately, three food pantries work to provide food to those who need it. Each of the three food pantries in Lexham Valley does quality work, but Haven Outreach is an exemplary food pantry, one that can serve as a model for ideas and improvement.

Revision: With the vast resources this country has, it is surprising that there are thousands of people, often children, who go hungry or who do not have adequate food supplies for good nutrition. But hunger is still a reality in the United States. Fortunately, many cities have food pantries that help to meet the nutritional needs of those who are less fortunate. While all food pantries are to be commended for the work they do, some of them excel at the business of feeding the hungry. By evaluating local food pantries, organizations can identify the practices that result in excellence. Each of the three food pantries in Lexham Valley does quality work, but Haven Outreach is an exemplary food pantry, one that can serve as a model for ideas and improvement.

Finishing

To finish your paper from a writer's mindset, keep your audience in mind throughout editing and formatting, the remaining stages of the writing process.

Editing. During the editing stage, focus on errors in grammar, spelling, and mechanics. Use the tools readily available to you, such as spell-checkers and grammar checkers, but also look at previous papers to see the errors you are likely to make. Check for those errors in your paper and make corrections.

Formatting. Use your instructor's guidelines for formatting and submitting your paper. Tierra formatted her paper in MLA style, the style required by her instructor.

Tierra Delgado, A Food Pantry Worth Admiring (Final Draft)

Here is Tierra's final draft, presented in MLA style.

Tierra Delgado
Mr. Colton
ENGL 1420
10 February 2021

A Food Pantry Worth Admiring

With the vast resources this country has, it is surprising that there are thousands of people, often children, who go hungry or who do not have adequate food supplies for good nutrition. But hunger is still a reality in the United States. Fortunately, many cities have food pantries that help to meet the nutritional needs of those who are less fortunate. While all food pantries are to be commended for the work they do, some of them excel at the business of feeding the hungry. By evaluating local food pantries, organizations can identify the practices that result in excellence. Each of the three food pantries in Lexham Valley does quality work, but Haven Outreach is an exemplary food pantry, one that can serve as a model for ideas and improvement.

Lexham Valley is lucky enough to have three local food pantries: Everyone Eats, Hope Shelter, and Haven Outreach. Lexham's newest food pantry, Everyone Eats, is sponsored by Lexham Methodist Church and is run out of their basement on Saturdays. Hope Shelter is a nonprofit organization located on the South side of Lexham and run by volunteers. Haven Outreach, a food pantry associated with Lexham College's downtown campus, is staffed by volunteers and administered by the Lexham College School of Social Work. All three food pantries serve a tremendous need in Lexham, but each operates somewhat differently.

Everyone Eats is open only on Saturdays, and it is housed at Lexham Methodist Church, a church in the Northwest suburbs of Lexham. While Everyone Eats is serving the needs of the hungry in the Northwest suburbs, many of the people who might benefit from it do not have the transportation to get to it. According to a recent socioeconomic survey, the population that is most likely to suffer from hunger is located in the Southwest quadrant of the city, approximately twenty miles from Everyone Eats (Villa). The fact that this food pantry is open only on Saturdays is another factor that limits its usefulness.

While Everyone Eats is geographically isolated, anyone—regardless of income or employment status—is welcome. Its eligibility policies are lenient, although clients may not receive more than one parcel per week. The facility is squeaky clean, and procedures to ensure food safety are top notch. Marta Jaramillo, the Operating Director, is well-equipped to enforce high standards. As a former hospital food service director, Jaramillo brings years of experience to Everyone Eats. While Jaramillo is happy with the facilities, she is not overjoyed with the offerings the pantry has at present. "I'm hopeful that within the year, we can start to bring in more fresh meats, fruits, and vegetables. While we have some of those items, we do not have a steady enough supply to meet the needs of our clients. We really depend on dried foods and canned goods, but we are hoping that will change." Patrons of Everyone Eats are provided with a box of food each Saturday. The box contains canned meats, peanut butter, grains, milk when it is available, and mainly nonperishable items.

A more centrally located food pantry, Hope Shelter, serves the needs of many clients on the South side of town. The shelter is open every day except for Sundays, and it was the first food pantry in town, having been established in 1972. Its South side location makes it convenient for many people, but because it is three blocks from the nearest bus station, some clients have to walk a significant distance, carrying food all the way.

While Hope Shelter is more convenient than Everyone Eats, it is also more selective. To be eligible for food pantry items, patrons are screened using the income guidelines set by the U.S. Department of Agriculture. In addition, patrons must live within the city limits of Lexham. In spite of being the oldest food pantry in town, Hope Shelter ironically serves a smaller percentage of Lexham's hungry than the other two food pantries. The citizenship requirement is partly to blame for this, as is the fact that no transportation between the nearest bus stop and the Hope Shelter exists. Age has not helped Hope Shelter in terms of its cleanliness. In April, 2020, Hope Shelter received a Health Department warning for failing to maintain proper temperatures for refrigerated items. No other food pantry in town has received a citation. Managing Director Patrick Lewkowski explains, "We were understaffed and overwhelmed; someone just dropped the ball."

One thing that Hope Shelter has excelled in is providing fresh food for patrons. Through an arrangement with local dairy farmers, fresh milk is always available. Eggs are almost always available, also, and customers are usually able to pick and choose the vegetables and fruits their families enjoy. Haynes points out that because Hope Shelter maintains strict income and citizenship requirements for its services, they are capable of providing higher quality foods to a smaller portion of customers.

Both Hope Shelter and Everyone Eats are helping to meet the needs of the hungry in Lexham. Haven Outreach, the third food pantry to open its doors in Lexham, has changed the game—not only for Lexham but for other food pantries across the nation that have been modeled after Haven Outreach. Operated by Dr. Sherry Denn, a professor of Social Work at Lexham College, and governed by a 12-panel board of directors, Haven Outreach provides not only food, but educational services—including cooking classes—to anyone, free of charge. Open Monday through Saturday and conveniently located in downtown Lexham, Haven Outreach is easy to get to via local busses. Its impeccably clean and organized kitchen is a model of efficiency and modern hygiene. Denn explains, "Our faculty who teach food science courses have been invaluable in their direction here. Not only did they help us plan the cleanest, most efficient kitchen possible, but they are often here, helping us come up with new and better ways to handle food."

Haven Outreach provides fresh fruit, produce, meat, and dairy products to its patrons, and each fresh item comes with instructions for storing and preparing. There are even videos available online produced by students and volunteers to help patrons learn more about preparing healthy meals with the produce and fresh foods they take home. The quality of food, availability of products, and policies of Haven Outreach make it a popular food pantry. Suri Patel, a volunteer, said, "I have volunteered at all three food pantries, and I've never seen people line up the way they do at Haven Outreach. It's just a great place."

Any organization that offers food to the hungry—free of charge—is doing a vital service for a community. However, some organizations simply do it better, and Haven Outreach is one of them. By focusing on education, providing the freshest food possible, and offering their services to all—regardless of income or address—Haven Outreach has managed to offer the impossible: a true haven to help the hungry.

Wells 4

Works Cited

Denn, Sherry. Personal interview. 1 Feb. 2021.

Jaramillo, Marta. Personal interview. 1 Feb. 2021.

Lewkowski, Patrick. Personal interview. 4 Feb. 2021.

Patel, Suri. Personal interview. 1 Feb. 2021.

Villa, Evan, and C. R. Johnson. "What the Numbers Say." *Lexham Tribune* [Lexham, PA], 14 Mar. 2020, 4B.

YOUR TURN: Analyzing Delgado's Rhetorical Strategies

1. How can you tell that Delgado's essay is an evaluation?
2. Where in the essay does Delgado provide support for her judgment about the best food pantry?
3. Why does Delgado choose to use interviews as sources? Could other sources have been as effective as interviews? Explain your answer.
4. How does Delgado organize her evaluation?
5. How does Delgado establish a tone of respect and goodwill for the food pantries in her town?

Reflecting to Develop a Writer's Mindset

When writing an evaluation, why is it important to keep the audience in mind? In what ways does the audience affect the way you evaluate? Explain your answer.

FAQ ORGANIZING AN EVALUATIVE COMPARISON

A comparative evaluation can be organized in one of two ways: (1) block (subject-by-subject) arrangement or (2) point-by-point arrangement.

1. How do the block (subject-by-subject) and point-by-point arrangements differ?

In the block arrangement, a writer organizes the discussion by subject, covering all the relevant points, first for subject A and then for subject B.

In the point-by-point arrangement, the writer organizes the discussion by the points of comparison, writing about the first point for both subjects A and B, then about the second point for both subjects A and B, and so on. For example, imagine writing a text that evaluates two options: buying a car versus leasing a car. The writer bases the evaluation on these criteria: monthly payments, mileage limits, warranty considerations, and ownership. The chart that follows shows how this evaluative text would be structured in a block arrangement and in a point-by-point arrangement.

Block arrangement	Point-by-point arrangement

Subject 1: Buying
    Monthly payments
    Mileage limits
    Warranty
    Ownership
Subject 2: Leasing
    Monthly payments
    Mileage limits
    Warranty
    Ownership
	Point 1: Monthly payments
	    Buying
	    Leasing
	Point 2: Mileage limits
	    Buying
	    Leasing
	Point 3: Warranty
	    Buying
	    Leasing
	Point 4: Ownership
	    Buying
	    Leasing

TRY IT!

Mia is writing a comparative evaluation of Mexican restaurants in her town. She plans to evaluate four restaurants: The Tortilla & Sopapilla Company, Cierra's Taco Shack, Poblito's, and Taco Soleada. She plans to evaluate the restaurants based on their food quality, service, price, and atmosphere. Create a simple outline for Mia's evaluation using either the block or point-by-point arrangement.

CREDITS

Page 178. Folstein, Maddy. Review: "'Hostiles' Tries to Revise History and Western Film Traditions." January 29, 2018. Used with permission.

Page 180. Stanford History Education Group. "Executive Summary of Evaluating Information; The Cornerstone of Civic Online Reasoning." Used with permission.

9 Writing to Persuade

Teaching Suggestion
This chapter is intended to provide a brief introduction to persuasive writing. For in-depth coverage of the topics in this chapter, see the chapters in Part 4.

Connect Adaptive Learning Assignment
Consider assigning Connect's Adaptive Learning Assignments to support this chapter.

Teaching Resources
See the Instructor's Manual (IM) for suggestions about how to teach this chapter, and consider assigning this chapter's test-bank quiz.

CHAPTER OBJECTIVES

You will learn to:
- Identify key rhetorical concerns of persuasive writing.
- Analyze persuasive texts.
- Compose a persuasive text.

Persuasive writing seeks to convince a reader that a point is true or believable. Persuasion sometimes takes the form of long texts, such as researched arguments and books, but it can also be found in shorter texts, such as newspaper opinion pieces, blogs, letters, and the like. In this chapter, we present a brief introduction to persuasive writing focused on creating short, persuasive texts; in the second half of this text, we present an in-depth guide to argument that complements this chapter.

WARM-UP
Read each of the three rhetorical situations that follow. In what ways will the writers in these situations be engaging in texts that attempt to persuade?

1. Laken is writing a letter to her apartment manager to explain why she should not be charged a fee for a broken appliance.
2. Tyler is creating a persuasive pamphlet for a marketing class. Its purpose is to persuade students to join an on-campus club.
3. Abby is writing a memo proposing a new, more efficient work procedure to her boss.

PERSUASIVE WRITING FROM A WRITER'S MINDSET

As you have seen, rhetorical skills are necessary to accomplish a wide variety of communication goals, including informing, analyzing, and evaluating. However, much of the study of rhetoric has focused on the strategies for persuasion, the subject of this chapter. You may be familiar with persuasive research papers—often called argument papers. These in-depth attempts to persuade make use of a wide variety of rhetorical strategies and almost always include the use of sources. But persuasive texts are not always lengthy, and persuasion can be found in a wide variety of genres. The three scenarios you examined in the Warm-Up present writing tasks that result in brief texts that have as their goal persuasion, but each text represents a different genre. Laken's letter will need to convince her apartment manager that she is not responsible for the damaged appliance. Tyler's marketing pamphlet must be designed to persuade students to participate in a club. Abby's memo requires her to persuade her boss to revise a procedure. All three rhetorical situations require the use of persuasive writing. In this chapter, we examine the elements of brief persuasive texts, and you will have the opportunity to compose a text with the goal of persuasion.

Key Elements of Persuasive Texts

One way to recognize a text that is persuasively focused is to examine the writer's thesis statement. A persuasive text presents a main idea that is debatable. It is important to remember that a writer can discuss an arguable issue without trying to persuade readers. The examples that follow demonstrate how the same topic may be presented for two different purposes: to inform and to persuade.

Thesis statement that is informative: *Laws about keeping wild animals as pets vary across the United States.* This is a fact, not an arguable issue. An essay on this topic would present information about the laws in question.

Thesis statement that is debatable: *Keeping wild animals as pets should be illegal.* This statement is an opinion; thus, it is debatable. Such a thesis statement is called a claim.

In general, persuasive writing consists of three main parts: a claim, reasons, and support.

1. The **claim** is the writer's thesis statement: it is the writer's assertion of an arguable point: Keeping wild animals as pets should be illegal.
2. **Reasons** are the main supporting points that make the claim believable. For example, a reason that keeping wild animals as pets should be illegal is that such animals present a threat to the community should they escape captivity.
3. **Support** consists of the explanations, examples, or evidence that provides proof for a reason. In research papers, support usually consists of information from sources. When sources are not used, support is provided often in the form of explanations and examples. For example, to support the reason that wild animals present a threat to a community, a writer might discuss an episode when a tiger escaped its cage and menaced a

> **Teaching Suggestion**
> See Chapter 14 for more information on the elements of argument.
>
> **Teaching Resources**
> Consider using the PowerPoint "An Introduction to Toulmin Analysis."

claim: The thesis statement of a persuasively oriented text; a statement of the writer's opinion or assertion of an arguable point.

reason: A main point that helps make the claim true or believable.

support: Explanations, examples, or evidence that provide proof for a reason.

neighborhood, requiring a massive effort by police and animal control to find the animal before it harmed someone.

counterargument: an argument that opposes the writer's claim or one of the writer's reasons.

rebuttal: A response to a counterargument that refutes it but may also concede to any part of it that is correct.

refutation: A writer's attempt to show the flaws in the counterargument; part of a rebuttal

concession: An acknowledgment that part of an opposing argument is correct; part of a rebuttal.

An additional element in most argument essays is a **counterargument**, an opposing argument. Writers often include the opposing argument and then attempt to provide a rebuttal. A **rebuttal** is a response to a counterargument. It consists primarily of a **refutation**: an attempt to show where the opposing view is weak or flawed. For instance, in the case of keeping wild animals as pets, the counterargument might be something like this: Reasonable regulations that would keep the public safe from wild animals kept as pets could be created and enforced. The rebuttal to this counterargument may be that the danger posed by many wild animals is so great that reasonable regulations would not be adequate.

A rebuttal can also include a concession when part of the counterargument is correct. A **concession** acknowledges that part of the opposing viewpoint is correct, but that the opposing argument is still wrong or weak. For example, a writer may concede that reasonable regulations may work in the case of wild animals that do not pose a threat to human life, such as small mammals. Concessions are often followed by refutations or a restatement of the writer's claim. For example, this concession would probably be followed by the refutation: Even though small, wild mammals might be reasonably kept as pets, there are no reasonable regulations that can govern animals capable of killing a human being. Therefore, dangerous wild animals should not be kept as pets. The elements of this argument are shown in Figure 9.1.

Co-requisite Teaching Tip
Consider using the co-requisite section as a writing workshop in which students plan a persuasive letter. The worksheet "Planning an Argument" leads students through this process.

Teaching Suggestion
Consider assigning the Power of Process assignment, "Identifying an Argument's Elements," in Connect.

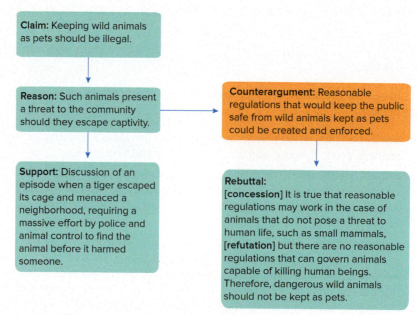

FIGURE 9.1 The elements of the "wild animals as pets" argument.

▶ **ACTIVITY 1** **Planning the Elements of a Persuasive Text**

In the Warm-Up, you read that Laken was writing a letter to her apartment manager. In Laken's letter, what might be a claim, a reason, support for the reason, and a counterargument or rebuttal that she could use to convince the manager that Laken is not responsible for the damage to an appliance?

Three Appeals: Logos, Ethos, and Pathos

Writers generally use three types of support for their claims: logical appeals, ethical appeals, and emotional appeals. An appeal is a rhetorical strategy that taps into one of three areas: logical reasoning (logos), goodwill or credibility (ethos), or feelings (pathos). These appeals are covered in depth in Chapter 15, and we provide a brief overview of them here.

Appeals to Logos. The Greek word *logos* can be translated as *logic*. Thus, **appeals to logos** present reasonable, or logical, explanations. For example, if it is raining outside, it is reasonable to argue that your friend should take her umbrella with her when she leaves for work. Another example is to argue that people should avoid getting into debt because debt leads to decreased financial options in life. Logical appeals often make use of text patterns such as cause and effect and comparison-contrast.

Appeals to Ethos. *Ethos* is a word from Greek rhetoric that refers to support that functions by tapping into the credibility and goodwill of the writer. In addition to logical appeals, writers also try to assure readers of their good intentions—that they are sincere, honest, and fair, and that they have the readers' interests and concerns in mind. Writers may also show that they are knowledgeable enough to speak authoritatively on the subject, or they may use the testimony of knowledgeable experts to bolster their credibility. **Appeals to ethos** consist of support that convinces us of the writer's trustworthiness, impartiality, expert knowledge, and goodwill.

Appeals to Pathos. A third type of support appeals to our emotions and is called **appeals to** *pathos*, a word that means *feelings*. Emotions are powerful; they can convince us to believe things and to take actions. For example, advertisements often tap into our emotions to sell products. A pair of name-brand, expensive athletic shoes may be the same quality as a pair of no-name sneakers, but wearing the expensive shoes gives us a feeling that the cheap shoes cannot provide. Appealing to our emotions can also mean appealing to our sense of shared values. In a written argument, we might tell the story of a child who is always hungry to make the claim that people should support a government supplemental food program because no child should have to suffer hunger. Emotional appeals can provide strong reasons for believing a claim or for taking an action.

Teaching Suggestion
See Chapter 15 for more information on the three appeals.

Teaching Resources
Consider using the PowerPoint "Three Appeals" to introduce ethos, pathos, and logos.

Teaching Suggestion
Consider assigning the Power of Process assignment, "Identifying an Argument's Appeals," in Connect.

appeals to logos: a rhetorical strategy that uses logical reasoning to attempt to persuade.

appeals to ethos: a rhetorical strategy that uses the writer's authority, good character, good intentions, or the authority of others to attempt to persuade.

appeals to pathos: a rhetorical strategy that taps into the readers' emotions to attempt to persuade.

Teaching Resources
After students have completed Activity 2, consider having them critique two versions of Laken's letter.

▶ **ACTIVITY 2** Choosing Appeals for a Persuasive Text

Think about the letter Laken is writing. She is considering using the following rhetorical strategies to persuade her manager not to charge her for the damaged appliance. Consider each strategy and identify whether it appeals to logos, ethos, or pathos.

A. She plans to point out that she has been an exemplary tenant in that she has never been late with any payment and has always complied with the requests of management.

B. She plans to quote a section from her rental contract to show she is not legally responsible for the damage.

Audience Analysis

Perhaps more than any other writing purpose, writing to persuade requires a keen analysis of one's audience. It requires careful planning to select the rhetorical strategies that will lead readers to persuasion. Using the questions in Rhetorical Toolbox 9.1 will help you plan a persuasive text, keeping your audience in mind.

Co-requisite Teaching Tip
Consider having students practice developing reasons that tap into ethos, pathos, and logos. Students can do this by devising reasons to support a particular claim, such as this one: "It should be illegal for anyone under the age of 18 to operate all-terrain vehicles."

RHETORICAL TOOLBOX 9.1
The Rhetorical Concerns of Persuasive Writing

1. **Claim.** What claim do you hope to persuade readers to believe or accept?
2. **Audience.** Who is the audience? What are the audience's values?
3. **Reasons**. Examining the list of reasons you could use to support the claim, which reasons are most aligned with the audience's values? Consider using those reasons.
4. **Appeals**. Which appeals—logos, ethos, or pathos—would be the most effective for getting your audience to agree with your claim? What content could you include in your text to help you appeal to ethos, pathos, and/or logos?
5. **Counterarguments**. What are the most powerful counterarguments to your claim or to any of your reasons?
6. **Rebuttal.** Will you need to make concessions or refutations of counterarguments to convince your audience of your claim?

By thinking about your specific audience, you can more successfully create a text that taps into their values and is persuasive.

▶ **ACTIVITY 3** Analyzing the Audience for a Persuasive Text

In the Warm-Up, Abby is writing a memo to try to persuade her boss to adopt a new procedure. Her boss oversees fifteen employees. What kinds of reasons might be persuasive to a supervisor? Are these reasons based on logic (logos), credibility (ethos), or emotions (pathos)?

MODELS OF PERSUASIVE WRITING

It's Time to Decriminalize Sex Work
David Rosen

The purpose of the following article is to persuade readers that legalizing prostitution is a good idea. David Rosen, a writer based in New York, is the author of Sin, Sex & Subversion: How What Was Taboo in 1950s New York Became America's New Normal *(Skyhorse, 2016). This piece was published in* The Progressive, *a magazine for general readers. The magazine presents a progressive–often liberal–point of view and describes itself as "a voice for peace, social justice, and the common good." As you read the article, notice the annotations in the right-hand column that point out the features in this persuasively focused text. In addition, notice that the claim is found in the last paragraph.*

> **Teaching Suggestion**
> For additional models of persuasive writing, see Part 6, An Anthology of Readings.

Donald Trump's presidency could mark a new phase in how America deals with prostitution, long considered the oldest profession. On April 11, 2018, the president signed an act that reconciled the Senate's "Allow States and Victims to Fight Online Sex Trafficking Act" and the House's "Stop Enabling Sex Traffickers Act." His action was aimed at restricting internet advertising of commercial sex services.

But for many Americans, prostitution has shifted from a moral issue, "sin," to a legal one, "consent." A May 2016 Marist poll found that 49 percent of Americans felt commercial sex between two consenting adults should be legal, and 44 percent opposed it. In addition, six in ten respondents opposed criminal prosecution of those arrested for prostitution, while 53 percent believed decriminalizing prostitution would minimize risks to sex workers by providing regulation.

Prostitution is legal at about 20 brothels operating in seven rural counties in Nevada, and has long been generally accepted by a significant part of the populace. Rhode Island decriminalized sex work for six years, from 2003 to 2009, and saw a significant decline in sexually transmitted diseases and rapes.

There are growing calls to decriminalize prostitution. Sex-worker advocacy groups like COYOTE (Call Off Your Old, Tired Ethics) as

Reason: Popular opinion supports decriminalization.

Appeal to logos: polling statistics

Reason: Some states have already decriminalized it.

Appeal to logos: examples of decriminalization

well as the World Health Organization have called to decriminalize non-trafficked—i.e., "consensual"—prostitution. And there have been legal challenges, like the lawsuit brought by San Francisco's Erotic Service Providers Legal Education and Research Project challenging California's laws against prostitution. It was not successful.

In October 2017, two city council members in Washington, D.C., introduced a bill to decriminalize sex work; it is still pending. New York State's former chief judge, Jonathan Lippman, headed a special commission on Criminal Justice and Incarceration Reform that advocated for reclassifying prostitution as a civil offense rather than a criminal one.

One thing we know for certain: Criminalizing prostitution has not made it go away. Revenues for sex work in the United States are estimated at $14.6 billion a year. The Fondation Scelles estimated in 2012 that there were one million prostitutes operating across the country.

Decriminalization protects sex workers, reducing instances of STDs and sexual assaults while also curbing sex trafficking and the need for risk-laden street prostitution. More broadly, it allows the government to save money on enforcement while creating new tax revenue.

We live in an era when gun ownership is a Constitutionally guaranteed right; when 30 states have decriminalized medical marijuana and nine states allow its recreational use by adults; the Supreme Court has just ruled that sports gambling is legal; and the commercial sex industry—sex toys, porn, enhancement drugs and more—is a multi-billion operation and an accepted part of American life.

It's time to decriminalize sex work.

Margin annotations:
- Additional support for the reason: Popular opinion supports decriminalization.
- Reason: Some lawmakers are in favor of decriminalization.
- Appeal to logos: revenue figures
- Reason: Criminalizing prostitution is ineffective. Appeal to logos
- Reason: Decriminalizing results in positive effects.
- Comparison with other decriminalized activities—appeal to logos
- Claim

Analyzing Rosen's Rhetorical Strategies

1. **What claim does Rosen hope to persuade readers to believe or accept?** He states his claim in the title and in the final sentence: "It's time to decriminalize sex work."

2. **Who is the audience?** The piece is written for a general audience, but since it was published in a liberal-leaning magazine, the audience is probably progressive (often liberal) in their orientation.

3. **What are the audience's values?** Many readers of *The Progressive* are liberal. They value the ideals valued by the magazine: "peace, social justice, and the common good."

4. **Which of the writer's reasons are most aligned with the audience's values?** The reasons in this section align with the values of many of the readers of the magazine: "Decriminalization protects sex workers, reducing instances of STDs and sexual assaults while also curbing sex trafficking and the need for risk-laden street prostitution. More broadly, it allows the government to save money on enforcement while creating new tax revenue."

5. **Which appeal—logos, ethos, or pathos—does the writer include?** The appeals are primarily appeals to logos.

6. **Does the writer include a counterargument and rebuttal? If so, what are they? If not, can you think of a counterargument the writer could have refuted to make the argument stronger?** Rosen does not address the counterargument. One counterargument he could have addressed is that prostitution objectifies and victimizes women. He could have addressed this objection to make his argument stronger.

Standardized Test Requirement Should Be Removed from College Admissions

Kyle Sheehy

The opinion piece that follows was written by Kyle Sheehy in 2019 when he was a freshman economics major at the University of Nebraska. The article was printed in the Daily Nebraskan, *the student newspaper of the University of Nebraska-Lincoln. As you read Sheehy's article, identify the main reasons he uses to support his claim. Think about whether most student newspaper readers would find the reasons convincing.*

Teaching Resources
This reading is available as a Power of Process assignment in Connect.

Most four-year universities require applicants to take either the ACT or the SAT, meaning high school students across the country must wake up early on a Saturday morning, trudge over to a local high school and fill out a bunch of circles that will determine much of their future.

However, Creighton University President Rev. Daniel Hendrickson announced last week the university would be getting rid of the standardized test requirement from its admissions process. Students will still be able to submit their ACT and SAT scores on their application, but it will be optional, not required.

Creighton's website says the change is to be implemented with the goal of, "expanding upon strategic initiatives and diversity and inclusion efforts." The goal of the strategic initiatives is to upgrade the university's selection process to admit more successful students and thus improve the university. They will do this by prioritizing four years in the classroom over four hours of a single test, believing this will give the administration a more holistic view of a student's academic career. The goal of diversity and inclusion efforts is to increase the number of "disadvantaged candidates" or people who are affected by implicit biases in tests, such as non-white students or those of a lower socioeconomic status.

By eliminating standardized test requirements, Creighton will improve the predictability of applicants' four-year college outcomes, increase diversity and encourage long-term success and dedication instead of short-term prowess. Because of these reasons, other universities should follow suit and remove their test requirements.

Creighton is switching from using standardized test scores as the main metric for screening applicants to using grade point average. This will likely help the school in its search for students who will do well in college, as GPA is actually a better indicator of college outcome than SAT scores. This is because the SAT and other standardized test scores only measure aptitude or general academic ability, and there is a lot the score leaves out.

The ACT, for example, cannot measure motivationally determined outcomes or outcomes which require additional work other than the ability to score well on a single test. GPA, on the other hand, gives a better picture of a student than test scores because it can track qualities such as motivation, work ethic and study habits.

The difference in judging a student's college readiness using GPA rather than standardized tests is similar to the difference between determining how big someone is by how much they weigh rather than how much they ate in a single day. Both will give you information to help answer the question, but the former takes into account accumulated, long-term factors that a day's worth of data will not provide. GPA and the number on the scale are more detailed and robust pieces of information. The better the information provided, the better and more accurate the decision.

Making standardized test submissions optional and focusing more on GPA will also foster more diversity on campuses. Dropping test requirements has been a growing trend across American universities. Institutions such as the University of Chicago, DePaul University, the University of Arizona and Arizona State University have dropped their requirements for the same reason: there are demonstrated racial biases in testing. These biases lead to considerable disparities in test results; white, Asian and high-income students perform much better than other ethnic minorities and low-income students, meaning measuring applicants by their test scores inhibits the diversification of student bodies. Dropping the test requirement has been shown to increase diversity at universities who have tried it and prioritizing GPA will help correct these biases by removing the distorted measure that is the SAT.

Most importantly, on a general societal level, the decision to remove testing requirements enforces the idea that larger bodies of work should speak louder than smaller ones. Society as a whole, including universities, should make judgments based on long-term observations of people, not one-time occurrences. A human being's worth should not be callously determined by circles on a scantron. Viewing people holistically is not only the most equitable way to measure their abilities, but also their intelligence.

The fact that high school GPA is a better predictor of college success than standardized tests is probably surprising to most people. The conventional wisdom goes that colleges need some kind of an objective way to measure applicants because GPA is arbitrary and incomparable across high schools. These claims are not supported by research though; GPA is a better predictor of college completion than standardized test scores.

It is also worth noting that removing test requirements and focusing on applicants' GPA will likely only increase ethnic and racial diversity, not socioeconomic.

> Extensive studies have shown there is a similar disparity between income classes in high school GPA as there is in SAT scores. While this is not ideal, increasing racial and ethnic diversity is still a positive move for universities, even if achieving socioeconomic diversity is still a ways away.
>
> Standardized tests only measure students based on one morning of filling out circles, wiping out four years of hard work and dedication. It is a distorted, flawed and biased measure that shows relatively little about the students it needlessly torments. Creighton is wise in removing its test requirement and other colleges and universities should do the same.

YOUR TURN Analyzing Sheehy's Rhetorical Strategies

Explain your answer for each question in two or three sentences. Use examples from the text to support your points.

1. What claim does Sheehy hope to persuade readers to believe or accept?
2. Who is the audience? What are the audience's values?
3. Which of the writer's reasons are most aligned with the audience's values?
4. Which appeal—logos, ethos, or pathos—does Sheehy include?
5. Does Sheehy include a counterargument and rebuttal? If so, what are they? If not, can you think of a counterargument the writer could have refuted to make the argument stronger?

CHAPTER PROJECT Writing to Persuade

Teaching Suggestion
See the IM for additional persuasive writing projects.

The three projects that follow require you to write a persuasive text. The first project asks you to find your own topic, while the next two projects provide more guidance about what to write. Select one of the following topics, or use a topic assigned by your instructor, and compose a persuasive text.

PROJECT 1 Find Your Own Topic

Teaching Resources
The chapter writing projects are available as writing assignments in Connect.

Write a persuasive essay on any topic in which you are personally interested. Make sure that you identify the target audience for your persuasive text. For example, a target audience may be your classmates, your community, a special interest magazine, and so on. Here are some ideas:

- Should college and university campuses completely ban the use of tobacco products?

- Should vaping products require FDA approval?
- Should single-use plastic bags and bottles be banned?
- Is there still a need for affirmative action policies?

Use research if you need to know more about the subject or if you need to find evidence. Cite your research according to the citation style specified by your instructor. Use Rhetorical Toolbox 9.1 as you plan and compose your persuasive essay.

PROJECT 2 A Letter to the Editor

A longstanding tradition in newspaper publishing is to publish letters sent in by readers. These letters are often persuasive in nature: they provide readers an opportunity to voice their opinions on the issues that matter to them. Examine your local newspaper or your college's newspaper. Read a few of the letters to the editor to get a sense of what such letters contain and how they are constructed.

Next, select a debatable topic about which you feel strongly, and write a persuasively oriented letter to the editor of your city's or college's newspaper. In your letter, urge readers to believe your point of view or to take an action. Be intentional in your use of rhetorical strategies. Use the steps of the writing process to plan, draft, revise, and edit your analysis. Keep in mind the Rhetorical Toolbox questions in this chapter so that you are writing with an audience—and a clear message—in mind.

Teaching Suggestion
See the IM for links to well-written letters to the editor that students can use as models.

PROJECT 3 A Persuasive Pamphlet

Identify a club, organization, or student resource (such as a tutoring lab) on your campus, and create a pamphlet that aims to increase the number of students who use the resource, or join the organization.

Write your persuasive pamphlet. Use the steps of the writing process to plan, draft, revise, and edit your text. Keep in mind the Rhetorical Toolbox questions in this chapter so that you are writing with an audience—and a clear message—in mind.

Teaching Suggestion
Consider assigning the parts of Chapter 18 that present visual rhetoric in conjunction with this assignment.

In the remaining pages of this chapter, you will follow the thinking and writing process of Jesse Martinez, a student in a composition class. Jesse is writing a persuasive essay on the topic of paying college athletes. As you complete your own persuasive writing project, use Jesse's process as a model.

Selecting a Topic

Thinking rhetorically about potential topics for a persuasive text requires you to think about the assignment conditions and the rhetorical situation. For instance, if the assignment is to write a letter to be published in a newspaper, the audience consists of the newspaper's readers. If you are creating a pamphlet to increase membership in a club, the audience consists of students at your college or university. Make sure the topic you select is relevant to the readers involved in the rhetorical situation.

You will also need to make sure the topic you select is arguable. Jesse, for instance, is interested in the issue of whether college athletes should be paid. Because he has friends who are college athletes, he might be tempted simply to tell their stories. Such a focus would not result in a persuasively oriented paper. Instead, Jesse could make the case that college athletes should receive compensation. The aim of such an approach would be to persuade readers of his point of view on the topic.

Teaching Note
At the time of writing, the NCAA is deciding how to implement rules that allow college athletes to receive some types of payment. Instructors may wish to review the topic to discuss the rulings the NCAA may make.

> **Jesse, on choosing a topic:** "As an avid sports fan, I really wanted to tackle the topic of paying college athletes. Two of my friends got full-ride basketball scholarships and may end up playing pro. Right now, they are as poor as I am. That just doesn't seem fair, so I want to change people's minds on this issue of paying college athletes. I could pick any topic and write for a general audience, and this was the topic that interested me most."

Planning

Think about these rhetorical considerations as you plan your project.

- **Speaker or Writer.** To have all the information you need on the topic, do you have to do research? What type of sources do you need, and where will you find them?
- **Audience.** Who is the audience? What are the values of the audience? How can you tap into these values to persuade them of your claim?
- **Message.** What is your claim? How resistant to the claim will your audience likely be? Are there counterarguments you should refute in your persuasive text?

Teaching Suggestion
When students do research to learn about multiple points of view, they are sometimes tempted to write papers that present differing points of view on the topic instead of persuasive texts that articulate a single point of view. Consider discussing this issue and helping students handle working with diverse viewpoints.

Use these strategies to plan your project:

1. **Use a method of prewriting to generate ideas.** You might brainstorm, list, cluster, free write, discuss the issue with friends, and so on. If you need to learn more about the topic, find high-quality research (see Chapters 10–12 for more information). Read the research and allow it to guide your thesis statement. In other words, avoid forming an opinion before you read. Read with an open mind and form an opinion only after you have read the best arguments from the different perspectives on the issue. Use a prewriting method to generate ideas, or write down ideas as you read the research. Focus your prewriting on identifying the best reasons for your position and on identifying the counterarguments that are most important to refute.

2. **Draft a claim.** The claim is your point about the topic. A claim will usually consist of one complete sentence but may be stated in two sentences, if necessary.

> **Jesse's claim:** College athletes are not like other college students and deserve compensation.

3. **Create an outline.** Create an outline that includes your claim, the reasons you will use to support it, and the plan you have for developing each of those reasons. Use these tips:

- **Introduction.** How will you start your persuasive text? What kind of introduction might be effective to make the topic relevant and to encourage readers to keep reading? Jot down ideas on your outline.
- **Claim.** Put your claim on your outline, aware that you may need to revise the wording of the claim later.
- **Reasons.** Identify and list the reasons you believe will be the most effective for the audience to support the claim.
- **Support.** For each reason, make a list of the explanations, examples, and evidence you will use as support. Make sure you choose support that the audience will find convincing.
- **Counterargument and rebuttal.** If you will be refuting the counterargument or making concessions, make a note on your outline. Show where you will refute it, and jot down the support you will use in your refutation.
- **Organization.** How will you organize your project? In what order will you present reasons? Where will you place refutations of the counterargument?

Create an outline based on your answers to these questions, noting where you will use research.

Jesse's Rough Outline

Ideas for Introduction: Start with a question like, "What could be more fun than college sports?"

Claim: College athletes are not like other college students and deserve compensation.

Reason 1: College sports make a lot of money and can afford to pay student athletes.

- Explanation of how the money is made
- Who makes the money

Counterargument: College athletes get free housing, tuition, and books, so they do not deserve additional payment.

Refutation: Explain why college athletes aren't like other students.

Reason 2: Another reason to pay athletes is to keep corruption out of college athletics.

- The disconnect between celebrity status and an empty bank account
- Examples of bribery
- How much advertisers can make

Conclusion: Repeat thesis statement?

Co-requisite Teaching Tip

Developing writers sometimes struggle when they try to include a counterargument and refutation. Consider discussing this skill and having students work through the "FAQ: Conceding a Point without Confusing Readers" in Chapter 21.

Drafting

One of the best ways to craft a persuasive text is to determine the reasons that persuade readers; however, during the drafting stage, you may encounter other rhetorical issues that can make your text more persuasive. Keep these tips in mind:

- **The critical reader.** Imagine the most critical reader. What objections might he or she raise? Drafting with this reader in mind helps you produce a better text.
- **Organization**. As you draft, think about the order in which you are presenting ideas. Would the most critical reader respond more positively if you first addressed potential objections (counterarguments) before stating your claim? Should some reasons come before others?
- **Outline**. As you draft, make changes to your outline. You may find the need to add or delete reasons, provide more evidence, and so on.
- **Clarity**. Work on sentence clarity as you draft, keeping readers in mind.
- **Reread**. Occasionally, read your paper from the beginning and make changes. Doing this greatly improves the quality of your sentences if you take the time to make revisions.

Consider using terms and phrases that guide readers through the information you are presenting, as suggested in the Drafting Toolbox.

DRAFTING TOOLBOX

Terms and Phrases for Texts that Persuade

It is clear that . . .
One [another, an additional] reason for . . . is . . .
Experts agree that . . .
The evidence supports the idea that . . .
Although some people believe . . ., this idea is mistaken.
One of the arguments against *x* is. . . . However, this argument is wrong because . . .

Thinking Recursively in the Writing Process

Recursive writing means that the writer goes back to previous stages in the writing process to make changes. For instance, a writer may return to the introduction to change it after writing a first draft, or a writer may return to the planning stage to reword the claim and find different research. Recursive writing requires a willingness to go back when things are not working out. Using a recursive process ensures that you are doing your best work, not merely finishing the task quickly.

> **Jesse, on recursive writing:** "I tried to write this without using sources, but I found that my paper was weak. I really needed to show how much money is potentially involved; that way, readers could see why bribery is such an issue. So I went back and did more research, and I found info I could use that really strengthened my argument."

Revising

To revise a persuasive text, imagine your most critical reader. Keeping this reader in mind, follow these steps:

1. **Try to put yourself into the reader's position.** Skim your text. What are the first impressions you have? Are any of these impressions negative? If so, use them to guide revision.
2. **Read each reason you have provided.** Are any reasons questionable in terms of logic? For more information on creating logically sound reasons, see Chapter 16.
3. **Check for appeals to ethos (credibility/goodwill) or pathos (emotions).** If there are none, would adding these appeals to your text improve its persuasiveness? For more information on ethos, pathos, and logos, see Chapter 15.
4. **Check for relevancy and purpose.** Can readers figure out how the topic is relevant to their lives? Is the persuasive intent of your text evident?
5. **Check the organization.** Examine the order in which you place the claim, reasons, and if applicable, counterarguments and refutations. Would a different sequence increase effectiveness?
6. **Read the introduction and conclusion.** Does the introduction engage the reader? Does the conclusion provide a sense of closure? Revise to improve, if necessary.
7. **Revise at the sentence level.** Good writing starts with clearly written sentences. Read each sentence for clarity. Are there sentences in your paper that should be revised so that they are clear? Are there sentences that contain many different ideas? Consider creating multiple sentences so that each idea is clearly articulated.
8. **Reread the assignment.** Does your paper meet all of the requirements of the assignment? If not, revise.
9. **Use peer review to help you make revision decisions.** The following questions will help a peer read your paper and give you constructive suggestions.

> **Co-requisite Teaching Tip**
> Consider having students work through these suggestions to revise their papers.

PEER REVIEW TOOLBOX: PERSUASIVE WRITING

1. What is the writer's purpose? Does the writer make this purpose clear?
2. Which of the reasons is strongest? Should this reason remain where it is, or should it be placed earlier or later in the composition?
3. Which of the reasons is weakest? Should the writer replace this with a different reason?
4. If the writer includes a counterargument and rebuttal, does the writer effectively disprove the counterargument?
5. Is anything missing from the text that might make the text more persuasive? For example, should the writer include more research? Should the writer add explanations? Does the writer need to add transitions to help you follow the thinking?

Jesse, on his revision decisions: "At first I tried to make the point that there is too much incentive for bribery, but I had not used any research. Without research, I really could not effectively support the reason or explain my thinking. So I did research and added examples. Doing that made my point about bribery much stronger, in my opinion."

Draft: Another reason to pay athletes is to keep corruption out of college athletics. While an amazing college athlete will certainly enjoy his or her share of fame, that fame does not result in a full bank account. In fact, the disconnect between enjoying celebrity status and having an empty bank account may contribute to the temptation to accept illegal gifts or bribes. But even gifts are forbidden: athletes who accept gifts or money can get banned from playing their sport. Even accepting a few dollars to buy some food or accepting a free tattoo can result in a stiff penalty. Nonetheless, bribery and illegal gifting in college athletics continue. Big sports companies have been known to offer bribes, as well as individuals who can benefit from a college athlete's potential fame.

Revision: Another reason to pay athletes is to keep corruption out of college athletics. While an amazing college athlete will certainly enjoy his or her share of fame, that fame does not result in a full bank account. In fact, the disconnect between enjoying celebrity status and having an empty bank account may contribute to the temptation to accept illegal gifts or bribes. But even gifts are forbidden: athletes who accept gifts or money can get banned from playing their sport. Even accepting a few dollars to buy some food or accepting a free tattoo can result in a stiff penalty. Nonetheless, bribery and illegal gifting in college athletics continues.

Marty Blazer, a financial advisor, is a case in point. In 2014, the FBI learned Blazer had given money to college athletes who pledged that when they became NBA athletes, they would use Blazer for financial services (Hobson). Blazer decided it would be in his best interest to become a witness for the FBI, and in doing so, he revealed the identity of many others who were bribing students, including "four assistant basketball coaches at Division I schools and a top Adidas executive accused of arranging six-figure bribes for basketball recruits." In a wire-tapped call, one of these men explained the reason for such bribery: " 'You can make millions off of one kid,' sports agent Christian Dawkins said" (qtd. in Hobson). The incentives to bribe college athletes are obvious, but if athletes were paid enough to live comfortable lives while they attended college, these bribes would not be so appealing.

Jesse: "When I reread my section that included the counterargument, I realized it may confuse readers. I had not spent enough time refuting it, and the way I plopped it into my essay made it seem like I actually agreed with the counterargument!"

Draft: College athletes do get free housing, tuition, and books, so they do not deserve additional payment. This argument is a common one and it is used to defend the decision to not compensate college athletes. But these athletes may not have enough money to live the life of an ordinary college student. After all, they cannot work a regular part-time job in most cases.	**Revision:** The argument goes something like this: college athletes get free housing, tuition, and books, so they do not deserve additional payment. At first glance, the argument seems to make sense, but what this argument does not consider is that those same athletes do double the work of regular college students. Practices start at 5:00 a.m., and even in the off season, these athletes are training. Out of town games complicate an athlete's study schedule; they make it impossible to work a part-time job. Let's face it: college athletes are not living the same lives as typical college students. They are the workhorses for college fame and notoriety, yet they are paid nothing for their contributions.

Jesse: "After I reread my draft, I realized that the claim I wrote needed to be revised somewhat, so I changed it."

Draft claim: College athletes are not like other college students and deserve compensation.	**Revised claim:** College athletes are not paid for their talent, dedication, and time, and failing to pay them is something that must change.

Finishing

To finish your work, keep your audience in mind throughout editing and formatting, which are the remaining stages of the writing process.

Editing. During the editing stage, spend time finding any errors in grammar, spelling, and mechanics. Use the tools readily available to you, such as spell-checkers and grammar checkers, but also look at previous papers to see the errors you are likely to make. Check for those errors in your paper and make corrections.

Formatting. Use your instructor's guidelines for formatting and submitting your paper. Jesse has formatted his paper in MLA style.

Jesse Martinez, Should College Athletes Be Paid? (Final Draft)

Jesse's final draft is presented in MLA style.

Jesse Martinez
Prof. Grossman
ENGL 300
15 March 2020

Should College Athletes Be Paid?

What is more fun than watching college football? For many people, college football is more popular than professional football. The enthusiasm for college sports such as football is responsible for bringing in billions of dollars to colleges each year. But what about the athletes? College athletes are not paid for their talent and dedication, and failing to pay them is something that must change.

College sports, like professional sports, are big businesses. They are extremely profitable, bringing in millions of dollars to colleges and universities every year. Coaches for major schools are paid handsomely, and television networks, sports clothing manufacturers, and souvenir sellers have all managed to get a piece of the college football pie. Everyone seems to be making money except the people who are doing all the work: the players. How can this possibly be a fair arrangement?

The argument goes something like this: college athletes get free housing, tuition, and books, so they do not deserve additional payment. At first glance, the argument seems to make sense, but what this argument does not consider is that those same athletes do double the work of regular college students. Practices start at 5:00 a.m., and even in the off season, these athletes are training. Out-of-town games complicate an athlete's study schedule; they make it impossible to work a part-time job. Let's face it: college athletes are not living the same lives as typical college students. They are the workhorses for college fame and notoriety, yet they are paid nothing for their contributions.

Another reason to pay athletes is to keep corruption out of college athletics. While an amazing college athlete will certainly enjoy his or her share of fame, that fame does not result in a full bank account. In fact, the disconnect between enjoying celebrity status and having an empty bank account may contribute to the temptation to accept illegal gifts or bribes. But even gifts are forbidden: athletes who accept gifts or money can get banned from playing their sport. Even accepting a few dollars to buy some food or accepting a free tattoo can result in a stiff penalty. Nonetheless, bribery and illegal gifting in college athletics continues.

Marty Blazer, a financial advisor, is a case in point. In 2014, the FBI learned Blazer had given money to college athletes who pledged that when they became NBA athletes, they would use Blazer for financial services (Hobson). Blazer decided it would be in his best interest to become a witness for the FBI, and in doing so, he revealed the identity of many others who were bribing students, including "four assistant basketball coaches at Division I schools and a top Adidas executive accused of arranging six-figure bribes for basketball recruits." In a wire-tapped call, one of these men explained the reason for such bribery: "'You can make millions off of one kid,' sports agent Christian Dawkins said" (qtd. in Hobson). The incentives to bribe college athletes are obvious: if athletes were paid enough to live comfortable lives while they attended college, these bribes would not be so appealing.

Clearly, paying our athletes is the right thing to do. These students deserve the money, and the future of college athletics depends on dealing with the corruption that can damage sports and students' lives. Perhaps college athletes should begin to boycott their sports if colleges don't start paying them. After a few canceled games, the universities will gladly agree to start sharing some of their massive wealth.

Work Cited

Hobson, Will. "How College Hoops Corruption Became a Federal Investigation, and Why It Might Get Bigger." *Washington Post*, 27 Sept. 2017, https://www.washingtonpost.com/sports/colleges/how-college-hoops-corruption-became-a-federal-investigation-and-why-it-might-get-bigger/2017/09/27/dfdfa6e0-a3d6-11e7-ade1-76d061d56efa_story.html?noredirect5on.

YOUR TURN Analyzing Martinez's Rhetorical Strategies

1. Does the writer know enough about the subject or have enough research to analyze the subject?
2. What is the purpose of the essay?

3. Who is the intended audience, and what knowledge does this audience have about the topic?
4. What rhetorical strategies help readers follow the logic of Jesse's argument or understand the points he makes?

Reflecting to Develop a Writer's Mindset

This chapter presents rhetorical strategies writers use in persuasive texts. What are these strategies? Which ones have you used before? Which would you feel comfortable experimenting with, and why?

FAQ IDENTIFYING ARGUABLE ISSUES

As you plan persuasive writing projects, you will need to identify topics that are arguable, those that lend themselves to persuasive writing.

1. How can you recognize whether a topic is arguable?

One way to recognize an arguable topic is to turn the topic into a question. An arguable topic is one that can be stated as a question whose answer is debatable—that is, it can be considered from multiple perspectives. Here are some topic questions whose answers are *not* arguable.

Question: What is COVID-19?

Arguable or not? This question is not arguable because the answer is universally agreed on. Medical professionals know what COVID-19 is. Thus, a paper that answers this question will simply inform, not persuade.

Question: What kinds of college financial aid are available for veterans?

Arguable or not? The answer to this question requires some research, but the answer is easily found and is clear-cut. We do not have to argue about the kinds of financial aid available for veterans because there is an authoritative answer to this question. A paper on this topic will inform, not persuade.

2. How can topic questions be refocused as arguable issues?

Although the questions above are not arguable as they are stated, we can refocus them as arguable issues. To do so, we simply ask, "About what aspects of this topic might people disagree?" Notice how refocusing can result in arguable issues:

Refocused: When a vaccine becomes available, should the United States require people to be vaccinated against COVID-19?

Arguable or not? The issue is now arguable. People will disagree on whether the vaccine should be required by law.

Refocused: Should veterans be given more financial aid than nonveterans?

Arguable or not? Now the issue is arguable. Some people will think the answer is yes, and others will disagree.

TRY IT!

The following topics are not arguable as stated. Refocus them in question form to make them appropriate for persuasive writing:

1. Some people think that because of the internet and digital texts, public libraries are no longer important.
2. Firearm training has been offered to teachers in many school districts across the nation.

CREDITS

Page 205. Rosen, David, "It's Time to Decriminalize Sex Work," *Progressive*, August 14, 2018. https://progressive.org/op-eds/its-time-to-decriminalize-sex-work-180814/. ©2017 The Progressive Inc. Used with permission.

Page 207. Sheehy, Kyle, "Standardized Test Requirement Should Be Removed from College Admissions." *The Daily Nebraskan*. February 20, 2019. http://www.dailynebraskan.com/opinion/sheehy-standardized-test-requirement-should-be-removed-from-college-admissions/article_adb65926-34a7-11e9-8225-d73f5b7f7ada.html. ©2019, The Daily Nebraskan. Used by permission.

PART 3 Research Strategies

10 Conducting Research

CHAPTER OBJECTIVES

You will learn to:
- Use an effective research process to keep sources organized.
- Use effective searching strategies when conducting research.
- Evaluate the quality and appropriateness of sources.
- Create an annotated bibliography.

Connect Adaptive Learning Assignment Consider assigning Connect's Adaptive Learning Assignments to support this chapter.

Teaching Resources See the Instructor's Manual (IM) for suggestions about how to teach this chapter, and consider assigning this chapter's test-bank quiz.

Many college and workplace writing tasks require research. To complete them, you need to be able to find high-quality sources and use them ethically. Any time you use sources, you should use a research process that helps you to stay organized and avoid plagiarism. In this chapter, we follow Tori Manning, a student who is writing a research paper on anorexia for a composition course, as she conducts research. As you observe Tori's research strategies, you will learn how to do research efficiently and effectively.

WARM-UP

A student is writing a research paper for an English class. His paper is due in two hours, and he has written most of it. But he's concerned about the works-cited page. He knows he has very little time to find all the information for the entries and assemble them. He is also concerned about accidentally plagiarizing and putting his grade in jeopardy. He copied and pasted from sources and did not always create in-text notes that give credit to the authors. What could this student have done to avoid this situation?

DEVELOPING AN EFFECTIVE RESEARCH PROCESS

Because researching is such a complex task, it is easy to become disorganized. In the Warm-Up, you were asked to think about the ways a student could have avoided the stressful situation in which he found himself. Obviously, he did not allow himself enough time to put together his works-cited page. But even if he had started earlier, the student would still face difficulties. He did not use a research and drafting method to make the bibliographic information he needed readily available. The problem with the student's lack of organization is not only

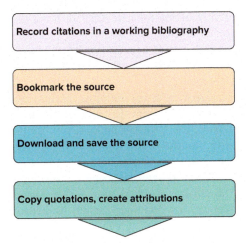

FIGURE 10.1 A method for handling each source.

the stress it creates but the real possibility that his works-cited page is incorrect or that he accidentally plagiarized from a source.

You can use many different methods to stay organized during the research process. The method that follows includes four simple steps that, if used consistently with each source, will enable you to keep track of your sources, quickly create works-cited pages, and avoid plagiarism (see Figure 10.1).

Recording Citations in a Working Bibliography

While you are finding sources, you need not take the time to read each source word for word. You should, however, read enough of the source (especially the abstract, if you are using an article from a database) to be reasonably sure the source applies to your specific topic and may be useful. Once you have found a source you want to keep, start by obtaining an MLA (or APA if you are using that style) citation for the source. If you are using online databases from a library, you often have the option to see a citation for the source (see Figure 10.2). Each database is different, but most include such a tool.

Once you have the citation, copy and paste it into your working bibliography, a file you keep on your laptop or other device. A **working bibliography** is a

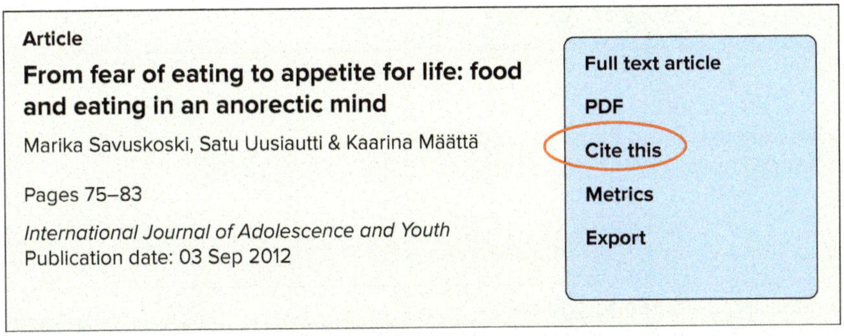

FIGURE 10.2 Viewing an article's citation in an online database.

Co-requisite Teaching Tip
Consider addressing the most challenging parts of finding good sources: using databases effectively, keeping track of sources and bibliographic information, and finding appropriate sources.

working bibliography: A list of citations for sources one may use in a research project.

Teaching Resources
See the IM for more information about individual databases and their citation tools.

collection of sources you are using or considering for use. Keep in mind that you will still need to check the accuracy of the citations generated by databases. When you copy and paste each new citation, use alphabetical order. When you create your final works-cited page, you can simply delete the sources you have not used. What remains is your works-cited page.

For sources that are not electronic, such as books or print journals and magazines, you can take photos of the pages that present the bibliographic information needed for a works-cited entry. Next, you have two options: you can use an online database or a library catalog to find the source online and search for a previously created citation, or you can simply create a citation yourself.

Take the time to record each citation in your working bibliography, even if you are not sure you will use the source. You usually have more time at this stage of the research process than at the final stage, so use that time carefully to prepare.

Bookmarking Sources

If the source is available electronically, use a bookmarking system for easy access to the source. Many libraries offer a system that allows you to save sources from multiple databases to a temporary file. Once you are finished researching, you can export the temporary file into a researching program such as RefWorks, EasyBib, and others (see Figure 10.3A). For a less technical method, simply create a file for your sources on your device, or send yourself an email with the pertinent information and link for each source you find, as shown in Figure 10.3B.

> **Teaching Suggestion**
> Online "free" citation generation sites have become increasingly commercialized. For best practices for using these sites and for alternative sites you can share with students, see the IM.
>
> **Teaching Suggestion**
> Helping students learn how to use an online referencing tool such as RefWorks may be worthwhile. These tools are readily available and easy to use. See the IM for more information.

A. Exporting a source to a researching program.

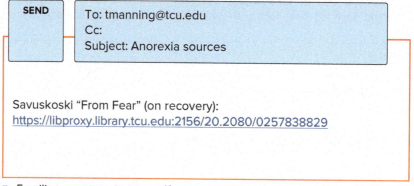

B. Emailing a source to yourself.

FIGURE 10.3 Two methods of bookmarking sources.

Downloading and Saving Sources

Information from websites and online databases can be downloaded easily and saved for future use. It is important, however, to be organized when saving files. Start by creating a folder for the paper or project, and then create subfolders for the topics you plan to cover in your paper and for which you will find research. Tori has predicted that she will need articles covering four aspects of anorexia, so she has created folders for each aspect, as Figure 10.4 shows. As Tori finds articles, she will save them in the appropriate folder. You can also save the files to a cloud-based file system, such as Dropbox, Google Drive, or Microsoft OneDrive.

Even sources you access in hard copy can be saved using a similar process. For instance, if you are examining a library book and find information you would like to use in your paper, take a picture of the book's title and copyright pages and any pages that you might use for research eliminate comma and save those pictures to the same project folder, selecting the appropriate subfolder. Tori's organization methods demonstrate how she used several of these suggestions to create her own, personalized process.

> **Tori, on staying organized:** "I'm the queen of 'cut and paste,' so I use that method as my primary organization system. I copy and paste the entire article into a Word document, and I include the bibliographic citation provided by the database. Then I save this doc with the writer's last name and the first three title words. I use Google Drive for everything so I can have easy access to all the articles I have found. One other thing I do is that when I use a source in my paper, I immediately copy and paste the bibliographic citation into my works-cited page."

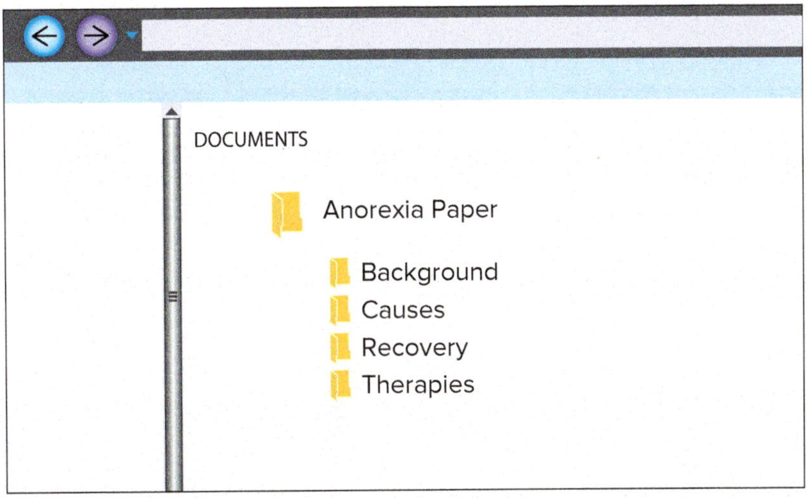

DOCUMENTS

- Anorexia Paper
  - Background
  - Causes
  - Recovery
  - Therapies

FIGURE 10.4 Creating folders for a research paper's subtopics.

Co-requisite Teaching Tip
Consider using the co-requisite section for hands-on research activities to support the skills in this chapter.

Teaching Suggestion
Consider using the assignment, "Creating Your Personal Cloud-Based College Organization System," available as a Word document.

Co-requisite Teaching Tip
Consider creating graded assignments for micro-tasks involved in the research process. See the IM for more information.

▶ **ACTIVITY 1 Using an Organized Research Process**

Decide where to store the sources you find and then create a project folder and topic subfolders for the sources you will need. Take a screenshot, and explain why you have chosen to organize your research in the way you have selected.

Copying Quotations and Creating Attributions

After you have found sources, read them and select the ones to use in your paper. Use these strategies to stay organized:

1. **Delete useless sources.** When you read a source and decide *not* to use it in your paper, delete it from your working bibliography. If you are reluctant to delete it because you may later want to use it, simply cross it out.

2. **Highlight useful material.** When you find a quotation you want to use or a part of the source to which you may want to refer when you draft your paper, highlight the quote or section. Make a note to remind yourself of how you might use the highlighted section. Tori has annotated a potential quotation as a reminder to herself later:

Within the net of anxiety

Use to show anxiety connection

As a human being is starving, moods change dramatically. One easily develops an inner state of anxiety. The participants of this research talked about a bad feeling that resembled mental malaise similar to anxiety and depression. Quite often, anxiety starts from the feeling of shame toward one's body and from the fear of food (Michel & Willard, 2003). Over one-half of the participants in this research reported some sort of depression-like state and malaise during their illness.

---

3. **Use in-text citations and attributions.** Finally, when you draft your paper, take the time to create the parenthetical in-text reference and attribute the quotation or idea to the writer. Doing so will help you avoid plagiarism and avoid confusion about the sections of your paper that are quoted. Notice how Tori gives credit to the author in this draft of one of her paragraphs.

A common cause of anorexia is anxiety. However, becoming anorexic actually causes anxiety to increase. In a study by Marika Savuskoski and her colleagues, interviews with women who have overcome anorexia help to

> explain how anxiety increases: "As a human being is starving, moods change dramatically. One easily develops an inner state of anxiety. The participants of this research talked about a bad feeling that resembled mental malaise similar to anxiety and depression" (78).

Imagine how using this four-step organization method would have improved the experience of the student in the Warm-Up activity. Using an effective process to stay organized and avoid plagiarism will help you focus on writing a good paper.

SELECTING SOURCE TYPES

From scholarly articles to music lyrics, a source is any work you consult for research purposes. The types of sources you use for a project depend on the project's purpose, the message, and the audience. Once you have analyzed the rhetorical situation of your project, you can select from a wide variety of sources.

Before you start searching for specific sources, figure out what kinds of sources will be most effective for your writing purpose. By the time you begin research, you will have selected a topic. To make sure you find the best research for the topic, create a topic question. A topic question is the central question you hope your research will answer. For example, Tori hopes her research will answer this question: *What are the most effective treatments for anorexia nervosa?* By keeping that question in mind, she can focus her research on sources that are relevant.

Teaching Suggestion
Give students a question to research in class using their smartphones. Have students make a list of the different types of sources they encounter so that they can begin to classify sources.

> **Tori, on selecting source types:** "My interest in anorexia came from reading an article in *Cosmopolitan*. It was written by a woman who had struggled with anorexia, and I originally wanted to use that article. But I wasn't really sure how I would focus my paper. By writing a research question, I realized that I was really interested in how anorexia is treated. I realized that there were much better articles I could use than the one I had initially read, so I focused on finding articles written by experts."

Teaching Resources
Consider using the PowerPoint "Low Quality Research vs. High Quality Research."

Becoming familiar with three types of research—primary sources, secondary sources, and field research—will help you choose the sources that are most appropriate for your purpose.

Primary Sources

A **primary source** consists of first-hand information you use in your paper. If you are analyzing or using a work of literature, a law, a court document, an argument, a film, song lyrics, a website, an interview, or some other first-hand source, you must list it in your works-cited page.

If you conduct your own field research, a topic we cover later in this chapter, that research is considered a primary source as well.

primary source: A source consisting of first-hand information or direct evidence; for example, a work of art, the text of a law, or an eyewitness report.

Secondary Sources

secondary source: A source consisting of second-hand information about a topic or a primary source; for example, a journal article.

A **secondary source** consists of information about your topic or about your primary source. For example, if you are analyzing a novel in your paper, the novel is the primary source. You may consult articles that others have written about the novel. These are secondary sources.

A wide variety of secondary sources is available: books, articles, information from journals, magazines, encyclopedias, and so on. Because so much information is available online, writers must carefully choose sources. Some sources attempt to present objective information or well-researched opinions. These sources rely on information that has been researched and well documented. For example, peer-reviewed journals present the best research in an academic field. On the other end of the spectrum are sources such as commercial websites. A vitamin manufacturer's website will extol the virtues of the vitamins they produce. There will probably be no dissenting opinions offered about the vitamins they sell. In general, objective sources are preferable to subjective sources. Table 10.1 presents a variety of secondary sources and some of the special concerns to keep in mind when selecting that type of source to use for your project.

TABLE 10.1 Types of Secondary Sources

Source Type	Examples	Special Concerns
Peer-reviewed journals	*Journal of Global Economics* *Health Systems and Policy Research*	The articles in peer-reviewed journals are generally trustworthy because of the process used in selecting the articles for publication. Using an anonymous process, scholars submit high quality articles for consideration. A panel of experts in the field examine the articles and select the best ones for publication. Peer-reviewed articles are considered credible and are among the highest quality sources you can use as research.
Academic books	*Poe* by James M. Hutchisson, University of Mississippi Press	Books published by scholars and researchers are generally good sources of information. While such books are not all peer-reviewed, academic publishers usually have high standards for the quality of the books they select to publish.
Statistical information (from government and organizational sites or periodicals)	Centers for Disease Control and Prevention (www.cdc.gov) *Monthly Bulletin of Statistics* (published by the United Nations)	Several websites and publications offer reliable statistical information that can be used as secondary sources.
Ebooks (available to the public)	Google Books Amazon Lulu	Most ebooks are simply electronic versions of books that are found in hard copy. Academic books may be published as ebooks, for example. Other ebooks, however, may simply be self-published manuscripts. While some self-published books are high quality, others are not.

Source Type	Examples	Special Concerns
National newspapers	*The New York Times* *The Wall Street Journal*	National newspapers generally enforce high-quality standards and carefully research the articles they publish.
Local newspapers	*The Daily Astorian* (Astoria, Oregon)	Local newspapers also try to publish high-quality material, but there is wide variation in the quality of the articles.
Trade publications	*Automotive Industries* *Adweek*	Journals, books, and newsletters that are geared toward a niche audience—such as auto mechanics, realtors, or investors—can present helpful information but are written for audiences that are familiar with their field.
General interest magazines	*Reader's Digest* *National Geographic*	Magazines written for the general public vary widely in their quality. Some, such as *Harper's* and *The Atlantic*, are well-respected for their selectiveness. Other magazines, however, publish lower-quality content.
Academic websites	The Center for Responsible Business at Berkeley	Websites associated with or sponsored by a university often provide higher-quality materials than websites from .com and .org domains.
Government websites	usa.gov maine.gov	State and federal government websites often have URLs that end in .gov. These sites attempt to present reliable information.
Organizational/ institutional websites	The Brookings Institute The American Cancer Society	The websites for nonprofit organizations and research institutions often provide information that can be helpful for a variety of research purposes. Be aware that nonprofits may be biased.
Corporate and industry websites	Peanut Growers Association National Rifle Association	Corporate and industry websites seek to promote the companies or industries they represent. As such, the information on these sites is often biased in favor of the industry or product.
Blogs and personal websites	Lifehacker.com JenMackBC's Blog	The information published in blogs and on personal websites varies greatly in quality.

Field Research

Field research consists of your own surveys, interviews, observations, and studies. Usually field research is focused on human behavior and responses. For instance, to understand attitudes about anorexia, a field researcher may create a survey and distribute it, collate the results, and use the findings as a source. Before you embark on field research, consult a field research guide to understand the best way to collect and use data.

field research: Data collection through first-hand observation, surveys, interviews, and so on.

Rhetorical Toolbox 10.1 presents some helpful questions to determine the kinds of sources you will need for your research project.

> **RHETORICAL TOOLBOX 10.1**
>
> ## Selecting Source Types by Analyzing the Rhetorical Situation
>
> 1. **Research question.** What question will your research answer?
> 2. **Primary sources.** Will your research require the use of any primary sources? If so, what are they and how will you obtain them?
> 3. **Field research.** To answer your research question, will field research be necessary or helpful? If so, how will you conduct field research?
> 4. **Secondary sources.** What kind of secondary sources—such as peer-reviewed articles, data or statistics, books, and so on—will you need to answer your research question?
> 5. **Audience.** What kind of support will be the most valuable for your particular audience? For example, in a paper on recovering from anorexia written for the general public, first-hand accounts from people who overcame anorexia might be more valuable than dense, scientific papers about the disease and strategies for recovery. If you are writing for medical professionals, scientific sources will be more highly regarded than personal stories.
> 6. **Argument and counterargument.** If you are writing an argument, will you need to find sources that present the counterargument? What kind of sources will you need to fairly present the counterargument?

▶ **ACTIVITY 2 Selecting Appropriate Source Types**

For each scenario that follows, identify a type of source that would be appropriate. Explain your answers.

A. Jen is writing a paper for a nursing class. In her paper, she will present the most commonly used cardiac medications.

B. Kaysha is writing a paper for her English class in which she discusses the "Boomer versus Millennial" debate. She will read her paper to the class, and her classmates include both Boomers and Millennials.

C. Jonathan is writing an argument that answers this question: "Is it ever right to euthanize a pet?" He plans to publish his argument in the local newspaper.

USING EFFECTIVE SEARCH STRATEGIES

Once you have determined the kinds of sources you will use, it is time to find specific potential sources. When you search for sources, you will also need to evaluate them to determine whether they are credible and useful. Although

Teaching Resource
See the PowerPoint "Finding Good Sources" to reinforce the ideas.

searching skills and evaluating skills are often used at the same time, we will first focus on searching and then discuss evaluating the sources you find.

Effective searches do not necessarily require a lot of time (although they may!). Rather, effective searches are a result of using sound search techniques. Follow the tips below to find exactly the sources you need.

Conducting Library Database Searches

The library at your college or university is usually the best place to search for information. Librarians and instructors have carefully curated the best books, periodicals, and databases for students. Beyond the library's collections, the best resource is a reference librarian. Reference librarians can help you with research strategies that will make quick work of finding the best sources.

Using your library's online databases is one of the most effective ways to find sources. Your library's online catalog is a database; it lists the books and periodicals available in hard copy (and often in digital format) from your library. Other popular databases, such as EBSCOhost, WilsonWeb, and ProQuest, provide full-text (access to the entire article) copies of sources.

Whether you are searching for books, articles, or other information, you will need to use effective database searching strategies. While all databases vary to some degree in the way they handle searches, using the following searching tips will help you find the information you need.

Teaching Suggestion
Consider using a team-based collaborative, competitive activity to help students learn to find good sources. See the IM for more information.

1. **Use the best database for your purposes.** Libraries offer hundreds of online databases. The first step to finding sources is to select the database that is the most likely to contain the kind of information for which you are searching. For example, by clicking on the alphabetized list of databases from her community college library, Tori can see that eight databases are available. The descriptions that follow each database will help her to determine which ones are most appropriate for her search.

    - **Academic Search Complete (EBSCO).** A comprehensive scholarly, multi-disciplinary full-text database, with more than 5,300 full-text periodicals, including 4,400 peer-reviewed journals, and conference proceedings.
    - **Acceda Noticias.** Acceda Noticias is a NewsBank collection providing online access to the complete full-text of more than fifty Spanish-language newspapers, newswires, magazines, and transcripts from major U.S. cities and Spanish-speaking countries.
    - **Agricola.** Agricola contains the records of the National Agricultural Library through the U.S. Department of Agriculture. This database has over 5 million records related to agricultural topics.
    - **AHFS Consumer Medication Information.** AHFS Consumer Medication Information is a trusted source and recognized standard for patient drug information, available in both English and Spanish.
    - **Alt HealthWatch.** Alt HealthWatch provides in-depth coverage across the full spectrum of subject areas covered by complementary and alternative medicine dating back to 1990.

- **America's News Magazines.** This NewsBank collection provides over thirty national magazines and newspapers that focus on business, politics, and science and technology.
- **ArticleFirst.** ArticleFirst is a citation database from OCLC and is accessed on the FirstSearch interface. The index contains bibliographic citations of more than 13,000 journals in science, technology, medicine, social science, business, the humanities, and popular culture.

If your library has a search bar that allows you to search several databases at once, start with that search bar. You may find that you have to narrow your search to specific databases, however, to find the best information.

2. **Experiment with keywords, synonyms, and phrases.** The most common reason for not finding good sources is failure to experiment with search terms. For example, if you are writing a paper on the dangers of concussions for youth who play football, you can use a variety of search terms. The most obvious term is "concussions," but a search for only that term results in 11,972 results, far too many to examine. By adding search terms, you can narrow those results significantly. The search shown in Figure 10.5 resulted in twenty-six records. Additionally, if one term does not produce the right results, find a synonym and use it instead. For example, to find research about working from home, you can use a variety of synonyms, each resulting in differing numbers of results:

   "working from home" = 9,962 results

   "telecommuting" = 6,840 results

   "remote working" = 662 results

Boolean operators: Words that limit or expand the scope of a keyword search; primarily AND, OR, and NOT.

3. **Use Boolean operators.** *Boolean operators* are words that help you to limit or expand the scope of a search. The most common are AND, OR, and NOT.
   - Using AND to connect two terms means that the results of the search must contain both terms.

     Example: *concussion AND football* = sources that contain both keywords
   - Using OR to connect two terms enables you to find sources with either keyword or with both keywords.

     Example: *planes OR airplanes* = sources that contain either or both words

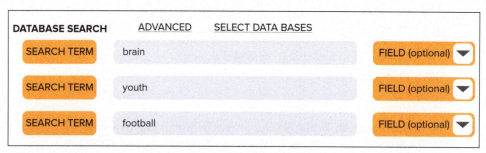

FIGURE 10.5 Narrowing a keyword search for "concussions."

- Using NOT excludes results that contain the prohibited word.

  Example: *planes NOT airplanes* = sources that contain "planes" but not "airplanes"

4. **Use search filters effectively.** Most databases have an advanced search tool, and in this tool, filters are available to help you narrow the results. Options for filtering differ for each database, but some of the most common options for filtering include these:
   - Limit results by document format (full text, pdf, html).
   - Limit results by document type (review, scholarly article, pamphlet, conference proceeding, etc.).
   - Limit results by publication type (peer-reviewed journal, magazine, newspaper, book, etc.).
   - Limit results by publication (a list of publications follows from which you can select).
   - Limit results by publication date.

> **Tori, on searching effectively**: "I had a really hard time searching at first because I didn't know enough to use the right keywords. I was trying to find all the treatment methods for anorexia, and I kept finding articles about particular treatment methods. I finally found an encyclopedia article that listed the various treatments. I could then use the names of those treatments as keywords, and that's when my research really got productive."

▶ **ACTIVITY 3 Using Keywords Effectively**

Imagine you are working on a research project to answer this question: *How can you tell if a charity is legitimate?* What keywords would you use in a search? Next, go to a database and use those keywords. How many results did you get? Were any of the results appropriate? How might you narrow your search by using additional (or different) keywords?

Teaching Suggestion
Have students do this activity in class by using their phones. Consider making this a group activity. Discuss the importance of varying keywords when the search results are not appropriate or adequate.

Searching for Statistics and Factual Information

Some institutions have as their missions the collection of data, and some of their databases are probably available in your library's database collection. Others can be found on the internet. Table 10.2 summarizes database sources that generally offer reliable statistical and factual information.

Finding Reliable Sources on the Internet

While your college library's reference librarian and database tools are often all you need to find high-quality sources, sometimes using the internet also yields quality sources. For example, many of the statistical databases in Table 10.2 are on the internet. However, because of the vast number of sources on the internet, special care must be taken to make sure the sources you find are high quality. Internet sites may offer intriguing information, but that information is only useful if it is credible.

TABLE 10.2 Databases of Statistics and Factual Information

Database Type	Examples
Federal data	**Data.gov.** This comprehensive database offers users data from a wide variety of governmental sources. The graphic that follows presents some of the types of data provided by the Data.gov website. *Categories (U.S. General Services Administration): Agriculture, Climate, Consumer, Ecosystems, Education, Energy, Finance, Health, Local Government, Manufacturing, Maritime, Ocean, Public Safety, Science & Research.* **The U.S. Census Bureau.** Provides statistical data about demographics and the nation's economy. **Statistical Abstract of the United States.** Social, political, and economic statistics related to the United States.
Crime	**Bureau of Justice Statistics.** Provides data about crime in the United States. **Uniform Crime Reports (FBI).** Provides statistics on crime and is maintained by the FBI.
Education	**Digest of Education Statistics.** A database that provides statistics about the state of education in the United States. **National Center for Education Statistics.** A database for educated-related data.
Facts and polling	**American Fact Finder.** A database of facts regarding geography, economics, living conditions, and population. **Gallup Poll.** A research organization's database on a variety of cultural issues. **Pew Research Center.** A nonpartisan research organization providing data on cultural issues and changes.
Health	**CDC Wonder.** A health database created and maintained by the Centers for Disease Control and Prevention. **National Center for Health Statistics.** Another CDC-maintained database that provides statistics regarding health.
Population	**City-Data.** A database presenting statistical information for U.S. cities. **U.S. Census Bureau.** A federal database offering statistical information about demographics.

> **Teaching Suggestion**
> Have students add to the list of "sources and sites not to use" by doing research in class and discussing their findings.

In addition to using the evaluation methods that we discuss in the next section, you will find more reliable information on the internet by knowing the kinds of sites to avoid.

- Avoid using sites where anyone can post an answer to a question, such as Quora, Yahoo Answers, and Reddit.
- Avoid using .com sites; opt instead for .edu or .gov sites.

Additional websites should be used with caution:

- Use caution when you choose .org websites that are highly biased and do not present both sides of an issue. For example, the website of **PETA** (People for the Ethical Treatment of Animals) presents information to support the viewpoint that animal testing should never be conducted. Using this site is fine—as long as you realize you are getting only one perspective on the issue.

- Use caution when selecting personal websites or social media to use as sources. For example, some writers, politicians, artists, and organizations and others communicate via social media, and you may wish to quote from these sources. On the other hand, a personal website or a friend's tweet may not be as authoritative or credible as a source should be. Use your judgment.

EVALUATING SOURCES

A crucial step in selecting research is evaluating a source for its credibility and appropriateness. Using a source that is not credible is worse than using no source at all because it shows a lack of care, or knowledge, on the part of the writer. Evaluating a source requires two activities: internal evaluation and external evaluation. Internal evaluation means looking inside the source to judge its quality. External evaluation means doing research outside the source to find information that will help you justify the quality of the publication, the author, and so on. For example, to judge the quality of a website, you would need to look at the elements on the site's homepage, but you would also need to open a new tab and do some research about the source itself to learn about its reputation, its authors' reputations, and so on. The evaluative activities that follow will require both internal and external evaluation.

Examining Authors

One way to assess the credibility of a source is to evaluate the author. What makes the author believable? Is he or she an expert in the field? If the author is a journalist, has the journalist cited experts on the topic? Judging whether the author is knowledgeable enough to speak authoritatively on the topic will help you to evaluate the quality of the source. Even if a source includes an author's biography, it is wise to do a search for the author's name. The information you find will either confirm or call into question the impression presented by the biography.

While analyzing the author is important in evaluating any source, doing so is especially important when you are evaluating a website. Reputable websites go to some trouble to be transparent about who runs them and who writes for them. If you cannot find information about the source of the information on a website, be wary about using it for research. If you learn only that an article on a site is authored by Millard Wentworth, for example, you have not really learned anything (unless the name Millard Wentworth is meaningful to you!). If author

Teaching Suggestion Consider presenting the evaluative methods discussed in "Lateral Reading and the Nature of Expertise: Reading Less and Learning More When Evaluating Digital Information." At the time of writing, this paper by Sam Wineburg and Sarah McGrew has not yet been published but will appear in Teachers College Record. A pre-publication version is available now at https://purl.stanford.edu/yk133ht8603.

biographies are provided, you have more information and can rank the site a bit higher in terms of credibility. To determine more about a site's author or sponsoring organization, conduct an external search for information about them.

Examining Audiences

Examining the potential audience for a source adds to your understanding and helps you detect biases. Consider an article about diabetes that appears in a journal for doctors. The writer has made certain assumptions about the medical knowledge of the audience. When you read the article, you may need to consult dictionaries or other sources to understand it. You will see later that readability is another factor to consider when selecting sources. If a source is so technical or difficult that it is hard to understand, the source will be of little use to you. Find sources that are written for a general audience rather than an audience of experts.

Examining Date and Historical Context

Another aspect of the source to consider is when it was published. If the source is not current, consider its historical context. Suppose you are reading an article about the oil industry that was written in 1976. If you know that the United States experienced an energy crisis in the mid-1970s, you will better understand the issues discussed in the article. If you read a 2006 article about hurricane preparedness, you will have more insight into the article by realizing that Hurricane Katrina—one of the most deadly hurricanes to hit the United States—occurred in 2005. However, unless a source is important or ground-breaking in its field (for example, a classic work on psychology by Sigmund Freud) or your topic is historical, use sources written within the last five years.

Examining Bias and Credibility

A source is biased if it advocates or promotes a particular viewpoint or opinion on an issue. For example, suppose you want to determine whether high-fructose corn syrup is good for you. If you look at the website of a company that produces high-fructose corn syrup, you would expect to find information that is biased in favor of the product and the many ways it improves foods and beverages. Likewise, it is unlikely that you would find arguments against the product. Therefore, you would be unwise to base your determination solely on the evidence of that biased website.

Note that having a bias does not necessarily mean a source is disreputable; it simply tells you the source is not neutral. At times, using biased sources might suit your writing task. For instance, in a persuasive essay, you might want to present the viewpoint of the corn syrup company as well as the viewpoint of those opposed to the wide use of corn syrup as a sweetener (a viewpoint that is also biased). Comparing these two biased sources may be helpful in such a paper. Often, however, writers are best served by looking for sources that are neutral and do not have an interest in promoting a particular point of view.

Detecting Bias. Sources may come from general magazines, scholarly journals, websites, and a variety of other publications. Knowing a source's origin will help you predict potential biases. Some journals and magazines directly reveal their biases. For example, the name of *The American Conservative* gives you a clue about the magazine's political orientation. If you go to the magazine's website, you will find a definitive statement of the magazine's biases. The magazine says, "To solve the country's seemingly intractable—and, in the long-term, lethal—strategic, economic, and socio-cultural problems requires a rediscovery of traditional conservatism. That's the mission of *The American Conservative*." Similarly, if you do an internet search on book publishers, you also may be able to detect biases. Ignatius Press, for example, describes itself as the "primary publisher in U.S. of Pope Benedict XVI's books." We can expect books from Ignatius Press to have a Roman Catholic bias.

Determining the bias of websites can be a bit trickier. One way to do so is to examine its domain name—the last part of its Web address. Common domain names are .com, .gov, .edu, and .org. If a website address ends in .com, it is a commercial website, and you should suspect it will contain biases in favor of the product or service it is selling. Websites whose domain is .org (meaning that it represents an organization) may be less biased, but .org sites often promote ideas. For example, PETA has this on its home page (www.peta.org): "Animals are not ours to eat, wear, experiment on, use for entertainment, or abuse in any other way." The bias of PETA's organizational website is clearly stated.

Websites sponsored by federal, state, and local governments have the domain .gov. Much of the information on government websites—in particular, statistical information—is simply factual. However, the website of a particular agency or department (for example, the United States Environmental Protection Agency) may advocate for activities such as conservation and more regulation, which other organizations (for example, energy companies) do not favor. Additionally, individual senators and congressional representatives have websites that end in .gov. These sites are biased because they present the senator's or representative's point of view.

Websites that end in .edu are educational—that is, associated with colleges, universities, and other recognized educational institutions. While these sites may be less biased than .com sites, it is important to remember that professors and even students often have personal websites sponsored by their institution. Those personal websites often present points of view about issues. Thus, these sites also present bias.

Always conduct an external evaluation of a website by opening another tab and learning more about the site. In the end you, as a consumer of information, must always be the one to make a careful choice about the bias of a particular website or source. Bias is not necessarily a bad thing, but as a researcher, you must know whether your sources are biased or take a neutral point of view.

Evaluating Credibility. One way to determine the credibility of a source—its trustworthiness—is by examining its origin. For example, we expect articles in well-established newspapers such as *The New York Times* and *The Wall Street Journal* to be written ethically and credibly. Similarly, we expect articles that appear in peer-reviewed journals (journals that have a stringent process for selecting what they publish) to be credible. On the other end of the credibility spectrum are tabloids that present celebrity gossip and news items that are often unverifiable—ranging from accounts of alien landings to reports of six-headed babies. You can often do an internet search of a source's name to learn more about its reputation and credibility.

To assess a source that comes from a website, you must assess the website itself. First, a credible website is well edited and does not contain errors in spelling or grammar. Second, a credible website will probably not carry advertising. There is one exception to this rule. Newspapers have historically depended on advertisements as a source of income. The presence of advertisements in newspapers is not an indication of bias. Some credible websites do allow advertising, but unless you are looking at reputable newspapers online, look for sites that do not permit advertising. Advertising is a sign that the owner of the website wants to make money by luring people to the site; thus, the owner may decide to post the content that draws in the most people, which may not necessarily be the most authoritative content on a subject. Finally, a credible website offers support for the information it posts. For example, some websites provide bibliographies to show the sources the authors consulted, a practice that allows readers to evaluate the credibility of the information.

Evaluating the credibility of websites can be challenging. Examine the website in Figure 10.6 and notice the factors that should trigger caution. Clearly, the website is biased, but its bias is not the problem. The real question is whether we should regard its writer, Kenneth Dislais, as a credible or qualified source for

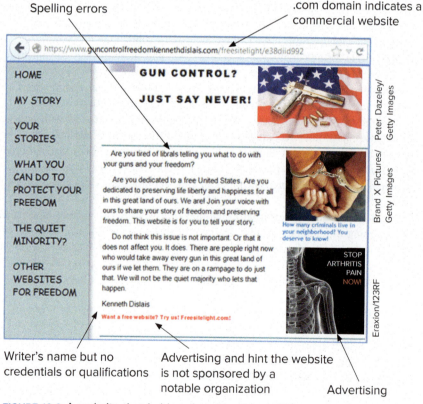

FIGURE 10.6 A website that is biased and is *not* credible.

FIGURE 10.7 A website that is biased but is also credible.

information about gun control. He offers no biographical information about himself; in fact, we have no information about the sponsors of the website either. The only information we have is that it was created by means of a free website generator. Why should we believe that Kenneth Dislais knows anything about the issue of gun control? We do know one thing: he did not use a spell-checker to proofread his website! Further, the site includes advertisements that are not related to the content. In summary, when you encounter sites like this one, question the value of the information. Can you verify that it is anything other than a mouthpiece for one unknown individual? If not, the site lacks credibility and is a poor source.

Now, take a look at another website for an organization that opposes gun control (see Figure 10.7). Notice that this site, sponsored by Citizens for Responsible Gun Ownership, is biased but credible. The website goes to some trouble to let viewers know who sponsors it, where the organization is located (its physical address), and the group's philosophy and mission. Also, the clear identification of the site's founder and president and easy availability of information about its supporters (board members) lend it credibility. Moreover, the site provides ways for the sponsoring organization to be contacted, which suggests that the group is well-established. While we know that the site is biased because it exists to promote the rights of gun owners, we can have some confidence that it may ultimately prove to have trustworthy information.

Finally, let's examine a website that is both credible and unbiased regarding the issue of gun ownership (see Figure 10.8). Notice the characteristics of this objectively oriented site. Its name suggests that we will learn about both sides of the issues. The site confirms this idea by providing a neutral introduction to the issue of carrying concealed guns and then offering both sides of the argument. Also, the website enhances its credibility by giving resources and bibliographies. We can see that Yes-or-No.org is a nonprofit educational organization that

FIGURE 10.8 A website that attempts to avoid bias and is credible.

depends on donations and is not funded by people on a particular side of an issue. These facts help establish the site as both credible and objective.

To facilitate the task of evaluating sources, use Rhetorical Toolbox 10.2.

> **RHETORICAL TOOLBOX 10.2**
> ## Questions for Evaluating Sources
>
> 1. **Author.** Does the author have the authority to write on the subject? What credentials make the author qualified to speak on the topic? Will readers think the author of the source is believable?
> 2. **Website.** If you are evaluating a website, is an author provided? Who sponsors the website? When you do some research about the website, what do you learn? Given what you learn about the website's author or sponsor, is the website likely to be biased?
> 3. **Audience.** Who is the intended audience for the source? Given the intended audience, might the writers be biased? Given the intended audience, is the source likely to contain jargon or highly technical information that is difficult for the average reader to understand?
> 4. **Date.** What is the date of the source? Given the publication date, is the source still relevant to the topic?
> 5. **Purpose.** What is the writer's purpose? Is the purpose to persuade, to inform, to analyze, to evaluate, to entertain or reflect? Is the source written with a bias or is it intended to be an objective presentation of information? If the source is written with a bias, how credible is the source for your research purposes?
> 6. **Red flags.** Does the source contain any "red flags" (such as advertising, spelling errors, incomplete information, lack of sources or references) that suggest it is not credible?

▶ **ACTIVITY 4** **Evaluating the Credibility of a Website**
Using internal and external evaluation, find a website you consider credible and a website that you believe is not credible. Explain your reasoning for your evaluation of each site.

Teaching Suggestion
See the IM for links to websites you can have students analyze for credibility in class.

CREATING AN ANNOTATED BIBLIOGRAPHY

Once you have selected sources, your instructor may ask you to create an annotated bibliography. There are two types of annotated bibliographies: descriptive and critical.

Descriptive Annotated Bibliography

The purpose of a descriptive annotated bibliography is simply to provide a brief summary of the sources you are using in your research. The descriptive annotated bibliography includes an entry for each source that contains several elements as shown in this excerpt from Tori's annotated bibliography.

Teaching Suggestion
Consider discussing the purpose of abstracts and how they should be used in the research process.

Tori's Descriptive Annotated Bibliography Entry

Conti, Janet E. "Recovering Identity from Anorexia Nervosa: Women's Constructions of Their Experiences of Recovery from Anorexia Nervosa Over 10 Years." *Journal of Constructivist Psychology*, vol. 31, no. 1, Jan. 2018, pp. 72–94.

Citation in MLA style

What does it mean to recover from anorexia? This is the question posed by Janet Conti, and she presents an answer to this question by interviewing and exploring the recovery journeys of 21 Australian women. Conti suggests that the traditional notion that recovery means returning to a pre-illness state of mind is not a helpful one. Instead, the women she interviewed suggested that thinking about recovery as a journey to a greater understanding of one's self is a better way to define recovery and facilitate it. Conti suggests that by rethinking recovery as a journey of self-discovery that honors the struggles women have been through, treatments for anorexia may change and be more effective.

Presentation of the research focus.

Presentation of the writer's main idea.

Recommendations made in the article.

Critical Annotated Bibliography

A critical annotated bibliography goes a step beyond describing to critique the sources being discussed. This critique may focus on any relevant aspect of the article. For instance, if the purpose of the critical annotated bibliography is to identify the highest quality research on a topic, the critique portion of the entry may address any failures or inadequacies in the source. The example that follows—this time presented in APA format—shows how a critical annotated bibliography includes both a summary and criticism. It is based on Tori's descriptive entry, above.

Citation in APA style

Conti, J. E. (2018). Recovering identity from anorexia nervosa: Women's constructions of their experiences of recovery from anorexia nervosa over 10 years. *Journal of Constructivist Psychology, 31*(1), 72-94.

Presentation of the research focus

What does it mean to recover from anorexia? This is the question posed by Janet Conti, and she presents an answer to this question by interviewing and exploring the recovery journeys of 21 Australian women.

Presentation of the writer's main idea

Conti suggests that the traditional notion that recovery means returning to a pre-illness state of mind is not a helpful one. Instead, the women she interviewed suggested that thinking about recovery as a journey to a greater understanding of one self is a better way to define recovery and facilitate it.

Recommendations made in the article

Conti suggests that by rethinking recovery as a journey of self-discovery that honors the struggles women have been through, treatments for anorexia may change and be more effective.

Critique

Unfortunately, Conti's work with these women does not result in any concrete suggestions for improving the treatment of anorexia. While Conti seems to suggest her research has important implications, she does not explain what these implications are. Her research, on the other hand, is helpful in that it presents actual interviews with patients who have recovered from anorexia.

CHAPTER PROJECT Creating an Annotated Bibliography

For each source in your annotated bibliography, create a bibliographic entry that presents the source in the style—MLA or APA—required by your instructor. Follow each source with a paragraph similar to the ones above. Use these guidelines to compose your annotated bibliography:

A. Put your bibliography in alphabetical order.
B. Do not copy and paste a source's abstract. The summary you write should be in your own words.

C. Do not quote from the source.

D. In the summary, present the main idea in the source, the support for that idea, and any other information readers may need to understand the source's focus and topic.

E. If the annotated bibliography is critical in nature, include your own criticism of the source.

F. Use the appropriate style manual's guidelines to format your paper.

Reflecting to Develop a Writer's Mindset

Reflect on the following statement: *Finding the best sources for your purpose requires rhetorical thinking.* What does the statement mean? How can you use rhetorical thinking in the research process? In previous research projects, have you used rhetorical thinking? Explain your answer.

FAQ TIME MANAGEMENT FOR RESEARCH PROJECTS

A research project cannot be completed in a day: it requires careful planning and sound time-management skills. If you struggle with time management, for any reason, use these tips to manage your research project and stay on track.

1. **What are the tasks involved in doing a research paper?**

    A research paper usually consists of these tasks, arranged in phases:

    Step 1. Understanding the project (asking questions, getting a clear idea of the assignment, planning time, making a research plan)

    Step 2. Conducting research (finding sources, doing field research)

    Step 3. Analyzing research (reading and annotating sources, creating a working bibliography, returning to Step 2 when you need more sources)

    Step 4. Writing a draft (using your ideas and research to compose a draft)

    Step 5. Revising the draft (rethinking ideas, organization, and the like; this step may include going back to Step 2)

    Step 6. Producing a final draft by editing and formatting (creating a final document in the documentation style specified by your professor, free from grammatical errors)

2. **How can you estimate the time needed for each step?**

    The best way to estimate is to actually start doing the task. For instance, to estimate how long it will take you to find sources, set a timer for twenty minutes. See how much you can accomplish in twenty minutes.

You can then use that information to estimate how much time you will need to find sources. Do this for each step.

3. **How can you set up a task calendar?**

   Working backward from the due date, and keeping your time estimates in mind, create a task calendar. Include a few extra days at the end of your calendar for unexpected delays, obstacles, and events that might occur during the project. For example, if your due date is May 1, and if you have three weeks before the due date, a task calendar may look like the one shown in Figure 10.9. Keep in mind that the calendar may need to be revised as you go along.

5	6	7	8	9	2 Hrs Step 1: Analyze Task 10	11
12	2 Hrs Step 2: Conduct Research 13	2 Hrs 14	3 Hrs Step 3: Analyze Sources 15	3 Hrs Step 3: Analyze Sources 16	3 Hrs Step 3: Analyze Sources 17	18
19	2 Hrs Step 4: Write a Draft 20	2 Hrs Step 4: Write a Draft 21	2 Hrs Step 4: Write a Draft 22	2 Hrs Step 5: Revise 23	2 Hrs Step 5: Revise 24	25
26	2 Hrs Step 6: Edit and Format 27	2 Hrs Step 6: Edit and Format 28	29	30	Submit Paper May 1	2

FIGURE 10.9 Planning tasks for a research paper.

4. **What else can you do to stay on track?**

   Having someone to help you monitor your progress can be very effective. You can work with a classmate or friend to plan priorities, tasks, and calendars, and keep each other on track. Working together in the library or even sending periodic updates to each other can also help keep you on track.

   TRY IT!

   Imagine the date is March 1, and you have been given a research paper assignment. You must use at least ten sources in your paper, and most of them must come from library databases. Your paper is due on April 1. Make a calendar that shows a time management plan for this project.

11 Using Sources Accurately and Ethically

CHAPTER OBJECTIVES

You will learn to:
- Use sources rhetorically as support for your own ideas.
- Use an effective method for working with sources.
- Quote, paraphrase, and summarize sources appropriately and grammatically.
- Use sources properly to avoid plagiarism.

Many, if not most, college and workplace writing assignments involve the use of source materials. How can you use sources rhetorically? When should you refer to sources in your writing? How can you connect a source's ideas with your own ideas? How can you integrate quotations and references smoothly? What must you do to avoid plagiarizing? These are a few of the questions we consider in this chapter to help you use sources accurately, ethically, and effectively.

WARM-UP

Johanna worked diligently on her research paper. She used many sources, made sure they were credible, and wrote a paper that was well organized, grammatically correct, and properly formatted. She carefully avoided plagiarism. Each paragraph of her paper summarized what a different source said about the topic. Her paper included at least two quotations for each body paragraph. Johanna thought that by summarizing and quoting each source, she would effectively support her thesis statement. However, the grade she received was a C. What could Johanna have done differently to improve her paper's effectiveness?

USING SOURCES FROM A WRITER'S MINDSET

Most research-based writing projects use sources to support the writer's points. In other words, the writer's voice is the dominant voice in the paper, and research exists to support that voice. In the Warm-Up, Johanna worked hard but received

Connect Adaptive Learning Assignment
Consider assigning Connect's Adaptive Learning Assignments to support this chapter.

Teaching Resources
See the Instructor's Manual (IM) for suggestions about how to teach this chapter, and consider assigning this chapter's test-bank quiz.

a disappointing grade on a research-based essay. You may have already figured out that she did everything well except for one thing: she did not use her sources properly. By summarizing and quoting from each source in individual paragraphs, Johanna's paper resembled a list of source materials rather than a unified and coherent essay. Johanna's voice was lost in her paper. As a writer, your voice should be the primary voice in the paper. Sources are used to bolster the writer's voice, not replace it. You can avoid the mistake Johanna made by using sources effectively—skills we discuss in this chapter.

While using sources is a practical way to support your points, it is also a rhetorical strategy. The use of sources enables a writer to support his or her voice with authoritative information from experts, studies, statistics, and so on. Thinking rhetorically about how you use sources means asking questions such as these: *When will readers demand more support for my ideas than I can personally provide? When will an expert's voice be needed? When will objective data—such as statistics and facts—make my paper more effective?* In this chapter you will learn about rhetorical and practical ways to use sources to write an effective paper.

In Chapter 10, "Conducting Research," you saw how Tori, a student writing a research paper, planned her project and selected sources. In this chapter, you will see additional choices Tori made as she continued to work on her paper. Use the guidelines in the next sections to help you determine *when* to use a source, as well as *how* to use the source.

When to Use a Source

These guidelines will help you figure out when using a source is rhetorically helpful. Keep the rhetorical situation in mind, especially the audience, as you use these guidelines.

- **Use a source to show that you understand the history or background of the topic.** Often, you will need to do some research to understand the context of the idea or topic you are discussing. By showing that you understand what has been said about the issue or idea, you can establish credibility as a writer. You will need to cite the sources that gave you this background knowledge. Keep in mind that readers, too, may need this background information, so plan with readers in mind.

- **Use a source to provide support for an idea.** When you think that readers will demand more than you can personally provide in order to understand or believe an idea, use a source.

- **Use a source to show you understand the multiple sides of an issue.** If you are writing an argument, you may want to cite sources that present opposing viewpoints. You will need to provide a rebuttal to these sources, as Chapters 9 and 14 explain.

- **Use a source to appeal to the authority of experts.** If you are not an expert on the topic you are discussing, your writing will be more believable if you cite experts in the field.

- **Use a source to equip readers with a way to get further information on a point.** Sometimes writers refer to a related issue or make a point about existing research on the topic. Citing sources in this way provides readers with resources for finding more information.

- **Use a source when you wish to provide complex or technical explanations.** Sometimes only experts can explain complex phenomena. Carefully select quotes or summarize information when an expert can offer a better explanation than you can.

- **Use a source when using your own wording of a concept or idea would not be as effective as quoting the source's wording.** When you find a source that expresses an idea perfectly, it is fine to quote that source as long as you give credit properly.

- **Use a source to provide information that is not common knowledge.** Any time you present information that is not commonly known, you need to refer to a source. Since the information is not common knowledge, readers expect to see where the information comes from, and citing a source allows you to show them. For more information on common knowledge, see "FAQ: Recognizing Common Knowledge" at the end of this chapter.

Teaching Resources
Students often struggle to understand this concept. To help explain the idea of common knowledge, use the PowerPoint "When to Use Sources."

How to Use Sources

As a writer, you also have choices about how you use sources in your paper. You can choose to create a direct quotation, an indirect quotation, a summary, or a paraphrase, but how can you determine which method is best for your purpose? Following the guidelines below will help you use sources appropriately.

- **Use a variety of methods for incorporating sources.** Remember that in addition to creating direct quotations, you can also create indirect quotations, summaries, and paraphrases. An indirect quotation puts a writer's ideas into your own words, whereas a summary presents a passage or even an entire article in your own words. A paraphrase provides a sentence-by-sentence rewording of an original passage.

- **Use a lengthy quote only when you have a very good reason to do so.** Quotations, especially those that are more than two or three sentences long, take up a lot of space. You may be tempted to fill your paper with long quotations (and thus more easily reach a required word count), but do not yield to this temptation.

- **Avoid using direct quotations too often.** If you pepper your essay with too many quotes, your voice will be lost, and you will not communicate your message effectively.

- **Avoid starting a paragraph with a quotation.** Take ownership of the paragraphs in your paper by starting them with your own words.

- **Follow a quotation with an explanation in your own words.** Do not assume that readers will see the significance of the quotation. Tie the quotation to your ideas by explaining or making a comment.

Co-requisite Teaching Tip
Consider working directly with students on using sources. Provide formative feedback for the first two uses of a source and have students finish the rest on their own.

> **Tori, on using sources rhetorically:** "I knew I would need sources because I'm writing about a health topic—anorexia treatments—and I'm not a health-care professional. What I thought I would struggle with is finding information that was not too technical. I knew that a general audience would need basic information without a lot of medical jargon."

Teaching Resources
Consider assigning the exercise "Making Choices About Sources."

Use the questions in Rhetorical Toolbox 11.1 to help you determine *when* to use a source, as well as *how* to use the source.

RHETORICAL TOOLBOX 11.1
When and How to Use Sources

When to Use Sources

1. **Evidence.** Does a passage need evidence—other than explanations you can provide—in order for readers to believe or understand it? If so, consider using a source.
2. **Background.** Are you demonstrating a knowledge of the history or background of the topic? If so, consider using a source.
3. **Experts.** Will readers demand an expert to back up your ideas? If so, consider using a source.
4. **Further information.** Might readers need to find more information on a point that you will not be elaborating on in great depth? If so, consider using a source.
5. **Complicated explanations.** Do you need to provide complex or technical explanations? If so, consider using a source.
6. **The best expression.** Is there a concept or idea that would be best presented in the words found in a source? If so, consider using a source.
7. **Common knowledge.** Have you obtained information that is not common knowledge? If so, use a source.

How to Use Sources

1. **Your voice.** Does the majority of your paper consist of your own words? If not, reduce the number of direct quotations in your work.
2. **Varied presentation.** Have you used a variety of methods for referring to sources, such as direct quotes, indirect quotes, summaries, and paraphrases? If not, revise.
3. **Quotations.** If you have used any lengthy quotes, would a reader believe these quotes were absolutely necessary? If not, revise to use a brief direct quote, summary, or paraphrase.
4. **Paragraphs.** Have you started any paragraphs with a quote? If so, revise to begin the paragraph with your own words.
5. **Explanations.** Have you followed all quotations with explanations in your own words? If not, add explanations or comments.

▶ **ACTIVITY 1 Planning How to Use Sources**

Matthew is writing a paper about the electoral college. He is arguing that the electoral college system is not the most effective way to elect a president and should be changed. How might Michael need to use sources to write this paper for a general audience? What kind of information would he need to find that he could not provide without using a source? Why would readers need this information?

PRACTICAL STRATEGIES FOR WORKING WITH SOURCES

From reading and annotating your sources to integrating quotations into your paper, several practical strategies will help you make the most of the sources you are using.

Annotating Effectively

For most students, the best way to work with sources is to print them for easier reading and annotating. Read the source, marking the ideas that seem to be important. In a dense text, it is often difficult to recognize the most important ideas the first time you read it, so read the source a second time, making additional notes. Mark the major supporting points, the thesis statement, and nuggets of information you find interesting or useful for quotations or summaries. If you are reading more than one source, make annotations about the connections you find between them. Keep in mind that your paper should not include many lengthy quotations. If a lengthy passage is important, make a note to summarize it.

Co-requisite Teaching Tip Consider discussing annotation skills. See the PowerPoint "Effective Annotation Strategies."

Creating a Source Chart

One way to keep track of the ideas in the sources you read is to create a chart. A source chart enables you to jot down the main points from your sources. In Chapter 10, we followed the work Tori did as she started to plan a paper on recovery from anorexia nervosa. In the example that follows, you will see how Tori has created a chart that lists her sources and records the most important information from each source; she adds a column for each new source she consults. You can use Tori's chart as a model for your own. Keep in mind that it is not possible to know exactly which quotes will best support the points you are making in your paper until you are drafting. Record any quotations that you think may be helpful, but be aware that you may need to return to a source to find a more appropriate quotation.

Tori's Source Chart		
	Franko, "Predictors of Long-Term Recovery . . ."	Calugi, "Intensive Enhanced . . ."
Thesis	". . . binge eating and purging behaviors were poor prognostic indicators and that comorbidity with depression is particularly pernicious in AN. Treatment providers might pay particular attention to these issues in an effort to positively influence recovery over the long-term."	"Inpatient enhanced cognitive behavioral therapy (CBT-E) is a viable and promising treatment for patients with severe and enduring anorexia nervosa (SE-AN)."

(Continued on next page)

(Continued from previous page)

	Franko, "Predictors of Long-Term Recovery . . ."	Calugi, "Intensive Enhanced . . ."
Support	Based on research study	Based on research study
Issues addressed	Binge eating and purging (assoc.w/anorexia) Depression (assoc.w/anorexia)	Using BMI to measure success Using CBT-E to treat SE-AN
Reminder notes	Good article to examine why treatment can be complicated	Good in-depth look at how CBT-E works in the treatment of SE-AN. Good to quote for info about CBT.
Citation	Franko, Debra L., et al. "Predictors of Long-Term Recovery in Anorexia Nervosa and Bulimia Nervosa: Data from a 22-Year Longitudinal Study." *Journal of Psychiatric Research*, vol. 96, Jan. 2018, pp. 183–188. doi:10.1016/j.jpsychires.2017.10.008.	Calugi, Simona, et al. "Intensive Enhanced Cognitive Behavioural Therapy for Severe and Enduring Anorexia Nervosa: A Longitudinal Outcome Study." *Behaviour Research and Therapy*, vol. 89, Feb. 2017, pp. 41–48. doi:10.1016/j.brat.2016.11.006.

Co-requisite Teaching Tip
Consider reinforcing each step of the research process by assigning mini-research tasks and giving separate grades for each one. See the IM for more ideas on how to teach a research project in a co-requisite course.

Notice that Tori added quotation marks to any words she took directly from the sources. This practice will help her to avoid unintentional plagiarism by reminding her that the words came from the source and that she must give credit to the authors.

> **Tori, on annotating and creating a source chart:** "I tend to highlight too many things. So instead of using a highlighter, I used a pen and wrote notes in the margins. I used a highlighter only for the places I might quote, and I tried to limit my quotes to three for each article. On the source chart, I included only one quote, but I wrote reminder notes to help me to remember other items I might want to use from the source."

Incorporating Sources into Your Paper's Outline

By analyzing each source and its potential usefulness, you can create a detailed outline of your paper in which you note the sources you will use to support each point. What follows is a detailed outline that helps Tori develop her essay with the right amount of support.

> **Tori's Detailed Outline**
>
> **Thesis statement:** Several therapies have been shown effective at helping women recover from anorexia nervosa.

Introduction: Present the core problem: anorexia is difficult to treat. <u>Use Clavy and Franko to explain this problem</u>. End with thesis statement.

Body

Paragraphs on major supporting point 1—medical interventions: Some medical interventions have proven themselves effective at restoring BMI, but they are not long-term recovery treatments. <u>Use Davidson and Granger sources.</u>

Paragraphs on major supporting point 2— psychotherapies: Cognitive behavioral therapy and other forms of psychotherapy are the most commonly used methods for treating anorexia, and their effectiveness is mixed. <u>Use Monroe and Canto sources. Summarize CBT by using the Juarascio source.</u>

Paragraphs on major supporting point 3—alternative approaches: Alternative treatment approaches include hypnotherapy, yoga, body awareness therapy, acupuncture, and biofeedback, and these approaches have shown limited success. <u>Use Jackson, Monroe, and Juarascio.</u>

Paragraphs on major supporting point 4—in-patient holistic approach: The most successful way to treat anorexia is to begin with a team-based, in-patient holistic approach. <u>Use quotes from Kavanaugh, Berman, and Canto.</u>

Conclusion: Explain the increase in anorexia, and urge that a solution be found. <u>Use Simmons source for statistics on the increase.</u>

INTEGRATING SOURCES ACCURATELY AND CORRECTLY

To integrate source materials well, be sure that you present sources fairly, accurately, and grammatically.

Representing the Source Fairly and Accurately

When you quote, paraphrase, or summarize a source, you are providing readers with another person's ideas, and you must do so fairly and accurately. Be thoroughly familiar with the entire source—the main idea, major supporting points, minor supporting details, examples, and so on—so that you do not misrepresent the writer's ideas.

Using Attributive Tags

An attributive tag gives credit to the author of the quote, paraphrase, or summary you are using in your essay. These tags can be used to introduce, interrupt, or conclude source material, and they can provide information about the author's credibility or viewpoint, as the examples in Table 11.1 show. Note that a writer's degree or job title and position or affiliation are sometimes included the first time the source is used. Also, note that the author's full name is used in the first reference, but in subsequent references, only the last name is used. (Never refer

---

Teaching Resources
Consider assigning "Using Sources Effectively," an exercise that presents students with an article to read, annotate, and use as a source for a hypothetical assignment.

TABLE 11.1 Using Attributive Tags

Attributive Tag (and Its Placement)	Example	Comments
According to (before the source material)	According to Deondre Jackson, professor of psychology at the University of North Texas, the use of cognitive behavioral therapy is the most effective method for treating anorexia (54).	The attributive tag emphasizes the speaker and the speaker's credentials.
As . . . writes, *As . . . says,* *As . . . contends,* *As . . . notes,* *As . . . states,* *As . . . remarks,* *As . . . shows,* (before the source material)	As researchers Max Hinzie and Ramie Goldstein show, helping women write narratives of their struggles can be of therapeutic value (343).	The attributive tag emphasizes the speaker and the speaker's credentials.
. . . claims. *. . . according to . . .* *. . . as . . . writes.* (after the source material)	"Understanding the neurological underpinnings of anorexia is vital," neurologist Casey Hunt claims (67).	The sentence begins with the source material, emphasizing it, and ends with the attributive tag.

to authors by first name only.) The numbers in parentheses are the page numbers of the source where the information can be found.

Teaching Resource
For practice integrating direct and indirect quotations, assign the worksheet "Integrating Direct and Indirect Quotations."

Integrating Direct Quotations

A quotation consists of the exact words of a source. Even if the writer of the source made a grammatical error, you must reproduce the words exactly, errors included. You will also need to use a method for giving credit to the source's writer, a skill covered in Chapter 12. In the first example, the attributive tag begins the sentence, the quoted words follow, and the quote's page number is placed in parentheses at the end of the sentence, followed by a period. **Note:** Sources from electronic databases sometimes do not show the original pagination. In such cases, page numbers are not included.

> **Example of a direct quote:** Jane Henderson writes, "The signs of anorexia become visible long before the disorder begins to affect the body" (377).
>
> **Example of a direct quote with errors in original and no original page numbers:** In an article about her recovery, Christine O'Campo explained her disgust: "Although I was only 115 pounds, I felt like a fat blobb [sic] of jelly."
>
> *Note:* The Latin word *sic*, meaning "thus," in brackets after an error indicates that the error is in the original quoted material.

By using the guidelines that follow, you can form quotations that are grammatically correct.

1. **Use a period inside the quotation mark to end a quotation at the end of a sentence.** When no page number follows the quotation, end punctuation goes inside the quotation marks.

   > Example: "A therapy that holds promise," said Dr. Crawley in an interview, involves "the combination of acupuncture and yoga."

2. **Use a period outside the quotation mark if a parenthetical reference to a source or page number ends a sentence.** If you quote something and include a page reference, the page reference is outside the quotation.

   > Example: A therapy that holds promise, according to Dr. Crawley, involves "the combination of acupuncture and yoga" (45).

3. **Punctuate question marks appropriately.** If a question mark is part of the quotation, put it inside the quotation marks.

   > Example: She asked, "Should we really rely on therapies that have not been proven effective after twenty years of research?" (56).

4. **Punctuate quotes within quotes appropriately.** When using a quote within a quote, use single quotation marks for the internal quote, and double quotation marks for the outer one.

   > Example: According to Marilyn Jackson, "Two patients called the treatment 'inhumane and demeaning' but the rest of the patients responded in more positive terms" (78).

5. **Avoid run-on sentences and sentence fragments when using quotes.** Formatting quotations incorrectly can result in run-on sentences, comma splices, and sentence fragments. Use these rules.

   A. **When the quote is a complete sentence, do not add it to another complete sentence.** Use correct punctuation to separate the two complete sentences.

> **Incorrect (with comma splice):** Jose B. Sanchez, a psychologist and clinical researcher at the University of California, would like to see increased education for parents and teachers, "If parents and teachers were more educated about the early symptoms of anorexia, interventions could be offered and we might see fewer cases develop" (324).
>
> **Corrected by creating two complete sentences:** Jose B. Sanchez, a psychologist and clinical researcher at the University of California, would like to see increased education for parents and teachers. "If parents and teachers were more educated about the early symptoms of anorexia, interventions could be offered and we might see fewer cases develop," Sanchez contends (324).
>
> *Note:* When you quote complete sentences, capitalize the first word of the quoted sentence.

B. **When a quote is not a complete sentence, it cannot stand on its own, even with an attributive tag.** Add your own words to the fragment to make it into a complete sentence.

> **Incorrect, with fragment:** Sanchez cites evidence of neurological changes that result from eating disorders. "Significant changes in brain structure" (321).
>
> **Corrected by adding words to make a complete sentence:** Sanchez cites evidence of "significant changes in brain structure" due to eating disorders (321).
>
> *Note:* Do not capitalize fragments that you quote.

6. **Use attributive tags grammatically.** You can interrupt a quote with an attributive tag, but you cannot put a complete sentence on one side of the attributive tag and a complete sentence on the other side.

> **Incorrect, with a comma splice:** "The idea that body image issues will simply go away is dangerous," according to Sanchez, "Body image issues

have a way of affecting long-term emotional development, especially if those issues develop in the pre-teen years" (325).

Corrected by inserting a period and an attributive tag: "The idea that body image issues will simply go away is dangerous," according to Sanchez. "Body image issues have a way of affecting long-term emotional development, especially if those issues develop in the pre-teen years," she notes (325).

7. **Use ellipses correctly.** An ellipsis is a mark made up of three spaced dots (. . .) that indicates the omission of words from quoted material. Study the examples that follow to see how to use ellipses correctly. If you have additional questions about the use of ellipses, refer to a style manual such as the *MLA Handbook* or the *Publication Manual of the American Psychological Association*.

Original source: On the voyage to the Americas, illness was a common cause of death.

Material to omit from the middle of the sentence: On the voyage [to the Americas,] illness was a common cause of death.

Use an ellipsis to show omission: "On the voyage . . . illness was a common cause of death" (89).

Original source: With little to no medicine available, not much could be done for those who became ill.

Material to omit from the end of the sentence: With little to no medicine available, not much could be done [for those who became ill].

Use an ellipsis to show omission: "With little to no medicine available, not much could be done. . . . " (89).

Original source: On the voyage to the Americas, illness was a common cause of death. With little to no medicine available, not much could be

> done for those who became ill. Consequently, mariners had to solve the problem of disposing of the dead.
>
> **Entire sentence to be omitted:** On the voyage to the Americas, illness was a common cause of death. [With little to no medicine available, not much could be done for those who became ill.] Consequently, mariners had to solve the problem of disposing of the dead.
>
> **Use an ellipsis to show omission:** "On the voyage to the Americas, illness was a common cause of death. . . . Consequently, mariners had to solve the problem of disposing of the dead" (89).
>
> *Note:* If you omit a sentence but continue the quotation, put a period after the third ellipsis point, as the above example shows.

Creating and Integrating Indirect Quotations

An indirect quotation enables you to express a writer's ideas but to do so in your own words. In the example, the writer's name begins the indirect quote, and the page on which the information appeared ends the quote.

> **Example of an indirect quote:** Jane Henderson notes that even before anorexia causes physical harm, there are symptoms that are noticeable (377).

Creating and Integrating Summaries

A grammatically correct summary consists of your own rewording of a particular passage or whole text (see Chapter 2 for guidelines for writing a summary). Notice that some bibliographic information (the date and the writers' names) is provided, but the title of the article is not provided. Readers can look at the works-cited list to learn the title, if they so choose. In addition, because Tori is summarizing the whole article, she does not need to include a page number.

Example of a summary: In a 2018 article about the historical development of treatments for eating disorders, researchers Michael Lieberman and Kelly Swain show that treatments over the last thirty years have increasingly come to depend on a team-based approach.

Creating and Integrating Paraphrases

Paraphrases help readers understand dense text or difficult ideas. To create and integrate a paraphrase, you must rewrite the original text in your own words. For example, notice how the paraphrase of the passage that follows helps nonexpert readers understand the source being used:

Original	Paraphrase
"Given that depression at intake was a unique predictor of a chronic course in AN-R and that this was not true for intake diagnoses of AN-BP or BN, there may be etiologic and nosologic implications of these findings as well" (Franko 188).	In some types of anorexic patients (subtype AN-R), having symptoms of depression before the onset of anorexia was shown to have significance. Other patients with subtypes AN-BP or BN seemed to have different reasons for the development of anorexia, and this may affect its classification, according to Franko (188).

Referring to Repeated Sources

If you continue to use information from the same source, make sure that you consistently give credit to the source. Do not move between your own ideas and the source's ideas without making it clear where the source's ideas start and end. In the next example, notice how the added highlighted phrase and page numbers clarify which ideas come from Brennan and which from the writer.

Unclear attribution	Clear attribution
Christa Brennan writes that the symptoms of anorexia in the early stages are often psychosocial in nature. For instance, a pre-teen girl may begin to wear baggy clothes to hide her developing figure. She may use language to describe herself that reveals body dysmorphia. Parents who are aware of these psychosocial symptoms can intervene and may be able to help guide their children to healthier ways of thinking about their bodies.	Christa Brennan writes that the symptoms of anorexia in the early stages are often psychosocial in nature (44). For instance, Brennan notes that a pre-teen girl may begin to wear baggy clothes to hide her developing figure and may use language to describe herself that reveals body dysmorphia (44). Parents who are aware of these psychosocial symptoms can intervene and may be able to help guide their children to healthier ways of thinking about their bodies.

▶ **ACTIVITY 2 Integrating Sources**

Using information from an online source (such as the Centers for Disease Control and Prevention), write a short paragraph in which you explain how the use of face masks helps control infectious respiratory illnesses. In your paragraph, include a brief direct quotation and at least one indirect quotation.

AVOIDING PLAGIARISM

plagiarism: Using another person's ideas, words, or works without giving proper credit.

Teaching Suggestion See the IM for ideas about how to teach students to recognize and avoid plagiarism.

Teaching Resources Consider using the PowerPoint "Avoiding Plagiarism" and assigning the exercise "Recognizing and Avoiding Plagiarism."

Plagiarism—using another person's words or ideas without giving proper credit—is a serious offense in academic writing. Obviously, if a writer wants to create a believable, credible text, the first principle to follow is to avoid plagiarism. In addition to losing one's audience, plagiarism can lead to failing grades and even dismissal from college. Certainly, submitting a paper you have not written and claiming it as your own work is plagiarism, and professors can recognize such intentional plagiarism right away. But plagiarism can also be unintentional; it can result from paying insufficient attention to how you credit your sources. To avoid plagiarism, you must make sure that every source you use in your essay is credited both in the text itself and in a list of sources at the end of the essay. Neglecting to properly credit sources is plagiarism, even if you do not intend to plagiarize. Follow these guidelines to avoid plagiarism in your paper:

- **Give credit to the author of the source.** Any time you use a writer's idea—even when you put it into your own words—you must give the writer credit. You can give the writer credit by using an attributive tag or by putting the writer's name in parentheses after the idea. For example:

    A. Jane Smith, a researcher at Johns Hopkins University, explains that antimicrobial soaps can lead to antibiotic-resistant bacteria (33).

    B. Methicillin-resistant staphylococcus aureus (MRSA) is an example of a bacterium that has evolved over time to become resistant to a wide variety of common antibiotics (Smith, 33).

- **Reread your entire paper to find source material.** Underline each section where you used an idea or a quote from a source. Now, for each of these underlined sections, answer the following questions:

    A. Have you provided the necessary attribution so that it is clear to readers where the quotation or idea came from?

    B. Have you provided a parenthetical reference for the source that will enable readers to find the corresponding entry in your works-cited or references list?

- **Make a list of the sources you used in your paper.** Is there an entry with complete information for each source on the works-cited or references list?

- **Think rhetorically.** If you are writing for an instructor, he or she will be alert to potential plagiarism. Any passages in your text that seem to come from sources will be suspect unless you cite sources for them. As you read your paper, imagine a reader asking, "Where did this information come from?" If you have a source for that information, you must cite the source.

> **Tori, on avoiding plagiarism**: "I was honestly petrified that I'd plagiarize without realizing it. In a paper like mine, where so much information is technical, I depended a lot on my sources. I reread my paper several times to make sure that any time I had gotten info from a source, I had cited the source."

CHAPTER PROJECT Creating a Source Chart

In this chapter, you saw Tori's source chart, which presents information about each source she planned to use. Create a source chart like Tori's for your research project. Include these elements in your chart, making sure you provide the same information for each source you plan to use.

Source Chart	
	Source 1
Source	Write the author's last name and abbreviated title of source.
Thesis	Write the source's thesis here.
Support	Note how the thesis is supported here.
Issues	Make a list of the issues addressed in the source.
Reminder notes	Make notes about how you will use this source.
Citation	Put a works-cited or references entry for the source here.

Reflecting to Develop a Writer's Mindset

What does it mean to use sources rhetorically? Explain in a paragraph, and provide an example of how a writer might use a source rhetorically. What are some of the practical strategies you can use to work with sources? How might they help you write a better paper?

FAQ RECOGNIZING COMMON KNOWLEDGE

Many students wonder whether they need to cite sources for well-known ideas, or common knowledge. A student may write, for instance, that football is a dangerous sport. Because many others have said the same, this is common knowledge; she does not have to cite other people who have made this general statement. In contrast, a statistic on the number of head injuries in football would need to come from a cited source because a statistic is not common knowledge.

1. What is common knowledge?

Common knowledge, then, is information that an ordinary person would be expected to know. Here are some examples:

- The earth orbits the sun.
- Public education is offered free of charge to all students in the United States.
- A carnivore is an animal that eats meat.

Common knowledge also includes adages and clichés that are in frequent use, such as these:

- A bird in the hand is worth two in the bush.
- Absence makes the heart grow fonder.

2. What should you do if you are unsure whether something is common knowledge?

When you use common knowledge, you do not have to provide a source. However, judging whether an idea is common knowledge can be difficult. For example, imagine that you have diabetes and know all about the disease. You are writing a paper on the disease for a college class. Your instructor does not necessarily share your knowledge. You cannot assume that knowledge of diabetes is common; thus, you should cite a source when you provide information about the disease, even if you are very familiar with the information. In short, if you are unsure whether your instructor will expect a source to be cited, then cite one!

TRY IT!

Evaluate each of the items that follow and determine whether the item should include the citation of a source.

1. Stagnant ponds and lakes can harbor dangerous microorganisms.
2. A common microorganism in stagnant water is *escherichia coli*.
3. Some scientists study water use, contamination, and conservation.
4. The average annual salary of a hydrologist is $80,000.
5. The Great Salt Lake is in Utah.

12 Documenting Sources in MLA and APA Style

CHAPTER OBJECTIVES

You will learn to:
- Explain what style manuals are and the purposes they serve.
- Locate bibliographic information needed to document a source.
- Use MLA style to document sources and format your paper.
- Use APA style to document sources and format your paper.

Manuals of style such as the *MLA Handbook* and the *Publication Manual of the American Psychological Association* present rules that guide how writers document sources and format papers. While following these rules can be tedious, doing so serves two important functions: it helps readers understand where to find the sources you've used in your paper, and it helps you, as a writer, to avoid plagiarism. Styles provide consistency and standardization, qualities that allow an audience to anticipate the ways in which they can find information in a paper. In this chapter, you will learn how to use an appropriate manual of style to create in-text documentation, to provide works-cited or references pages, and to format your paper.

Connect Adaptive Learning Assignment
Consider assigning Connect's Adaptive Learning Assignments to support this chapter.

WARM-UP
Do a quick online search for the style manual your professor uses: either the Modern Language Association's *MLA Handbook* (MLA) or the *Publication Manual of the American Psychological Association* (APA). Scan the manual's table of contents. Find one thing in the table of contents that you didn't expect would be included in the manual and that you might find helpful when you write a researched paper.

Teaching Resources
See the Instructor's Manual (IM) for suggestions about how to teach this chapter, and consider assigning this chapter's test-bank quiz.

THE IMPORTANCE OF STYLE GUIDES

Preparing your work for readers requires rhetorical thinking: you need to anticipate readers' needs and expectations. Questions of style—such as how to format your paper, how to refer to the sources you use, and how to provide readers with a list of those sources—are also important. In the same way that a potential employer expects a resume to be formatted in a certain way and to contain particular information, your instructors expect your papers to conform to a certain style. A style guide will help you understand and use the stylistic conventions of the discipline in which you are writing. Style manuals provide consistency in the way writers handle their sources and format their papers.

Different style manuals are used in different academic disciplines.

- **English.** When you write a paper for an English class, you will probably use MLA style.
- **Psychology.** When you write a paper for psychology, you will most likely use APA style.
- **History, art, or business.** A paper written for a history, art, or business class might be written according to the *Chicago Manual of Style*, a style we do not cover in this chapter.

The value of writing in the style of a particular discipline is that readers in that field who know the style will be able to easily navigate your paper. For example, a reader familiar with MLA style will know that to find a source referred to in your paper, he or she must go to the works-cited page and search by last name (or by the title word you used in the parenthetical reference).

Both of the styles we study in this chapter—MLA and APA—work by prescribing a method for documentation. MLA and APA require the use of in-text references (a type of shorthand used within a text to help guide readers to the source in the bibliography), as well as a final bibliography of the sources used in the paper. But manuals of style present more information than students sometimes realize. In the Warm-Up, you were asked to examine the *MLA Handbook* or the *Publication Manual of the American Psychological Association* to see the kind of information these manuals contain. You may have been surprised to see that in the *MLA Handbook*, plagiarism is clearly defined, and there is a section on evaluating sources. The APA manual contains a section for new users of APA style and a variety of sample papers formatted in APA style. Having the actual handbook nearby as you write a paper is ideal, but the brief guidelines in this chapter will provide you with the basic information you need to document sources and format your paper in MLA or APA style. For more information about each style, see these resources:

- *MLA Handbook*, Eighth Edition, published by the Modern Language Association of America, 2016, or the MLA style website: style.mla.org
- *Publication Manual of the American Psychological Association*, Seventh Edition, published by the American Psychological Association, 2019, or the APA style website: https://apastyle.apa.org/

▶ **ACTIVITY 1** Finding Online Style Resources

In addition to the resources above, you can find several websites that provide instructions for using a manual of style. Select the manual of style your instructor requires, and find one website that presents information about the style or tools that might help you use the style. Write a few sentences about how you might use the website.

Co-requisite Teaching Tip
Have students compile their own notebook of guidelines for MLA or APA style. This notebook should include detailed information on how to format their papers, create in-text references, and cite sources. See the IM for more information.

Teaching Suggestion
Consider making this a competitive assignment. Ask students to work in groups to find the *best* supplementary site for the style guide and then judge the groups' selections.

LOCATING BIBLIOGRAPHIC INFORMATION

When you use a source, you will need to have bibliographic information for the source in order to document it properly. The location of this information depends on the type of source and the way you accessed the source. Specifically, you will need to know the following:

- Author(s) and any additional contributors, such as translators or editors
- Title of source
- Title of publication (such as the journal, website, or book in which the material was found)
- Version, edition, volume number, issue number
- Publisher
- City of publication
- Publication date
- Page numbers, if you are using specific pages from a larger source (such as a chapter from an anthology), if available
- DOI (digital object identifier), a unique string of numbers and letters that helps readers find the source
- Database, if you used one to find the source

Use the following tips to locate the bibliographic information you will need.

Finding Bibliographic Information in an Online Database

Any time you use your library's online databases, you have access to a source's bibliographic information. Often, you can click on the source and the information will be listed, as Figure 12.1 demonstrates with an article in an online database.

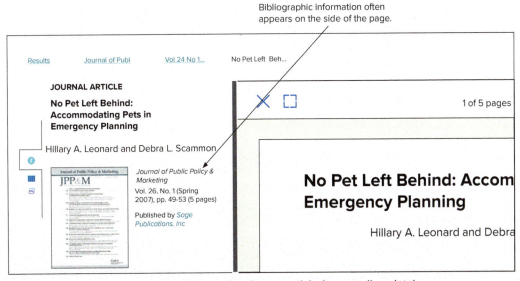

FIGURE 12.1 Finding bibliographic information for an article in an online database.

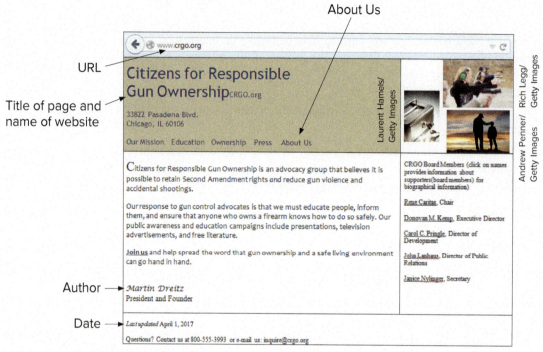

FIGURE 12.2 Finding bibliographic information on a website.

Teaching Resources
Consider assigning the worksheet "Finding Bibliographic Information."

Finding Bibliographic Information for Websites

Finding bibliographic information on websites can be tricky. Use these tips to locate the information you need.

1. Look for a menu item that indicates it will give you information about the website. Sometimes this is labeled "About Us" or something similar.
2. Scroll to the bottom of the website's homepage and click on the links provided to see if one supplies bibliographic information.
3. Click on the main title on the website's homepage. Sometimes bibliographic information is accessible through this means.

Figure 12.2 points out some of the many locations where you may find bibliographic information on a website.

Finding Bibliographic Information for Books

Books printed in hard copy usually have a page or two devoted to providing bibliographic information. The title page of a book presents the title and authors, but the publication information is usually on the next page, the copyright page. A textbook's copyright page lists the city, publisher, and date of publication, while the title page lists only the title and authors (see Figure 12.3).

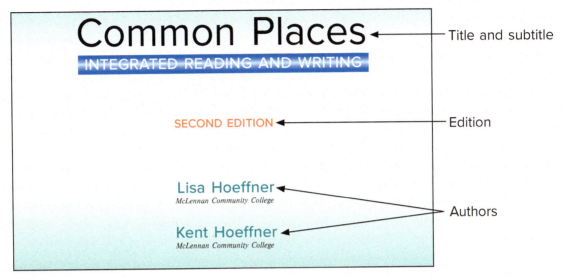

A. Title Page of a Book

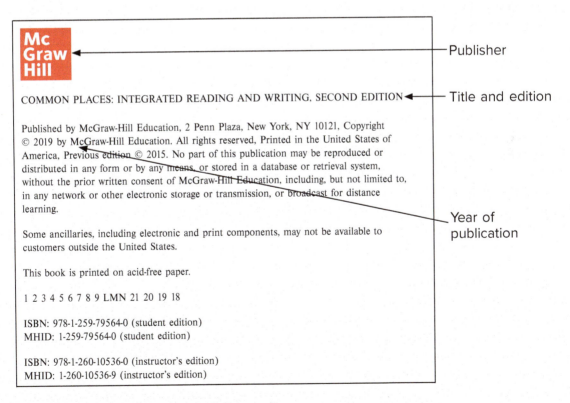

B. Copyright Page with Bibliographic Information

FIGURE 12.3 Finding bibliographic information for a book on the title page (A) and the copyright page (B).

Journal of Ethnography and Literature

April, 2020
Volume 115, No. 2

Ethnography Association of the Southwest
155 Canyon
Mesa, Arizona 85210

JEL 115.2 / April, 2020

Jania J. Trinh

Structured Identities in Pavelka's *Iron Flats* Trilogy

Long before Simone Pavelka's published her first ethnographic novel, *The Thing About Treaties*, the seeds for her ethnographic masterpiece, *Iron Flats*, had been sown. Indeed, the years Pavelka spent in Manila as a Peace Corps volunteer and the insights she gained from that experience

FIGURE 12.4 Finding bibliographic information for an article in a print journal.

Finding Bibliographic Information for Journal Articles in Print

On the title page of a journal, you will often find important bibliographic information such as the journal's name, volume, issue number, and date (Figure 12.4). Note that not all journals are organized by volume or issue number. Some journals are quarterly, meaning they appear four times a year, often organized by season (winter, spring, summer, fall). In addition to the journal's title page, you will need to have the article's name and the writer's name. This information is available on the first page of the article itself.

USING MLA STYLE

Three important skills in learning to use MLA style are (1) mastering the construction of in-text citations, (2) creating an accurate works-cited list, and (3) formatting your paper properly.

Teaching Resources
Consider using the PowerPoint "Creating In-Text Citations in MLA Style."

Creating In-Text Citations

An in-text citation is an abbreviated reference to a source in the body of your paper. The in-text citation tells readers which source was used and how to find the full citation of the source in the works-cited list at the end of the paper. Any time you use a source—even if you use the source only for an idea—you must provide an in-text citation. Use the following rules and examples to create in-text citations.

- The content in the in-text citation must exactly match the first word or two in the corresponding entry on the works-cited page. For example, if the in-text citation refers to a writer's last name, such as Browne, the name Browne must appear first in the entry on the works-cited page. In the examples that follow, notice how the content in the in-text reference matches the works-cited entry.
- If you use the author's name in the text you write, do not use the name in a parenthetical in-text citation; conversely, if you do not use the name in the text, use the name in the in-text citation.
- If a source has no author listed, use the name of the source (its title or the name of the web page) in the parenthetical reference.
- Use page numbers to show the exact page from which you obtained the information, but use page numbers only when you are able to view the source as it was originally published. In other words, if you are examining the journal article from the journal itself and can see the original page numbers, use those numbers. Do NOT use page numbers if you obtain the source from an online database that does not provide the original page numbers.

Teaching Resources
Consider assigning the MLA Documentation Quiz.

- Follow the rules for punctuating in-text citations. Notice the punctuation tips in the examples that follow.
- When summarizing or paraphrasing your sources, use attributive tags to refer to the source (see Chapter 11), or create an in-text citation.

In the examples that follow, notice how the in-text citation contains the name or word that begins the works-cited entry.

In-text Citation: One Author

Ted Genoways explains that Spam was created, in part, because "Paying high wages for slow-selling products was eating up Hormel's profits" (11).

OR

Spam was created, in part, to help Hormel maximize profits and continue to pay workers fairly (Genoways 11).

Punctuation tip: The period for the sentence goes *after* the last parenthesis mark.

Works-cited entry:

Genoways, Ted. *The Chain: Farm, Factory, and the Fate of Our Food.* Harper Collins, 2014.

In-text Citation: Two Authors

One of the reasons for the use of group psychotherapy is "the current health care climate with its emphasis on the efficacy and cost of services" (Ponech and McBride 33).

OR

Ponech and McBride point out that group psychotherapy is common because of "the current health care climate with its emphasis on the efficacy and cost of services" (33).

Works-cited entry:

Ponech, Heather, and Dawn Lorraine McBride. "Coming Together to Calm the Hunger: Group Therapy Program for Adults Diagnosed with Anorexia Nervosa." *Journal of Groups in Addiction & Recovery*, vol. 8, no. 4, 2013, pp. 309-328, doi:10.1080/1556035X.2013.836879.

In-text Citation: Three or More Authors

Social consensus intervention is "based on social influence whereby individuals tend to endorse values, beliefs, opinions, attitudes, or actions consistent with social norms" (Yan et al. 63).

OR

Yan et al. point out that social consensus intervention is "based on social influence whereby individuals tend to endorse values, beliefs, opinions, attitudes, or actions consistent with social norms" (63).

Punctuation tip: The term *et al.* means "and others," and it is always followed by a period because *al.* is an abbreviation for the Latin word *alia*.

Works-cited entry:

Yan, Yuwen, et al. "Reducing the Stigma Associated with Anorexia Nervosa: An Evaluation of a Social Consensus Intervention among Australian and Chinese Young Women." *International Journal of Eating Disorders*, vol. 51, no. 1, Jan. 2018, pp. 62-70. EBSCOhost, doi:10.1002/eat.22808.

In-text Citation: More than One Work by the Same Author

Roxanne Henkin points out that "So many of the bullying programs and safe school initiatives are inadequate and don't address the realities that LGBTQ

(Continued on next page)

(Continued from previous page)

> and bullied students face in high schools and middle schools today" ("Confronting Bullying" 111). Henkin's chronicle of the history of AGLIA, the Assembly on Gay and Lesbian Academic Issues Awareness, part of the National Council of Teachers of English, makes clear that even in academia, LGBTQ faculty face issues similar to those our students face ("Creating a Safe Zone" 76).
>
> *Works-cited entries*
>
> Henkin, Roxanne. "Confronting Bullying: It Really Can Get Better." *The English Journal*, vol. 101, no. 6, 2012, pp. 110-113.
>
> —. "Creating a Safe Zone: LGBTQ Work in NCTE." *The English Journal*, vol. 101, no. 1, 2011, pp. 76-79.

In-text Citation: No Author, or Published by an Organization or Website

> As the *Feeding America* website shows, "nutrition-related illnesses disproportionately affect food-insecure people" ("Leading the Movement").
>
> *Works-cited entry:*
>
> "Leading the Movement to Solve Hunger." *Feeding America*, www.feedingamerica.org/our-work/our-approach/leading-the-fight. Accessed 19 Oct. 2020.

In-text Citation: Indirect Quotation.

The abbreviation *qtd. in* stands for "quoted in" and indicates that the content was quoted from another source. In this example, Cody was quoted in Orlando's work, and Orlando is listed in the works-cited entry.

> Diablo Cody points out that "if the era of Facebook and Twitter has fed any monsters, it's those of vanity, self-obsession, and immaturity" (qtd. in Orlando).

Works-cited entry:

Orlando, Emily J. "Edith Wharton and the New Narcissism." *Women's Studies,* vol. 44, no. 6, Sept. 2015, pp. 729-752.

Creating the List of Works Cited

At the end of a paper in MLA style, a works-cited page lists all the sources used in the paper. Each source is presented as a works-cited entry, and each entry is formatted in a precise manner. As a writer, you are ultimately responsible for creating accurate and correctly formatted works-cited entries, but there are tools that can help. Most online databases contain links that show you how to cite articles in a variety of styles, including MLA and APA. In addition, citation generation websites enable you to enter bibliographic information and create a citation. Always check the citations you get from databases or online generators to make sure they are formed correctly.

The *MLA Handbook* suggests using a template to identify the core elements for each works-cited entry (Table 12.1). The template asks you to gather key pieces of information that are necessary to create a works-cited entry. Additionally, the template lists the information in the order in which it should appear in the entry you compose. What follows is a template similar to the one provided in the *MLA Handbook*, Eighth Edition. Use the template to find the information you need to create an entry, and then look up the particular type of source for more information about how to format it for the works-cited page.

Note that a source may have two "containers." For example, an article may appear in a scholarly journal (container 1), which in turn appears in an online

TABLE 12.1 MLA Template of Core Elements

Who is the author?
What is the title of the source?
What is the title of the container? (The *container* is the journal, or website, or book or other "holder" in which the source appears.)
Who are the other contributors (such as editors or translators) to the source?
What version is the source?
What number does the source have?
Who is the source's publisher?
What is the publication date?
Where was the source published (city, state)?

database (container 2). You'll need information for both containers. Here is an example with two containers:

> Bayerlein, Leopold, and Debora Jeske. "Student Learning Opportunities in Traditional and Computer-Mediated Internships." *Education & Training*, vol. 60, no. 1, Jan. 2018, pp. 27-38. EBSCOhost, doi:10.1108/ET-10-2016-0157.

Once you have located as much information as you can to fill in the template, find the type of source (article, book, interview, etc.) in the list below. Use the example as a guide to create your work-cited entry for the source. If you need additional information, consult the *MLA Handbook* or visit the *MLA Handbook*'s website.

A Note about Multiple Authors. Regardless of the type of source, you will need to know how to account for one, two, or multiple authors as you create works-cited entries. Use these examples.

> **One Author**
>
> Sharkey, Lauren. "Work and Family Demands May Impact Women's Heart Health." *Medical News Today*, MediLexicon International, 19 Oct. 2019, www.medicalnewstoday.com/articles/326721.php#1.
>
> **Two Authors**
>
> Ponech, Heather, and Dawn Lorraine McBride. "Coming Together to Calm the Hunger: Group Therapy Program for Adults Diagnosed with Anorexia Nervosa." *Journal of Groups in Addiction & Recovery*, vol. 8, no. 4, 2013, pp. 309-328, doi:10.1080/1556035X.2013.836879.
>
> **Three or More Authors**
>
> Yan, Yuwen, et al. "Reducing the Stigma Associated with Anorexia Nervosa: An Evaluation of a Social Consensus Intervention among Australian and Chinese Young Women." *International Journal of Eating Disorders*, vol. 51, no. 1, Jan. 2018, pp. 62-70. EBSCOhost, doi:10.1002/eat.22808.

Works Cited: Articles. To create an entry for an article, you need several pieces of bibliographical information. One of the newer ways to identify a source is to include a digital object identifier, commonly referred to as a DOI. The DOI for an article or book is a string of numbers and letters. Each DOI is unique and leads to a specific document. However, not all articles and books have DOIs. When a source does have one, include it in your works-cited entry. Some of the examples that follow include a DOI.

Journal Article in Print

Carter, Shani D. "Comparison of Student Learning Outcomes Assessment Practices Used Globally." *Athens Journal of Education*, vol. 2, no. 3, Aug. 2019, pp. 179-191.

Journal Article Online (or from an Online Database)

Bayerlein, Leopold, and Debora Jeske. "Student Learning Opportunities in Traditional and Computer-Mediated Internships." *Education & Training*, vol. 60, no. 1, Jan. 2018, pp. 27-38. EBSCOhost, doi:10.1108/ET-10-2016-0157.

Newspaper Article in Print

Lind, Michael. "Saving Democracy from the Managerial Elite." *The Wall Street Journal*, 11-12 Jan. 2020, p. C1.

Newspaper Article Online

Weiss, Bari. "The World's Wokest Sports League Bows to China." *The New York Times*, 7 Oct. 2019, www.nytimes.com/2019/10/07/opinion/nba-china-hong-kong.html.

Magazine Article in Print

Ying, Ding. "Revitalizing History." *Time Magazine*, vol. 194, no. 21, 11 Nov. 2019, pp. 4-5.

Magazine Article Online

Pritchard, Mary. "This Is Why Anorexia Might Be So Difficult to Treat." *Fitness Magazine*, Meredith Women's Network, 31 Mar. 2017, www.fitnessmagazine.com/mind-body/image/the-surprising-reason-anorexia-might-be-so-difficult-to-treat/.

Article from a Website

Brazier, Yvette. "Anorexia Nervosa: Symptoms, Causes, and Treatment." *Medical News Today*, MediLexicon International, 19 Jan. 2018, www.medicalnewstoday.com/articles/267432.php.

Works Cited: Books

Book in Print

Strathern, Marilyn. *The Gender of the Gift: Problems with Women and Problems with Society in Melanesia*. U of California P, 1988.

Ebook

Yan, Weikai. *Crop Variety Trials: Data Management and Analysis*. Wiley, 2014. ProQuest Ebook Central, doi:10.1002/9781118688571.

Book from a Multivolume Set

Flower, Elizabeth, and Murray G. Murphey. *A History of Philosophy in America*. Vol. 2, Capricorn, 1977.

Reprinted Work

Shelley, Mary. *Frankenstein*. 1818. Edited by Johanna M. Smith, Bedford Books, 1992.

Dictionary or Encyclopedia Entry

Davidson, Tish, and Deborah L. Nurmi. "Anorexia Nervosa." *The Gale Encyclopedia of Mental Health*, edited by Brigham Narins, 4th ed., vol. 1, Gale, 2019, pp. 95-101. Gale eBooks, https://libproxy.library.unt.edu:8026/apps/doc/CX2491200036/GVRL?u=txshracd2679&sid=GVRL&xid=a259a80c.

Work in an Anthology

"Sir Gawain and the Green Knight." *The Broadview Anthology of British Literature*, edited by Joseph Laurence Black, 3rd ed., Broadview Press, 2015, p. 296.

Unpublished Dissertation or Thesis

Conners, Duane. "Inseparable Identities or Not? Twin Studies Reexamined." Dissertation. U of Houston, 2020.

Sacred Text

The New Jerusalem Bible. Standard ed., Doubleday, 1999.

Works Cited: Internet Sources

Web Page

"Anorexia Nervosa." *The Center for Eating Disorders at Sheppard Pratt Health*, 2015, www.sheppardpratt.org/knowledge-center/condition/anorexia-nervosa/.

Blog

Jefferson, Travon. "If Your Students Can Relate, They Can Read, So Give Them Culturally Relevant Texts." *Education Post*, 26 Sept. 2019, educationpost.org/if-your-students-can-relate-they-can-read-so-give-them-culturally-relevant-texts/.

YouTube or Other Streaming Video

Miller, Brooke. "Anorexia Nervosa—Causes, Symptoms, Diagnosis, Treatment and Pathology." *YouTube,* 25 Mar. 2019, www.youtube.com/watch?v=olIz9MqtW-U.

Social Media Posting

@narendramodi. "I want to unequivocally assure my fellow Indians that CAA does not affect any citizen of India of any religion. No Indian has anything to worry regarding this Act. This Act is only for those who have faced years of persecution outside and have no other place to go except India." *Twitter,* 16 Dec. 2019, 12:34 a.m., twitter.com/narendramodi/status/1206492850378002432.

Podcast

Bryant, Charles, and Josh Clark, hosts. "What's a Gap Year Anyway?" *Stuff You Should Know Podcast,* iHeart Radio, 5 Dec. 2019, www.iheart.com/podcast/105-stuff-you-should-know-26940277/episode/whats-a-gap-year-anyway-53486926/.

Streaming Television (Entire Series)

Waller-Bridge, Phoebe, creator. *Fleabag.* Two Brothers Pictures, 2016-2019.

Streaming Television (Specific Episode)

"Episode 3." *Fleabag,* season 1, episode 3, 4 Aug. 2016. BBC, www.bbc.co.uk/programmes/b07v3164.

Email

Rosetti, Lisa. "Evaluation of Employees." Received by Holly Towns, 1 Oct. 2020.

Works Cited: Miscellaneous Sources

Conference Presentation

Hawkins, Macy. "Adjusting Pedagogy for Dialects." 10th Annual Literacy K-12 Conference, Syracuse, NY, 10 May 2019.

Lecture

Oldman, Ruth "Meg." "SGGK Chivalric Code." *Sir Gawain and the Green Knight*. Medieval Literature Class, 3 Oct. 2020, Stephenville, Tarleton State University.

Movie

Coen, Joel, director. *The Big Lebowski.* Working Title Films, 1998.

Advertisement

M&M Commercial. 30 Jan. 2019. YouTube, www.youtube.com/watch?v=5CCRNmmnG3c.

Brochure

Association of Women in Farming. *Crop Yields*. DBB Publications, 2019.

Congressional Legislation

United States, Congress, House, Homeland Procurement Reform Act, 2019.
    116th Congress.

Court Case

United States District Court. Brown v. Board of Education.
    17 May 1954. *Our Documents*, www.ourdocuments.gov/doc.
    php?flash=false&doc=87&page=transcript.

Government Publication

"Anorexia Nervosa." *MentalHealth.gov*, U.S. Department of Health and
    Human Services, 22 Aug. 2017, www.mentalhealth.gov/what-to-look-for/
    eating-disorders/anorexia.

Map

Britton, Peter. "Map of Egypt at 3500 BC." *Time Maps,* 2019, www.
    timemaps.com/history/ancient-egypt-3500bc/.

Painting/Photo/Other Work of Art

Van Gogh, Vincent. *Starry Night*. 1889, Museum of Modern Art,
    New York City.

Performance

The Phantom of the Opera. 8 Oct. 2019, The Majestic Theater, New York City.

Personal Interview

Albright, Stephanie. Personal interview. 28 Feb. 2020.

Raw Data

"International Programs." United States Census Bureau, 2019, www.census.gov/
    data-tools/demo/idb/region.php?T=13&RT=0&A=both&Y=2019&C=GR&R=.

> **Report**
>
> Srinivasa, Preeti, et al. "Case Report on Anorexia Nervosa." National Center for Biotechnology Information Search Database, 2015, www.ncbi.nlm.nih.gov/pmc/articles/PMC4418263/.

▶ **ACTIVITY 2 Understanding MLA Style**

Indicate whether each of the following statements is true or false. If a statement is false, correct it.

1. When referring to the volume of a journal, abbreviate and capitalize "volume," like this: Vol.
2. Use a comma between the author and the page number in a parenthetical reference, like this: (Aronsen, 114).
3. When using a source by three or more authors, list the first author's name in the works-cited entry followed by *et al.*, like this: Jameson, Timothy, et al.
4. If you read a source but do not use it in your paper, you must still include it on the works-cited page.
5. The following parenthetical reference is correctly punctuated:

    Survivors claimed the chemical exposure left them permanently disabled. (Konech 52).

Formatting a Paper in MLA Style

What follows is a sample paper that has been formatted according to MLA guidelines. For more detailed information, consult the *MLA Handbook*, Eighth Edition.

Tori Manning, Finding a Treatment for Anorexia (Sample Paper in MLA Style)

Tori Manning
Dr. Stein
ENGL 1301.16
11 November 2020

Finding a Treatment for Anorexia

In a world dominated by images of thin supermodels, eating disorders among women are common. Because eating disorders are not exotic diseases, it may seem that they are not all that dangerous. Nothing could be further from the truth. The Eating Disorders Coalition (EDC), an advocacy group that attempts to raise awareness about eating disorders, has compiled some statistics that make clear how serious these disorders are. Among adolescent girls, eating disorders are the "the 3rd most common chronic illness" ("Facts About Eating Disorders"). Even more alarming, "Every 62 minutes at least one person dies as a direct result from an eating disorder" ("Facts About Eating Disorders").

These statistics are worrisome; the prevalence of eating disorders and their potential harm cannot be overstated. Unfortunately, recognizing the problem does not necessarily mean there are ready solutions for eating disorders. One of the most common disorders, anorexia nervosa, is particularly challenging to cure. Anorexia nervosa is a "psychiatric disorder characterized by an unrealistic fear of weight gain, conspicuous distortion of body image, and self-starvation. Individuals with this disorder are obsessed with becoming increasingly thinner and limit food intake to the point at which health is compromised" (Davidson and Nurmi 95). Because anorexia is so devastating and because it affects so many adolescent girls, it is imperative that healthcare providers find therapies that actually work to aid recovery. Despite being notoriously difficult to treat, anorexia nervosa patients have been shown to respond to several therapies.

One of the challenges faced by those who seek to treat anorexia is the fact that patients often deny having the disease. Because they do not feel thin enough, they are unable to see their bodies objectively (Davidson and Nurmi 99). When a patient

Manning 2

is in denial, treatment is difficult. The patient may not comply with the advice offered by healthcare providers. It is easy to see how treating the mental condition of the patient might be the first step to take. Those who advocate a psychological approach to treating anorexia nervosa often do so for this reason. M. Irene Sharkey-orgnero, for example, points out that the belief systems of some people who suffer from anorexia are an inherent part of the problem of finding a treatment that works: "Many patients with anorexia nervosa describe how, through penitence and self-denial, they will be rewarded with a complete and permanent happiness that is almost heavenly" (182). Sharkey-orgnero goes on to point out that "the religiosity of this belief is added to by culturally accepted attitudes that describe fasting as good (righteous) and satiety as bad (weak)" (182). Countering such a belief can be difficult and can take years of therapy.

One of the mental health treatments most commonly used to help those suffering from anorexia nervosa is cognitive behavioral therapy (CBT). Cognitive behavioral therapy:

> . . . is an action-oriented form of psychosocial therapy that assumes that maladaptive, or faulty, thinking patterns cause maladaptive behavior and "negative" emotions. (Maladaptive behavior is behavior that is counter-productive or interferes with everyday living.) The treatment focuses on changing an individual's thoughts (cognitive patterns) in order to change his or her behavior and emotional state. (Ford-Martin 378)

The idea behind the CBT approach is that if a therapist can help a client see how behaviors and faulty thinking result in the disease, the patient can change the way he or she thinks and behaves; in turn, the disease is cured. It is easy to see how a person who is in denial about the diagnosis of anorexia would *not* necessarily benefit from CBT. While CBT is often used to treat anorexia, the technique has not been shown to be superior to other therapies (Galsworthy-Francis and Allan).

A different form of CBT, called *enhanced* cognitive behavioral therapy (CBT-E), has been deemed "a viable and promising treatment for patients with severe and enduring anorexia nervosa" (Calugi et al. 42). The disease is classified as severe and enduring anorexia (SE-AN) when a patient has been anorexic for more than seven years. Patients who have struggled with anorexia for this long often face significant medical complications and the real possibility of dying from the disease (Touyz et al.). The focus of CBT-E for these patients is *not* on recovery: instead it is on enhancing the patient's quality of life (Calugi et al. 44). What researchers found, however, is that enhanced cognitive behavioral therapy that is focused on quality of life—rather than recovery—had surprisingly positive effects. First, the patients stayed in the program, and that is a significant factor since lack of participation is so often the cause for a remedy's failure. Second, participants "achieved a substantial increase in BMI, and significant improvements in eating-disorder and general psychopathology" (Calugi et al. 45). Finally, "between baseline and 12-month follow-up, the majority of patients changed status from extreme to mild current level of AN severity" (Calugi et al. 45). In-patient enhanced cognitive behavioral therapy seems to hold promise as an effective treatment for anorexia nervosa.

Another mental health therapy—group counseling and variations of it—holds more promise in the treatment of anorexia nervosa. Ponech and McBride point out that group counseling has an advantage over individual counseling because of the personal contact involved (10). Participants gain a sense of shared experiences, and the dialogue that goes on within group counseling sessions seems to help participants come to terms with their disorders and be more willing to accept the need for treatment (10). One of the greatest challenges in treating anorexia is retaining patients. A new type of group therapy, multi-family therapy group (MFTG) shows promise in its ability to retain patients and to treat anorexia successfully. In MFTG, five to seven anorexic patients, as well as their families, come together for counseling, discussing, goal-setting, and support (Tantillo et al. 950). Because these patients and their families get to know each other and develop friendships during sessions, a sense of trust is established. Patients are able to openly talk about their disorders, and families learn the best methods for intervening to help their loved ones. Tantillo et al. recruited and retained ten patients and their families for the study. The patients made progress in gaining weight and in showing an increased understanding of the factors that motivate anorexic tendencies. In short, "This pilot study demonstrated that R4R [the Reconnecting for Recovery program] is a promising intervention for young adults with AN" (Tantillo et al. 953). While more research is needed, the use of multi-family therapy groups seems to be one of the most promising treatments for anorexia.

In addition to treating anorexia by addressing mental health, there has been some research on alternative therapies that can affect anorexia. These therapies include hypnotherapy, yoga, body awareness therapy, acupuncture, massage, and biofeedback. While each therapy claims some success, there is not enough research to support the idea that these therapies are generally useful. For example, in a limited study of the use of massage and acupuncture, Stephen Eddey found that participants had increases in their BMI (body mass index) which indicated weight gain, as well as a self-reported decrease in their eating-related concerns. But this study included only 26 patients, and its author acknowledges that more research is needed to confirm the results (Eddey). The ancient Chinese Hua tuo treatments are a type of massage that some practitioners believe can be helpful to treat the anxiety that often causes anorexic behaviors (Xia et al.46). The results of Hua tuo treatments were "at least comparable with [other] alternative treatments" (Xia et al. 49), but since other alternative treatments have had limited success, there is little reason to hope Hua tuo will be curative. Nasim Furoughi and his fellow researchers examined the most commonly used alternative treatments for anorexia, and they found that although people had great faith in these treatments, there is little evidence suggesting alternative therapies are effective (179).

Finally, the most acute cases of anorexia must be treated by focusing on the physical aspects of the disease. Because anorexia is a disease that can be fatal, medical interventions focus on increasing BMI (body mass index) and treating the issues that occur as a result of malnutrition. Patients who have been admitted to a hospital for acute and life-threatening anorexia may be treated using the MARSIPAN protocol. MARSIPAN stands for "Management of Really Sick Patients with Anorexia Nervosa" (Robinson 5). As Paul Robinson and Dasha Nicholls explain, the protocol advised by this group involves taking care of the most serious medical issues to treat the patient. For instance, a patient may need to be given serum electrolytes, nutritional supplements administered via food or a nasogastric tube, and strict oversight to make sure that a common medical complication called "refeeding syndrome" does not occur (6).

The goal of any anorexia treatment program is to completely cure the disease so that a patient's condition will not progress to the need for an in-patient hospital stay. Perhaps the best treatment for recovery from anorexia consists of a combination of

Manning 5

the available remedies. By examining a wide variety of studies, researchers have identified certain factors that predict successful recovery from the disease. First, those who recover successfully have found a way to manage their mood and anxiety symptoms (Keski-Rahkonen and Tozzi 84-85). Because anorexia is so often driven by anxiety about body weight, helping patients figure out how to manage that anxiety seems to be a crucial part of recovery. The use of cognitive behavioral therapy is one way to teach patients to manage anxiety. While CBT was not shown to be a totally effective treatment for anorexia, combining it with other treatments may make the therapy more successful. In addition to managing anxiety and mood, developing positive personality traits is also associated with recovery (Franko 185). One way patients can learn about their personality and how it affects their disease is to participate in multi-family therapy groups (MFTG). In such groups, leaders can facilitate discussions about how personality tendencies—such as perfectionism—can contribute to anorexic tendencies. If an alternative therapy such as massage or biofeedback contributes to less anxiety, that therapy should also be used in tandem with CBT and MFTG.

Anorexia is a stubborn disease. It is difficult to treat, and the research shows that there is no one therapy that is effective for all patients. By experimenting with and using a combination of available therapies, healthcare practitioners may be able to help patients recover from the disease before it becomes life-threatening.

Manning 6

Works Cited

Calugi, Simona, et al. "Intensive Enhanced Cognitive Behavioural Therapy for Severe and Enduring Anorexia Nervosa: A Longitudinal Outcome Study." *Behaviour Research and Therapy*, vol. 89, Feb. 2017, pp. 41-48. EBSCOhost, doi:10.1016/j.brat.2016.11.006.

Davidson, Tish, and Deborah L. Nurmi. "Anorexia Nervosa." *The Gale Encyclopedia of Mental Health*, edited by Brigham Narins, 4th ed., vol. 1, 2019, pp. 95-101. Gale eBooks, libproxy.library.unt.edu:8026/apps/doc/CX2491200036/GVRL?u=txshracd2679&sid=GVRL&xid=a259a80c.

Eddey, Stephen. "Media Watch: The Treatment of Anorexia Nervosa Using
    Acupuncture and/or Massage." *Journal of the Australian Traditional-Medicine
    Society*, vol. 20, no. 1, Mar. 2014, p. 57.

"Facts About Eating Disorders." Eating Disorders Coalition, 2019, www.
    eatingdisorderscoalition.org/inner_template/facts_and_info/facts-about-eating-
    disorders.html.

Ford-Martin, Paula Anne, et al. "Cognitive-Behavioral Therapy." *The Gale
    Encyclopedia of Mental Health*, edited by Brigham Narins, 4th ed., vol. 1, 2019.
    Gale eBooks, libproxy.library.unt.edu:8026/apps/doc/CX2491200116/
    GVRL?u=txshracd2679&sid=GVRL&xid=96d8c89e.

Foroughi, Nasim, et al. "The Perceived Therapeutic Benefits of Complementary
    Medicine in Eating Disorders." *Complementary Therapies in Medicine*, vol. 43,
    2019, pp. 176-80. ProQuest, doi:10.1016/j.ctim.2019.01.025.

Franko, Debra L., et al. "Predictors of Long-Term Recovery in Anorexia Nervosa and
    Bulimia Nervosa: Data from a 22-Year Longitudinal Study." *Journal of Psychiatric
    Research,* vol. 96, Jan. 2018, pp. 183-88. EBSCOhost, doi:10.1016/j.
    jpsychires.2017.10.008.

Galsworthy-Francis, Lisa, and Steven Allan. "Cognitive Behavioural Therapy for
    Anorexia Nervosa: A Systematic Review." *Clinical Psychology Review*, vol. 34, no.
    1, 2014, pp. 54-72.

Keski-Rahkonen, Anna, and Federica Tozzi. "The Process of Recovery in Eating
    Disorder Sufferers' Own Words: An Internet-based Study." *International Journal
    of Eating Disorders,* vol. 37, no. S1, 2005, pp. S80-S86.

Ponech, Heather, and Dawn Lorraine McBride. "Coming Together to Calm the
    Hunger: Group Therapy Program for Adults Diagnosed with Anorexia Nervosa."
    Journal of Groups in Addiction & Recovery, vol. 8, no. 4, 2013, pp. 309-28, doi:
    10.1080/1556035X.2013.836879.

Robinson, Paul H., and Dasha Nicholls, Eds. *Critical Care for Anorexia Nervosa: The Mar-
    sipan Guidelines in Practice.* Springer, 2015. ProQuest Ebook Central, ebookcentral.
    proquest.com/lib/unt/detail.action?docID=1974107.

Sharkey-orgnero, M. I. "Anorexia Nervosa: A Qualitative Analysis of Parents'
    Perspectives on Recovery." *Eating Disorders*, vol. 7, no. 2, 1999, pp. 123-41.

Manning 8

Tantillo, Mary, et al. "A Pilot Study of Multifamily Therapy Group for Young Adults with Anorexia Nervosa: Reconnecting for Recovery. *International Journal of Eating Disorders*, vol. 52, no. 8, Aug. 2019, pp. 950-55.

Touyz, Stephen, et al. "Is the Neglect of Exercise in Anorexia Nervosa Research a Case of 'Running Out' of Ideas or Do We Need to Take a 'LEAP' of Faith into the Future?" *Journal of Eating Disorders*, vol. 5, no. 1, 2017, doi:10.1186/s40337-017-0157-z.

Xia, Qiao C., et al. "Evaluating the Efficacy of Tui Na in Treatment of Childhood Anorexia: A Meta-Analysis." *Alternative Therapies in Health and Medicine*, vol. 20, no. 5, 2014, pp. 45-52.

Checking MLA Style

You are now aware of the basic requirements for formatting a paper in MLA style. Rhetorical Toolbox 12.1 can serve as a handy guide as you document and format your work in MLA style. Keep in mind that this chapter presents only an overview of the most fundamental elements of MLA style.

RHETORICAL TOOLBOX 12.1
Checking for MLA Style

Mark each instance in your paper in which you have used a source, and answer the following questions:

1. Have you created an in-text citation for the source?
2. Is the in-text citation correctly formed and punctuated?
3. Have you created a works-cited entry for the source?
4. Is the works-cited entry correctly formed and punctuated?
5. Does the information in the in-text citation match the wording on the works-cited page?
6. Is your paper formatted according to MLA style? Specifically, are each of these items formatted correctly?
   A. Margins
   B. Heading
   C. Title
   D. Header
   E. Line spacing
   F. Works-cited page formatting

USING APA STYLE

Teaching Resources
Consider using the PowerPoint "Creating In-Text Citations in APA Style."

Like the Modern Language Association, the American Psychological Association provides a handbook of style. While there are many differences in MLA and APA style, both rely on the use of in-text citations that match the bibliographic entries at the end of the paper. The guidelines that follow will show you how to create in-text citations as well as a reference list, a list of the sources used in the paper.

- When you use a source in a paper written in APA style, you need to create a parenthetical reference in the body of the paper.
- The parenthetical reference provides enough information so that readers can find the source in the list of references at the end of the paper.
- In APA style, the date on which a source was published is used in both the in-text citation and the bibliographic entry on the references list.

Creating In-Text Citations

An in-text citation is a reference to a source designed to show the information you used from a source. Readers should be able to look at the content within the parenthesis and use that content to find the source on the list of references. Any time you use a source—even if you use the source only for an idea—you must provide an in-text citation. The following rules and examples will help:

- The content in the in-text citation must match the content on the references page. For example, if the in-text citation lists "(Browne)," the name *Browne* must appear on the references page.
- If you use the author's name in the text you write, do not use the name in the in-text citation; conversely, if you do not use the name in the text, use the name in the in-text citation.
- If a source has no author listed, use the name of the source (its title or the name of the web page) in the parenthetical reference.
- Use page numbers to show the exact page from which you obtained the information, but use page numbers only when you are able to view the source as originally published. In other words, if you are examining a journal article from the journal itself and can see the original page numbers, use those numbers. Do NOT use page numbers if you obtain the source from an online database that does not provide the original page numbers. (APA also provides a method for citing paragraph numbers or sections. Consult your instructor to see if you will need to follow the APA's guidelines for this kind of citation.)
- Follow the rules for punctuation for in-text citations. Notice the punctuation tips in the examples that follow.
- When summarizing or paraphrasing your sources, use attributive tags to refer to the source (see Chapter 11) or to create an in-text citation.

In the examples that follow, notice how the in-text citation contains the name or word that begins the entry on the references page.

In-text Citation: One Author

Ted Genoways explains that Spam was created, in part, because "Paying high wages for slow-selling products was eating up Hormel's profits" (2014, p. 11).

OR

Spam was created, in part, to help Hormel maximize profits and continue to pay workers fairly (Genoways, 2014, p. 11).

Punctuation tip: The period for the sentence goes *after* the last parenthesis mark. Also, note that a comma is used after the writer's last name and after the date.

References entry:

Genoways, T. (2014). *The chain: Farm, factory, and the fate of our food.* Harper Collins.

In-text Citation: Two Authors

One of the reasons for the use of group psychotherapy is "the current health care climate with its emphasis on the efficacy and cost of services" (Ponech & McBride, 2013, p. 33).

OR

Ponech and McBride point out that group psychotherapy is common because of "the current health care climate with its emphasis on the efficacy and cost of services" (2013, p. 33).

References entry:

Ponech, H., & McBride, D. L. (2013). Coming together to calm the hunger: Group therapy program for adults diagnosed with anorexia nervosa. *Journal of Groups in Addiction & Recovery, 8*(4), 309–328. https//doi.org/10.1080/1556035X.2013.836879

In-text Citation: Three or More Authors

Social consensus intervention is "based on social influence whereby individuals tend to endorse values, beliefs, opinions, attitudes, or actions consistent with social norms" (Yan et al., 2018, p. 63).

OR

Yan et al. point out that social consensus intervention is "based on social influence whereby individuals tend to endorse values, beliefs, opinions, attitudes, or actions consistent with social norms" (2018, p. 63).

Punctuation tip: The term *et al.* means "and others," and it is always followed by a period because *al.* is an abbreviation for the Latin word *alia.*

Reference entry:

Yan, Y., Rieger, E., & Shou, Y. (2018). Reducing the stigma associated with anorexia nervosa: An evaluation of a social consensus intervention among Australian and Chinese young women. *International Journal of Eating Disorders, 51*(1), 62–70. https://doi.org/10.1002/eat.22808

In-text Citation: More than One Work by the Same Author

Roxanne Henkin points out that "So many of the bullying programs and safe schools initiatives are inadequate and don't address the realities that LGBTQ and bullied students face in high schools and middle schools today" (2012, p. 111). Henkin's chronicle of the history of AGLIA, the Assembly on Gay and Lesbian Academic Issues Awareness, part of the National Council of Teachers of English, makes clear that even in academia, LGBTQ faculty face issues similar to those our students face (2011, p. 76).

References entries:

Henkin, R. (2011). Creating a safe zone: LGBTQ work in NCTE. *The English Journal, 101*(1), 76–79.

Henkin, R. (2012). Confronting bullying: It really can get better. *The English Journal, 101*(6), 76–79.

In-text Citation: No Author, or Published by an Organization or Website

> As the Feeding America website shows, "nutrition-related illnesses disproportionately affect food-insecure people" (Leading the movement, 2019).
>
> *References entry:*
>
> Leading the movement to solve hunger. (2019). Feeding America. https://www.feedingamerica.org/our-work/our-approach/leading-the-fight

In-text Citation: Indirect Quotation

> Diablo Cody points out that "if the era of Facebook and Twitter has fed any monsters, it's those of vanity, self-obsession, and immaturity" (as cited in Orlando, 2015).
>
> *References entry:*
>
> Orlando, E. J. (2015). Edith Wharton and the new narcissism. *Women's Studies, 44* (6), 729–752. https//doi.org/10.1080/00497878.2015.1045690

Creating the References List

APA style requires writers to compile a list of the sources they use in their papers. This references list is placed at the end of the paper. Each source is presented as a references entry, and each entry is formatted in a precise manner. You may find it helpful to compile the same bibliographic information for an APA entry as you would for an MLA entry. Using the MLA template can help you to remember the information to find.

Once you have located as much information as you can to fill in the template, find the type of source (article, book, interview, etc.) in the list below. Use the example as a guide to create your references entry for the source. If you need additional information, consult *The Publication Manual of the American Psychological Association*, Seventh Edition, or the organization's website.

A Note about Multiple Authors. Regardless of the type of source, you must know how to account for a work written by a single author or multiple authors. Use these examples:

Teaching Resources
Consider assigning the APA Documentation Quiz.

One Author

Brazier, Y. (2018, January 19). Anorexia nervosa: Symptoms, causes, and treatment. *Medical News Today.* https://www.medicalnewstoday.com/articles/267432.php

Two Authors

Ponech, H., & McBride, D. L. (2013). Coming together to calm the hunger: Group therapy program for adults diagnosed with anorexia nervosa. *Journal of Groups in Addiction & Recovery, 8*(4), 309-328. https//doi.org/10.1080/1556035X.2013.836879

Three to Twenty Authors

All authors' names—up to and including twenty—should be listed in the author area of the entry. The last author's name is preceded by an ampersand (&).

Murcia, M. J., Rocha, H. O., & Birkinshaw, J. (2018). Business schools at the crossroads? A trip back from Sparta to Athens. *Journal of Business Ethics, 150*(2), 579-591. https//doi.org/10.1007/s10551-016-3129-3

Twenty-One or More Authors

If there are more than twenty-one authors, use ellipses points (. . .) after the nineteenth author. End the ellipses points with the name of the last author, skipping those in between.

Paresi, M., Wade, P., Morales, P. Z., Johnson, C. B., Sokolovsky, K., del Fontana, J., Lopez, J. C., Deister, V. G., Blanco, N., Santos, P. L., Kent, M., Raboso, P. M., Olarte Sierra, M. F., Chavez, A. F., del Castillo Hernández, A. D., Bergamo, F. A., Leone, P. J., Escavino, N. P., Bortolini, M. C., . . . García Deister, V. (2015). Nation and race in Latin American languages. *Current Linguistics, 56*(5), 356-381.

References: Articles. To create an APA style entry for an article, you will need several pieces of bibliographic information. By including a digital object identifier, commonly referred to as a DOI, you will enable readers to easily access the document. The DOI for an article is a string of numbers and letters. Each DOI is unique and leads to a specific document. However, not all articles have DOIs.

When an article does have one, you must include it. Readers should be able to click on it and go directly to the source.

Journal Article in Print

Carter, S. (2019). Comparison of student learning outcomes assessment practices used globally. *Athens Journal of Education*, *2*(3), 179–191.

Journal Article Online (or from an Online Database)

The database name is not needed unless it is absolutely necessary to locate the article. Most articles are available in multiple databases.

Bayerlein, L., & Jeske, D. (2018). Student learning opportunities in traditional and computer-mediated internships. *Education & Training*, *60*(1), 27–38. https://doi.org/10.1108/ET-10-2016-0157

Newspaper Article in Print

Lind, Michael. (2020, January 11–12). Saving democracy from the managerial elite. *The Wall Street Journal*, C1.

Newspaper Article Online

Weiss, B. (2019, October 7). The world's wokest sports league bows to China. *The New York Times*. https://www.nytimes.com/2019/10/07/opinion/nba-china-hong-kong.html

Magazine Article in Print

Ying, D. (2019, November 11). Revitalizing history. *Time Magazine*, *194*(21), 4–5.

Magazine Article Online

Pritchard, M. (2017, March 31). This is why anorexia might be so difficult to treat. *Fitness Magazine*. https://www.fitnessmagazine.com/mind-body/image/the-surprising-reason-anorexia-might-be-so-difficult-to-treat/

Article from a Website

Facts about eating disorders. (2019, April). Eating Disorders Coalition. http://eatingdisorderscoalition.org.s208556.gridserver.com/couch/uploads/file/edc-fact-sheet-revised.pdf

References: Books

Book in Print

Strathern, M. (1988). *The gender of the gift: Problems with women and problems with society in Melanesia.* University of California Press. https://doi.org/10.1525/ae.1989.16.3.02a00310

Ebook

Database information is not necessary. Include a doi if there is one.

Yan, W. (2014). *Crop variety trials: Data management and analysis.* Wiley. https://doi.org/10.1002/9781118688571

Book from a Multivolume Set

Flower, E., & Murphey, M. (1977). *A history of philosophy in America* (Vol. 2). Capricorn Books. https://doi.org/10.1093/0199260168.001.0001

Reprinted Work

Shelley, M. (1992). *Frankenstein* (J. M. Smith, Ed.). Bedford Books. (Original work published 1818)

Dictionary or Encyclopedia Entry

Davidson, T., & Nurmi, D. (2019). Anorexia nervosa. In *The Gale encyclopedia of mental health.*

Work in an Anthology

Sir Gawain and the green knight. 2015. In J. L. Black (Ed.), *The Broadview anthology of British literature* (3rd ed., p. 296). Broadview Press.

Unpublished Dissertation or Thesis

Conners, D. (2019). *Inseparable identities or not? Twin studies reexamined* [Unpublished doctoral dissertation]. University of Houston.

Sacred Text

The New Jerusalem Bible: Standard edition (1999). Doubleday.

References: Internet Sources

Web Page

Anorexia nervosa. (2015). Sheppard Pratt Health System. https://www.sheppardpratt.org/knowledge-center/condition/anorexia-nervosa/

Blog

Jefferson, T. (2019, September 26). If your students can relate, they can read, so give them culturally relevant texts. *Education Post*. https://educationpost.org/if-your-students-can-relate-they-can-read-so-give-them-culturally-relevant-texts/

YouTube or Other Streaming Video

Miller, B. (2019, September 9). *Anorexia nervosa—causes, symptoms, diagnosis, treatment & pathology* [Video]. YouTube. www.youtube.com/watch?v=olIz9MqtW-U

Social Media Posting

Modi, N. [@narendramodi]. (2019, December 16). *I want to unequivocally assure my fellow Indians that CAA does not affect any citizen of India of any religion. No Indian has anything to worry regarding this Act. This Act is only for those who have faced years of persecution outside and have no other place to go except India* [Tweet]. Twitter. https://twitter.com/narendramodi/status/1206492850378002432

Podcast

Bryant, C., and Clark, J. (Hosts). (2019, December 5). What's a gap year anyway? [Audio podcast episode]. In *Stuff you should know*. https://www.iheart.com/podcast/105-stuff-you-should-know-26940277/episode/whats-a-gap-year-anyway-53486926/childrens-book-panel/

Streaming Television (Entire Series)

Waller-Bridge, P. (Executive Producer). (2016–2019). *Fleabag* [TV series]. Two Brothers Pictures.

Streaming Television (Specific Episode)

Waller-Bridge, P. (Writer & Executive Producer). (2016, August 4). (Season 1, Episode 3) [TV series episode]. In P. Waller-Bridge (Executive Producer), *Fleabag*. Two Brothers Pictures.

Email

Do not put an email on the references page. Rather, cite it only in the text.

References: Miscellaneous Sources

Conference Presentation

Hawkins, M. (2019, May 10). *Adjusting pedagogy for dialects* [Paper presentation]. 10th Annual Literacy K-12 Conference, Syracuse, NY, United States.

Lecture

Oldman, R. (2020, October 3). *SGGK chivalric code* [Lecture]. Tarleton State University, Stephenville, TX, United States.

Movie

Coen, E. (Producer), & Coen, J. (Director). (1998). *The big Lebowski* [Film]. Working Title Films.

Advertisement

M&M Mars. (2019, January 30). M&M'S chocolate bar Super Bowl commercial [Advertisement]. YouTube. https://www.youtube.com/watch?v=5CCRNmmnG3c

Brochure

Costa Rica Tourism Board. (2019). *Essential Costa Rica* [Brochure].

Congressional Legislation

Homeland Procurement Reform Act. (2019). House, 116th Cong.

Court Case

Brown v. Board of Educ., 347 U.S. 483 (1954).

Government Publication

U.S. Department of Health and Human Services. (2017). *Anorexia nervosa*.

    https://www.mentalhealth.gov/what-to-look-for/eating-disorders/anorexia

Map

Britton, P. (2019). *Map of Egypt at 3500 BC* [Map]. https://www.timemaps.

    com/history/ancient-egypt-3500bc/

Painting/Photo/Other Work of Art

Van Gogh, V. (1889). *Starry Night* [Oil on canvas]. Museum of Modern Art,

    New York, NY, United States.

Performance

The phantom of the opera. (2019, October 26). Live performance at the

    Majestic Theater, New York, NY, United States.

Personal Interview

Cite personal interviews in the body of the paper, not the references list.

Raw Data

United States Census Bureau. (2019). *International programs* [Data set].

    https://www.census.gov/data-tools/demo/idb/region.php?T=13&RT=0&

    A=both&Y=2019&C=GR&R=

Report

Srinivasa, P. et al. (2015). Case report on anorexia nervosa. National Center

    for Biotechnology Information Search Database. www.ncbi.nlm.nih.gov/

    pmc/articles/PMC4418263/

▶ **ACTIVITY 3** **Understanding APA Style**

Indicate whether each of the following statements is true or false. If a statement is false, correct it.

1. When referring to the volume of a journal, abbreviate and capitalize "volume," like this: Vol.
2. Use a comma between the author and the page number in a parenthetical reference, like this: (Aronsen, 114).
3. When using a source by three or more authors, list the first author's name in the references entry followed by *et al.*, like this: Jameson, T., et al.
4. If you read a source but do not use it in your paper, you must still include it on the references page.
5. The following parenthetical reference is correctly punctuated:

    Survivors claimed the chemical exposure left them permanently disabled. (Konech, 52).

Formatting a Paper in APA Style

In addition to providing guidelines for in-text citations and for the list of references, APA style specifies how a paper is to be formatted. The following paper is written in APA style. Notice the formatting conventions. For more detailed information, consult the *Publication Manual of the American Psychological Association,* Seventh Edition.

Tori Manning, Finding a Treatment for Anorexia (Sample Paper in APA Style)

Finding a Treatment for Anorexia

Tori Manning

Department of English, McLennan Community College

ENGL 1301.16

Dr. Stein

November 11, 2020

2

Finding a Treatment for Anorexia

In a world dominated by images of thin supermodels, eating disorders among women are common. Because eating disorders are not exotic diseases, it may seem that they are not all that dangerous. Nothing could be further from the truth. The Eating Disorders Coalition (EDC), an advocacy group that attempts to raise awareness about eating disorders, has compiled some statistics that make clear how serious these disorders are. Among adolescent girls, eating disorders are the "the 3rd most common chronic illness" (*Facts about eating disorders*, 2019). Even more alarming, "Every 62 minutes at least one person dies as a direct result from an eating disorder" (*Facts about eating disorders*, 2019).

These statistics are worrisome; the prevalence of eating disorders and their potential harm cannot be overstated. Unfortunately, recognizing the problem does not necessarily mean there are ready solutions for eating disorders. One of the most common disorders, anorexia nervosa, is particularly challenging to cure. Anorexia nervosa is a "psychiatric disorder characterized by an unrealistic fear of weight gain, conspicuous distortion of body image, and self-starvation. Individuals with this disorder are obsessed with becoming increasingly thinner and limit food intake to the point at which health is compromised" (Davidson & Nurmi, 2019, p. 95). Because anorexia is so devastating and because it affects so many adolescent girls, it is imperative that healthcare providers find therapies that actually work to aid recovery. In spite of being notoriously difficult to treat, anorexia nervosa has been shown to respond to several therapies.

One of the challenges faced by those who seek to treat anorexia is the fact that patients often deny having the disease. Because they do not feel thin enough, they are unable to see their bodies objectively (Davidson & Nurmi, 2019. When a patient is in denial, treatment is difficult. The patient may not comply with the advice offered by healthcare providers. It is easy to see how treating the mental condition of the patient might be the first step to take. Those who advocate a psychological approach to treating anorexia nervosa often do so for this reason. M. Irene Sharkey-orgnero (1999), for example, points out that the belief systems of some people who suffer from anorexia are an inherent part of the problem of finding a treatment that works: "Many patients with anorexia nervosa describe how, through penitence and self-denial, they will be rewarded with a complete and permanent happiness that is almost heavenly" (p. 182). Sharkey-orgnero goes on to point out that "the religiosity of this belief is added to by culturally accepted attitudes that describe fasting as good (righteous) and satiety as bad (weak)" (p. 182). Countering such a belief can be difficult and can take years of therapy.

One of the mental health treatments most commonly used to help those suffering from anorexia nervosa is cognitive behavioral therapy (CBT). Cognitive behavioral therapy

> . . . is an action-oriented form of psychosocial therapy that assumes that maladaptive, or faulty, thinking patterns cause maladaptive behavior and "negative" emotions. (Maladaptive behavior is behavior that is counterproductive or interferes with everyday living.) The treatment focuses on changing an individual's thoughts (cognitive patterns) in order to change his or her behavior and emotional state. (Ford-Martin et al., 2019)

The idea behind the CBT approach is that if a therapist can help a client see how behaviors and faulty thinking result in the disease, the patient can change the way he or she thinks and behaves; in turn, the disease is cured. It is easy to see how a person who is in denial about the diagnosis of anorexia would *not* necessarily benefit from CBT. While CBT is often used to treat anorexia, the technique has not been shown to be superior to other therapies (Galsworthy-Francis & Allan, 2014).

A different form of CBT, called *enhanced* cognitive behavioral therapy (CBT-E), has been deemed "a viable and promising treatment for patients with severe and enduring anorexia nervosa" (Calugi et al., 2017, p. 42). The disease is classified as severe and enduring anorexia (SE-AN) when a patient has been anorexic for more than seven years. Patients who have struggled with anorexia for this long often face significant medical complications and the real possibility of dying from the disease (Touyz et al., 2017). The focus of CBT-E for these patients is *not* on recovery: instead it is on enhancing the patient's quality of life (Calugi et al., 2017). What researchers found, however, is that enhanced cognitive behavioral

4

therapy that is focused on quality of life—rather than recovery—had surprisingly positive effects. First, the patients stayed in the program, and that is a significant factor since lack of participation is so often the cause for a remedy's failure. Second, participants "achieved a substantial increase in BMI, and significant improvements in eating-disorder and general psychopathology" (Calugi et al., 2017, p. 45). Finally, "between baseline and 12-month follow-up, the majority of patients changed status from extreme to mild current level of AN severity" (Calugi, 2017, p. 45). In-patient enhanced cognitive behavioral therapy seems to hold promise as an effective treatment for anorexia nervosa.

Another mental health therapy—group counseling and variations of it—holds more promise in the treatment of anorexia nervosa. Ponech and McBride (2013) point out that group counseling has an advantage over individual counseling because of the personal contact involved. Participants gain a sense of shared experiences, and the dialogue that goes on within group counseling sessions seems to help participants come to terms with their disorders and be more willing to accept the need for treatment (Ponech & McBride, 2013). One of the greatest challenges in treating anorexia is retaining patients. A new type of group therapy, Multi-Family Therapy Group (MFTG), shows promise in its ability to retain patients and to treat anorexia successfully. In MFTG, five to seven anorexic patients, as well as their families, come together for counseling, discussing, goal-setting, and support (Tantillo et al., 2019). Because these patients and their families get to know each other and develop friendships during sessions, a sense of trust is established. Patients are able to openly talk about their disorders, and families learn the best methods for intervening to help their loved ones. Tantillo et al. recruited and retained ten patients and their families for the study. The patients made progress in gaining weight and in showing an increased understanding of the factors that motivate anorexic tendencies. In short, "This pilot study demonstrated that R4R [Reconnecting for Recovery program] is a promising intervention for young adults with AN" (Tantillo et al., 2019, p. 953). While more research is needed, the use of Multi-Family Therapy Groups seems to be one of the most promising treatments for anorexia.

In addition to treating anorexia by addressing mental health, there has been some research on alternative therapies that can affect anorexia. These therapies include hypnotherapy, yoga, body awareness therapy, acupuncture, massage, and biofeedback. While each therapy claims some success, there is not enough research to support the idea that these therapies are generally useful. For example, in a limited study of the use of massage and acupuncture, Stephen Eddey (2014) found that participants had increases in their BMI (body mass index) which indicated weight gain, as well as a self-reported decrease in their eating-related concerns. But this study included only 26 patients, and its author acknowledges that more research is needed to confirm the results (Eddey, 2014). The ancient Chinese Hua Tuo treatments are a type of massage that some practitioners believe can be helpful to treat the anxiety that often causes anorexic behaviors (Xia, 2014). The results of Hua Tuo treatments were "at least comparable with [other] alternative treatments" (Xia, 2014, p. 49), but since other alternative treatments have had limited success, there is little reason to hope Hua Tuo will be curative. Nasim Furoughgi and his fellow researchers (2019) examined the most commonly used alternative treatments for anorexia, and they found that although people had great faith in these treatments, there is little evidence suggesting alternative therapies are effective.

Finally, the most acute cases of anorexia must be treated by focusing on the physical aspects of the disease. Because anorexia is a disease that can be fatal, medical interventions focus on increasing BMI (body mass index) and treating the issues that occur as a result of malnutrition. Patients who have been admitted to a hospital for acute and life-threatening anorexia may be treated using the MARSIPAN protocol. MARSIPAN stands for "Management of Really Sick Patients with Anorexia Nervosa" (Robinson & Nicholls, 2015, p. 5). As Paul Robinson and Dasha Nicholls explain, the protocol advised by this group involves taking care of the most serious medical issues to treat the patient. For instance, a patient may need to be given serum electrolytes, nutritional supplements administered via food or a nasogastric tube, and strict oversight to make sure that a common medical complication called "refeeding syndrome" does not occur (Robinson & Nicholls, 2015).

The goal of any anorexia treatment program should be completely curing the disease so that a patient's condition will not progress to the need for an in-patient hospital stay. Perhaps the best treatment for recovery from anorexia consists of a

6

combination of the available remedies. By examining a wide variety of studies, researchers have identified certain factors that predict successful recovery from the disease. First, those who recover successfully have found a way to manage their mood and anxiety symptoms (Keski-Rahkonen & Tozzi, 2005). Because anorexia is so often driven by anxiety about body weight, helping patients figure out how to manage that anxiety seems to be a crucial part of recovery. The use of cognitive behavioral therapy is one way to teach patients to manage anxiety. While CBT was not shown to be a totally effective treatment for anorexia, combining it with other treatments may make the therapy more successful. In addition to managing anxiety and mood, developing positive personality traits is also associated with recovery (Franko et al., 2018). One way patients can learn about their personality and how it affects their disease is to participate in multi-family therapy groups (MFTG). In such groups, leaders can facilitate discussions about how personality tendencies—such as perfectionism—can contribute to anorexic tendencies. If an alternative therapy such as massage or biofeedback contributes to less anxiety, that therapy should also be used in tandem with CBT and MFTG.

Anorexia is a stubborn disease. It is difficult to treat, and the research shows that there is no one therapy that is effective for all patients. By experimenting with and using a combination of available therapies, healthcare practitioners may be able to help patients recover from the disease before it becomes life-threatening.

7

References

Calugi, S., et al. (2017). Intensive enhanced cognitive behavioural therapy for severe and enduring anorexia nervosa: A longitudinal outcome study. *Behaviour Research and Therapy, 89*, 41–48. https//doi.org/10.1016/j.brat.2016.11.006

Davidson, T. (2015). Anorexia nervosa. In J. L. Longe (Ed.), *The Gale encyclopedia of medicine* (5th ed., Vol. 1, pp. 282–286). Gale.

Eddey, S. (2014, March). Media watch: The treatment of anorexia nervosa using acupuncture and/or massage. *Journal of the Australian Traditional-Medicine Society, 20*(1), 57.

8

Facts about eating disorders. (2019, April). Eating Disorders Coalition. http://eating-disorderscoalition.org.s208556.gridserver.com/couch/uploads/file/edc-fact-sheet-revised.pdf

Ford-Martin, P. A., Weidman, C., & Lerner, B. W. (2019). Cognitive-behavioral therapy. In B. Narins (Ed.), *The Gale encyclopedia of mental health* (4th ed., Vol. 1, pp. 378-382). Gale.

Foroughi, N., Zhu, C. Y., Smith, C., & Hay, P. (2019). The perceived therapeutic benefits of complementary medicine in eating disorders. *Complementary Therapies in Medicine, 43,* 176-180. https://doi.org/10.1016/j.ctim.2019.01.025

Franko, D. L., Tabri, N., Keshaviah, A., Murray, H. B., Herzog, D. B., Thomas, J. J., . . . Eddy, K. T. (2018). Predictors of long-term recovery in anorexia nervosa and bulimia nervosa: Data from a 22-year longitudinal study. *Journal of Psychiatric Research, 96,* 183-188. https://doi.org/10.1016/j.jpsychires.2017.10.008

Galsworthy-Francis, L., & Allan, S. (2014). Cognitive behavioural therapy for anorexia nervosa: A systematic review. *Clinical Psychology Review, 34*(1), 54-72. https://doi.org/10.1016/j.cpr.2013.11.001

Ponech, H., & McBride, D. L. (2013). Coming together to calm the hunger: Group therapy program for adults diagnosed with anorexia nervosa. *Journal of Groups in Addiction & Recovery, 8*(4), 309-328. https://doi.org/10.1080/1556035X.2013.836879

Robinson, P., & Nicholls, D. (Eds.) (2015). *Critical care for anorexia nervosa: The marsipan guidelines in practice.* Springer.

Sharkey-orgnero, M. I. (1999). Anorexia nervosa: A qualitative analysis of parents' perspectives on recovery. *Eating Disorders, 7*(2), 123-141. https://doi.org/10.1080/10640269908251191

Tantillo, M., McGraw, J. S., Lavigne, H. M., Brasch, J., & Le Grange, D. (2019). A pilot study of multifamily therapy group for young adults with anorexia nervosa: Reconnecting for recovery. *International Journal of Eating Disorders, 52*(8), 950-955. https://doi.org/10.1002/eat.23097

Touyz, S., Hay, P., & Noetel, M. (2017). Is the neglect of exercise in anorexia nervosa research a case of "running out" of ideas or do we need to take a "LEAP" of faith into the future? *Journal of Eating Disorders, 5*(1). https://doi.org/10.1186/s40337-017-0157-z

> Xia, Q. C., Feng, Z. X., & Ping, C. X. (2014). Evaluating the efficacy of Tui Na in treatment of childhood anorexia: A meta-analysis. *Alternative Therapies in Health and Medicine, 20*(5), 45–52.

9

Reflecting to Develop a Writer's Mindset

How can following the instructions in a style guide affect your credibility as a writer? In other words, what does it say about a writer when he or she makes errors in style? What impression is made by a writer who makes no errors in style? How might the use of stylistic conventions affect your reputation in non-academic writing scenarios, such as the workplace?

FAQ TWO DOCUMENTATION SHORTCUTS

Two tools can be especially helpful when writing a research paper: online citation generators and plagiarism checking services. Sometimes these are free services and may even be provided by your college or university.

Co-requisite Teaching Tip
Consider spending time to help students select citation generators and use them effectively.

1. **What are citation generators?**

   Instead of creating a works-cited or references page entry yourself, you can let your computer do it for you. Citation generators are online tools that enable you to enter information about a source and create a works-cited or references page entry for the source. Of course, the responsibility for checking the accuracy of the citations is ultimately yours, but having a tool at your disposal may make the process of creating entries easier. The following list presents two methods you can use to generate citations online.

   - Use the citation creation tools within online databases. When you find an article or book in an online database, you are often given the option to create a citation for the source. Usually, you can click on "cite" or "create citation." You are then prompted to enter the style manual you are using (APA, MLA, or others), and the program automatically generates a citation.

- Independent citation creation sites prompt you to enter information or the address of a website and can then create a citation for your source. For instance, EasyBib is a citation generator that uses the information inputted to build a citation. To find additional citation generators, do an internet search for "create citation." Some of these sites may require a fee, but most are free.

2. **What are plagiarism checking services?**

   If your college or university uses a learning management system—such as Blackboard, Canvas, Moodle, or BrightSpace—you may have access to a plagiarism checking service. Turnitin is an example of a plagiarism checking service that is built into some of the learning management systems commonly used. Such services allow you to upload your paper and to receive a report on whether or not there is any plagiarism in the paper. Of course, you are ultimately responsible for checking for plagiarism, but using a service can give you a head start. For more information about the services available to you, ask your instructor, a tutor in your campus's writing center, or a librarian.

   ### TRY IT!

   Find either an online citation creator or a plagiarism checking service. Use the tool, and then write two or three sentences explaining the advantages and any potential disadvantages of the tool.

PART 4 Arguments in Depth

13 Recognizing Arguments

CHAPTER OBJECTIVES

You will learn to:
- Define argument.
- Identify arguments by recognizing claims and reasons.
- Identify arguments by examining the rhetorical situation: speaker, genre, and purpose.
- Write a brief rhetorical analysis that focuses on claims, reasons, and rhetorical situations.

We live in a country that is always changing and evolving. Some of the changes represent real progress: slavery is illegal, women can vote, people with disabilities are protected by law, and so on. In hindsight, it may be tempting to say, *Of course, slavery is illegal, women can vote, and people with disabilities should be protected!* But these hallmarks of progress were not "of course" issues in the past. We have this progress only because people argued that things had to change. Argument is key to progress because argument disrupts the status quo and suggests—or more accurately, insists—that change is necessary.

Clearly, arguing effectively has real-world value in all three domains of life: academic/professional, public, and personal. We use argument to change society for the better and to make decisions in the workplace that affect the productivity and value of our companies. Argument has personal value, too. The person who argues well is the one who is listened to, the one who thinks critically enough to find the real issues involved in any debate, the one who can figure out the most effective words to get people to listen. The person who argues well has the power to make real change happen, whether that change is at work, in personal life, or in the world. In short, having a strong set of argument skills is invaluable.

In the first parts of this text, you have seen how thinking rhetorically can help you to analyze and critique what you read, and in turn, use your insights to become a better writer. Thinking rhetorically helps you make sound writing decisions and equips you with a variety of tools you can use to convey your

Connect Adaptive Learning Assignment
Consider assigning Connect's Adaptive Learning Assignments to support this chapter.

Teaching Resources
See the Instructor's Manual (IM) for suggestions about how to teach this chapter, and consider assigning this chapter's test-bank quiz.

Teaching Suggestion
The study of argument often gives rise to contentious debates, especially when the topics are hot-button issues. Teaching students to analyze dispassionately is important, and using advertisements is a good way to begin. See the IM for more information.

message to an audience. Studying argument will help you further develop a writer's mindset so that when you write to persuade, you can select the most effective rhetorical strategies. You will begin to see that argument is everywhere, and you will begin to understand how arguments are constructed—and how they can be dismantled by keen analysis. The rhetorical analysis of arguments will help you evaluate more critically the many persuasive messages you encounter each day.

WARM-UP

As early as the 1940s, tobacco companies were beginning to realize the dangers of smoking. When the ad shown in Figure 13.1 was created in 1946, the companies knew that there was a link between smoking and lung cancer and that cigarette smoke was carcinogenic. With this background in mind, examine the ad and then answer the questions that follow.

1. What methods does the ad use to try to sell Camel cigarettes?
2. Why do you think the ad creators selected the details in the ad, including the graphics, given the growing awareness that smoking leads to lung cancer?

WHAT IS AN ARGUMENT?

As you may have already realized, the word *argument* has different meanings. In its popular use, an *argument* is an angry exchange; it is something usually to be avoided. However, in academic and public domains, an argument is simply a type of communication in which a speaker conveys a point of view by providing reasons to support it. Written academic arguments, such as persuasively oriented research papers, are one type of argument. In a courtroom, an attorney may deliver an *opening argument*, a brief summary showing why the defendant is innocent. On the showroom floor, a car salesperson will subtly use argument to suggest a shopper should buy a certain vehicle. When we interview for a job, the clothes we wear, behaviors we exhibit, and words we choose function as support for the argument that we should be hired. In brief, any time we hope to convince an audience of some point, we make an argument.

Research papers, trial lawyers' speeches, and sales pitches are clearly arguments, but some communications that may not seem like arguments may, indeed, also be classified as such. Think about a news article, for example. We expect a news article to present facts, but *which facts*? By presenting certain facts and withholding others, a news article may actually be presenting an argument.

Even a story can present an argument. The way the story is told can suggest meanings that go beyond the story itself. If you have ever watched a program such as *20/20* or *Dateline*, you have seen that *how* a story is told—the content choices that are made, the background information that is provided, the tone the speaker uses, and even the music—can lead viewers to conclusions about the mystery (or crime) being presented. One technique these programs often use is first to present the story from one point of view and to follow that original presentation with details that were originally left out. The second telling of the story

Teaching Suggestion
To help students see the arguments in news stories, select two news articles on the same topic, one from a conservative source and one from a liberal source. Have students identify how the articles differ and how even the presentation of news involves argument.

> **Teaching Resources**
> If you would like to have students analyze a more current advertisement, consider using the exercise "Analyzing an Advertisement."

FIGURE 13.1 Cigarette advertisement, 1946.

helps viewers see that the issue is actually more complex, and the solution is not as simple as it first appears.

When we fail to see the arguments around us, we can succumb to faulty thinking that has real-world implications. We might accept an argument without considering its merits, and the results can be costly. In the Warm-Up activity, you examined a cigarette advertisement that attempts to sound like a presentation of facts, not an argument. We could critique the "data" presented in the ad in numerous ways: while the ad refers to "a recent Nationwide survey," no sources are presented and no information about who was surveyed is provided. We have no idea whether the survey was conducted by the cigarette company or by a twelve-year-old, and no details about the supposed "study" are presented. Instead of providing this information, the ad brings up an issue that seems irrelevant: women's accomplishments. Obviously, the ad writers hope to suggest that successful women smoke Camel cigarettes. We can infer that the ad writers anticipate an audience of female readers. By linking cigarettes to successful women, the ad writers hope that more women will start smoking. In addition, the profession of the successful woman in the picture is significant: she is a doctor. If doctors smoke Camels, the ad writers imply, then smoking Camels must be okay for one's health! Tobacco companies knew that cigarettes were deadly, but they argued for years—in advertisements, articles, and reports—that there was no harm in smoking. How many lives could have been saved if people had questioned that argument?

When we analyze an argument in the way the last few sentences do, we are producing a rhetorical analysis. A *rhetorical analysis* is an analysis of the choices a writer makes to produce a text. For instance, one of the choices made by the creators of the Camel ad was to use pseudo-scientific language. Why do the writers use such language? Which particular words make the text sound scientifically authoritative? Does the ad merely *sound* authoritative or is the evidence truly trustworthy? These are the kinds of questions you will ask and answer in a rhetorical analysis. Each chapter in Part 4 develops your ability to write a complete rhetorical analysis of an argument. In this chapter, we focus on the first step: how to identify an argument.

IDENTIFYING AN ARGUMENT BY ITS CLAIM AND REASONS

Earlier, we defined argument as a belief or point of view a speaker hopes to convey by providing reasons. We will now introduce a new term and modify this definition a bit: an **argument** is a claim supported by reasons. One way to identify an argument is to look for two essential elements: a claim and the reasons that support the claim. Let's examine claims and reasons in more depth.

Claims

A *claim* is a statement that is debatable. Here are some claims:

- Understanding math at a deep level is important.
- The federal government should require all states to create welfare-to-work programs.
- Basic internet access should be provided free of charge to all households.

All three statements present ideas that are debatable. More importantly, we cannot refute (disprove) these claims simply by looking up a fact or a piece of data. These claims present opinions that require support and deliberation. For example, it may or may not be true that a deep-level understanding of math is important. In addition, no one will ever be able to prove beyond the shadow of a doubt that understanding math at a deep level is important. Because the claim is not *provable*, we must create an argument to support it. The reasons we present may be convincing enough for a reader to agree with the claim.

We can now add to the definition of a claim: a **claim** is not only a debatable statement, but it is also a statement for which no definitive or absolute proof exists; it is a statement that depends on support to be accepted.

claim: The thesis statement of a persuasively oriented text; a statement of the writer's opinion or assertion of an arguable point.

What Is Not a Claim? Let's take a look at two types of statements that are not claims, that is, not debatable and not provable: personal preferences and facts.

Personal preferences. *Living in California is better than living in Vermont.* No one can argue with a preference, so in our study of argument, we will not label statements of personal preference as claims.

Additional examples of personal preferences include:

- Sleeping late on a rainy Saturday is wonderful.
- Oregano has an enticing aroma.

Basic facts. *Olive oil is used in Mediterranean cuisines.* This statement could be easily proven by looking at evidence. Any statement that can be supported by evidence that most people accept as true or scientific can be considered a basic fact.

Additional examples of facts include:

- The Declaration of Independence was signed in 1776.
- COVID-19 is a type of coronavirus.
- Oxygen is flammable.

Explicit and Implicit Claims. So far we have discussed explicit claims—those that are stated directly. When a claim is stated in a sentence, it is the thesis statement of the argument. An implicit claim, however, is not stated; it is implied by the details of the text. When a text does not include an explicit claim, you can infer it, or figure it out, and put it in your own words. If you have trouble inferring claims, see "FAQ: Making Accurate Inferences" at the end of this chapter.

Here is an example of a simple argument with an implicit claim.

Argument with an Implicit Claim

Recent studies show that children who have been bullied are at greater risk for mental health problems when they grow older. Being the victim of bullying also correlates with a higher risk of unemployment. These studies confirm the findings of earlier research that showed just how damaging bullying can be to students. Teachers are in a unique position to be able to reduce incidences of bullying.

Putting the Claim into Your Own Words

Teachers should do what they can to prevent bullying.

Recognizing claims is the first step toward identifying arguments. Try your hand at recognizing claims in the exercise that follows.

Teaching Resources
Consider using the exercise "Identifying Arguable Statements."

▶ **ACTIVITY 1 Recognizing Claims**

Examine the statements that follow. Which are claims? Which are not? Why? Justify your answer for each statement.

  A. Spanking is an ineffective type of punishment.
  B. Spanking should be illegal.
  C. Some parents who spank their children have been investigated by Child Protective Services.
  D. I prefer to use time-out sessions rather than spankings.

Reasons

To be an argument, a claim must be followed with support. This support consists of reasons that explain why the claim is true. The reasons motivate the audience to believe or act on the claim. Here is an example of one of the claims we examined earlier followed by reasons:

Claim

Basic internet access should be provided free of charge to all households.

Reasons

- Internet access makes equality more attainable.
- Internet access contributes to the ability of ordinary people to monitor their governments' actions and respond appropriately.
- Access to the internet contributes to the education of millions of people.
- Internet access provides vital, life-saving information.
- Access to the internet equips people with a means for finding jobs and generating income, contributing to a higher quality of life.

By examining the reasons, you can tell that reasons themselves require support. A reason will need to be explained and supported with evidence such as examples, facts, statistics, and other types of information.

Arguments consist of more than claims and reasons, but the first step to identifying an argument is to find these two vital elements. When expressed in an argument essay, a claim is the thesis statement of the essay, and the reasons are presented in the body of the argument. For now, we consider arguments as texts that *at the very least* consist of a claim supported by reasons.

Teaching Resources
Consider using the argument essays in Part 6 as additional texts for analysis. See the IM for more information and a list of the argument texts available.

▶ **ACTIVITY 2 Identifying Arguments by Finding Claims and Reasons**

Read the passage that follows. What is the claim? What reasons are given to support the claim? Is the passage an argument?

Year-round schooling should replace the "summers off" model of public education. When students take off the summer, they stop using their newly acquired learning and skills for nearly twelve weeks. Brain science has demonstrated that learners need constant, regular practice to truly master a skill or commit information to long-term memory. Summer breaks interrupt the learning process, making it necessary to reteach concepts when school begins again in the fall.

IDENTIFYING ARGUMENTS BY EXAMINING THE RHETORICAL SITUATION

You may remember from Chapter 1 that the rhetorical situation of a communication consists of three essential elements—the writer or speaker, the message, and the audience—and four related elements: immediate situation, broader context, genre, and purpose (see Figure 13.2). Analyzing the parts of the rhetorical situation will help you decide whether or not a text presents an argument.

Analyzing the Writer or Speaker's Credentials and Bias

One way to identify an argument is to consider the person who is speaking or writing. Examine the writer's credentials. Credentials include facts such as the writer's qualifications (job, position, degrees, experience) and reputation. Additionally, if you can identify the writer's interests or the focus of the writer's work, you may be able to make some predictions about the writer's opinions and biases. You can then examine the text to see if it presents the writer's opinions.

Once you have analyzed the writer's credentials and interests, look over the text's language to see if it contains bias. The word *bias* sometimes has negative connotations. You have probably heard statements such as "The judge was biased" or "I'm proud of Maria, but I'm her mom, so I'm biased." These

> **Teaching Suggestion**
> Consider discussing the issue of objectivity. While writers may attempt to be objective, very few can write without revealing a bias. Help students to identify these biases by closely examining texts and authors. For more information, see the IM.

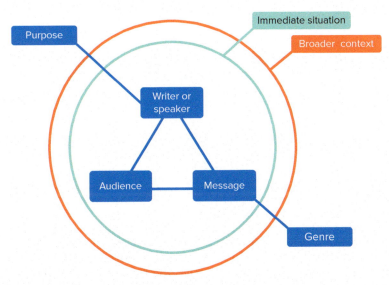

FIGURE 13.2 The rhetorical situation.

bias: In argument, a point of view or opinion.

statements imply that being biased is somehow wrong or bad, but in the study of argument, we use the word *bias* in a neutral way. A **bias** is simply a point of view. If a person does not care about (or know about) an issue, the person has no bias. On the other hand, a person who holds an opinion on an issue is biased. In argument, being biased is not good or bad: it simply means that one has an opinion.

As you look for bias, keep in mind who the speaker is and what the speaker stands for. If, for instance, you are reading an argument written by the president of a teachers union, you can expect the writer to be biased about issues affecting education. On the other hand, if you are reading a newspaper article by a journalist, you may not be able to find out enough about the journalist to expect any bias.

Teaching Resources Consider using the PowerPoint "Identifying Biases."

Analyzing the Writer or Speaker's Tone and Voice

A text can be written with a subjective or objective tone. A subjective tone allows the writer's voice to be heard. The writer may use personal pronouns such as *I* and *my,* and the writer's personal opinions may be evident. An objective tone, on the other hand, is often used in texts that present facts and information without aiming to convince or persuade a reader. A writer attempts to be objective by presenting a subject fairly, by not offering a personal point of view or opinion, and by removing personal commentary from the text as much as possible. This removal of the writer's voice is accomplished in part by using the third person point of view. Table 13.1 demonstrates the features of each type of tone.

Analyzing the Writer or Speaker's Purpose

Another way to identify an argument is to identify the writer or speaker's purpose. If the purpose is to debate the merits of a claim, to convince, or to urge

TABLE 13.1 Subjective versus Objective Tone

Subjective Tone	Objective Tone
• May use first person (*I, my, mine, we, our, ours*) • May use second person (*you, your, yours*) • May use opinion-revealing adjectives: for instance, *moral, good, bad, reliable, honest, evil, right, wrong* • May include passages that reveal the writer's emotions	• Uses third person (*one, they*) • Avoids the use of opinion-revealing adjectives • Uses neutral and factual language • Uses little to no emotional language
Example: Some people think that adults who are in prison because they committed murder as juveniles should be released and given a second chance. This idea is ridiculous. I know that I would not want to live next door to an adult who killed his parents when he was thirteen.	*Example:* Some people think that adults who are in prison because they committed murder as juveniles should be released and given a second chance. They claim that the crime was committed long before the child could mature; thus, they believe that re-examining the case after the child has matured is necessary.

an action or behavior, the text is probably an argument. Consider each of the following purposes that arguments serve:

- **We use argument to explore the merits of a claim.** Some arguments exist to further the discussion of a claim by examining its reasons. For instance, recent measles outbreaks have resulted in some cities passing ordinances that *require* everyone to be immunized against measles. Should individuals have the right to refuse to be vaccinated? A paper in which this question is discussed and debated may not result in a clear answer; however, the reasons for the claim that everyone should be vaccinated will be examined and evaluated. This kind of argument helps to clarify an issue, to bring the best reasons to the table, to discredit reasons that are weak, and to reach some tentative conclusions about the subject. For example, a paper about vaccinations may conclude with the claim that more immunological research is required before communities should mandate universal vaccinations.

- **We use argument to convince others of a claim.** In arguments that attempt to persuade readers, the writer's goal is to provide the reasoning that an audience would need to believe or accept the writer's claim. The goal of such an argument is to provide a case so compelling that the audience must agree with the writer's claim. The arguments created by attorneys when they represent clients in court are good examples of using argument to convince. A defense attorney will craft an argument by using the best reasons, the highest-quality research, the testimonies of experts, and so on, to convince a jury that their client is not guilty.

- **We use argument to motivate others to take action or change behaviors.** Some arguments exist to urge the audience to do something. For instance, some educators believe that year-round schooling (swapping a long summer break for shorter, more frequent breaks throughout the year) is a better way to administer public education; thus an advocate may use argument to urge schools to adopt a year-round schedule. The goal of such an argument is to motivate change: the implementation of a new scheduling plan.

Often, when we communicate, we are trying to accomplish multiple purposes. For example, a lawyer arguing a case needs to inform jurors about the facts of the case in order to persuade them that the defendant is guilty or innocent. You may have even seen lawyers attempt to entertain jurors. Entertaining jurors may help the lawyer form a positive bond with them, and this bond may help the lawyer accomplish their primary purpose: to persuade.

When you examine a text to identify whether or not it is an argument, look for the writer's purpose. If the purpose is to debate the merits of a claim, to convince or persuade, or to urge an action or behavior, the text is probably an argument.

Analyzing the Genre and Publication

A text's genre can give important clues that will help you determine whether it presents an argument. In fact, some genres are dedicated to presenting

Teaching Suggestion
Not all students are familiar with positions on the political spectrum and terms such as *liberal, conservative, left-leaning, radical, right-wing,* and so on. Consider presenting an overview of these terms and concepts.

Teaching Resources
Consider using the PowerPoint "Political Biases" to provide background information about positions on the political spectrum.

arguments. For instance, editorials are articles that, by definition, present a writer's opinion and support for that opinion. Similarly, letters to the editor and comments posted on a news website often present arguments. On the other hand, encyclopedia entries are meant to be informative. They are written with an objective tone, and the writers do not explicitly reveal their opinions.

It is important to note that because everything written has come from the mind of a person, no text can be one hundred percent objective. As we mentioned earlier in this chapter, even a news story is a kind of argument because the writer has chosen which facts to present. Some genres, however, are almost exclusively dedicated to arguing about issues. Study Table 13.2 to learn about the writing genres that are most likely to contain explicit arguments.

Identifying a work's genre provides helpful information if the work is in the first or third category, but for works in the second category, we need more information. Analyzing the reputation of the publication in which a text appears can help you identify arguments. For example, a writer of an article published in *The National Review,* a news source that calls itself "the leading conservative magazine and website covering news, politics, current events, and culture," is likely to have a conservative bias. An article in *The Progressive,* a magazine that promotes progressive (liberal) politics, is likely to be written from a liberal perspective. These magazines may include articles that do not advocate a conservative or liberal viewpoint, but by knowing that the publications themselves are biased toward a particular point of view, you can be more aware of the likelihood that the articles found in these publications will reveal a bias—and constitute arguments.

TABLE 13.2 Genres and Argument

Genres That Aim for Objectivity and Are Not Likely to Include Argument	Genres That May or May Not Include Argument	Genres Likely to Include Argument
• encyclopedia entry • dictionary entry • meeting minutes • summary • abstract • biographical summary • instructional guide (how-to writing)	• textbooks • business correspondence • personal letters • reports • research papers • news reports • analyses • annotated bibliographies • scientific reports	• writing in a personal journal • personal letters • personal blogs and websites • autobiographies • editorials • letters to the editor, website comments • commentaries and opinion pieces • evaluations • reviews • proposals • speeches • advertisements • literary analyses • rhetorical analyses

Rhetorical Toolbox 13.1 presents questions that help you identify arguments. After you read through the Toolbox questions, keep reading for an explanation of how to use them.

RHETORICAL TOOLBOX 13.1
Identifying Arguments

1. **Claim and reasons.** Does the text have a claim and reasons supporting the claim? If so, the text may be an argument.
2. **Speaker.** Who is the speaker? Does the rhetorical situation suggest that the speaker is making an argument? Are there passages that reveal the speaker's bias? Is the tone subjective? If you can answer *yes* to any of these questions, the text may be an argument.
3. **Purpose.** Does the writer try to convince readers to believe or do something? Does the writer make tentative claims or refute the claims of others? If you can answer *yes* to either question, the text may be an argument.
4. **Genre.** Is the genre or the publication in which you have found the text one in which you might expect to find an argument? If so, the text may be an argument.

▶ **ACTIVITY 3 Using the Rhetorical Situation to Identify Arguments**

Read each brief passage and, using the Rhetorical Toolbox 13.1 questions, determine whether it is an argument.

A. In my family, we love to debate. In fact, last night we sat around the dinner table talking about whether cable television is worth the cost.

B. There are so many alternatives to cable television that are affordable and that have rich content. No one should pay for cable television any more.

C. Streaming devices, such as Roku and the Amazon Fire TV Stick, have given consumers a choice about how they purchase their entertainment. Whereas cable television used to be the only option, there are far more options these days.

MODEL ARGUMENT AND INTRODUCTION TO RHETORICAL ANALYSIS

One way to understand arguments is to write a rhetorical analysis, or study, of how the argument is constructed. The first step is to find an argument's claim and reasons, and briefly introduce its rhetorical situation (the bibliographic information about the writer, the place of publication, the date, and so on). When you identify an argument and begin to analyze it, you may have a personal response to the ideas you encounter. To analyze an argument objectively, you will need to put aside your personal reactions and your viewpoints on the topic. The goal of identifying and analyzing arguments is understanding what the writer is claiming and how they are supporting the claim. By dissecting the argument, you will be in a better position if you later want to create a personal response to it. Dissecting an argument will also help you become familiar with an argument's structure and with strategies writers can use to support their claims. This familiarity will help you when you write your own arguments.

In the article that follows, the annotations identify the major portions of Mark Greene's argument. As you read, think about not only *what* Greene is arguing but also *how* he is supporting his claim. Highlight one or two strategies Greene uses to help readers believe his claim.

Why Manning Up Is the Worst Thing to Do
Mark Greene

Mark Greene writes and speaks on men's issues for *The Good Men Project*, *The Shriver Report*, *The New York Times*, *Salon*, the *BBC*, and the *HuffPost*. As you read Greene's argument, notice how the annotations point out the structure of Greene's thoughts, including the claim and the major reasons he uses to support the claim.

Background information that helps us understand the broader rhetorical situation

The traditional rules about how to be a "real man" in America are breaking down. Economic upheaval has shifted wage earning from men to their wives or partners. The rise of men as primary caregivers of their children is challenging our most fundamental assumptions about gender. The gay rights and trans rights movements are creating expansive new definitions of masculinity. Millennials are leading a much broader acceptance of diversity.

This generation is witness to a collision between traditional masculinity and a new wave, one that values intimacy, caregiving, and nurturing. But many of us have spent our lives under immense pressure to stifle emotional expression of any kind. And we're learning there's a cost: Men are suffering higher rates of life-threatening disease, depression, and death. Simply put, the suppression of emotional expression in men is damaging their health and well-being.

If you've grown up in the United States, then you're familiar with the Man Box, the longstanding rules of how to walk, talk, and sound like a man in America:

Presentation of the problem: rules for manliness (the "Man Box")

1. Real men don't express a wide range of emotions. They limit themselves to expressing anger or excitement.
2. Real men are breadwinners, not caregivers.
3. Real men are "alphas" and natural leaders.
4. Real men are authoritative and make all final decisions.
5. Real men are physically tough and sexually dominant.

These rules take hold early in our lives. Boys 4 and 5 years old are told to shake it off, man up, don't be a crybaby, and, worst of all, don't be a girl. This is because the Man Box devalues any form of emotional expression traditionally deemed to be feminine. A devastating result of this anti-feminine bias is that women, gays, and trans people face epidemic levels of bullying, rape, misogyny, homophobia, and violence.

The Man Box robs our sons of a lifetime of opportunities to develop their emotional capacities. Instead, they grow into emotionally isolated men who wall themselves off from the social connectivity central to healing and creating community. The resulting health effects are undeniable.

"Man Box" rules result in emotional and social isolation.

One in three men aged 45 or older reported himself to be lonely or socially isolated, according to a 2010 survey conducted by AARP. The consequences of that social isolation can be fatal. Between 1999 and 2010, suicide among men aged 35–64 rose by nearly 30 percent, as reported by the Centers for Disease Control and Prevention. Although rates have been rising for both sexes, the study found that middle-aged men are three times likelier than women to end their own lives—27.3 deaths versus 8.1 (per 100,000).

Reason 1: Social isolation has negative effects.

But the risks of social isolation are not just psychological; the absence of robust social relationships has a direct measurable impact on men's physical health. A 2004 medical study based in Sweden showed that for middle-aged men, having a strong social network and sense of belonging lowered their risk of heart attack and fatal coronary heart disease; inversely, low social support predicted a risk.

The study further confirms that the risk of mortality for poor social relationships is comparable to risk factors like smoking and alcohol consumption, writes Niobe Way, author of Deep Secrets and professor of applied psychology at New York University. "This point underscores the fact that friendships are not simply a feel-good issue—they are a life-or-death issue."

Reason 2: Emotional isolation has negative effects.

Add to this epidemic of emotional isolation the physical impact of unresolved trauma in men's lives, and the combined effects are devastating. In *The Body Keeps the Score*, psychiatrist and PTSD researcher Bessel van der Kolk explores his decades-long work treating victims of catastrophic trauma. In 1978, he joined the Boston Veterans Administration Clinic as a staff psychiatrist. There, working with veterans of the Vietnam War, van der Kolk began to see the patterns that mark our modern-day understanding of trauma.

How much unresolved trauma do men carry after decades of emotional suppression?

He learned that the human body, when confronted with trauma, can etch horrific memories in the brain, literally reorganizing our perceptions and imagination. The most harmless sounds can trigger flashbacks. One veteran, upon hearing a baby crying, "found himself suddenly flooded with unbearable images of dying children in Vietnam." He was stuck, in effect, in a terrible loop, revisiting the events over and over again.

One of the many physiological responses to trauma can be seen in a region of the brain called Broca's Area, which freezes up during flashbacks. This region of the brain is where we construct language to define and interpret our experience of the world. Is it any wonder people find it deeply challenging to put their experiences of trauma into words? Our own physiology is telling us it's better to remain silent, making trauma all the harder to share or process.

And what exactly qualifies as trauma? Is it only present after catastrophic events or can it also take hold in the smaller brutalities of daily life, on playgrounds or in locker rooms? How much unresolved trauma do men carry after decades of emotional suppression?

I can recall, as a 7-year-old, seeing my home disappear out the back window of a car as a bitter divorce and my mother's new marriage drew me away. I recall my brother taking out his shock and rage on me for 15 years afterward. I still flash back to the suffocating bullying and violence that ran rampant throughout my years of school and Scouts. And yet, when is any man encouraged to share such stories? For generations, talking about such things was antithetical to our culture's insistence on male toughness. Thankfully, this is changing. As an editor for the *Good Men Project*, a website devoted to modern masculinity, I see thousands of men's stories being told. But we need to hear more. Millions more.

Trauma and the Man Box are mutually reinforcing. If, as men, we do not share our feelings, we will accrue decades of painful hidden stories, some of which will play over and over, triggering depression, fear, and unresolved anger toward ourselves and those we love. Van der Kolk writes, "Everything about us—our brains, minds, and our bodies—is geared toward collaboration in social systems. This is our most powerful survival strategy, the key to our success as a species, and it is precisely this that breaks down in most forms of mental suffering."

If we are to empower our sons and improve men's lives—and their health—we must tear down the walls of the Man Box, encouraging boys and men to express their full emotional range. — Claim (thesis statement)

The path forward begins in our homes. In small, ongoing daily conversations, we can encourage our sons to explore their internal emotional landscapes, sharing those profound discoveries of life. The result will be countless authentic human moments, strung out across decades, each one growing the rich tapestry of human connection and capacity.

The cost of failing to do so is incalculable. Without the robust social networks that emotional expression creates, men will continue to suffer social isolation and shorter, sicker lives. Van der Kolk defines humans as powerfully resilient and resourceful creatures, able to move beyond the challenging events of our lives and heal. But to do so, men must collaborate, connect, and share our stories, no matter how difficult they may be to tell.

And everyone else? They need to listen.

Co-requisite Teaching Tip
Consider using the models of student writing for practice. Give students an argument to analyze and then have them write paragraphs similar to those in the models. See the IM for more information.

Speaker, genre, purpose

Greene's claim

Greene's reasons

Thesis statement of rhetorical analysis

Model of an Introductory Paragraph for a Rhetorical Analysis

Now that you have read Greene's article, examine the introductory paragraph to a rhetorical analysis of this article.

> In his article, "Why Manning Up Is the Worst Thing to Do," writer Mark Greene confronts the issue of "manning up" and its effects. Greene hopes to persuade readers that the traditional rules of manliness result in trauma to men. Specifically, Green argues, "If we are to empower our sons and improve men's lives—and their health—we must tear down the walls of the Man Box, encouraging boys and men to express their full emotional range." He defines the "Man Box" as a set of five unwritten rules that not only harm men but also have negative effects on all of society. Greene supports his claim by providing two main lines of support: following "Man Box" rules results in social and emotional isolation. Greene's primary rhetorical strategies consist of appeals to logos and pathos.

In Chapter 14, we discuss how to analyze and discuss the reasons writers use to support a claim, as well as other strategies writers use to help persuade readers.

CHAPTER PROJECT Writing the Introductory Paragraph of a Rhetorical Analysis

Teaching Suggestion
In Chapter 21, students are prompted to return to this chapter and to use the introductory paragraph they have written for a complete rhetorical analysis. See the IM for more information about how to teach this chapter in tandem with Chapter 21.

Using these writing guidelines, write the introductory paragraph to a rhetorical analysis of an excerpt from "The Moral Case for the Fossil Fuel Industry," reprinted below or of another argument assigned by your instructor.

Writing Guidelines

Before Reading

1. Actively preview the text by focusing on rhetorical situation questions:
    A. Who is the author? Based on the author's credentials, can you figure out what point of view they are likely to have?
    B. Where was the text published? Is it a website? Was it published in a peer-reviewed journal? What might the venue in which the article was published tell you about the writer's purpose or point?

2. Think about this historical context and the topic. Is the writer responding to a current debate? What has already been said about this topic?
3. Read the first and last paragraphs. Based on the information in these paragraphs, can you predict the author's claim? Write it on a sheet of paper.

While Reading

4. Read the entire text for understanding. The goal of this first reading is to simply understand what the writer is saying.
5. Do a second reading, this time making annotations. Start by finding and underlining the claim. If you cannot find the claim, put the claim in your own words and jot it down. Sometimes the claim is apparent. If so, you can then specifically search for reasons that support the claim. When the claim is not immediately apparent, start by finding the reasons (step 6) and then return to the claim.
6. Ask, "What reasons does the writer present to support this claim?" Every time you see a reason, circle or underline it. Sometimes reasons are explained but not stated in a concise sentence. If you do not find a particular sentence that states a reason, write your own sentence to express the reason.

After Reading

7. When you finish reading, look back at the article and make a list of the reasons you marked. Do some of these reasons seem the same? If so, you may have made a mistake in identification.
8. Next, without looking at the text, ask this question: *What reasons does the writer provide for the claim?* Put these reasons into your own words. You may find reasons that you did not note in your annotations.
9. Once you have finished reading and analyzing the article, write the introduction paragraph using the model above as an example.

The Moral Case for the Fossil Fuel Industry

Alex Epstein

The excerpt that follows is part of a longer text, *The Moral Case for Fossil Fuels: The Key to Winning Hearts and Minds*. It was written by Alex Epstein, founder of the Center for Industrial Progress, and its intended audience is oil and gas company executives and marketers.

> What does it mean to be moral?
> This is an involved philosophical question, but for our purposes I will say: an activity is moral if it is fundamentally beneficial to human life.

By that standard, is the fossil fuel industry moral? The answer to that question is a resounding yes. By producing the most abundant, affordable, reliable energy in the world, the fossil fuel industry makes every other industry more productive—and it makes every individual more productive and thus more prosperous, giving him a level of opportunity to pursue happiness that previous generations couldn't even dream of. Energy, the fuel of technology, is opportunity—the opportunity to use technology to improve every aspect of life. Including our environment.

Any animal's environment can be broken down into two categories: threats and resources. (For human beings, "resources" includes a broad spectrum of things, including natural beauty.)

To assess the fossil fuel industry's impact on our environment, we simply need to ask: What is its impact on threats? What is its impact on resources?

The moral case against fossil fuels argues that the industry makes our environment more threatening and our resources more scarce.

But if we look at the big-picture facts, the exact opposite is true. The fossil fuel industry makes our environment far safer and creates new resources out of once-useless raw materials.

Let's start with threats. Schoolchildren for the last several generations have been taught to think of our natural environment as a friendly, stable place—and our main environmental contribution is to mess it up and endanger ourselves in the process. Not so. Nature does not give us a healthy environment to live in—it gives us an environment full of organisms eager to kill us and natural forces that can easily overwhelm us.

It is only thanks to cheap, plentiful, reliable energy that we live in an environment where the air we breathe and the water we drink and the food we eat will not make us sick, and where we can cope with the often hostile climate of Mother Nature. Energy is what we need to build sturdy homes, to purify water, to produce huge amounts of fresh food, to generate heat and air-conditioning, to irrigate deserts, to dry malaria-infested swamps, to build hospitals, and to manufacture pharmaceuticals, among many other things. And those of us who enjoy exploring the rest of nature should never forget that oil is what enables us to explore to our heart's content, which preindustrial people didn't have the time, wealth, energy, or technology to do.

The energy we get from fossil fuels is particularly valuable for protecting ourselves from the climate. The climate is inherently dangerous (and it is always changing, whether we influence the change or not). Energy and technology have made us far safer from it.

The data here are unambiguous. In the last 80 years, as CO_2 emissions have risen from an atmospheric concentration of .03% to .04%, climate-related deaths have declined 98%. Take drought-related deaths, which have declined by 99.98%. This has nothing to do with a friendly or unfriendly climate, it has to do with the oil and gas industry, which fuels high-energy agriculture as well as natural gas-produced fertilizer, and which fuels drought relief convoys.

Fossil fuels make the planet dramatically safer. And dramatically richer in resources.

Environmentalists treat "natural resources" as a fixed pile that nature gives us and which we dare not consume too quickly. In fact, nature gives us very little in the way of useful resources. From clean water to plentiful food to useful medicines, we need to create them using ingenuity. This is certainly true of energy. Until the Industrial Revolution, there were almost no "energy resources" to speak of. Coal, oil, and natural gas aren't naturally resources—they are naturally useless. (Or even nuisances.) Those who first discovered how to convert them into energy weren't depleting a resource, they were creating a resource. The world was a better place for it.

It is obscene to call today's new resource creators in the shale energy industry and the oil sands energy industry "exploiters" when they have turned stone and sludge into life-giving energy—a feat that may ultimately extend to trillions of barrels of once inaccessible oil (in all of human history we've used just over a trillion barrels). The fact that oil is a "finite" material is not a problem, any more than the "finite" supply of rare-earth metals is a black mark against windmills. Every material is finite. Life is all about taking the theoretically finite but practically limitless materials in nature and creatively turning them into useful resources. The fossil fuel industry does it, the "renewable"—actually, the "unreliable"—energy industry doesn't. End of story. "Renewables" are no more the ideal form of energy than wood is the ideal material for skyscrapers.

And by creating the best form of energy resource, the fossil fuel industry helps every other industry more efficiently create every other type of resource, from food to steel.

Your industry is fundamentally good. It minimizes environmental threats and maximizes environmental resources. Understanding that—really understanding that, root and branch—is the key to winning hearts and minds.

Reflecting to Develop a Writer's Mindset

Write a paragraph in which you reflect on what you read in this chapter by answering these questions:

A. Why is it important to recognize arguments?

B. Think of a time when you believed an argument without critically evaluating it. What was the result? Which methods presented in this chapter for identifying arguments do you find most helpful? How could using those methods help you evaluate issues?

FAQ MAKING ACCURATE INFERENCES

Co-requisite Teaching Tip
Consider using the exercise "Inferring Claims and Reasons in Argument Analysis."

When a writer does not explicitly state a claim, you will need to infer it. Writers may also provide paragraphs of details to support a reason for the claim but may not state the reason in any sentence. In this case, you will also need to infer the reason and put it into your own words. Making inferences can be tricky. Answer these questions to make accurate inferences:

1. **What are the details, and what do they suggest?**

    Read the following passage and notice the details that are underlined. In the second column, read the inference suggested by the passage.

Apartheid was a legal system of segregation and institutionalized racism in South Africa. It began officially in 1948, although South Africa had discriminated against people of color since the Dutch colonial period. One of the most <u>prominent and influential critics of apartheid was Nelson Mandela.</u> Born in 1918, Mandela came of age during the institutionalization of apartheid. Mandela <u>practiced nonviolent resistance to apartheid. He was a natural leader.</u> Although he spent twenty-seven years in prison for an alleged plot to overthrow the racist government, he <u>eventually became president of South Africa</u> in 1994.	*What do these details suggest?* Nelson Mandela was instrumental in ending apartheid in South Africa.

For a conclusion to be considered a sound inference, you must always be able to support the inference with details from the text. Sometimes we add our own opinions or attitudes or interpretations to the text, and the inferences we then make are not backed up by *only the text*.

2. **How can reasons be used to infer unstated claims?**

Some arguments present reasons but do not present an explicit claim. In these arguments, readers are expected to infer the claim, to figure it out using the details in the text. Here is an example of a claim that is inferred by analyzing the reasons.

Reasons:
- Most vaping and e-cigarette products contain nicotine, and nicotine is highly addictive.
- Nicotine is also a toxic substance, and it increases one's chances of having a heart attack or stroke.
- The products used in vapes and e-cigarettes are not regulated by the FDA and can contain hazardous substances.

Inferred claim:
- The use of vapes or e-cigarettes is a risky practice.

To infer the claim, we examined each reason and determined that each one addresses a concern associated with vaping or using e-cigarettes. And each one presents a risk. Thus, we can infer the claim and support it with the reasons.

TRY IT!

Read the following paragraph and infer the writer's claim:

> Having well-developed researching skills can help people find health-care information on the Web, information that is more authoritative than ordinary consumer websites might offer. Researching skills also can have a positive effect on finances. From learning about loan terms to finding the best investments, the number of research sources for financial literacy is vast. In the area of parenting, research skills are vital. Such skills can help parents find educational information and parenting advice.

CREDITS

Page 316. Greene, Mark, "Why Manning Up Is the Worst Thing to Do," *YES! Magazine*, Winter 2016, pp 27-28. Reprinted by permission of Positive Futures Network.

Page 321. Epstein, Alex. "The Moral Case for Fossil Fuels: The Key to Winning Hearts and Minds." Center for Industrial Progress. Used by permission.

14 Analyzing an Argument's Elements

CHAPTER OBJECTIVES

You will learn to:
- Identify the elements of the Toulmin model of argument: claims, qualifiers, reasons, grounds, warrants, backing, and rebuttals.
- Conduct a Toulmin analysis of an argument.
- Write a Toulmin analysis of an argument's elements.

Arguments are often complex. Perhaps you have been in an argument and found yourself getting lost in your reasoning or not fully understanding the other person's reasoning. Or maybe you thought you had a clear idea of your position on an issue, only to learn that the issue is far more complicated than you thought—and your opinion may actually not be correct.

Analyzing arguments requires a well-developed level of critical thinking. One way to improve your ability to understand arguments and to argue more effectively is to use **Toulmin analysis**, a system developed by Stephen Toulmin, a British philosopher. The Toulmin model of argument can help you more clearly understand the parts of an argument and how they work together. In this chapter, you will learn how to use the Toulmin model to analyze an argument. In a later chapter, you will use your knowledge of Toulmin analysis to create and evaluate your own argument.

Connect Adaptive Learning Assignment
Consider assigning Connect's Adaptive Learning Assignments to support this chapter.

Toulmin analysis: A system of analyzing the parts of an argument and how they work together developed by British philosopher Stephen Toulmin.

WARM-UP
Read the following very brief argument. Why might John's argument fail to persuade Nanette to use Tres Amigos to cater a conference?

Nanette: We need to find the best Mexican restaurant in the city to cater our conference.

John: The best Mexican restaurant is Tres Amigos because they have the best margaritas.

AN OVERVIEW OF TOULMIN ANALYSIS

Before we examine the elements of a Toulmin analysis, consider the argument in the Warm-Up activity. Nanette may not be persuaded by John's argument for several reasons. One of these reasons is that John assumes that the quality of

Teaching Resources
See the Instructor's Manual (IM) for suggestions about how to teach this chapter, and consider assigning this chapter's test-bank quiz.

margaritas is an important factor—in fact, he implies, the most important factor—in selecting a Mexican restaurant. If Nanette does not share John's assumption, she might respond: "Okay, yes, they have great margaritas, but it's more important that we find the restaurant that makes the best Mexican food."

Notice that John never stated his assumption that margaritas are the most important criterion directly. It is an unstated, but very important, part of his argument. In Toulmin analysis, the unstated assumption is called the *warrant*. By naming this very important part of an argument, as well as six other parts, Toulmin analysis helps you analyze an argument in more depth than you might otherwise. The seven elements from Toulmin analysis that we focus on are claims, qualifiers, reasons, grounds, warrants, backing, and rebuttals. To accurately examine these elements, you must have already analyzed the rhetorical situation, especially the audience. In the example of John and Nanette, John's argument may have worked if he had been talking to someone who also shared the assumption that the quality of margaritas is the most important factor in selecting a restaurant to cater the conference. By examining these elements in the context of a rhetorical situation, you can see why arguments fail or succeed, and you can then write your own arguments with more clarity and effectiveness.

Figure 14.1 displays the seven elements of analysis in the Toulmin model. As you study these parts in the sections that follow, refer to the diagram to reinforce your understanding of how they work together.

Claims and Qualifiers

A claim, as you already know, is the debatable statement that is the main point of an argument. Claims can be called other names: thesis statements, conclusions, propositions, and assertions. All claims are arguable propositions that need support to be believed or accepted. John's assertion that Tres Amigos should cater the conference is a claim. Here are some additional examples of claims:

> People should be required by law to be vaccinated against measles.
>
> The city council should rezone the land along the river as commercial property.
>
> Single-use plastic bags should be illegal in this state.

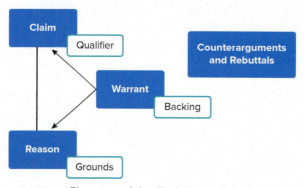

FIGURE 14.1 Elements of the Toulmin model of argument.

Sometimes a claim needs a qualifier. A **qualifier** is a word or phrase that limits a claim. Words such as *many, most, almost, partly, some, very few,* and the like are qualifiers. Using a qualifier makes a claim more precise and helps to avoid overgeneralizations. Notice the difference in meaning in these two claims:

qualifier: A word or phrase that limits a claim.

Claim: People should be required by law to be vaccinated against measles.

Claim with qualifier: *Most* people should be required by law to be vaccinated against measles.

The claim with the qualifier *most* helps the writer avoid overgeneralizing. There will be some people for whom the measles vaccine should *not* be required. By using the qualifier, the writer ensures that the audience will not be able to object to the claim on the basis that it overgeneralizes and that there are exceptions to the rule—such as people who may be allergic to the vaccine.

Reasons and Grounds

To form an argument, a claim must be followed by a reason. A **reason** is an idea that supports a claim. The reason itself may also need support, such as data, statistics, and evidence. **Grounds** consist of the support for the reason. Notice how a reason and grounds support a claim:

reason: An idea that provides support for a claim.

grounds: Support for a reason in an argument.

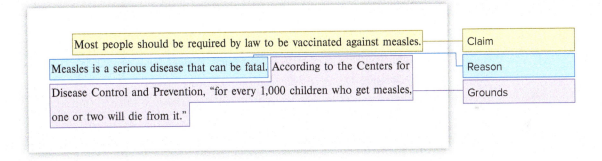

Warrants

A **warrant** is the assumption that connects the reason to the claim. It is often a belief or value that is implicit; that is, the arguer holds this belief or value but may not necessarily say it out loud. When people disagree, they often disagree about these foundational beliefs or values. Thus, identifying the warrants in an argument is crucial. Let's examine the previous example to identify the warrant:

warrant: The assumption, belief, or value that ties a reason to the claim of an argument.

Claim: Most people should be required by law to be vaccinated against measles.

Reason: Measles is a serious disease that can be fatal.

To find the warrant, ask questions such as these: "How does the reason lead one to believe the claim? What is the unstated assumption? What value or belief must I hold for the reason to make sense as support for the claim?" In the vaccination argument, the warrant is a commonly held belief:

Warrant: We should prevent fatal diseases.

Teaching Suggestion
Identifying warrants is often the most difficult part of Toulmin analysis. Consider using the PowerPoint "Identifying Warrants," and have students do the PowerPoint exercises collaboratively.

> **Co-requisite Teaching Tip**
> Toulmin analysis is difficult for most students. Consider using these supplemental worksheets and exercises: "Toulmin Analysis--Step by Step," "Finding Warrants and Backing: More Practice," and "Warrants, Grounds, and Backing: How They Differ."

Many people will agree with this warrant. Even so, the argument may not be convincing. Some people who do not vaccinate against measles often value another warrant more. Their argument goes something like this:

Claim: People should not be required by law to be vaccinated against measles.

Reason: Some religions prohibit vaccinations, so a law requiring vaccination would infringe on religious freedom.

Warrant: We value religious freedom.

A person may believe both warrants—that preventing disease is important and that religious freedom is important—but may value one belief more than the other. By figuring out an argument's warrants, you will be better able to understand the logic behind the claim and reasons. As a writer, you can analyze the warrants for your reasons to predict whether or not readers are likely to accept the warrants, and thus, your argument. Use the tips that follow to accurately identify warrants.

Remember that the warrant is often a value. Values are beliefs about the worth or importance of something. Here are some examples:

Getting a college education is important.

Saving money is important.

Being clean is valuable.

Use this question to identify the warrants: *What must someone value for this reason to make sense?* Here are two examples:

Claim: You should exercise at least thirty minutes a day several days a week.

Reason: Doing so will help prevent heart disease.

Question to identify warrant: *What must someone value for this reason to make sense?*

Warrant: Good health is important.

Claim: Our city should offer curbside recycling.

Reason: Curbside recycling will help more people participate in recycling.

Question to identify warrant: *What must someone value for this reason to make sense?*

Warrant: Recycling is a worthwhile practice.

Don't confuse the warrant with the reason. A common mistake is to see a reason and to assume that the reason is the warrant. The warrant is always more general than the reason. Reasons are so specific that they must be stated. Warrants are often so general that we take them for granted. These two examples provide more explanation:

Claim: McKinney High is the best high school in the city.

Reason: Its football team almost always wins first place in the district. (Notice how specific the reason is.)

Question to identify warrant: *What must someone value for this reason to make sense?*

Warrant: Winning at football is important. (Notice that the warrant is more general; it is a statement that could be used for many different arguments.)

Claim: We must find a solution to the opioid crisis.

Reason: Deaths from opioid overdoses have significantly increased over the last three years.

Question to identify warrant: *What must someone value for this reason to make sense?*

Warrant: We value the health of others (public health). (Again, the warrant is more general; it is a statement that could be used for many different arguments.)

Remember that the warrant is not always stated. Because the warrant is an assumption or a commonly held belief, it is often unstated. You will have to put it in your own words. Thus, don't be tempted to find a sentence in the text that articulates the warrant. Such a sentence may exist, but you will have an easier time finding it by first putting the warrant in your own words and then by looking to see if the writers ever state the warrant explicitly.

▶ **ACTIVITY 1 Identifying Claim, Reason, and Warrant**

State claim, reason, and warrant for each of these brief arguments.

1. We should put speed bumps on this road because children play here.
2. We should put speed bumps on this road because too many people use it as a shortcut.
3. Martha's house is the best place to have the party. Martha has a pool.
4. Martha's house is the best place to have the party. It can accommodate at least twenty-five people.
5. You should finish college. You'll be much more likely to find a high-paying job with a college degree.
6. You should finish college. Your parents saved money for years to put you through college.

Backing

If you anticipate that the audience might not accept a warrant, you can explain or justify the warrant itself in your argument. The justification, or defense, of the warrant is called **backing**. Here is an example:

backing: Support for a warrant in an argument.

> The twenty-five acres of land that surround the river in the middle of our downtown region sit vacant. This real estate could be really valuable if it were zoned commercial. In fact, some developers have presented plans for

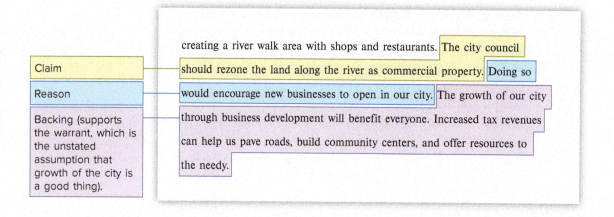

The claim is straightforward: "The city council should rezone the land along the river as commercial property." It is followed by the reason: "Doing so would encourage new businesses to open in our city." The warrant, however, is not stated. The speaker assumes that the growth of the city is a good thing. Not everyone will agree with that assumption. Some people want their cities to remain the same size; others may want green space, such as the twenty-five acres surrounding the river, to remain green and natural. To support the warrant, the writer provides backing in the last two sentences. These sentences defend the warrant by explaining why a city's growth is good. When a writer thinks readers may disagree with the warrant, providing backing can help readers see why the assumption in the warrant is justified.

▶ **ACTIVITY 2** Providing Backing

Read the following argument. What kind of information might the writer include as backing?

Claim: We should make higher education free.

Reason: Doing so will increase the number of people who get a college education.

Warrant: Education is valuable.

Backing: ?

Counterarguments and Rebuttals

counterargument: an argument that opposes the writer's claim or one of the writer's reasons.

rebuttal: A response to a counterargument that refutes it but may also concede to any part of it that is correct.

concession: An acknowledgment that part of an opposing argument is correct; it is part of a rebuttal.

Effective arguments often include a discussion of the opposing point of view. By including this discussion, the speaker shows that he or she considered other points of view and has found them unconvincing. The opposing viewpoints are called **counterarguments**. To deal with counterarguments, writers often include a **rebuttal**, an attempt to address a counterargument by conceding to part of it and/ or refuting it. In a rebuttal, writers may include two elements: concessions and refutations.

When part of the counterargument is correct, a speaker may include a **concession**. A concession is a writer's acknowledgment that under some conditions, the claim would not apply. For example, let's consider this counterargument: Making higher education free would cause significant problems because colleges and university admissions would skyrocket, requiring increased staffing and facilities. A writer may offer a concession:

Claim: We should make higher education free.

Counterargument: Making higher education free would cause significant problems because college and university admissions would skyrocket, requiring increased staffing and facilities.

> **Concession:** It is true that making higher education free would increase the staffing and facilities needs of colleges and universities.

The writer makes this concession because she realizes this opposing point is correct. To determine whether to include a concession, a writer must think about exceptions, situations in which the claim may not apply. Often these exceptions are part of the opposing argument, as is the case in the example about increased enrollments. By thinking about reasonable opposition to the argument, a writer can anticipate counterarguments and can create concessions when necessary.

Regardless of whether a concession is included, addressing a counterargument in a rebuttal requires the writer to offer a refutation. A **refutation** is a writer's attempt to show that the counterargument is wrong, even if a concession has been made. The example that follows shows how a writer can anticipate the opposing argument and refute it:

Claim: We should make higher education free.

Counterargument: Making higher education free would cause significant problems because college and university admissions would skyrocket, requiring increased staffing and facilities.

> **Refutation:** Making college free would not simply mean paying for tuition: it would include increased support for institutions so that needs in staffing and facilities were covered.

If part of the counterargument is correct, a writer may include both a concession and a refutation. The example that follows shows how a writer can anticipate the opposing argument and refute it:

Claim: We should make higher education free.

Counterargument: Making higher education free would cause significant problems because college and university admissions would skyrocket, requiring increased staffing and facilities.

> **Rebuttal including concession and refutation:** It is true that making higher education free would probably result in increased numbers of students, thus resulting in institutional needs for increased staffing and facilities. But these concerns would be addressed by the same legislation that would ensure a free college education. Making college free would not simply mean paying for tuition: it would include increased support for institutions so that needs in staffing and facilities were covered.

Teaching Suggestion
Consider using "friendly debate" to help students see potential counterarguments. Have students identify the warrants for each position and the backing that could support those warrants. See the IM for questions that lend themselves to "friendly debate."

refutation: A writer's attempt to show the flaws in the counterargument—part of a rebuttal.

▶ **ACTIVITY 3** **Identifying Counterarguments, Concessions, and Refutations**

Read the following argument and identify the counterargument, the concession, and the refutation.

> The city should not ban single-use plastic bags. Those in favor of a ban claim that single-use plastic bags harm the environment, but recent research has shown that the situation is more complicated than it appears. It is true that the production of plastics has a negative impact on the environment, but the alternative is actually worse. The process and raw materials required for making nonplastic bags—such as canvas bags and paper bags—do more damage to the environment than the process and raw materials for making plastic bags.

CONDUCTING A TOULMIN ANALYSIS OF AN ARGUMENT

The purpose of a Toulmin analysis is to identify and discuss the elements in an argument so that you can understand and explain how a writer's argument works. As you begin analyzing arguments, be aware of three potential areas of confusion: implied elements, the order of elements, and the similarities of elements.

Problem Spot 1: Identifying Implied Elements

Teaching Resources
Consider using the exercise "Avoiding Problems in Toulmin Analysis" to give students hands-on practice using the tips in this section of the chapter.

You already know that warrants are often implied. As surprising as it may seem, claims can also be implied. Consider this scenario: You are about to walk out the door, and your friend says, "Hey, wait; it's supposed to rain today!" She has given you a reason for an implied claim: *You should grab your umbrella.* In this simple example, you can see how some claims can be inferred from the reasons that support them. Let's look at a longer example:

> According to the organization, *Start School Later,* the majority of American high schools start before 8:30 a.m. Ten percent start before 7:30 a.m., with most beginning at 8:00 a.m. While these are early start times, they tell only part of the story. Students who attend these schools have to wake up even earlier, of course. If a student rides a school bus, he or she may have to catch the bus as early as 5:00 a.m.
>
> Scientists who study circadian rhythms know that sleep cycles vary according to age. Adolescents begin to have difficulty with early bed times because their sleep cycles shift. "Typical sleep cycles begin around 11 p.m. for teenagers and continue through 8 a.m." according to research cited by the *Start School Later* organization. Having to wake up early interrupts this natural sleep cycle. Instead of getting the nine hours of sleep their developing brains need, teens who must wake up early for school often get far less. In fact, "nearly 3/4 get under 8 hours of sleep per night, and 2/5 get 6 or fewer" hours of sleep.

Without stating the claim explicitly, the writer argues that high schools should not begin at early morning hours. If you cannot find an explicit claim in an argument, write one in your own words. Make a list of the argument's reasons and then create the claim that they support.

Problem Spot 2: Identifying "Out of Order" Elements

It would be convenient if writers presented arguments in a predictable way, but writers organize arguments in the most effective way possible. This means that you cannot expect to find a claim followed by a reason, and so on. As you analyze arguments, be aware that there is no "normal" sequence in which elements appear. In the example that follows, the argument starts with a stated warrant, followed by backing and grounds, and then concludes with the claim and the reason.

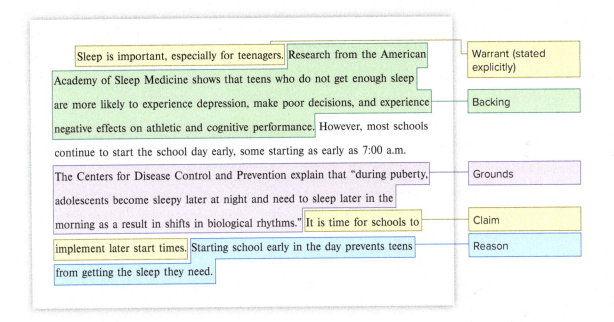

The best way to identify elements of an argument is to read the argument in its entirety. First, find the reasons; next, determine the claim they support. Alternatively, if the claim is obvious, look for the reasons. Once you have figured out reasons and claim, you can find the remaining elements. (Are you finding Toulmin analysis difficult? For more examples, see "FAQ: Becoming Familiar With Toulmin Analysis" at the end of this chapter.)

Problem Spot 3: Distinguishing between Similar Elements

It can be easy to confuse some of the Toulmin elements. Use the suggestions that follow to avoid confusing similar elements.

Avoid confusing claims and reasons. Some reasons are actually arguable, so they can look like claims. The argument's claim, however, is the central idea that all the reasons support. As you analyze reasons, ask whether they present the main idea of the argument or whether they support an idea that is broader than they are. For example:

> Adults should avoid drinking milk. The human body was not made to digest milk.

While both statements are arguable, the second sentence provides support for the first. Thus, the second sentence is a reason, and the first is the claim.

Avoid confusing qualifiers and concessions. Both qualifiers and concessions limit a claim, but they do so in different ways. Qualifiers are words or phrases that are added to the claim to narrow it, while concessions present exceptions to the claim.

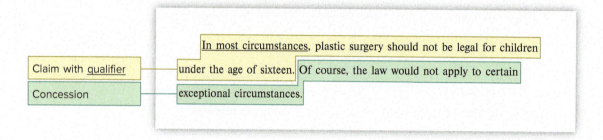

The qualifier, *in most circumstances,* limits the claim. The concession is the sentence highlighted in green after the claim, and it explicitly acknowledges that the claim should be set aside in certain instances.

Avoid confusing grounds and backing. Grounds provide proof for a reason, and backing provides proof for a warrant. Both grounds and backing offer additional evidence, and that is why they can easily be confused. To avoid this, follow these steps:

1. Identify the claim, reason, and warrant. Remember, the warrant may not be stated directly. You may have to infer it.

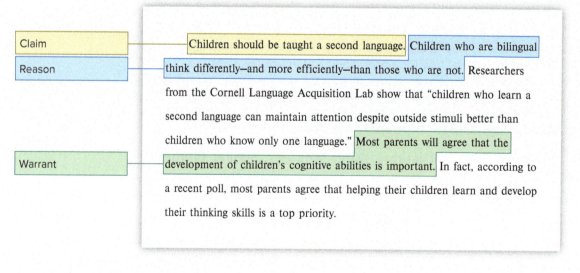

2. Next, analyze the supporting material to see whether it supports the reason or the warrant. If it supports the reason, it is grounds. If it supports the warrant, it is backing.

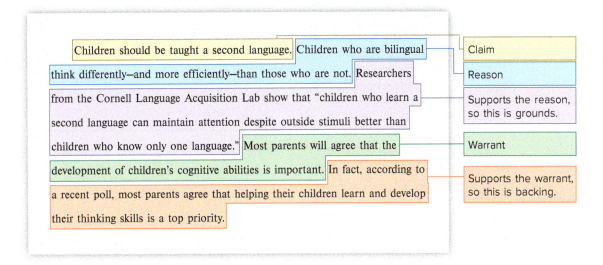

Both grounds and backing provide the additional evidence needed as support, but as the example shows, grounds support reasons, and backing supports warrants.

Using Questions to Identify Toulmin Elements

Rhetorical Toolbox 14.1 presents questions you can use to identify the elements of an argument.

RHETORICAL TOOLBOX 14.1

Identifying the Toulmin Elements of an Argument

Read the entire argument, keeping the rhetorical situation in mind, and then use these questions to help identify Toulmin elements.

1. **Reasons.** What are the reasons presented in the argument? Make a list.
2. **Claim.** What is the claim these reasons support? Either find the claim, if it is stated explicitly, or write it in your own words if it is not.
3. **Qualifiers.** As you analyze the claim, do you see any qualifiers?
4. **Rebuttals of counterarguments.** Does the writer address opposing points of view? If so, does the writer present any concessions (situations that would call for the claim to be set aside) or acknowledge the legitimacy of any of the opposing side's points? Does the writer present any refutations, attempts to show where the counterargument is incorrect?
5. **Grounds.** As you examine a reason, does the writer provide evidence or additional support for the reason? If so, these are grounds.
6. **Warrants.** As you examine a reason, what is the warrant? Look for the belief, value, or assumption that ties the reason to the claim. Put the warrant in your own words if it is not directly stated in the argument.
7. **Backing.** Does the writer offer any support for the warrant? If so, this is the backing.

MODEL OF A TOULMIN ANALYSIS OF AN ARGUMENT

Student Sarit Fisher is writing a Toulmin analysis of an argument about the use of tracking apps. Read the argument she is analyzing and then follow her thinking and writing process and final draft.

Why Parents Should Think Twice About Tracking Apps for Their Kids

Joel Michael Reynolds

Joel Michael Reynolds is a professor of philosophy at the University of Massachusetts–Lowell. This piece was published on The Conversation, *a global network of newsrooms, in 2019. As you read it, notice the annotations. These annotations will be important as we move from reading and analyzing the argument to reading the analysis essay.*

The use of self-tracking and personal surveillance technologies has grown considerably over the last decade. There are now apps to monitor people's movement, health, mindfulness, sleep, eating habits and even sexual activity.

Some of the more thorny problems arise from apps designed to track others, like those made for parents to track their kids. For example, there are specific apps that allow parents to monitor their child's GPS location, who they call, what they text, which apps they use, what they view online and the phone number of their contacts.

As a bioethicist who specializes in the ethics of emerging technologies, I worry that such tracking technologies are transforming prudent parenting into surveillance parenting.

Here are three reasons why.

1. Companies are tracking for profit.

> *The first reason: Companies track for profit (and may endanger children).*

The first reason has to do with concerns over the tech itself.

Tracking apps are not primarily designed to keep children safe or help with parenting. They are designed to make money by gathering loads of information to be sold to other companies.

A 2017 report from a marketing research firm estimates that self-monitoring technologies for health alone will reach gross revenues of US$71.9 billion by 2022. [Grounds]

The lion's share of the profit is not in the device itself, but in the data drawn from its users.

To get as much data as they can, these apps work hard to keep one constantly using them via push notifications and other design techniques. [Warrant (unstated): Parents should not expose their children to dangers.]

This data is then often sold to other companies — including advertising agencies and political campaign firms. The primary aim of these devices is not people's well-being, but the profit that can be made off of their data.

When parents track children, they help companies maximize their profits. Should a child's information become de-anonymized and fall into the wrong hands, this could put one's child at risk.

2. Risks of leaking private data

[Reason: Parents risk privacy when they use tracking apps.]

There are also significant privacy risks.

A 2014 study by the security firm Symantec found that even devices that do not appear to be traceable can still be tracked wirelessly, as a result of insufficient privacy features. [Grounds]

That same year, a study by computer scientists at the University of Illinois at Urbana-Champaign found that many Android mobile health applications, for example, send unencrypted information over the Internet. Nearly all of these apps monitor one's location. Researchers at MIT and the Catholic University of Louvain found that just four time-stamped locations could uniquely identify 95% of individuals, making promises of anonymity hollow.

Information related to people's whereabouts can reveal valuable data about them. In the case of children, their tracking data could very easily be used by someone else. [Warrant (unstated): Parents should not expose their children to dangers.]

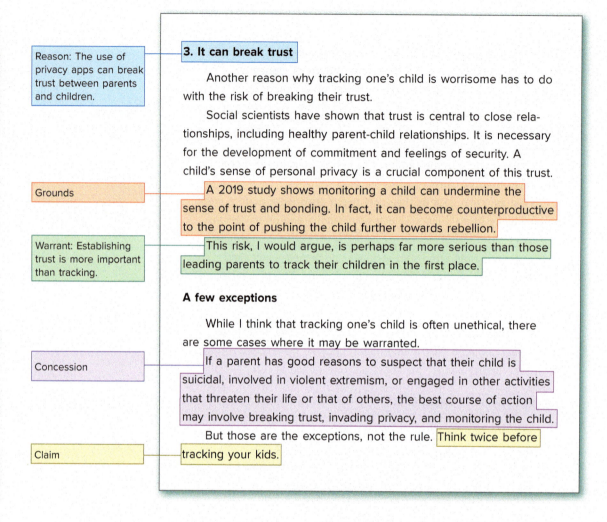

3. It can break trust

Another reason why tracking one's child is worrisome has to do with the risk of breaking their trust.

Social scientists have shown that trust is central to close relationships, including healthy parent-child relationships. It is necessary for the development of commitment and feelings of security. A child's sense of personal privacy is a crucial component of this trust. A 2019 study shows monitoring a child can undermine the sense of trust and bonding. In fact, it can become counterproductive to the point of pushing the child further towards rebellion. This risk, I would argue, is perhaps far more serious than those leading parents to track their children in the first place.

A few exceptions

While I think that tracking one's child is often unethical, there are some cases where it may be warranted. If a parent has good reasons to suspect that their child is suicidal, involved in violent extremism, or engaged in other activities that threaten their life or that of others, the best course of action may involve breaking trust, invading privacy, and monitoring the child. But those are the exceptions, not the rule. Think twice before tracking your kids.

Sarit Fisher, A Toulmin Analysis of an Argument (Final Draft)

Read Sarit's Toulmin analysis, annotated to show the parts of her essay.

Sarit, on organizing her paper: "Since the purpose of a Toulmin analysis is to identify and discuss the elements of argument, I decided to first discuss the claim and then the reasons, the grounds associated with the reasons, the warrants associated with the reasons, and any backing for warrants that I could find. I decided to put the counterargument and my rebuttal after the discussion of reasons and their associated elements."

Fisher 1

Sarit Fisher
Dr. Blevins
ENGL 1302.44
15 June 2020

A Toulmin Analysis of an Argument

    In an article about tracking apps, Joel Michael Reynolds, professor of philosophy at University of Massachusetts–Lowell, argues that parents should not use tracking apps to monitor the movements of their children. Reynolds begins his argument with background information to explain the power of tracking apps. He hints at his claim when he writes that, as a bioethicist, he worries "that such tracking technologies are transforming prudent parenting into surveillance parenting." It is not until the end of his argument, however, that he explicitly states his claim: "Think twice before tracking your kids." To support his claim, he presents three reasons.

    First, Reynolds argues that companies track for profit. While this may not seem like a relevant reason, Reynolds hopes readers will infer that tracking for profit may mean ignoring dangers to children. Reynolds cites a "2017 report from a marketing research firm" that "estimates that self-monitoring technologies for health alone will reach gross revenues of US $71.9 billion by 2022." He explains that the revenue from such apps comes from the data they produce, data which is then sold to other companies. Reynolds writes, "the primary aim of these devices is not people's well-being, but the profit that can be made off of their data." The warrant, which Reynolds does not explicitly state, is that parents should not expose their children to dangers. Because most people would agree with this warrant, Reynolds does not provide backing. By showing that tracking companies are more interested in profits than well-being, Reynolds hopes readers will agree with his claim that parents should not use tracking apps.

    The second reason Reynolds offers is very similar to the first and, in fact, may be seen as a continuation of the first reason. He claims that parents take privacy risks when they use tracking apps.

Bibliographic information

Claim

Discussion of the first reason, associated grounds, warrant, and backing

Fisher 2

To prove this, Reynolds points out that the companies that create and maintain such apps use the data for profit, not for ensuring the safety of children. He provides grounds by pointing to a 2014 study by Symantec that found tracking technologies to have "insufficient privacy features." He provides additional grounds by citing a study conducted by the University of Illinois that showed "just four time-stamped locations could uniquely identify 95% of individuals, making promises of anonymity hollow." Although Reynolds does not explicitly state a warrant, the warrant is clear: Parents should not expose their children to dangers. Since most people would agree with this warrant, Reynolds does not provide backing.

A third reason Reynolds offers is that the use of tracking apps can break trust between parents and children. As support, he offers grounds: "A 2019 study shows monitoring a child can undermine the sense of trust and bonding." Reynolds also offers a warrant for this reason: "This risk [of breaking trust], I would argue, is perhaps far more serious than those leading parents to track their children in the first place." As backing for this warrant, Reynolds writes, "Social scientists have shown that trust is central to close relationships, including healthy parent-child relationships."

In addition to providing reasons, Reynolds does acknowledge that there are conditions under which his claim would not apply. He offers specific concessions when he claims that if a child "is suicidal, involved in violent extremism, or engaged in other activities that threaten their life or that of others" then parents may be justified in using tracking apps. He is quick to say, however, that "those are the exceptions, not the rule." He ends his argument by explicitly stating his claim: "Think twice before tracking your kids."

Discussion of the second reason, associated grounds, warrant, and backing

Discussion of the third reason, associated grounds, warrant, and backing

Discussion of concessions

Fisher 3

Work Cited

Reynolds, Joel Michael. "Why Parents Should Think Twice about Tracking Apps for Their Kids." *The Conversation*, 31 Oct. 2019, theconversation.com/why-parents-should-think-twice-about-tracking-apps-for-their-kids-114350.

CHAPTER PROJECT Writing a Toulmin Analysis

Using Rhetorical Toolbox 14.1, read and analyze "How Football Can Wreck a University" or an argument assigned by your instructor. Next, write a Toulmin analysis of the argument. Use the Toulmin model in this chapter for guidance.

How Football Can Wreck a University
Robert Zaretsky

Robert Zaretsky is a professor of English at the University of Houston. His article was originally printed in The Chronicle of Higher Education, *a journal that describes itself as "the nation's largest newsroom dedicated to covering colleges and universities."*

In its most-recent game, the University of Houston football team notched its sixth loss. Not only does this fare poorly against its win column—three victories against mostly risible rivals—it also fares poorly against the exorbitant salary of Coach Dana Holgorsen.

Signed last year to a five-year, $20-million contract, Holgorsen was hired to create a football powerhouse, one that would fill the university's largely empty stadium that Houston built a few years ago to the tune of $125 million. Those 40,000 seats will remain sparsely filled for the rest of the season.

Teaching Suggestion
Consider spending time as a class investigating the rhetorical situation of this article, including the football program at the University of Houston and the journal publishing the article (*Chronicle of Higher Education*) and its readership.

Did Houston's leadership wake up on Sunday morning with buyer's remorse? Only they, of course, can answer that question. But this story does raise other and more urgent questions about the colossal role played by football programs at state universities. Is the insatiable appetite of these behemoths luring universities from their traditional duty, which is not to win games but to educate students? By creating football programs too big to fail, have universities created academic programs too small to succeed?

In Billion-Dollar Ball, his blistering account of the university-athletic complex, Gilbert M. Gaul dissects the motivations of large and midsize state universities that invest dazzling sums of money to build successful football teams. In part, Gaul suggests, it is a case of "football envy." Given the sheer size and financial sway of NCAA football—for the first time, in 2017, the organization's total revenue justified its moniker as a "billion-dollar industry"—such envy is explicable, perhaps even inevitable. But this does not mean it is reasonable.

Defenders of collegiate football play the "front porch" card to justify the expense and prominence of football programs. There are few better ways, they claim, to attract prospective students and donors. Build the porch, in effect, and they will come.

They might have a point, though the porch metaphor is too quaint for the 21st century. In an age where the omnipresent electronic screen has become the arbiter of reality, what was once a game has become a spectacle, one that is endlessly looped and layered by the satellite, social, and traditional media. A football program has become less a porch than a perch in programming, one whose prominence depends on wins and losses.

Yet there is a problem with focusing on curbside appeal. Invest too much money in the porch and you might not have much left for the house just behind it. The likelihood of neglect is all the greater in an era where decreasing state support makes universities increasingly desperate to grow, or simply maintain, revenue streams. Blitzed by hostile legislators and hawkish regents, scrambling university presidents are turning to their football program as a kind of Hail Mary pass. And why wouldn't they? In Texas alone, two universities—the University of Texas and Texas A&M—have each generated more than $200-million in annual revenue through their athletic programs. Along with a dozen other programs, including those at LSU, Alabama, Auburn, Ohio State, and Notre Dame, they raked in well over $1 billion in 2017.

Those high-profile success stories notwithstanding, the brutal fact is that only an elite group of universities actually profit from their athletic programs. Yet many are nevertheless betting their futures on football not despite funding cuts imposed by their state legislatures but because of them. Rather than falling over one another for star scholars, universities do that for star coaches. Houston's Holgorsen is not the only one to benefit from an astronomical pay raise; mid-level universities like Western Kentucky and Florida Atlantic have also doubled the salaries of incoming coaches.

While the elite programs pay for themselves, most others seek new ways to nickel and dime students through a variety of fees, as well as shift institutional funds to keep the lights on and Jacuzzis whirling in their state-of-the-art training facilities. (Last year, student fees at Houston funneled more than $8 million into the athletic program, while the university coughed up $17 million more to keep the program afloat. And yet, plans for a new office building for the football staff are on the drawing board.) These administrators take for gospel the observation made by a former athletic director at Texas: "Football is the train. You ride it for all it's worth." For most colleges, though, this particular train leads not to dazzling riches but dizzying debt. Even Michigan's program, despite its glorious history and devoted fans, is teetering on the edge of potentially catastrophic debt.

Nevertheless, dozens of state universities continue to tax students and transfer funds in order to keep the gridirons green. As for the groves of academe, they are less green. What might this mean for the university's ability to educate its students? When Tilman Fertitta, chairman of Houston's Board of Regents, was asked if the athletic program's $100-million debt harmed the university's academic activities, he replied, "Not at all." Of course, adjuncts without health benefits, academic coordinators without classrooms, and department chairs without tenure lines might disagree.

> So, too, might students without an inkling of how to write. Universities have long emphasized that a core task is to teach the entwined skills of clear writing and critical thinking. It is a laudable goal; it is a vital goal; it is a goal that merits the necessary resources. Yet the resources often are lacking. Conversations with colleagues at several universities reveal that their administrations talk the talk but rarely walk the walk when it comes to the funding of writing programs. At my own institution, there is a rightly well-regarded Writing Center dedicated to this very task. But a glimpse of contrasting numbers reflects our actual priorities. With about 85 active players and 31 full-time coaches, assistant coaches, and trainers, the student-teacher ratio for our football team is about 2.5 to 1. Over at the Writing Center, there is a staff of five, plus 25 "consultants"—part-time tutors who are either still students or recent graduates. They and the full-time staff have a potential clientele of more than 40,000 students, or one instructor for every 1,300 students. The math is as simple as its lesson: Our future lies with an educated citizenry, not an entertained one.

Reflecting to Develop a Writer's Mindset

You have spent some time learning Toulmin analysis. How might your knowledge of Toulmin analysis help you to make better life choices? Explain and provide an example of how you might use such analysis to make a choice in the future.

FAQ BECOMING FAMILIAR WITH TOULMIN ANALYSIS

Finding the elements of an argument is challenging because we do not always think analytically. These questions and answers will help you become more familiar with Toulmin analysis.

1. **Do you completely understand Toulmin terminology?**

   If you cannot define *backing,* for example, you will not be able to find backing in an argument. The words you should be able to define, from memory, are listed here:

claim	reason	grounds	warrant	qualifier	backing
rebuttal	concession	refutation	conditions of rebuttal	counterargument	

2. **Can you correctly identify the writer's claim and reasons?**

   If you do not identify these correctly, your entire analysis will be incorrect. For more help with identifying a writer's thesis and support (which is what you are doing when you find the claim and reasons), see "FAQ: Outlining a Text" in Chapter 2, and see Handbook 1, Improving Your Reading Skills.

3. **Can you explain why each Toulmin element is so identified in an argument?**

   Study the two examples of Toulmin analysis in Table 14.1. For each element, ask yourself, "Why is this called [the element it is labeled]?"

TABLE 14.1 Examples of Toulmin Elements

	Example A	Example B
Claim	Children should be encouraged to play team sports.	Working a part-time job during high school is not wise.
Reason	Team sports teach children to work productively with others.	Working takes time that could be used for studying.
Grounds	A study showed that adults who participated in team sports as children were more productive team members at their jobs.	According to experts, students who work more than nine hours per week sacrifice study time to do so.
Warrant	Having good teamwork skills is important.	For high school students, studying is important.
Backing	Seventy percent of employers interviewed in a recent study said that teamwork skills are important for employees.	In a recent study, researchers learned that high school students who set aside at least two hours a day to study were more likely to graduate with a college degree later in life.
Counterargument	There are many ways to develop teamwork skills other than participating in team sports.	Students can *both* work a part-time job and study for classes, if they are dedicated enough.

| Rebuttal of Counterargument (concession and refutation) | It is true that there are other ways to build teamwork skills, but participating in team sports is an option that is readily available to most children and that most children enjoy. | Most students are not dedicated enough to *both* work a part-time job and study for classes. |

Practice using the Toulmin elements to plan your own arguments. If you can begin to think about your own arguments in Toulmin terms, you will find it easier to use Toulmin analysis to examine the arguments of others.

TRY IT!

Create an Example C to add to Table 14.1. Use a claim of your own, or select one of these:

- Parents should not (or should) use physical punishment.
- Elementary school children should (or should not) have smartphones.
- Households that do not recycle should (or should not) be fined.

CREDITS

Page 338. Reynolds, Michael Joel, "Why Parents Should Think Twice About Tracking Apps for Their Kids," *The Conversation*, May 16, 2019. https://theconversation.com/why-parents-should-think-twice-about-tracking-apps-for-their-kids-114350. Used with permission.

Page 343. Zaretsky, Robert. "How Football Can Wreck a University." The *Chronicle of Higher Education*, November 12, 2019. Used by permission.

15 Understanding an Argument's Appeals

CHAPTER OBJECTIVES

You will learn to:
- Explain the purpose of appeals to ethos, pathos, and logos.
- Define and identify appeals to ethos.
- Define and identify appeals to pathos.
- Define and identify appeals to logos.
- Analyze the rhetorical appeals of an argument.
- Write a rhetorical analysis of an argument's appeals.

What persuades us to start running, to buy a certain outfit, or to donate blood? It may be tempting to think that we make these decisions by logically analyzing our alternatives and making reasonable choices. The study of rhetoric, however, reveals that our motivations are more complex. A person may start running so that they can lose weight; this is a perfectly logical reason to run. But the same person may buy a certain outfit, *not* because they need clothes but because the new outfit makes the person feel fit, healthy, and attractive. The decision to donate blood is logical—people need blood—and donating can result in a feeling of satisfaction. But such a decision is also motivated by goodwill, by the desire to see good things happen to others.

One way to create an effective argument is to tap into factors that influence people. In the study of rhetoric, we call these factors **appeals**. Three types of appeals that help to create persuasion are appeals to the reader's values, emotions, and logic. In this chapter, we will examine these three appeals to gain an understanding of how they are used in argument. In a later chapter, you will be prompted to create appeals to support your own argument.

Connect Adaptive Learning Assignment
Consider assigning Connect's Adaptive Learning Assignments to support this chapter.

Teaching Resources
See the Instructor's Manual (IM) for suggestions about how to teach this chapter, and consider assigning this chapter's test-bank quiz.

appeal: An attempt to gain support for a claim by using logic, emotions, or credibility.

WARM-UP

The things we buy can be divided into two categories: needs and wants. Needs are those things we must have to survive—such as food and housing—while wants are those extra things—such as movie tickets or a new jacket—that are fun to have but not required for survival. Think of a "want" you would like to purchase, and list three reasons why you'd like to purchase it. You will analyze these reasons in the paragraphs that follow.

AN OVERVIEW OF THE THREE APPEALS

Teaching Resources
Consider using the PowerPoint "Three Appeals" to introduce ethos, pathos, and logos.

Three types of appeals—factors that motivate persuasion—are appeals to ethos, appeals to pathos, and appeals to logos (see Figure 15.1).

- **Appeals to ethos tap into our values.** The Greek word *ethos* is closely related to the word *ethical*. An appeal to ethos uses the good character, good intentions, expertise, or authority of the writer or others to make a text's message believable or credible.
- **Appeals to pathos tap into our emotions.** They urge us to believe a claim or take an action based on our feelings.
- **Appeals to logos are based on logic.** They motivate us to believe something or do something because the belief or action is logical and reasonable.

Co-requisite Teaching Tip
Students tend to have an easier time coming up with appeals to ethos, pathos, and logos rather than identifying them in the arguments of others. Consider working with students to analyze advertisements to find examples of the three appeals.

Scholars Ruth Anne Robbins, Steve Johansen, and Ken Chestek summarize the power of the three appeals like this: "Logos makes your audience *think* you are right; pathos makes your audience *feel* you are right; and ethos makes your audience *trust* you are right."[1]

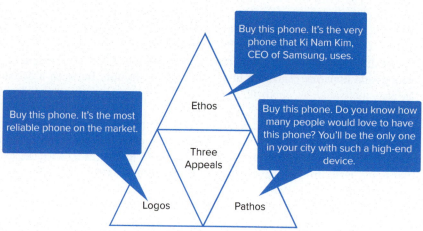

FIGURE 15.1 The three appeals to ethos, pathos, and logos.

---

[1] Robbins, Ruth Anne, Steve Johansen, and Ken Chestek, *Your Client's Story: Persuasive Legal Writing*. New York: Wolters Kluwer Law and Business, 2013, 21.

Imagine that you upgraded your phone to the newest model. Most people buy new phones, not because their phones stop working, but because they are enticed by the latest bells and whistles. We may try to make a logical case for buying a new phone by rationalizing: *The battery on my phone is getting old and may soon go out. Plus, I'll use the apps on the new phone to be more productive!* Rationalizing means creating logical reasons for an action or behavior to make it seem like the action or behavior is justified. Some logical reasons are legitimate: if your phone doesn't work anymore, it is logical to buy another phone (or to get yours repaired).

In the Warm-Up, you were asked to consider a recent "want" that you would like to purchase. As you listed the reasons why you want the item, which reasons were based on logic? Did you use any rationalization to justify the purchase? If you did not find any rationalization or logical reasons, the "want" may be based on its emotional appeal. Let's return to the decision to buy a new phone. If your existing phone works just fine yet you buy a new one, emotional desires may drive your purchase. If you are the only one in the room who has to flip open your phone, you may *feel* like an outsider. You may experience negative feelings about your wealth or social status. To feel better, you want a new phone, one that doesn't flip. Which of the reasons you generated in the Warm-Up were based on the emotional appeal of the "want"?

While many purchases that are "wants" are based on emotions, we are also motivated by appeals to ethos. If you were to buy a smartphone because your brother, an expert on technology, advised you to do so, you would be motivated by his ethos, his authority to offer sound advice because of his experience or education. As you consider the reasons for your purchase, were any of them based on what experts have said about the reputation and reliability of the make or model?

A mixture of appeals to ethos, pathos, and logos affect the choices you make and the arguments you find compelling. In most written arguments, we find a mix of appeals. Identifying the appeals that go along with an argument is a major step in being able to analyze them. Once you analyze the appeals, you are in a better position to determine whether to accept or reject the argument. Later, when you are constructing your own argument, you can determine the appeals that might work best for your audience and message.

Teaching Resources
Consider assigning the worksheet "Identifying Appeals to Ethos."

APPEALS TO ETHOS

A television commercial advertising pain medication says, "More doctors recommend PainAway than any other ointment!" A research paper on the topic of international trade policies starts with six pages that summarize the views of experts. A lawyer calls a prominent pathologist to testify on behalf of her client. Each of these rhetorical strategies appeals to ethos, the knowledge and/or good character of the speaker. An **appeal to ethos** is a rhetorical strategy that uses the writer's own authority, good character, and good intentions or the authority of others to make a text's message believable or credible.

Appeals to ethos take several forms. A sentence or passage that establishes the writer's ethical character (his or her character as a person who is good or

appeal to ethos: A rhetorical strategy that uses the writer's authority, good character, and good intentions or the authority of others to attempt to persuade.

moral), believability, fairness, objectivity, or authority to speak on the subject can be an appeal to ethos. You can identify appeals to ethos by looking for passages that make you trust the writer.

Appealing to Ethos by Demonstrating Knowledge

The following strategies appeal to ethos by helping writers prove that they are knowledgeable enough to be trusted.

- **Using one's reputation, degree, affiliations, or experiences to gain trust.** Sometimes writers do not explicitly write about their knowledge because they do not have to. For example, when a Supreme Court justice writes an opinion, he or she does not have to explain in writing why the opinion is believable; the position of the writer, in this case, is already established. When the affiliations or experiences of a writer are not well-known, the writer may refer to them explicitly to gain trust.

- **Demonstrating an accurate and thorough understanding of the topic.** Writers can appeal to ethos by presenting a topic so well—so accurately and thoroughly—that their presentation makes readers trust them.

- **Quoting authorities and experts.** A writer may not have enough personal knowledge on a subject to be trustworthy; in such cases, quoting experts can appeal to ethos. Journalists, for example, are professional writers—not experts in a discipline—so to add credibility to their work, journalists often quote experts.

Teaching Suggestion
An effective way to help students recognize ethical appeals is to contrast a news item presented by a "shock jock" with the same news item presented by an ethical journalist.

Appealing to Ethos by Demonstrating Fairness and Respect

Because we value fairness, writers who appear fair-minded are often judged more believable than those who are clearly one-sided. Writers can appeal to ethos by demonstrating fairness in several ways.

- **Presenting multiple perspectives.** A writer may be seen as fair-minded by including the perspectives of his or her opponents. By presenting the viewpoints of others, the writer shows they have considered the subject from enough perspectives to write fairly about the topic. Presenting multiple perspectives does not mean the writer agrees with them; often, the writer shows that the viewpoints of others are ultimately flawed in some way. The fact that the writer can accurately articulate the viewpoints of others means that they have studied, researched, or listened to opposing ideas; ultimately, this makes the writer seem more fair-minded.

- **Using an objective tone when possible.** Fairness and objectivity are closely linked, so using an objective tone can help a writer sound fair. An objective tone is established by avoiding first and second person and by avoiding judgmental adjectives (good, ugly, evil, wonderful, and so on).

- **Demonstrating respect.** Writers who use name-calling or disrespectful language may not be seen as believable; demonstrating respect for others can make the writer seem trustworthy, professional, and fair-minded.

Appealing to Ethos by Demonstrating Good Character

It is difficult to agree with someone we dislike. Writers use the following strategies to establish a positive relationship with the audience and present themselves as likeable:

- **Presenting noble intentions.** When a speaker is not self-interested, we are more likely to believe what the speaker has to say. Salespeople sometimes have difficulty establishing ethos because they are clearly self-interested: they need to sell their products. We are more likely to believe a person who has a noble goal, such as finding out the truth about a matter or promoting a course of action that is good for everyone, than a person who is arguing out of self-interest. Thus, when a passage of text reveals the noble intentions of the writer, the passage may be an appeal to ethos.

- **Using an open or friendly tone.** When speaking in person, an appeal to ethos can be established by behaviors, including body language and tone of voice. Writers have fewer tools available to them to establish their likeability, but writing in a tone that is not condescending, hostile, or angry, and showing respect for opposing viewpoints can contribute to an open and friendly tone. When a speaker seems open-minded, the audience is more likely to think of the speaker as fair-minded and less biased. Openness and fairness contribute to the establishment of ethos.

▶ **ACTIVITY 1 Identifying Appeals to Ethos**

In what ways does the writer of the following example appeal to ethos? Use the items discussed in this section to find the specific methods the writer uses.

> Over the twenty years I have worked as a pediatrician, I have seen thousands of children and their concerned parents. Most of the parents who refuse to immunize their children are not bad people: in fact, they are the opposite. They worry so much about their children that they let fear—and sometimes a misunderstanding of the facts—cloud their judgment. Fortunately, when I share the research about vaccines with these parents, many of them change their minds and decide to vaccinate their children.

APPEALS TO PATHOS

Rhetorical strategies that appeal to pathos tap into the emotions of the reader. While we like to think we make decisions logically, emotions play a great role in persuasion and decision making. Advertisers are masterful at using emotional

Teaching Resources
Consider assigning the worksheet "Identifying Appeals to Pathos."

appeals to sell their products. To sell alcohol, advertisements do not point out all the logical reasons for drinking: there are very few! Instead, these advertisements sell a feeling: this drink will make you feel like you are in the islands; that drink will make you feel sophisticated. **Appeals to pathos** are often called *emotional appeals* because they encourage a belief or action based on the reader's emotions.

A primary function of the appeal to pathos is to create empathy. Empathy helps readers understand and share the feelings of others; this sharing can help readers to be receptive to a writer's claim. For instance, if a writer is arguing that something should be done to stop separating families who try to immigrate into the United States, the writer may tell the story of an immigrant family's experience to create empathy. The same story may appeal to anger by arousing the reader's indignation about how the immigrant family was treated. Both of these appeals to pathos can motivate readers to agree with the claim that families seeking entrance to the United States should not be separated.

The following strategies help writers create appeals to pathos:

- **Using details that trigger emotional responses.** Consider this example: *The outlines of the dog's ribs were visible through his thin skin, and he could not make eye contact with me or come near to me, probably because of years of abuse.* The writer could have simply said that he encountered a dog that had been abused, but by adding details about the dog's ribs, thin skin, and lack of eye contact, the reader may experience an emotional response.
- **Sharing stories to evoke emotions.** A writer may tell the story of his or her experience or the experience of another person to create empathy. This empathy may lead readers to accept the argument's claim.
- **Inciting fear.** Fear is a powerful emotion, and writers can tap into their readers' fears to stress the importance of an idea or desired behavior.
- **Using figurative language to evoke emotion.** A writer may use metaphors, similes, imagery, personification, and other types of figurative language to appeal to the emotions. For instance, describing a child's home as a "house of horrors" is figurative language (a metaphor) to help readers feel sympathetic for the child.

appeal to pathos: A rhetorical strategy that taps into readers' emotions to attempt to persuade.

▶ ACTIVITY 2 **Identifying Appeals to Pathos**

In what ways does the writer of the following example appeal to pathos? Use the items discussed in this section to find the specific methods the writer uses.

One parent refused to believe that vaccines are worth the risk. I treated her son, Benjamin, from the moment he was delivered until, sadly, he left my care at age ten for the 24-hour treatment facility he required. Benjamin had

> developed subacute sclerosing panencephalitis (SSPE), a rare complication from measles. His parents helplessly watched as their once vibrant, smart child developed seizures that were uncontrollable. "Why is this happening to me, Dr. P?" Ben asked tearfully after his third seizure. Countless tests revealed the truth: SSPE had taken over Benjamin's brain. His parents and I stood by his side throughout the painful journey that ended with Ben's death at age twelve.

APPEALS TO LOGOS

An **appeal to logos** provides sound reasons, objective data (such as statistics), or logical explanations to support a claim. Writers may or may not include appeals to ethos or pathos in their arguments, but appeals to logos—the logical reasons that support a claim—are almost always included in the support for an argument's claim.

An appeal to logos is based on rational thought. It presents a reasonable, logical rationale for a claim. Writers use a variety of methods to appeal to logos. These are some of the most common ones:

- **Using objective data.** Writers appeal to logos by using facts, statistics, research studies, and data.
- **Using reasons.** Any reason that can be logically proven can be an appeal to logos. For instance, all of these reasons for purchasing Best Brand Vitamins are based on logos:
  A. Best Brand Vitamins are inexpensive.
  B. Best Brand Vitamins are available locally.
  C. Best Brand Vitamins have been certified organic.
  D. Best Brand Vitamins are gluten-free.
- **Providing reasonable comparisons.** When situations are similar, it is logical to come to conclusions by making comparisons.
- **Providing reasonable explanations of causes and/or effects.** A writer may appeal to logos by explaining what caused an event or situation or by what effects an event or situation may generate.
- **Providing definitions.** Creating or providing a definition can be a logical strategy if doing so helps the writer support a point.
- **Classifying, organizing, and ordering information.** Presenting the logic of organization and classification can help a writer communicate ideas and argue points.

appeal to logos: A rhetorical strategy that uses logical reasoning to attempt to persuade.

Teaching Resources
Consider assigning the worksheet "Identifying Appeals to Logos."

For more help with analyzing the appeals, see "FAQ: Misidentifying and Overlooking Appeals" at the end of this chapter.

▶ **ACTIVITY 3 Identifying Appeals to Logos**

In what ways does the writer of the following example appeal to logos? Use the bulleted lists to find the specific methods the writer uses.

> Parents need to vaccinate their children against measles, not because vaccinations are perfect, but because vaccinations carry very little risk, and because measles outbreaks can result in death. Additionally, according to the Centers for Disease Control and Prevention, measles is highly contagious: "It is so contagious that if one person has it, up to 90% of the people around him or her will also become infected if they are not protected." Outbreaks of measles are on the rise; it is not a disease that has been eradicated.

ANALYZING RHETORICAL APPEALS

To more fully understand how appeals to ethos, pathos, and logos work, analyze them in an argument. Use the questions in Rhetorical Toolbox 15.1 to help you analyze rhetorical appeals in the argument that follows.

RHETORICAL TOOLBOX 15.1

Analyzing Rhetorical Appeals

1. **Claim.** What is the writer's claim?
2. **Audience.** Who is the intended audience?
3. **Appeals to ethos.** Will the intended audience need the writer to establish ethos to be convincing? If so, how does the writer establish ethos? Are there appeals to ethos in the argument?
4. **Appeals to pathos.** What appeals to pathos does the writer use to help the audience find the claim convincing? Are there appeals to pathos in the argument?
5. **Appeals to logos.** What are the logical reasons that support the claim? Are these reasons appeals to logos and not appeals to ethos or pathos? Are they convincing?

"Juvenile Lifers" Deserve Second Chance

Jody Kent Lavy

The following article presents an argument on the topic of juvenile offenders. Specifically, the writer, Jody Kent Lavy, argues that juveniles who receive life without parole should be given a second chance after they have had time to rehabilitate—and grow up—in prison. Jody Kent Lavy is the executive director of Fair Sentencing for Youth, an organization that works to abolish sentences of life without parole for juvenile offenders. As you read the article, you will notice that the claim and three appeals—one to ethos, one to pathos, and one to logos—have been identified in annotations. The argument contains additional appeals to ethos, pathos, and logos, but these have not been annotated. Read and analyze the argument and annotations that are provided. Annotate any additional appeals you can find.

The men, ranging in age from late teens to early 60s, were all told that they would die in prison.

All were teenagers at the time of their crimes. All were tried as adults and convicted of murder—some felony murder, meaning they weren't the primary perpetrators and may not have even known the crime would take place.

<mark>The United States is the only nation in the world that sentences children to life in prison without parole.</mark> — Appeal to logos

These men, whom I visited at San Quentin State Prison in mid-July, are not just doing their time. <mark>They are determined to reflect on their crimes, acknowledge the harm they caused, and better themselves.</mark> — Appeal to ethos They are part of an innovative program called Kid CAT—"Kid" because they were kids at the time of their offenses, and "CAT" for Creating Awareness Together.

Kid CAT was developed by a group of "juvenile lifers" who hope to one day convince a judge or parole board that they deserve a second chance at life. Those approved to participate grapple to understand the factors that led to their crimes. They work to address the traumas of their childhoods—childhoods that would be unrecognizable to most children in this country, wracked by violence, neglect, poverty and the lure of gangs.

They even do community outreach, meeting weekly with "at-risk" youth from the Bay Area, to help them identify and manage some of their potentially dangerous, yet normal emotions—such as anger, sadness, and loss—so those feelings do not lead to destructive behavior.

<mark>During my visit, the men talked about meeting with people whose loved ones were killed. They shed tears of remorse.</mark> [Appeal to pathos] They shared their art, their writing, their innovative ideas for joining my group's efforts to end life sentences for children. They inquired about everything, from how I came to work for this cause to the intricacies of laws passed around the country.

These men are working hard to become better people. They have overcome challenges most of us could never imagine. They are devoted to ensuring other children don't make the mistakes they made. Thankfully, they are imprisoned in a state that has seen meaningful reforms in recent years that give them hope of a second chance.

California's reforms and recent U.S. Supreme Court decisions limiting the practice of sentencing children to life without parole are spurring others to act. Seventeen states do not sentence children to life without parole, and another five have banned it in most cases. There is bipartisan support to end draconian sentences that fail to account for the differences between children and adults.

State policymakers would be wise to follow this national trend. <mark>We must ban life sentences for children and ensure that others have opportunities to participate in programs like Kid CAT.</mark> [Claim] These men demonstrate that we are all more than the worst thing that we have ever done and that children—even those who have made grave mistakes—possess a capacity for change and rehabilitation.

▶ **ACTIVITY 4** **Analyzing Rhetorical Appeals**

Annotate one additional appeal to ethos, pathos, and logos in the Lavy article, and explain how the appeal works.

CHAPTER PROJECT Analyzing Rhetorical Appeals

You have learned how to write a rhetorical analysis in which you identify and critique the elements of a writer's argument. You can add to your rhetorical analysis skills by discussing the appeals in an argument. For this assignment, you will read "Equal When Separate," by Ernest Owens (reprinted in the pages that follow) or an argument assigned by your instructor, and identify appeals to ethos, pathos, and logos using Rhetorical Toolbox 15.1. You will then write the body paragraphs of a rhetorical analysis essay. Each body paragraph should present one appeal and discuss the appeal using the four-step process described in the steps that follow. (Each step is illustrated with an example showing an analysis of Lavy's article.)

Step 1. In your paper, identify the passage you believe contains the appeal.

> Lavy's description of her visit helps to humanize the men. She writes, "During my visit, the men talked about meeting with people whose loved ones were killed. They shed tears of remorse."

Step 2. Name the appeal, if you have not already done so.

> This passage presents an appeal to pathos.

Step 3. Support your assertion that the passage is, indeed, the appeal you say it is.

You can do this by pointing out how the passage functions to build trust (appeal to ethos), tap into feelings (appeal to pathos), or present a logical reason (appeal to logos).

> Specifically, Lavy wants readers to empathize with the men by presenting them as humans, capable of emotions and remorse. By showing how the men talked about their victims' families and "shed tears of remorse," Lavy hopes readers will feel sympathetic.

Step 4. Tie it all together: explain why the writer uses this appeal to support the claim.

In other words, explain how this appeal might help readers to believe the claim.

> Lavy hopes that the appeal to pathos will help soften readers' opinions about giving juvenile offenders a second chance.

Use these guidelines to analyze the appeals in the following argument.

Equal When Separate
Ernest Owens

As a contributing writer for Philadelphia Magazine *and* The Grio, *Ernest Owens writes on a range of social issues, including race relations, social media and policy, and entertainment. His work has also appeared on* CNN, The New York Times, MTV News, *and* NPR. *"Equal When Separate" appeared in* The Daily Pennsylvanian *on September 13, 2012.*

Some of my favorite moments at Penn have happened at 1920 Commons—most of them on a Saturday morning over brunch with friends.

We usually laugh loudly and take comical jabs at one another—each more intense than the last. But then comes a moment when our antics dim and someone in the group points out the fact that we're the only black students in the room and shouldn't be so loud about it.

Someone usually says, "I wonder what they think about us being so loud and black over here . . . we are being so self-segregating."

For a long time, I felt the same way. Was I being culturally limiting by eating brunch every weekend with my black peers? Was this self-segregation?

Then I looked around the other tables at Commons and saw separate groups of white students and Asian students congregated over waffles and bacon. That made me wonder: do they ever have the same discussion that I just had with my friends?

I bet they don't. Otherwise, we would all mingle over pancakes every weekend like they do at the United Nations cafeteria. Fantasy aside, minorities on campus shouldn't feel a sense of guilt when they choose to hang out with friends from a similar background.

It didn't take a UMOJA, Makuu or Black Student League event for me to get together with my friends. We just found each other as a group of black students looking to kick start the weekend together.

Debates about self-segregation are nothing new. W.E.B. Du Bois, Penn's honorary emeritus professor of sociology and Africana studies, was a strong proponent of developing economic enterprises exclusive to blacks.

Coretta Scott King, however, spoke out vocally against the practice when she said that segregation "is still wrong when it is requested by black people."

This idea is also explored at length in one of my favorite novels, *Invisible Man* by Ralph Ellison, published in 1952.

While the media and politicians attempt to convince us that we live in a post-racial society, the truth is, self-segregation persists and is a natural instinct.

Not everyone is going to get along all the time. It is normal for people to gravitate toward those who are similar. It is necessary for each of us to find a "safe space" where we feel accepted and immune from misunderstandings.

Most Quakers devote a substantial amount of their time and energy to others. We're always working on group projects with people we'd rather never see again. Or we're involved in six different student groups where we have to interact with students from all walks of life.

While there is a lot to be learned from interacting with diverse people, the question arises: when can we take a step back from the face we strive so hard to display and be ourselves?

The fabric of Penn life is woven by strings of separate communities. While we work together to produce equality, especially in an academic setting, each community is distinct. Most of our successes have come from different groups that worked hard to achieve a goal.

There is something aesthetically and socially pleasing about seeing the internal workings of these individual groups. When I go to Hillel for lunch, it always amazes me to see a close-knit circle of Jewish students. I also appreciate the ability to see groups of exchange students from Germany, Israel, and China occupy the floors of Du Bois College House every semester.

In essence, we should stop attempting to sacrifice our identities and embrace self-segregation.

By virtue of being members of the Penn community, we have already made strides to produce a more equal society. But in the words of Malcolm X, "We cannot think of uniting with others until after we have first united among ourselves."

> ### Reflecting to Develop a Writer's Mindset
>
> Think about the appeals—ethos, pathos, and logos—you learned about in this chapter. How might recognizing these appeals in the arguments and advertisements you encounter in life help you to make better decisions?

FAQ MISIDENTIFYING AND OVERLOOKING APPEALS

Identifying appeals can be tricky. Let's look at each appeal in more depth to see how to solve some of the problems you might encounter as you try to identify appeals.

1. **When are words used as appeals to pathos?**

   Some words may make you think about emotions. Words such as *anger, joy,* and *anxiety* are nouns that name emotions. And words such as *surprising, excitedly,* and *uncontrolled* may bring emotions to mind. However, not every word that brings an emotion to mind is used as an appeal to pathos. Consider this passage:

   > After the vice president was fired, the university was in a state of turmoil. Many people were upset and worried about how the change in power would affect the institution.

   To figure out whether this passage contains an appeal to pathos, think about the writer's purpose. Is the writer trying to evoke an emotional response from the reader? The answer is *no*. The writer is reporting how people felt to convey information. Contrast the passage with this one:

   > Faculty, staff, students, and anyone who loves this university should be worried by the vice president's firing. They should fear that the radical hirings and firings of this university might be the beginning of this institution's demise. Our university has changed—for the worse—overnight.

   In contrast to the first passage, the second passage attempts to support the claim that something bad is happening to the university. The second passage is not merely informative; it is an attempt to persuade; thus, it is an appeal to pathos.

2. **What are the purposes of appeals to ethos?**

   Appeals to ethos are often overlooked rather than misidentified. For instance, consider this passage:

> Most people understand the facts about donating blood. They know that donating saves lives, that they themselves may benefit from blood donations in the future, and that donating is quick and easy. What people sometimes forget is that we each have a moral obligation to each other. Donating blood contributes to the good of humanity, and we should donate simply because *it is the right thing to do.*

This passage is an appeal to ethos, but recognizing the appeal may be tricky. The passage starts with logical reasons why people should donate blood, but it ends with an ethical reason: it is the right thing (the moral and ethical thing) to do. These words appeal to *the reader's* morality and ethical sensibility. We sometimes think of ethos as applying only to the writer or to those the writer quotes and uses as authority. Appeals to ethos can also tap into the ethical values and character of readers.

To more easily find appeals to ethos, look for passages that attempt to achieve one of these goals:

- To motivate readers to accept the claim on the basis of their own goodness, morality, or ethics
- To show that the writer is good, moral, or ethical
- To show that those who support the writer are good, moral, or ethical
- To show that the writer's claim contributes to goodness, fairness, or some other ethical value
- To show that the writer, those who support the writer, or the writer's claim are believable or credible
- To show good intentions

3. How can you recognize appeals to logos?

An appeal to logos works because it is logical. When something is logical, it is reasonable. For instance, if you hear thunder, it is reasonable to conclude that it may rain. Many of the reasons used in arguments are based on logic. One way to identify an appeal to logos is to ask, "Is there a logical connection between the reason (or appeal) and the claim?"

The most common error in analyzing appeals to logos is failing to recognize them. Consider the following passage:

> One reason to support legalized gambling in this state is to examine its effects in the states where it is legal. A close look at the criminal activity rates in those states shows that gambling has a negligible effect on crime.

When you examine the reason, you will find that it is a comparison. The reason goes something like this:

> X has Y, and X doesn't have any problems; therefore we should have Y.

To determine whether this is an appeal to logos, ask these questions: What is the reasoning here? Can I explain the logical connection between the reason and the claim? If you can find reasoning, then the appeal is probably an appeal to logos. In this case, a comparison is a reasonable way to support a claim if (and only if) the comparison involves two similar things. In the United States, the states are similar enough to be able to make comparisons about what might happen if a new law is created. Thus, it is reasonable to suggest that because one state has legalized gambling and has reasonable crime rates, another state will not experience a great increase in crime if gambling is legalized.

Sometimes, however, a comparison is made as an appeal to ethos or an appeal to pathos. For example, an ad that compares feeding a child soda to feeding a child motor oil is designed to evoke emotions. No one would want to hurt a child in such a way; the shock value of such an ad is an emotional appeal designed to persuade. Clearly, no reasonable person would give motor oil to a child to drink; thus, the ad is not an appeal to logos but an appeal to pathos.

Using Rhetorical Toolbox 15.1 as a guide for analysis will help you accurately identify appeals to ethos, pathos, and logos.

TRY IT!

Read the following paragraph. You will find two types of appeals. Identify each one and make a few notes explaining why you believe the passage you have identified is the appeal you have named.

> Parents of high school–aged children should consider teaching their children how to drink alcohol responsibly. This proposal may sound ridiculous since the legal drinking age in most states is twenty-one, but the idea is actually very reasonable. Most older teens will experiment with alcohol, regardless of the drinking age. And this experimentation can be deadly. By allowing older teens to drink alcohol under the close supervision and instruction of a parent, teens can learn how much is too much, and they can learn the signs of intoxication in the safety of their own homes. Dr. Suri Patel, a pediatrician in private practice, supports this idea. She writes, "Teens who go to college with no knowledge of how to responsibly drink alcohol are at a disadvantage, and their health can suffer. Many of the alcohol poisoning–related deaths of young college students could have been prevented if parents had taken the time to actually teach their children *how* to drink alcohol."

CREDITS

Page 357. Lavy, Jody Kent, "'Juvenile Lifers' Deserve Second Chance," *The Progressive*, July 28, 2016. https://progressive.org/op-eds/juvenile-lifers-deserve-second-chance/. Used with permission.

Page 360. Owens, Ernest, "Equal When Separate," *The Daily Pennsylvanian*, September 13, 2012. Used with permission.

16 Recognizing Fallacies

CHAPTER OBJECTIVES

You will learn to:
- Identify fallacies.
- Analyze fallacies in an argument.
- Write a fallacies analysis.

Most people do not use the term *fallacy* in everyday discussions with friends. Nonetheless, we do encounter fallacies every day. **Fallacies are errors in reasoning that, if detected, can weaken an argument.** For instance, Marjorie wants to buy a laptop computer. Her friend tells her about a sale on XKP laptops. Marjorie replies that she will never buy an XKP because a friend had one, and after six months, the hard drive gave out. Marjorie's thinking is fallacious: the fact that one XKP computer had a faulty hard drive doesn't mean that *most* XKP laptops will be faulty. This kind of erroneous thinking is a fallacy. In this chapter, you learn how to identify fallacies in arguments, how to explain why the passages you identify are fallacious, and how to avoid fallacies in your own thinking and writing.

fallacy: An error in reasoning.

Connect Adaptive Learning Assignment Consider assigning Connect's Adaptive Learning Assignments to support this chapter.

Teaching Resources See the Instructor's Manual (IM) for suggestions about how to teach this chapter, and consider using this chapter's test-bank quiz.

WARM-UP
In an interview, a candidate for Congress says, "We can either require more physical education in our schools or expect obesity rates among children to continue to skyrocket." What is wrong with the candidate's reasoning?

IDENTIFYING FALLACIES

If you do an internet search for the word *fallacy*, you will find a wide variety of results. Most writers agree that fallacies are errors in reasoning, and these errors are often given names. However, not everyone agrees on the same terminology. For instance, in the Warm-Up, a candidate for Congress offered two choices: either (1) "require more physical education in our schools" or (2) "expect obesity rates among children to skyrocket." You may have figured out the fallacy: there are more than two choices! We can change the lunch menus in schools to offer more healthy choices, for instance, or we can create education programs to encourage healthy eating and physical activity. By acting as if we have only two choices and by making one of the choices undesirable, the candidate tries to manipulate voters into thinking they must support increased physical education. Some people call this fallacy in thinking a *false dilemma*, and others call it the *either/or fallacy*. However, the most important skill in analyzing fallacies is not naming the fallacy; rather, it is the ability to explain why the reasoning is faulty.

Of course, using fallacies might sometimes be beneficial. Often speakers can manipulate unsuspecting—and uncritical—audiences by using fallacies. Listen to any political candidate's speech and you will hear plenty of fallacies. Why? Political candidates know that fallacies can be persuasive because many voters simply do not analyze the reasoning of candidates. In fact, many people do not know how to critically analyze the rhetoric they encounter. That is one reason why developing a writer's mindset is so important: it helps you ask critical questions about the reasoning you hear, and by questioning, you can think more clearly and make better decisions. Of course, politicians are not the only ones who use fallacious reasoning: we all do on occasion. In a spat with her significant other, Tina says, "You don't want to buy a house because you're such a tightwad. You're just like your parents!" This statement, probably spoken in anger, is unreasonable. Finances may be one reason why her partner does not want to buy a house, but there may be other reasons. Even if finances are an issue, calling her partner a "tightwad" and comparing him to his parents are unfair moves, both designed to make him *feel* bad about himself and thus change his mind about buying a house.

Ideally, arguments should be free from fallacies. An argument's reasons should be strong enough that fallacious, manipulative strategies are not necessary. When you write arguments for college and work, readers will often be more critical and more aware of the fallacies you use than when you talk with friends and family. Resorting to fallacies to sell a claim to an audience who can detect those fallacies will cause you to lose credibility. Your ethos in an argument is important: if speakers believe that you want to win the argument at any cost—even by using fallacious reasoning—your ethos will suffer. As a result, your argument may not even be considered. Learning to detect and analyze fallacies in the arguments of others helps you avoid using them in your own arguments.

The first step in analyzing fallacies is recognizing them (see Table 16.1). One way to recognize fallacies is first to identify the argument strategy a speaker is using (as the column on the left displays). You can then look for fallacies associated with the speaker's strategy. These are presented in the right-hand column. Of course, writers can accomplish many of the tasks in the left-hand column *without* using fallacies. In this chapter, we examine each of the argument strategies in more depth to see how particular fallacies can result and how fallacies can be avoided.

Presenting Causes or Effects

Slippery Slope. The **slippery slope** fallacy occurs when a speaker makes a prediction that something undesirable will result if certain actions are (or are not) taken. A slippery slope is often used to evoke unreasonable fear. An arguer may use a slippery slope to try to scare the audience into accepting a claim.

Teaching Suggestion Consider having students follow one politician or political candidate on Twitter for the semester and find fallacies in the politician's tweets.

Teaching Resources Use the PowerPoint "Recognizing Fallacies" to help students identify and name fallacious reasoning.

Teaching Suggestion Consider assigning the worksheet "Finding Fallacies."

slippery slope: A fallacy in which it is predicted that something undesirable will happen as a result of an action (or inaction).

TABLE 16.1 Recognizing Fallacies

Argument Strategies When a writer . . .	Potential Fallacies . . . these fallacies may result:
Presents causes or effect	Slippery slope *Post hoc* Correlation error
Refers to or characterizes others	*Ad hominem* False authority Guilt by association
Summarizes the position of others	Strawman Sweeping generalization
Presents options or choices	Either/or
Uses language in tricky ways	Begging the question Loaded language
Theorizes about a group of things, people, results, etc.	Hasty generalization Sweeping generalization
Diverts attention or changes the subject	Red herring *Tu quoque*
Presents irrelevant reasons	Bandwagon *Non sequitur*
Makes a comparison	Weak analogy
Uses emotional appeals	Manipulative appeal to emotion (fear, pity, patriotism, and so on)
Uses data or statistics	Sampling bias Cherry picking

Teaching Resources
Consider assigning the worksheet "Avoid Causal Errors" to help students both identify cause-and-effect fallacies and create fallacy-free causal analyses.

Teaching Suggestion
Consider having students analyze these examples of potentially fallacious cause-and-effect thinking:

Vaping is touted as a great alternative to cigarette smoking, but it's really just a gateway to cigarettes.

After Trinity started college, she lost all interest in going to church. College professors must have had this effect on her.

Example: Strengthening gun control laws will lead to the eventual confiscation of all firearms.

Explanation: The writer does not provide any proof that such a drastic result—*confiscation of all firearms*—will come from strengthening gun control laws. The goal of this faulty reasoning is clearly to scare the reader by predicting dire consequences. By scaring the reader, the writer hopes the reader will accept the claim and reject efforts to strengthen gun control laws.

Avoiding the slippery slope fallacy: Not all predictions are fallacious. Make sure the prediction is grounded in evidence. For instance, someone may argue that if a sizeable number of people refuse vaccinations, diseases such as polio and smallpox could kill thousands, if not millions. The arguer can use research to show this dire prediction is true; thus, there is no fallacy.

Post Hoc, Ergo Propter Hoc. This Latin phrase means "after this, therefore because of this." A ***post hoc, ergo propter hoc*** error occurs when someone asserts that *x* caused *y* because *x* happened first and then *y* happened—but without enough evidence to support a causal connection. This fallacy is often used to blame or praise.

post hoc, ergo propter hoc: A fallacy in which it is argued that *x* caused *y* because *x* occurred before *y* without a proof of a causal connection. The Latin means "after this, therefore because of this."

Example: The college hired a new president, and a year later, the nursing program lost its accreditation. Clearly, the new president was not a good hire!

Explanation: The writer provides no proof that the president's hiring was a direct cause of the nursing program's lost accreditation. It is true that the president was hired a year before the nursing program lost accreditation, but there is no reasoning provided to show that the president was responsible for the loss. Thus, this is fallacious reasoning.

Avoiding the *post hoc, ergo propter hoc* fallacy: A writer can reasonably assert that x caused y as long as there is ample evidence to support that claim. For example, someone may argue that a change in the ownership of a restaurant led to its closing. If the person produces evidence that the new owners raised prices, reduced the wait staff, and started serving poor quality food, the causal claim is not a fallacy. It is still a debatable claim, but the writer provides ample support.

Correlation Error. A **correlation error** is a claim that there is a causal connection between two events in a correlation without producing evidence that one event caused the other.

> **correlation error:** A fallacy in which it is claimed that two events are related causally, but in fact the two events are simply correlated or take place at the same time.

Example: During a three-month period, air pollution levels in a city were very high. During that same period, there was an increase in suicides. Clearly, when air pollution goes up, we should be aware that suicides may also increase.

Explanation: A correlation exists when two things happen at the same time, whereas a *post hoc* exists when one thing happens and then another happens. Recognizing a correlation is fine, but claiming that there is a causal connection between the two events in a correlation is a problem unless you can show real evidence that one event caused the other. Claiming that there is a causal connection between air pollution and suicide is illogical. It is true that both phenomena increased during the three month period, but there is no evidence that one had an effect on the other.

Avoiding the correlation error: Before asserting that two events are causally connected, make sure you have evidence that proves one caused the other. If you do not have such evidence, call the relationship a correlation, and acknowledge that identifying a correlation is not strong enough to infer causality.

Referring to Others

False Authority. In the **false authority** fallacy, the writer uses someone as an authority who is not qualified to be an authority.

> **false authority:** A fallacy in which someone is represented as an authority on an issue when in fact he or she is not qualified to be an authority.

Example: To support a health-related argument, Kendra quotes a blogger who has written about the importance of fasting.

Explanation: The blogger has no expertise—no degrees, no experience—in the field of health. Thus, she is not a real authority on the subject. The same is true for celebrities who endorse products.

Avoiding the false authority fallacy: To use a person as an authority, quote only people who are genuine experts in their fields.

Ad Hominem.
An *ad hominem* fallacy is an attack on the speaker instead of the argument. The fallacy calls out the speaker's flaws instead of addressing the merits of the speaker's claim and reasons.

> **Example:** I wouldn't believe a word Senator Brown says about foreign trade. Everyone knows she's an alcoholic.
>
> **Explanation:** Senator Brown's character flaws are not the issue: the issue is foreign trade. The senator may be fully qualified to speak about foreign trade. Referring to a person's qualities, history, personality traits, or flaws as a method for discrediting the person's argument is never acceptable in argument.

Avoiding the *ad hominem* fallacy: Focus on the message unless there is a legitimate reason for focusing on the speaker.

ad hominem: A fallacy in which a speaker or writer is attacked personally rather than his or her argument. The Latin means "to the person."

Guilt by Association.
Guilt by association occurs when a person is discredited because of his or her associations, such as memberships in a group, nationality, ethnicity, religion, gender, and so on.

> **Example:** Senator Rodriguez's father was a pharmaceutical executive. We cannot trust him to make objective decisions about pharmaceutical regulations.
>
> **Explanation:** Guilt by association is a fallacy because it assumes the person is unduly influenced by his or her associates without providing proof of that influence. There are times when people *are* unduly influenced by their associates, but in general, it is unfair to judge a person's argument by his or her affiliations.

Avoiding the guilt-by-association fallacy: Focus on the argument of the person, not the person's affiliations, unless you have evidence that the person's associations have created a bias or influenced the person in a way that affects the argument.

guilt by association: A fallacy in which a person is discredited because of his or her affiliations with others rather than on the merits of his or her argument.

Teaching Suggestion
Consider having students analyze these examples of fallacious errors that could occur when referring to others:

Dr. B should not get a teaching award. He has been divorced six times because of his infidelity.

Dr. B is friends with his neighbor, Tom. I personally know that Tom is a racist, so I would not trust Dr. B to be fair.

Dr. B is the most brilliant chemist I've ever met. He told me that he is going to vote for Martindale. I think I will too.

▶ **ACTIVITY 1 Identifying Fallacies**

Read each of the passages that follow and determine whether it contains a fallacy from this set:

slippery slope	post hoc ergo propter hoc	correlation error
ad hominem	guilt by association	

If the passage contains a fallacy, identify the fallacy and defend your assertion that the fallacy exists. If a passage does not contain a fallacy, write "okay."

> **A.** I could never have voted for Hilary Clinton. Any woman who could stay married to Bill Clinton must have something wrong with her.

B. After repeated scientific studies, the researchers found that every time the rats were given Drug X, the rats' heart rates nearly doubled. Because the drug causes this increase in heart rate, we must do more research before considering clinical trials.

C. If the Affordable Care Act is repealed, eventually Medicare and Medicaid will be repealed too. The elderly and the disadvantaged will simply start dying off.

Summarizing the Position of Others

Strawman. When a speaker inaccurately presents the argument of those who have opposing opinions, a **strawman** fallacy occurs.

> **Example:** People who are in favor of legalizing same-sex marriage would like to see traditional marriages come to an end.
>
> **Explanation:** People who are in favor of legal same-sex marriage do not claim that traditional marriage should end. This is a misrepresentation of their argument: a strawman. This fallacy is called "strawman" because fighting a man made of straw is easy, but fighting a real man is difficult. In the same way, misrepresenting the opposing argument makes it easy to beat the argument.

Avoiding the strawman fallacy: Be fair when you summarize the argument of opponents. Present their best reasons.

Presenting Options or Choices

Either/Or Fallacy. The **either/or fallacy** (sometimes called the false dilemma) presents fewer choices than are actually available so that only one choice is appealing.

> **Example:** You can either buy an overpriced new car or buy a reasonably priced used car.
>
> **Explanation:** This is a fallacy because there are more than two options available. Some new cars are not overpriced, and some used cars *are* overpriced! In addition, a person can decide to lease a car. The options presented are thus too limited and not accurate.

Avoiding the either/or fallacy: There are almost always more than two choices. Be fair when you present the actual choices people have.

Using Language in Tricky Ways

Loaded Language. **Loaded language** consists of words that have powerful negative or positive connotations. Loaded terms *suggest* ideas that are not necessarily reasonable or merited.

> **Example:** We cannot allow Trisha Maxwell and her socialist agenda to influence this nation. We need to elect Mark Simmons, a true patriot.
>
> **Explanation:** The words "socialist" and "patriot" are loaded words. "Socialist" is loaded with negative connotations, while "patriot" is loaded with positive connotations. The speaker provides no real reason for

---

strawman: A fallacy in which the argument of the opposition is falsely represented.

Teaching Suggestion
Consider having students analyze this fallacy.
My mother constantly nags me to lose weight. She is intent on making me miserable.

either/or fallacy: A fallacy in which two options are presented as the only options when there are others; also called the *false dilemma*.

Teaching Suggestion
Consider having students analyze this fallacy.
You can either buy an overpriced new car or buy a reasonably priced used car.

loaded language: words with powerful negative or positive connotations

electing Simmons over Maxwell, only loaded language that suggests meanings that may or may not be true.

Avoiding loaded language: Use reasons, not loaded words, as support for your argument.

Begging the Question. A form of circular reasoning, **begging the question** occurs when a speaker uses an idea to support another similar idea.

> **Example:** John cannot have murdered his wife! John is not a murderer.
>
> **Explanation:** The proof offered for the first claim (John is not a murderer) is not proof at all; it is a restatement of the original claim. The second statement does not add a reason. It does not provide any proof. It is simply a rewording of the first statement. Consider this additional example: You can't go wrong when you buy a Toyota; Toyota is the best car ever made. The second statement sounds like evidence, but it is really a mere restatement of the first statement.

Avoiding the begging-the-question fallacy: When making a claim, offer a reason to support it. Make sure the claim and the reason are different in their content.

Theorizing About a Group of Things, People, and So On

Hasty Generalization. A **hasty generalization** is a conclusion based on a set of evidence that is faulty in some way; there is not enough data in the set of evidence to support a conclusion.

> **Example:** I have visited New Orleans three times, and every time I visited, it rained. New Orleans is one of the rainiest cities in the United States.
>
> **Explanation:** The generalization is hasty because the speaker is basing it on only three visits to New Orleans. A hasty generalization can occur when there is not enough evidence or when the evidence is flawed in some way (biased, out of date, etc.).

Avoiding the hasty generalization fallacy: Make sure there is sufficient and appropriate evidence before using a set of data to support a conclusion.

Sweeping Generalization. A **sweeping generalization** is a statement about a group of people or things when the evidence applies to only some of the group members.

> **Example:** Teenagers are irresponsible; they have to learn responsibility the hard way.
>
> **Explanation:** It is unfair to say that all teens are irresponsible and have to learn responsibility the hard way. Some teens may be irresponsible, but to suggest that they all are is a sweeping generalization. The sweeping generalization can also pertain to things, such as this statement: *Computer games are addictive.* Some games are, and some are not. To make such a broad statement is to create a sweeping generalization.

---

begging the question: A fallacy in which an unproven or questionable premise is used as support for a claim. Also called circular reasoning.

Teaching Suggestion
Consider having students analyze these fallacies:

Have you stopped your self-destructive eating habits yet?

I'm voting for Adams. He's a true patriot.

hasty generalization: A fallacy in which a conclusion is drawn on insufficient evidence.

Teaching Suggestion
Consider having students analyze this fallacy:

My Brazilian neighbors have made some of the best food I've ever eaten. Those people in Brazil really know how to cook!

sweeping generalization: A fallacy in which a statement is made about a group when the evidence applies to only some of its members.

Avoiding the sweeping generalization fallacy: Use qualifiers such as *some, most, sometimes,* and so on. Avoid making statements about gender groups, ethnic groups, age groups, and others.

▶ **ACTIVITY 2 Identifying Fallacies**

The following passages contain at least two fallacies from this set:

| strawman | either/or | loaded language |
| begging the question | hasty generalization | sweeping generalization |

Identify the passages that contain fallacies, and identify the fallacies. Then explain why the passage has the fallacy you have identified.

A. Cutting off trade with China is the only way we are going to have a fair relationship with the Chinese.

B. One of the most notorious serial killers in American history was an illegal alien. Opening the border to immigrants is simply welcoming foreign rapists, murderers, and child molesters.

C. The people who vote for increased gun control really want all guns to be taken away. They dream of living in a world where the only ones with guns are the government.

Pointing Out a Lack of Evidence

> **argument to ignorance:** A fallacy in which a claim is made on the basis that there is no evidence to prove the claim untrue.
>
> **Teaching Suggestion** Consider having students analyze these fallacies:
>
> *Vaping is perfectly safe. No one has demonstrated otherwise!*
>
> *I've never seen a UFO, so they must not exist.*
>
> **red herring:** A fallacy in which distraction or a change of subject is used to shift attention away from the issue at hand.

Argument to Ignorance. An **argument to ignorance** occurs when a speaker makes the claim that something is true because there is no evidence showing it is not true.

Example: In spite of multiple attempts, no one has been able to prove Bigfoot does not exist. Clearly, Bigfoot is out there.

Explanation: Failing to disprove is not the same as proving something. To make the statement that Bigfoot exists, the speaker needs evidence that proves such existence. It is not sufficient to say that no one can prove otherwise.

Avoiding the argument-to-ignorance fallacy: Make sure claims are supported by positive evidence.

Diverting Attention or Changing the Subject

Red Herring. A **red herring** occurs when a speaker changes the subject or presents distracting information to support a false conclusion.

Example: A parent asks her son how he did on his chemistry test. He responds by talking about how unfair his chemistry teacher has been to him.

Explanation: The son's response is an attempt to shift attention away from the question at hand—how he did on the test—by talking about his teacher's unfairness.

Avoiding the red herring fallacy: Stick to the argument under consideration. Do not introduce other issues unless you have a good reason for doing so.

Tu Quoque. Literally, "you too," the *tu quoque* fallacy occurs when someone tries to divert blame or criticism by criticizing the accuser.

> **Example:** A citizen's review board criticizes the city council for not doing enough to promote tourism in a city. A councilmember responds, "Well, you could be promoting tourism yourselves instead of forming review boards to criticize the city council!"
>
> **Explanation:** Criticizing the speaker is another way of diverting attention from the issue.

Avoiding the *tu quoque* fallacy: Stay on topic and respond to the argument at hand.

tu quoque: A fallacy in which an opponent is criticized to divert attention from one's own actions. The Latin means "you too."

Teaching Suggestion
Consider having students analyze this fallacy:
> You asked me why I want to quit college. Let me ask you: Did you enjoy your college classes?

Presenting Irrelevant Reasons

Bandwagon. This fallacy can be summarized in a few words: Everyone else is doing it! Additionally, using the ideas or preferences of the majority as proof that an idea or preference is sound constitutes a **bandwagon** fallacy. A bandwagon fallacy appeals to popularity to support a claim.

> **Example:** We should buy a new car. All of our friends bought new cars in the last year.
>
> **Explanation:** The fact that others have done something is often irrelevant, as is the case in the example. There may be times, though, when what others are doing is a valid reason. For example, "The threat of the volcano erupting is apparently real; everyone is leaving town! As tourists, we should trust the locals and leave too." In this case, doing what the majority is doing may be legitimate since the speaker does not know the area and the dangers.

Avoiding the bandwagon fallacy: Present reasons for supporting a claim, not irrelevant facts about what others are doing.

Non Sequitur. This is one of the most generic fallacy names because, literally, a *non sequitur* is a conclusion that *does not follow* from the evidence.

> **Example:** Raj, the owner of Furniture King, is one of the nicest guys I know. Furniture King is a great place to buy your new mattress.
>
> **Explanation:** The facts that Raj is a nice guy and owns a furniture store do not mean that his store is the best place to buy a mattress. The conclusion does not follow from the facts presented. Many of the more specific fallacies are also *non sequiturs*. For example, a slippery slope is a *non sequitur* in that the dire prediction the speaker makes does not follow from the scant evidence provided. Label a fallacy a *non sequitur* only when a more specific fallacy name is not appropriate.

Avoiding the *non sequitur* fallacy: Make sure any conclusion (or claim) you present is supported by relevant reasons and evidence.

bandwagon: A fallacy in which a claim is supported by the idea that "everyone does it" rather than by sound reasons or evidence.

Teaching Suggestion
Consider having students analyze this fallacy:
> Three of my best friends agree: grading students for doing group projects is wrong.

non sequitur: A fallacy in which a conclusion is drawn that does not follow from the evidence. The Latin means "it does not follow."

> **Teaching Suggestion**
> Consider having students analyze these potential analogies to determine whether they are weak:
>
> *Failing to exercise is like eating a half gallon of ice cream every night after dinner.*
>
> *Feeding homeless people is similar to feeding squirrels in the park. The homeless get used to handouts and come to expect them.*

Making a Comparison

Weak Analogy. A weak analogy is a comparison of two or more things that are not similar enough to lead to the speaker's conclusion.

> **Example:** Homeless people are like the seagulls on the shore. They gather around because they expect to be fed and supported. If we didn't feed or support them, they would not be such a nuisance.
>
> **Explanation:** There are too many ways in which people and seagulls differ to suggest that we can treat them similarly. This comparison is faulty. All comparisons involve two things that are different to some extent; otherwise, we would not be able to make a comparison at all. It is fine to compare how one state's experiences in legalizing recreational marijuana compares to another state's experiences; but it is fallacious to compare two things that are *so unlike* that it would be impossible to draw a meaningful conclusion from the comparison.

Avoiding the weak analogy fallacy: Think critically about comparisons. Make comparisons only when the things being compared are in the same category (state compared to another state, not animal compared to human) and when such comparison can be justified.

Using Emotional Appeals

> **Teaching Suggestion**
> Consider having students analyze this example of a manipulative appeal to emotions.
>
> *Mom, I can't tell you how stupid I feel when I have to use the free computer in the dorm lobby while all my other friends sit on their beds with their laptops.*

Manipulative Appeal to Emotion. A manipulative appeal to emotion attempts to evoke emotion that may not normally be warranted for the situation. All appeals to emotion are somewhat manipulative: speakers use emotional content to manipulate the audience to agree with the claim. But when a speaker has no other basis for the claim—no logical reasons to support it, for instance—the use of emotional appeals can be manipulative. The emotional appeal is manipulative when it is used to replace more substantive evidence, evidence that may not exist.

> **Example:** A candidate for Congress creates a television advertisement targeted to elderly people. In the advertisement, the candidate shows an elderly person suffering because she cannot afford her prescription medications. The candidate accuses his opponent of not caring about the welfare of the elderly.
>
> **Explanation:** This appeal to emotion is manipulative. To solicit votes, the candidate preys upon the fear of elderly people instead of presenting hard facts and logical reasons why he should be elected. Appeals to emotion are common in arguments. Sometimes those appeals seem more manipulative than reasonable.

Avoiding the manipulative-appeal-to-emotion fallacy: Some appeals to emotion are reasonable. For example, when we see suffering because of famine or when we look at the plight of refugees, it is reasonable to appeal to sympathy in order to support a claim that we should help these people. As a writer, be aware of reasonable appeals to emotions versus manipulative uses of emotional appeals.

▶ **ACTIVITY 3 Identifying Fallacies**

The passages that follow contain at least two fallacies from this set:

bandwagon	*non sequitur*	weak analogy	argument to ignorance
tu quoque	red herring	manipulative appeal to emotion	

Identify the passages that contain fallacies, and identify the fallacies. Then explain why the passage has the fallacy you have identified.

A. In the U.S., children ages fourteen or older can play paintball because children these ages have shown themselves capable of responsibly handling paintball guns. This shows that children age fourteen or older should legally be able to purchase handguns.

B. Candidate Johnson didn't ask for your opinion because she doesn't need it. As a Harvard-educated elitist, she already thinks she's better than you.

C. People who do not smoke should avoid using e-cigarettes. The nicotine in cigarettes is addictive, but people can also become psychologically addicted to using a device—a cigarette—to reduce stress. In the same way, an e-cigarette (which can contain nicotine) can produce a calming effect and can therefore become addictive.

Using Faulty Data or Statistics

Sampling Bias. Collecting data on a sample that is not truly representative is called **sampling bias**.

> **Example:** Jennifer is conducting field research. She has created a survey to measure student attitudes toward campus dining selections. She interviews every student in her MWF 11:00 a.m. class. She uses the results to speak for students at her school and to argue that campus dining selections are adequate.
>
> **Explanation:** Jennifer's research is flawed by sampling bias. She has not interviewed night students or weekend students, and there are *no* campus dining options during those times. As such, Jennifer's research does not accurately represent the students at her school.

Avoiding the sampling bias fallacy: Make sure the sample is diverse and does not exclude populations that should be surveyed.

sampling bias: A fallacy in which data is collected on a nonrepresentative selection of subjects.

Cherry Picking. **Cherry picking** is a type of sampling bias but deserves special attention here because it is so often a problem in argument. Cherry picking occurs when a speaker selects only evidence that supports his or her claim.

> **Example:** Matthew is writing a paper on why football rules should be changed because of potential traumatic head injury issues. He creates a thesis statement and then searches only for research that supports his thesis statement.

cherry picking: A fallacy in which only the evidence that supports a claim is considered; other evidence is ignored.

> **Teaching Suggestion**
> Consider having students analyze these examples of fallacious errors that could occur when using data or statistics:
>
> *Ninety percent of people believe that plastic surgery for cosmetic purposes is justified. The Plastic Surgery Physicians Group interviewed all their patients and found this amazing statistic.*
>
> *High fructose corn syrup is simply another sugar, not an evil product. Here are three sources that back up my point. Case closed.*

Explanation: Matthew has cherry-picked his evidence. Instead of approaching the topic with an open mind, he looked only for evidence that supported his claim.

Avoiding the cherry picking fallacy: Find evidence from all viewpoints. Weigh all of the evidence, and let the evidence guide the claim.

▶ **ACTIVITY 4 Identifying Faulty Uses of Data or Statistics**

Read the following paragraph. What is the problem with the use of data or statistics?

> I've heard that the people who live here in Carlton are divided on the issue of building a new football stadium, but I haven't seen any proof. I recently interviewed every person who lives on my street, and every single one was in favor of the new stadium. Where's all the division the newspaper keeps talking about?

ANALYZING FALLACIES IN AN ARGUMENT

Part of the analysis of arguments consists of identifying and analyzing fallacies. The first step is to find the fallacies in the argument. Use Rhetorical Toolbox 16.1 as a guide for identifying the fallacies in "Thinking of Getting a Tattoo? Think Again" or another argument assigned by your instructor.

> **RHETORICAL TOOLBOX 16.1**
> ### Identifying and Analyzing Fallacies
>
> 1. **Slippery slope.** Does the writer make predictions? If so, are the predictions founded on evidence? Are the predictions intended to scare the reader? If so, check for the slippery slope fallacy.
> 2. **Post hoc, ergo propter hoc.** Does the writer assert that *x* caused *y*? If so, make sure the writer's causal assertion is founded on evidence. Check for the *post hoc, ergo propter hoc* fallacy.
> 3. **False authority.** Does the writer use others to support the argument? If so, make sure those people have the authority to speak on the subject. Check for false authority.
> 4. **Ad hominem and guilt by association.** Does the writer make derogatory statements about his or her opponents? If so, check for *ad hominem* and guilt by association.
> 5. **Either/or (false dilemma).** Does the writer offer a limited number of options? If so, check for either/or.
> 6. **Loaded language.** Does the writer use terms that have strong emotional connotations? If so, check for loaded language.
> 7. **Begging the question.** Does the writer word a reason in such a way that the reason seems like the claim? If so, check for begging the question.

8. **Hasty generalization, sampling bias, and cherry picking.** Does the writer come to a conclusion without adequately surveying all the evidence? If so, check for hasty generalization, sampling bias, and cherry picking.
9. **Sweeping generalization.** Does the writer make a broad assertion about a group (of people, ideas, etc.)? If so, check for sweeping generalization.
10. **Argument from ignorance.** Does the writer use a *lack of evidence* as proof for something? If so, check for argument from ignorance.
11. **Bandwagon and *non sequitur*.** Does the writer use evidence that seems irrelevant or off topic? Check for bandwagon and *non sequitur*.
12. **Red herring and *tu quoque*.** Does the writer change the subject or turn the blame back onto the opponent? If so, check for red herring and *tu quoque*.
13. **Faulty comparison.** Does the writer make a comparison? If so, make sure the comparison is fair and not faulty.
14. **Manipulative emotional appeal.** Does the writer appeal to emotions? If so, check to see if the emotional appeal is manipulative.

The following article contains several fallacies. One fallacy has been annotated. Mark any additional fallacies you see as you read it. Use Rhetorical Toolbox 16.1 as a guide.

Thinking of Getting a Tattoo? Think Again
Martina Velez

Gone are the days when tattoos were only for outlaws and criminals. Yes, those people still get them, but so do countless others. Regardless of whether one is a Baby Boomer, Gen Xer, Millennial, or too young to care about generations, tattoos are all the rage. It is not uncommon to see elderly people getting inked these days. So why not get a tattoo?

Actually, there are quite a few reasons why you should think twice before settling down to be permanently branded. The most serious of these is safety. According to a Mayo Clinic article, "Think Before You Ink," unclean equipment used in the tattooing process leads to diseases such as hepatitis B, hepatitis C, and methicillin-resistant Staphylococcus aureus (MRSA). The scariest of these is

Teaching Suggestion
The wording in this article suggests that diseases are inevitable. Consider pulling up the Mayo Clinic article and having students analyze how Velez misrepresents the Mayo Clinic by failing to use a qualifier.

probably MRSA, a disease that can easily kill you. The Sepsis Alliance explains the urgency: "Unchecked MRSA may develop into sepsis. Sometimes incorrectly called blood poisoning, sepsis is the body's often deadly response to infection. Sepsis kills and disables millions and requires early suspicion and rapid treatment for survival."

D'Andra Anderson can vouch for the deadly nature of tattoos. After receiving a tattoo on her shoulder, Anderson's arm began to swell. She eventually learned that she had contracted MRSA, a life-threatening and very difficult to treat infection. And this infection did not go away on its own. Anderson was in the hospital for three months, and fortunately, after thousands of dollars of medical care and spending some time at death's doorway, she recovered, but not everyone is so lucky. "I would never do it again," a tearful D'Andra said. "It will take me at least ten years to pay off my medical bills." Do you have enough money to pay off the potential medical bills you might receive if you get a bad tat?

So let's imagine you know the tattoo artist is super clean and feel confident you won't get a disease. You should still avoid getting a tattoo—if you value working! ==You can have a great job or a tattoo, but you can't have both.== [**Fallacy: Either/or**] Think about it. If you were hiring for a reputable company and you had two equally qualified candidates, one all inked up and the other fresh-faced and clean, which would you prefer? And think about the high-level executives you have met. Do they have tattoos? Probably not. Hailey Ventrano graduated from an Ivy League university with a degree in accounting, but work did not come easy. It took Ventrano a year to find a job. Her impressive degree didn't seem to matter much to employers when they saw the "Life is Good" tattoo on her neck. One poor decision led to countless rejection letters.

The decision to get a tattoo will probably lead to other bad decisions. Yes, it's true that people with tats these days are not all biker gang rebels, but getting a tattoo (and not getting ill from it) leads a person to wonder, *what other things can I get away with?* What will be next? Drug experimentation? Petty theft? Getting a tattoo is like taking that first hit of marijuana. And we all know where that leads: next thing you know, doing cocaine doesn't sound so off limits.

Finally, you may be interested in tattoos now, but later, as a parent, you'll regret your decision. Any parent knows the importance of teaching children to obey laws and submit to authority. How can a tatted-up parent reinforce these messages if he or she has obviously not submitted to authority? Tattoos tell children to rebel, not submit. Take it from Katarina Madison. "I allowed my high school son, Caleb, to get a tattoo his sophomore year. Little did I know I had accidentally told my son that it's okay to be a rebel. Caleb didn't even make it through his junior year. He dropped out, and now he's working low-paying jobs instead of going to college. I really think that if I had said no to the tattoo, he would be in college right now."

Let's take a minute to be really honest. People who choose to bow to the pressure to get a tattoo are weak-minded. We all know that. Why do we insist on acting like following the crowd is okay to do in this one case? According to "Tattoo Statistics," about 20% of Americans have tattoos. Obviously most people think more critically than the minority that chooses to get inked up. If 80% of Americans refuse to get tats, there must be some wisdom in that decision. Following the crowd is never okay, and in the case of getting a tattoo to do so, you may be choosing a life of unemployment, or worse, an early death.

Works Cited

"Tattoo Statistics—How Many People Have Tattoos?" *Historyoftattoos.net*, 2012, www.historyoftattoos.net/tattoo-facts/tattoo-statistics/.

"Think Before You Ink: Tattoo Risks." *Mayo Clinic*, 2018, www.mayoclinic.org/healthy-lifestyle/adult-health/in-depth/tattoos-and-piercings/art-20045067.

CHAPTER PROJECT Analyzing Fallacies in an Argument

Analyze three fallacies (other than the either/or fallacy already identified) in Velez's argument, and write a fallacies analysis using the writing guidelines below.

Writing Guidelines

- Using Rhetorical Toolbox 16.1 as a guide, look for fallacies in Velez's argument.

- Select three fallacies.
- For each fallacy, compose a paragraph. Use the four-step process in this section as a guide for your writing.

As you write your analysis, keep in mind that your task is to *prove* that the argument contains a fallacy. Do not expect a reader to agree; offer evidence for your assertion that *x* passage is a fallacy. You can use the following plan to write an analysis of the fallacies in an argument.

Step 1: Cite the passage that contains the fallacy. You may have to provide some background information so that the passage makes sense. You may quote the passage if it is brief, or you may summarize it.

Step 2: Name the fallacy. What fallacy do you claim is presented in the passage? Tell readers.

Step 3: Defend your judgment. Assume that readers will not see the passage as fallacious. Why do you believe it is a fallacy? Explain your reasoning. This part of your analysis may take several sentences or—for complex arguments—paragraphs.

Step 4: Tie the fallacy to the writer's purpose and claim. What does the writer hope to gain by using a fallacy? Explain how the fallacy might lead unsuspecting readers to accept the claim.

Reflecting to Develop a Writer's Mindset

We have all been guilty of fallacious reasoning at one time or another. It is easy to develop lazy thinking habits that lead to fallacies. Reflect on the fallacies presented in this chapter. Which ones have you succumbed to as a thinker? Which have you used in arguments you have created? How can a deeper understanding of fallacies improve your life?

FAQ AVOIDING COMMON ERRORS IN IDENTIFYING AND ANALYZING FALLACIES

Identifying fallacies can be difficult. What follows are suggestions on how to avoid three common errors in fallacy analysis.

1. How can you avoid finding a fallacy where one does not exist?

At the beginning of this chapter, you were presented with a chart that lists argument strategies on one side and potential fallacies on the other side (see Table 16.1). It is important to remember than not every strategy in the left-hand column results in a fallacy. For instance, a writer can present a cause and effect explanation reasonably by explaining the logic that connects the cause to the effect. If the explanation is reasonable—which is something that you as a critical thinker must determine—there is no fallacy. To avoid finding fallacies where they do not exist, look for the reasons behind the argument. If the writer presents evidence or explanations that support the reasoning, there may not be a fallacy in the passage.

Example: A writer may assert that when a college increased their tuition costs by fifty percent, enrollment dropped. If the writer provides sound evidence that this increase in tuition was, indeed, the reason for the drop in enrollment, and if the writer shows that other factors were not involved, the argument is sound. There is no *post hoc* fallacy.

2. **How can you avoid confusing similar fallacies?**

   The list that follows presents some of the fallacies in this chapter that are easily confused, as well as strategies for avoiding such confusion.

   - *Post hoc* **and slippery slope.** Both of these fallacies involve cause and effect. *Post hoc* deals with an event in the past, while slippery slope predicts what will happen in the future.
   - **Either/or and slippery slope.** Many either/or fallacies are predictions. If an argument is focused on giving readers only two choices, you are pretty safe to call it an either/or fallacy (if you can think of other choices readers have). If an argument focuses on negative consequences that will result if an action is taken or not taken, it is a slippery slope unless the writer presents adequate evidence that these consequences will indeed follow.
   - **Hasty generalization and sweeping generalization.** A hasty generalization is a conclusion that is drawn from insufficient evidence. There may not be enough evidence, or the evidence may be biased. A sweeping generalization is a broad statement about a group of people or things, a statement that does not necessarily apply to everyone or everything in the group. To avoid confusing these, ask yourself, *Is the writer using evidence—such as interviews, data, statistics, examples, instances—to reach a conclusion?* If the answer is yes, then the problem may be a hasty generalization and not a sweeping generalization. If, however, the subject is a group of things or people (all men, Hispanics, uses of technology, colleges), and the writer is making a statement that applies to everyone or everything in the group, the problem is a sweeping generalization.

3. **Should you assume the reader will agree with your fallacy identification?**

   When you assert that a writer has used a fallacy, do not expect your reader to agree with you. The most significant and lengthy part of an analysis of a fallacy is the defense you provide for your assertion. For instance, if you believe a writer's prediction is a slippery slope, you must prove to your reader that the prediction is indeed the fallacy you have named it— slippery slope. Make your case by offering in-depth explanations. What makes the passage a slippery slope? Explain your reasoning. By imagining that the reader will disagree, you may be able to write a more fully developed explanation that provides a good defense of your assertion.

TRY IT!

James is analyzing an argument to find fallacies. He believes this passage presents a *post hoc* error.

> Before Mark Williams was elected as mayor, the city's crime rate was low. Now, only two years after Williams came to office, crime is up 12 percent. This increase is a direct result of having such an incompetent mayor.

If you were James's tutor, how would you help him determine whether the passage is a *post hoc* or a slippery slope?

17 Writing a Rhetorical Analysis

CHAPTER OBJECTIVES

You will learn to:
- Explain the purpose of a rhetorical analysis.
- Describe how to conduct, organize, and draft a rhetorical analysis.
- Write a rhetorical analysis.

In the previous four chapters, you learned several rhetorical skills: you can identify arguments; describe their elements; recognize appeals to ethos, pathos, and logos; and identify fallacies. You have also seen that once you identify the rhetorical features of a text, you can analyze and critique them. In this chapter you will learn how to write a rhetorical analysis, an examination of the rhetorical strategies a writer uses to make his or her argument successful. Writing a rhetorical analysis gives you a chance to produce a comprehensive analysis of a writer's attempt to create a persuasive argument.

WARM-UP

Imagine you have just returned from seeing a long-awaited movie sequel. Your friend, Sarah, who is unfamiliar with the series, asks, "What was it about?" Another friend, Marco, who knows the series well, asks, "So what's your judgment of the new movie?" How would the responses to these two questions differ? In other words, what kind of information would you give Sarah, and what kind of information would you give Marco?

ANALYZING ARGUMENTS

The purpose of a rhetorical analysis is twofold. First, analyzing the rhetorical strategies used by a writer to produce an argument helps you to understand more fully how an argument works. When you write an analysis, your mind actively constructs knowledge: you figure out things—how appeals work, whether fallacies undermine the argument, and so on. Second, by writing an analysis of an argument, you become more aware of the rhetorical strategies you can use in your

---

Connect Adaptive Learning Assignment
Consider assigning Connect's Adaptive Learning Assignments to support this chapter.

Teaching Resources
See the Instructor's Manual (IM) for suggestions about teaching this chapter, and consider assigning this chapter's test-bank quiz.

own arguments. You also become more aware of the flaws that can weaken arguments and therefore can avoid them in your own writing.

In the Warm-Up, you were asked to think about how you would respond to two different questions about a movie. You would probably respond to Sarah's question by providing a simple plot summary. Marco's question, on the other hand, requires more than a summary. He wants your judgment of the film, and judgment requires analysis. To respond to Marco, you might offer a judgment and then support it. For instance, if you found the movie disappointing, you might explain how some of the director's choices—in casting, production, and so on—did not work well. Answering Marco's question requires a different kind of thinking than the thinking necessary to answer Sarah's.

Writing a rhetorical analysis essay is more like answering Marco's question than answering Sarah's. A rhetorical analysis goes beyond mere summary. In the same way you might discuss the features that contribute to a movie's quality (or that make a movie disappointing), a rhetorical analysis focuses on key features—rhetorical strategies—of an argument. As you will see, you can discuss any of the writer's rhetorical strategies as long as you can show how the strategies help—or hinder—the writer as he or she seeks to create a convincing argument.

▶ **ACTIVITY 1** Defining Rhetorical Analysis—In Your Own Words

What is a rhetorical analysis? Why do you think your instructor wants you to be able to write a rhetorical analysis?

ANALYZING AN ARGUMENT RHETORICALLY

Analysis is both a process and a product.

- As a process, analysis consists of the critical thinking you do to understand the argument, identify the significant rhetorical strategies, and explain how those strategies work.
- As a product, a rhetorical analysis presents the insights you have gained into the writer's strategies to create a persuasive argument.

In the text that follows, you will see how Jacob Trinh, a student in an English composition class, analyzed an argument and composed a rhetorical analysis essay. The Rhetorical Toolboxes included in this section will help you to think rhetorically and to create your own rhetorical analysis later in the chapter.

We begin by examining the article and Jacob's annotations.

Co-requisite Teaching Tips
Many students struggle to find rhetorical strategies to discuss in a rhetorical analysis. Consider having students work backwards from Jacob's analysis at the end of this chapter. Have students read his finished paper first, and then return to this section to dissect Jacob's thought processes.

Teaching Suggestion
Consider spending some time in class to research the elements of the rhetorical situation of Bentley's essay.

The CDC Botched Its Vaping Investigation and Helped Spark a National Panic
Guy Bentley

Guy Bentley is director of consumer freedom at the Reason Foundation, a nonprofit think tank advancing liberty and free markets. Bentley's work has been featured in

USA Today, Forbes, Time, Business Insider, The Daily Beast, The New York Post, *and many other publications in the United States and the United Kingdom. The article that follows first appeared in 2019 on the website of RealClear Policy, a media company that focuses on U.S. domestic policy.*

The Centers for Disease Control and Prevention (CDC) finally identified a primary suspect in the wave of vaping-related lung illnesses and deaths. Examining lung tissue samples of patients hospitalized with vaping-related illnesses, CDC found 100 percent tested positive for vitamin E acetate, which is often used to cut marijuana oils. This finding was not a surprise to those who have been arguing that the cause of these illnesses is not the commercial e-cigarette market, but the illicit market for THC vapes.

For the past three months, the CDC's data showed a clear pattern. Those getting sick have been vaping illicit or adulterated THC, the main psychoactive component in cannabis. A tiny minority of patients claimed to have vaped just nicotine but were often found to be lying, most likely due to the fact that marijuana is still a schedule one substance.

It should have been obvious to CDC that regular e-cigarettes were not and could not have been causing these illnesses. Commercial nicotine e-cigarettes have been on the American and European markets for more than a decade and are used by tens of millions of people.

In Europe, there is no such outbreak of vaping-related illnesses, nor is there one in Canada. According to the deputy director of CDC, Anne Schuchat, the agency doesn't believe these illnesses were occurring in previous years but being underreported. Instead, on Oct. 25, Schuchat told journalists on a telebriefing, "We [CDC] think something riskier is in much more frequent use."

Instead of conducting a reasonable investigation and giving consumers useful advice, CDC has been deliberately ambiguous and helped spark a national panic over vaping. This contrasts sharply with CDC's actions on *E. coli* last year.

On April 10, 2018, CDC announced an *E. coli* outbreak with the source unknown. Just eight days later, the agency determined the cause was romaine lettuce from a specific region.

Margin annotations:

- Suggests CDC was behind in their research
- Background information
- Reason 1: No outbreaks elsewhere or at other times in history. Support for Reason 1: history of vaping
- Support for Reason 1: no outbreak in Europe or Canada
- Support for Reason 1: even CDC admits illnesses are anomaly
- Claim
- Comparison/contrast to CDC's *E. coli* response

CDC reacted differently	The primary factor for their speedy conclusion was interviews with people who had gotten sick. They found that 93 percent ate romaine lettuce. Although no common grower, supplier, distributor, or brand of romaine lettuce had been identified, the CDC didn't tell consumers to stop eating lettuce. Instead, the CDC recommended: "If the romaine lettuce is not labeled, do not buy, serve, sell, or eat it."
Reason 2 (implied): CDC overgeneralized. Comparison points out the fallacy of overgeneralization Quote showing overgeneralization	Contrast this to CDC's advice on vaping, where more than 80 percent of patients interviewed admitted to using THC. "Since the specific compound or ingredient causing lung injury are not yet known, the only way to assure that you are not at risk while the investigation continues is to consider refraining from use of all e-cigarette, or vaping, products."
Reason 3: Other health authorities disagree. Appeal to ethos (authority) of NASEM and the Royal College of Physicians	No commercial e-cigarettes have been associated with these illnesses in the U.S. or anywhere else in the world. But the CDC is telling consumers to stop vaping altogether, even though the National Academies of Sciences Engineering Medicine (NASEM) says there is conclusive evidence that e-cigarettes are less toxic than combustible cigarettes. According to the Royal College of Physicians, the risks of e-cigarettes are unlikely to exceed five percent of combustible cigarettes.
Reason 4: Devastating consequences Evidence: poll	The consequences of the CDC's advice have been devastating. More Americans now incorrectly believe e-cigarettes are just as or more dangerous than combustible cigarettes. A Morning Consult poll conducted in September shows the majority of people blame e-cigarettes, like Juul, for the outbreak rather than black market THC or marijuana cartridges.
Slippery slope? Dire consequences predicted if e-cigarette flavors are banned Loaded language The language of failure	E-cigarette sales have slowed, and the decline in cigarette sales has weakened. The Food and Drug Administration (FDA) may soon ban all e-cigarette flavors, which could put more than 100,000 people out work, deny safer alternatives to adult smokers, and spark a never-before-seen black market in flavored nicotine.
International consequences (India)	The CDC's communication failure has even spilled over into the rest of the world. As a direct consequence of the CDC's miscommunication, India banned the sale of e-cigarettes entirely. India has 12 percent of the world's smokers and suffers one million tobacco-related deaths every year.

> But thanks to a moral panic and mass confusion, a country that suffers more than most from smoking-related diseases, banned the most effective alternative to cigarettes ever invented. If the Trump administration or Congress moves ahead with a ban on e-cigarette flavors, the only e-cigarettes left in America will likely be in tobacco flavors sold by tobacco companies. This calamitous situation is in no small part, thanks to the deliberate ambiguity of the CDC.
>
> It should be a source of embarrassment that the public would be better informed on this issue if they listened to a vape shop owner or a cannabis website rather than the nation's top public health authority.

Sarcastic tone

Irony (country that suffers more. . . . Banned the most . . .)

Hyperbole? "most effective alternative to cigarettes ever invented"

Loaded language

Irony

Attempt to shame CDC

Analyzing the Rhetorical Situation

As you already know, any rhetorical analysis must start with a clear understanding of the rhetorical situation. The rhetorical strategies a writer chooses largely depend on the context: the message, the audience, the event or situation that motivated the argument, and so on. To begin any rhetorical analysis, use the questions in Rhetorical Toolbox 17.1 to analyze the rhetorical situation.

Teaching Resources Consider using the handout "Planning a Rhetorical Analysis."

RHETORICAL TOOLBOX 17.1
Rhetorical Situation Questions

Use these questions to gain deeper insight into the rhetorical situation of any communication.

1. **Speaker or writer.** Who is the speaker or writer? What values, beliefs, or personal interests of the speaker or writer can help you understand the message?
2. **Message.** What is the message? What is the purpose of the message? In other words, what does the speaker or writer hope to accomplish with this message? What is its immediate situation? What is the broader context?
3. **Audience.** Who is the intended audience? How does the speaker or writer attempt to meet the audience's needs or craft the message for this specific audience? What genre does the speaker or writer select for a message to this audience? Why is the genre appropriate?

> **Jacob, on analyzing the rhetorical situation:** "I had heard about the deaths from vaping, so I knew a little about the broader context. I Googled the author and learned that he often writes about smoking and vaping, and he contributed to a report called 'Sinnovation: How markets can solve public health problems—but government gets in the way.' Reading that title gave

> me some insight into what Bentley's claim might be. Since Bentley was writing for RealClear Policy, I also Googled that site. I learned that it's a clearinghouse for articles—other websites go there to pick up articles to use. So Bentley knew he was writing for a general, national audience. He probably decided to write in language the general public could understand and use references they might be familiar with (such as the comparison with the *E. coli* outbreaks)."

Analyzing Claim, Reasons, and Other Elements

Once you have a firm grasp of the rhetorical situation, you can focus on the elements of argument. While you do not have to analyze each element, a rhetorical analysis should include an analysis of at least the claim and the reasons used to support it. To be effective, a speaker must select reasons that will work to help the particular audience believe or act on the message.

As you analyze reasons, try to imagine how the audience may regard each reason. A reason may be problematic for a variety of causes:

- A writer may not provide enough grounds.
- The warrant may be questionable; and if it is, backing may be needed.
- The backing provided may be insufficient.

Use Rhetorical Toolbox 17.2 as a guide to analyze the elements of the argument. If necessary, review Chapter 14, "Analyzing an Argument's Elements."

Teaching Suggestion
Students may need a review of Toulmin analysis if you plan to have students analyze reasons as part of their rhetorical analysis. See Chapter 14.

RHETORICAL TOOLBOX 17.2
Identifying the Toulmin Elements of an Argument

Read the entire argument, keeping the rhetorical situation in mind, and then use these questions to help identify Toulmin elements:

1. **Reasons.** What are the reasons presented in the argument? Make a list.
2. **Claim.** What is the claim these reasons support? Either find the claim, if it is stated explicitly, or write it in your own words if it is not.
3. **Qualifiers.** As you analyze the claim, do you see any qualifiers?
4. **Rebuttals of counterarguments.** Does the writer address opposing points of view? If so, does the writer present any concessions (situations that would call for the claim to be set aside) or acknowledge the legitimacy of any of the opposing side's points? Does the writer present any refutations, attempts to show where the counterargument is incorrect?
5. **Grounds.** As you examine a reason, does the writer provide evidence or additional support for the reason? If so, these are grounds.
6. **Warrants.** As you examine a reason, what is the warrant? Look for the belief, value, or assumption that ties the reason to the claim. Put the warrant in your own words if it is not directly stated in the argument.
7. **Backing.** Does the writer offer any support for the warrant? If so, this is the backing.

> **Jacob, on analyzing the reasons.** "Most of the argument is based on logical reasons (appeals to logos), so I thought I would take a closer look at them and make sure there weren't any fallacies. I found it interesting that two long paragraphs are devoted to a comparison of how the CDC treated the *E. coli* outbreak. I think the comparison is fair, and the interesting thing is that Bentley was actually doing his own rhetorical analysis! He was showing that the CDC's statement about vaping was an overgeneralization."

Analyzing Appeals

Once you have analyzed the reasons, you will have found many of the writer's logical reasons, but there may be additional places where the writer uses logic to support his or her claim. Find the appeals to ethos and pathos, as well. When you find an appeal, think about why the writer included it. How does the writer hope the appeal will work? Can you tell whether the appeal was crafted with a particular audience in mind? Rhetorical Toolbox 17.3 can help you analyze the argument's appeals. If necessary, review Chapter 15, "Understanding an Argument's Appeals."

RHETORICAL TOOLBOX 17.3

Analyzing Rhetorical Appeals

1. **Claim.** What is the writer's claim?
2. **Audience.** Who is the intended audience?
3. **Appeals to ethos.** Will the intended audience need the writer to establish ethos to be convincing? If so, how does the writer establish ethos? Are there appeals to ethos in the argument?
4. **Appeals to pathos.** What appeals to pathos does the writer use to help the audience find the claim convincing? Are there appeals to pathos in the argument?
5. **Appeals to logos.** What are the logical reasons that support the claim? Are these reasons appeals to logos and not appeals to ethos or pathos? Are they convincing?

Teaching Suggestion
Students are sometimes unaware that rhetorical analyses are subjective. They forget that they must argue that *x* passage is *y* strategy. See the IM for suggestions on how to help students defend their rhetorical analyses.

> **Jacob, on analyzing the appeals.** "Most of the reasons were appeals to logos, but Bentley also talks about two other respected health agencies and their views on vaping. He does this to appeal to ethos and call into question the CDC's actions and words. When I saw Bentley make the prediction that black markets for flavored vape products might be a result of a ban, I thought that he might be appealing to fear. The language he used just seemed a bit exaggerated."

Analyzing for Fallacies

As you examine the writer's reasoning, you may find areas that could potentially be fallacies. Using Rhetorical Toolbox 17.4, examine the argument for fallacies. If you find fallacies, consider including them in your analysis. For more on fallacies, see Chapter 16, "Recognizing Fallacies."

Teaching Suggestion
In Chapter 16, students are prompted to look for fallacies by looking for certain writing moves (Table 16.1). See the IM for more information about using this approach to identifying fallacies.

RHETORICAL TOOLBOX 17.4
Identifying and Analyzing Fallacies

1. **Slippery slope.** Does the writer make predictions? If so, are the predictions founded on evidence? Are the predictions intended to scare the reader? If so, check for the slippery slope fallacy.
2. *Post hoc, ergo propter hoc.* Does the writer assert that *x* caused *y*? If so, make sure the writer's causal assertion is founded on evidence. Check for the *post hoc, ergo propter hoc* fallacy.
3. **False authority.** Does the writer use others to support the argument? If so, make sure those people have the authority to speak on the subject. Check for false authority.
4. *Ad hominem* **and guilt by association.** Does the writer make derogatory statements about his or her opponents? If so, check for *ad hominem* and guilt by association.
5. **Either/or (false dilemma).** Does the writer offer a limited number of options? If so, check for either/or.
6. **Loaded language.** Does the writer use terms that have strong emotional connotations? If so, check for loaded language.
7. **Begging the question.** Does the writer word a reason in such a way that the reason seems like the claim? If so, check for begging the question.
8. **Hasty generalization, sampling bias, and cherry picking.** Does the writer come to a conclusion without adequately surveying all the evidence? If so, check for hasty generalization, sampling bias, and cherry picking.
9. **Sweeping generalization.** Does the writer make a broad assertion about a group (of people, ideas, etc.)? If so, check for sweeping generalization.
10. **Argument from ignorance.** Does the writer use a *lack of evidence* as proof for something? If so, check for argument from ignorance.
11. **Bandwagon and** *non sequitur.* Does the writer use evidence that seems irrelevant or off topic? Check for bandwagon and *non sequitur.*
12. **Red herring and** *tu quoque.* Does the writer change the subject or turn the blame back onto the opponent? If so, check for red herring and *tu quoque.*
13. **Faulty comparison.** Does the writer make a comparison? If so, make sure the comparison is fair and not faulty.
14. **Manipulative emotional appeal.** Does the writer appeal to emotions? If so, check to see if the emotional appeal is manipulative.

> **Jacob, on analyzing for fallacies**. "Most of the reasons seemed to be based on sound logic, but I did think that Bentley's prediction about the black market might be a slippery slope. I also wasn't sure that his comparison to the *E. coli* outbreak was a sound comparison. I'm not sure if I'm right about these, so I need to go back and study them in more depth."

As you read, annotate, reread, and mark strategies, you will begin to find rhetorical strategies to discuss in a written rhetorical analysis. The next section demonstrates the kind of thinking involved in creating such an analysis, as well as the work Jacob Trinh does to write his analysis.

Organizing and Drafting a Rhetorical Analysis

When you have found the writer's rhetorical strategies, you can plan, organize, and draft a rhetorical analysis essay.

Planning. A good way to start planning is to survey the rhetorical strategies you found when you analyzed the argument. You will need to choose some of these to discuss in your written rhetorical analysis. To choose strategies, consider starting with those that are most obvious or those that are most successful in your opinion. Alternatively, think about finding the strategies that do not work so well (such as logical fallacies or missing information). Also, keep in mind that you will need to discuss and explain each rhetorical strategy thoroughly. Even if you do not yet know what you will say about the strategies, select strategies you believe are significant enough so that you could write at least a paragraph about them.

Teaching Suggestion
Many students have never written a rhetorical analysis. Understanding the reason for analyzing an argument rhetorically will help students get a clearer sense about how to approach this assignment.

It might be helpful to remind students that each student's rhetorical analysis will probably be different in that students will select different strategies they wish to discuss.

> **Jacob, on selecting rhetorical strategies to discuss:** "For this step, I made a list of the rhetorical strategies I thought I would discuss in my analysis essay. Eventually, I decided not to include all of these and to put some of them together."

> **Jacob's Notes**
> - Suggestive language: ("should have been obvious," "deliberately ambiguous," "communication failure," "calamitous situation," "source of embarrassment")
> - Use of logos: No outbreaks in other countries or in history of vaping, response was an overgeneralization, other health authorities disagree, dire consequences followed
> - Bentley uses comparison with CDC's *E. coli* response to show overgeneralization error

- Appeal to ethos: comparison to other agencies' responses
- Appeal to pathos: fear evoked by prediction of a "never-before-seen black market in flavored nicotine"
- Possibly slippery slope; possible weak analogy
- Irony
- Attempt to shame CDC

Creating a Thesis Statement and Outline. As you get further into planning your rhetorical analysis, you will want to create a thesis statement and an outline. It is helpful to remember that the purpose of a rhetorical analysis is to convince your audience that you have accurately identified and understood the rhetorical strategies a writer has used to create an argument. You might not be able to discuss every single rhetorical strategy you find. Instead, you will need to focus on the ones you have selected.

A thesis statement for a rhetorical analysis should focus on the strategies you plan to discuss. For instance, as you will see in Jacob's rhetorical analysis essay, he wrote a two-sentence thesis statement that presented the writer's claim and the strategies Jacob planned to analyze.

In addition to writing a thesis statement, creating a simple outline can help you think about how to organize your analysis. Typically, rhetorical analysis essays include these parts:

Teaching Suggestion
Help students to see how analyzing the rhetorical situation gives them content they can use for the introductory paragraph.

- **An introduction paragraph.** In the introduction, include basic source information, the same kind of information you would use in a summary, and include the writer's main idea and basic information about the rhetorical situation, such as the title of the argument, where it was published, the date, and the audience (if known).
- **Body paragraphs.** Write at least one body paragraph for each rhetorical strategy you discuss. You may need to write additional paragraphs to discuss complex rhetorical strategies. In the discussion of a rhetorical strategy, include this information:
    1. The specific word, phrase, sentence, or section that suggests a rhetorical strategy
    2. The name of the strategy in the passage
    3. A defense and explanation: in this section, defend your point that x passage $=y$ strategy. This will be the lengthiest part and will be where you present your analysis of the rhetorical strategy in question.
    4. A sentence that ties the rhetorical strategy to the writer's claim. If it is not already clear, make sure you show how the strategy could help readers accept the writer's claim.
- **A simple conclusion paragraph.** Bring your essay to a close in a few sentences.

> **Jacob, on creating a thesis statement and an outline:** "I found that I needed two sentences to write the thesis statement. The first sentence presents the writer's claim, and the second one tells readers what I'm going to talk about in the rhetorical analysis. For my outline, I wasn't sure how many paragraphs I would write for each of the rhetorical strategies so I just created four body 'parts.' That way, I could write as many paragraphs as I needed for each part."

Jacob's Outline

Introduction paragraph: Give bibliographic info and state my thesis

Part 1: Language of Failure

- "should have been obvious," "deliberately ambiguous," "communication failure," "calamitous situation," "source of embarrassment"
- Irony

Part 2: Appeals to Logic

- No outbreaks in history or in other countries; warrant: history precedent matters and what happens in other countries is relevant in the sphere of health
- Response was an overgeneralization; warrant: CDC should make decisions that are based on sound logic, not fallacies.

Part 3: Appeal to Ethos

- Other health agencies point out merits of vaping; warrant: CDC should be in line with other agencies (discuss the ethos of these other agencies)

Part 4: A Slippery Slope Fallacy

- Unprecedented black market will develop

Conclusion

Drafting. As you start drafting, keep in mind your purpose for writing a rhetorical analysis. Your instructor probably wants to see that you can identify and correctly analyze an argument. Above all, your draft must demonstrate these skills. The goal of a rhetorical analysis is *not* to merely provide a summary. You may need to summarize some of the parts of the argument, but summary should only be included when it is necessary for your analysis. As you write your analysis, remember that readers may not necessarily agree with you. Keeping this in mind can help you to thoroughly explain and defend the points you are making. For instance, if you find a passage and believe it is an appeal to ethos, you need to make the case for readers that the passage *is indeed* an appeal to ethos. You also need to be able to explain how using such an appeal may help readers accept the writer's claim.

> **Jacob, on creating a rough draft:** "I was a little stumped by what a rhetorical analysis was when writing the introduction. I was trying to write a really engaging introduction, but my instructor helped me realize that the focus of the rhetorical analysis is really to show that I can analyze. So I wrote a very basic introduction and conclusion and focused on the body paragraphs where I analyzed the piece."

Revising. In addition to using a sound revision process that helps you rethink ideas and their development, you can improve the draft of your rhetorical analysis by examining some specific concerns.

Most important, make sure your analysis is primarily an analysis, not a summary. When you analyze, you have to refer to the original text, but referring to the original text is different than summarizing it. In addition, do not offer your opinion about the argument's issue and claim. Write your analysis in third person and use an objective tone. The examples in Table 17.1 help clarify these instructions.

TABLE 17.1 Revising a Rhetorical Analysis

Dos and Don'ts	Example
Don't: Summarize without analyzing	**Summary without analysis:** A few paragraphs later, Bentley writes, "It should have been obvious to CDC that regular e-cigarettes were not and could not have been causing the illness." Later he calls the CDC "deliberately ambiguous" in their messaging about vaping and suggests that the ambiguity "helped spark a national panic." Bentley claims that the CDC was responsible for a "communication failure," and such failure resulted in a "calamitous situation."
Do: Provide a brief summary—when necessary—along with analysis	**Summary with analysis:** To support his claim that the CDC was irresponsible when it recommended a complete ban on the use of vaping products, Bentley uses words and phrases that suggest the CDC has failed, and worse, is inept. He begins his article with a mild indictment when he says that the CDC "finally" realized that Vitamin E acetate was the culprit responsible for so many deaths. Adding that "This finding was not a surprise" suggests that the CDC was not as competent as other research agencies who had already reached that conclusion. A few paragraphs later, Bentley writes, "It should have been obvious to CDC that regular e-cigarettes were not and could not have been causing the illness." The words "should have been obvious" contribute to a tone of disdain Bentley is establishing through language choices. Later he calls the CDC "deliberately ambiguous" in their messaging about vaping and suggests that the ambiguity "helped spark a national panic." Bentley claims that the CDC was responsible for a "communication failure," and such failure resulted in a "calamitous situation." The connotations of such phrases are negative; they suggest that the CDC is incompetent. In fact, the most powerful descriptor Bentley uses is his description of the CDC as a "source of embarrassment." Bentley chooses words with strong negative connotations, and these words contribute to a tone of disdain.

Don't: Offer your opinion about the issue and claim	Bentley is correct in his condemnation of the CDC's statement. The CDC needs to be more responsible and to realize that when it issues a recommendation, that recommendation will have serious consequences.
Do: Use an objective tone and present only the writer's thoughts and ideas	Bentley condemns the CDC's statement. He hopes readers will agree that the CDC needs to realize that their recommendations will have serious consequences.

- Make sure your analysis is as objective as possible. A rhetorical analysis focuses on the writer's strategies to support a claim. A rhetorical analysis should not include your opinion on the topic itself.
- Make sure your analysis includes enough explanation. Each rhetorical strategy you present must be discussed thoroughly. For example, if you find a passage you consider to be a slippery slope, you must explain why the passage is, indeed, the fallacy you are calling it.

> **Jacob, on revising.** "I'm glad I checked for summary because in my first draft, I had summarized too much. I also realized that at the end of the paper, I had slipped in my own viewpoint on vaping. I took these parts out when I revised my paper."

Jacob Trinh, A Rhetorical Analysis: The CDC Botched Its Vaping Investigation and Helped Spark a National Panic (Final Draft)

Trinh 1

Jacob Trinh
Dr. Phillips
ENGL 1302.87
20 March 2020

A Rhetorical Analysis:
"The CDC Botched Its Vaping
Investigation and Helped Spark a National Panic"

In an article titled "The CDC Botched Its Vaping Investigation and Helped Spark a National Panic," Guy Bentley makes the argument that the Centers for

Disease Control and Prevention (CDC) was irresponsible when it suggested "refraining from use of all e-cigarette, or vaping, products." Bentley is director of consumer freedom at Reason Foundation, and his previous work clearly focuses on smoking and vaping related issues. His article was published first on the website of RealClear Policy, a media group focused on making good policies for the United States. In his article, Bentley hopes to convince readers that the CDC failed when it recommended a complete ban on the use of vaping products. He uses the language of failure, along with appeals to logos and ethos, to support his claim, and he makes one potentially fallacious prediction.

    To support his claim that the CDC was irresponsible when it recommended a complete ban on the use of vaping products, Bentley uses words and phrases that suggest the CDC has failed, and worse, is inept. He begins his article with a mild indictment when he says that the CDC "finally" realized that Vitamin E acetate was the culprit responsible for so many deaths. Adding that "This finding was not a surprise" suggests that the CDC was not as competent as other research agencies who had already reached that conclusion. A few paragraphs later, Bentley writes, "It should have been obvious to CDC that regular e-cigarettes were not and could not have been causing the illness." The words "should have been obvious" contribute to a tone of disdain Bentley is establishing through language choices. Later he calls the CDC "deliberately ambiguous" in their messaging about vaping and suggests that the ambiguity "helped spark a national panic." Bentley claims that the CDC was responsible for a "communication failure," and such failure resulted in a "calamitous situation." The connotations of such phrases are negative; they suggest that the CDC is incompetent. In fact, the most powerful descriptor Bentley uses is his description of the CDC as a "source of embarrassment." Bentley chooses words with strong negative connotations, and these words contribute to a tone of disdain.

    In addition to these negative words and phrases, Bentley uses irony to further establish his point that the CDC was reckless and irresponsible. He writes, "But thanks to a moral panic and mass confusion, a country that suffers more than most from smoking-related diseases, banned the most effective alternative to cigarettes ever invented." Bentley's irony centers on the idea that the country that suffers most has simultaneously banned the most effective cure. The use of "most" twice in the sentence points out the irony; we would expect the country that suffers most from smoking-related diseases and death to embrace—not ban—the most effective alternative to cigarettes. Another example of Bentley's use of irony occurs when he writes, "It should be a source of embarrassment that the public would be better informed on this issue if they listened to a vape shop owner or a cannabis website rather than the nation's top public health authority." One would not expect a vape shop owner or cannabis websites—clearly entities that are not public health experts—to have more accurate information than the Centers for Disease Control and Prevention. If they do, that is ironic. Bentley's use of irony is a rhetorical strategy designed to help readers understand why he claims the CDC was irresponsible in its proclamation against vaping products.

Bentley's use of connotative language and irony helps set a tone of disdain, but his criticism of the CDC is also supported with appeals to logos and ethos. First, he supports the claim that the CDC was incompetent by showing that there have been no vaping-related deaths in the history of vaping. The warrant for this reason is that historical precedents matter, and most readers would agree. The reasoning goes like this: if vaping has been safe for decades, then why now, all of a sudden should *all vaping* be declared unsafe? He hopes readers will see his logic, and to support his assessment of the CDC, he also points out that other countries have not had the same outbreak of deaths from vaping. The warrant is that it is reasonable to make international comparisons when doing health research, and most readers would find such comparisons logical, so Bentley does not offer explicit backing for this warrant.

Another logical strategy Bentley uses is to criticize the CDC for using a logical fallacy. Specifically, Bentley wants to show that the CDC overgeneralized when it recommended ceasing the use of *all* vaping products. To explain this fallacy, Bentley contrasts the way the CDC handled *E. coli* outbreaks to the way it treated the vaping health issues. He shows that the CDC used a conditional statement about romaine lettuce: "[T]he CDC didn't tell consumers to stop eating lettuce. Instead, the CDC recommended: "If the romaine lettuce is not labeled, do not buy, serve, sell, or eat it." Only if the lettuce was unlabeled was it off limits. In contrast,

Bentley shows that the CDC's urging to refrain "from use of all e-cigarette, or vaping, products" is unconditional, and thus, an overgeneralization. As Bentley points out early in the article, the CDC was aware that only those vaping liquids made from Vitamin E acetate were causing illness. By calling out the logical fallacy of overstatement, Bentley hopes readers will agree with him that the CDC was irresponsible.

In addition to these logical appeals, Bentley appeals to ethos by citing the viewpoints of two other well-respected health organizations. Specifically, he notes that the National Academies of Sciences Engineering Medicine (NASEM) shows that e-cigarettes are "less toxic than combustible cigarettes" and that the Royal College of Physicians finds that e-cigarettes' risks "are unlikely to exceed five percent of combustible cigarettes." This appeal to ethos is designed to work by having the reader call into question the CDC's recommended ban—given that the two agencies noted have seemed to endorse e-cigarettes. The weakness, however, is that Bentley does not mention what these two agencies have said about the current issue—the fact that people have died because of a type of vaping.

Finally, Bentley attempts to appeal to logos by claiming that the CDC's statement may lead to "a never-before-seen black market in flavored nicotine." The language alone is a bit suspect. The descriptor, "never-before-seen," is an attempt to make readers wonder just how big the black market can get. And, of course, any time the phrase "black market" is used, negative connotations attend its use. Readers are supposed to imagine anyone and everyone creating homemade vaping concoctions with no oversight and no safety controls. Such a market is supposed to strike fear in the reader, and if the CDC is responsible for such a market, Bentley's claim about the CDC's irresponsibility is easily accepted. However, this is not a true appeal to logos; instead, it is a slippery slope. Bentley supplies no proof that this terrible black market will develop. In fact, the CDC's statement suggests that their recommendation is temporary: "Since the specific compound or ingredient causing lung injury are not yet known, the only way to assure that you are not at risk while the investigation continues is to consider refraining from use of all e-cigarette, or vaping, products." If the recommendation is, indeed, temporary, then it is not logical to assume a black market will develop. A more logical assumption is that the cause for

Trinh 5

the illnesses will be identified (and as Bentley notes, it has been) and that e-cigarette products will be made safer.

    Bentley's article presents a strong critique of the CDC, and for the most part, Bentley avoids logical fallacies and uses reasons with warrants readers will probably find acceptable. His argument would be stronger if he avoided the slippery slope fallacy. In addition, Bentley might write a more convincing argument if he had identified what other health agencies he cites said about the issue at hand instead of vaping in general. His carefully established tone of disdain helps him call the CDC's statement into question and challenges them to be more careful when they issue statements in the future.

Trinh 6

Work Cited

Bentley, Guy. "The CDC Botched Its Vaping Investigation and Helped Spark a National Panic." *Reason Foundation*, 4 Dec. 2019, reason.org/commentary/the-cdc-botched-its-vaping-investigation-and-helped-spark-a-national-panic/.

CHAPTER PROJECT Writing a Rhetorical Analysis

Using the rhetorical analysis process and examples outlined in this chapter, write a rhetorical analysis of the argument that follows.

Teaching Resources
See the IM for additional articles that lend themselves to subject essays for student rhetorical analyses.

Public Health First
Robert Reich

The opinion that follows was written by Robert Reich as a post on his blog, Robertreich.org. Reich is a well-known economist, author, and political commentator who served as secretary of labor from 1993 to 1997. He is the author of The Work of Nations, Reason, Saving Capitalism, *and many other books. This blog post was published on March 30, 2020, when Americans were debating when to reopen the economy during the early months of the COVID-19 pandemic.*

Dick Kovacevich, former CEO of Wells Fargo Bank, thinks most Americans should return to work in April, urging that we "gradually bring those people back and see what happens."

Lloyd Blankfein, former CEO of Goldman Sachs, whose net worth is $1.1 billion, recommends "those with a lower risk of the diseases return to work" within a "very few weeks."

Tom Galisano, founder of Paychex, whose net worth is $2.8 billion, believes "the damages of keeping the economy closed could be worse than losing a few more people. . . . You're picking the better of two evils."

Donald Trump is concerned that a prolonged lockdown might harm his chances of reelection. "We cannot let the cure be worse than the problem," he said last week. On Sunday he backed off his Easter back-to-work deadline, saying social distancing guidelines would remain in place until the end of April.

But senior public health officials including Dr. Anthony Fauci, director of the National Institute of Allergy and Infectious Diseases, think this may be too soon.

America already leads the world in coronavirus cases. Dr. Fauci believes we haven't yet felt the worst of the pandemic.

It may seem logical to weigh the threat to public health against the accumulating losses to the economy, and then at some point decide economic losses outweigh health risks. As Stephen Moore, who is advising the White House, warns: "You can't have a policy that says we're going to save every human life at any cost, no matter how many trillions of dollars you're talking about."

But whose "trillions of dollars" of costs are we talking about?

Workers typically bear the biggest burdens during economic downturns, especially if they lose their jobs and don't have enough money to pay the bills. Eighty percent of Americans live paycheck to paycheck.

Late last week, lawmakers made an important step to prevent such hardships. The $2.2 trillion coronavirus bill provides jobless Americans an extra $600 in unemployment benefits per week for four months, and includes contract and gig workers.

The bill was almost scuttled when Republican lawmakers objected that this would boost incomes of some job losers higher than their pay when they worked.

Apparently, these lawmakers hadn't noticed that the pay of the typical working American has stagnated for decades, adjusted for inflation. So a temporary boost in pay in order to get people to stay home and thereby help slow the spread of Covid-19 is hardly unseemly.

Here's what *is* unseemly. The "economy" that the bankers and billionaires are eager to restart had been growing rapidly before the pandemic. But most of its gains had gone into corporate profits, as shown by the meteoric rise of the stock market until a few weeks ago.

The bankers and billionaires now urging Americans [to] get back to work own a huge share of that stock market. The richest 1 percent of the population owns roughly half of the value of all shares of stock. (The richest 10 percent own more than 80 percent.)

So when they recommend Americans get back to work for the sake of the "economy," they're really urging that other people risk their lives for the sake of restoring the bankers' and billionaires' stock portfolios.

While it's true that we can't save every human life at any cost, and at some point may have to end the lockdown of America and accept some additional coronavirus casualties, we need to keep in mind which Americans we are talking about.

The trade-off average Americans might make between getting back to work and exposing themselves to the virus is likely to be quite different from the trade-off bankers and billionaires make, especially if average Americans have enough income support to get through the crisis.

Even four months of extra unemployment benefits may not be enough. The richest nation in the world surely has enough resources to keep its people safe at home for as long as it takes.

> ### Reflecting to Develop a Writer's Mindset
>
> At this point, you have studied rhetorical analyses, and you may have even written one. What is the purpose of analyzing the rhetoric of a writer? What can you gain from the process that helps you as a student? What can you gain from the process that helps you in life?

FAQ SELECTING CONTENT AND DRAFTING A THESIS STATEMENT FOR A RHETORICAL ANALYSIS

Selecting what to include in your analysis can be challenging, and writing a good thesis statement can also be an issue. Use the suggestions that follow to help with both tasks.

1. **How can content for a rhetorical analysis be selected and organized?**

    One way to select content is to group your thoughts about the argument into categories of similar elements. Let's look at an example. When Sasha read and annotated an argument essay about car seats for children, she found these elements:

    > - appeal to ethos: writer talks about his experience and education
    > - the use of direct quotes to show the emotional intensity of the situation
    > - use of a story to help us feel for the victims
    > - two faulty predictions (slippery slopes)
    > - no grounds provided for his second reason
    > - warrant for reason 1: we care about the safety of children (taps into emotional values)
    > - use of loaded words in paragraph 14
    > - bandwagon appeal in paragraph 17
    > - several appeals to logos (comparison in paragraph 6, definition in paragraph 7, explanation of law in paragraph 8)

Sasha knew that she had too many elements in her list to cover all of them, so she grouped together elements that were similar in some way. Sasha created two groups and eliminated some of the elements she found that did not fit into these groups:

- Strategies that appeal to ethos:
  - writer talks about his experience
  - writer mentions his education
- Strategies that appeal to readers' emotions:
  - the use of direct quotes to show the emotional intensity of the situation
  - use of a story to help us feel for the victims
  - warrant for reason 1: we care about the safety of children (taps into emotional values)
  - use of loaded words in paragraph 14
- ~~two faulty predictions (slippery slopes)~~
- ~~no grounds provided for his second reason~~
- ~~bandwagon appeal in paragraph 17~~
- ~~several appeals to logos (comparison in paragraph 6, definition in paragraph 7, explanation of law in paragraph 8)~~

Since Sasha has so many examples of appeals to readers' emotions, she decided to fully explore how the writer uses this rhetorical strategy. She decided that adding the writer's appeals to ethos to her discussion provided just the right amount of analysis for her paper.

2. **What should the thesis statement of a rhetorical analysis say?**

   Sasha wrote a thesis statement that included the two elements her rhetorical analysis presented:

In the article, "One Child Too Many," physician John LeBlanc relies on appeals to ethos and pathos to persuade parents to use car seats.

TRY IT!

Imagine that you have analyzed an article in which the writer, Sandra Jones, argues that cloning of humans should never be legal. You have found several rhetorical strategies and have listed them in the following box. Organize these rhetorical strategies by creating at least two groups of content. Eliminate any strategy that does not fit into the groups you create. Next, write a thesis statement for the content you selected.

- Reason #1 rests on a faulty assumption (warrant): the belief that scientific facts cannot be overturned.
- Reason #2 rests on a faulty assumption (warrant): the idea that in most situations, people are honest. (This is questionable, and not everyone will believe it.)
- There is an appeal to ethos in paragraph 1.
- There are loaded words in paragraph 3.
- The writer does not address any counterarguments, making the argument rather one-sided.
- The writer has cherry-picked information.
- There is a weak analogy in paragraph 5.
- The writer appeals to logos in paragraphs 6 and 7 when she cites Supreme Court decisions.

CREDITS

Page 384. Bentley, Guy. "The CDC Botched Its Vaping Investigation and Helped Spark a National Panic." Reason Foundation, December 4, 2019. Used by permission.

Page 399. Reich, Robert. "Public Health First." https://robertreich.org/post/614042606348943360. Used by permission of ICM Partners.

18 Classical, Rogerian, and Visual Arguments

CHAPTER OBJECTIVES

You will learn to:
- Identify the purposes of classical, Rogerian, and visual arguments.
- Explain the features of classical argument.
- Explain the features of Rogerian argument.
- Explain the features of visual argument.

What is the best way to make an argument? Would a visual argument have an impact, given the message you wish to send and the audience? Would a written argument—such as a letter to your college newspaper—be more effective for your message and audience? When you plan an argument, you have a variety of options, and by choosing the best option, you can effectively craft a persuasive argument. By becoming familiar with three styles of argument—classical, Rogerian, and visual—you can choose the best type of argument for any rhetorical situation.

> **Connect Adaptive Learning Assignment**
> Consider assigning Connect's Adaptive Learning Assignments to support this chapter.

WARM-UP
Considering the rhetorical situation of each scenario that follows, what purpose—or goal—does each speaker have? How do these goals differ?

A. A defense attorney delivers a closing argument in a criminal trial.

B. A manager has to decide whether to use seniority or productivity as a basis for offering overtime. The employees are bickering about this issue. The manager writes an email to employees, acknowledging the merits of both sides of the argument and presenting a final opinion.

C. An automobile advertiser creates a television commercial that shows how their vehicle helped a young family avoid a wreck that would have almost certainly been fatal.

> **Teaching Resources**
> See the Instructor's Manual (IM) for suggestions about how to teach this chapter, and consider assigning this chapter's test-bank quiz.

ARGUMENT STYLES

Most of the arguments you encounter in college are based on a modified version of classical argumentation. The purpose of a **classical argument** is to persuade, so when persuasion is the goal of argument, using a classical structure may be

> **classical argument:** A form of persuasive argument with a five-part structure that originated with the ancient Greeks.

Rogerian argument: A form of argument that seeks to establish common ground rather than to persuade.

visual argument: A form of argument that uses images or graphics to persuade.

a sound choice. In the Warm-Up, you analyzed three rhetorical situations. Clearly, the defense attorney's argument is intended to persuade the jury, so using some form of classical argumentation may be wise. Sometimes, however, persuasion is not the sole purpose of an argument. The manager who has to make a decision about overtime needs to persuade her employees to accept her decision, but she also needs to help employees calm down, understand the merits of the other side of the argument, and accept the new overtime policy. For her purposes, a different kind of argument is needed. She can use **Rogerian argument**, a type of argument that helps opposing sides establish common ground.

Neither of these argument types, however, would work for the automobile advertiser creating a commercial. The advertiser will use **visual argument**, a form of argument that is everywhere and that has tremendous power. Visual argument is most appropriate for the advertiser's rhetorical situation. Selecting the most appropriate argument type is an important step in accomplishing your purpose.

Selecting the appropriate argument style depends on many factors, but most of them can be analyzed by examining the rhetorical situation. If your purpose is to persuade the audience of your claim, a classical argument is more appropriate than a Rogerian argument. A visual argument may also be effective, depending on the audience and the message. On the other hand, if you are not aiming to persuade the audience but are hoping to achieve more common ground and cooperation, Rogerian argument is probably the best choice. You can use the questions in Rhetorical Toolbox 18.1 to help in the selection of an argument style. As you study the three argument styles in the following pages, refer to Rhetorical Toolbox 18.1 as needed.

RHETORICAL TOOLBOX 18.1
Selecting an Argument Style

1. **Rhetorical situation.** What is the rhetorical situation of your argument? Specifically, what message are you communicating? Who is the audience, and what characteristics of the audience can help you figure out the best style of argument? Will the audience view you as an authority on the issue? If not, how will you establish credibility?
2. **Purpose.** Is your purpose persuasion, or do you simply hope to achieve common ground and help opponents understand your point of view?
3. **Effectiveness.** Given the rhetorical situation and your purpose, which style of argument—classical, Rogerian, or visual—will be best for achieving the purpose of your argument?

CLASSICAL ARGUMENT

Teaching Resources
See the PowerPoint "Classical Argument."

The term *classical* in the context of rhetoric refers to the rhetorical theory of the ancient Greeks of Athens. The Greeks developed a system of justice that included trial by jury. In Greek courts, citizens did not have lawyers; ordinary people had

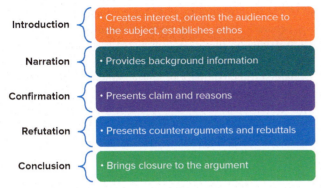

FIGURE 18.1 The five parts of classical argument.

to present their arguments and their defenses themselves. Professional speech writers helped Athenian citizens write the speeches that would be necessary in court, and in so doing, these speech writers contributed to a growing body of knowledge that would come to be known as the art of rhetoric. In addition, politicians, teachers, and military leaders regularly engaged in public discourse and needed speaking skills. Thus, there was intense interest in mastering persuasive speech.

Much of what we know about the Greek rhetorical tradition comes from Aristotle's famous treatise, *On Rhetoric*. In this work, Aristotle presents a model for argument that we call classical argumentation. Classical argument consists of five parts: introduction, narration, confirmation, refutation, and conclusion, as shown in Figure 18.1.

The Introduction

Classical argument begins with an introduction that fulfills several functions.

- **An introduction creates interest.** Speakers can do this by making the audience aware that the issue is relevant to them, or by explaining why the issue is important at the time of the speech (or writing).
- **An introduction orients the audience.** Aristotle writes, "[A] foretaste of the theme is given, intended to inform the hearers of it in advance instead of keeping their minds in suspense. Anything vague puzzles them: so give them a grasp of the beginning, and they can hold fast to it and follow the argument." Orienting the audience means, additionally, presenting one's claim in straightforward, unambiguous language.
- **An introduction establishes ethos.** Ethos can be established by creating a tone of respect, demonstrating one's knowledge of the subject, or alluding to one's experience or education to speak on the subject. An appeal to ethos makes an audience more receptive to the argument.

If you have ever heard a defense attorney's opening argument (also called *opening statements*), you have experienced the importance of a powerful introduction. After careful analysis of the jurors—the audience—an attorney will

Teaching Resources
Consider assigning "Analyzing a Classical Argument" for extra practice.

Teaching Suggestion
See the IM for a classical argument you can use as a handout and that students can analyze as you present the parts of classical argumentation.

Co-requisite Teaching Tip
The classical argument form may imply a linear progression from the introduction to the narration, and so on, but arguments are seldom that linear. Consider working with co-requisite students to analyze arguments that do not proceed in linear fashion.

carefully craft each word of the introduction so as to begin to cultivate the trust of the jury and eventually persuade them. In an opening statement, an attorney will usually state the claim explicitly. In classical arguments written for other purposes, writers may choose to state the claim in the introduction or to strategically wait to state the claim in another part of the argument. To analyze a classical introduction—and to create one yourself—use the questions that follow.

Thinking Rhetorically to Analyze an Introduction

- **Value.** How does the speaker help the audience to see the value of listening to the argument that is about to be presented?
- **Interest.** How does the speaker create interest in the issue?
- **Claim.** Does the speaker present the claim in the introduction? What rhetorical reasons might the speaker have for waiting to present the claim later or for placing the claim where it is placed?
- **Ethos.** Does the speaker attempt to establish his or her ethos in the introduction? If so, what strategies does he or she use?

Thinking Rhetorically to Create an Introduction

- **Value.** Who is your audience, and how can you show that this issue is relevant to them?
- **Interest.** What can you say that might make your audience want to know more about this subject?
- **Claim.** Should you state your claim in the introduction, or would it be more effective to state it elsewhere—according to the rhetorical situation?
- **Ethos.** How important is it that you, as a speaker, establish ethos? What will help this audience judge you as competent to speak on this topic?

The Narration

narration: In classical argument, a presentation of the background or back story that provides information necessary for the audience to understand the claim and its support.

In a courtroom setting, the **narration** tells what led up to the court case; it presents the main characters (the defendant and the plaintiff), as well a brief account of what happened. In modern argument, we often think of narration as part of the introductory material. The narrative includes the background information the audience needs to know to understand the claim. Sometimes the claim, too, is included in the narration, but it is more commonly found in the confirmation.

To analyze the narration and to create the narration for a classical argument you are writing, use the questions that follow.

Thinking Rhetorically to Analyze a Narration

- **Context.** What information does the speaker include about the context of the argument? Why is including this information important? Why do you think the writer places it where it is placed?
- **Story.** Does the speaker create a background story? How might putting background information in the form of a story be an effective rhetorical strategy?

Thinking Rhetorically to Create a Narration

- **Context.** What background information does the reader need to understand why this topic is important or relevant?
- **Story.** Is there a background "story" the reader needs to hear? Should you include this story in the introduction or weave it into the argument?

The Confirmation

Once the argument is introduced, the claim is often stated if it has not already been. At this point, the speaker must set about the hard work of proving the claim is true. In the **confirmation** of an argument, the speaker confirms the claim by providing proof. This is the section where the reasons that support the claim are presented, along with evidence for each reason. A classical argument does not include refutation of opposing viewpoints in the confirmation section. Modern arguments sometimes include reasons as well as refutations of the counterarguments to those reasons in the same section.

confirmation: In classical argument, the presentation of the claim and its support.

Use the questions that follow to analyze and create rhetorical strategies for the confirmation part of classical arguments.

Thinking Rhetorically to Analyze a Confirmation

- **Reasons.** Which reasons did the speaker choose to use for support?
- **Values.** Do the reasons seem to be chosen to correspond with the audience's values? To what extent did the speaker consider the audience in selecting reasons?
- **Appeals.** Which kinds of appeals (logos, ethos, pathos) does the writer use? Why do you think he or she chose these appeals for the given audience?
- **Support for reasons.** Consider each reason and the support the speaker uses for it. Why did the speaker choose the support?

Thinking Rhetorically to Create a Confirmation

- **Reasons.** What are all the possible reasons you could use to support the claim?
- **Values.** Given the audience's values, which reasons for your claim may be most effective?
- **Appeals.** Which kinds of appeals (logos, ethos, pathos) would be most effective for the audience?
- **Support for reasons.** Consider each reason. What support will the audience need to believe the reason or find it persuasive?

The Refutation

In the **refutation**, the writer first presents the best arguments of the opposing side and then refutes those arguments. The writer may concede a point but will still show how his or her argument is superior to that of the opposition.

refutation: In classical argument, presenting and then arguing against counterarguments.

To analyze the narration and to create the refutation for a classical argument you are writing, use the questions that follow.

Thinking Rhetorically to Analyze a Refutation

- **Opposing arguments.** Which of the opposing arguments are included in the argument? Why do you think the writer chose the particular opposing arguments that he or she chose?
- **Refutation.** Does the writer effectively refute the opposing arguments? If so, how?
- **Concession.** Does the writer concede to any of the opposition's points? How does the writer include a concession yet still firmly argue the claim?

Thinking Rhetorically to Create a Refutation

- **Opposing arguments.** Which of the opposing arguments would the audience need to have refuted so as to accept your argument?
- **Refutation.** How can you refute the opposing arguments?
- **Concession.** Are there parts of these arguments to which you can concede? If so, would there be advantages in including a concession to these parts?

The Conclusion

The conclusion is the final part of a classical argument. In much the same way an attorney presents a closing argument, the conclusion in classical argument summarizes the strongest support in the argument. It may remind the audience of the counterarguments that were refuted. In addition, the conclusion may urge the audience to do something. Above all, the conclusion is an attempt to leave the audience with the strongest points of the argument so that they will keep these in mind as they judge the argument.

Analyze the conclusion of a classical argument and plan a conclusion for an argument you are writing by using the questions that follow.

Thinking Rhetorically to Analyze a Conclusion

- **Reasons.** Does the writer include any reasons in the conclusion? If so, why do you believe the writer chose to conclude with these reasons?
- **Refutation.** Does the writer include a refutation of the counterargument in the conclusion? If so, is this strategy effective? If not, would the argument have been more effective if the writer had reminded readers of the refutation?
- **Concluding thoughts.** What ideas does the writer hope to leave in readers' minds? How might these ideas help readers accept the argument?

Thinking Rhetorically to Create a Conclusion

- **Reasons.** What are the strongest reasons for your claim? Which ones of these would you most like readers to contemplate as they judge the merits of your argument?

- **Refutation.** Would your conclusion be more effective if you reminded readers of your refutation of counterarguments?
- **Concluding thoughts.** What thoughts do you hope readers will leave with? How can you get those thoughts into the conclusion of your argument?

You can see that classical argument is similar to most of the arguments you have been reading in this text. Although modern arguments vary somewhat from the strict classical form, most still include the five parts that Aristotle identified so many years ago.

Model of a Classical Argument

The letter to the editor that follows uses the classical argument style to present the writer's opinion about a proposed citywide ban on single-use plastic shopping bags. As you read it, notice the parts of a classical argument.

To the Editor:

Should single-use plastic bags be banned in Seacrest? This is the question our city council must decide, and there is no shortage of opinions on the issue.

The issue of banning single-use plastic bags is not unique to our seaside town. Many big cities such as New York, Los Angeles, and San Francisco have bans on single-use bags, and as David Funkhouser from the Earth Institute at Columbia University points out, over 300 cities in the U.S. have such bans.

Seacrest is right to join the growing number of cities that have banned these harmful plastic bags. According to Funkhouser, *one hundred billion* single-use plastic bags are thrown away each year. In numerals, that is 100,000,000,000. They often end up in our oceans, in the bellies of animals, and in other places where they can do irreparable environmental damage. Additionally, these bags do not biodegrade; instead they break down into micropieces that enter the food chain, and we do not yet know the long-term effects on humans.

Here in Seacrest, many people are concerned that a ban on single-use plastic bags will have negative effects on tourism because of the

Introduction

Narration

Confirmation

Refutation

> inconvenience shoppers will face. Frankly, this is a rather weak argument. Shops will still have the option to *sell* bags to customers, so those customers who truly need a bag can buy it. Think about it for a moment. If Disney World banned single-use plastic bags, would you avoid the place? Do bags really matter that much to tourists? I doubt it.
>
> Conclusion
>
> What really matters to tourists is that Seacrest is beautiful. It is a place that manatees, sea turtles, and starfish call home. It is a town where tourists know they can enjoy the pristine pleasures of the ocean. And we need to keep it that way.
>
> —Elena Baricelli

▶ **ACTIVITY 1 Analyzing a Classical Argument**

Return to the questions in the lists labeled "Thinking Rhetorically to Analyze . . ." for the various parts of a classical argument. Analyze Elena Baricelli's letter by jotting down answers for each of the questions.

Teaching Resources
See the PowerPoint "Rogerian Argument."

ROGERIAN ARGUMENT

There are some situations in which persuasion is simply not possible, at least not immediately. For example, in the Warm-Up, a manager had to decide whether to use seniority or productivity as a basis for determining which employees were given the option to work overtime. Employees who had seniority argued that they should be given priority. Newer employees argued that productivity is more important than seniority and that the employees who are most effective at their jobs should be offered overtime first. The manager is in a tough position. Regardless of what she decides, some employees will be unhappy.

One way the manager can handle this dilemma is by using the principles of Rogerian argumentation to communicate her decision. Rogerian argument focuses not on winning an argument but on helping the two parties find common ground. Carl Rogers, an American psychologist, focused much of his work on the need to be understood. Rogers emphasized the importance of listening in such a way that each person in a conversation—or argument—feels like he or she has been heard. But being heard is not enough. Rogers also pointed out the need for empathy, for truly understanding where the other party is coming from. These principles, when applied to argument, help foster a greater understanding of the areas where both parties agree and the common values they share. This mutual understanding helps both sides cooperate, even when they continue to disagree.

Rogerian argument does not prescribe a particular structure, as classical argument does. Instead, what differentiates Rogerian argument from classical argument are other features.

- **A tone of respect and goodwill.** Rogerian argument is not combative. Because the speaker does not plan to win the argument or convert the audience to his or her view, the goal is to soothe the disagreement instead of emphasize the differences between the parties. For example, the manager who has to decide on the overtime issue must reassure each side that she cares about both parties, and that newer workers are valued just as much as workers with seniority, regardless of her decision about the issue.

- **An accurate and respectful expression of the opposing argument.** In the same way that Carl Rogers emphasized the importance of truly *hearing* what another person is saying, Rogerian argument must show that the speaker has listened and has accurately understood the opposing viewpoint. The manager, in this case, must be able to recount each side's arguments accurately. Doing this shows she has really listened and considered her employees' viewpoints.

- **A focus on concessions.** If there are concessions the speaker can make to some points made by the opposing side, these concessions are freely made. Making concessions to certain points does not mean the speaker agrees with the opposing view; it merely means that there are some points on which both sides agree. In the case of the manager, if the newer employees argue that employees with seniority receive many more benefits than they do, the manager might acknowledge the truth of that assertion. She might concede that it is indeed true that newer employees need to be given more privileges. This concession does not mean that newer employees will necessarily win the overtime argument, but it does show these employees that the manager has heard with one of their points.

- **A focus on common ground.** Rogerian argument seeks to find the points on which both sides agree so that, even with their differences, the parties can continue to dialogue and work together. Common ground can include concessions, but it can also include shared values. For example, the workers all value the extra income that comes with overtime. Since they share this value, the manager might find additional ways workers can earn extra income other than working overtime, such as taking on additional responsibilities, working on short-term projects, and so on.

- **A focus on the value of cooperation and dialogue.** Rogerian argument does not seek to persuade the opposing side to change its point of view; rather, it focuses on how two opposing sides can cooperate in spite of their differences. The manager might explain that if the two battling sides can work together toward a common goal—an increase in productivity—everyone will get a small raise. The focus on cooperation does not require the parties to change their minds but rather refocuses their energies on what can be accomplished by recognizing shared values.

Teaching Suggestion
Students sometimes undervalue the importance of a conciliatory tone. Consider having students analyze emails, especially professional emails or emails sent to professors, to help students understand the power of tone. See the IM for examples and additional suggestions.

Teaching Suggestion
Consider helping students find situations in their lives where Rogerian argument would be more effective than arguing to win a point. See the IM for suggestions and examples.

Rogerian argument is an excellent approach to situations that demand resolution without persuasion or conviction. These kinds of situations are common: congressional representatives disagree on an issue but need to find a compromise; a wife and husband take opposite sides in an argument and realize they must find a resolution that honors both of their viewpoints; a work team has to complete a project, but team members disagree on the process to use. When people can honestly listen to each other and find the common values and viewpoints they share, agreement on the issue at hand may not be necessary.

- **Analyzing and Creating Rogerian Arguments**

By thinking rhetorically about Rogerian arguments, you can learn how they work and can use Rogerian argumentation when it is appropriate for a rhetorical situation. The questions that follow will serve as a guide.

Thinking Rhetorically to Analyze a Rogerian Argument

- **Common ground.** How can you tell the writer's purpose is to seek common ground or cooperation instead of persuasion? Given the rhetorical situation, why do you think the writer chose Rogerian argument instead of classical argument?
- **Tone of goodwill and respect.** How does the writer create a tone of goodwill and respect? Find the words, ideas, and expressions that help the writer create this tone.
- **Shared values.** Where, in the argument, does the writer tap into the audience's values, assumptions, or goals and show that he or she shares them?
- **Concessions.** Are there concessions in the argument? If so, what function do they serve?

Thinking Rhetorically to Create a Rogerian Argument

- **Common ground.** Who is the audience? What is their opposing point of view? Why are you seeking common ground rather than trying to persuade them?
- **Tone of goodwill and respect.** What words, ideas, or expressions help you to convey a tone of goodwill and respect to this audience?
- **Shared values.** What values, assumptions, goals, or other points do you have in common with those who oppose your viewpoint? How can you use these commonalities to invite the opposing side to cooperate?
- **Concessions.** To which reasons offered by those with an opposing viewpoint can you concede? Would offering a concession aid you in your purpose for this Rogerian argument?

Teaching Resources
Consider using the assignment "Analyzing a Rogerian Argument."

Model of a Rogerian Argument

Like the model classical argument you read, the argument that follows is also a letter to the editor. While the writer is also in favor of a ban on single-use plastic bags, her letter is written using Rogerian argument style. As you read the letter, notice the features that make the argument Rogerian rather than classical.

To the Editor:

The Seacrest city council has a difficult task in deciding whether to ban single-use plastic bags, and I would like to take a moment to remind readers of a few salient points.

First, we all agree that tourism is important to our community. Shop owners and others who argue against the ban are concerned about tourism, and to be fair, they are rightly worried. Tourists are often unaware of city ordinances, and many will be surprised that plastic bags are not free and readily available. This surprise—at the cash register—may become unpleasant, and no shop owner wants a customer to leave unhappy.

However, I am quite certain that shop owners are also concerned about the environment. As residents of a beach community, we all know the value of preserving the environment that makes this place so special. After all, it's the beach and the beauty of Seacrest that brings in those tourists and that makes commerce possible. Seeing plastic bags all over the shoreline and knowing what those plastics do—over time—to the environment is a real concern, not only to the environmentalists among us but to the shop keepers, locals, and tourists.

While we may have real differences of opinion, I believe we can create a policy that is fair and that respects the concerns of both sides. Creating a reasonable policy for single-use plastic bags would mean compromising. But to compromise, we must admit that it is in our best interest—as a community—to find a solution to this problem. For instance, shops could offer plastic bags for a nominal fee, such as fifty cents. Such a solution would enable us to sharply reduce the number of single-use plastic bags in this community, but it would give tourists—who may not be equipped with their own shopping bags—a way to tote around the items they purchase. This idea is only one of many that we should consider. But we will be able to consider these compromises only if we come together as a community, a community that ultimately must stick together to keep our home the thriving seaside town that it is.

—Lourdes Alvarez

Establishment of common ground

Accurate presentation of one side of the argument

Additional common ground

Accurate presentation of a second side of the argument

Focus on compromise and cooperation

▶ **ACTIVITY 2** Using Features of Rogerian Argument

Jennifer believes children should clean their plates. Her wife, LaChelle, disagrees. Because they are co-parents, they must find a way to deal with this disagreement. How might the features of Rogerian argument help these two parties to work together productively, in spite of their disagreements?

VISUAL ARGUMENT

Teaching Resources
See the PowerPoint presentation "Visual Argument."

Teaching Suggestion
Have students find a meme that presents a visual argument, and discuss the argument it presents.

Rhetoric is not confined to words. Visual argument is the intentional use of images to influence or persuade an audience. Visual argument can be powerful, as advertisements demonstrate. But advertisements are not the only forms of visual argumentation. Memes, videos, and still images can be persuasive. Charts, graphs, and diagrams can provide persuasive proof for an argument. And if we expand the concept of visual argument even further, it is not difficult to see how one's choice of clothing for a job interview consists of a visual argument. Any visual medium can present an argument. Let's look in more depth at a few of the more common visual arguments: wordless images, images with minimal text, and images that support text.

Images without Words

Some images speak for themselves. They do not need words. Symbols and photographs depend on shared meanings in a culture to convey a message.

Symbols. The symbols in Figure 18.2 present tacit arguments. Can you figure out the meaning of each one? The first symbol is recognized as a symbol of radiation danger. The symbol presents an implied argument: *Be careful; there is radiation here.* The second symbol is the peace sign, and although this symbol has multiple meanings, it is most often associated with the 1960s movement that called for peace and unity among all people. Both symbols present implied arguments.

Photographs. In addition to symbols, photos can function as wordless arguments. Examine the photo in Figure 18.3. What argument does it express?

Bananaboy/Shutterstock Creative icon styles/Shutterstock

FIGURE 18.2 Symbols as argument.

FIGURE 18.3. A photograph as argument.

Without a single word, this photo presents an argument: irresponsible use of plastic bags threatens sea life. A photo can present an argument even more effectively than words can if it helps readers visualize the subject and develop empathy.

Images with a Few Words

Some visual arguments, such as memes and advertisements, present an image and include just enough text to help readers understand the argument.

Memes. Memes are a fun example of this kind of visual argument. Examine the meme in Figure 18.4. Can you figure out the argument this meme presents? We may laugh at memes, but they actually present viewpoints. The common "first world problem" meme points out the irony of complaining about things—such as free wifi—that are often viewed as luxuries in other parts of the world.

Advertisements. Most advertisements are also minimal-text visual arguments. Consider the advertisement in Figure 18.5. Even though you may not be able to read the ad—since it is in Italian—the dominant impression comes from the image. Notice that the words are very small compared to the image. This advertisement makes its claim—that circuses should not use live animals—by presenting an alarming image, one that is very likely to capture the audience's attention and even to elicit an emotional response.

Images That Support Text

Finally, visual aids can present support for arguments and sometimes can function as entire visual arguments themselves.

FIGURE 18.4 A meme as argument.

Infographics. Infographics are often used as additional support for a written argument. They both support the argument's claim as well as present it visually. The infographic shown in Figure 18.6 appears on the website of the Centers for Disease Control and Prevention (CDC). While articles on the CDC's website present the same information, the infographic provides a brief visual argument about the risks involved in using e-cigarettes.

Charts and Graphs. A simple chart or graph can also present an argument or provide support for a written argument. Can you figure out the argument presented in Figure 18.7? Without overtly stating anything, the chart shows that education correlates with one's employment status and weekly earnings. The information in the chart may be summarized in words, but *reading* all the information would probably be tedious, whereas providing a graph or chart makes it easy to see how much an education matters in terms of employment and wages.

Analyzing and Creating Visual Arguments

Use the questions that follow as a guide for analyzing the visual arguments you encounter and for creating a visual argument of your own. If you need help to create a visual argument, see "FAQ: Using Technology to Create Visual Arguments," at the end of this chapter.

Teaching Suggestion
See Part 6 of this text for additional visual arguments for analysis.
Consider using the assignment "Analyzing a Visual Argument."

CHAPTER 18 Classical, Rogerian, and Visual Arguments 419

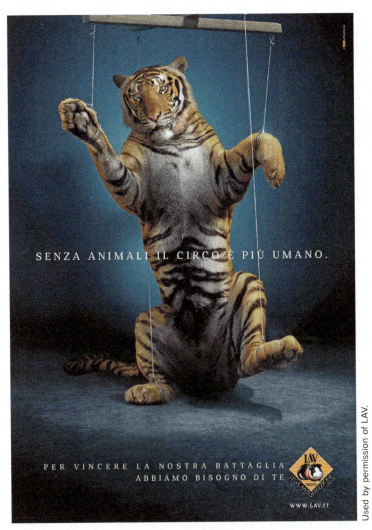

FIGURE 18.5 An advertisement as argument.

Thinking Rhetorically to Analyze a Visual Argument

- **Rhetorical situation.** Analyze the rhetorical situation. Why does the creator choose to make a visual argument? Do you think this is a sound choice?
- **Use of words.** Are there any words used in the visual argument? If so, why are the particular words significant? If not, is the visual argument unambiguous in its message? Would the use of words help—or hinder—the argument?
- **Details.** Why does the writer choose the particular visual content to create the argument? What details in the visual content are intended to make the argument effective?
- **Documentation.** Does the creator use the visual aids ethically by giving credit to their sources?

WHAT ARE THE HEALTH EFFECTS OF USING E-CIGARETTES?

SCIENTISTS ARE STILL LEARNING ABOUT THE LONG-TERM HEALTH EFFECTS OF E-CIGARETTES. HERE IS WHAT WE KNOW NOW.

1 Most e-cigarettes contain nicotine, which has known health effects
- Nicotine is highly addictive.
- Nicotine is toxic to developing fetuses.
- Nicotine can harm adolescent brain development, which continues into the early to mid-20s.
- Nicotine is a health danger for pregnant women and their developing babies.

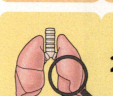

2 Besides nicotine, e-cigarette aerosol can contain substances that harm the body.
- This includes cancer-causing chemicals and tiny particles that reach deep into lungs. However, e-cigarette aerosol generally contains fewer harmful chemicals than smoke from burned tobacco products.

3 E-cigarettes can cause unintended injuries.
- Defective e-cigarette batteries have caused fires and explosions, some of which have resulted in serious injuries.
- In addition, acute nicotine exposure can be toxic. Children and adults have been poisoned by swallowing, breathing, or absorbing e-cigarette liquid.

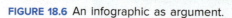

FIGURE 18.6 An infographic as argument.

Thinking Rhetorically to Create a Visual Argument

- **Rhetorical situation.** Who is the audience for the argument? Would a visual argument be more effective for the audience than a written argument?
- **Use of words.** Will the visual argument consist of a wordless image, an image with minimal text, or an image that supports a text?
- **Details.** What visual content enables you to communicate your claim and reasons to an audience?
- **Documentation.** Where can you find the visual aids you plan to use? If you find visual aids that have already been created, be sure that you are mindful of copyright law before using them. All visual aids have authors; to use a visual aid, you need to obtain permission from its creator. Alternatively, you can take your own photographs or create your own artwork, charts, graphs, or diagrams.

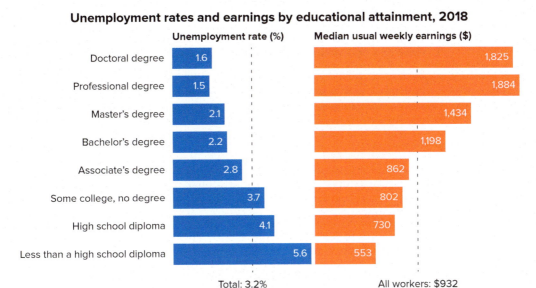

FIGURE 18.7 A chart as argument.

▶ **ACTIVITY 3 Choosing a Type of Visual Argument**

Imagine that your goal is to present a visual argument in which you claim that students should join student organizations. Your research shows that doing so will give them a sense of belonging, expose them to diverse people and ideas, and increase their network of friends and contacts. What kind of visual argument would be most effective for this audience? Why? What would your visual argument look like?

Reflecting to Develop a Writer's Mindset

Think of the three types of argument presented in this chapter. How do they differ? How are they the same? Think of three situations in which you might use each argument type, and explain why the argument type would fit the situation.

FAQ USING TECHNOLOGY TO CREATE VISUAL ARGUMENTS

It may be tempting to use an internet image in a visual argument, but doing so is often illegal, unless you have the written permission of the person who created the image and the people in the image. As an alternative to using someone else's work, you can create your own visual aids by using the methods that follow.

1. **How can you acquire photos that you can use?**

   Most smartphones are equipped with high quality cameras. You can take your own pictures and use them any way you wish. Be sure, however, that you do not take pictures of people, because you need their permission if you want to use those photos for your own work.

   When you determine the subject of the photo, take several shots. You can choose the best one later and use photo-editing software to make changes to it. As you create your visual argument, think about how you want your photo to appear. Would your photo be more realistic if it were in color rather than black and white? Would using a sepia tone change the way readers experience the photo? Would cropping the photo make it a more effective visual aid? As you edit the photo, make the choices that contribute to the argument you are hoping the photo will make.

2. **How can you create an infographic?**

   Most infographics rely on artwork, so even if you create your own infographic, you still need to be careful about the artwork you choose for it. If you have the ability, draw your own images. A quick internet search will take you to websites that explain how to master some basic drawing skills. If you do not feel competent to draw your own images, consider using clip art. While clip art cannot usually be used for commercial purposes, you can use it for academic projects without worry about copyright infringement.

3. **How can you create a chart or a graph?**

   You can use the tools in Microsoft Word, Microsoft Excel, Microsoft PowerPoint, Google Slides, or Google Sheets to create charts and graphs. All five of these programs provide methods for creating visual aids.

TRY IT!

Create a visual aid—such as a photo, infographic, or chart—to make a statement about an issue that concerns you. For example, you might take a photo of food waste in the cafeteria to illustrate how much food we regularly throw away, or you might create a chart to show that young teens are increasingly addicted to their smartphones.

CREDITS

Page 420. U.S. Department of Health and Human Services, Center for Disease Control and Prevention. "Electronic Cigarettes: What the Bottom Line?" https://www.cdc.gov/tobacco/basic_information/e-cigarettes/pdfs/Electronic-Cigarettes-Infographic-508.pdf

Page 421. U.S. Bureau of Labor Statistics. "Unemployment rates and earnings by educational attainment." https://www.bls.gov/emp/chart-unemployment-earnings-education.htm

PART 5 Writing a Researched Argument

19 Planning an Argument

CHAPTER OBJECTIVES

You will learn to:
- Select a topic and issue question for an argument.
- Create a guidance rubric for an argument.
- Identify research needs and find sources.
- Explain diverse viewpoints on an issue.
- Write a claim for an argument.
- Evaluate and select reasons to support a claim.

In many college classes, you are asked to take a position on an issue and support that position with research. Such assignments go by many names: position papers, research papers, theses, persuasive papers, argument papers, and so on. Whatever the assignment is called, an effective argument demonstrates your ability to form a well-stated claim and support it with the best evidence possible. In Chapters 19 through 22, we present a research and writing process that guides you through the thinking, planning, and composing involved in creating an effective argument. In this chapter, you will select a topic and begin planning your argument by working through the following assignments:

- Argument Assignment 1: Selecting a topic and writing an issue question
- Argument Assignment 2: Creating a guidance rubric
- Argument Assignment 3: Identifying your research needs and finding sources
- Argument Assignment 4: Analyzing your research and creating a viewpoints chart
- Argument Assignment 5: Drafting a claim
- Argument Assignment 6: Evaluating and selecting reasons

Connect Adaptive Learning Assignment
Consider assigning Connect's Adaptive Learning Assignments to support this chapter.

Teaching Resources
See the Instructor's Manual (IM) for suggestions about how to teach this chapter, and consider assigning this chapter's test-bank quiz.

PART 5 PROJECT Writing a Researched Argument

Use an argument project your instructor assigns, or select one of the three argument projects that follow.

PROJECT 1 An Argument in Your Field of Study

Write a researched argument on an arguable issue related to your major or to a field in which you are interested. Write your paper for undergraduate students who may be considering the major or field. The topic must be appropriate for an argument paper. If you are unsure of a topic, do some research to learn about the controversial issues in your major or field of study. Here are some examples of topics. (*Note:* These topics lend themselves to a variety of writing aims, such as informing, analyzing, and so on. You will need to select an aspect of the topic about which you can make an argument.)

- **Humanities and social sciences:** immigration policy, Confederate monuments, food scarcity, cost of higher education
- **Science and technology:** stem cell research, uses of drones, gene-editing, computer privacy and security
- **Health:** how to effectively manage a pandemic (such as COVID-19), pharmaceutical advertising, universal health care, funding for mental health
- **Education:** bilingual education, physical education requirements, using technology as teaching tools, behavioral policies
- **Business and economics:** paid-leave policies, minimum guaranteed income, effectiveness of tariffs, using alternate currencies

PROJECT 2 A "Mythbuster" Argument

A myth is an idea that many people believe but that is not true. For this assignment, you will select a widely held belief and compose a researched argument showing that the belief is not true. Your audience will be a general audience that includes people who believe the myth is true. Here are some examples of widely held beliefs for which ample evidence to the contrary exists:

- Most highly successful people skipped college.
- Vaccines cause autism.
- Women are more emotional, and men are more logical.
- Global warming is a natural occurrence that will not affect human life.
- Physical punishment is effective.
- The death penalty is a deterrent to crime.

PROJECT 3 A Visual Argument for a Social Change

Think about the social changes you would like to see happen. Perhaps you would like to see more people with disabilities get high-quality jobs; maybe you would like to change policies that affect policing; perhaps you would like to change the way people regard and treat animals. Select an

---

Teaching Suggestion
To help students select a topic, consider pointing them to research sites such as EBSCO's Point of View Reference Center. For additional resources, see the IM.

Teaching Suggestion
See the IM for resources to support this assignment, including websites and articles.

Teaching Suggestion
See the IM for a list of visual arguments that advocate for social change.

issue that calls for social change, research the issue, and create a visual and textual argument for a general audience. Follow these instructions:

1. Select a topic.
2. Select the type of visual argument—such as a slideshow, an advertisement, a webpage, a video, or a brochure—that is best for your topic and audience.
3. Create your argument. Use the steps in Chapters 19 to 22, and review the elements of effective visual arguments in Chapter 18.

To write the best argument possible, it is important that you use a process of academic inquiry that starts with *learning* instead of *asserting*. Asserting means stating a claim or opinion. If you create a claim before you learn everything you need to know about the topic, you run the risk of creating a failing argument. Creating a claim before doing research also leads to cherry-picking: selecting only sources and evidence that support your argument. As you know from previous chapters, cherry-picking will make your argument fallacious.

Academic inquiry starts by asking a research question and then learning everything you can to answer that question. It requires that you keep an open mind throughout the learning phase and that you allow the research to influence you as you determine the claim you will argue. Asserting a thesis statement or claim happens *after* you have read the research, weighed the evidence, and come to a conclusion.

As we discuss the process of planning and writing an argument, we will follow Jada Spalding, a student in a college writing class, as she plans and writes an argument paper using the Project 1 assignment.

SELECTING A TOPIC AND WRITING AN ISSUE QUESTION

Because a researched argument involves many hours of work, selecting a topic and asking a good issue question are crucial tasks. Think about topic selection as a part of the research process. You may need to examine several topics by doing some preliminary reading before you find the best one for your purposes. The topic you choose needs to meet several criteria.

- **A good topic for an argument is one in which you are interested.** If you are not interested in the topic, do not select it. If you are interested in a topic, you will be much more likely to engage in high-quality research and write a paper others will find interesting.
- **A good topic for an argument is a topic that is debatable.** Some topics are simply not debatable. For instance, an informative paper about the signs of stroke is not an argument. Select a topic for which alternative points of view can be supported. The topic of how to provide affordable health care for Americans is debatable because research supports various points of view.

Co-requisite Teaching Tip
Developing writers are sometimes reluctant to embrace the uncertainty that comes with learning about a topic—instead of immediately asserting a thesis. Consider spending time helping students learn about issues before creating a claim for an argument. See the IM for more information.

Teaching Suggestion
Consider requiring students to propose three argument topics instead of one. Consider also having students do at least 1-2 hours of research on the topics and summarize what they have learned. Doing so helps students propose topics about which they can find sufficient information.

Teaching Resources
Consider using the exercise "How About These Topics?"

- **A good topic for an argument is one on which ample research exists.** When you have an idea for a topic, do a preliminary search to see if enough research exists to support different points of view on the issue. Since your assignment is to produce a research-based argument, you will need to find sources that support your point of view, as well as other points of view on the issue.

- **A good topic is one on which you can keep an open mind.** Do not choose a topic that is so important to you that you would never change your mind about it. Ideally, the topic you select will be something you are *not* sure about so that the research you do can guide your opinion.

Once you have selected a topic, turn the topic into a specific issue question. Topics, by nature, are broad. An issue question is more focused and narrow than a topic; keeping a specific issue question in mind helps you limit the scope of your argument. In turn, limiting the scope will help you to avoid overgeneralization. By writing a question instead of a thesis statement, you can focus on finding research that answers the question from diverse viewpoints. Here are some examples of topics and issue questions. For your argument, you would select only one of the issue questions:

Topic: Online dating

Issue question: Should online dating companies be held legally liable for safe matchmaking?

Issue question: Should impersonation on an online dating site be punishable by law?

Topic: Mass shootings

Issue question: Would increased mental health services have an effect on the prevalence of mass shootings?

Issue question: Should teachers be trained in the use of firearms and carry guns?

Topic: Policing

Issue question: Should modern policing make use of different tactics and policies?

Issue question: What measures can be implemented to decrease the need for policing?

> **Jada, on choosing a topic for her researched argument project:** "Honestly, I dreaded writing this paper. But picking a topic that I was interested in helped. I've always been interested in the work-from-home trend, but after the COVID-19 quarantines, I really got curious. I wanted to know whether employers benefit when their employees work from home. My hunch was that employees who work from home are just as productive as those who work on site."
>
> **Jada's issue question:** Do companies benefit when employees work from home?

ARGUMENT ASSIGNMENT 1
Selecting a Topic and Writing an Issue Question

Using the guidelines in this section and Jada's work as a model, select a topic and write an issue question.

CREATING A GUIDANCE RUBRIC

Your instructor may give you a rubric, and if so, you should use it as your guidance rubric. If not, you can create your own guidance rubric. A guidance rubric lists the qualities and features you believe are important for the assignment. This rubric is just for your use, not your instructor's, but it will help you make sure your paper has everything in it, and because it is a personalized rubric, you can add your own personal notes to it. If you are unsure about how to create a rubric, see Chapter 3 for more information.

Your guidance rubric should be a chart that lists the assignment requirements. Add any other expectations your instructor may have, and if you know your grammatical weaknesses, list those too. Keep the guidance rubric handy throughout the research and writing process so that you can make sure you are meeting requirements.

Jada's Guidance Rubric					
	How Well I Met the Requirement (5 best, 1 worst)				
Requirement	5	4	3	2	1
Topic must lend itself to argument.					
Must concern a controversial issue related to my field of study.					
Must include logical reasons and avoid logical fallacies.					
Must address counterarguments.					
Must be 2,000 to 2,500 words.					
Must include a visual aid such as a chart or graphic, if appropriate.					
Must use at least 10 sources.					
Must be in MLA style.					
Note to self: Check spelling and look for fragments!					
Note to self: Double check for accidental plagiarism.					

Notice that Jada's guidance rubric includes the Project 1 requirements, her instructor's specific requirements, and her own notes. Jada includes reminders to check for spelling errors, fragments, and accidental plagiarism because she has struggled with those issues in the past.

ARGUMENT ASSIGNMENT 2
Creating a Guidance Rubric

Using your argument assignment and Jada's rubric as a model, create a guidance rubric for your essay.

IDENTIFYING YOUR RESEARCH NEEDS AND FINDING SOURCES

Before you start searching for books, articles, and other kinds of sources, take some time to figure out the types of research that will help you answer the issue question. Keep in mind that your goal should be to find the most credible and useful sources. Use Rhetorical Toolbox 19.1 to figure out your research needs.

> **RHETORICAL TOOLBOX 19.1**
> ### Identifying Your Research Needs
>
> 1. **Types of sources.** What kind of research should you do to fully understand the topic? What kind of sources will you need to understand and explain technical aspects of the issue, if applicable? What kind of information will you need to understand the issue's historical background? What other types of research will you need in order to write authoritatively about the issue?
> 2. **Points of view.** What points of view (opinions) do you anticipate finding? What kinds of sources will help readers believe that you have a complete understanding of the most significant opinions on the topic? How will you gain an understanding of the diverse viewpoints on the topic?
> 3. **Experts.** Who are the most authoritative experts on the issue you are arguing? What kind of research from experts would you like to have, and where might you find it?

Depending on your issue, you can choose to research a wide variety of sources. Because finding credible, appropriate sources is a complex skill, we devoted Chapter 10 to this topic. Be sure to use the guidelines in that chapter as you conduct research.

To conduct research for an argument assignment, the best place to start is your college library. Using online databases such as EBSCOhost, Gale, ProQuest, NewsBank, and others will help you to learn the particular keywords that apply to your topic. Jada learned that working from home is often abbreviated WFH, and she learned other names used to describe WFH such as "remote working" and "telecommuting."

The first phase of your research is all about learning. Your first few searches may not be productive, so you will need to adjust search terms and search strategies until you start finding the information you need. You may even find that your research question needs to be revised. Remember that the writing process

Co-requisite Teaching Tip Consider spending time to analyze potential sources, especially to help students judge the value of potential articles.

is recursive. Being flexible and making changes as you learn about your issue will help you create a better argument.

Select only the very best sources for your issue question. Before you select a source, examine it. Determine whether it is applicable to your topic. Figure out how technical the source is. Some highly technical sources are of limited use because they are too difficult for nonexperts to understand. Remember that you must read and carefully analyze every source you select, so choose only sources that help you answer your issue question.

Additionally, you will need to find sources from multiple viewpoints. For instance, to become fully knowledgeable about the topic, Jada needs to find sources that show both the advantages and disadvantages of allowing employees to work from home. If she searches only for sources that promote working from home, her research will be cherry-picked and she will not be able to fairly evaluate the issue. If you need help finding multiple viewpoints on your issue, see "FAQ: Finding Research from Multiple Viewpoints" at the end of this chapter.

> **Jada, on conducting research:** "When I did a search on my topic, I found many blogs by people who started working from home during the COVID-19 quarantines. Those were interesting, but they were not exactly what I needed. People who were forced to work at home without adequate preparation have different experiences than those whose companies have fully developed WFH programs. I imagined a skeptical business owner reading my paper and demanding solid evidence about telecommuting so I wanted to find info about those well established WFH programs. I decided to look for studies that showed productivity rates. I found several case studies of companies that permit WFH, and those will be important as I make my argument. My biggest challenge was finding multiple points of view. At first, I was finding a lot of grumbling about WFH, especially from people who were forced into it. By changing my search strategies, I found some excellent sources about how even well-prepared employees face challenges when they work from home."

ARGUMENT ASSIGNMENT 3
Identifying Your Research Needs and Finding Sources

Use the questions in Rhetorical Toolbox 19.1 to identify your research needs, and then, using sound researching strategies, find sources to meet those needs. Use the guidelines in Chapter 10 to conduct your research.

ANALYZING YOUR RESEARCH AND CREATING A VIEWPOINTS CHART

Once you gather sources, you will need to analyze what you have found. Analysis starts with a full understanding of each source. A common error in argument papers is to misread or misrepresent sources. This error often comes from not reading sources carefully enough. As you read and analyze your sources, imagine that your audience—and your instructor—will be reading those sources too. If necessary, reread a source multiple times until you are certain you understand it.

After a thorough analysis of a source, you may decide it is not usable in your argument. For example, you may find that a source does not address your issue question as well as you thought it might, or it is simply too focused on the scientific parameters of the case study its authors conducted. Any number of factors can make a source less than perfect. In such cases, go back to the research process and find a better source.

You may also find, upon a more thorough reading of your sources, that you lack research that addresses an aspect of your issue question. Or you may find that an article you thought was presenting an opposing point of view actually does not do so. Again, return to the research process and find other sources. Plan to go back to the research process at least three times. It is common to conduct research only to learn that you need something different for your purposes.

Your sources should present multiple viewpoints and reasons for those viewpoints. Creating a Viewpoints Chart will enable you to map the viewpoints of the writers, record their reasons, and look at the whole of your research efforts. Doing this will help you keep the sources organized, select the right sources to support your claim, and recognize whether your research has equipped you with viewpoints from both (or multiple) sides of the issue.

To create a Viewpoints Chart, make a table that has a column for each source and five rows for notes. The example here is for only three sources; you will need a column for each source, so a Viewpoints Chart will probably take more than a single page.

Viewpoints Chart			
	Source #1 Author/Title	Source #2 Author/Title	Source #3 Author/Title
Claim			
Reasons			
Issues Addressed			
Reminder Notes			
Citation			

Teaching Suggestion
Students sometimes view the Viewpoints Chart as busy work, but it is not. It requires careful, analytical thinking about sources. Consider working together to analyze Jada's chart, or to create a chart column together. See the assignment "Creating a Viewpoints Chart."

1. **Claim.** For each source, write the writer's claim. If you use any direct quotes, be sure to use quotation marks and note the page number.
2. **Reasons.** Next, write the main reasons the writers use to support their claim in the appropriate row. Again, be sure to use quotation marks around any words you take directly from the articles.
3. **Issues Addressed.** List keywords to summarize the issues the authors discuss.
4. **Reminder Notes.** Write anything that will help you remember the distinguishing characteristics of the source or the features from the source you may use.
5. **Citation.** Finally, enter the article's citation into the citation row. See Chapter 12 for more information on how to cite sources.

Part of Jada's Viewpoints Chart is shown here.

Jada's Viewpoints Chart (excerpt)

	Bloom, "Does Working from Home Work?"	Felstead, "Assessing the Growth of Remote Working"
Claim	In a large research study, the authors show that working from home (WFH) resulted in greater productivity and "is worth further exploration."	Remote working has benefits for employers because it increases productivity, but it presents some challenges to remote employees.
Reasons	"[T]he performance of the home workers went up dramatically, increasing by 13% over the nine months of the experiment." ". . . [A]ttrition fell sharply among the home workers, dropping by 50% versus the control group." ". . . [O]ne downside of WFH appears to be that, conditional on performance, it was associated with reduced rates of promotion of about 50%."	Remote workers "agree that their job requires them to work very hard, that they work beyond formal working hours to get the job done, and that they put a lot of effort beyond what is required." "Remote workers also display more positive attitudes towards the employing organisation." ". . . [R]emote working is associated with higher organisational commitment, job satisfaction and job-related well-being; these benefits come at the cost of work intensification and a greater inability to switch off."
Issues Addressed	Productivity Cost/benefit Job satisfaction Attrition Promotion	Problems for employees Job satisfaction Attitudes Productivity
Reminder Notes	Very scholarly, mathematical article with some good charts/graphs. Huge research study.	This article deals with both the advantages and disadvantages but focuses more on advantages.
Citation	Bloom, Nicholas, et al. "Does Working from Home Work? Evidence from a Chinese Experiment." *Quarterly Journal of Economics*, vol. 130, no. 1, Feb. 2015, pp. 165–218, doi:10.1093/qje/qju03.	Felstead, Alan, and Golo Henseke. "Assessing the Growth of Remote Working and Its Consequences for Effort, Well-Being and Work-Life Balance." *New Technology, Work & Employment*, vol. 32, no. 3, Nov. 2017, pp. 195–212, doi:10.1111/ntwe.12097.

> **Jada, on creating her Viewpoints Chart:** "This chart was much more work than I realized it would be, but it was the most helpful thing I did to write this paper. I was not used to being so analytical about my sources. Having all this info in a chart made it easy to know which source said what. I also used some of the quotes in my paper, as well as the citations. Ultimately, the time it took to create the chart was well worth it because it saved time when I wrote the draft."

You can create a Viewpoints Chart as you find sources, or you can wait until you have all your sources and then put them into a chart. The benefit of creating the chart as you go is that you will be able to see whether the research you have is sufficient or whether you need different kinds of articles, such as articles expressing opposing points of view. The advantage of creating the Viewpoints Chart after finding your research is that you may have a greater sense of the relationships among your sources.

ARGUMENT ASSIGNMENT 4
Analyzing Your Research and Creating a Viewpoints Chart

Create a Viewpoints Chart to organize the analysis of your sources. Consider using a word processor or spreadsheet so that you can easily cut and paste quotations and citations from your Viewpoints Chart into your draft.

DRAFTING A CLAIM

Teaching Resources
Consider using the exercise "Evaluating Claims."

Once you have thoroughly analyzed the research, you will need to reexamine the issue question in light of what you have learned from your sources. Sometimes the research will cause you to refocus the question. Sometimes you may even decide to change the issue question after reading the research. If that is the case, be sure to write the new question so that you can maintain your focus and find additional research that answers it, if necessary.

Once you are certain about the issue question, you can write a claim. The claim is your answer to your current version of the issue question. The claim presents your arguable proposition—the main idea that you will advocate. When you write a rough draft of your paper, you may find that you need to revise the claim. The first draft of your claim is always preliminary; you can change it later if necessary.

Using Qualifiers in Claims

The strength of a claim can be increased when qualifiers are used appropriately. A claim that lacks qualifiers may be considered *absolute*; that is, the claim applies to all situations. For example, consider this claim:

> **Unqualified claim:** Children in the foster-care system benefit from being reunited with their parents.

Because the claim lacks a qualifier, the claim is absolute: it applies to all foster children. Obviously, children whose parents are abusive would not benefit from reunification, so using a qualifier to limit the scope of this claim increases the likelihood that readers will agree:

> **Claim with qualifier:** *Many* children in the foster-care system could benefit from being reunited with their parents.

Some claims are intentionally absolute. For example, a person who believes that there are no circumstances under which killing an animal is acceptable may want to create a claim that is absolute. In most cases, however, arguers can think of exceptions and will choose to qualify their claims. The chart that follows presents common qualifiers that can be used in claims.

Circumstance	Qualifiers
To limit by quantity	Some, most, many, a few
To limit by certainty	May, might, could, probably, possibly, unlikely, improbable, doubtful
To limit by frequency	Rarely, infrequently, seldom, often, frequently, usually, sometimes, repeatedly

Identifying Claim Types

You will be able to think more clearly about your claim and the support it needs by identifying the type of claim you are making. Most claims fall into one of five categories: claims of fact, claims of definition, claims of policy, claims of cause and/or effect, and claims of value. Later, you will be prompted to think about your claim type to select the best support for it.

Claims of Fact. These claims assert that *something is the case.*

Example: *Student loan debt is manageable and does not adversely affect financial stability.*

Claims of Definition. These claims define or categorize by asserting that *x is y.*

Example: *Prayer in schools is the institutionalization of religion.*

Claims of Policy. As the name suggests, these claims assert that a policy change should be enacted. The word *should* is often found in claims of policy.

Example: *Basic internet access should be provided by the government for all households.*

Claims of Cause and/or Effect. These claims about causality often take the forms of *x caused y* or *if x, then y will result.*

Example: *If laws are not created to regulate genetic experimentation, irreversible damage will result.*

Claims of Value. These claims present a statement of value and often take the form of *x is better* (or *best*). Claims of value may be moral in nature, taking a form such as *x is wrong*; but they are often assertions of worth, as the example here shows.

Example: *The benefits of hybrid and electric vehicles are well worth the costs of those vehicles.*

> **Jada, on writing a claim:** "When I started my research, I thought I would learn that working from home is advantageous to both the employer and the employee. I learned that working from home actually does raise productivity, but there are a number of issues that can cause working from home to not turn out so well. Clearly, employees who were forced to work at home because of the pandemic struggled to make everything work. In addition, not all businesses benefit from work-from-home policies. So when I wrote my claim, I used the qualifier 'most' to communicate that idea. I tried to imagine what a reader might say about my claim, and that helped me come up with the need for a qualifier. I realized that my claim is a claim of policy."
>
> **Jada's claim:** Most employers should create work-from-home options for employees.

ARGUMENT ASSIGNMENT 5
Drafting a Claim

Draft your claim, using qualifiers as appropriate. Identify the type of claim you have written.

SELECTING AND EVALUATING REASONS

A claim can be defended by many reasons. One of the most important parts of planning an argument is to figure out the reasons that will be most effective for a particular audience. Of course, you have already read sources that present sound reasons, and you probably want to use some of those reasons. But it is helpful to think more generally about the reasons you will use and to select those that both fit your claim type and appeal to readers.

Selecting Reasons by Claim Type

Table 19.1 presents some of the types of reasons that are commonly used for each claim type. You will probably think of additional types of reasons to support your claim, but you can use this chart as a starting point for planning your reasons.

> **Jada, on selecting reasons by claim type:** "I am arguing a claim of policy, so the types of reasons that applied most were that an effective work-from-home policy will save money, produce the results a company desires, increase happiness, and has shown itself to work in similar situations."

Selecting Reasons That Appeal to Readers

Once you have a list of reasons you can use to support your claim, you can think about which of them will be most effective for your audience. In Jada's case, she is writing a paper for an English class, so she knows that her primary audience is her instructor. However, Jada can imagine a broader audience that might be

TABLE 19.1 **Claim Types and Reasons**

Claim Type	Reasons
Fact: X is the case because . . .	• Statistics and data prove it to be . . . • Research shows that it is . . . • Authorities say that it is . . . • Personal experiences show that it is . . . • Most people agree that it is . . .
Definition: X is/is not Y because . . .	• X is/is not similar enough to be considered Y. • An accepted practice (precedent) supports this definition. • An accepted authority supports this definition. • In a comparable situation, X is/is not considered Y. • Using this definition is expedient, practical, fair, and so on.
Policy: We should do X because . . .	• X is the moral thing to do. • X will save money. • X will produce the results we desire. • X will increase happiness. • X will be the least expensive and most effective policy. • X has worked in the past. • X works in similar situations.
Cause and effect: The causes of X are . . . The effects of X are . . .	• Statistics and data prove it to be . . . • Research shows that it is . . . • Authorities say that it is . . . • Personal experiences show that it is . . . • Most people agree that it is . . .
Value: X is better because . . .	• It is more effective/practical/admirable/dependable (insert any other value judgment). • It costs less than other options. • It is morally right. • It is endorsed by authorities and experts.

interested in her research, one composed of employers who are considering creating a work-from-home policy. So Jada hopes to find reasons that this broader audience—as well as her instructor—will value. She makes a list of her reasons, and keeping this audience in mind, she selects the five reasons that she believes will provide the most effective support.

> **Jada's Reasons**
>
> *Claim*: Most employers should create work-from-home (WFH) options for employees.
>
> - Research shows that WFH increases productivity.
> - Workers' attitudes were more positive when they worked from home.
> - WFH programs are trendy and show that a company thinks progressively.
> - Having a WFH system makes a company prepared for emergencies, such as COVID-19.

- WFH programs show that employers understand employees' needs (for flexibility, family time, convenience, etc.)
- Employees respond favorably to the option of working from home.
- WFH policies reduce facilities-related costs.
- WFH policies reduce absences due to sick leave.
- WFH programs make a company a more desirable place to work, so higher quality recruiting is possible.

Jada, on selecting audience-based reasons: "When I analyzed my reasons, I could see that several of them would appeal to employees. Since my focus is on employers, I selected the reasons I thought would appeal the most to them. I thought about using the COVID-19 preparedness reason, but I imagined skeptical employers who might say that circumstances like that are rare. I imagined writing for a skeptical employer, and that helped me select the best reasons."

Evaluating Reasons

Once you have selected the reasons you think will be effective, take the time to evaluate those reasons by using Rhetorical Toolbox 19.2. Evaluating reasons requires you to look closely at each reason to identify its strengths and weaknesses. If you find that a reason has some serious weaknesses, consider replacing it.

Teaching Suggestion
Review the elements of argument presented in Chapter 14, if necessary.

RHETORICAL TOOLBOX 19.2
Evaluating Your Argument's Reasons

For each of your reasons, answer these questions:

1. **Grounds.** How will you provide grounds for the reason? Grounds consist of the evidence needed to prove the reason is true.
2. **Warrant.** What is the warrant—the assumption—that ties the reason to the claim?
3. **Backing.** Will most of the audience accept the truth of the warrant? If not, can you provide backing and proof that the warrant is true?
4. **Objections.** What possible objections might the audience offer to your reason? Are these objections legitimate? Will you address these objections in your paper?
5. **Strength of reason.** Based on your answers to Questions 1–4, how strong is the reason you are evaluating? Might there be a better reason to use for your argument? If so, what would that reason be?

> **Jada, on evaluating reasons:** "Once I looked more closely at the reasons I had chosen, I figured out that the reason about improved employee attitudes was not a very strong reason. When I evaluated this reason, I realized that the warrant was the problem. The warrant is that employees' attitudes matter when creating new policies. While that may be true, the effect a policy will have on an employee's attitude is not nearly as important to most employers as the costs and benefits of the policy. I am not going to include this reason."

Jada's evaluation led her back to her list of reasons to find a replacement for the one she eliminated. By using this evaluative process for all the reasons you have identified, you will be able to select the reasons that will be most effective for your audience.

ARGUMENT ASSIGNMENT 6
Evaluating and Selecting Reasons

After evaluating your reasons, identify three to five of the strongest reasons. Restate your claim with the strongest reasons that you selected. This is the basic outline of your argument.

Analyzing your research, writing a claim, and selecting reasons are three of the most important steps in writing your argument. Since writing is always a recursive process, you will probably need to make changes to your claim and reasons, and you may even have to find additional research. Making changes is an important part of improving the quality of your argument, so do not hesitate to revise any part of your argument as you continue the research and writing process.

Reflecting to Develop a Writer's Mindset

This chapter guides you through the thinking processes required to plan an argument. What are those processes? How might thinking in the way this chapter suggests result in a higher quality argument than would merely finding sources that agree with your thesis statement? Explain your answer.

FAQ FINDING RESEARCH FROM MULTIPLE VIEWPOINTS

If a topic is suitable for an argument, you should be able to find several viewpoints on it. The more controversial the topic, the easier it will be to find multiple viewpoints. A topic like Jada's is controversial, but it is not highly controversial. Even more challenging, there has not been a great deal of research on it. So Jada has to use some creative strategies to find multiple viewpoints. The strategies that follow will help you find sources that present differing opinions on your topic.

1. **How can you figure out the best search terms?**

   Obviously, the keywords you use have a great impact on your search results. Sometimes you have to start researching to discover the best terms to use. Jada was having difficulty finding viewpoints that showed the disadvantages of remote working, but changing her search terminology produced the results she needed. A search in the Business Abstracts (H. W. Wilson) from EBSCOhost resulted in a wide variety of results depending on keywords, as the chart here shows:

Search Terms	Results
Remote working disadvantages	12 results
Working from home disadvantages	7 results
Telecommuting disadvantages	12 results
Telecommuting issues	34 results
Telecommuting policy	84 results

   The last item on the chart, "telecommuting policy," presented some articles that were not applicable to Jada's argument. However, some of the articles *did* address the negative aspects of telecommuting because policy development must account for potential problems.

   Simply changing the search terms can result in a much greater number of sources from which to choose. For more information about finding sources, see Chapter 10.

2. **What are the advantages of using different databases?**

   Academic libraries subscribe to hundreds of databases. The chart in Question 1 shows search results for one database, H. W. Wilson (from EBSCOhost). Notice how the search results differ when different databases are used to search for "telecommuting issues":

Database	Results
Regional Business News (from EBSCOhost)	12 results
Small Business Reference Center	2 results
Gale Databases (search all)	50 results
WorldCat	578 results
ABI/Inform Global (from ProQuest)	6967 results

   Of course, if you get too many results, you will need to narrow the search terms or filter the results so that you can view the most appropriate articles. If you are unsure of the database to use, ask a librarian for help.

3. **How can you find opposing viewpoints?**

   You often can find opposing viewpoints in the bibliographies of the sources that support your claim. For example, you may think that an article that promotes working from home would be of no help in finding opposing viewpoints, but you may be wrong. Read the article carefully and see if the writers acknowledge opposing viewpoints. Sometimes writers cite studies that present viewpoints opposite of their own so that they can show how those studies are flawed or incorrect. If a writer does acknowledge the opposing arguments, you can find those original sources in an online database and use them as part of your research.

TRY IT!

Using the researching tips presented here, find two articles that express one point of view and two articles that express the opposite point of view on the following issue question:

> **Issue Question:** Would bans on single-use plastics have a positive effect on the environment?

20 Selecting Evidence and Drafting Reasons

CHAPTER OBJECTIVES

You will learn to:
- Outline your argument.
- Evaluate and select good evidence to support each reason.
- Organize and draft the reasons that support your claim.
- Check for fallacies.

Connect Adaptive Learning Assignment
Consider assigning Connect's Adaptive Learning Assignments to support this chapter.

A claim is only as strong as the reasons that support it. In turn, each reason in your argument needs its own support—evidence that is appropriate, credible, and convincing. In this chapter, we focus on using the best evidence possible to support each reason. You will continue to make progress on your argument project by completing the following assignments:

- Argument Assignment 7: Creating an outline for your argument.
- Argument Assignment 8: Selecting the best evidence for each reason.
- Argument Assignment 9: Organizing and drafting the reasons that support your claim.
- Argument Assignment 10: Checking for fallacies.

Teaching Resources
For suggestions about how to teach this chapter, see the Instructor's Manual (IM), and consider assigning this chapter's test-bank quiz.

CREATING AN OUTLINE

Sketching a basic outline for your argument will give you an overview of your argument. As you create an outline, you will make choices about what elements to include and how to organize them. Will you put your strongest reason first? Will you include a discussion of the counterargument, as well as a rebuttal? Make these choices with your readers' needs in mind.

Jada's basic outline is a simple list of the reasons she plans to use. As she does more planning, she will think rhetorically about how to organize these ideas and what additional elements her argument will include.

To write a detailed outline, Jada will have to make a number of decisions. For instance, she will have to figure out how much background information to

> **Jada's Basic Outline**
>
> **Claim:** Most employers should create work-from-home (WFH) options for employees.
> **Reason 1:** Productivity increases when employees work from home.
> **Reason 2:** Employee absences decrease when employees work from home.
> **Reason 3:** The costs associated with maintaining office space decrease when employees work from home.
> **Reason 4:** Employers can attract higher quality candidates by offering WFH options.

provide for readers. She will have to determine which counterarguments to address and where to address them. She will need to decide the best evidence for each reason, and when to use direct quotes, summaries or paraphrases, and graphics. As Jada makes these decisions, she makes notes on her basic outline. Eventually, her basic outline becomes a detailed outline on which she has noted every element in her argument.

> **Jada, on creating basic and detailed outlines:** "Starting with a basic outline helped me keep track of my ideas. I actually put each reason on a separate sheet of paper and jotted down the quotes I'd use to support the reason. I did the same for the counterargument I planned to include. When I transferred my thoughts into the outline, I experimented with a few different organizations. Eventually, I settled on an organization that I think will help even the most skeptical reader see why WFH programs are beneficial to employers."

We will see Jada's detailed outline after we examine the reasons she chose and the rhetorical thinking that informed her choices. As you work on your argument, start with a basic outline and add to it so that you eventually have a fully detailed outline of your paper.

ARGUMENT ASSIGNMENT 7
Creating an Outline for Your Argument

Create a basic outline for your argument. Include your claim and each reason you plan to use as support. As you identify additional elements you will use in your paper, add them to your outline.

SELECTING EVIDENCE TO SUPPORT REASONS

A reason can often be stated in a single sentence. Obviously, a reason alone is not enough support for a claim. The reason itself needs support. In fact, some reasons are arguable statements and function as miniature arguments, requiring their own support. For example, one of Jada's reasons for advocating for work-from-home options is that doing so will attract higher quality applicants. This reason is not a fact: it is an arguable statement. Jada will have to prove that, indeed, higher quality candidates apply for jobs that allow them to work from home.

To prove a reason, you will need to find evidence that readers will accept. While many people think of evidence as coming from books or articles, there are many other types of evidence you can use to support an argument, such as statistics, laws, case studies, interviews, and field research. For more information on selecting appropriate types of evidence, see Chapter 10, "Conducting Research."

The evidence you choose to support a reason should be authoritative. What makes evidence authoritative? Think about the evidence used in courtrooms. Obviously, physical evidence and eye-witnesses testimony are important, but so is testimony from subject-matter experts. If an expert is good at communicating, he or she is an especially valuable source of evidence. An articulate expert may help a jury understand a difficult concept, whereas an expert who is not very good at communicating may be brilliant but may not be the best person to put on the stand.

The same is true for the evidence you use to support your arguments. Evidence should come from respected sources, but it should also be clearly expressed. Using an obscure or difficult-to-understand quote from a source is like putting someone who has poor communication skills on the stand to testify. Let's look in more depth at the criteria for good evidence.

> **Teaching Suggestion**
> Consider using the PowerPoint "What Is Good Evidence?"

1. **Good evidence is appropriate.**

   Imagine writing an argument about terrorism prevention but using sources that were published before the World Trade Center terrorist acts in 2001. The world changed so much after 9/11 that anything written about terrorism prior to that date is almost irrelevant. Good evidence must be timely to be appropriate. But the issue of timeliness is not always as simple as looking for sources that are less than a few years old. A person writing about animal rights would be remiss to not mention Peter Singer's 1974 treatise, *Animal Liberation*. Appropriateness is determined by both timeliness and relevancy. Singer's ideas about the treatment of animals are still debated; thus, his works are relevant, regardless of the date of their publication.

2. **Good evidence is authoritative.**

   The internet provides millions of potential sources, but many sources are simply not authoritative enough to use as evidence. The issue of authority is more important today than ever because so much questionable "news" and misinformation is spread through social media and online outlets. The strength of an argument is affected by the authority and credibility—in short, the ethos—of its writer and the sources the writer uses. A source can be deemed authoritative if it meets one of these conditions:

- **It is published in a peer-reviewed journal.** The articles published in peer-reviewed journals are selected by experts in the journal's field of study. Researchers submit papers, and, to prevent bias, other experts read the papers without knowing the authors' names; only the best research is selected.

- **Its authors are experts in the field.** For instance, a science article written by a scientist is more authoritative than one written by a science reporter. Nonetheless, a reporter's article may also be authoritative if the reporter uses credible sources. Always check the authors' expertise to make sure that they are authoritative in their own right or that they rely on authorities in the field.

- **Its authors or publishers have a reputation for integrity in their research methods and publication practices.** For example, the Brookings Institution is a "nonprofit public policy organization" whose mission "is to conduct in-depth research that leads to new ideas for solving problems facing society at the local, national and global level." Like many other think tanks, the Brookings Institution is respected for its research methods. You may have to do some research to determine whether an institution or publication is reputable. See Chapter 11 for more information on judging the credibility of sources.

3. **Good evidence is comprehensible.**

   In the same way that putting a poor communicator on the stand is not a good idea in a court of law, quoting from an article that is difficult to understand will not add value to your argument. The best evidence expresses its ideas well; it is comprehensible, and the quotes you use are readable and clear.

4. **Good evidence provides satisfactory proof.**

   The evidence you choose will have to satisfy readers' needs for proof. Readers will need *enough* evidence. If you cite a small study that involved ten participants, that study may not satisfy readers' needs. Citing two large studies from two different sources is more likely to be deemed sufficient evidence. Similarly, using a personal story to support a point may lend authenticity to an argument, but one person's experience is not enough evidence to provide satisfactory support for most reasons.

Teaching Suggestion
Sometimes students try to find the very best research by consulting peer-reviewed journals, but the articles they find are too technical or require too much background knowledge for comprehension. Help students learn to vet articles by assessing the sources' accessibility.

> **Jada, on selecting evidence:** "While the blogs I read about working from home were interesting, I knew that they wouldn't count as high-quality evidence. I found several studies that measured productivity, and most of these met the four criteria for good evidence. I plan to use these studies to support my reasons. The only reason that did not have a scientific study available as support was the fourth one—WFH programs attract higher quality candidates. I had to find a different way to support this reason."

ARGUMENT ASSIGNMENT 8
Selecting the Best Evidence for Each Reason

Select the best evidence for each of your reasons. Make sure the evidence you select meets all four of the criteria for good evidence.

ORGANIZING REASONS AND DRAFTING CONTENT

As you begin drafting content, you will quickly realize the importance of organization. How will readers follow your argument? Which reasons should come first? Why? How would your argument be affected if you reordered the reasons? Keeping these questions in mind will help you organize reasons and draft content effectively.

Organizing Reasons

> **Teaching Resources**
> Consider using the exercise "Outlining a Paper Rhetorically" to reinforce the ideas in this section.

In what order will you present the reasons that support your claim? This is a crucial question you need to answer as you draft content for each reason. A few different organizing strategies are common:

- **Use reader-based reasons first.** Find the reason that is the most likely to appeal to readers and start with it. Which reason appeals most to readers' values? Obviously, answering this question requires thinking about what readers find important. For instance, Jada is writing with a skeptical business owner in mind as her primary reader. Business owners are likely to value actions that can help them improve productivity, save money, and so on. But owners may also value having contented employees. Thinking about the readers' values will help you determine the reason that will most appeal to readers. When you start with that reason, readers may be predisposed to accept the claim

- **Use a reason that appeals to ethos, pathos, or logos.** Depending on the issue and the audience, you can start with a reason that makes use of a powerful appeal, one that your audience will value. If your primary audience is comprised of economists, starting with the strongest logical reasons makes sense since economists often argue in terms of costs and benefits. If your audience is comprised of the general public, a reason that appeals to ethos or pathos may be a better way to start. For example, in a paper about ending hunger in the United States, one of the reasons you might use is that ending hunger is the right thing to do. The support for this reason can appeal to ethos by discussing why we should do what is moral and right, or to pathos by discussing, for example, the case of a malnourished American child. Presenting the plight of a single child might help readers humanize the issue.

- **Organize your reasons to end with your strongest one.** In some types of arguments, such as candidates' speeches and criminal cases, "finishing strong" is important. Saving the strongest reason for last enables you to slowly build a case for your claim and to leave readers thinking about the most powerful reason you have offered. This strategy is especially important when you believe the audience may not remember all of the finer points of your argument, as might be the situation in long court cases.

Regardless of how you decide to organize your reasons, keep an open mind as you draft your paper. You may find that reorganizing them makes sense. Do not be afraid to rethink organization as you draft.

Drafting Content

The reasons for your claim are in many ways the most crucial parts of your argument. Drafting the content for each reason before you write the introduction or conclusion will enable you to fully make your case—your argument. You may end up making changes during the drafting process, so waiting until body paragraphs are finished to write the introduction and conclusion can help you create a more unified paper.

The support for each reason will need to include your ideas—your explanations, reasoning, and so on. It will also include information you get from sources. For more information about how to integrate sources properly and avoid plagiarism, see Chapter 11, "Using Sources Accurately and Ethically." Consider using a variety of methods for integrating sources, including summarizing, paraphrasing, and quoting directly from the source.

Summaries. When you want to present the main idea of a source, providing a quick summary is often an effective method. Summarizing also helps you to avoid using too many quotations in your paper. To support the idea that working from home increases productivity, Jada discusses two studies in detail, and she uses brief summaries to present the findings of two additional studies.

Paraphrases. When you paraphrase, you put the ideas of a source into your own words. Paraphrases are more detailed than summaries. A paraphrase may take a dense text and provide a sentence-for-sentence rewording to make the dense text more readable or comprehensible. Jada uses paraphrasing when she presents one of the major studies to support her reason. Doing so helps her to make the passage more comprehensible without quoting too frequently.

Direct Quotations. Use direct quotations when doing so is rhetorically important. Avoid the temptation to quote excessively. Any time you consider quoting, think about whether a quote is really necessary. Could you put the ideas into your own words and express them just as effectively? If so, do so. There are times, however, when a quote is more effective than a summary or a paraphrase.

- If the passage you are quoting is particularly well-expressed, use a direct quote. Jada quotes the phrase "400 business decision makers throughout Europe" passage because she does not know how she would communicate the idea it expresses in her own words.

- If the source is a well-known authority on the subject, a direct quote may be more powerful than a summary or paraphrase.

Co-requisite Teaching Tip
Students sometimes write research papers that resemble annotated bibliographies: they simply summarize articles rather than use those articles to support their own voices. Remind students to use sources as support. Refer to Chapter 11 for more information.

- If you want to emphasize important parts of your evidence, a direct quote can be effective. When Jada presents the results of important studies, she uses direct quotations. These quotes emphasize the results and help readers know with certainty that the source is reporting the results, not the arguer.

If you quote too frequently, your paper will sound like a collection of research instead of an argument *you* are making. Your argument should primarily be comprised of your words: your thoughts, your explanations, your reasoning, and so on. Be especially careful about using long quotations. Always have a good reason for including a long quote, such as the need for a detailed explanation for which a summary would not suffice. Your instructor wants to know that you have understood and synthesized your sources. Providing summaries and paraphrases shows your understanding; direct quotes do not necessarily demonstrate your understanding of a source.

Organizing Support for Reasons

Since you will probably use a combination of your own words, direct quotes, summaries, and paraphrases to support each reason, you may end up with a significant amount of information. You will need to make decisions about how best to present this information so that readers can understand it. Should the reason be developed in a single paragraph? Should it be developed in multiple paragraphs? In researched arguments, reasons often need to be developed in more than one paragraph because reasons are usually supported by more than one piece of evidence. One of Jada's primary reasons for advocating for work-from-home policies is that such policies increase productivity. As you read Jada's support for this reason, notice where and how she uses evidence to support the reason.

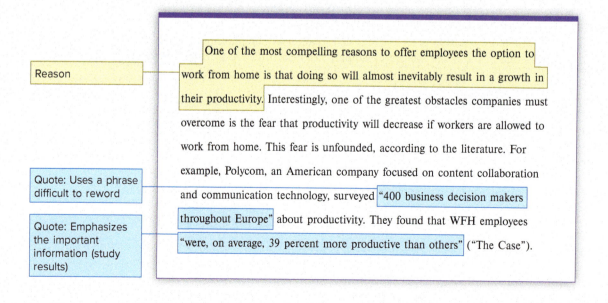

CHAPTER 20 Selecting Evidence and Drafting Reasons   447

The increase in productivity is documented in numerous other studies. CTrip, the largest travel agency in China, was interested in the possibility of allowing employees to work from home, but managers worried that employees would not be as productive as their in-office coworkers (Bloom 167). Thus, the company created a nine-month randomized controlled study in which over one hundred employees worked from home, and a control group worked from CTrip's corporate offices (Bloom 168-69). The company designed the study carefully so that incidental variables were limited. The workers in both locations "used the same IT equipment, faced the same work order flow . . . , carried out the same tasks, and were compensated under the same pay system" (Bloom 169). The findings of this large, carefully constructed experiment confirm the fact that productivity increases in WFH scenarios:

> We found several striking results. First, the performance of the home workers went up dramatically, increasing by 13% over the nine months of the experiment. This improvement came mainly from a 9% increase in the number of minutes they worked during their shifts (i.e., the time they were logged in to take calls). This was due to reductions in breaks, time off, and sick days taken by the home workers. (Bloom 169)

Even greater productivity resulted when, after the study, CTrip evaluated employees who worked from home and reassigned those with the lowest productivity rates. When they did this, productivity almost doubled, rising from 13% to 22% (Bloom 170).

Several additional studies are consistent with Polycom's findings and the CTrip study. Brittany Harker Martin and Rhiannon MacDonnell conducted a meta-analysis of studies and found that working from home increases productivity (602). Similarly, in a study of telecommuting employees from Kentucky American Water Company, researchers E. Sonny Butler, Cheryl Aasheim, and Susan Williams noted that productivity increased and that the

Annotations:
- New paragraph for a new source of evidence
- Paraphrase
- Quote: Details that Jada cannot put into her own words without plagiarizing
- Quote: Emphasizes the important information (study results)
- Summary
- Summary

> increase was sustained over time (103). Almost all of the studies that reported increased productivity make an attempt to explain why the increase occurs. One reason is that employees often perceive working from home as a privilege. As such, WFH employees are motivated to do their jobs well. In the CTrip study, only those WFH employees who showed increased productivity were allowed to continue working from home. Because of the link between motivation and productivity, employers who are considering WFH options can feel more confident that offering such options will not decrease productivity. In fact, employers can be relatively certain that, if carefully planned, a WFH policy may cause productivity to increase.

Since Jada wrote three paragraphs to support one reason, must she write three paragraphs for her other reasons? In general, readers value balance. If you can offer roughly the same amount of support for each reason, do so. If you cannot, determine whether the reason you are presenting is worth including in your argument. In other words, if you cannot create much support for a reason, is the reason really the best one to support your claim? Or will readers think the reason isn't well developed? Consider swapping a reason for which you have little evidence for a different reason supported by ample evidence.

> **Jada, on drafting content for a reason:** "I was surprised how much material I had. Originally, I had put all the support in one paragraph, but that paragraph went on for several pages, so it was clear that I should break it into several paragraphs. I did make the mistake of relying too much on the evidence in the first draft. My professor warned us to not simply list sources, so I made sure to go in and discuss the evidence for why productivity increased in WFH scenarios."

Use Rhetorical Toolbox 20.1 as a guide for drafting the content for each reason.

Introducing Evidence

You may have noticed that many writers use the same conventions for introducing evidence. For example, to introduce a quote, a writer may use a phrase such as "researcher X claims that" or "in a large study, researchers found that." Having these conventional phrases handy as you draft paragraphs for each reason can be helpful. The Drafting Toolbox presents templates you can use as you summarize or quote from sources. (Since paraphrases provide a sentence by sentence rewording of a source, there are no templates for paraphrases. See Jada's sample earlier in this chapter for a model of a paraphrase.)

RHETORICAL TOOLBOX 20.1
Organizing Reasons and Drafting Content

Think about the most skeptical person who might read your argument. What does that reader value? With that reader and his or her values in mind, work through the following questions.

1. **Type of evidence.** For each reason, what kind of evidence (research studies; explanations; quotations, interviews; stories; appeals to ethos, pathos, and logos; and so on) would provide the best support?
2. **Amount of evidence.** How much evidence will be required for readers to think you have adequately explained and supported each reason? How many sources will you use to support each reason?
3. **Integrating sources.** How will you use sources to support each reason? Will you present direct quotes? Summaries? Paraphrases? How will you make sure you are not using too many direct quotations or long quotations?
4. **Sequence of reasons.** Which method of ordering your reasons will readers find most effective? Why?

DRAFTING TOOLBOX
Templates for Introducing Evidence

Templates for Summaries

To provide an overview of research that shows similarities:

- Many of the researchers have shown that . . .
- A survey of the research suggests that . . .
- Most researchers agree that . . .

To provide an overview of research that shows differences:

- While some of the research suggests . . ., other studies show . . .
- The research has produced conflicting results. Some studies show. . . . Other studies show . . .

To provide a summary of one source:

- [Name], a researcher from Boston University, claims that . . .
- In [Name's] study, researchers found that . . .
- [Name] shows that . . .

Templates for Direct Quotations

Quotes that focus on or introduce the source's author (for the first time):

- [Full name], a researcher from Boston University, explains that " . . . ."
- According to [full name], a researcher from Boston University, " . . . ."
- As researcher [full name], a scientist from Boston University, shows, " . . . ."

(Continued on next page)

(Continued from previous page)

> Quotes that provide information from a source without using the author's name:
> - [Your point]: "...."
>
>   Example: Working from home is becoming more common in private industry: "...."
>
> **Attributive Tags to Introduce Quotations**
> - John Smith shows . . .
> - John Smith contends . . .
> - John Smith argues . . .
> - John Smith notes . . .
> - According to John Smith . . .
> - According to researchers at . . .
>
> **Attributive Tags to End Quotations**
> - . . . as John Smith has noted
> - . . . as Smith and others have shown
> - . . . according to Smith and others

ARGUMENT ASSIGNMENT 9
Organize and Draft the Reasons that Support Your Claim

Organize your reasons, and then write a draft for each reason that supports your claim. Include summaries, paraphrases, and direct quotations as appropriate, and provide correct in-text documentation using the style your instructor requires. For more details on using sources ethically, avoiding plagiarism, and documenting sources properly, see Chapter 11, "Using Sources Accurately and Ethically" and Chapter 12, "Documenting Sources in MLA and APA Style."

AVOIDING FALLACIES

You have spent considerable time researching, reading, analyzing, planning, and drafting. There is one more step that will help you make sure you created the best support possible: checking for fallacies. As you know from Chapter 16, a fallacy is an error in reasoning. Make sure your reasons do not contain fallacies by using the questions in Rhetorical Toolbox 20.2. For a review of fallacies and for more explanation about how to use the Toolbox, review Chapter 16.

> **Jada, on checking for fallacies:** "When I reviewed my draft for fallacies, I realized that someone might think I had cherry-picked only the evidence that supported each reason. I went back and revised my paper to acknowledge that there were exceptions to my claim."

RHETORICAL TOOLBOX 20.2
Identifying and Analyzing Fallacies

1. **Slippery slope.** Does the writer make predictions? If so, are the predictions founded on evidence? Are the predictions intended to scare the reader? If so, check for the slippery slope fallacy.
2. *Post hoc, ergo propter hoc.* Does the writer assert that *x* caused *y*? If so, make sure the writer's causal assertion is founded on evidence. Check for the *post hoc ergo propter hoc* fallacy.
3. **False authority.** Does the writer use others to support the argument? If so, make sure those people have the authority to speak on the subject. Check for false authority.
4. *Ad hominem* **and guilt by association.** Does the writer make derogatory statements about his or her opponents? If so, check for *ad hominem* and guilt by association.
5. **Either/or (false dilemma).** Does the writer offer a limited number of options? If so, check for either/or.
6. **Loaded language.** Does the writer use terms that have strong emotional connotations? If so, check for loaded language.
7. **Begging the question.** Does the writer word a reason in such a way that the reason seems like the claim? If so, check for begging the question.
8. **Hasty generalization, sampling bias, and cherry picking.** Does the writer come to a conclusion without adequately surveying all the evidence? If so, check for hasty generalization, sampling bias, and cherry picking.
9. **Sweeping generalization.** Does the writer make a broad assertion about a group (of people, ideas, etc.)? If so, check for sweeping generalization.
10. **Argument from ignorance.** Does the writer use a *lack of evidence* as proof for something? If so, check for argument from ignorance.
11. **Bandwagon and** *non sequitur.* Does the writer use evidence that seems irrelevant or off topic? Check for bandwagon and *non sequitur.*
12. **Red herring and** *tu quoque.* Does the writer change the subject or turn the blame back onto the opponent? If so, check for red herring and *tu quoque.*
13. **Faulty comparison.** Does the writer make a comparison? If so, make sure the comparison is fair and not faulty.
14. **Manipulative emotional appeal.** Does the writer appeal to emotions? If so, check to see if the emotional appeal is manipulative.

Teaching Suggestion
Consider spending a day in class during which each student presents one reason and classmates critique the reason. See the IM for more details.

ARGUMENT ASSIGNMENT 10
Checking for Fallacies

Using Rhetorical Toolbox 20.2 as a guide, read the paragraphs you drafted for each reason and check for fallacies. Make revisions if necessary.

> ### Reflecting to Develop a Writer's Mindset
>
> How is drafting reasons a rhetorical activity? In your experience, which parts of the drafting process require the most rhetorical attention? Explain your answer.

FAQ USING A TEMPLATE TO PLAN THE BODY OF AN ARGUMENT

There are so many parts of an argument that outlining can be confusing. One way to start the outlining process is to use a template.

1. **How can a template be used to plan the reasons for a claim?**

   The template that follows is not a definitive outline, one that you will stick to no matter what. Instead, it provides you with a place to start. Keeping these points in mind, use the following template to sketch out your ideas. Repeat the process for each reason.

   Your claim: State your claim.

   Reason 1: State your first reason.

   - What kind of discussion will you provide in your own words to support this reason? Explain.
   - List at least three quotations, summaries, and/or paraphrases you will use as evidence for this reason.
   - Will you address potential counterarguments to this reason? If so, what are these counterarguments? Will you concede to any part of the counterarguments? If so, which ones? How will you show that, in spite of your concession, your claim still holds? (For more information on addressing counterarguments, see Chapters 14 and 21.)
   - Will you refute these counterarguments? If so, how will you refute them? Will your refutation require the use of evidence? If so, what kind of evidence will you use?

2. **What do you do once you have templates for each reason?**

   Once you have used the template for each reason, determine the order in which you plan to present the reasons. You can then use the templates—in sequence—to draft body paragraphs for the reasons.

TRY IT!

Select one of the reasons you plan to use to support your claim. Use the questions in "FAQ: Using a Template to Plan the Body of an Argument" to plan your draft of this reason, and then draft the reason and supporting evidence.

21 Drafting Counterarguments, Introductions, and Conclusions

CHAPTER OBJECTIVES

You will learn to:
- Identify counterarguments and create rebuttals.
- Compose rhetorically effective introductions and conclusions.

In previous chapters, you developed the main elements of your argument—the claim and the reasons that support it—as well as evidence for the reasons. In this chapter, you will learn how to address counterarguments, those opposing viewpoints that can keep readers from being convinced. You will also learn how to write an introduction that engages readers in your argument and a conclusion that provides a sense of closure and helps convince readers of your claim. If you address counterarguments and write effective introductions and conclusions, even readers who hold opposing views are likely to listen to your argument in a more open-minded way.

In this chapter, you will complete the following assignments:

- Argument Assignment 11: Identifying and rebutting counterarguments.
- Argument Assignment 12: Writing an engaging introduction.
- Argument Assignment 13: Writing a convincing conclusion.

Connect Adaptive Learning Assignment Consider assigning Connect's Adaptive Learning Assignments to support this chapter.

Teaching Resources See the Instructor's Manual (IM) for suggestions about how to teach this chapter, and consider assigning this chapter's test-bank quiz.

ADDRESSING COUNTERARGUMENTS

A counterargument is an opposing argument. For instance, the claim that the minimum wage should not be increased has a counterargument: the minimum wage should be increased. When you write an argument, you need a keen knowledge of all the counterarguments—their claims and their reasons—that threaten to dislodge your own point of view. You can identify counterarguments by conducting research on viewpoints that differ from yours. To fully understand each counterargument, you need to find sources that accurately express each one.

Once you identify counterarguments, you can craft a rebuttal based on careful rhetorical thinking. Which of the counterarguments will the audience be most familiar with? How important is it to rebut these counterarguments? What kind

Teaching Suggestion
To help students predict counterarguments, require them to find articles (and their abstracts) that articulate the opposing viewpoints. Students can read the abstracts to become familiar with the most powerful counterarguments.

Co-requisite Teaching Tip
Consider offering extra help with counterarguments to co-requisite students by working through the end-of-chapter FAQ, which presents solutions to a common error in addressing counterarguments.

of rebuttal will be convincing to the audience? Thinking rhetorically about how to create a convincing rebuttal will help you argue more persuasively.

A rebuttal includes a refutation—an explanation of why the counterargument is wrong—and it may also include a concession—an agreement that part of the counterargument has merit or is correct. You can review Chapter 14 for an in-depth explanation of rebuttals. As you think about the viewpoints of those who will oppose your argument, make a plan to deal with their counterarguments, keeping your audience in mind.

Basic Approaches for Dealing with Counterarguments

Once you have identified, read, and understood the points of view that oppose your argument, you must decide how to address them. If you are writing for a general audience, you can expect some readers to be familiar with the counterarguments, and in addition, to disagree with your argument. For such an audience, you will need to figure out the most popular counterarguments to rebut. If you are writing for a hostile audience, you can expect readers to be familiar with most of the counterarguments. In such a rhetorical situation, writers often focus primarily on rebutting counterarguments. In fact, some arguments are structured by offering multiple rebuttals—discussions of where the opposing arguments are wrong—before presenting the claim and reasons. The method you choose to deal with counterarguments depends on your audience (see Figure 21.1). If the audience is sympathetic to your point of view, you may not need to address the counterarguments at all because the audience will already be inclined to agree with you. Analyze your audience to select the most appropriate method for dealing with counterarguments.

1. **Present your claim and reasons as well as a rebuttal of the strongest counterarguments.** This approach is useful for a wide variety of arguments, especially those addressed to a general audience. This is the approach we illustrate in the Part 5 chapters and the approach that Jada uses. Writers using this approach can rebut the strongest counterarguments at the end of their argument, or they can present rebuttals throughout the argument. For instance, when presenting a reason, a writer may also include a counterargument for that reason and a rebuttal. It is logical to include the rebuttal in the part of the paper where the reason is presented.

2. **Rebut the counterarguments and then present your claim and reasons.** This approach is helpful when you are presenting an argument to an audience that is likely to disagree with your claim or an audience that is hostile. By addressing the audience's objections first, you may help them become more receptive to your claim.

3. **Present only your claim and reasons.** This approach results in a one-sided argument that does not even consider evidence contrary to the writer's claim. One-sided arguments may be effective if a writer knows the audience agrees with the claim, but such arguments seldom work for general or hostile audiences. One-sided arguments risk alienating the audience because these arguments show a narrow-minded focus on the writer's

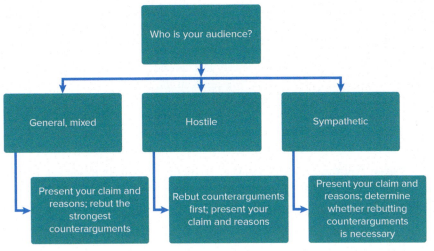

FIGURE 21.1 Three approaches to counterargument, depending on the audience.

claim with no regard for other points of view. A speaker is more convincing when he or she shows an understanding of the opposing point of view and shows—in a respectful way—where the opposing point of view falls short.

> **Jada, on addressing counterarguments:** "When I first started my research, I couldn't understand why employers would be hesitant to offer work-from-home options. Of course, I found info about how difficult it was to WFH because of COVID-19, but that really wasn't what I needed. That was a special situation. Eventually I found articles written from employers' perspectives about why they thought WFH programs wouldn't work. By reading these articles, I began to understand their worries and could figure out how to rebut their arguments. I decided that I needed to use Approach 1. I realized that I needed to deal with the counterargument that working from home will give employees a chance to slack off. I also realized that because of the recent quarantines, employers might be receptive—not hostile—to my ideas."

Developing Rhetorically Effective Rebuttals

As you know from Chapter 14, a rebuttal must include a refutation, the writer's attempt to show the flaws in the counterargument. A rebuttal may also include a concession—an acknowledgment that part of the counterargument is correct. Keep in mind that the purpose for a rebuttal is to effectively deal with a counterargument, and to do so, readers must be satisfied that you have fully understood the counterargument, made concessions where doing so is fair, and shown conclusively that the counterargument is not as strong as the argument you are making.

Teaching Resources
Consider using the PowerPoint "Developing Rhetorically Effective Rebuttals."

Refuting a Counterargument. Writers use a variety of strategies to create the refutation part of a rebuttal. Consider using one of these strategies for refutations:

1. **Refute by finding a "greater good."** The "greater good" concept asserts that we should do that which will result in the most good—the most happiness—for the most people. Will your argument result in more happiness—the greater good—than the counterargument? If so, you may wish to refute the counterargument by pointing out that your argument will have a greater positive effect than the counterargument.

   Claim: City Council should not rezone the riverside land downtown so that Walmart can build a new store.

   Counterargument: *Our community should rezone the land by the river so that Walmart can build a store. Businesses such as Walmart increase the city's tax revenues.*

   Refutation: It is true that if a Walmart were to be built, the city's sales tax revenues would increase. But do we really need an increase in sales tax revenues? The city ended last year with a surplus in the budget. Money is not the issue our city must deal with: it's lack of public spaces for recreation and city events. Nearly every acre downtown—except for the land by the river—has a building or parking lot on it. The only land available for recreation, festivals, and animal habitat is the land by the river. Money is important, but it is not as important as the last bit of land we have downtown for public use. Further, there is a Walmart only six miles away. The general public will benefit more by having this valuable greenbelt than by building yet another Walmart.

2. **Refute by showing grounds are insufficient.** Claims are supported by reasons, and reasons are supported by grounds. For instance, the claim that raising the minimum wage is a bad idea might be supported with the reason that such an increase will have negative effects on the economy. Grounds would present the evidence to prove that these negative effects are likely. When a counterargument does not include grounds, or when the grounds are inadequate, you can refute it by showing that the reason has not been supported with evidence.

   Claim: The average American does not need to take multivitamins.

   Counterargument: *Everyone should take a daily multivitamin. Most Americans do not get the nutrients they need from their diets. A multivitamin is comprised of nutrients that come from foods. Taking a daily multivitamin ensures that Americans get the nutrients they need.*

   Refutation: There is no proof that Americans lack necessary nutrients from their diets. In fact, there is some evidence that suggests multivitamins are unnecessary because, despite less-than-healthy eating habits, the average person gets all the nutrients he or she needs from food.

3. **Refute by identifying fallacies in the counterargument.** If you can find flaws in the reasoning of the opposing argument, you can refute the argument more easily. Look for errors in reasoning to show that the counterargument is based on fallacies and thus is not a reliable argument.

   Claim: We should not require students at our high school to wear uniforms.

   Counterargument: *Students should be required to wear uniforms. At Clement High School, the year uniforms were required was the very year that the math team won first place in the National Math Championship and the football team won the state championship. Uniforms contributed to an atmosphere of excellence that made these wins possible.*

   Refutation: The reason is a *post hoc* fallacy. The writer claims that requiring uniforms led to the success of the math and football teams, but no evidence is provided that there is a causal connection between these two events. A number of factors other than the wearing of uniforms could have been responsible for the success of these teams.

4. **Refute by identifying faulty assumptions on which the counterargument rests.** A claim is supported by reasons, and the often-unstated assumptions that tie claims to reasons are warrants. Identify the warrant for each reason. If the warrant is untrue or debatable, you can refute the argument by showing how the original claim and reason rest on a problematic warrant.

   Claim: We should allow public school students to have visible tattoos.

   Counterargument: *Public school students should not be allowed to reveal tattoos. Schools depend on a well-regulated, obedient student body.*

   Refutation: The assumption is that students who have visible tattoos detract from establishing an environment conducive to "a well-regulated, obedient student body." The problem with this assumption is that it is not based on facts or shared beliefs. Few people will agree that revealing tattoos leads to an unregulated, disobedient student body. Because this assumption is faulty, the argument itself is weak.

Conceding a Point. You have heard it said that there are two sides to every argument. The more subtle point is that even though you may disagree with a person's argument, there is often some merit to it. Including a concession in a rebuttal enables you to acknowledge that the counterargument does have some merit, although not enough. Obviously, a writer cannot concede *every* point of an opposing argument, but there may be specific points that the writer *does* agree with. (For more information about conceding a point without confusing readers, see "FAQ: Conceding a Point without Confusing Readers" at the end of this chapter).

Here is an example of a concession. In the debate about raising the minimum wage, one reason for doing so is that the working poor—those who are paid the least—will see a real increase in the amount of money they take home. A writer who is arguing against increasing the minimum wage may wish to concede this point, to agree, but also to show why his or her argument is still reasonable. The example that follows demonstrates that a rebuttal can include both a concession and a refutation:

Claim: Raising the minimum wage is not a good idea.

Counterargument: *A study by the Economic Policy Institute argues that the minimum wage should be raised to $15, and they support their claim with many reasons. One of the reasons they note is that such an increase would, on average, result in "an extra $3,000 a year—enough to make a tremendous difference in the life of a preschool teacher, bank teller, or fast-food worker who today struggles to get by on around $20,000 a year."*

Concession: It is true: raising the minimum wage would provide a bit more money for the lowest earners in society.

Refutation: However, these numbers do not tell the entire story. Many businesses will struggle to pay these higher wages, and that struggle can have negative effects on the average consumer. In an article for *Forbes*, Adam Millsap asserts that raising the minimum wage might result in a crisis for small businesses. To balance their budgets, Millsap explains, these businesses may have to charge more for their products, fire their less productive workers and retain only the very best workers (thus increasing unemployment), or even go out of business. When the cost of doing business increases, consumers ultimately pay for those costs. Of what good is an increase in the minimum wage if everyday groceries and goods also increase in price? While it is true that an increase in the minimum wage will result in higher wages for many of the working poor, it is not true that this increase will result in greater prosperity for these people.

You can use Rhetorical Toolbox 21.1 to make a plan for dealing with counterarguments.

> **Jada, on working with counterarguments:** "The main argument against working from home, surprisingly, is that remote workers often feel isolated and think that on-site employees don't value their work. I saw this more as an obstacle to be avoided than a compelling argument to not implement work from home programs, so I knew I wanted to address it in my paper. I decided to concede the point that there are some obstacles but to refute the idea that these obstacles cannot be overcome."

Jada drafted a paragraph in which she addressed the issue of social isolation. By citing a source and conceding a point, Jada shows that she has listened to the counterarguments. She also shows that this particular counterargument can be overcome. By doing this, she bolsters her own argument that work from home programs can be effective.

Teaching Suggestion Consider dividing students into two groups to argue about whether animal shelters should euthanize. (For an excellent reading on this topic, see "The Cruelty of Kindness" in Part 6, An Anthology of Readings.) Have each group create reasons, anticipate counterarguments, and create rebuttals for those counterarguments. Help students debate the issue respectfully.

RHETORICAL TOOLBOX 21.1
Addressing Counterarguments

Audience and message. Consider the rhetorical situation, especially the message and the audience. What predictions can you make about the audience's openness to the claim? Based on your predictions, is the audience more likely to be neutral or mixed (as most general audiences are), hostile, or sympathetic? Once you determine the answer, use the following questions to address counterarguments.

For a general, mixed audience
1. What are the counterarguments the audience might know about or believe?
2. Which of these counterarguments are most important to rebut?
3. For each counterargument you choose, what will you include in your rebuttal?
4. Is there part of the counterargument to which you will concede?
5. Where will you place the rebuttals of counterarguments in your argument?

For a hostile audience
1. What are the main counterarguments the audience will have toward your argument?
2. Which of these are most important to rebut? (Sometimes a writer must rebut all of the major counterarguments when the audience is hostile.)
3. Will the audience be more receptive to your argument if you rebut counterarguments before presenting your claim and reasons?
4. Are there parts of the counterarguments to which you will concede?
5. What will you say to this hostile audience to create a convincing rebuttal for the counterarguments you have chosen?

For a sympathetic audience
1. Although the audience is sympathetic, would rebutting counterarguments increase the audience's convictions?
2. Would rebutting the most powerful counterarguments help to educate the audience so that they, too, can rebut counterarguments?

Jada's Rebuttal

While working from home offers a wide variety of advantages to both employers and employees, **at least one large study found that employees who work from home often experience social isolation. The *Harvard Business Review* polled nearly 1,153 employees. Of these, 52% worked from home at least occasionally (Grenny). Those who worked from home reported that "they worry that coworkers say bad things** —— Counterargument

> behind their backs, make changes to projects without telling them in advance, lobby against them, and don't fight for their priorities" (Grenny). [Concession:] Employers are right to worry about this aspect of working from home. [Refutation:] However, companies can take positive steps to make sure employees who work from a distance do feel connected to their coworkers. The study's authors even say as much: "While managers may be tempted to respond to these findings by ending remote work programs and bringing everyone back to the office, we don't recommend that." Instead, they argue that such obstacles could be overcome by using strategies to strengthen human relationships among employees such as adding "water cooler" conversation time to meetings, prioritizing team building and camaraderie, and exploiting the interpersonal potential of technological tools (Grenny). During the COVID-19 quarantine, employers found a wide variety of camaraderie-building activities. For example, General Assembly, an education company, created a "video chatroom link . . . for workers to join in the morning for watercooler chat over coffee" as well as hosting an end-of-day virtual trivia game by using a chat channel online. The chat channel has nearly 150 members, so employees are clearly engaged (Liu). Although social isolation can be an issue, it is one that can be solved.

ARGUMENT ASSIGNMENT 11
Identifying and Refuting Counterarguments

Using Rhetorical Toolbox 21.1, identify the counterarguments that are important to rebut in your argument. Write rebuttals for these counterarguments. If appropriate, concede to the points with which you agree.

DRAFTING INTRODUCTIONS AND CONCLUSIONS

In addition to making choices about how—and where in your argument—you will address counterarguments, you will also have to make rhetorically effective decisions about how to start and end your argument. The opening words of any argument are crucial: if those words are off-putting or offensive, the audience may immediately sour to the writer's ideas. A conclusion is important because it presents the writer's final opportunity to convince readers. Thinking rhetorically about introductions and conclusions will help you write a more effective argument.

Teaching Suggestion
Consider analyzing the introductions and conclusions to the arguments "The Dog Delusion," "Urban Spaces and the Mattering of Black Lives," and "Mass Incarceration: The Whole Pie," available in Part 6.

Creating Introductions

If you have ever browsed a magazine, you know the importance of an article's introductory paragraphs. Those paragraphs often determine whether you read the article or not. In general, argument introductions work to engage the reader's attention, preparing the reader to hear the claim. Often, introductions end with the writer's claim—which functions as the argument's thesis statement. Sometimes, writers introduce a topic and wait to present the claim later in the paper. Regardless of where you choose to place the claim, an introduction is the first impression a reader gets.

An introduction can consist of one paragraph or several paragraphs. If the introduction presents background information, a writer may need to compose several paragraphs. On the other hand, a writer may be able to briefly summarize the issue and launch the argument in just one paragraph. The length of the introduction depends on the topic and what readers need to know to understand the argument and its context.

When deciding how to approach your introduction, consider your claim and your audience. Do readers need background information to understand your claim and reasons or the issue in general? Is the issue highly controversial? If so, readers may need to know you have fairly considered all sides. Would using an appeal to pathos engage readers and help them be more receptive to your claim? Thinking about questions such as these will help you choose one of the following methods of introduction.

1. **Provide background information needed by readers.** One function of an introduction is to provide background information that readers need in order to fully understand the writer's argument. Background information might include definitions, historical information, data and statistics, a recap of the current context of the issue, or other details that are important for readers to grasp before you present the argument. For instance, an argument about immigration reform would need to provide information about current immigration laws. Not every reader will know how the immigration system works, so providing this information in the introduction allows the writer to briefly inform readers before moving on to his or her argument.

2. **Present various points of view.** An introduction can also set the tone for the argument. If a writer hopes to be seen as fair-minded, he or she can use language that creates a tone of respect for the opposing point of view. A universal principle in psychology is that people want to be heard and understood. By writing an introduction that demonstrates the speaker has heard and understood the opposing argument, the introduction can help readers who already hold an opposing viewpoint to feel less defensive since the writer has listened to their ideas.

3. **Appeal to ethos by demonstrating credibility.** To be believable, a speaker must demonstrate that he or she has the knowledge, expertise, or experience to competently argue the issue. Student writers can develop ethos by presenting an excellent overview of the issue. This overview should demonstrate that the student has sufficient knowledge, of both sides of the issue, to be able to create a well-informed argument.

4. **Appeal to pathos.** In addition to providing background information and setting the tone, an introduction can provide a powerful start to an argument by appealing to emotion. Of course, the speaker must be sure that appealing to emotion is an effective strategy for his or her argument. If it is, a common way to help readers see the human side of an issue is to use a story. If a speaker has a powerful story that shows how important the issue is, even if the story is hypothetical, using a short narrative might be an effective way to appeal to pathos and create an introduction.

> **Jada, on composing an introduction:** "I have been guilty of using one method—asking a question—to start almost every paper I have ever written. Since this is an argument, I want the introduction to show that I am credible and know what I'm talking about. I decided to use data and background information to help readers see that I understand the issue and am qualified to write about it. I also want them to see how important this issue is. Hopefully, if they realize it is important, they will want to keep reading."

Jada's introduction is shown below. As you read it, notice how she uses the past and the present—as well as statistics—to help readers understand the background they need to grasp the topic's importance.

Jada's Introduction

Historical information with examples:

The world of work has changed significantly over the last fifty years. Fifty years ago, a doctor would not have dreamed of working from home. A secretary or administrative assistant would expect to report each day to an office and sit at a desk or cubicle for eight hours. Sales professionals would work the field but would return to the office at the end of the day.

Statistics to present the current situation:

Today's workplace is different. In 2014, as Laura Vanderkam notes, 34 percent of the business leaders who responded to a survey predicted that "more than half their company's full-time workforce would be working remotely by 2020." A more recent study produced by the International Workplace Group found that "70 percent of professionals work remotely—a phenomenon known as telecommuting—at least one day a week, while 53 percent work remotely for at least half of the week" (Browne). Of course, when the nation faced the COVID-19 pandemic, these statistics grew exponentially—and almost overnight. Clearly, even without a pandemic, working from home was beginning to grow in popularity.

> Working from home is quickly becoming a norm rather than a deviation. **Nonetheless, some employers are still hesitant to offer their employees the option to work from home.** Some employers are convinced that productivity will decrease when employees work from home. They believe that working from home is not a viable option because it will result in less commitment to the company, social isolation, and other perils. The evidence, however, suggests otherwise. In fact, the evidence suggests that working from home programs will actually benefit employers. **Because of the many benefits working from home offers to both employers and employees, most companies should create work-from-home options for employees.**

Narrowing and focusing the topic to working-from-home from an employer's perspective

Claim

ARGUMENT ASSIGNMENT 12
Drafting a Rhetorically Effective Introduction

Consider the rhetorical situation of your argument. Select a method of introduction that you believe will help you write an effective argument, and draft the introductory paragraph(s) of your argument.

Creating Conclusions

While the introduction of an argument prepares readers for the writer's claim, the conclusion presents the writer with a final opportunity to convince the reader. In courtrooms, closing statements are often the most powerful moments in a trial. They allow attorneys to emphasize the strongest parts of their argument, to create one final appeal to pathos or ethos, and to leave the jury with certain key words or ideas that support their arguments.

You can write an effective conclusion to an argument by using some of the same strategies found in the courtroom. Of course, any conclusion should provide readers with a sense of closure, a sense that the argument has been made and can end. But conclusions to arguments need to accomplish more than merely providing closure. Whatever method you choose to conclude your paper, avoid the temptation to use "in conclusion," one of the most overused phrases in writing. Think creatively about the words you can use to leave one final, important, lasting impression in readers' minds. The strategies that follow can be used to create memorable and effective conclusions.

1. **Summarize your strongest reasons.** One way to conclude is to summarize the strongest reasons in support of the claim. A claim may be supported by multiple reasons; some reasons will be stronger than others. Strong reasons are those that are hard to refute because of their logic or because of the strength of the evidence used to support them. Strong reasons also

include those that the audience is more likely to accept. Selecting and reiterating the strongest reasons of your argument in your conclusion allows you to refocus readers' attention on these reasons.

2. **Appeal to the audience's values.** Another strategy for concluding an argument is to appeal to the values of the audience. For instance, in an argument to improve the foster care system, a writer might appeal to a value that most people share: a desire to protect children. Emphasizing the value that the writer and readers hold in common might help readers to accept the argument.

3. **Appeal to pathos.** If one of the reasons for your argument requires readers to be empathic to the plight of others, consider reemphasizing the pathos appeal of your argument. Human persuasion is rarely based solely on logic; we are often moved by the stories of others and can be convinced when those stories are powerful. By using the story of an individual, you may be able to tap into the empathy of the audience. Writers often return to a story they began in the introduction to provide an ending for the story; doing so allows them to include appeals to pathos if such appeals are appropriate.

4. **Make predictions and call for action.** While reiterating the strongest reasons, calling upon shared values, and appealing to pathos can be effective strategies for arguments, two strategies that can be used for a variety of writing types can also be used for arguments. Writers can make predictions and can call for action. Making predictions can leave readers with ideas about what will happen if they fail to acknowledge the argument's claim, while calling for a plan of action can equip readers with concrete steps they can take, actions that would require agreeing with the writer's claim.

> **Jada, on writing a conclusion:** "When I reread my paper from the beginning, writing a conclusion was easy. I was able to summarize my strongest arguments, make a prediction, and then make a call to action. My conclusion is simple, but I think it's powerful."

Jada combines two conclusion methods: summarizing her strongest points and predicting. Notice how she brings closure to her paper by using these strategies.

Jada's Conclusion

The evidence is in. **[Summary of strongest points:** Working from home does not put a company's productivity in jeopardy: it increases productivity. While many employees who were forced to work from home because of the COVID-19 pandemic were unprepared to do so, it is clear that resourcefulness and high quality technological tools can make working from home more than possible. And with adequate preparation and training, employees who work from home are happier and highly productive. In addition, high-caliber candidates are more likely to gravitate to companies that allow the freedom and flexibility of working from home.

Because working from home seems to be the direction in which companies are headed, those companies that fail to offer this option may find themselves facing a shortage of employees. The future demands forward-thinking employers to make available working-from-home options where they are possible. Doing so just might make the difference between a business's success or failure. — Prediction and call to action

ARGUMENT ASSIGNMENT 13
Drafting a Rhetorically Effective Conclusion

Consider the rhetorical situation of your argument, and identify the most effective way to conclude. Draft a conclusion.

Reflecting to Develop a Writer's Mindset

Consider the following statement:

> Rebuttals, introductions, and conclusions serve rhetorical purposes.

What does that statement mean? Why is it important to see rebuttals, introductions, and conclusions as rhetorical elements? Explain your answer.

FAQ CONCEDING A POINT WITHOUT CONFUSING READERS

When you concede a point, you agree with or acknowledge the merit of one of the opposing side's ideas. Conceding a point requires careful wording.

How can you concede a point without conceding the whole opposing claim?

Readers need to know that although you are agreeing with one of the opponent's reasons, you are *not* agreeing with the opponent's whole claim. Unless you use careful wording, readers can get confused and wonder what your position is. The following examples show how confusion can be created and how to avoid it.

Claim: Zoos play a critical role in the protection of animals and deserve support.

Confusing concession: Some people argue that zoos should be closed because of the number of animal deaths that occur in zoos. Their concern is justified. Statistics show that some zoos are responsible for hundreds of animal deaths each year. No one likes seeing an animal get hurt or die.

This concession basically agrees with the opposing argument. Here is the revision, with a clearer, qualified concession.

Claim: Zoos play a critical role in the protection of animals and deserve support.

Clear, qualified concession: Some people argue that zoos should be closed because of the number of animal deaths that occur in zoos. No one likes seeing an animal get hurt or die. The truth is that keeping animals in zoos is not the problem. The problem lies in the handful of zoos that have substandard living situations or that do not care for the animals properly. The activists are right in this regard: such zoos should be shut down. But the fact that there is a small number of zoos that treat animals poorly does not mean that *all* zoos do so. In fact, the majority of zoos take excellent care of their animals.

TRY IT!

Draft a paragraph in which you concede a point without confusing readers.

Your claim: The local high school should receive funding to build a new band hall.

Counterargument: Funds should be spent on projects related to academics because academic knowledge is what matters when students take the ACT and SAT, not band.

1. What part of the counterargument can you concede?
2. What part can you refute?
3. Write a paragraph in which you concede a point, and offer a refutation that does not confuse readers.

22 Revising and Finishing Your Argument

CHAPTER OBJECTIVES

You will learn to:
- Use a guidance rubric for revising your argument.
- Revise your argument's development, unity, organization, and clarity for a general audience.
- Revise your argument with your most critical reader in mind.
- Finish your argument by editing, checking for plagiarism, and formatting.

Revision is one of the single most important processes in writing anything, but when you are composing an argument, revision is crucial. It is the stage of the writing process when thinking rhetorically is most important. How will readers experience your argument? What objections will they raise? How will you, as a writer, come across? These are only a few of the questions that can help you write the very best argument possible. In this chapter, you will revise and finalize your argument project by completing these assignments:

- Argument Assignment 14: Using a rubric for revision.
- Argument Assignment 15: Revising for a general audience.
- Argument Assignment 16: Revising for a critical audience.
- Argument Assignment 17: Finishing your argument.

Connect Adaptive Learning Assignment
Consider assigning Connect's Adaptive Learning Assignments to support this chapter.

USING A RUBRIC FOR REVISION

First, read your paper in its entirety. Although you are not in the editing stage, you can always correct minor errors that stand out. You will revise and edit more carefully later. For now, simply read your paper to get an overall sense of what you have drafted.

Next, reread the assignment. Make sure that the paper you wrote or the project you created conforms to the assignment instructions. When you began this argument project, you were prompted to analyze your instructor's rubric, if you received one, or to create your own guidance rubric (see Chapter 19). Using

Teaching Resources
See the Instructor's Manual (IM) for suggestions about how to teach this chapter, and consider assigning this chapter's test-bank quiz.

Co-requisite Teaching Tip
If time allows, have students work with classmates, swapping guidance rubrics and instructor rubrics and providing formative feedback on drafts.

the rubric throughout the writing process to help you stay focused on the assignment is important; equally important is using the rubric as a guide for revision. To use the rubric, check your paper against each requirement and note areas needing revision. If your paper is too long or too short, you'll need to cut it or develop it further (see "FAQ: Too Short? Too Long? Solving Length Problems" at the end of the chapter for help). Be as objective as you can. You will probably find some criteria that do not score as well as you would like. Take the time to revise your paper so that you improve in these areas.

Your guidance rubric should list assignment requirements, but it is also a place where you can include the rhetorical goals you want your paper to meet. Jada created a guidance rubric early in the writing process, but as she drafted her paper, she realized that some of her rhetorical goals were not on the rubric, so she added them. To use your guidance rubric for revision, first check to make sure it includes all the assignment criteria, and add any rhetorical goals you may have developed as you wrote your argument.

What follows is Jada's guidance rubric with her notes. Notice that the last two rows show the two rhetorical goals Jada developed as she drafted her argument.

Jada's Guidance Rubric					
	How Well You Met the Requirement (5 best, 1 worst)				
Requirement	5	4	3	2	1
Topic must lend itself to argument.	✓				
Must concern a controversial issue related to my field of study.	✓				
Must include logical reasons and avoid logical fallacies. *I need to check my predictions to make sure they aren't slippery slopes. I also need to make sure I haven't overgeneralized about the productivity increases in working from home.*					
Must address counterarguments.	✓				
Must be between 2,000–2,500 words. *I've gone over. Need to revise.*					✓
Must include a visual aid such as a chart or graphic, if appropriate. *I don't think a visual aid is necessary, but I need to see if there is a place where showing the data visually might be effective.*					
Must use at least 10 sources.	✓				
Must be in MLA style.	✓				
Note to self: Check spelling and look for fragments! *Still need to edit, especially for fragments.*					
Note to self: Double check for accidental plagiarism.	✓				
Rhetorical goal: Develop my ethos by showing that I understand both sides of the issue.	✓				
Rhetorical goal: Anticipate the objections of the most skeptical business owner and address them.	✓				

> **Jada, on using her guidance rubric:** "I actually used the guidance rubric several times when I was researching and drafting my paper. Adding the two rhetorical goals at the end was important because I figured out that my argument might not be convincing if I can't show that I'm thoroughly knowledgeable about the topic and if I can't overcome the objections of my worst critics. I ended up using the rubric a lot during revision. It helped me remember my goals and make changes that made my paper more effective."

ARGUMENT ACTIVITY 14
Using a Rubric for Revision

Using Jada's model as an example, make notes on your rubric for items that need revising, and check off requirements that you have met. If you have created additional rhetorical goals that are not on your guidance rubric, add them.

REVISING FOR A GENERAL AUDIENCE

Revising for a general audience requires examining your argument for elements that any audience would expect: a clearly articulated claim, well-developed support for the claim, content that is unified and organized, and an argument that is clear at both the level of ideas and sentences. As you revise for a general audience, you will check each of these elements.

Revising for Development

The main components of an argument are its claim and the support for the claim. Readers will expect to understand the idea you are advocating. If the claim is not obvious to readers, they will probably experience confusion. Readers need to find the claim, but they also need to see clear development. Developing the claim requires providing reasons. In turn, each reason needs to be developed with evidence, explanations, and the like. Use these questions to revise for development:

- **Claim.** Will readers be able to easily locate the claim? How will readers experience the claim's placement? Should it be provided earlier in the argument to help readers avoid confusion? Are there any places in the paper where readers may think the claim has shifted?
- **Reasons.** If readers were asked to list the reasons you offered as support, what would they list? Would skeptical readers be likely to think these reasons are sufficient support for your claim?
- **Support for each reason.** Would a skeptical reader believe you have offered enough explanation and evidence to fully develop each reason? What additional information might make the reason stronger or easier to understand? What objections or questions might a reader have? How can you answer these?

Teaching Suggestion
Research shows that formative feedback during the writing process helps students make more progress as writers than summative assessment. See the IM for more on how to support the revising process by using formative feedback.

Teaching Suggestion
Consider having students revise letters to the editor. For links to some letters to analyze, see the IM.

Revising for Unity and Organization

An argument consists of several parts, and these parts can be confusing to readers if an argument is not unified or well organized.

Unity. Unity results when all of the parts are in the right places. For the argument as a whole, if there are paragraphs that do not serve a precise function—such as providing a reason, evidence, background information, or a counterargument—those paragraphs may not need to be in your argument.

Similarly, each paragraph should demonstrate unity. One way that unity can be disrupted is by using a quotation without anchoring it to the ideas in a paragraph. In fact, some writers advise to never start a paragraph with a quotation because doing so does not provide a context for the quotation. Remember to comment on or explain the quotations you use. Additional elements in a paragraph—statistics, examples, anecdotes, explanations, and so on—must clearly support the paragraph's main idea so that the paragraph is unified.

Use these questions to revise for unity:

- **Purpose.** Will readers see the purpose for each of the paragraphs in the argument? For each paragraph, how would a reader answer these questions: *What is the paragraph's purpose? How does the paragraph relate to the claim?* If a paragraph's purpose is not clear, either eliminate the paragraph or revise to make its purpose obvious.

- **Relevance.** Are there any ideas that readers might see as irrelevant to the claim? If so, are these paragraphs relevant? Revise them to make sure their relevancy is obvious to readers.

- **Sources.** When a source is used, whether directly for a quotation or indirectly as a reference, is the source anchored to the rest of the information in the paragraph? For each instance in which you use a source, think about how readers might experience your argument. Will they understand why you are using the source? If not, revise to provide introductions for the source and commentary on the source when necessary.

Organization. Organization refers to the way the elements in the argument are ordered. A well-organized paper proceeds in a logical order; in addition, the reasons should be ordered from a rhetorical point of view. The questions that follow will help you to revise to make sure your argument is well organized.

One way to analyze the organization of your argument is to create a reverse outline. Unlike an outline you use to plan your argument, a reverse outline is an outline of the ideas in each paragraph, and it is created *after* your argument has been composed. The reverse outline shows what made it into your argument and can be a helpful tool to see the main structure of your argument.

To revise for organization, use these questions:

- **Elements of argument.** Examine your reverse outline. Based on your outline, do you see a claim, reasons, evidence for each reason, counterarguments, and rebuttals? Would a reader be able to analyze your paper and label these elements?

- **Purpose of current organization.** Why did you organize your paper in the way you did? How will readers experience your organization choices? Are any of these choices likely to confuse a reader?
- **Effectiveness of current organization.** Is there another, more effective way you might organize your argument in order to convince readers of your claim?

Revising for Clarity

When you revise for clarity, you assess how clearly your argument has been expressed. Revise for clarity in two ways: assessing clarity of the argument and assessing clarity of expression.

Clarity of Argument. An argument demonstrates clarity when readers can easily figure out the claim and the reasons that support it. Additionally, a writer may need to define new terms or provide necessary background information so that the audience can fully understand the writer's point. Another element that can be unclear is the discussion of counterarguments. Sometimes writers present counterarguments without clearly rebutting them, or writers may concede to a point in a confusing way. (See the FAQ at the end of Chapter 21 for tips on how to concede a point without appearing to agree with the counterargument.) Not exercising enough care in dealing with counterarguments can make a writer's claim confusing. The counterargument presents the opposite claim; thus, a writer must make sure that discussions of the counterargument do not lead readers to think the writer wholly accepts the opposing viewpoint.

Revise for clarity by asking these questions:

- **Claim and reasons.** Is each reason logically tied to the claim? In other words, can readers easily figure out how the reason supports the claim?
- **Audience needs.** Will readers have the definitions and background information necessary to understand the argument?
- **Rebuttals.** Are counterarguments, concessions, and refutations clear in their purpose? In other words, could the discussions of these elements lead readers to be confused about the writer's claim?

Clarity of Expression. Regardless of how clearly the reasons support the claim, if the sentences in an argument are hard to understand, clarity will be a problem. Clarity of expression occurs at the sentence level. Some people consider clarity of expression an editing activity because it requires you to look closely at how sentences are structured and whether sentences make sense. However, because clarity of expression affects meaning, we treat it as a revision topic.

Teaching Resources
Consider using the PowerPoint "Revising for Clarity of Expression" and the accompanying assignment "Writing Clearly."

Co-requisite Teaching Tip
Consider working with students on revising sentences for clarity. If students can master the skill of writing sound sentences, many grammar and mechanics issues will be resolved.

To revise for clarity of expression, read each sentence to determine whether the words work together logically to create meaning. Three types of revisions can help to create sentences that clearly express ideas:

1. **For the most part, express only one idea in a sentence, especially if the idea is complex.** To revise, use multiple sentences to express complex ideas.

   Original: The opioid crisis is complicated, in part, from several factors, including the fact that health-care providers cannot decide how to treat opioid addiction, as well as the fact that those who are addicted often lose their jobs and do not have insurance to aid in their treatments.

   Revised for clarity: The opioid crisis is a complex problem. One factor that affects the crisis involves health-care providers. Providers debate about the best way to treat opioid addiction. While they debate, however, those who are addicted suffer. In addition, because people who are addicted often lose their jobs, these people also lose their insurance, and not having insurance limits treatment options.

2. **Avoid vague terms.** Be concrete and specific about what you mean.

   Original: The craving for opioids is so strong that users often engage in certain illegal activities to be able to satisfy that craving.

   Revised for clarity: The craving for opioids is so strong that users often resort to stealing money or selling stolen goods in order to purchase drugs.

3. **Express ideas as simply as possible.** A simply worded sentence with a clear meaning is much better than a sentence with complicated wording and an unclear meaning.

   Original: The addiction of a person on opioids has deleterious effects for many within that person's sphere of influence, especially those who share a domicile with the user.

   Revised for clarity: The lives of those who live with opioid addicts are also affected by the addiction.

Use these questions to revise for clarity of expression:

- **Number of ideas.** Does any sentence express multiple ideas? If so, are those ideas expressed as clearly as possible? Would creating separate sentences for these ideas improve clarity?
- **Vagueness.** Do any sentences contain vague terms or expressions? How can you revise those terms or expressions to make the sentence clearer?
- **Simplicity.** Are there any sentences that could be reworded to express the ideas more simply?

Rhetorical Toolbox 22.1 combines these revising questions into a handy reference that you can use to revise your argument.

RHETORICAL TOOLBOX 22.1
Revising Your Argument for a General Audience

Revising for Development
- **Claim.** Will readers be able to easily locate the claim? How will readers experience the claim's placement? Should it be provided earlier in the argument to help readers avoid confusion? Are there any places in the paper where readers may think the claim has shifted?
- **Reasons.** If readers were asked to list the reasons you offered as support, what would they list? Would skeptical readers be likely to think these reasons are sufficient support for your claim?
- **Support for each reason.** Would a skeptical reader believe you have offered enough explanation and evidence to fully develop each reason? What additional information might make the reason stronger or easier to understand? What objections or questions might a reader have? How can you answer these?

Revising for Unity
- **Purpose.** Will readers see the purpose for each of the paragraphs in the argument? For each paragraph, how would a reader answer these questions: *What is the paragraph's purpose? How does the paragraph relate to the claim?* If a paragraph's purpose is not clear, either eliminate the paragraph or revise to make its purpose obvious.
- **Relevance.** Are there any ideas that readers might see as irrelevant to the claim? If so, are these paragraphs relevant? Revise them to make sure their relevancy is obvious to readers.
- **Sources.** When a source is used—whether directly for a quotation or indirectly as a reference—is the source anchored to the rest of the information in the paragraph? For each instance in which you use a source, think about how readers might experience your argument. Will they understand why you are using the source? If not, revise to provide introductions for the source and commentary on the source when necessary.

Revising for Organization
- **Elements of argument.** Examine your reverse outline. Based on your outline, do you see a claim, reasons, evidence for each reason, counterarguments, and rebuttals? Would a reader be able to analyze your paper and label these elements?
- **Purpose of current organization.** Why did you organize your paper in the way you did? How will readers experience your organization choices? Are any of these choices likely to confuse a reader?
- **Effectiveness of current organization.** Is there another, more effective way you might organize your argument in order to convince readers of your claim?

Teaching Suggestion
Rhetorical Toolbox 22.1 can be handy, but it can also be overwhelming. Suggest that students identify five or six bullet points that are the areas in their arguments most likely to need attention and to focus revision on those bullet points.

(Continued on next page)

> **Revising for Clarity of Argument**
> - **Claim and reasons.** Is each reason logically tied to the claim? In other words, can readers easily figure out how the reason supports the claim?
> - **Audience needs.** Will readers have the definitions and background information necessary to understand the argument?
> - **Rebuttals.** Are counterarguments, concessions, and refutations clear in their purpose? In other words, could the discussions of these elements lead readers to be confused about the writer's claim?
>
> **Revising for Clarity of Expression**
> - **Number of ideas.** Does any sentence express multiple ideas? If so, are those ideas expressed as clearly as possible? Would revising make the ideas more clear?
> - **Vagueness.** Do any sentences contain vague terms or expressions? How can you revise them to make the sentence clearer?
> - **Simplicity.** Are there any sentences that could be reworded to express the ideas more simply and clearly?

Jada, on revising for a general audience: "I had spent a lot of time writing and rewriting my reasons so that they were well-developed, but I had not thought carefully enough about unity. I had put some quotes in the wrong places, and when I reread my argument, I realized those quotes seemed disjointed, so I revised. I also found times when I started a paragraph with a quote and provided no other information to anchor it to the paragraph. I revised these sections. As far as clarity goes, I think my reasons pretty clearly supported my claim, so I focused on clarity of expression. I circled all the sentences that I didn't think were perfect, and I rewrote them. They are much better now!"

Examine one of the paragraphs from Jada's argument to see the revision choices she made.

Jada's First Draft Revision Notes

[Margin note: Start with my own words! Anchor the quote.]

[highlighted: Kristen Waters notes that "teleworking is being used to attract, retain, and motivate talented employees" (31).] As working from home continues to grow in popularity, employers might expect that the highest quality candidates will seek positions that offer the flexibility of working from home. Aline Masuda and others argue that "telecommuting availability is an observable action of the organization, which symbolizes that the organization cares for the employees' well-being." In the same way that employees may feel an increased commitment to a company that allows telecommuting, potential candidates are more likely to be attracted to a company that offers such flexibility. It may be in an employer's best interest to create options for telecommuting because doing so will put the company in a better position to hire the best candidates.

I need to comment on the quote

This is a super long sentence! Ideas getting lost. Revise.

Jada's Revised Paragraph

In addition to creating social commitment and increasing productivity, working-from-home options can also offer companies benefits that are not always obvious. First, the option of telecommuting often attracts higher quality candidates to a company. Kristen Waters notes that "teleworking is being used to attract, retain, and motivate talented employees" (31). As working from home continues to grow in popularity, employers might expect that the highest quality candidates will seek positions that offer the flexibility of working from home. Aline Masuda and others argue that "telecommuting availability is an observable action of the organization, which symbolizes that the organization cares for the employees' well-being." As Masuda seems to imply, offering work-from-home options is actually a public relations strategy. In the same way that employees may feel an increased commitment to a company that allows telecommuting, potential candidates are more likely to be attracted to a company that offers such flexibility. By creating telecommuting options where possible, employers put themselves in a better position to hire the brightest and the best.

New introduction anchors the quote

Comment on quote

Changed one long sentence into two sentences

ARGUMENT ACTIVITY 15
Revising for a General Audience

Using Rhetorical Toolbox 22.1 as a guide, revise your argument for a general audience by examining its development, unity, organization, clarity of argument, and clarity of expression.

Teaching Resources
Consider using the assignment "Revising for a Critical Audience."

REVISING FOR A CRITICAL AUDIENCE

Because you already know the counterarguments for your claim, you are in a good position to imagine what your worst critic would say about your argument. Ideally, you can articulate the very best arguments *against* your point of view and refute them. One way to revise your argument is to imagine your worst critic and to revise with that person in mind. Use Rhetorical Toolbox 22.2 as a guide for revising for critical readers.

RHETORICAL TOOLBOX 22.2

Revising Your Argument for a Critical Audience

1. **Weakest reason.** Which of your reasons is the weakest, and thus most susceptible to being refuted? What might a critic say about this reason? How can you strengthen this reason?
2. **Lack of evidence or support.** Which statements in your argument might a critic find in need of more evidence or support? How can you support these statements?
3. **Warrants.** What are the warrants for each of your reasons? Could a critic argue with these warrants? If so, revise to provide backing for each warrant that a critic might question.
4. **Counterarguments.** Could a critic show that you have not read enough to fully understand the opposing argument? If so, conduct more research and include more counterargument refutation in your paper.
5. **Fallacies.** Could a critic find areas where you have used fallacious reasoning? For instance, are discussions of cause and effect accurate and based on evidence? Have you avoided overgeneralizing? Look for logical fallacies and revise any that you find.
6. **Criticism.** What do you predict would be the strongest criticism of your argument? How can you revise to address that criticism?

Jada, on revising for her most critical reader: "When I started thinking about my most critical reader, I got nervous. Originally, in my outline, I had planned to write three long sections about how telecommuting is good for absenteeism, how telecommuting helps with a company's expenses, and how telecommuting helps with recruiting candidates. I just could not find enough info on these topics, so I put them into one section on the "less obvious" benefits of working from home. That way, I could pack a lot of support into one section, and that section would parallel the other two sections on productivity and organizational commitment. I also changed a section where I had used a prediction from the past. What I really needed was a prediction for the future, not a prediction that has already come and gone, so I changed that section."

Notice how Jada managed to work in a prediction without relying on the original quoted passage. We have included the date of Jada's paper to show why the prediction was a problem in her first draft.

Jada's First Draft Revision Notes

Jada Spalding
Dr. Wilson
ENGL 1302
12 June 2020

Why Employers Should Adopt Telecommuting Policies

The world of work has changed significantly over the last fifty years. Fifty years ago, a doctor would not have dreamed of working from home. A secretary or administrative assistant would expect to report each day to an office and sit at a desk or cubicle for eight hours. Sales professionals would work the field but would return to the office at the end of the day. Today's workplace is different. A recent study by International Workplace Group found that "70 percent of professionals work remotely—a phenomenon known as telecommuting— at least one day a week, while 53 percent work remotely for at least half of the week" (Browne). These percentages may seem astounding, but the truth is that working remotely is slated to increase even more in the future. Laura Vanderkam notes that, according to a survey administered to business leaders at the Global Leadership Summit, "34% said more than half their company's full-time workforce would be working remotely by 2020. A full 25% said more than three-quarters would not work in a traditional office by 2020." Of course, when the nation faced the COVID-19 pandemic, these statistics grew exponentially—and almost overnight. Even before COVID-19, working from home was growing in popularity.

The prediction is somewhat out of date. Revise.

This intro is long. Maybe break into 2 paragraphs.

Jada's Revised Introduction

The world of work has changed significantly over the last fifty years. Fifty years ago, a doctor would not have dreamed of working from home. A secretary or administrative assistant would expect to report each day to an office and sit at a desk or cubicle for eight hours. Sales professionals would work the field but would return to the office at the end of the day.

Today's workplace is different. In 2014, as Laura Vanderkam notes, 34 percent of the business leaders who responded to a survey predicted that "more than half their company's full-time workforce would be working remotely by 2020." A more recent study produced by the International Workplace Group found that "70 percent of professionals work remotely—a phenomenon known as telecommuting—at least one day a week, while 53 percent work remotely for at least half of the week" (Browne). Of course, when the nation faced the COVID-19 pandemic, these statistics grew exponentially—and almost overnight. Clearly, even without a pandemic, working from home was beginning to grow in popularity.

ARGUMENT ACTIVITY 16
Revising for a Critical Audience

Imagine your reader is an expert in the field who disagrees with you. How would he or she view your argument? Which parts would be most easily criticized? Revise these parts.

FINISHING YOUR ARGUMENT

You are almost finished with your argument. At this stage in the writing process, most students are tired of working with their papers. Ironically, the final touches you put on your paper can be really important. If you submit a paper that is not correctly formatted in MLA or APA style (depending on your instructor's preference), the first impression your paper will make will be a negative one. You have spent significant time creating a winning argument; do not neglect these final steps in the writing process. Leave enough time to edit your paper carefully, check for plagiarism, and format your paper properly.

Editing

Editing means looking for and correcting errors in grammar, spelling, and mechanics. You should always use a spell-checker, but be aware that such tools are not perfect. Read your paper to find misspellings or commonly confused words. The best way to find errors in grammar and mechanics is to know your writing weaknesses. By being aware of the errors you tend to make, you can look for those specifically. For more suggestions about editing strategies, see Chapter 3.

Formatting

Review any instructions your instructor has given you that specify the format of your paper. Your instructor will probably have specified a style—such as MLA or APA—for your paper. Consult Chapter 12 for more information about MLA and APA style so that you can make sure your paper is formatted properly.

Checking for Plagiarism

If your paper contains any plagiarism—whether accidental or not—all the work you have done to create an amazing argument will be meaningless. Use the guidelines in Chapter 11 to make sure you have avoided plagiarism.

> **Jada, on finishing her paper:** "I'm relieved I took the time to double check my paper for plagiarism. I actually found a whole sentence that I had forgotten to put in quotation marks. I knew those words weren't mine, but I guess I was just in a rush when I copied and pasted the quote!"

Jada Spalding (student), Why Employers Should Adopt Telecommuting Policies (final draft)

Spalding 1

Jada Spalding
Dr. Wilson
ENGL 1302
16 June 2020

Why Employers Should Adopt Telecommuting Policies

The world of work has changed significantly over the last fifty years. Fifty years ago, a doctor would not have dreamed of working from home. A secretary or administrative assistant would expect to report each day to an office and sit at a desk or cubicle for eight hours. Sales professionals would work the field but would return to the office at the end of the day.

Today's workplace is different. In 2014, as Laura Vanderkam notes, 34 percent of the business leaders who responded to a survey predicted that "more than half their company's full-time workforce would be working remotely by 2020." A more recent study produced by the International Workplace Group found that "70 percent of professionals work remotely—a phenomenon known as telecommuting—at least one day a week, while 53 percent work remotely for at least half of the week" (Browne). Of course, when the nation faced the COVID-19 pandemic, these statistics grew exponentially—and almost overnight. Clearly, even without a pandemic, working from home was beginning to grow in popularity.

Working remotely—usually from home—is quickly becoming a norm rather than a deviation. Nonetheless, some employers are hesitant to offer their employees the option to work from home. Some employers are convinced that productivity will decrease when employees work from home. They believe that working from home is not a viable option because it will result in less commitment to the company, social isolation, and other perils. The evidence, however, suggests otherwise. In fact, the evidence suggests that working from home programs will actually benefit employers. Because of the many benefits working from home offers to both employers and employees, most companies should create work-from-home options for employees.

Contrary to what some employers fear, productivity does not decrease when employees work from home; in fact, it increases. One of the most compelling reasons to offer employees the option to work from home is that doing so will almost inevitably result in a growth in their productivity. Interestingly, one of the greatest obstacles companies must overcome is the fear that productivity will decrease if workers are allowed to work from home. This fear is unfounded, according to the literature. For example, Polycom, an American company focused on content collaboration and communication technology, surveyed "400 business decision makers throughout Europe" about productivity. They found that WFH employees "were, on average, 39 percent more productive than others" ("Inbox").

The increase in productivity is documented in numerous other studies. CTrip, the largest travel agency in China, was interested in the possibility of allowing employees to work from home, but managers worried that employees would not be as productive as their in-office coworkers (Bloom 167). Thus, the company created a nine-month randomized controlled study in which over one hundred employees worked from home, and a control group worked from CTrip's corporate offices (Bloom 168-69). The company designed the study carefully so that incidental variables were limited. The workers in both locations "used the same IT equipment, faced the same work order flow . . . , carried out the same tasks, and were compensated under the same pay system" (Bloom 169). The findings of this large, carefully constructed experiment confirm the fact that productivity increases in WFH scenarios:

> We found several striking results. First, the performance of the home workers went up dramatically, increasing by 13% over the nine months of the experiment. This improvement came mainly from a 9% increase in the number of minutes they worked during their shifts (i.e., the time they were logged in to take calls). This was due to reductions in breaks, time off, and sick days taken by the home workers. (Bloom 169)

Even greater productivity resulted when, after the study, CTrip evaluated employees who worked from home and reassigned those with the lowest productivity rates. When they did this, productivity increases almost doubled, rising from 13 to 22 percent (Bloom 170).

Several additional studies are consistent with Polycom's findings and the CTrip study. Brittany Harker Martin and Rhiannon MacDonnell conducted a meta-analysis of studies and found that working from home increases productivity (602). Similarly, in a study of telecommuting employees from Kentucky American Water Company, researchers E. Sonny Butler, Cheryl Aasheim, and Susan Williams noted that productivity increased and that the increase was sustained over time (103). Almost all of the studies that reported increased productivity made an attempt to explain why the increase occurs. One reason is that employees often perceive working from home as a privilege. As such, WFH employees are motivated to do their jobs well. In the CTrip study, only those WFH employees who showed increased productivity were allowed to continue working from home. Because of the link between motivation and productivity, employers who are considering WFH options can feel more confident that offering such options will not decrease productivity. In fact, employers can be relatively certain that, if carefully planned, a WFH policy may cause productivity to increase.

Employers should also consider implementing WFH policies because of the positive effect such policies have on organizational commitment, an employee's sense of responsibility, and commitment to the company. Organizational commitment has an effect on productivity, but it is not the same as productivity; instead, organizational commitment can be called "a positive attitude toward the organization" (deVries 5).

Another way to explain organizational commitment is that it is an affective quality, one that results in "feelings of belonging, and a sense of attachment, to the organization" (deVries 5). Obviously, any company needs to create this sense of attachment in its employees to get the kind of buy-in required for success. But is organizational commitment possible when employees work from home?

In fact, organizational commitment is one of the positive results of telecommuting. To understand why, it is important to understand social exchange theory. Many of the researchers in this field point to social exchange theory as the underlying psychological process that increases organizational commitment. Social exchange theory is essentially a cost-benefit analysis applied to relationships. Tulane University's School of Social Work explains:

> Social exchange theory is a concept based on the notion that a relationship between two people is created through a process of cost-benefit analysis. In other words, it's a metric designed to determine the effort poured in by an individual in a person-to-person relationship. The measurement of the pluses and minuses of a relationship may produce data that can determine if someone is putting too much effort into a relationship. ("What")

Social exchange theory helps to explain why telecommuting employees may be more committed to an organization. Most employees view working from home as a privilege. Clearly, not having to go into an office allows a person to have more control over his or her time and schedule. It allows employees who are parents more flexibility in juggling the demands of raising children and working. Employees who work from home do not have to dress for the workplace or make a long commute. As Gould-Williams and Davis point out, because of these benefits, many people think of working from home as a privilege. As a result, they value an organization that allows them this privilege. Organizational commitment increases because working from home is so desirable (Gould-Williams). The employee feels a sense of commitment because of the social exchange of benefits: the employee gets the privilege of working from home, so he or she feels commitment to the company.

In addition to creating social commitment and increasing productivity, working from home options can also offer companies benefits that are not always obvious. Clearly, those companies that had established WFH programs in place before the COVID-19 pandemic were better prepared to conduct business as usual. Other less-obvious benefits

Spalding 5

include attracting high-quality candidates, minimizing absenteeism, and decreasing office costs. First, the option of telecommuting often attracts higher quality candidates to a company. Kristen Waters notes that "teleworking is being used to attract, retain, and motivate talented employees" (31). As working from home continues to grow in popularity, employers might expect that the highest quality candidates will seek positions that offer the flexibility of working from home. Aline Masuda and others argue that "telecommuting availability is an observable action of the organization, which symbolizes that the organization cares for the employees' well-being." As Masuda seems to imply, offering work-from-home options is actually a public relations strategy. In the same way that employees may feel an increased commitment to a company that allows telecommuting, potential candidates are more likely to be attracted to a company that offers such flexibility. By creating telecommuting options where possible, employers put themselves in a better position to hire the brightest and the best.

Another less obvious benefit is that absenteeism is minimized when employees are allowed to work from home. Obviously, when an employee can work from home, he or she is less likely to call in sick. No employer wants to force a sick person to work, but not all sicknesses are the same. With mild illnesses, it may be possible to work if a person is able to stay in his or her own home. If employees have only one choice—call in sick—then absenteeism results and productivity decreases. Schaufeli and others studied the reasons for absenteeism and divided those into two categories: sickness absenteeism and voluntary absenteeism. Sickness absenteeism is missing work for legitimate health reasons, while voluntary absenteeism, also called "withdrawal absenteeism" (Schaufeli) is a more complex issue. Drawing on the research of Farrell and others, Schaufeli explains that "employees who are low in job satisfaction and organizational commitment are more frequently absent than those who are more satisfied and committed" (894). Because employees who are allowed to work from home report higher job satisfaction, it is no surprise that their absenteeism decreases (Schaufeli 895).

Finally, an unexpected and less obvious effect of permitting employees to work from home is a decrease in the costs associated with maintaining office space. Obviously, employees who work from home do not need office space at a home office. These employees do not need office furniture; they do not require a parking spot; they do not need coffee. While these advantages may seem relatively small, when an employer rolls out telecommuting to a significant number of employees, the company may be able to move to a smaller facility, resulting in substantial savings not only in real estate but also in maintenance—cleaning, air conditioning, heating, and so on—of facilities.

While working from home offers a wide variety of advantages to both employers and employees, at least one large study found that employees who work from home often experience social isolation. The *Harvard Business Review* polled nearly 1,153 employees. Of these, 52 percent worked from home at least occasionally (Grenny). Those who worked from home reported that "they worry that coworkers say bad things behind their backs, make changes to projects without telling them in advance, lobby against them, and don't fight for their priorities" (Grenny). Employers are right to worry about this aspect of working from home. However, companies can take positive steps to make sure employees who work from a distance do feel connected to their coworkers. The study's authors even say as much: "While managers may be tempted to respond to these findings by ending remote work programs and bringing everyone back to the office, we don't recommend that." Instead, they argue that such obstacles could be overcome by using strategies to strengthen human relationships among employees, such as adding "water cooler" conversation time to meetings, prioritizing team building and camaraderie, and exploiting the interpersonal potential of technological tools (Grenny). During the COVID-19 quarantine, employers found a wide variety of camaraderie-building activities. For example, General Assembly, an education company, created a "video chatroom link . . . for workers to join in the morning for watercooler chat over coffee" as well as hosting an end-of-day virtual trivia game by using a chat channel online. The chat channel has nearly 150 members, so employees are clearly engaging (Liu). Although social isolation can be an issue, it is one that can be solved.

The evidence is in. Working from home does not put a company's productivity in jeopardy: it increases productivity. While many employees who were forced to work from home because of the COVID-19 pandemic were unprepared to do so, it is clear that resourcefulness and high quality technological tools can make working from home more than possible. And with adequate preparation and training, employees who work from home are happier and highly productive. In addition, high-caliber candidates are more likely to gravitate to companies that allow the freedom and flexibility of working from home. Because working from home seems to be the direction in which companies are headed, those companies that fail to offer this option may find themselves facing a shortage of employees. The future demands forward-thinking employers to make available working-from-home options where they are possible. Doing so just might make the difference between a business's success or failure.

Works Cited

Bloom, Nicholas, et al. "Does Working from Home Work? Evidence from a Chinese Experiment." *Quarterly Journal of Economics*, vol. 130, no. 1, Feb. 2015, pp. 165–218, doi:10.1093/qje/qju032.

Browne, Ryan. "70% of People Globally Work Remotely at Least Once a Week, Study Says." *CNBC*, 31 May 2018, www.cnbc.com/2018/05/30/70-percent-of-people-globally-work-remotely-at-least-once-a-week-iwg-study.html.

Butler, Sonny E., et al. "Does Telecommuting Improve Productivity?" *Communications of the ACM*, vol. 50, pp. 101–03, doi:10.1145/1232743.1232773.

de Vries, Hanna, et al. "The Benefits of Teleworking in the Public Sector: Reality or Rhetoric?" *Review of Public Personnel Administration*, Feb. 2018, doi:10.1177/0734371X18760124.

Gould-Williams, Julian, and Fiona Davies. "Using Social Exchange Theory to Predict the Effects of HRM Practice on Employee Outcomes: An Analysis of Public Sector Workers." *Public Management Review*, vol. 7, 2005, pp. 1–24.

Grenny, Joseph, and David Maxfield. "A Study of 1,100 Employees Found That Remote Workers Feel Shunned and Left Out." *Harvard Business Review*, 2 Nov. 2017, hbr.org/2017/11/a-study-of-1100-employees-found-that-remote-workers-feel-shunned-and-left-out.

"Inbox: The Case for Remote Working: Yahoo Recently Announced an End to Its Long-Standing Remote Worker Programme, Now Requiring Employees to Be Physically in the Office." *New Zealand Management*, 2013, p. 9.

Liu, Jennifer. "Virtual Happy Hours, Team Yoga Sessions: How Coworkers Are Staying Connected While They Work from Home." *CNBC*, 25 Mar. 2020, www.cnbc.com/2020/03/25/how-coworkers-are-staying-connected-while-they-work-from-home.html.

Martin, Brittany H., and Rhiannon MacDonnell. "Is Telework Effective for Organizations? A Meta-Analysis of Empirical Research on Perceptions of Telework and Organizational Outcomes." *Management Research Review*, vol. 35, no. 7, 2012, pp. 602–16. ProQuest, DOI:10.1108/01409171211238820.

Masuda, Aline D., Claudia Holtschlag, and Jessica M. Nicklin. "Why the Availability of Telecommuting Matters." *Career Development International*, vol. 22, no. 2, 2017, pp. 200–19, doi:10.1108/CDI-05-2016-0064.

Schaufeli, Wilmar B., et al. "How Changes in Job Demands and Resources Predict Burnout, Work Engagement, and Sickness Absenteeism." *Journal of Organizational Behavior*, vol. 30, no. 7, 2009, pp. 893–917. *JSTOR*, www.jstor.org/stable/41683873.

Vanderkam, Laura. "Will Half of People Be Working Remotely by 2020?" *Fast Company*, 13 Aug. 2014, www.fastcompany.com/3034286/will-half-of-people-be-working-remotely-by-2020.

Waters, Kristin A. "Teleworking in Higher Education: What Managers Should Know before Developing Teleworking Policies." *College and University*, vol. 90, no. 3, 2015, pp. 28–31, 34–38. *AACRAO*, www.aacrao.org/research-publications/quarterly-journals/college-university-journal/article/c-u-archive/c-u-vol.-90-no.-3-spring-2015-(.pdf).

"What Is Social Exchange Theory?" Tulane University, School of Social Work, 20 Apr. 2018, socialwork.tulane.edu/blog/social-exchange-theory.

ARGUMENT ACTIVITY 17
Finishing Your Argument

Prepare your final draft by editing, checking for plagiarism, and formatting.

> **Reflecting to Develop a Writer's Mindset**
>
> In what ways is revision a rhetorical act, an act that takes into consideration the speaker, audience, and message? Which of the suggestions in this chapter will help you revise in a way that improves the effectiveness of your argument? Explain your answers.

FAQ TOO SHORT? TOO LONG? SOLVING LENGTH PROBLEMS

Ideally, the length of an argument should depend on the rhetorical situation. The number of reasons you provide and the development of those reasons must be sufficient for the audience to accept the claim. And the length of your argument must be appropriate for the context. For instance, a letter to the editor will need to be brief, whereas a researched argument for a class may need to demonstrate depth and, thus, be lengthy. While you should always think about length as a rhetorical matter, you will sometimes have to meet length requirements. Many instructors give students a word count for each assignment. If you finish your argument and find that it is too short or too long, the following suggestions will help you revise your paper.

1. **What can you do if your paper is too short?**

   When a paper does not meet the length requirements, the argument may not be well-enough developed. Use these suggestions to improve:

   - **Examine each reason and add explanations.** Sometimes writers believe a reason "speaks for itself." Reasons never speak for themselves. They require explanation. Read each reason and ask, "Have I explained this reason in as much depth as readers will need?" If necessary, add more explanatory material. Imagine a reader who does not understand the reason. How could you explain it more clearly or in more depth?

   - **Examine each reason and add examples.** Examples help to make concepts more concrete, and they increase the development of body paragraphs. Read each reason and ask, "Can I give an example that might help readers understand this more thoroughly?" Remember, examples can be hypothetical.

   - **Examine each quotation and be sure to anchor and explain each one.** Quotations must always be connected to the text around them. If you include a quotation from an expert, be sure to start the quotation with information about the expert and provide anchoring material, such as an explanation of the quotation's meaning or significance, after the quote. Like reasons, quotations never "speak for themselves." They require the writer to unpack them and explain their significance.

   - **Use journalistic questions to develop body paragraphs.** *Who? What? Where? When? Why? How?* Reread each of your reasons and ask these six journalistic questions about the content you have written. Would your reason make better sense if you presented more information about one of these questions? If so, add that information.

2. **What can you do if your paper is too long?**

   When a paper is too lengthy, readers may tune out. Determining how much content to provide is tricky. Use these strategies:

   - **Cut or summarize quoted content.** Quotations add words for many reasons: they must be introduced, and they must be anchored to the text around them. Examine each quotation. Is the quote really necessary? If not, remove it. Can you summarize the quote (remembering to give credit to the source) and save words? If so, summarize it.

   - **Eliminate long, indented (block) quotations.** There are very few occasions on which long, indented quotations are necessary. Examine each block quotation. Can you use a shorter quotation? Can you put the ideas into your own words (remembering to give credit to the source)? Select one of these methods for handling block quotations.

- **Reword sentences for conciseness.** Long, rambling sentences and paragraphs can cause readers to lose interest or even worse, not understand the point you are making. The example that follows shows how condensing a long passage helps improve clarity:
  - **Original:** The growth in popularity of online websites used for dating is tremendous. Ten years ago, very few people used dating websites, but today, most single people have used such sites at least once. (33 words)
  - **Trimmed:** The use of dating websites has increased dramatically over the last ten years. Most single people have used a dating site at least once. (24 words)
- **Trim the introduction and/or conclusion paragraphs.** Scan the introduction and conclusion. If they are lengthier than necessary, remove content. Remember the function of these paragraphs: the introduction provides information readers will need to understand your claim, and the conclusion should leave readers with your most important points and provide a sense of closure. Remove any information that does not contribute to these objectives.

TRY IT!

1. Add content. The paragraph that follows came from a brochure for new college students designed to help students succeed. However, the paragraph is undeveloped and needs additional content. Revise the paragraph by adding information.

One strategy for making a high grade in a college class is to gain thorough knowledge of how the course works. By learning about how the course works and how grades are calculated, students will be in a better position to meet the requirements for an "A."

2. Subtract Content. The paragraph that follows appeared on a website designed to help students master study skills for foreign language classes. The paragraph is lengthier than it should be. Revise it by subtracting content and/or rewriting.

Learning a foreign language is a requirement for many degrees. It is a requirement that many students find challenging. Students who have not ever studied a foreign language are at a particular disadvantage, but those who have studied a foreign language during their years in high school have a slight advantage in that they know what to expect as one tries to acquire foreign language skills. In spite of the challenge, there are some strategies students can use to master a foreign language and to do well in a foreign language class. The most important strategy is to understand the importance of studying every single day and to set up and keep a studying schedule. Like algebra, foreign language acquisition is a process that requires mastery of one lesson before another can be mastered. For example, in the same way that in algebra one must learn how to multiply and divide fractions before certain algebraic functions can be used, foreign language requires students to understand some preliminary lessons, such as the types of verbs involved in the language or the most commonly used pronouns. Recognizing that each lesson builds on the prior lesson helps students figure out the need to thoroughly master one concept before going on to the next concept.

PART 6 An Anthology of Readings

1 Environmental Issues

The Fracking of Rachel Carson: Silent Spring's Lost Legacy, Told in Fifty Parts

Sandra Steingraber

An ecologist, author, and cancer survivor, Sandra Steingraber is the author of Living Downstream: An Ecologist's Personal Investigation of Cancer and the Environment *and* Raising Elijah: Protecting Children in an Age of Environmental Crisis. *"The Fracking of Rachel Carson: Silent Spring's Lost Legacy, Told in Fifty Parts" appeared in* Orion Magazine, *an environmental and nature publication, in 2013. It commemorated the fiftieth anniversary of the publication of* Silent Spring, *Rachel Carson's ground-breaking book about the effects of pesticide use on the environment. A slide show about the fracking of the place where Carson grew up in Pennsylvania—narrated by Steingraber—is available at the* Orion Magazine *website.*

Teaching Resources
For ideas about how to use the readings in Part 6, please see the Instructor's Manual (IM).

Teaching Suggestion
Consider using Steingraber's essay as a model of argument in the form of creative nonfiction.

---

1. Rachel Carson, the ecologist who kicked the hornet's nest, wrote a book that needed no subtitle. Published fifty years ago this September, *Silent Spring* rocketed to the top of the bestseller list, prompted a meeting with the president's science advisers, occasioned congressional hearings, and circled her neck with medals of honor. It also let loose swarms of invective from the pesticide industry. Throughout it all, Carson remained calm. Friends and foes alike praised her graceful comportment and gentle voice. Also, her stylish suits and trim figure. Nevertheless, her various publicity photos (with microscope; in the woods; outside her summer cottage in Maine; at home in Maryland) look as if the same thought bubble hovers above them all: *I hate this.*

2. In the later portraits, Carson was dying of breast cancer. It was a diagnosis she hid out of fear that her enemies in industry would use her medical situation to attack her scientific objectivity and, most especially, her carefully constructed argument about the role that petrochemicals (especially pesticides) played in the story of human cancer. But behind her unflappable public composure, Carson's private writings reveal how much physical anguish she endured. Bone metastases. Radiation burns. Angina. Knowing this, you can imagine her patience running out during

the interminable photo shoots. The wretched wig hot and itchy under the lights. The stabbing pains (cervical vertebrae splintered with tumors) that would not, would not relent.

3. In the iconic Hawk Mountain photo, Rachel Carson is truly beautiful. Her smile looks natural rather than forced. Posed on a rocky summit, she is wearing a badass leather jacket and wields a pair of leather-strapped binoculars. So armed, she scans the horizon. At her feet, the whole of Berks County, Pennsylvania, unfurls, forest and valley, field and mountain, like a verse from a Pete Seeger song.

4. Hawk Mountain, along the Appalachian flyway, is an officially designated refuge for raptors. As with so many sanctuaries, it started out as a hunting ground with bounties. By the mid-1930s, it had become *the* spot in Pennsylvania to witness the annual fall migration of hawks. Rachel Carson loved it here. She wrote about her experiences in a never-finished, never-published essay titled "Road of the Hawks." According to biographer Linda Lear—who gathered the fragments into the collection Lost Woods: *The Discovered Writing of Rachel Carson*—the essay is notable not only for its careful analysis of bird behavior and knowledge of geology but also because Carson traced the origin of her airy lookout to Paleozoic marine organisms.

5. *And always in these Appalachian highlands there are reminders of those ancient seas that more than once lay over all this land . . . these whitened limestone rocks on which I am sitting . . . were formed under that Paleozoic ocean, of the myriad tiny skeletons of creatures that drifted in its waters. Now I lie back with half closed eyes and try to realize that I am at the bottom of another ocean—an ocean of air on which the hawks are sailing.*

6. She sat on a mountaintop and thought about oceans.

7. The marine inhabitants of the ancient seas that once overlay Appalachia transformed, when they died, into gaseous bubbles of methane. Pressed under the accumulated weight of silt sifting down from nearby mountains, the seafloor solidified into what's now called the Marcellus Shale, a layer of bedrock that's located under thousands of feet of what we would call *the earth*, but the mining industry calls *overburden*: the material that lies between the surface and an area of economic interest. To extract methane bubbles from the area of economic interest, the natural gas industry is now blowing up the state of Pennsylvania.

8. High-volume, slickwater, horizontal hydrofracking would be considered a crime if the requirements of the Safe Drinking Water Act, which regulates underground chemical injections, pertained.

9. But they don't. In 2005, fracking was granted specific exemptions from the Safe Drinking Water Act. Fracking is also exempt from key provisions within the Clean Air Act and the Clean Water Act. Chemicals used in drilling and fracking operations can be claimed as trade secrets; public release of their identity is not mandated by federal right-to-know provisions. The Environmental Protection Agency has limited jurisdiction over fracking.

10. The Environmental Protection Agency credits *Silent Spring* for its existence.

11. You can think of fracking as a hostage exchange program. A drill bit opens a hole a mile deep, turns sideways, and then, like a robotic mole, tunnels horizontally through the shale bedrock for another mile or more. The hole is lined with steel pipe and cement. To initiate the fracturing process, explosives are sent down it. Then, fresh water (millions of gallons per well) is injected under high pressure to further break up the shale and shoot acids, biocides, friction reducers, and sand grains deep into the cracks. Trapped for 400 million years, the gas is now free to flow through the propped-open fractures up to the surface, where it is condensed, compressed, and sent to market via a network of pipelines. The water remains behind.

12. Within the rumply state of Pennsylvania is a place called Triple Divide, where three adjacent springs feed the watersheds of three mighty rivers: the Allegheny (which flows west to the Mississippi River); the Susquehanna (which flows east to Chesapeake Bay); and the Genesee (which flows north to Lake Ontario). This area of Pennsylvania—which is the sixth most populous state in the union, which sits upwind and upstream from the eleventh most populous state of New Jersey and the third most populous state of New York—lies in the heart of the ongoing fracking boom in the eastern U.S. According to the Pennsylvania Land Trust Association, drillers in the Marcellus Shale amassed 1,614 violations of state oil and gas laws between January 2008 and August 2010. In one incident, a well blowout near the Punxsutawney Hunting Club in Clearfield County sent 35,000 gallons of toxic effluent into a state forest over the course of sixteen hours. Campers were evacuated.

13. Rachel Carson was born on May 27, 1907, and grew up on the outskirts of Springdale, sixteen miles from Pittsburgh. Her lifelong devotion to the sea began as a small child when she discovered, on a rocky hillside near her family's farm, a fossilized shell. A sea creature in Allegheny County, Pennsylvania.

14. Actually, only some of the frack water stays behind in the shale. The rest, now mixed with brine and radioactivity, shoots up to the surface with the gas. Finding a safe place to dispose of this toxic flowback is an unsolved problem.

Sometimes, the waste from drilling is just dumped on the ground. That's illegal, but it happens. Sometimes the waste is dumped down other holes. In 2010, 200,000 gallons were poured down an abandoned well on the edge of Allegheny National Forest. Much of the flowback fluid is trucked to northeast Ohio, where it is forced, under pressure, into permeable rock via deep injection wells. This practice, the Ohio Department of Natural Resources has concluded, is the likely cause of the unusual swarm of earthquakes that shook northeast Ohio in 2011.

15. Most of the state's fracking operations are set to take place in Pennsylvania's forests. To be precise, 64 percent of Pennsylvania gas wells are to be drilled in forested land, which includes state forests and natural areas. For each well pad sited in a forested area, an average of nine acres of habitat are destroyed, says The Nature Conservancy's Pennsylvania chapter (each well pad can accommodate up to six wells). The total direct and indirect impact is thirty acres of forest for each well pad. This does not include acreage lost to pipelines. On average, each well pad requires 1.65 miles of gathering pipelines, which carry the gas to a network of larger transporting pipelines.

16. Somewhere between 60,000 and 100,000 wells are planned for Pennsylvania, to be built over the next few decades. The Nature Conservancy forecasts the destruction of 360,000 to 900,000 acres of interior forest habitat due to pipeline right-of-ways alone.

17. They are fracking Allegheny County.

18. They are sizing up Berks County, too.

19. Berks Gas Truth is a grassroots antifracking organization that focuses on human rights. The group is fond of quoting Article 1, Section 27, of the Pennsylvania Constitution:

The people have a right to clean air, pure water, and to the preservation of the natural, scenic, historic, and esthetic values of the environment. Pennsylvania's public natural resources are the common property of all the people, including generations yet to come. As trustee of these resources, the Commonwealth shall conserve and maintain them for the benefit of all the people.

20. Carson had a lot to say about human rights. In *Silent Spring*:

If the Bill of Rights contains no guarantee that a citizen shall be secure against lethal poisons distributed either by private individuals or by public officials, it is surely only because our forefathers, despite their considerable wisdom and foresight, could conceive of no such problem.

In congressional testimony (June 1963):

[I assert] the right of the citizen to be secure in his own home against the intrusions of poisons applied by other persons. I speak not as a lawyer but as a biologist and as a human being, but I strongly feel that this is or should be one of the basic human rights.

From her final speech (San Francisco, October 1963):

Underlying all of these problems of introducing contamination into our world is the question of moral responsibility. . . . [T]he threat is infinitely greater to the generations unborn; to those who have no voice in the decisions of today, and that fact alone makes our responsibility a heavy one.

21. Human rights were not always Carson's focus. Indeed, her bestselling trilogy of books about the sea—*Under the Sea Wind* (1941), *The Sea Around Us* (1951), *The Edge of the Sea* (1955)—gives an adventurous account of a world in which the human race scarcely appears. If we the readers could visualize the oceanic world below the waves—full of communities of interacting creatures that possessed agency and distinct personalities—we might, the author believed, experience wonder and humility. And wonder and humility, said Carson, "do not exist side by side with a lust for destruction." By contrast, the book she longed to begin at the time of her death was going to be all about environmental destruction—and the human rights violations that occur as a result. To halt the growing contamination of the oceans, to counteract a culture of conquest and annihilation, required more than humility, Carson had come to believe. It called for confrontation and witness. Nevertheless, she was also, at the time of her death, working on a book-length expansion of an essay titled "Help Your Child to Wonder."

22. The Springdale where Rachel Carson lived as a child was no preindustrial, Romantic garden. The stench of the local glue factory was horrible. By the time she left for graduate school at Johns Hopkins in 1929, two coal-burning power plants flanked the town and were plainly contaminating both the river and the air. "The memory of the defilement industrial pollution brought," said Linda Lear, would remain with Carson for the rest of her life.

23. To honor Carson (and promote tourism), the Springdale Team of Active Residents coined a new slogan for the town: *Where Green Was Born.*

24. According to a 2010 investigation by the *Pittsburgh Post-Gazette*, residents of Springdale have higher than average rates of death from lung cancers and heart ailments linked to air pollution. Quoted in the article, the then-director of the Rachel

Carson Homestead Association, Patricia DeMarco, said, "We're in a black hole here, where companies put out pollution and take in profits while the costs to our air and water quality are borne by the public." DeMarco characterized Springdale residents as being quick to accept pollution as normal.

25. *Silent Spring* predated the nation's cancer registry program, which came into being under Richard Nixon and mandated that all states track cancer incidence within their populations. Without registry data—and the information about the changing rates of cancer they provide—Carson was left with only case studies and mortality data to work with. She also lacked sophisticated geographic information systems (GIS) and computer mapping programs that can generate visually compelling pictures of potential cancer clusters and other spatial patterns for statistical analysis. In 1960, there were no right-to-know laws, pesticide registries, or Toxics Release Inventories. There were no statewide women's breast cancer groups that monitor public and academic research. Carson painstakingly pieced together the evidence available to her—reports of farmers with bone marrow degeneration, sheep with nasal tumors, spray-gun-toting housewives with leukemia—and concluded that cancer was striking the general population with increasing frequency. She believed that she was seeing the early signs of an epidemic in slow motion. She was especially concerned with the apparent rise in cancers among children. And she was right.

26. April 2012 was a silent spring in Pennsylvania. Funds for a statewide health registry—which would track illnesses in residents who live near drilling and fracking operations—were quietly removed from the state budget. At the same time, a new state law, Act 13, went into effect, which allows a physician in Pennsylvania access to proprietary chemical information for purposes of treating a possibly exposed patient—but only if he or she signs a confidentiality agreement. Confounded, Pennsylvania doctors began asking questions. Does that mean no contacting the public health department? What about talking to reporters or writing up case studies for the *New England Journal of Medicine*? Can a physician who signs the nondisclosure agreement (in order to treat a patient) and then issues an alert to the community at large (in order to fulfill an ethical obligation to prevent harm) be sued for breach of contract? The president of the Pennsylvania Medical Society registered her objections, to which Pennsylvania Speaker of the House Sam Smith furiously counter-objected. Denying that Act 13 constitutes a medical gag order, Smith's spokesman accused objecting doctors of yelling fire in a crowded theater.

27. Still waiting for the Pennsylvania Medical Society to point out that, verily, the theater is burning.

28. Rachel Carson was diagnosed with breast cancer in April 1960, although she would not find out until the following December. Her physician did not tell her the results of the biopsy. Her cancer rapidly metastasized. With her next surgeon, she insisted on full disclosure. She knew the news would not be good. Nevertheless, she wrote to him in February 1963, "I still believe in the old Churchillian determination to fight each battle as it comes. ('We will fight on the beaches—' etc.)"

29. In 2011, Chesapeake Energy, a top producer of natural gas, was a corporate sponsor of the Pennsylvania Breast Cancer Coalition. In response to questions about possible conflicts of interest, the coalition's executive director Heather Hibshman said, "I'm not a scientist. I'm not a researcher. I run a nonprofit. I'm going to leave it at that." Hibshman also said that she was unaware of any correlations between fracking and breast cancer.

30. Fracking for the cure.

31. In *Silent Spring*, Rachel Carson pointed out that pesticides were rapidly rolled out after World War II not because of some unmet pest-control need (like, say, farmers suddenly overrun with bugs and weeds). Rather, abundant leftover stockpiles from wartime use were in need of a domestic market. And so, with the help of Madison Avenue, one was created. DDT, a military weapon, was thus repurposed for domestic use without any premarket testing for safety. An abundance of former military planes that could be cheaply converted into spray planes—and an abundance of former military pilots who loved to fly them—helped seal the deal.

32. In March 2012, it was announced that the town of Monaca, in Beaver County, Pennsylvania (twenty-eight miles northwest of Pittsburgh), would be the site for a massive new ethylene cracker facility—the first in Appalachia—that will create chemical feedstocks for the plastics industry out of the other hydrocarbons that come up with the gas when Marcellus Shale is fracked. Most notably, ethane. This plant is being rolled out not because of some unmet need for more plastic. Rather, it is being built to solve a disposal problem for the energy industry and—of course—to create jobs. Petrochemical crackers are notorious air polluters, and the air of Beaver County, Pennsylvania, already exceeds legal limits for ground-level ozone (smog) and fine particles, which is the very sort of pollution that crackers create. Michael Krancer, Pennsylvania's Department of Environmental Protection secretary,

is not worried. "The plant will be state-of-the-art and built by a world-wide, world-class, environmentally responsible company."

33. That company would be Shell Oil.

34. The biggest repository for plastic waste is the ocean. It was Captain Charles Moore who discovered, in 1999, that the mass of plastic fragments in the central Pacific now outweighs the zooplankton by a factor of six. Sunlight and wave action break the fragments into smaller and smaller bits, but no one knows how small the bits can become or how long they last. It's possible that some common plastics never degrade in the ocean. It's possible that these plastic particles absorb organic toxicants. It's certain that plastic particles are consumed by marine organisms, including the fish that are then consumed by us. According to the National Oceanic and Atmospheric Administration, the best way for individuals to address the problem of plastic waste in our oceans is to use less and recycle more. Blocking a convoy of fracking trucks is not on its list of recommended actions.

35. Rachel Carson's final speech, "The Pollution of Our Environment," was delivered six months before her death. By then, her pelvis was pocked with tumors and she walked with great difficulty. To her audience, a convocation of 1,500 physicians and medical professionals, she asked *why*. Why, in the face of overwhelming evidence of human harm, do we continue to pollute? Why do we pretend that alternatives to defilement and risk do not exist, even when other courses of action are available to us? Or, to use Carson's framing, why do we behave "not like people guided by scientific knowledge, but more like the proverbial bad housekeeper who sweeps dirt under the rug in the hope of getting it out of sight"?

36. Says *Businessweek*, "The preferred way to dispose of the brine and fracking fluid . . . is to pump it out of sight, out of mind into deep, cavernous wells." At last count, Ohio, with its permeable bedrock, has 176 such wells into which 511 million gallons of flowback waste have been injected.

37. To her audience of doctors, an ailing Rachel Carson offered three explanations for our collective reluctance to give up on poisonous technologies. First, she said, we wait too long to evaluate the risks. Once a new technology is deployed and a vast economic and political commitment has been made, dislodging it becomes impossible.

38. Second, we fail to acknowledge that nature invariably has its own (unpredictable) way with harmful pollutants. Because ecosystems are dynamic, chemicals released into the environment do not stay where they are put, nor do they remain

in their original form. Instead, they are transported, metabolized, concentrated, oxidized, methylated, and otherwise reassembled. They enter cycles and pathways. They are sent up food chains and passed down generations. Look, said Carson (who delivered her remarks while seated), the earth is alive. And living things interact with their environments. There are no compartments.

39. Third, we act as though the evidence for harm in other animals does not apply to us even though we share biological ancestry and are thus clearly susceptible to damage from the same forces. This, in spite of the fact that "it would be hard to find any person of education who would deny the facts of evolution."

40. Oh, Rachel.

41. No comprehensive study on the human or animal health impacts of fracking has ever been conducted. However, using a case study approach, veterinarian Michelle Bamberger and Cornell biochemist Robert Oswald have been studying the impact of gas drilling on livestock, horses, pets, wildlife, and people who live in the gaslands of Pennsylvania. Nondisclosure agreements, trade secrets, litigation, and a general atmosphere of intimidation make their investigation difficult. So far, as described in a paper published in the environmental policy journal *New Solutions*, the team has documented widespread evidence of health and reproductive problems. In cattle exposed to fracking fluid: stillborn calves, cleft palates, milk contamination, death.

42. In cats and dogs: seizures, stillbirths, fur loss, vomiting.

43. In humans: headaches, rashes, nosebleeds, vomiting.

44. In a private letter, Rachel Carson suggested another explanation for the prevalence of pollution. Scientists are cowards. Especially scientists who work in government agencies. The ones who are privy to the disconnect between the state of the scientific evidence and the policies that ignore that evidence. The ones who stay silent when they should be blowing whistles.

45. Rachel Carson died in Silver Spring, Maryland, on April 14, 1964. Cause of death: breast cancer and heart disease. She was fifty-six.

46. In May 2012, Stephen Cleghorn, a farmer, scattered the ashes of his wife, Lucinda—who died of lung cancer—on their farm in Reynoldsville, Pennsylvania, which is in Jefferson County. The ceremony was unusual. It included a press conference, during which Cleghorn announced that, with this deposition of ash, he was hereby consecrating his land and declaring it off-limits to fracking in perpetuity. From here on out, the widower averred, "surface rights" (a concept whereby ownership of the surface land is separated from the mineral rights below) would refer to

the rights of all beings whose lives are sustained at the surface and depend upon the clear, clean water that runs upon and below it:

May she who was tender and close and loving of me—now made dust and distant from me by cancerous death—come now in these ashes to declare this farm forever inviolate of shale gas drilling or any other attack upon it as a living system. Here now she declares a new right of love on the surface and below this farm that no gas drill will ever penetrate.

The goats bore witness.

47. We will fight on the beaches—etc.

48. In February 2012, Berks Gas Truth brought financial analyst Deborah Rogers to the Episcopal Church in Kutztown, Pennsylvania. Rogers lives in Fort Worth, Texas, and serves on the Advisory Council for the Federal Reserve Bank of Dallas. To her audience in Kutztown, Rogers argued that the economic fundamentals of shale gas were shaky. Gas reserves were smaller than projected, life spans of producing wells shorter. The leasing frenzy and subsequent speculation had produced financial bubbles. She pointed out that solar panels on a tract of land the same size as a well pad would generate electricity for twice as long as a shale gas well would bring methane up from bedrock. Rogers also noted that 94 percent of the gas wells in the Barnett Shale play in Texas emit benzene. Three months after Rogers's lecture, researchers from the Colorado School of Public Health found elevated benzene levels in the ambient outdoor air of communities located near drilling and fracking operations in rural western Colorado. For residents living close to wells, benzene levels were high enough, according to the authors, to create acute and chronic health effects.

49. Memo to the Pennsylvania Breast Cancer Coalition: it's been known for some time that benzene exposure causes leukemia and birth defects. As for a link between benzene and breast cancer, that possibility was affirmed by the Institute of Medicine in December 2011.

50. *If, having endured much, we have at last asserted our "right to know," and if, knowing, we have concluded that we are being asked to take senseless and frightening risks, then we should no longer accept the counsel of those who tell us that we must fill our world with poisonous chemicals; we should look about and see what other course is open to us.*

—Rachel Carson, *Silent Spring*

QUESTIONS FOR CONSIDERATION

1. What is the main point Steingraber hopes to communicate in this essay? Defend your answer.
2. Which of these writing purposes (to reflect, inform, analyze, evaluate, or persuade) best characterize Steingraber's goals?
3. How do Steingraber's writing decisions—which result in a unique style—help her achieve her purpose(s)? Explain.
4. Steingraber could have presented the ideas in this piece in a more commonplace, straightforward essay. If she had, do you think your response to the content would have been different? Explain your answer.
5. Environmental concerns often result in partisan politics. Which of the issues Steingraber presents do you think all people—regardless of political affiliation—might find concerning?

IDEAS FOR WRITING

A. **A Reflection Assignment.** Steingraber's unique style in this article sets it apart from ordinary prose and results in a more poetic, creative approach to communicating the importance of the topic. Select a topic that is important to you. Using Steingraber's essay as a model, reflect on the topic "in fifty parts" (or twenty parts, or thirty, or whatever works best for your topic).

B. **A Rhetorical Analysis Assignment.** Steingraber uses a variety of methods to subtly present an argument. What is her claim? How does she develop this claim? What are the reasons she presents? What rhetorical strategies help her write an argument that might affect readers' opinions on the topic she presents?

C. **A Researched Argument Assignment.** It is easy to criticize oil companies for fracking, but most people who criticize also use crude oil: they use the plastics created from oil, they drive cars and enjoy air travel, and they depend on the asphalt roads that make travel possible. The need for oil seems like it will not go away. We know, however, that crude oil is a fossil fuel, and as such, it is a limited resource. And we also know that, as Rachel Carson has shown, extracting oil comes at a price, a price that affects humans, animals, and the earth. Given this situation, how can we balance our need for oil with our concern for health and the environment? Write a source-based argument in which you argue your point of view on this topic.

Teaching Suggestion
Calma's point of view in this article and Basav Sen's point of view in the next article present a sharp contrast to that of Alex Epstein's in "The Moral Case for Fossil Fuels" (Chapter 13). Assignment ideas include a comparative analysis of the ideas in these articles or a comparison of rhetorical strategies.

Big Oil Touts Offshore Drilling Jobs to Communities Most Harmed by Oil

Justine Calma

Justine Calma reports on the environment for **The Verge**, *an online magazine covering technology and news. Calma's reporting has been published by a variety of news outlets, including NBC News, PBS News, and others, and her writing has been* *published in* Quartz, Wired, Huffington Post, Mother Jones, *and many other magazines. Born in the Philippines, Calma immigrated to the United States and is now based in New York City.*

Earlier this month, the American Petroleum Institute, the biggest U.S. trade organization for oil and gas, launched a bipartisan effort to reach out to diverse communities across the Southeastern U.S. The group touts offshore drilling jobs for African American and Latino workers.

"We want to build support in minority communities because the message that increasing the supply of affordable energy and good paying jobs will resonate," API's Erik Milito told Reuters.

While the oil and gas lobby is billing offshore drilling as an economic boon, environmental justice leaders caution that it's peddling dangerous work to the very communities that Big Oil has hurt the most.

"We used to call that economic extortion—in order to have a job you needed to be in a dirty job," says Jose Bravo, the executive director of the Just Transition Alliance. Bravo, who organizes for clean jobs in California, says he's seen decades of false promises by the fossil fuel industry.

Refineries located near neighborhoods of color often promise to hire locally, he says, but then bring on employees from out of town. And oil jobs can be risky.

"There's a lot of potential damage both to the planet and to health," Bravo says, citing the Deepwater Horizon explosion off the coast of Louisiana that killed 11 people in 2010. He also points out that the damage eventually makes its way back to land: "Historically, when we bring that oil onshore, we're bringing it into communities of color."

Last year, the NAACP published a report that found that over a million African Americans live within a half-mile of oil and natural gas production, processing, or transmission and storage facilities, leading to elevated risks of cancer and asthma attacks from toxic air emissions.

To be sure, many local business organizations have joined API's effort, including the Florida Black Chamber of Commerce, the South Carolina African American Chamber of Commerce, along with Hispanic chambers of commerce from Florida, North Carolina, and Virginia, among others.

Another touchy subject has been the oil lobby's outreach to Hurricane Maria survivors. Julio Fuentes, president of Florida's Hispanic Chamber of Commerce, a partner in API's initiative, defended the push to hire locals in an email to Grist. "Florida has welcomed many of our friends from Puerto Rico, and it is important to provide secure, high-paying jobs for our residents and evacuees," he said. "Offshore exploration is one way we can do so."

Michelle Suarez with Organize Florida, a grassroots nonprofit group that has been assisting hurricane survivors, sees how Big Oil can make an appealing offer to an evacuee who has just lost so much. "We're in this crisis. And so I imagine that it's going to be tempting for families that are impacted to get some of those jobs," Suarez says.

Suarez doesn't think working in Big Oil, with its links to climate change and more frequent and severe superstorms, is the answer to helping evacuees recover. "We're talking about the industry that has been one of the causes of these disasters, indirectly through their work," says Suarez.

Both Suarez and Bravo say that their communities don't need to choose between jobs and a healthy community and environment.

"We need to switch from that narrative because we do need to take care of the earth. This is our home. We have to make it work so that we have jobs that are not extracting and destroying the environment," Suarez says.

Bravo believes the U.S. can still be a global leader in spurring careers in renewable energy.

"We are all for jobs but we're for jobs that don't pollute, we're for jobs that are clean, we're for jobs that are sustainable," Bravo says.

QUESTIONS FOR CONSIDERATION

1. What is Calma's purpose: to inform or to persuade? Explain your answer and defend it by citing parts of the article as evidence.
2. What is the rhetorical effect of using the term "Big Oil"?
3. Why does Calma quote Julio Fuentes? How does her inclusion of Fuentes' ideas affect your understanding of Calma's writing purpose?
4. Why are some communities harmed more by oil than other communities? Explain.
5. What does Jose Bravo mean when he uses the term "economic extortion"? Explain your answer.

IDEAS FOR WRITING

A. **A Summary and Response Assignment.** Write a summary of Calma's article. Next, respond to the ideas she presents. Are the jobs in the oil industry worth the health hazards they pose?

B. **An Analysis Assignment.** Think about the "dirty jobs" in your city or in a city with which you are familiar. In what part of the city are the industries most likely to pollute the environment? What is the demographic composition of those areas? Would Calma's point—that dirty jobs are often located in areas where more people of color live—be true for the city you are analyzing? Write an analysis in which you explain whether there is a connection between industrial areas that are likely to pollute the environment and communities where people of color live.

C. **A Researched Argument Assignment.** Write an essay in which you argue whether the economic benefits of working for an oil refinery (or coal-burning power plant or any other industry known for pollution) are worth the health risks. Use research to support your claim.

Want to Create More Jobs? Reduce Fossil Fuel Use
Basav Sen

Basav Sen has served as the climate justice project director for the Institute for Policy Studies (IPS) as well as a long-time campaign researcher for the United Food and Commercial Workers union. He writes extensively for the IPS. His article "Want to Create More Jobs? Reduce Fossil Fuel Use" was published on Counterpunch *in August 2018.*

1   We've all heard claims that fossil fuels such as coal, oil, and gas are major job creators. President Trump says so all the time.

2   But it turns out that developing and installing the technology to *reduce* fossil fuel use—known in the industry as "energy efficiency"—creates many more jobs than fossil fuels.

3   Energy efficiency jobs in the United States totaled 2.18 million in 2016, more than double the total of fossil fuel production and fossil-fuel based electricity generation combined.

4   They're growing at a much faster rate, too. From 2015 to 2016, there was 53 percent employment growth in advanced and recycled building materials, and

59 percent employment growth in Energy Star appliances. Compare that to just 9 percent growth in fossil fuel-based electricity generation.

These energy efficiency jobs are much cheaper to create. According to an academic study, every $1 million invested in energy efficiency creates 12 jobs, compared to just 4 or 5 for fossil fuel jobs.

These are good, well-paying jobs. For example, electricians have a median hourly pay of $26, and the corresponding numbers for heating, ventilation, and air-conditioning (HVAC) workers and carpenters are $22.64 and $21.71, respectively. (Compare that to the median hourly pay for all U.S. workers, $18.12.)

These jobs are more likely to be unionized, too. And they're a great way to lift up people who've been left out of the fossil fuel economy.

So it's no wonder that many states are working to grow their share of efficiency jobs, especially for traditionally excluded populations such as people of color and low-income people. I looked at a bunch of inspiring examples in a new report for the Institute for Policy Studies that will be out this week.

For example, Illinois has passed legislation requiring larger utilities to create renewable energy and energy efficiency job training programs, especially for people from economically disadvantaged communities—including youth of color, formerly incarcerated people, individuals who've been in the foster care system as children, and others.

Oregon is another success story. Forty-seven percent of new jobs created through Oregon's statewide residential energy efficiency program—and 55 percent of the hours worked—went to women and people of color. Median hourly wages for these jobs were 7 percent higher than the median hourly wage of $17.24 for all Oregon workers, and 81 percent of workers had health benefits.

These successes didn't happen by themselves—they were the product of setting goals and making serious efforts to meet them.

So energy efficiency creates more jobs than fossil fuels—and at a faster rate and a lower cost.

They're good jobs, with good wages and above-average rates of unionization. And states have taken concrete measures to make these jobs accessible to everyone and raise standards for energy efficiency workers.

Why, then, does the federal government lag behind? And worse still, why does it pursue fantasies such as bringing back coal? Sadly, the answer is bribes, bribes, bribes.

Fossil fuel interests pour money into congressional and presidential campaigns, and politicians return the favor by doing their bidding. The Trump administration's push for coal is driven by two billionaire coal oligarchs, Robert Murray and Joseph Craft. Both have pumped money into Trump's campaign and openly advocate for deregulating fossil fuels and bailing out coal.

If the federal government really cared about "jobs, jobs, jobs," they would follow the lead of Illinois and Oregon and make a big push to subsidize energy efficiency—instead of bailing out coal.

QUESTIONS FOR CONSIDERATION

1. What is Sen's main point about fossil fuels?
2. What is the writer's attitude about unions? Explain your answer and use passages from the article as support.
3. What is the author's purpose in writing this piece?
4. Sen provides figures for median wages, both overall and for specific occupations. What is his purpose in providing these figures? What effects on readers might Sen be hoping for?
5. Sen uses the word "oligarch" to refer to two coal billionaires in the next to last paragraph. What rhetorical effect do you think he hopes to achieve by using this word?

IDEAS FOR WRITING

A. **A Reflection Assignment.** Think about the things you have heard in conversations with family and friends, or your own beliefs about government regulation of businesses. What assumptions do people have about government regulation? Are these the same assumptions Sen has? Are these assumptions justified? Write a paper in which you reflect on what the government's role should be in regulating businesses.

B. **An Evaluative Assignment.** Sen makes certain assumptions throughout his essay, such as the idea that the government should have a hand in regulating the energy industry. Reread the article and identify at least one other assumption that is included in his work, then evaluate the evidence that Sen provides to support that assumption.

C. **A Rhetorical Analysis Assignment.** Write a rhetorical analysis of the strategies Sen uses to attempt to convince the reader of his final claim that the federal government needs to change its policies toward fossil fuel and renewable energy.

Thais Rally in Bangkok for Global Climate Strike (Photograph)

Lauren DeCicca

Lauren DeCicca is a documentary photographer based in Thailand. DeCicca's work has been published in The New York Times, The Wall Street Journal, *and numerous other journals and newspapers.*

This photo was taken at a rally on September 20, 2019, in Bangkok, Thailand, and was organized by Climate Change Bangkok. At the rally, hundreds of demonstrators participated in a "die-in" by lying on the ground and demanding a response to the climate crisis from the government. Specifically, participants demanded that the Ministry of Natural Resources acknowledge the climate crisis and make efforts to address it, in part by eliminating coal emissions.

Lauren DeCicca/Getty Images

QUESTIONS FOR CONSIDERATION

1. What message does the photograph communicate?
2. Which details in the photo help to communicate a message?
3. Consider the text on the poster the young woman is holding. What is one of the rhetorical strategies used by the poster's creator?
4. What is the photographer's purpose in taking this photograph? Can you tell from the photograph itself? What is the young woman's purpose? Are their purposes the same? Explain your answer.
5. Do you think this photo is effective at raising awareness of the climate crisis? Why or why not?

IDEAS FOR WRITING

A. **An Informative Assignment.** What is the larger context of the photograph? In other words, what happened in Thailand to cause the rally? Is there an even broader context that helps to explain the subject of the photograph? Write an informative essay in which you present the background information readers would need in order to more fully understand the photograph.

B. **An Evaluative Assignment.** What qualities must a photograph have to make a political statement? Identify these qualities, and then select three to four photographs and evaluate how effectively they communicate a political opinion. Use the qualities you have identified to evaluate the photos you select.

C. **A Rhetorical Analysis Assignment.** Use the photograph above or find a different photograph that communicates a political message. Write a rhetorical analysis in which you explain the rhetorical strategies used to present a visual argument.

2 Animal Welfare

Teaching Suggestion
Pedersen demonstrates that argument need not only concern hot button issues. Consider having students critique Pedersen's treatment of the counterargument.

The Dog Delusion
April Pedersen

April Pedersen has written and illustrated several pamphlets and books as a freelance artist, including "May the Farce Be with You." Her article "The Dog Delusion" appeared in the November/December 2009 edition of The Humanist.

There was a time when "Dog is my co-pilot" was merely a fun slap at the "God is my co-pilot" bumper sticker, and it was funny precisely because nobody would ever think to elevate their dog to such a height. Within the past decade, however, pets—primarily dogs—have soared in importance. ("Dog is my co-pilot" is now the slogan of *Bark*, a magazine of dog culture, and the title of an anthology—published by *Bark*'s editors—billed as essays, short stories, and expert commentaries that explore "every aspect of our life with dogs.") Canines, with their pack instincts and trainability, are by far the most likely pet to be

1

anthropomorphized as a family member, a best friend, or a "fur baby," treated accordingly with gourmet meals, designer apparel, orthopedic beds, expensive therapy, and catered birthday parties. Some people even feel (and in some cases, demonstrate) that their dogs are worth dying for. Others say the animal lovers are going too far.

"OH, IT'S A HUMAN BABY."

Pedersen/The Humanist/American Humanist Association

In a Pew Research Center study, 85 percent of dog owners said they consider their pet to be a member of their family. However the latest trend is to take that a step further in seeing the animal as a child. A company that sells pet health insurance policies has dubbed the last Sunday in April as "Pet Parents Day." Glance through magazines like *Bark*, *Cesar's Way* (courtesy of "Dog Whisperer" Cesar Millan), and other mainstream publications, and the term "pet parent" crops up regularly. The "my-dogs-are-my-kids" crowd isn't being tongue-in-cheek, either. They act on their beliefs, buying Christmas presents, photos with Santa, cosmetic surgery, and whatever-it-takes medical care for their animal. In fact having a puppy, claimed one "mother," is "exactly the same in all ways as having a baby." And while pushing a dog around in a stroller would have gotten you directions to a mental health facility twenty years ago, today it's de rigeur to see a canine in a stroller (or a papoose), and some passersby are downright disappointed to discover a human infant inside.

Who's to say what a pet's value is (aside from the purchase price)? Shouldn't people be free to spend whatever they want on things for their dog? What real harm is there in believing one's schnauzer is a "child who never grows up?" The implications are more ridiculous and far reaching than you might expect. Take the widely held notion that dogs give us unconditional love and nonjudgmental loyalty. Praising dogs for being incapable of acting like bad people is not only junk logic, it turns the animal into an idealized (godlike?) version of ourselves, to be rewarded with all manner of pampering. How can the comparatively complex human being compete with creatures said to exude unwavering faithfulness, forgiveness, trust, love, and innocence? Pets are pegged as more loving, more pure, more giving, more devoted. They are implied to be our moral superiors for not stealing money, starting wars, or judging people by their physical appearance. They accept us for who we are, while we come across as scheming, judgmental malcontents who love on condition only. I have quite a collection of misanthropic utterances from dog lovers, most along the lines of "I'll take dogs over humans any day," and "dogs love without having an agenda!" It's no surprise that many dog lovers would rather be stranded on an island with a dog than with their spouse (or with any other person for that matter). Then there's the CEO who said he doesn't trust clients who don't have pets. How sadly similar to the religious who say they don't trust nonbelievers.

"WHEN WE DO BAD, PEOPLE BLAME THEMSELVES; WHEN WE DO GOOD, WE GET THE PRAISE — ARE WE GODS OR WHAT!"

Pedersen/The Humanist/American Humanist Association

Further undermining humans, dogs trained for various tasks are routinely referred to as soldiers, officers, actors, therapists, heroes, or athletes. But a police dog simply can't know the moral difference between a stash of cocaine and an old sock. One of the most absurd examples of anthropomorphism I've seen was a funeral for a drug-sniffing dog. The sheriff's department went all out with a motorcade, flag-draped casket, bag pipers playing "Amazing Grace," a eulogy from a pastor, and a rose-adorned easel on which the dog's portrait rested. Officers from all across the Western United States paid their respects, and the service received heavy local media coverage. All this for an animal that couldn't even grasp what a "law" was.

"Dogs are for people who can't have kids," a gay newspaper columnist told me recently. It's true that homosexual (and straight) couples who can't or don't want children of their own often migrate towards dogs as child substitutes and view the arrangement as a different kind of family, but a family nonetheless. Such dog-based "families" may at first blush seem benign or even beneficial. After all, people with a family mentality are more likely to form stable, safe neighborhoods and have a vested interest in the community. Those without children may benefit from nurturing a living creature and learning to be less self-centered. But doesn't it make more evolutionary sense to want to care for the young of your own species over another species? Couples without kids for whatever reason could still opt to be foster parents, mentors, or Big Brothers/Sisters to make a positive difference in a child's life instead of funneling all their concerns into dogs. And what about devoting one's time to saving endangered species of animals (whose survival also affects that of humans)?

Yet each day dogs gain more and more importance, protection, and access to realms once reserved for humans. Michigan is considering a bill that would allow pet care as a tax write-off. What's next? Dogs counted as residents in the U.S. Census?

This shift in the status of dogs hasn't gone unnoticed by animal rights advocates. Already thirteen U.S. cities have ordinances that ditch "pet owner" for "pet guardian." The change is intended to be merely symbolic, its fans claim. If so, why make the effort? I worry it's a foot in the door to gradually desensitize society to the outlandish idea of pets being the equals of minor children. Allowing ourselves to glance down the slippery slope, we might foresee absurd lawsuits over injuries to pets, murder charges for those suspected of negligence in a pet's death, and laws requiring guardians to strap their fur kids into car seats, or to walk them twice a day, or giving any number of rights to the animals. Recently dog owners have begun to demand off-leash beaches and trails, under the premise that dogs have a "right" to run free. What's next, making spaying or neutering a crime, because pets should have the right to reproduce? Or allowing dogs to bite people or chase livestock in order to fulfill their right to behave as predators? Where would the "pet" line for special status be drawn? At gerbils? Ferrets? Canaries? Hermit crabs? The funny part is, not even the pet industry can decide if pets are children or property. In ads hawking pet supplies, dogs and cats are promoted as family members, loved ones, and babies. Yet the defense strategy, if sued over, say tainted pet food or a defective squeaky toy, is to focus only on the economic aspect of the pet.

Viewing dogs as our children extends to risking life and limb to save them as well. What would evolutionary psychologists make of healthy people of reproductive age leaping to their deaths into scalding hot springs, icy rivers, or smoke-filled infernos in an attempt to rescue a possibly neutered animal? Among surveyed pet owners, 93 percent, which includes the young and childless, would do just that. Of course, most dog owners fully expect their pet to save them, Lassie style, should the need arise. But if not trained for rescue work, most dogs would simply stare, hide, or eat the contents of their owner's picnic basket as their master sinks under the lake's surface. Cases abound where pets happen to save people from perilous situations, but they, the pets, were acting as animals, not as humans.

8

Pedersen/The Humanist/American Humanist Association

One can always argue that, from an environmental perspective, the pets-as-kids thing makes sense. With the human population reaching unsustainable numbers, pets can fill our desire to nurture without adding to the surplus of humans. Even so, dogs still eat a lot and produce a lot of waste (which has to be cleaned up unless the status lift requires potty training). And don't forget that dogs have to come from somewhere, and parents will show preferences for certain breeds. Puppy mills would be happy to meet the increased demand for dogs, if it can be considered ethical in the best of circumstances to take puppies away from their mothers and litter mates and give them to another species to raise them. Interestingly, our popular pets such as the domestic dog play no balancing role in any ecosystem; they are human-developed and human-maintained. Even feral dogs prefer to hang around our villages, urban areas, and garbage dumps instead of returning to the woods to dance with wolves. And if too many people opted against having children in favor of pets, the result couldn't be good for economies; children are the future workforce, consumers, voters, tax payers, innovators, you name it.

Let's outsmart dogs a little by cutting back on the over-the-top stuff. The dogs won't notice. Funds spent on a dog's blueberry facial or in-room canine massage at a swanky hotel ($130 an hour) are about as close to setting a pile of cash on fire in front of a destitute person as I can imagine. Ditto on buying a sweater for an animal covered in fur, or a carob-coated eclair for a scat eater, or personalized cookies for the species that can't read (that would be all species except us). Certainly dogs can't visualize themselves as Homo sapiens of any age, and are becoming obese and even ill-mannered at the hands of their besotted owners. It makes no sense whatsoever to pour so much time, money, and emotion into an animal whose main "goal" in life is to leave its scent on a tree. Think about it—how would you like to be a dog? To be unable to talk, write, or question. To look upon a masterpiece of art without an ounce of admiration, to gaze at the starry night without an iota of wonder, to see a book and have not the slightest inclination to open it, or stare without comprehension at a voting booth.

It's fine to enjoy a pet. I've had several myself, including a cat that lived eighteen years. When his kidneys failed, a $12,000 kidney transplant was off the radar (a case can be made that such surgery on an animal is unethical anyway), and I didn't consider him to be my son. This need not diminish pets. We can enjoy them for what they are, without the anthropomorphic delusion.

QUESTIONS FOR CONSIDERATION

1. Pedersen makes several minor points throughout her essay, all of which support one overarching claim. What is this claim, and in what one or two sentences is it most clearly stated?

2. Sarcasm plays a large role in this essay, with many paragraphs being almost entirely facetious or flippant. Does her use of humor affect your ability to follow her points or take seriously the argument she is making? How do the cartoons in the article contribute to the sarcasm in the article?

3. Think about your own experience with pets. What are the parallels, if any, between the behaviors Pedersen is arguing against and your own relationship with animals?

4. What do you make of Pedersen's claim that we are on a "slippery slope" to "pets being the equals of minor children"? Is she on a slippery slope herself, or does the evidence she provides support her point well enough to be believed?

5. Pedersen makes a broad comparison at the end of paragraph 3. Is it fair to equate people who say they trust their pets more than other people to religious believers who say they don't trust nonbelievers? Why or why not? How might this comparison affect readers?

IDEAS FOR WRITING

A. **A Summary and Response Assignment:** Using media forms such as memes, tweets, or other types of nontraditional language, summarize Pedersen's claims. These can be original or the work of others. Then respond to each of them, either from the pet owners' or the animals' points of view. Be sure to provide bibliographic information for any sources you use.

B. **A Reflection Assignment:** Almost everyone has had some experience with pets, whether they own or owned them themselves or had friends who had pets. Even people who never had pets probably have strong feelings about them, one way or the other. Write an essay in which you reflect on the role of pets in your life or the lives of others around you.

C. **A Persuasive Assignment:** Pick any "pet peeve" topic about which you feel strongly, in the same way that Pedersen clearly feels strongly about dog ownership. Write an essay using sarcasm in which you persuade readers that you are right to be bothered by the "pet peeve" you have chosen.

Teaching Suggestion
In this long article, Heinlein chronicles her thinking about how we treat animals. Her deliberative, first-person style may cause some students not to see that she is writing an argument. Consider having students analyze the ways in which Heinlein's writing has a persuasive focus.

The Cruelty of Kindness
Sabine Heinlein

Sabine Heinlein is the author of the nonfiction book Among Murderers: Life After Prison *and the recipient of many awards, such as a Pushcart Prize and a Margolis*

Award. Over a long career she has published in many journals and forums, including The New York Times, The Guardian, Longreads, *and* Die Zeit. *Her article "The Cruelty of Kindness" was published in* Aeon *in March 2016.*

In March 2013, my husband and I were on our way to a museum when we saw a sign advertising an adoption event at the Petco pet store on the Upper West Side in New York City.

"Should we adopt another cat?" my husband asked. We'd got our scaredy-cat Gilbert from the American Society for the Prevention of Cruelty to Animals (ASPCA) the year before: he was sweet and funny but so neurotic that we considered calling him Woody; a vet had suggested that a friend might ease his problems.

At Petco we were approached by Gisella McSweeny, the founder of Zani's Furry Friends, one of more than 150 rescue organizations that partner with the Mayor's Alliance for New York City's Animals, whose mission is to save as many animals as possible from the city-run Animal Care and Control of NYC (AC&C). Since 2003, the Alliance and its partners have held regular adoption events with cute monikers such as "Whiskers in Wonderland" and "Adoptapalooza" at Petcos across town.

When we told McSweeny about our Gilbert, she quickly led us to a cage housing two cats that were grooming each other. One was a fancy Maine Coon; the other, a grey-and-white, McSweeny assured us, was our cat. She rattled off his sad story: Zani's had pulled him and his brother from the city-run shelter and put them in one of their privately run foster homes. While the brother was adopted, this one was left behind. After McSweeny discovered that the foster "mom" was hoarding animals, she transferred him to a second foster mom. The cat was healthy and equipped with a microchip, a rice seed-sized tracking device implanted under the skin to identify animals. There was no need to check references or conduct a home visit, McSweeny said; the adoption fee for the two-year-old was only $125, a special deal.

On the way home, I mentioned to my husband that our new cat looked like a barn cat. "Why not name him Barnaby?" he suggested.

Barnaby was large and boney; he weighed only seven pounds. I noticed he smelled funny. He didn't seem scared of us, just indifferent.

It was clear from the start that something was seriously wrong with Barnaby. He sneezed, his eyes were runny, and his ears oozed a gooey brown substance.

His gums were bright red, he often had bloody diarrhea, and he threw up several times a week. A blood test revealed a severe Bartonella infection, more commonly known as cat-scratch fever because that's how it can be spread to humans.

Then, on one of multiple vet visits we learned that Barnaby hadn't been microchipped as McSweeny had told us. My husband and I emailed her and the AC&C, mentioning the missing chip. By email, a Jessica Van Brunt responded: "Kitten didn't get a microchp [sic]." I complained to the three people cc'ed on that email, adding that Barnaby also came with an eye infection, but I never received a response.

In a few months, we had spent around $1,500 on tests, dewormers, antibiotics and dental care for our rescue cat. But we still hadn't resolved his gastrointestinal issues or gotten him chipped.

Our experience was not unusual. Today, thanks to the animal rights movement launched in the 19th century and the no-kill movement of today, slightly more people adopt their cats and dogs from animal shelters and rescues than buy from breeders. With more and more shelters pressured to keep animals alive regardless of the circumstances, an estimated 10,000 private rescue groups pull animals from "high kill" city-run shelters and transfer them to private, supposedly temporary "no-kill" foster homes for a savior rate that the Humane Society estimates to be as high as 90 per cent. No-kill isn't necessarily zero-kill, but that's what its advocates aspire to.

No-kill advocates consider the killing of animals to combat overcrowding in shelters offensive and heartless. And sure enough, the "Adopt, Don't Shop" brand was originally based on a wholesome and noble sentiment. But with little to no oversight, it fosters an underbelly that has left the no-kill movement in crisis. The promise of life often leaves cats or dogs languishing in cages or transferred from foster home to foster home for years. Animals are given out sick, with minimal to no prior medical care. While numbers are still hard to come by, hardly a day goes by when a rescue or foster home isn't exposed for overcrowding, neglect or, notably, hoarding.

While we dress our pets in matching pajamas, saving, coddling and healing them, our ever-growing empathy for the furry has led us off the rails. As consumers, we are complicit in creating an inhumane and dangerous situation that leaves animals in pain, shelter staff overwhelmed, and pet owners burdened with

On Friday, December 19, 2014, approximately sixty dogs and other animals were rescued from atrocious conditions in Sequatchie County, Tennessee.
Kathy Milani/For The HSUS

unprecedented levels of financial and emotional stress. Struggling with Barnaby's illnesses, I couldn't help wondering who was benefitting from this tragic situation, and who was suffering the most?

I come from a different world. My two sisters and I grew up in the Bavarian countryside. Each fall, when the river by our house flooded the fields, we blew up our little inflatable boat and paddled out to rescue mice, rabbits and hedgehogs. The ones who survived were released back into the wild the following spring. Each kid had her own little menagerie. We had bunnies, a cat, a dog, lizards, and for a while my middle sister hid two pet rats in her room. I remember being praised by our country vet after I nursed a rabbit with a broken foot back to health. The foot, wrapped in gauze, needed to be soaked regularly for several weeks, a duty I took very seriously.

But there was more than rescuing animals in distress. My father is a hunter and he did not hide from us the deer he shot. He explained why he had killed it: the deer had lost its natural enemies, wolves and bears, and was now destroying the forest. We knew that what we had seen in the back of his truck would end up on the dinner table. One time, when a litter of bunnies developed seizures and we couldn't reach the vet, my father killed the babies with an iron rod right in front of us. I was horrified then—and still am today, as one should be when looking death in the eye—but I also understood his lesson: if death was inflicted fast and without suffering, it was nothing to be afraid of. Rescuing and killing were not mutually exclusive. It was the years we lived that counted, not the final two or three minutes before we expired.

Yet for centuries now, modernity, agriculture and the advance of industry have been turning that old world on its head. The British historian Keith Thomas described our increasing estrangement from nature and the longing it instilled in *Man and the Natural World* (1983):

The progress of cultivation had fostered a taste for weeds, mountains and unsubdued nature. The new-found security from wild animals had generated an increasing concern to protect birds and preserve wild creatures in their natural state. . . .

As time passed, more people promoted pets to family members. And by the mid-19th century, many began to see cats and dogs as sentient beings similar to humans, setting the stage for the newfangled concept of animal rights. Then, in 1866, the New York City philanthropist Henry Bergh founded the ASPCA to demand that animals receive kind and respectful protection under the law.

The changes worked their way through society slowly, and were felt more in some places than others. There was a time when, even within current memory, animals weren't kept solely for sentimental reasons, when they were eaten or used for work—or both. Dogs herded cattle, hunted fox and guarded the house; cats kept the grain free from rodents and the lap warm in the winter. A mix of utilitarian and sentimental attitudes can still be found in some cultures. On a recent trip to Peru, I noticed the prevalence of dogs on the streets. The dogs didn't seem to belong to anyone in particular, but most of them appeared clean and well-fed. "We keep them like this," said my cab driver, "because in the winter old people take the dogs to bed with them. Dogs are very good against arthritis pain. In Peru we say, treat your dogs like your children."

Yet by the time I found my way to Barnaby, the world of my childhood had been swept away. To understand how the US took the final step from protecting pets to becoming an aspiring no-kill nation, I spoke to Rich Avanzino, often referred to as the father of the no-kill movement and until quite recently, president of Maddie's Fund, America's most powerful no-kill organization.

Avanzino's story starts in 1976, when he took over San Francisco's city shelter. Chatty and personable, now in his 70s, Avanzino remembers how hundreds of pets each day were loaded into the Euthanair machine and killed through oxygen deprivation: "[Dead] animals were put in barrels. It was a very disconnected way of dealing with a species that is near and dear and precious."

Avanzino got rid of the killing machine on his third day at the shelter. Death suddenly became a more personal, intimate and painful experience for shelter staff, who now had to hold the individual animal and insert a needle intravenously to kill her with an overdose of anaesthetic.

In his fourth year at the San Francisco shelter, a little dog named Sido entered Avanzino's life. Sido's caregiver had died, leaving a will requesting that the dog be euthanized and buried beside her. "We wouldn't let the executor carry out her will," said Avanzino, who won the first animal-rights case in the state with a ruling that dogs are not property but sentient beings.

In saving Sido, Avanzino ignited an unprecedented movement that swept across the country. Admirably, millions of homeless cats and dogs have found homes.

Yet Avanzino's no-kill revolution has also caused a split that has left animal welfare groups sharply divided over one fundamental question: is each and every life worth saving, no matter its quality, or is it better to euthanize a large number of animals, sparing them the possibility of a life spent in a cage or an overcrowded foster home? No-kill advocates staunchly believe the former.

Avanzino thinks that the US is less than a year away from becoming a no-kill nation. His math goes like this: 29 million people will be adding a pet to their family this year; fewer than 2.4 million healthy and treatable dogs and cats will be killed this year. We just need to convince 2.4 million of those 29 million people to go to a rescue or shelter and take home an animal and we can stop the killing.

Avanzino added that even if the shelter "has horrible customer service, is in bad shape, is noisy and smelly and unattractive—go save a life because, in doing that, you are going to stop the killing of our family members on four legs. The message should be, it doesn't matter how good or bad the organization is, take a pet home, save a life. We do not kill family members," he added firmly. Then he drew what he believes to be an instructive parallel: "When we talk about homeless people, their life is less than perfect, but just because they are homeless we don't round them up and put them down. When we hear of foster homes that have been abusive to children, we don't take the child away and kill it."

After speaking to Avanzino, I contacted the Mayor's Alliance for New York City Animals, the umbrella non-profit that helps bridge the AC&C with rescues such as Zani's. Jane Hoffman, the Alliance's president, told me that to become an Alliance partner a shelter must sign a contract promising to follow certain rules. The contract states, among other things, that an Alliance partner can lose his or her privileges if an animal's care is compromised or if he or she engages in animal cruelty or hoarding.

Ensuring that members of the Alliance and other, similar umbrella groups can save and distribute pets nationwide is Maddie's Fund. Between 2005 and 2011, the Alliance received $26 million from Maddie's Fund. Part of the grant money was used for marketing, but part went to the rescue groups, which received between $500 and $2,000 for each animal adopted out, depending on age and health status.

When I asked whether the Alliance monitors the foster homes of its rescue organizations, Hoffman said: "You know what Ronald Reagan said about Russia? 'Trust but verify.' That's the motto. You can't work with partners unless you have a certain level of trust. If we hear a complaint we of course look into it." When I asked more directly whether there have been problems with overcrowding, Hoffman responded: "You seem a little focused on this issue. People have big hearts and sometimes they take on more than they can handle."

Who, if not cats like Barnaby, benefits from the money rescues receive from Maddie's Fund? If there is no independent entity to check on whether the cats are properly cared for, does that encourage, or at least permit, abuse?

31 Around the same time we adopted Barnaby, Hannah, an acquaintance, rescued a scruffy, black terrier from Heavenly Angels Animal Rescue, a non-profit in Queens, New York. Hannah said Pepper was one of countless dogs in a room "that smelled intensely." She saw carriers and wire crates stacked up to the ceiling, and wanted to get Pepper out as quickly as possible. Because the rescuer refused to take a check or credit card, Hannah paid cash. Pepper not only suffered from heartworm, which cost Hannah more than $1,000; he also bit her mother in the face, and her boss's husband, drawing blood and sending him to the ER. "If we hadn't been friends with my boss, I am sure he would have sued us," Hannah said. Essentially, Hannah had three choices: having Pepper euthanized, returning him into the shelter system, or hiring a dog trainer. Hannah went with the trainer.

32 I, for my part, could not *not* hear Barnaby's suffering. I could make out his stomach's gurgling from across the room. Sometimes, when we picked him up after breakfast, he struggled to keep in his food. While the antibiotics improved his Bartonella infection, his gastrointestinal symptoms continued unabated. One day while researching his condition, I learned about Tritrichomonas foetus, a parasite that is not well-known because it remains undetected in regular stool tests and fails to respond to regular dewormers.

33 A study that examined gastrointestinal illnesses in cats kept in hoarding situations found that roughly 40 percent were infected with T foetus, 88 percent with the coronavirus, and 49 percent with Clostridium. Barnaby's PCR test for DNA evidence of the infections came back positive for all of them; symptom-free Gilbert also carried T foetus, and needed treatment too.

34 After another $1,000 for tests and treatment, Barnaby was finally symptom-free. We had now spent $2,500 on our rescue cat.

35 Barnaby's and Pepper's stories of disease and neglect from hoarding are hardly isolated. The week of 25 March 2015 was typical: nearly 100 dogs were seized from the no-kill shelter Dogs Deserve Life Rescue in Jacksonville, Florida. The same day, Carol Merchant and Russell Goodell, the owners of the Vermont rescue known as Pink Palace, were arrested and charged with multiple counts of animal cruelty. Authorities found the house filled with clutter and feces. Later, authorities cited Benny Terry, an operations manager at a Georgia Humane Society, on 57 counts of cruelty to animals; Terry had about five-dozen dogs and cats at his

home living in "unacceptable" conditions. In February 2016, the ASPCA pulled a record number of 700 neglected and sick animals from an unlicensed rescue in North Carolina. And while there are no definite numbers on animal hoarding cases nationwide, veterinarian Gary Patronek and sociologist Arnold Arluke, both from the Hoarding of Animals Research Consortium at Tufts University in Massachusetts, estimate a minimum of 5,100 such cases affecting perhaps a quarter of a million animals annually.

Animal-hoarding experts distinguish between the overwhelmed caregiver, the rescuer hoarder, and the exploiter hoarder. The overwhelmed caregiver initially provides adequate care for her animals but later loses control of the situation due to financial or medical difficulties. The rescuer hoarder, who works within the network of animal welfare people, has a compulsive need to rescue animals from euthanasia, believing that she is the only one who can adequately care for them. Often the line between these two categories is blurry. And there are times when those in a malevolent third category, the narcissistic and manipulative exploiter hoarder who runs a moneymaking enterprise to serve her own needs, can blend in as well. Regardless of category, the typical hoarder is a woman in her 50s, socially isolated and raised in a difficult and chaotic home environment filled with loss; often, her earliest attachment was with animals, not people.

"Generally speaking, it's people who don't find human relationships very reliable," said Christiana Bratiotis, a private clinician and researcher at the University of Nebraska. With her colleague Catherine Ayers of the University of California, San Diego, Bratiotis is conducting the first-ever neurocognitive study on animal hoarders. "It is not uncommon to hear people who hoard animals say that the animals don't let them down in the same way that human beings might," she adds.

Research about what instigates an individual's hoarding behavior is just beginning, but what's clear is that hoarders would never be able to inflict such massive harm alone. "Within the rescue community, there is a whole underground network where people know who to call so that animals aren't taken to a shelter where their lives may be threatened. Rescuers know other rescuers in communities across the nation," Bratiotis says.

One of the most outspoken organizations against the pitfalls of the no-kill movement is People for the Ethical Treatment of Animals (PETA). A leader of the animal-rights movement, PETA provides no-cost spay and neuter services, and fights testing on animals, as well as the use of animals in entertainment.

"It's like a religion, to kill or not to kill," PETA's president Ingrid Newkirk told me. She explained that many owners in Virginia, where PETA's headquarters are located, can't afford a hefty euthanasia bill. In a sea of no-kill shelters that turn people down, PETA will euthanize your pet for free. But this policy outrages its opponents. "We get threats of physical violence, we get animal organs sent to us in the mail. We got a deer head thrown on our front parking lot, all sorts of nastiness."

Why would someone who hates euthanasia throw deer heads? Newkirk has a theory. "The no-kill movement is linked to the meat industry," she explained, referring to the Center for Consumer Freedom, a right-wing non-profit that started the website petakillsanimals.org, and is supported by major US meat producers such as Cargill and Tyson Foods, as well as the Ringling Brothers circus, and the tobacco and fast-food industries. To Newkirk, the hypocrisy behind the Center for Consumer Freedom's attacks is obvious: Tyson and Cargill contribute an enormous amount of meat to the pet-food industry; they both also offer their own pet product lines. Never before have Americans owned so many carnivores; the pet industry has tripled in the past two decades, and it is estimated that Americans now spend more than $23 billion a year to feed their pets.

"Are they no-kill of cats or just no-kill?" Newkirk asked. "What do they think is humane?"

Gilbert and Barnaby are a happy couple. Barnaby turned out to be an exceptionally smart and sweet cat who accepted neurotic Gilbert without any problems—and Gilbert started to come around, too. He became more confident and independent, playfully chasing and grooming Barnaby and cuddling up to him on the couch. Barnaby spends hours running up and down the stairs playing fetch and, after a few months with us, he took on a little morning routine: lying beside us on the couch and turning on his back to have his belly stroked.

I wondered what would have happened had we not had the money to pay for Barnaby's medical care. What if he had been adopted by someone less fortunate? Would he have been returned to the rescue and transferred to yet another foster home? Would he have been dropped off at the city shelter and put to sleep? Or, left untreated, would his illness have caused a slow and painful death?

I also wonder whether our endless trips to the vet, all that probing, cutting and being poked with needles, was really worse than euthanasia could have ever been. Perhaps our focus on keeping pets alive, no matter the consequences, is really more about us humans than about a desire to spare animals suffering.

QUESTIONS FOR CONSIDERATION

1. Heinlein raises several issues in this article. What is her main point?
2. Heinlein uses her personal experiences to support her main idea. What rhetorical effect does her choice to use her personal experiences have on the persuasiveness of the article?
3. Around paragraph 20, Heinlein refers to a conversation she had with Rich Avanzino. Avanzino makes several analogies. How strong—or weak—are Avanzino's analogies? What might be Heinlein's purpose in including these quotes from Avanzino?
4. What rhetorical effects are produced by including the photo that accompanies the article?
5. What is your position on pet euthanasia? Given the information you have learned in this article, has your position on pet euthanasia changed?

IDEAS FOR WRITING

A. **An Informative Essay.** How are stray animals treated in your city? Are there competing interests—such as no kill shelters and shelters that euthanize—at play in your community? Write an essay in which you present your community's options for handling stray pets. Write for readers who need this information to make a decision about their own pets.

B. **A Rhetorical Analysis.** What rhetorical strategies does Heinlein use to support her point? Write a rhetorical analysis in which you discuss at least four rhetorical strategies Heinlein uses. Include in your analysis an evaluation of their effectiveness.

C. **A Researched Argument Assignment.** Select one of the following questions and write a research-based argument in which you support your point of view.

- Are animals sentient beings?
- Is the no-kill movement the most humane way to deal with unwanted pets?
- What should be done to mitigate the damage caused by hoarders who shelter pets for their own economic advantage?

How Zoos Help Preserve the World's Species for the Future

Liz Sanchez

When she wrote this article in 2019, Liz Sanchez was staff writer for the annual Mosaic Journalism Workshop, an event organized for high school students in the San Francisco Bay Area. The workshop is sponsored by San Jose State University's journalism department and allows high school students to report on real stories and to have their work published.

Zoos around the United States draw millions of people every year, who come to see and learn about exotic animals like giraffes, elephants, lemurs and jaguars. And while animal rights organizations are critical of the treatment of animals in zoos, professionals who work with those animals have a different point of view.

Two zoos in the Bay Area make efforts to provide their animals with extra care and even work to save endangered species.

The Oakland Zoo, which opened in 1922, has more than 750 animals, including four elephants and at least two giraffes. It's been accredited by the Association of Zoos and Aquariums since 1988. Oakland Zoo President and CEO Joel Parrott said the zoo monitors the behavior of its animals and provides "enrichment" for animals like elephants to provide them with exercise and keep them interested in their day.

"We give them good food, toys to play with, games to play, a swimming pool and mud baths," he said.

Another Oakland Zoo resident, a reticulated giraffe named Benghazi, was an artist, creating paintings with a brush he held in his mouth. But the last of his paintings was auctioned on June 15—World Giraffe Day—following Benghazi's death in May. The giraffe was euthanized at the zoo after his quality of life declined because of lower back injuries. The average lifespan of a giraffe in the wild is around 25 years, and he was 23.

Benghazi's death could be seen as supporting the position of animal rights organizations like People for the Ethical Treatment of Animals (PETA), which says living in any zoo can be harmful for animals. According to a PETA issues statement, "Even the best artificial environments can't come close to matching the space, diversity, and freedom that animals want and need." Instead, PETA recommends people skip the zoos and instead help rescue operations associated with the Global Federation of Animal Sanctuaries, a non-profit group that provides certification for animal sanctuaries.

However, many zoos, including Happy Hollow Park and Zoo in San Jose and the Oakland Zoo, also lend a hand in saving endangered animals. They do this through their own conservation programs and being involved with others like the Species Survival Plan, started by the Association of Zoos and Aquariums in 1981, or the U.S. Fish and Wildlife Service's California Condor Reintroduction Program. They also work with other institutions to save these animals.

"Twenty-five percent of the approximated amount of animals we have here are a part of the SSP (Species Survival Program), so we, a credible zoo, reach out to an animal coordinator to get another mate for an animal to repopulate our endangered species," said Kevin Hertell, zoo manager at Happy Hollow Park, which houses two jaguars, a red panda, lemurs, meerkats and an American alligator.

Parrott cited the Oakland Zoo's work with California condors as one of the ways it supports endangered species.

"We worked with the Cal Condor Reintroduction Program and at one point, the Condor species population was down to 22 left—and after 30 years, we helped bring the population up to 400," he said.

And while these conservation efforts are important to the zoo, it is facing a battle against natural forces. The planet is experiencing the sixth mass extinction, a process that has been going on for thousands of years and is believed to be caused by human activity and climate change. At least 75% of species are expected to become extinct within a geologically short amount of time. Hertell said this has had a big impact on how people look at animals, too.

"Zoos are not what they used to be," he said. "We are much more conservation-minded. I believe this sixth mass extinction has affected not just zoos, but the broader community as well, which is why we teach and mentor kids of the future to make a difference."

QUESTIONS FOR CONSIDERATION

1. Why does Sanchez believe zoos are beneficial?
2. Does Sanchez show that she fully understands the arguments of those who are opposed to zoos? Explain your answer. If necessary, do some research to learn what the counterarguments are.
3. What point does Sanchez make by telling the story of Benghazi?
4. Do you find Sanchez's article convincing? Why or why not?
5. Why do many people believe the survival of species is important? If necessary, do some research.

IDEAS FOR WRITING

A. An Informative Assignment. Sanchez writes, "At least 75% of species are expected to become extinct within a geologically short amount of time." Is this true? If so, why? Write an informative essay in which you discuss what scientists have to say about the state of endangered species.

B. An Evaluative Assignment. Sanchez and others believe that zoos provide essential services in helping to preserve species. But not all zoos are equally diligent in their efforts to provide for the animals they keep or in their preservation attempts. How are zoos evaluated? In other words, what differentiates a good zoo from one that should be shut down? Identify the criteria used to evaluate the quality of zoos, and then select a zoo in your city or a nearby city. Using the criteria you have identified, evaluate the zoo and write an evaluative essay to share your assessment.

C. A Researched Argument Assignment. Write an argument in which you answer this question: Do zoos do more harm than good? Use research to support your claim. Write for a mixed, general audience, and include rebuttals for the strongest counterarguments.

South Africans Protest against Rhino Poaching (Photograph)

This photograph was taken in Cape Town, South Africa, where activists from OSCAP—Outraged South African Citizens Against Poaching—gathered to protest the poaching of rhinos.

Teaching Suggestion Consider having students compare this photograph to "Thais Rally in Bangkok for Global Climate Strike" (Photograph), earlier in this anthology. Analyzing these images can lead to a discussion of protest rhetoric.

Gallo Images/Getty Images

QUESTIONS FOR CONSIDERATION

1. Which detail in the photo do you find most powerful or thought-provoking?
2. What impression do the activists hope to create? How do these impressions support the text in the ad?
3. Why do you think there are chalk lines drawn around the activists?
4. How does the use of color help the activists convey their message?
5. If you were going to communicate the idea that poaching is unethical and must stop, what method might you use other than a protest? Explain how this method might be effective.

IDEAS FOR WRITING

A. **A Reflective Assignment.** The protesters in the photo obviously have strong feelings about the issue of poaching. Think of an issue that would motivate you to participate in a rally or public protest. Why is the issue so important to you? What factors in your life influenced the way you feel about the issue? Write a reflective essay about the issue and how it has affected you personally.

B. **An Informative Assignment.** What is the larger context of the photograph? Was there a trigger event that caused activists to protest? What broader context might help explain the photograph? Write an informative essay in which you present the background information readers would need in order to more fully understand the photograph.

C. **A Rhetorical Analysis Assignment.** The activists pictured in the photo are participating in a rhetorical act: an attempt to persuade onlookers that rhino poaching is unethical. What rhetorical strategies do they use in this attempt? Write a rhetorical analysis based on the photo.

3 Diversity

Teaching Suggestion
Moore presents a definition of a "just city." Consider having students analyze Moore's use of definition as a foundation for his argument.

Urban Spaces and the Mattering of Black Lives
Darnell L. Moore

Darnell L. Moore is writer-in-residence at the Center on African American Religion, Sexual Politics and Social Justice at Columbia University. He serves as senior editor for Mic, *a news and media company, and he is a co-managing editor of* The Feminist Wire, *a news outlet with a mission "to provide socio-political and cultural critique of anti-feminist, racist, and imperialist politics pervasive in all forms and spaces of private and public lives of individuals globally." Moore's article was published on the website of The Nature of Cities, an "idea hive" focused on creating cities that are "better for both people and nature."*

It was close to midnight. A youngish, jovial-looking white woman with russet colored hair ran by me with ostensive ease. She donned earphones and dark, body-fitting jogging attire. I was walking home from the A train stop and along Lewis Avenue, which is a moderately busy thoroughfare that runs through the Bedford-Stuyvesant neighborhood in central Brooklyn, where I live.

Lewis runs parallel to Marcus Garvey. Black. Two avenues to the right is Malcolm X Boulevard. It's Black. Fulton Street. Atlantic Avenue. The B15 bus. Bedford Avenue. Marcy Projects. Brownstoners. The C train. Working class renters. Peaches Restaurant. June Jordan. Livery taxis. Restoration Plaza. Jay-Z. Bed-Stuy is quite black. I am, too.

Encountering the strange sight of a white woman running without care on a street in a section of our borough once considered an unredeemable "hood" terrified me. She ran past the new eateries and grocery shops that sell organic and specialty foods. Within a span of a few blocks, residents and visitors now have their choice of premium Mexican eats, brick oven pizza or freshly baked scones with artisan coffee. Citi Bike racks and skateboard riding hipsters adorn the now buzzing thoroughfare. To many, our part of Bed-Stuy may appear safer, cleaner, and whiter.

And, yet, I was still terrified. It was midnight. Black boys and men have been killed throughout the history of the U.S. for being less close to and observant of white women's bodies as I was that late evening.

Shortly after I passed by with the white woman jogger, my close friend, Marcus, who lives in walking distance from me—closer to a densely populated public housing development—lamented about the lingering tremors of gentrification. Citing the presumed changes in racial demographics, renovated housing options, and increased business development efforts, Marcus hinted at the frustration of black communities undergoing rapid and contested transformation.

He came upon a flier that was fastened to a tree. According to Marcus, the New York Police Department (NYPD) precinct near his building created a "wanted" sign that was posted not too far from where he lived. The "wanted" were a few black men who allegedly robbed a neighbor. The neighbor was white.

Never before, in the several years Marcus had lived in Bed-Stuy, had he seen anything similar. There were no signs made after black teens were shot or robbed. There were no cries for the "wanted" after black women and girls were sexually assaulted or followed home by a predator. There was no indication of concern for black people besides the ever-present anxiety black bodies seem to cause both to the state and to white people when they dwell en masse in the hood. A cursory review of NYPD's data on the disproportionate and deleterious impact of stop, question and frisk procedures and broken windows policing on black communities is but one example. Marcus's critique resonated because it illuminated the ways the state and its citizenry afford value to white lives.

Hence, the reason for selecting the vignettes I've opened with here. In both scenes, white bodies signify worth and, therefore, are always centered in our collective imagination. They are esteemed commodities, especially in black spaces—that is, neighborhoods and other publics mostly inhabited and culturally shaped by a majority black populace. Thus, any dreamed and invented "just city" that is structured by a set of race ideologies that do not factor in the hyper-mattering of white lives and the perceived worthlessness of black and brown lives is not "just" at all. That is why catch phrases like "community development" or "urban planning and design" can be counterproductive if, in fact, one's praxis is not guided by a commitment to a type of transformative work grounded in the belief that black lives actually matter.

The connection between space and race became clearer to me after visiting Ferguson, MO, shortly after 18-year-old Mike Brown, Jr. was fatally shot by police officer Darren Wilson. Standing in the same street where Brown's bloodied body had been left uncovered for four hours—in view of his family and neighbors—forced me to question the extent to which ideas about race and space collude to create precarious lives for black and brown people. In an essay titled "The Price of Blackness: From Ferguson to Bed-Stuy" originally published at The Feminist

Wire shortly after my return, I wrote, "Changes in the racial composition of towns precipitate changes in the ways black bodies are policed and valued in many neighborhoods."

I was drawn to the horrific events unfolding in Ferguson because it occurred to me that Ferguson—like some neighborhoods in New York City, Chicago, Oakland and elsewhere—have not only experienced shifts in its racial composition, but also have undergone changes in government leadership, laws, policing practices and economics that inevitably impact black and poor people.

Mike Brown's death was a unique tragedy that occurred within a specific place and time, but the conditions within which it took place are mundane and, seemingly, quintessential characteristics of gentrified black spaces. This led me to postulate, "Black lives and white lives are differently valued and are, therefore, differently impacted under the conditions of white racial supremacy across the country." Thus, beyond the noticeable changes—such as the movement of more white people into otherwise black neighborhoods—the insidious aspect of gentrification is the seeming logic of white significance and black worthlessness that underwrites the process.

"My brief time in Ferguson prompted me to consider the many ways Mike Brown's death, and life, was warped by the structural conditions mentioned above—all emanating from what scholar George Lipsitz aptly calls the 'possessive investment in whiteness,'" I concluded upon my return from Ferguson. "Such investments in whiteness, which impact everything from access to housing markets to points of educational access for black people across the country, must also be considered alongside the mundane incidents of police violence and hyper criminalization in the U.S."

But police violence is one lens through which we can assess the connection between race and space, whether in Ferguson or Brooklyn. 16-year-old Kimani Gray was shot and killed by a member of the NYPD in the Flatbush neighborhood of Brooklyn in March 2013. Flatbush is not too far from Bed-Stuy. Like Bed-Stuy, it is a neighborhood that has experienced an increase in its white populace. While some may argue that the increased number of white people in black spaces is the singular problem, I contend the public should be concerned with the problematic ways whiteness functions as a signifier. As I've written elsewhere:

The more insidious problem is the belief that whiteness at all times and in all places signifies safety and bounty and, therefore, represents a site of investment: new stores selling expensive items begin emerging; the same stores stay open (the doors and not just side windows) twenty-four hours; realtors finally begin to take an interest in property sales; nameless and faceless 'investors' begin leaving cheap flyers on stoops or in mailboxes promising cash for homes. Safety becomes a relative experience when gentrification occurs. The presence of white people almost always guarantees the increased presence of resources, like police, which does not always guarantee safety for black people in those same spaces.

A "just city," then, is a space where one's hued flesh does not determine one's full or limited access to equity and safety in communities where she or he lives and works. To vision and create the type of city that is not a built rendition of the biased ideologies we maintain requires a liberated imagination, but we can only free our minds from the chains of anti-blackness and classism when we first acknowledge each has its hold on us. An expanded public dialogue is necessary for us to arrive at this set of shared understandings.

The current movement for black lives is a perfect backdrop for a conversation on reimagined cities that needs to move from the halls of think tanks and municipal development offices to the streets and neighborhoods where all manner of black people dwell.

Imagine dialogues on neighborhood development and urban design occurring among protest participants. Imagine planned public talks hosted on neighbors' stoops or in the foyers of housing projects. Imagine democratized approaches to urban planning that begins with the people, not the corporate class. Imagine the embedding of urban planners within movement collectives combatting anti-black racism and state sanctioned violence from Ferguson to Flatbush. That type of work is characteristic of the critical first steps needed to inform the creation of the "just" city.

We have reached a critical juncture in the U.S. Indeed, if the Black Lives Matter iteration of the long struggle for black liberation in this country has done nothing else, it has reminded us that the fight for a new, black-loving and just world is an ideological and material struggle. Our public ethos begets our public spaces. And we need unjust spaces no more.

Instead, we need neighborhoods where the value afforded to inhabitants is not based on the color of their skin, or presumed or actual gender expression and sexual identity. Integrated neighborhoods are beautiful expressions of community when, in fact, all members are seen as worthy of police protection or respect from business owners.

In my imagination, a safe and materially just black space is one where residents, whether homeowners or renters, are actually asked about the changes they'd like to see occur. Citi Bike representatives would knock on doors and assess residents' levels of comfort and desires before placing hordes of bikes on street corners where car services would previously park in wait for residents en route to their jobs, the market, or doctors' offices. I heard that particular complaint on my block.

In a "just city" residents can actually afford food at eateries and wares sold at businesses in their neighborhoods and, even more, they are provided access to services so they too can create businesses in the very locales they reside.

I want to live in a neighborhood where mostly white police officers do not see or treat me like a potential threat when walking home while my new white neighbors are offered respect regardless of their too loud parties or strong smell of marijuana coming from their direction. I've experienced or witnessed all of the above.

I imagine neighborhoods my physically disabled friends can maneuver through with greater ease. My South African wheelchair-bound mentee could not visit me in New York City because it would have been hard for him to make it through most of the city, including my neighborhood, without encountering a range of obstacles.

A safe and equitable space is one that centers the needs and desires of all residents regardless of race, gender, ability, income, or sexual identity. And in the cases when design and redevelopment revolve around those typically centered in the public imagination—characteristically white, sometimes heterosexual, nearly always abled-bodied people with wealth or access to other forms of capital—the work must be recalibrated. Yet the only way these forms of erasure can be assessed is by ensuring the group assembled at the planning table is as diverse as the communities it aims to reimagine and rebuild.

The public and private sectors will remain complicit in the creation of inequitable communities as long as both benefit from the structural inequities that surface as a result of race, class, and other forms of stratification. And that is not just.

QUESTIONS FOR CONSIDERATION

1. In what ways does Moore's article support the mission of the website—the Nature of Cities—on which it appeared? (See the headnote for more information about the website's mission.)
2. According to Moore, what would be a "just city"?

3. What is Moore's purpose in writing this article? What kind of readers might Moore have had in mind?
4. Moore would like to see "democratized approaches to urban planning." What does he mean by this phrase?
5. How does Moore link the issue of "just cities" with the Black Lives Matter movement? What are the connections?

IDEAS FOR WRITING

A. **A Summary and Response Assignment.** Summarize Moore's article, and then respond to the ideas he presents. Do you agree with Moore? Which ideas make sense to you, and which need rethinking?

B. **A Reflection Assignment.** Think about the city in which you live. Is it a "just city"? Why or why not? Are there other cities you have visited that do a better job at providing equity for all citizens? Present your reflective thoughts in an essay.

C. **An Evaluative Assignment.** Write an essay in which you compare two or three cities or towns with which you are familiar to determine which of these is the most "just city." Select criteria you will use to judge the cities you analyze, and write an essay in which you present the results of your comparative evaluation.

Teaching Suggestion
To provide the historic context for this article, consider assigning "What Is Affirmative Action," published in *The Economist*. https://www.economist.com/open-future/2018/06/15/what-is-affirmative-action.

I Am an Asian-American Who Benefits from Affirmative Action

Andrew Ham

Andrew Ham *is a student at Harvard University and editor of* The Harvard Crimson *editorial page. This article appeared in* The Harvard Crimson *in 2019.*

Diversity may be a buzzword to many; for me, it has always been an alien concept.

Growing up in South Korea, a nation that is essentially ethnically homogenous, meant that I was always surrounded by people who looked like me, spoke the same language, and shared the same culture. In Korea, I was never uncomfortable, my identity was never challenged, and I always felt safe. I always counted this as a blessing. At the same time, however, I could never get rid of the nagging feeling that I wasn't truly Korean, even after living all 18 years of my life in the heart of Seoul.

Speaking English at home and attending an international, American-styled school meant that my Korean was noticeably clumsy, my vocabulary was at a sixth-grade level, and English mixed incoherently with Korean when I spoke more often than I wished. In my home country, I was asked why I wasn't "Korean" by my neighborhood friends whenever I forgot a basic word or when they learned I was an American citizen. During my summers in the United States, however, I learned that I also wasn't "American" by the way people would look at my brother and me on the streets of suburban Maryland and ask us, with a strange combination of suspicion and politeness, where we were from.

I have always wished that I could label myself conveniently, that I didn't have to explain my nationality and identity. In my first few months at Harvard, however, I have met countless people who struggle to label and identify themselves, just like I do. It was the diversity that exists in Harvard's student body that, ironically enough, allowed me to feel at home for the first time in my life. This is why I cannot disavow affirmative action, both as a policy and as an ideal, even though the recent lawsuit against Harvard alleges that my university has been discriminating against people like me for years.

My response to the admissions lawsuit is simple. Although there may have been instances of discrimination in the admissions process, affirmative action remains a goal and policy worth pursuing. Discrimination against Asian-Americans is in no way a product of affirmative action; it is the result of centuries-old, deeply-rooted racism that has persisted ever since the first Asian immigrants came to America. Of course, biases in Harvard's admissions process must be investigated, tackled, and resolved; but to even pretend that demolishing a policy designed to promote historically excluded groups will somehow achieve racial equality is absurd and counterproductive. Ultimately, arguments against affirmative action amount to an excuse used by those in power to maintain traditional structures of privilege. The fact that racial biases plagued Harvard's admissions process only further demonstrates the need for race-conscious education and training—in other words, discriminatory admissions processes constitute an argument against structural and institutional racism, certainly not against a policy designed to tackle it.

Importantly, affirmative action also celebrates the idea that diversity is a fundamental good in college communities, an idea I have personally come to appreciate these past few months. During my short tenure as a Harvard student, I have heard Farsi, Serbian, and Russian from my friends, eaten food and listened to music I never tasted or heard before, and most importantly, met people who have revolutionized my way of thinking just by being who they are.

Last semester, for the first time in my life, I talked about religion and my struggle in understanding it when a Muslim friend discussed her faith with me for hours past midnight. I learned so much about public service and struggle in the week I spent with community organizers, activists, and passionate fighters during my pre-orientation program. I have been more vulnerable in this community than I have ever before—the openness and inclusivity that the Harvard community promotes is derived from the idea that there is no one correct way to think, no one correct way to live, and no one correct way to "be" a Harvard student. The diversity of experiences and perspectives that every student brings to Harvard is what prevents the institution from becoming even more isolated from the average American experience than it already is. It is this diversity that sparks intellectual discourse and allows for such a vibrant extracurricular life to thrive. Ultimately, diversity means that the true teachers at Harvard are often the students, constructing a community that is always learning from itself.

Having lived my entire life alone in a sea of familiar people, I am not an Asian-American who is harmed by affirmative action; quite the opposite, in fact. I benefit every day from living in a community that is so rich, so strange and quirky and interesting and wonderful, and one that I can confidently call home.

QUESTIONS FOR CONSIDERATION

1. What is Ham's purpose in writing this essay? Explain your answer, citing parts of his essay as support.
2. What does Ham mean when he says that diversity has "always been an alien concept"? Why do you think he might start the essay off with this sentence?
3. Do we know from this essay if affirmative action was actually a factor in Ham's acceptance to Harvard? Does this issue matter? Why or why not?
4. Think about your own initial experiences on a college campus or in a new environment. How does it compare with the experiences that Ham describes in the last several paragraphs, and how does that comparison make you feel?
5. Does it matter that Ham never really describes his family situation in concrete terms, that we do not know why he speaks English at home and has American citizenship? Explain your answer.

IDEAS FOR WRITING

A. **A Summary and Response Assignment.** Go to the *Harvard Crimson* webpage where this article is published, and read some of the responses to Ham's claims. Summarize either the negative or the positive ones and then write a response to them.

B. **A Reflection Assignment.** Take some time to think about your own comfort level with yourself, your ethnicity, and your culture. Compare your experiences to those Ham describes in the first two paragraphs. Write an essay in which you relate your experience with feeling comfortable or uncomfortable with your identity, using specific examples to illustrate your points.

C. **An Informative Assignment.** Ham refers to a lawsuit against Harvard regarding its use of affirmative action, but he does not give any more information about it. Research the lawsuit, and write an essay explaining the claims of the suit, its current status, and how Ham's piece either does or does not address the lawsuit's issues.

Pervasive Myths about Immigrants
Laura Collins

A former practicing attorney, Laura Collins is the director of the Bush Institute-SMU Economic Growth Initiative at the George W. Bush Institute. She has been active in Republican politics through both the Republican National Committee and the Texas State Legislature. Her article "Pervasive Myths about Immigrants" appeared in The Catalyst *in 2018.*

Teaching Suggestion
As the director of the Bush Institute—SMU Economic Growth Initiative, Laura Collins' point of view on immigrants may be surprising to some students. Consider using this article as an introduction to an assignment focused on attitudes toward immigration.

---

1   If you want to take America's temperature, few issues are more revealing than immigration. Americans who feel anxious or insecure about the economy or their community are quick to blame a flow of new people into the United States. They do so despite consistent evidence that immigrants do not cause their problems.

2   Unfortunately, these concerns are as old as the Founding Fathers. While the Declaration of Independence argued for the American colonies' right to populate through immigration, Benjamin Franklin expressed misgivings about the German immigrants to Pennsylvania. He complained that they would never assimilate to the culture and customs established by the English colonists.

3   It is easy to laugh at his prediction today: Germans are America's largest ethnic group. All of these citizens, presumably, are as American as their neighbors of other origins.

Still, it is disheartening to realize that nearly identical arguments have been made about successive groups of immigrants since Franklin's time. These arguments correspond more with broader social and economic anxieties than with particular characteristics of the immigrant groups to which they are directed.

Don't blame the economy

Animosity toward immigrants and anxiety about immigration levels correspond particularly to two phenomena: politicians discussing immigration in negative terms, or a poor economic outlook.

The culprit couldn't be the economy because it strengthened significantly in 2017. True, many Americans feel that they personally have not recovered from the Great Recession. And wage growth is tepid, while millennials are predicted to be the first generation in U.S. history that will be worse off than their parents. Yet our economy is running at full employment. GDP growth has been higher lately. And consumer confidence has increased.

The culprit is instead political rhetoric. Politicians at all levels make negative statements about immigration, but the 2016 presidential election was a low point in recent years for rhetoric on immigration and immigrants themselves. Unfortunately, negative statements continue, increasing public anxiety that eventually gets released against immigrants.

The red-hot language has created a storm of anger towards immigrants. Facts do not support the desire to blame them, but attitudes about immigration tend to reflect our collective psyche. We want someone to blame, especially if we feel that no one else is below us on the economic ladder.

That frustration often leads some to believe that the solution is to drastically reduce the number of immigrants we allow annually into the U.S. They also want to reduce the current undocumented population through stronger interior enforcement and deportation efforts.

The frustration may be real, but immigrants are not the source of the problem. Take wages. Take-home pay may have grown at a paltry rate since the 2008 financial crisis, but economic studies of the effect of immigrants on wages show an incredibly modest negative effect on low-wage workers in the short run only. Actually, the impacted low-wage workers are often recent immigrants, not native-born American workers.

This isn't to say there is no pain associated with lackluster wage growth. But many factors contribute to the slow and unsatisfactory growth, particularly among lower-skilled workers. The solutions lie in domestic policy reforms that encourage economic growth that in turn drives wage growth. Restricting immigration is not one of those policies, and continually directing energy towards this as a solution is wasting opportunities to address the real roots of the problem, such as declining worker mobility and a lower rate of new business formation.

The truth is that American workers have more to fear from technology than from immigration. Technology has dramatically increased the productivity of the American worker since the early 2000s. Manufacturing is an excellent example. Productivity in manufacturing increased so much between 2000 and 2010 that the U.S. would have required an additional 20.9 million workers if productivity had remained steady since 2000. Because of the dramatic increase in productivity, the U.S. manufacturing sector only required 12.1 million workers in 2010. Continually acquiring new skills will alleviate the anxiety that workers understandably feel.

Robots working on cars on an assembly line. *Rainer Plendl/Shutterstock*

And here's another reality: studies show that immigrants do not steal jobs from Americans. *America's Advantage: Handbook on Immigration and Economic Growth*, a recent Bush Institute report, reveals that immigrants are more likely than native-born workers to create jobs. They start businesses at nearly twice the rate of native-born Americans and are more likely to be self-employed. Immigrant-owned businesses with employees other than the owner employ, on average, 11 additional workers.

Of course, the common misperception is that immigrants do take away jobs. This only adds to the anguish over losing a job and promotes fear and hostility to immigrant labor.

The labor market, however, is not a fixed pie. A new worker like an immigrant who enters the labor market does not need to displace a currently-employed worker in order to find a position. In fact, immigrants often are not perfect substitutes for native-born American workers and are therefore not competing directly with each other for the same positions.

Their skills typically complement native-born workers' skills, seeking positions where there is a scarcity of native born labor. This complementarity happens for immigrant workers at all skill levels.

And immigrants aren't driving the budget deficit

Another common myth is that immigrants put a strain on the federal budget. Here, too, the reality is different. Immigrants are not the strain on the federal budget they are made out to be.

Consider entitlement programs like Medicaid, Medicare, and Social Security, which are the biggest items in the federal budget. Immigrants cannot unduly burden these programs because they are limited in their access to them.

Legal immigrants, for example, do not qualify for federal entitlement benefits for five years after their arrival in the U.S. Once they do qualify, they only use them at lower rates than native-born Americans. And undocumented immigrants cannot receive any federal entitlement benefits, although their U.S.-citizen children do qualify.

So, even with millions of immigrants in the U.S., they simply cannot use enough benefits to strain the budget. The fact that they, overall, add value to the economy reduces or negates any fiscal burden they might put on the federal budget.

The fiscal costs they do impose are mostly borne at the state and local level. As an example, immigrants without health insurance are likely to burden public hospitals, just as native-born Americans in the same situation are likely to do.

Our country undoubtedly faces challenges over the next several years—fiscal irresponsibility, the growth of entitlements, technological disruption in the workforce, and many more. These problems require tough solutions.

But the problems are not about immigration. Instead, the U.S. owes a great deal to the immigrants who built America and made our nation great. That's the ultimate reality we should remember.

QUESTIONS FOR CONSIDERATION

1. What is Collins's main claim in this essay? Name at least two ways in which she supports this claim.
2. Does the fact that she cites a recent report from the Bush Institute, the organization for which she works and which published this article, skew your feelings about her argument? If so, in what way?
3. Would the article be more persuasive if there were more specific examples used, for instance, if some of the "red-hot" language that she references was quoted or explained here? Why or why not?
4. Think about the ways in which you have heard your family and friends discussing immigration recently, or your own thoughts. How does Collins's argument mesh with or conflict with your previous experience?
5. Collins references the Founding Fathers and claims that immigration has been a persistent source of political strife in this country since its beginning. Why do you think immigration causes so much tension? Explain your answer.

IDEAS FOR WRITING

A. **An Informative Assignment:** Collins seeks to debunk myths by providing information. Select a myth and write an informative essay, using Collins's article as a model, in which you debunk the myth.
B. **An Analytical Assignment:** Collins analyzes myths (viewpoints that are not based in fact) that are, in part, responsible for some of the animosity related to immigration. Pick any other topic in the news recently about which misinformation (information not based in facts) contributes to animosity. Write an essay in which you show how misinformation contributes to the problem you are analyzing.

C. A Researched Argument Assignment: Collins's argument is only loosely supported with data; its tone is similar to that of an opinion piece. Find at least five sources that use data to either support or rebut her claims that immigrants are not a problem for the American economy but rather a benefit. Write an argument in which you argue—based on the data you find—that Collins's argument is correct, partially correct, or incorrect.

Black Walnut: A Sweet Blood History
Linda Hogan

Teaching Suggestion
Linda Hogan's writing makes use of description to present a reflection. Challenge students to emulate Hogan's strategies that evoke sensory perceptions.

The current Chickasaw Nation Writer in Residence, Linda Hogan has been writing poetry, short stories, and novels for over forty years. She has received many awards for her environmentally themed works, including the 2016 Thoreau Prize from PEN and the two-time Colorado Book Award for Solar Storms *(1996) and* The Book of Medicines *(1993). "Black Walnut: A Sweet Blood History" was published in* Cold Mountain Review *in the Fall 2016 issue.*

1 From one seed of childhood memories, I recall a stormy night and seeing my grandfather ride his horse toward home through a thunderstorm. I watched through the leaves of a large tree. In each flash of lightning as he came closer, the world was also a bright display of daylight green grass and trees.

2 Even through the strong odor of rain, from the open window I smelled the powerful soul of the black walnut tree near the window. It had an odor that was unique, a medicinal scent of herb and something fragrant I couldn't name.

3 I had an affinity for that tree, a love that eventually grew to contain other trees. By day, I liked to put my small fingers in the dark, furrowed bark and let them travel. I considered this particular tree my own in some way, its long leaves that held other leaves and shaped something like a fern, the green cluster of nuts together in young groups until ready to fall. It even had its own unique sound as the warm winds passed through its leaves.

4 But it was the odor of this tree that really distinguished it from others. It had a beautiful smell I believed. It was strong enough that broken layers of shells or even the leaves kept insects from entering the house.

5 This one tree grew outside the old, small unpainted home where my grandparents moved after the Great Depression. It was a land of great silences and the

dappled light of many trees. I played in the movement of that light, and sometimes I tried to open the two layers of walnut shell, a child seeking mysteries with tools, a hammer or another utensil, but I usually only managed to stain my hands and clothing. That is, until my father stepped in to help. He was gifted enough to impeccably open the shells and remove the meat.

6   Memory is filled with presences made large, and we were part of a big Chickasaw family with large memories. Our people were strongly those of the land who once cared for grasses, gardens, and trees. We had long been keepers of the Southeastern forests, and nuts were a primary food, so the many nut trees received much attention and care.

7   In my child's imagination, that particular Oklahoma black walnut tree may have been one of many nut trees growing in the area. It is possible that it permitted other trees to grow in its presence. In all the singular peculiarity of this species, it is a tree with roots stretching far and wide, holding the tree solid while they send out a toxin (juglans) that kills many other trees and brush. A black walnut is choosy about which certain plants and understory are permitted to thrive near or beneath its shadows.

8   In those young days I didn't know about the ways of plants or their keen intelligence. Looking back now, it seems that we were mostly the keepers of stories, not forests. Our lives were created by stories. Many were told at night, without electricity, as we sat outside and listened to the older people talk. Even now, there are times I feel I grew up during the Great Depression, the closing of the banks, and the loss of our lands. I lived through numerous acts of federal corruption and local thefts. I survived living in Indian Territory before it was the state of Oklahoma and the famous thieves and gangs passed through. There they were safe from the law, and they sought refuge in the caves nearby. Many years later, some of my very young students, two cousins, each individually wrote about their family members saving Bonnie and Clyde from the law, so I wasn't alone in this lived experience of story and our history and its effects on children.

9   Invariably, as we sat and listened, someone told about the time my grandfather bought a car from his brother. It turned out to be stolen. It was the only car he ever bought. After that he drove only two horses with a wagon to fill the large milk container with water from the community pump. The pump was for the Indians who lived without a source of water. My sister and I rode along and while he filled the milk cans outside, we went inside the general store for a soda or other treat.

But despite that experience of ours, my father told me the story that influenced me greatly. Before land thefts and losses, their own first home had been a large ranch. It was on our family's original allotment land and my grandfather was the kind of man who'd part with no parcel of earth and never a healthy tree. But during the time of war, black walnut was the most valuable wood because it was in great demand for gunstock.

The family went to town one day, and I believe they stopped to visit relatives. Perhaps they stayed to eat. In those days, no one left another home hungry. They might even have spent the night. When they returned, their beautiful black walnut trees had been cut and taken away. It was a terrible loss, and I understood that the loss of the trees mattered not so much financially, but that their disappearance was a loss to the heart, and it was also one more theft from an Indian family who'd lost much already.

All this happened before I was born, when my father was young. But the pain over this loss was never remedied. Even after the last trace of the older generation was gone, the ghosts of the stolen trees have remained with me. They were the trees of my heart, too.

Some time later, the smaller home of my grandmother burned down. By then my grandfather was gone, so my grandmother moved to a small town to be near one of my aunts. Several years later, my father and I were on a journey of memory, collecting oral histories and visiting our family. I wanted to stop at my grandmother's old home, even though it had burned. To our surprise, not far from the black shadow that had been their home, the black walnut tree was still there. It stood older, larger, and shaped a bit differently by the changed currents of air.

After that, I began research on our very long Chickasaw history, including our lives before the explorers and invaders arrived in 1541. Those first violent Europeans wrote about how amazed they were at our forests, how we cared for them, groomed them, and lived from their many offerings. Their botanists wrote the most, so the trees and plants were well documented. Nothing similar existed at the time in Europe. Numerous botanists arrived to take samples back to Europe. They had boxes large enough for trees and smaller boxes for medicinal and other important plants. Few of their samples survived in European conditions, even though greenhouses with controlled temperatures were built for them. I imagine the soil was long dead, missing nutrients and micronutrients necessary to feed and nurture trees or plants from any of the continents they visited.

Perhaps some intuition informed me that forests and plants beyond compare had lived in my blood centuries ago. Then I discovered that black walnut trees were even a larger part of our history. In a book called *The Global Forest*, Diana Beresford-Kroeger wrote about the large city of the Mississippians called Cahokia, people from which I come. While called a city in history and anthropology books, it was primarily more of a gathering place. What's important is that the population of this place considered a city was larger than London or Paris at the same time in history, from 800–1200 C.E.

Southeastern tribal peoples were mound builders and earth-workers. Our ancestors built numerous effigy mounds, some in the shape of animals and other mysteries, some to accommodate the sky, the sun and moon and constellations. Numbers of these are still in existence, even if little known to many people. Most popular now is the "city" named Cahokia, which is a region of many mounds. A pyramid there is larger than any found in Egypt or the Yucatan. Of over a hundred mounds, one that's most frequently visited is named "Monk's Mound" because French Trappist monks lived there for a time.

For me, the most fascinating fact about this pyramid is that it was completely encircled by black walnut trees. The people who lived there knew these intelligent trees were able to repel certain animals, insects, and parasites. At the same time, the trees attracted others that were beneficial. With their strong scent, they were a valuable presence and may have permitted medicine plants, berries, and other foods to grow beneath them. Their magnificent underground roots spread out a long distance to hold the moist bottomland soil intact. These trees preferred earth near waterways like those where great rivers meet, land given to flooding and easily washed away. This green bottomland is the perfect home for black walnut trees. They held it strong, even during seismic activity, such as the Great Madrid earthquake of 1812 that reversed the direction of the Mississippi River.

…

The odor I loved of the black walnut tree is the language, maybe even the labor, of this tree. Each tree has its own intelligence. This one dwells among the higher minds.

Its intelligence isn't only the root system, or how many parts of a tree might work together to keep it alive in a complex ecosystem. It draws to it the monarch butterflies that make their migration through this location to feed from this favored tree, the black walnut. So do over two hundred other species of butterfly and moths, including the rare Luna moth. The deer are attracted to its shade, and in these shadows, healing plants like swamp weed, milkweed and wild ginger grow.

Some of these mounds are mysteries. Classes were attended here, and so were performances of drama and music. Some areas were only for worship of our sky and our ancestral beings. Some mounds held the ancestors. One body was found with a tablet in her hand. On one side was a butterfly and on the other were a panther and snake. Constellations and something that appeared to be writing were also there. These were only part of the collected life known by the people, but nothing was known as well as the trees. The black walnut trees were groomed of insects by numerous but now extinct heath hens and passenger pigeons. Other birds protected the trees from those who might break into the sweet liquid inside the bark, once used as a sweetener or syrup for the people.

Because of this tree, the region remained free of unwanted insects, attracted food, and kept the unwanted wildlife at bay, while bringing close the animals that were desirable. The root system, in a riverine bottomland, kept the land intact, and held the world of mounds in place during seismic activity.

Perhaps it is history, but I believe it is truth, that trees are part of the sacred life. The fluid that passes through all things that have lived on our small and amazing planet continues to pass into other lives. It is a world that may be too great for us to take in with only a simple human mind.

Unknown to me, the first tree I remember was a long part of our history through time.

I still think of the black walnut tree I knew as a girl and wonder how many may once have existed in the rich forests of Oklahoma, earlier called Indian Territory, in the time before great deforestation. What I believed was a beautiful, intriguing scent was actually a toxic smell that said, "Keep away," to many other trees, to animals, and to insects that might otherwise have harmed it.

Trees are still my sacred world. They are beautiful people. I try to remember to acknowledge them, especially the grandmother and grandfather pine that have grown tall here where I live, old growth trees that have shaped themselves and rooted so perfectly that they've withstood great snows over the years, with branches perfectly spaced to allow air currents to move around them, healthy enough to withstand infestations, and to have remained standing even after the great flood of 2013 created devastation all around them.

As a child, I never knew about nitrogen-fixing plants or trees, or potassium, or the table of elements that is part of our world. I only knew the sound of the wind passing through leaves and carrying the breath of all of the life around us. As it turned out, there were stories older than the ones I heard sitting outside at night, listening to the family speak about older times.

Now I know that all trees are sacred. They are not speechless. It's just that you have to listen with your heart, and at night you may see the stars through branches and know it is all one cosmos, the sky, the ground beneath, and the way sweet fluid moves through our lives.

QUESTIONS FOR CONSIDERATION

1. Hogan covers a lot of ground in this essay, with personal reflection, Chickasaw history and politics, and ecological concerns all playing a part. Is there a central claim, and if so, what do you think it is?
2. Is this essay a political essay, a personal reflection, or something else? Explain your answer.
3. What do you think Hogan means when she says that the tree had a smell she "believed" (paragraph 4)?
4. At one point, Hogan claims that the black walnut trees that were cut down from her grandfather's property before she was even born "remained" with her as "the trees of my heart" (paragraph 12). What does she mean by this claim, and is it supported throughout the essay?
5. Does the larger history embedded throughout the essay—the names and dates and facts—contribute to your understanding of the story Hogan is trying to tell about her family's history, or does it detract? Why?

IDEAS FOR WRITING

A. **A Reflection Assignment:** Reread the essay, focusing on all the ways in which the smell of the tree is used, referenced, and imagined. Think about something that appeals to your senses or about a memory that involves sensory perceptions. Write an essay in which you communicate to readers the sensory perceptions you have experienced, and help readers understand their significance.

B. **An Evaluative Assignment:** Hogan draws many parallels between her family's history, the larger concerns such as Native American relations, and the place of Native American culture in world history.

Evaluate the effectiveness of Hogan's essay in terms of the connections she seeks to make between her family's history and relationship with the black walnut to the larger concerns of Chickasaw and Native American history.

C. **A Rhetorical Analysis Assignment:** Hogan's essay might be characterized as a reflective piece; however, her essay might also be framed as an argument. In what ways is Hogan's essay an argument? What is her claim, and what support does she provide for that claim? In what ways do her personal stories support her claim? Write a rhetorical analysis in which you focus on the rhetorical strategies Hogan uses to create her argument.

4 Crime and Punishment

Teaching Suggestion
Reginald Dwayne Betts' poetry and life story are worth having students read in conjunction with this article. See http://www.dwaynebetts.com/ for additional resources.

Only Once I Thought about Suicide
Reginald Dwayne Betts

Reginald Dwayne Betts is an award-winning American poet and writer, and he is also an attorney. Betts holds a BA from the University of Maryland, an MFA from Warren Wilson College, where he was a Holden Fellow, and a JD from Yale Law School. At the age of 16, Betts was sentenced to over eight years in prison, an experience that helped to shape his political and personal interests and that formed the basis for the following article that appeared in the Yale Law Journal.

I.

Every prison and jail in Virginia has a series of cells used for solitary confinement. Fairfax County Jail had three units for solitary confinement. None had windows. The R-Cells had ceilings so high that a tall man could not reach them by jumping. The other had a door so thick and heavy that when it closed no sounds escaped. The third looked like the cells for the general population.

At Southampton Correctional Center, an entire building had been converted to hold men in solitary. The cells looked just like those housing the general population, except the doors only opened to take you to the shower once every three days, or to the kennel-like cages where you periodically had an hour to pace the fifteen steps back and forth, to do push-ups, jumping jacks, to stare out the window into the open countryside that taunted you.

Some of the cells in solitary confinement at Red Onion State Prison faced what people called the gutted side of a mountain. Three times a week guards would shackle and cuff prisoners and escort them, under the watchful eye of a guard holding a shotgun, to the showers.

Sussex 1 State Prison, like Southampton, had units initially constructed for general population converted into solitary confinement units. Men could stare from their cell into the yard and watch men going about the work of doing time, the basketball games, the circling the yard, the fights. At Sussex, they also held death row prisoners, and on occasion, while being walked to the shower, you would glimpse a man preparing to die.

At Coffeewood Correctional Center, the solitary confinement unit had about a dozen cells. The windows were so high up that a tall man would have to leap to glimpse the green of the outside grass. Of all these prisons, only Southampton's units had windows wider than an open palm or taller than a man's arm.

II.

In 1996, when I was sixteen, a fifteen-year-old friend and I carjacked a man in Virginia. Shortly after being arrested, I confessed. Back then, I did not know what it meant to be transferred to criminal court. But I would learn. Following John DiLulio's super-predator theory, state prosecutors began to rely increasingly on statutory mechanisms that allowed them to transfer children from juvenile to criminal court, where, if found guilty, they would be exposed to the same punishments and same prisons as people eighteen or older. In Virginia, carjacking carries a minimum sentence of fifteen years and a maximum of life in prison. Five months after my crime, after pleading guilty to carjacking and a weapons charge, I stood before the Honorable Judge Bach to be sentenced. Before sentencing me to nine years, he said, "I am under no illusion that sending you to prison will help, but you can get something out of it if you want." It should not have been a surprise to anyone that part of what I got out of my time in prison was nearly a year and a half of solitary confinement.

For a time, I called cells in the solitary units of the Fairfax County Jail, Southampton Correctional Center, Red Onion State Prison, Sussex 1 State Prison, and

Coffeewood Correctional Center home. Inside those cells, I counted everything: days, weeks, months, birthdays, and frequently the tiny markings on the wall. All told, I spent more than fourteen months in isolation at these various institutions. Author Jack Abbott, reflecting on his time spent in solitary confinement, wrote that it could "alter the ontological makeup of a stone." I know that what it does to men and women is far worse.

III.

A hundred and fifty years is a good spell of time to let pass without learning a lesson, but a case as secure as a cell in the hole attests to our modern failure. Jack Abbott's adage was old news a century before he penned it. The world's first prison kept all of its prisoners in solitary confinement. Built in 1829, Eastern Penitentiary's enabling act required that "the principle of solitary confinement of prisoners be preserved and maintained." Describing this system, Samuel Wood, Eastern's first warden, explained that "no prisoner is seen by another, after he enters the walls." The effects were obvious. One official observer, British Penal Authority William Crawford wrote, "[t]he whip inflicts immediate pain, but solitude inspires permanent terror." For some, including Crawford, this was a good thing; others knew better.

When Charles Dickens toured the facility, he described its system as "rigid, strict, and hopeless solitary confinement" and denounced its horrors as "a secret punishment which slumbering humanity is not roused up to stay."

The ASCA-Liman *Time-In-Cell* report provides the numbers that underscore the significance of this discussion. According to the report, between eighty and a hundred thousand men are in restrictive housing. Over thirty thousand are in administrative segregation. The report focuses on the latter group. By arguing that the practice is overused, the report addresses the issue of isolation as a form of social control within the contemporary prison—and raises serious questions about the legitimacy of the practice. But the report leaves equally important work to be done by future scholars. The absence of the voices of men and women who have experienced administrative segregation means that the ontologically troubling questions that pervade all practices involving isolation, whether they be done within a prison (in the form of administrative segregation) or through the use of supermax facilities or solitary confinement units, are not fully confronted.

IV.

Why, nearly two centuries after Dickens, does it still take studies like this one to make us consider the human beings who suffer and whose lives are often extinguished in these cells? How does a system that critics, prisoners, and correction officials all recognize as akin to torture remain intact today? The answer is simple: we justify prison policy based on our characterizations of those confined, not on any normative belief about what confinement in prison should look like.

The era of the "supermax"—or super-maximum security prison—arguably began with Marion Penitentiary. In 1983, Marion gained notoriety in the federal system after prisoners connected to the Aryan Brotherhood gang killed two correctional officers while being escorted from their cells in shackles and cuffs. Marion prison officials responded by returning to the philosophy of Eastern Penitentiary and locking the entire institution down. For the next twenty-three years, men spent twenty-three hours in their cells for every hour they were allowed outside of them. Over the next two decades, more institutions followed Marion's approach. One was Red Onion State Prison, which Virginia opened sixteen years after Marion went on total lockdown. Billed as the state's toughest prison, Red Onion was meant to house the "worst of the worst"—a common catchphrase used to legitimate the harsh treatment of inmates. The *Washington Post* claimed Red Onion had been built for "inmates so dangerous that it's better to forget about rehabilitation and simply warehouse them." If only this were true. I arrived at the place we all called "the Onion" months before the *Post* article appeared. By then I was many things—barely eighteen years old, frail, young, terrified—but far from the worst of the worst.

The continued use of solitary confinement as a punitive measure suggests the correctional officers fail to recognize its negative side effects. But scholars and medical experts have extensively documented them. One such expert, Dr. Craig Haney, concluded in 2003 that "[t]here are few if any forms of imprisonment that appear to produce so much psychological trauma and in which so many symptoms of psychopathology are manifested." Others in the field overwhelmingly agree. Dr. Hans Toch has argued that "[t]he most extreme punitive confinement—such as supermaximum isolation—most heavily taxes limited coping competence, and leads, literally, to points of no return. . . . [P]rison cells become filled with prisoners who have withdrawn from painful reality and quietly hallucinate." But even Dr. Toch does not capture how overwhelmingly oppressive a cell becomes when the door never opens. These quotes from his work, too, erase as they reveal. Because inside his quotes are the lives of men whose stories are lost. Some of them are lost inside my head. And the ones that are not lost, images of men screaming as guards in riot gear rushed into their cells, the makeshift nooses—these, even in their horror, fail to capture how time in a cell can haunt and ruin you.

Fortunately, there have been scholars who have used their research to get the voices of prisoners into this difficult conversation. In an effort to address mental health issues among inmates, ethnographer Lorna Rhodes spent eight years interviewing prisoners in Washington state penitentiaries. In one interview, a prisoner told Rhodes that "[t]he experience [of solitary confinement] stays with you . . . A strong person with a strong will, if it's not breaking them it's gonna make them into something with a lot of violent potential, a lot of hostility." The men in administrative segregation are both visible and invisible. The conditions of their confinement are "concealed from public and even internal scrutiny behind layers of security precautions" while "representations of criminals and television documentaries of maximum-security prisons highlight the ritualized procedures that contain the dangerousness of the supermax inmate."

Narratives from prisoners reinforce what researchers have found. Rhodes explored the artwork of Todd Tarselli, a then-prisoner in a Pennsylvania supermax, to emphasize the way in which administrative segregation "plays a role in producing or exacerbating mental illness in prison. . . ." In "Decompensation," named after the psychiatric term for the failure to generate coping mechanisms in response to stress, Tarselli illustrates a man slowly losing the ability to recognize who he is and assert himself as an individual. Another powerful story comes from poet Etheridge Knight, who wrote about his experience in the hole:

I am being shoved into the Hole. I am stripped naked. . . . I am given a blanket, and the steel door behind me is shut and locked. It is dark and chilly in the Hole. . . . I pace the dark space, do push-ups, masturbate, curse the guards and the gods. Five or six days pass. . . . I begin to slow down, and the smothering starts. . . . After being in the Hole for a couple of weeks, not knowing night from day, I begin to lose track of time.

These stories, too often untold, animate the ways that time in the hole and in administrative segregation ruins people.

V.

Today there is no question that solitary confinement and administrative segregation create psychological problems in prisoners. By emphasizing the immense number of people in administrative segregation, the *Time-In-Cell* report creates an opportunity for us to discuss the stories of prisoners that would not have otherwise received mainstream attention—that would have gone untold. Eight years and four months in prison, two six month long stretches in solitary, and four shorter stints in the solitary give me an abundance of evidence to draw from.

19   On February 21, 1997, I was transferred from the Fairfax County Juvenile Detention Center to the Fairfax County Jail. At the time, my friend and codefendant was housed in the jail's only juvenile unit. To prevent us from housing together, the deputies placed me in administrative segregation. For ten days I awaited a cell in general population. For the first eight of those ten days, I was denied a mattress, a pillow, or a sheet. Given only a small gray blanket, I slept on a concrete slab covered in dried mucus and the grime of years without cleaning. The guy in the cell across from me spent all day talking to himself. Arguing with himself. Guards and nurses alike ignored his disintegration.

20   Later, while in administrative segregation at Sussex 1 State Prison, I watched men strapped down at four points, both arms and both legs. One old white man refused to shower. Periodically, they opened his cell door and forced him to bathe. I was in cell 5. The man in cell 6, he was afraid to go into general population.

21   At Coffeewood Correctional Center, I remember the exact moment when the man in the cell next to me lost himself. On the verge of being released to the general population, he changed his mind, turned around, and demanded to go back inside the cage that had held him. Once inside, he slammed a plastic chair against the door, again and again.

22   The hole broke some men. Others, it didn't. But while many of their stories are buried, hidden, this is not always true.

23   A short time ago, I walked into a local barbershop with a sheaf of papers. My barber knows that I am a writer and a law student, but he did not know about the time I spent in prison. That morning the papers I carried were a printed copy of *De Profundis*, Oscar Wilde's book about the time he spent in solitary confinement. Staring at it, my barber asked if the sheaf of papers was the start of a new book. I told him no, and explained that I was writing an essay about solitary confinement. "Why would you be writing that?" he asked. When I told him about the time I'd spent in prison, in solitary confinement, and how it has long informed my study of the law, he was silent for a second. Over the next few minutes, he and I began a dance where we exchanged a fact at a time, slowly admitting our mutual intimacy with the

darkness of the hole. In *De Profundis*, Wilde wrote, "[m]any men on their release carry their prison along with them into the air, and hide it as a secret disgrace in their hearts, and at length, like poor poisoned things, creep into some hole and die." After I told him about the long stretches I spent in solitary, he told me that the hole had almost crushed him. It reminded me of when I was sixteen, alone in the hole, nearly broken.

24 When I was sixteen years old and had only been in general population at the Fairfax County Jail for a few days, the ten-person block where I was assigned seemed like a scene from *Blood In Blood Out* or *The Shawshank Redemption*. I wanted out and asked to be moved, arguing that the frequent lockdowns kept me from attending school. They called it writing yourself out the block. It was a coward's move, what men who couldn't protect themselves did. When a deputy came and informed me that I was being moved to a different unit, I balked. By this time, I'd lost my earlier fears, and feared more the stigma that would come from writing myself out the block. In the hierarchy of shame, only checking into protective custody trumped asking to be moved from one block to another out of fear. The deputy threatened to put me in the hole if I did not move. I touched his arm, a childhood gesture. I was trying to say: I will move, no need for the handcuffs. But before I could speak, he slammed me against a brick wall. Handcuffed me. Dragged me to a cell in the hole for assaulting an officer. They tossed me in a cell with a door so thick that no sound escaped. I was sixteen years old. Each morning they took my mattress from me so that I could not sleep during the day. How do I explain this? Each day, I lost a little bit of what made me want to be free. I've never told this story. Those were the longest days of my sentence. One afternoon, in a fit of panic, I slammed my right fist against the wall. I fractured my pinky. I thought about suicide. I almost disappeared.

25 All around us, there are men and women made invisible, their spirits wiped out by policies that we don't notice. The *Time-In-Cell* report forces us to grapple with their narratives in a way that Due Process and Eighth Amendment challenges brought to court do not, because the majority of the thirty thousand people in administrative segregation will never be represented in a lawsuit. But their stories, if we listen, can be found. And those are the stories that demand change.

QUESTIONS FOR CONSIDERATION

1. What is Betts's purpose in writing this article?
2. How does the article benefit from Betts's first-hand knowledge of the prison environment?
3. If Betts had not had first-hand experiences to share, what other writing strategies could he have used to make his message compelling?
4. What role does the title of the article have in helping readers understand Betts's point?
5. How does Betts use emotional appeals to support his point?

IDEAS FOR WRITING

A. **A Reflective Assignment.** Reflect on the ideas presented in Betts's article. Did the stories relayed in the article help you feel differently about prisoners? Did they confirm ideas you already had, or did they give you new insights into prison life? Explain your answer. Based on Betts's article, would you advocate that solitary confinement be eliminated? Explain your answer.

B. **A Rhetorical Analysis Assignment.** Betts's article presents an argument. What is the claim? What are the reasons? How does Betts use appeals to pathos, ethos, and logos to support his claim? Write a rhetorical analysis in which you answer these questions and discuss any other significant rhetorical strategies in Betts's article.

C. **A Persuasive Essay Assignment.** Betts uses personal experiences to make an argument about a social practice—the treatment of inmates—that he believes needs to be changed. Write a persuasive letter to the editor of your local newspaper in which you use your personal experiences to support a change you believe should be made. Use additional evidence to support your claim, if necessary.

Yes, Black America Fears the Police. Here's Why.
Nikole Hannah-Jones

Nikole Hannah-Jones is a staff writer for The New York Times. *She recently received a Pulitzer Prize for her contributions to the development of* The 1619 Project, *a multimedia examination of the legacy of slavery. She has published in a wide variety of journals and writes on issues of racial injustice and civil rights. She has received numerous other awards for her writing, including a 2017 MacArthur Genius Fellowship. The article that follows appeared in* ProPublica, *a news outlet whose mission is "to expose abuses of power and betrayals of the public trust by government, business, and other institutions, using the moral force of investigative journalism to spur reform through the sustained spotlighting of wrongdoing."*

Teaching Suggestion
Consider discussing with students one of Nikole Hannah-Jones's writing purposes: establishing empathy. A good companion piece to assign is https://www.nytimes.com/guides/year-of-living-better/how-to-be-more-empathetic.

Last July 4, my family and I went to Long Island to celebrate the holiday with a friend and her family. After eating some barbecue, a group of us decided to take a walk along the ocean. The mood on the beach that day was festive. Music from a nearby party pulsed through the haze of sizzling meat. Lovers strolled hand in hand. Giggling children chased each other along the boardwalk.

Most of the foot traffic was heading in one direction, but then two teenage girls came toward us, moving stiffly against the flow, both of them looking nervously to their right. "He's got a gun," one of them said in a low voice.

I turned my gaze to follow theirs, and was clasping my 4-year-old daughter's hand when a young man extended his arm and fired off multiple shots along the busy street running parallel to the boardwalk. Snatching my daughter up into my arms, I joined the throng of screaming revelers running away from the gunfire and toward the water.

The shots stopped as quickly as they had started. The man disappeared between some buildings. Chest heaving, hands shaking, I tried to calm my crying daughter, while my husband, friends and I all looked at one another in breathless disbelief. I turned to check on Hunter, a high school intern from Oregon who was staying with my family for a few weeks, but she was on the phone.

"Someone was just shooting on the beach," she said, between gulps of air, to the person on the line.

Unable to imagine whom she would be calling at that moment, I asked her, somewhat indignantly, if she couldn't have waited until we got to safety before calling her mom.

"No," she said. "I am talking to the police."

My friends and I locked eyes in stunned silence. Between the four adults, we hold six degrees. Three of us are journalists. And not one of us had thought to call the police. We had not even considered it.

We also are all black. And without realizing it, in that moment, each of us had made a set of calculations, an instantaneous weighing of the pros and cons.

As far as we could tell, no one had been hurt. The shooter was long gone, and we had seen the back of him for only a second or two. On the other hand, calling the police posed considerable risks. It carried the very real possibility of inviting disrespect, even physical harm. We had seen witnesses treated like suspects, and knew how quickly black people calling the police for help could wind up cuffed in the back of a squad car. Some of us knew of black professionals who'd had guns drawn on them for no reason.

This was before Michael Brown. Before police killed John Crawford III for carrying a BB gun in a Wal-Mart or shot down 12-year-old Tamir Rice in a Cleveland park. Before Akai Gurley was killed by an officer while walking in a dark staircase and before Eric Garner was choked to death upon suspicion of selling "loosies." Without yet knowing those names, we all could go down a list of unarmed black people killed by law enforcement.

We feared what could happen if police came rushing into a group of people who, by virtue of our skin color, might be mistaken for suspects.

For those of you reading this who may not be black, or perhaps Latino, this is my chance to tell you that a substantial portion of your fellow citizens in the United States of America have little expectation of being treated fairly by the law or receiving justice. It's possible this will come as a surprise to you. But to a very real extent, you have grown up in a different country than I have.

As Khalil Gibran Muhammad, author of *The Condemnation of Blackness*, puts it, "White people, by and large, do not know what it is like to be occupied by a police force. They don't understand it because it is not the type of policing they experience. Because they are treated like individuals, they believe that if 'I am not breaking the law, I will never be abused.'"

We are not criminals because we are black. Nor are we somehow the only people in America who don't want to live in safe neighborhoods. Yet many of us cannot fundamentally trust the people who are charged with keeping us and our communities safe.

As protest and revolt swept across the Missouri suburb of Ferguson and demonstrators staged die-ins and blocked highways and boulevards from Oakland to New York with chants of "Black lives matter," many white Americans seemed shocked by the gaping divide between law enforcement and the black communities they are supposed to serve. It was no surprise to us. For black Americans, policing is "the most enduring aspect of the struggle for civil rights," says Muhammad, a historian and director of the Schomburg Center for Research in Black Culture in New York. "It has always been the mechanism for racial surveillance and control."

In the South, police once did the dirty work of enforcing the racial caste system. The Ku Klux Klan and law enforcement were often indistinguishable. Black-and-white photographs of the era memorialize the way Southern police sicced German shepherds on civil rights protesters and peeled the skin off black children with the force of water hoses. Lawmen were also involved or implicated in untold numbers of beatings, killings and disappearances of black Southerners who forgot their place.

In the North, police worked to protect white spaces by containing and controlling the rising black population that had been propelled into the industrial belt during the Great Migration. It was not unusual for Northern police to join white mobs as they attacked black homeowners attempting to move into white neighborhoods, or black workers trying to take jobs reserved for white laborers. And yet they strictly enforced vagrancy laws, catch-alls that gave them wide discretion to stop, question and arrest black citizens at will.

Much has changed since then. Much has not.

Last Fourth of July, in a few short minutes as we adults watched the teenager among us talking to the police, we saw Hunter become a little more like us, her faith a little shaken, her place in the world a little less stable. Hunter, who is biracial and lives with her white mother in a heavily white area, had not been exposed to the policing many black Americans face. She was about to be.

On the phone, she could offer only the most generic of suspect descriptions, which apparently made the officer on the other end of the line suspicious. By way of explanation, Hunter told the officer she was just 16. The police called her back: once, twice, then three times, asking her for more information. The interactions began to feel menacing. "I'm not from here," Hunter said. "I've told you everything I know."

The fourth time the police called, she looked frightened. Her interrogator asked her, "Are you really trying to be helpful, or were you involved in this?" She turned to us, her voice aquiver.

"Are they going to come get me?"

"See," one of us said, trying to lighten the mood. "That's why we don't call them."

We all laughed, but it was hollow.

My friend Carla Murphy and I have talked about that day several times since then. We've turned it over in our minds and wondered whether, with the benefit of hindsight, we should have called 911.

Carla wasn't born in the United States. She came here when she was 9, and back in her native Barbados, she didn't give police much thought. That changed when she moved into heavily black Jamaica, Queens.

Nikole Hannah-Jones, at front, with her friends Carla Murphy, left; Monifa Bandele; and her husband, Faraji Hannah-Jones, in Bedford-Stuyvesant, Brooklyn.

Ben Baker/Redux

28   Carla said she constantly saw police, often white, stopping and harassing passersby, almost always black. "You see the cops all the time, but they do not speak to you. You see them talking to each other, but the only time you ever see them interact with someone is if they are jacking them up," she said. "They are making a choice, and it says they don't care about you, it tells you they are not here for your people or people who look like you."

29   Carla herself was arrested at a young age—because she was present when her cousin pushed through a subway turnstile without paying. The teenagers were cuffed, thrown in a paddy wagon, booked and held overnight. At 15, Carla, then a

student at The Dalton School, a prestigious private academy in Manhattan, had an arrest record.

That experience, along with many others, informed Carla's decision on July 4.

"I am a responsible adult, but I really can't see having a different reaction. Isn't that weird?" she told me. "By calling the police, you are inviting this big system—that, frankly, doesn't like you—into your life. Sometimes you call and it is not the help that comes."

"So, no, I wouldn't call the police," she said. "Which is sad, because I want to be a good citizen."

I moved to the historic Bedford-Stuyvesant neighborhood of Brooklyn in 2011. Before then, I had been living in Portland, Oregon, and when I chose my new home in the gritty big city, it was partly because it was only a block away from a police precinct. That proximity made me feel safer—I figured crime would be less common with so many police nearby. Inadvertently, however, I also picked a prime target area of the city's stop-and-frisk program—a system of policing that caught so many innocent black and brown men in its dragnet that a federal judge found it unconstitutional in 2013.

My block is fairly typical of Bed-Stuy. My neighbors, until recently, were all black and included everyone from laborers to college professors. Both immaculately kept brownstones and boarded-up townhouses line my street. We have block meetings and a community garden. Police are a constant presence, speeding down the street to the precinct or walking the beat. Sometimes, I escort my daughter to the store underneath police watchtowers with tinted windows that pop up around the neighborhood with no warning, then disappear just as suddenly—their entire existence ambiguous yet alarming. I have witnessed from my window, countless times, police stopping someone, usually a young man, who is walking down the street. These men are often searched and questioned as they go to the bodega or head home from work or school.

A few months ago, a police officer approached my neighbor as he was leaving the bodega and began questioning him. My neighbor is quiet and respectful, but he also is poor and transient. He tends to look disheveled, but the worst thing I've seen him do is drink beer on the stoop.

When he asked why he was being stopped, the police grabbed him and threw him to the ground. As someone recorded the incident on a cellphone, police shot my neighbor with a Taser gun and then arrested him.

He was never told why police stopped him. The only thing they charged him with was resisting arrest. But this arrest cost him his job and a fine he will struggle to pay. If he doesn't pay, a judge will issue a bench warrant, and instead of preventing crime, the police will have created a criminal.

Across the street and a few doors down from me, my neighbor Guthrie Ramsey has his own story. Guthrie was born in Chicago and grew up in a family that did not emphasize the obstacles their children would face. "I was socialized to believe that the police were our friends," he said.

Yet one night, some years ago, while driving his teenage son to a soccer game, Guthrie was pulled over by police. Within minutes, he and his son were sprawled on the ground, with guns drawn on them. The police believed Guthrie fit the description of a suspect. Guthrie, a short, easy-going guy with a contagious laugh, managed to point the police to his University of Pennsylvania faculty ID. That's right: He's an Ivy League professor. And a noted musician.

"It was so frightening. It was humiliating. You get so humiliated that it's hard to even get to the anger," he told me. "You just don't get to experience interactions with the police as a garden-variety circumstance."

These types of stories in black communities are so ubiquitous as to be unremarkable. If my husband is running very late and I cannot get hold of him, my mind does not immediately go to foul play. I wonder if he's been detained.

This fear is not unjustified. Young black men today are <u>21 times</u> more likely to be shot and killed by police than young white men. Still, it's not that black Americans expect to die every time they encounter the police. Police killings are just the worst manifestations of countless slights and indignities that build until there's an explosion.

Since 1935, nearly every so-called race riot in the United States—and there have been more than 100—has been sparked by a police incident, Muhammad says. This can be an act of brutality, or a senseless killing. But the underlying causes run much deeper. Police, because they interact in black communities every day, are often seen as the face of larger systems of inequality in the justice system, employment, education and housing.

In the months since Ferguson, many pundits have asserted that black Americans deserve this type of policing, that it is a consequence of their being more likely to be both the perpetrators and victims of violent crime. "White police officers wouldn't be there if you weren't killing each other," former New York Mayor Rudy Giuliani argued on *Meet the Press* as the nation awaited the grand jury decision in the Michael Brown shooting. It should be noted that Giuliani oversaw the NYPD during two of the most notorious cases of police brutality in recent memory, the sodomy of Abner Louima and the death of Amadou Diallo, who was unarmed, in a hail of 41 bullets. Both were black men.

What Giuliani was saying, in essence, is that law-abiding citizens deserve to be treated with suspicion because they share racial traits with the tiny number among them who commit crimes.

Black communities want a good relationship with law enforcement because they want their families and property to be safe. After all, it is true that black communities often face higher rates of crime; in 2013, more than 50 percent of murder victims across the country were black, though only 13 percent of the total population is. But it's also true that crime reduction efforts by black people in black communities have contributed to the recent, historic drop in crime across the country.

So why are black Americans still so often denied the same kind of smart policing that typically occurs in white communities, where police seem fully capable of discerning between law-abiding citizens and those committing crimes, and between crimes like turnstile-jumping and those that need serious intervention?

"You can be protected and served," Muhammad says. "It happens every day in communities across America. It happens all the time in white communities where crime is happening."

During the height of the "Black Lives Matter" protests, a mentally ill man shot and killed two police officers a few blocks from my home. I lay up that night thinking about those two men and their families. No one wants to see people killed. Not by police, not by anyone. The next morning, my husband and I took food and flowers to the grim brick precinct right around the corner from us that the officers were working out of when they were killed.

The officer at the front desk did not greet us when we came in. And he looked genuinely surprised by our offering, his face softening as he told us we didn't have to do this, but thank you. That people who should be allies somehow felt like adversaries troubled me.

The next day, I drove by the precinct on my way to the store. It had been cordoned off with metal barricades. Two helmeted officers stood sentry out front, gripping big black assault rifles, and watching. The message felt clear.

They weren't standing out there to protect the neighborhood. They were there to protect themselves from us.

QUESTIONS FOR CONSIDERATION

1. Hannah-Jones presents a variety of issues in this article, all of which relate to the main idea she is presenting. What is the main idea?
2. Hannah-Jones chooses to start her essay with a story. What effect did this choice have on you as a reader?
3. What is the relationship between the Black Lives Matter movement and the story Hannah-Jones uses to start the essay?
4. Why does Hannah-Jones discuss history in the essay? In other words, what is the rhetorical function of this discussion of historical events and attitudes?
5. Hannah-Jones wrote this article in 2015, long before the sweeping protests of police violence that resulted from George Floyd's death in 2020. How does her article contribute to the conversations about policing that we are having today? What changes could be made to policing to improve the situation?

IDEAS FOR WRITING

A. **A Summary and Response Assignment.** Write a summary of the article, and then respond to the ideas Hannah-Jones has presented. What experiences have you had with police? Do you think your ethnicity or your neighborhood's location have affected the way police have treated you? Explain your answer.

B. **A Persuasive Essay Assignment.** Examine the social issues involved in policing in your city or town. Write a letter to the editor of your local newspaper in which you advocate ideas that can help citizens and police work together cooperatively.

C. **A Researched Argument Assignment.** Hannah-Jones presents a number of statistics as support for her ideas. Conduct research to answer this question: Under what conditions (environments, neighborhoods, and so on) is unwarranted police violence the most widespread? In other words, are there conditions that lend themselves to an overly zealous police force? What can be done to change these conditions and to curb the violence?

Mass Incarceration: The Whole Pie
Wendy Sawyer and Peter Wagner

Wendy Sawyer, research director at the Prison Policy Initiative, has worked as an investigator for the Civilian Complaint Review Board in New York City and a research associate for Northeastern's Institute on Race and Justice. She has written extensively on criminal justice issues, including women's incarceration, pretrial detention, and probation.

Peter Wagner is the executive director of the Prison Policy Initiative, an organization he co-founded to reveal the debilitating effects of mass incarceration. He has received numerous awards for his work.

Teaching Suggestion
This report is an excerpt from a larger report, available at https://www.prisonpolicy.org/reports/pie2020.html. The report online contains multiple graphics. Consider using this report as a springboard into creating graphics to present data.

Can it really be true that most people in jail are being held before trial? And how much of mass incarceration is a result of the war on drugs? These questions are harder to answer than you might think, because our country's systems of confinement are so fragmented. The various government agencies involved in the justice system collect a lot of critical data, but it is not designed to help policymakers or the public understand what's going on. As public support for criminal justice reform continues to build, however, it's more important than ever that we get the facts straight and understand **the big picture**.

This report offers some much needed clarity by **piecing together this country's disparate systems of confinement**. The American criminal justice system holds almost 2.3 million people in 1,833 state prisons, 110 federal prisons, 1,772 juvenile correctional facilities, 3,134 local jails, 218 immigration detention facilities, and 80 Indian Country jails as well as in military prisons, civil commitment centers, state psychiatric hospitals, and prisons in the U.S. territories. This report provides a detailed look at where and why people are locked up in the U.S.,

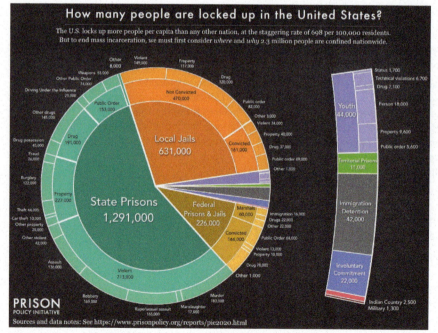

Wagner, Peter, and Wendy Sawyer. "Mass Incarceration: The Whole Pie 2019." Prison Policy Initiative, March 19, 2019. Used with permission.

and dispels some modern myths to focus attention on the real drivers of mass incarceration, including exceedingly punitive responses to even the most minor offenses.

This big-picture view allows us to focus on the most important drivers of mass incarceration and identify important, but often ignored, systems of confinement. The detailed views [not shown] bring these overlooked systems to light, from immigration detention to civil commitment and youth confinement. In particular, local jails often receive short shrift in larger discussions about criminal justice, but they play a critical role as "incarceration's front door" and have a far greater impact than the daily population suggests.

While this pie chart provides a comprehensive snapshot of our correctional system, the graphic does not capture the **enormous churn** in and out of our correctional facilities, nor the far larger universe of people whose lives are affected by the criminal justice system. Every year, over 600,000 people enter *prison* gates, but people go to *jail* 10.6 million times each year.

Jail churn is particularly high because most people in jails have not been convicted.

Some have just been arrested and will make bail within hours or days, while many others are too poor to make bail and remain behind bars until their trial. Only a small number (about 160,000 on any given day) have been convicted, and are generally serving misdemeanor sentences under a year. At least 1 in 4 people who go to jail will be arrested again within the same year—often those dealing with poverty, mental illness, and substance use disorders, whose problems only worsen with incarceration.

With a sense of the big picture, the next question is: *why* are so many people locked up? How many are incarcerated for drug offenses? Are the profit motives of private companies driving incarceration? Or is it really about public safety and keeping dangerous people off the streets? There are a plethora of modern myths about incarceration. Most have a kernel of truth, but these myths distract us from focusing on the most important drivers of incarceration.

Five myths about mass incarceration

The overcriminalization of drug use, the use of private prisons, and low-paid or unpaid prison labor are among the most contentious issues in criminal justice today because they inspire moral outrage. But they do not answer the question of why most people are incarcerated, or how we can dramatically—and safely—reduce our use of confinement. Likewise, emotional responses to sexual and violent offenses often derail important conversations about the social, economic, and moral costs of incarceration and lifelong punishment. Finally, simplistic solutions to reducing incarceration, such as moving people from jails and prisons to community supervision, ignore the fact that "alternatives" to incarceration often lead to incarceration anyway. Focusing on the policy changes that can end mass incarceration, and not just put a dent in it, requires the public to put these issues into perspective.

The first myth: Releasing "nonviolent drug offenders" would end mass incarceration

It's true that police, prosecutors, and judges continue to punish people harshly for nothing more than drug possession. Drug offenses still account for the incarceration of almost half a million people, and nonviolent drug convictions remain a defining feature of the federal prison system. Police still make over 1 million drug possession arrests each year, many of which lead to prison sentences. Drug arrests continue to give residents of over-policed communities criminal records, hurting their employment prospects and increasing the likelihood of longer sentences for any future offenses.

Nevertheless, 4 out of 5 people in prison or jail are locked up for something other than a drug offense—either a more serious offense or an even *less* serious one. To end mass incarceration, we will have to change how our society and our justice system responds to crimes more serious than drug possession. We must also stop incarcerating people for behaviors that are even more benign.

The second myth: Private prisons are the corrupt heart of mass incarceration

In fact, less than 9% of all incarcerated people are held in private prisons; the vast majority are in publicly-owned prisons and jails. Some states have more people in private prisons than others, of course, and the industry *has* lobbied to maintain high levels of incarceration, but private prisons are essentially a parasite on the massive publicly-owned system—not the root of it.

Nevertheless, a range of private industries and even some public agencies continue to profit from mass incarceration. Many city and county jails rent space to other agencies, including state prison systems, the U.S. Marshals Service, and

Immigration and Customs Enforcement (ICE). Private companies are frequently granted contracts to operate prison food and health services (often so bad they result in major lawsuits), and prison and jail telecom and commissary functions have spawned multi-billion dollar private industries. By privatizing services like phone calls, medical care and commissary, prisons and jails are unloading the costs of incarceration onto incarcerated people and their families, trimming their budgets at an unconscionable social cost.

The third myth: Prisons are "factories behind fences" that exist to provide companies with a huge slave labor force

Simply put, private companies using prison labor are not what stands in the way of ending mass incarceration, nor are they the source of most prison jobs. Only about 5,000 people in prison—less than 1%—are employed by private companies through the federal PIECP program, which requires them to pay at least minimum wage before deductions. (A larger portion work for state-owned "correctional industries," which pay much less, but this still only represents about 6% of people incarcerated in state prisons.)

But prisons do rely on the labor of incarcerated people for food service, laundry and other operations, and they pay incarcerated workers unconscionably low wages: our 2017 study found that on average, incarcerated people earn between 86 cents and $3.45 *per day* for the most common prison jobs. In at least five states, those jobs pay nothing at all. Moreover, work in prison is compulsory, with little regulation or oversight, and incarcerated workers have few rights and protections. Forcing people to work for low or no pay and no benefits allows prisons to shift the costs of incarceration to incarcerated people—hiding the true cost of running prisons from most Americans.

The fourth myth: People in prison for violent or sexual crimes are too dangerous to be released

Particularly harmful is the myth that people who commit violent or sexual crimes are incapable of rehabilitation and thus warrant many decades or even a lifetime of punishment. As lawmakers and the public increasingly agree that past policies have led to unnecessary incarceration, it's time to consider policy changes that go beyond the low-hanging fruit of "non-non-nons"—people convicted of non-violent, non-serious, non-sexual offenses. If we are serious about ending mass incarceration, we will have to change our responses to more serious and violent crime.

Recidivism data do not support the belief that people who commit violent crimes ought to be locked away for decades for the sake of public safety. People convicted of violent and sexual offenses are actually among the least likely to be rearrested, and those convicted of rape or sexual assault have rearrest rates 20% lower than all other offense categories combined. More broadly, people convicted of *any* violent offense are less likely to be rearrested in the years after release than those convicted of property, drug, or public order offenses. One reason: age is one of the main predictors of violence. The risk for violence peaks in adolescence or early adulthood and then declines with age, yet we incarcerate people long after their risk has declined.

Despite this evidence, people convicted of violent offenses often face decades of incarceration, and those convicted of sexual offenses can be committed to indefinite confinement or stigmatized by sex offender registries long after completing their sentences. And while some of the justice system's response has more to do with retribution than public safety, more incarceration is not what most victims of crime want. National survey data show that most victims want violence prevention, social investment, and alternatives to incarceration that address the root causes of crime, not more investment in carceral systems that cause more harm.

The fifth myth: Expanding community supervision is the best way to reduce incarceration

Community supervision, which includes probation, parole, and pretrial supervision, is often seen as a "lenient" punishment, or as an ideal "alternative" to incarceration. But while remaining in the community is certainly preferable to being locked up, the conditions imposed on those under supervision are often so restrictive that they set people up to fail. The long supervision terms, numerous and burdensome requirements, and constant surveillance (especially with electronic monitoring) result in frequent "failures," often for minor infractions like breaking curfew or failing to pay unaffordable supervision fees.

In 2016, at least 168,000 people were incarcerated for such "technical violations" of probation or parole—that is, not for any new crime.

Probation, in particular, leads to unnecessary incarceration; until it is reformed to support and reward success rather than detect mistakes, it is not a reliable "alternative."

Offense categories might not mean what you think

To understand the main drivers of incarceration, the public needs to see how many people are incarcerated for different offense types. But the reported offense data oversimplifies how people interact with the criminal justice system in two important ways: it reports only one offense category per person, and it reflects the outcome of the legal process, obscuring important details of actual events.

First, when a person is in prison for multiple offenses, only the most serious offense is reported. So, for example, there are people in prison for violent offenses who were also convicted of drug offenses, but they are included only in the "violent" category in the data. This makes it hard to grasp the complexity of criminal events, such as the role drugs may have played in violent or property offenses. We must also consider that almost all convictions are the result of plea bargains, where defendants plead guilty to a lesser offense, possibly in a different category, or one that they did not actually commit.

Secondly, many of these categories group together people convicted of a wide range of offenses. For violent offenses especially, these labels can distort perceptions of individual "violent offenders" and exaggerate the scale of dangerous violent crime. For example, "murder" is an extremely serious offense, but that category groups together the small number of serial killers with people who committed acts that are unlikely, for reasons of circumstance or advanced age, to ever happen again. It also includes offenses that the average person may not consider to be murder at all. In particular, the felony murder rule says that if someone dies during the commission of a felony, everyone involved can be as guilty of murder as the person who pulled the trigger. Acting as lookout during a break-in where someone was accidentally killed is indeed a serious offense, but many may be surprised that this can be considered murder in the U.S.

Lessons from the smaller "slices": Youth, immigration, and involuntary commitment

Looking more closely at incarceration by offense type also exposes some disturbing facts about the 52,000 youth in confinement in the United States: too many are there for a "most serious offense" that is **not even a crime**. For example, there are over 6,600 youth behind bars for technical violations of their probation, rather than for a new offense. An additional 1,700 youth are locked up for "status" offenses, which are "behaviors that are not law violations for adults, such as running away, truancy, and incorrigibility."

Nearly 1 in 10 youth held for a criminal or delinquent offense is locked in an adult jail or prison, and most of the others are held in juvenile facilities that look and operate a lot like prisons and jails.

Turning to the people who are locked up criminally and civilly for **immigration-related reasons**, we find that 11,100 people are in federal prisons for criminal convictions of immigration offenses, and 13,600 more are held pretrial by the U.S. Marshals. The vast majority of people incarcerated for criminal immigration offenses are accused of illegal entry or illegal re-entry—in other words, for no more serious offense than crossing the border without permission.

Another 39,000 people are civilly detained by U.S. Immigration and Customs Enforcement (ICE) not for any crime, but simply for their undocumented immigrant status. ICE detainees are physically confined in federally-run or privately-run immigration detention facilities, or in local jails under contract with ICE. An additional 3,600 **unaccompanied children** are held in the custody of the Office of Refugee Resettlement (ORR), awaiting placement with parents, family members, or friends. While these children are not held for any criminal or delinquent offense, most are held in shelters or even juvenile placement facilities under detention-like conditions.

Adding to the universe of people who are confined because of justice system involvement, 22,000 people are **involuntarily detained or committed** to state psychiatric hospitals and civil commitment centers. Many of these people are not even convicted, and some are held indefinitely. 9,000 are being evaluated pre-trial or treated for incompetency to stand trial; 6,000 have been found not guilty by reason of insanity or guilty but mentally ill; another 6,000 are people convicted of sexual crimes who are involuntarily committed or detained after their prison sentences are complete. While these facilities aren't typically run by departments of correction, they are in reality much like prisons.

Beyond the "Whole Pie": Community supervision, poverty, and race and gender disparities

Once we have wrapped our minds around the "whole pie" of mass incarceration, we should zoom out and note that people who are incarcerated are only a fraction of those impacted by the criminal justice system. There are another 840,000 people on parole and a staggering 3.6 million people on probation. Many millions more have completed their sentences but are still living with a criminal record, a stigmatizing label that comes with collateral

Beyond identifying how many people are impacted by the criminal justice system, we should also focus on **who is most impacted and who is left behind** by policy change. Poverty, for example, plays a central role in mass incarceration. People in prison and jail are disproportionately poor compared to the overall U.S. population.

The criminal justice system punishes poverty, beginning with the high price of money bail: The median felony bail bond amount ($10,000) is the equivalent of 8 months' income for the typical detained defendant. As a result, people with low incomes are more likely to face the harms of pretrial detention. Poverty is not only a predictor of incarceration; it is also frequently the outcome, as a criminal record and time spent in prison destroys wealth, creates debt, and decimates job opportunities.

It's no surprise that people of color—who face much greater rates of poverty—are dramatically overrepresented in the nation's prisons and jails. These racial disparities are particularly stark for Black Americans, who make up 40% of the incarcerated population despite representing only 13% of U.S residents. The same is true for women, whose incarceration rates have for decades risen faster than men's, and who are often behind bars because of financial obstacles such as an inability to pay bail. As policymakers continue to push for reforms that reduce incarceration, they should avoid changes that will widen disparities, as has happened with juvenile confinement and with women in state prisons.

Equipped with the full picture of how many people are locked up in the United States, where, and why, our nation has a better foundation for the long overdue conversation about criminal justice reform. For example, the data makes it clear that ending the war on drugs will not alone end mass incarceration, though the federal government and some states have taken an important step by reducing the number of people incarcerated for drug offenses. Looking at the "whole pie" also opens up other conversations about where we should focus our energies:

- Are state officials and prosecutors willing to rethink not just long sentences for drug offenses, but the reflexive, simplistic policymaking that has served to increase incarceration for violent offenses as well?
- Do policymakers and the public have the stamina to confront the second largest slice of the pie: the thousands of locally administered jails? Will state, county, and city governments be brave enough to end money bail without

imposing unnecessary conditions in order to bring down pretrial detention rates? Will local leaders be brave enough to redirect public spending to smarter investments like community-based drug treatment and job training?

- What is the role of the federal government in ending mass incarceration? The federal prison system is just a small slice of the total pie, but the federal government can certainly use its financial and ideological power to incentivize and illuminate better paths forward. At the same time, how can elected sheriffs, district attorneys, and judges—who all control larger shares of the correctional pie—slow the flow of people into the criminal justice system?

- Given that the companies with the greatest impact on incarcerated people are not private prison operators, but service providers that contract with public facilities, will states respond to public pressure to end contracts that squeeze money from people behind bars?

- Can we implement reforms that both reduce the number of people incarcerated in the U.S. and the well-known racial and ethnic disparities in the criminal justice system?

Now that we can see the big picture of how many people are locked up in the United States in the various types of facilities, we can see that **something needs to change**. Looking at the big picture requires us to ask if it really makes sense to lock up 2.3 million people on any given day, giving this nation the dubious distinction of having the highest incarceration rate in the world. Both policymakers and the public have the responsibility to carefully consider each individual slice in turn to ask whether legitimate social goals are served by putting each group behind bars, and whether any benefit really outweighs the social and fiscal costs.

34

QUESTIONS FOR CONSIDERATION

1. In this report, the writers make several claims. What is their main claim?
2. What is the purpose of discussing myths about incarceration?
3. Based on the report, why are so many people incarcerated?
4. The pie chart included in this selection is only one of the graphics that are included in the full report. Examine the graphics in the full report (https://www.prisonpolicy.org/reports/pie2020.html). What function do the graphics serve? Could the graphics tell the whole story of the report, or is written explanation required for readers to fully understand the message? Explain your answers.

5. Near the end of the report, the writers claim that "reflexive, simplistic policymaking" is, in part, to blame for mass incarceration. What do the writers mean by this?

IDEAS FOR WRITING

A. **A Summary and Response Assignment.** Write a summary of the report. Select an idea from the report that you found personally interesting, and write a response to that idea. Do you agree with the idea? Why or why not?

B. **A Reflective Assignment.** Consider the five myths about incarceration, and reflect on your own beliefs about people who are in prison. How have your life experiences shaped your beliefs about incarceration? Write a reflective essay to share your insights.

C. **A Persuasive Assignment.** One of the ways the writers provide support for their claim that mass incarceration is a serious social problem is to debunk five myths about incarceration. Select a social issue you feel strongly about, and identify myths people have about the issue. Write a persuasive essay in which you debunk the myths and argue for social change.

5 Media and Culture

Breaking Down the Anti-Vaccine Echo Chamber
Rachel Alter and Tonay Flattum-Riemers

Rachel Alter, MD, is a research affiliate for the Vaccine Confidence Project in New York. Her research and writing focus on disease eradication, epidemic/pandemic control, health communication, bioterrorism, and vaccination. Tonay Flattum-Riemers is a graduate research assistant at the Columbia National Center for Disaster Preparedness, where he focuses on epidemiology and infectious disease. Alter and Flattum-Riemers both manage the social media pages concerning vaccine-related issues for March for Science.

Teaching Suggestion
Consider assigning this article in conjunction with the myth-busting argument assignment in Chapter 19.

The rhetoric around vaccination is generally black and white: vaccines are good or vaccines are bad. In these days of Facebook and Twitter, it is easy enough to block out the opinions of those you disagree with, and only associate with people whose voices reinforce your own opinions. These echo chambers have real-world implications; currently, the U.S. is in the midst of its largest measles outbreak in decades. That's why it's important to find ways to communicate across the divide.

While the overwhelming majority of the scientific and medical communities (including the authors of this article) agree that vaccines are extremely safe and effective, and that the benefits far outweigh the risks, it is important to note that there have been, on rare occasions, events where certain vaccines have been recalled, and there are very rare occasions when anaphylactic events can occur after vaccination. Failing to admit that these events can occur fuels the anti-vaccination community further in their dangerous rhetoric and pushes them deeper into the echo chambers that exacerbate vaccine denialism. It is important for vaccine advocates to stop completely discounting these fears as impossible and to reframe their argument in a way that acknowledges the fears but underscores the importance, efficacy, and safety of vaccination on the whole, despite the risks.

Many who are on the fence about vaccination are worried about the potential consequences of vaccines; they've heard stories about children having severe immunologic reactions or dangerously high fevers after their shots; they're enticed by anecdotes about children who were vaccinated one day and severely impaired the next. Most of these stories come from a misunderstanding of the common scientific axiom, "correlation does not equal causation," and carry little to no weight in arguments against vaccinating. Many of the stories are also lies fabricated by the most vocal vaccine deniers and profiteers seeking to further their own dangerous agendas.

But every once in a while, a story will carry some legitimacy, and it does vaccine advocates no good to dismiss them as impossible. Instead of outright dismissing the claims, it would benefit the pro-vaccine community to acknowledge that sometimes, albeit rarely, mistakes occur, and to focus on what the scientific community does to ensure safety, how infrequent these events actually are, and how the benefits of vaccines still significantly outweigh the risks. In fact, when mistakes do occur, the products are removed from the market immediately and the kinks are worked out, further evidence that the system works well.

Vaccine advocates should feel comfortable with these conversations and instead of shutting them down; those whose fears are dismissed will look for another outlet to vent their frustration, convinced the medical community and government are engaging in a conspiratorial cover-up, and if they cannot find a place to have a civil discussion about it in an evidence-driven environment, they will often seek confirmation from those whose agendas are nefarious: enter the anti-vax echo chambers.

Many of these echo chambers—like Facebook's "Vaccine Resistance Movement," "Vaccine Re-education Discussion Forum," and "Vaccine Truth Movement" groups, for example—have tens of thousands of followers. Where do they come from? Much of the blame can be placed on profiteers: those who seek to profit off the ignorance and fears of parents and others.

Andrew Wakefield, whose retracted *Lancet* article claimed there was a link between the MMR vaccine and autism, is a textbook profiteer who intended to profit from his own measles vaccine and treatment, for which he filed a patent application. Even after his medical license was revoked because of fraudulent, unethical methods and conflict of interest, he continues to profit from his hoax. In 2016, he and other big-name anti-vaccine profiteers directed the propagandistic documentary *Vaxxed*, which makes the same spurious claims as Wakefield's original *Lancet* article and raked in almost $1.2 million.

Or consider Larry Cook, who runs a group called Stop Mandatory Vaccination. He has made almost $80,000 from anti-vaccination GoFundMe campaigns, which he freely admits go "directly" to his bank account and "may be used to pay [his] personal bills."

Profiteers are responsible for gatekeeping many of the staunch anti-vaccine communities found on social media, where anyone who expresses an opinion contrary to theirs is attacked and banned from the group in order to keep the echo chamber as tight as possible. It is through these echo chambers that profiteers continue profiting; they sell their own books and alternative lifestyles and bankroll from GoFundMe campaigns. Any dissenting voice is a threat to their finances, so they encourage intense groupthink and mob mentality.

It is our goal as public health professionals—and should be the goal of every scientifically-minded, pro-evidence person—to keep those on the fence about vaccines as far away from the echo chambers as possible. Foresight is important: understand the commonly used tropes they may use, and know how to combat them with evidence and reason instead of shutting them down.

Unfortunate as it may be, it is on all of us to steer the conversation in the direction science has told us is safe and effective for decades. We must do what we can to prevent the echo chambers from growing.

QUESTIONS FOR CONSIDERATION

1. What do the writers advocate in this article?
2. Why do you think the writers acknowledge that vaccines have been recalled in the past and that anaphylactic shock has sometimes resulted from vaccinations? How does such an admission serve a rhetorical purpose?
3. What do the writers mean when they discuss the axiom "correlation does not equal causation"?
4. How and why is antivaccination misinformation spread, according to the writers?
5. What do the writers mean by "echo chambers"?

IDEAS FOR WRITING

A. **An Informative Assignment.** The writers point out that social media outlets function to propagate misinformation for personal gain. How does misinformation—fake news, for example—benefit those who spread it? Write an informative essay in which you explain the connections between personal gain and the spreading of misinformation.

B. **An Evaluative Assignment.** Write a comparative analysis in which you evaluate the risks of receiving a vaccine (select a specific type of vaccine, such as the MMR [measles, mumps, and rubella]) and the risks of driving without a seatbelt or driving while slightly intoxicated.

C. **A Persuasive Assignment.** Write a letter to the editor of your local newspaper in which you attempt to persuade readers to be vaccinated against flu. Use reasons that general readers would find the most convincing.

Teaching Tip
Many students will be unfamiliar with Gloria Steinem, and although students have heard the term "feminism," not all students have a clear idea of what is meant by it. Consider having students do research to answer the question, "What is feminism?" To introduce Steinem, consider using this article: "How Gloria Steinem Became the World's Most Famous Feminist," https://www.nationalgeographic.com/culture/2019/03/how-gloria-steinem-became-worlds-most-famous-feminist/#close.

Erotica and Pornography
Gloria Steinem

Gloria Steinem (b. 1934), writer, activist, and co-founder of **Ms.** *magazine, has been working for many decades to increase public awareness of gender inequities. Today she is perhaps the best-respected and most prominent feminist writer and thinker at work in the United States. The article that follows was first published in 1978 in* **Ms.** *magazine.*

1   Human beings are the only animals that experience the same sex drive at times when we can—and cannot—conceive.

2   Just as we developed uniquely human capacities for language, planning, memory, and invention along our evolutionary path, we also developed sexuality as a

form of expression, a way of communicating that is separable from our need for sex as a way of perpetuating ourselves. For humans alone, sexuality can be and often is primarily a way of bonding, of giving and receiving pleasure, bridging differentness, discovering sameness, and communicating emotion.

We developed this and other human gifts through our ability to change our environment, adapt physically, and in the long run, to affect our own evolution. But as an emotional result of this spiraling path away from other animals, we seem to alternate between periods of exploring our unique abilities to change new boundaries and feelings of loneliness in the unknown that we ourselves have created; a fear that sometimes sends us back to the comfort of the animal world by encouraging us to exaggerate our sameness.

The separation of "play" from "work," for instance, is a problem only in the human world. So is the difference between art and nature, or an intellectual accomplishment and a physical one. As a result, we celebrate play, art, and invention as leaps into the unknown; but any imbalance can send us back to nostalgia for our primate past and the conviction that the basics of work, nature, and physical labor are somehow more worthwhile or even moral.

In the same way, we have explored our sexuality as separable from conception: A pleasurable, empathetic bridge to strangers of the same species. We have even invented contraception—a skill that has probably existed in some form since our ancestors figured out the process of birth—in order to extend this uniquely human difference. Yet we also have times of atavistic suspicion that sex is not complete—or even legal or intended-by-god—if it cannot end in conception.

No wonder the concepts of "erotica" and "pornography" can be so crucially different, and yet so confused. Both assume that sexuality can be separated from conception, and therefore can be used to carry a personal message. That's a major reason why, even in our current culture, both may be called equally "shocking" or legally "obscene," a word whose Latin derivative means "dirty, containing filth." This gross condemnation of all sexuality that isn't harnessed to childbirth and marriage has been increased by the current backlash against women's progress. Out of fear that the whole patriarchal structure might be upset if women really had the autonomous power to decide our reproductive futures (that is, if we controlled the most basic means of production), right-wing groups are not only denouncing prochoice abortion literature as "pornographic," but are trying to stop the sending of all contraceptive information through the mails by invoking obscenity laws. In fact, Phyllis Schlafly recently denounced the entire Women's Movement as "obscene."

Not surprisingly, this religious, visceral backlash has a secular, intellectual counterpart that relies heavily on applying the "natural" behavior of the animal world to humans. That is questionable in itself, but these Lionel Tigerish studies make their political purpose even more clear in the particular animals they select and the habits they choose to emphasize. The message is that females should accept their "destiny" of being sexually dependent and devote themselves to bearing and rearing their young.

Defending against such reaction in turn leads to another temptation: To merely reverse the terms, and declare that all non-procreative sex is good. In fact, however, this human activity can be as constructive or destructive, moral or immoral, as any other. Sex as communication can send messages as different as life and death; even the origins of "erotica" and "pornography" reflect that fact. After all, "erotica" is rooted in eros or passionate love, and thus in the idea of positive choice, free will, the yearning for a particular person. (Interestingly, the definition of erotica leaves open the question of gender.) "Pornography" begins with a root meaning "prostitution" or "female captives," thus letting us know that the subject is not mutual love, or love at all, but domination and violence against women. (Though, of course, homosexual pornography may imitate this violence by putting a man in the "feminine" role of victim.) It ends with a root meaning "writing about" or "description of" which puts still more distance between subject and object, and replaces a spontaneous yearning for closeness with objectification and a voyeur.

The difference is clear in the words. It becomes even more so by example.

Look at any photo or film of people making love; really making love. The images may be diverse, but there is usually a sensuality and touch and warmth, an acceptance of bodies and nerve endings. There is always a spontaneous sense of people who are there because they want to be, out of shared pleasure.

Now look at any depiction of sex in which there is clear force, or an unequal power that spells coercion. It may be very blatant, with weapons or torture or bondage, wounds and bruises, some clear humiliation, or an adult's sexual power being used over a child. It may be much more subtle: A physical attitude of conqueror and victim, the use of race or class difference to imply the same thing, perhaps a very unequal nudity, with one person exposed and vulnerable while the other is clothed. In either case, there is no sense of equal choice or equal power.

The first is erotic: A mutually pleasurable, sexual expression between people who have enough power to be there by positive choice. It may or may not strike the sense-memory in the viewer, or be creative enough to make the unknown seem real; but it doesn't require us to identify with a conqueror or a victim. It is truly sensuous, and may give us a contagion of pleasure.

The second is pornographic: Its message is violence, dominance, and conquest. It is sex being used to reinforce some inequality, or to create one, or to tell us the lie that pain and humiliation (ours or someone else's) are really the same as pleasure. If we are to feel anything, we must identify with conqueror or victim. That means we can only experience pleasure through the adoption of some degree of sadism or masochism. It also means that we may feel diminished by the role of conqueror, or enraged, humiliated, and vengeful by sharing identity with the victim.

Perhaps one could simply say that erotica is about sexuality, but pornography is about power and sex-as-weapon—in the same way we have come to understand that rape is about violence, and not really about sexuality at all.

Yes, it's true that there are women who have been forced by violent families and dominating men to confuse love with pain; so much so that they have become masochists. (A fact that in no way excuses those who administer such pain.) But the truth is that, for most women—and for men with enough humanity to imagine themselves into the predicament of women—true pornography could serve as aversion therapy for sex.

Of course, there will always be personal differences about what is and is not erotic, and there may be cultural differences for a long time to come. Many women feel that sex makes them vulnerable and therefore may continue to need more sense of personal connection and safety before allowing any erotic feelings. We now find competence and expertise erotic in men, but that may pass as we develop those qualities in ourselves. Men, on the other hand, may continue to feel less vulnerable, and therefore more open to such potential danger as sex with strangers. As some men replace the need for submission from childlike women with the pleasure of cooperation from equals, they may find a partner's competence to be erotic, too.

Such group changes plus individual differences will continue to be reflected in sexual love between people of the same gender, as well as between women and men. The point is not to dictate sameness, but to discover ourselves and each other through sexuality that is an exploring, pleasurable, empathetic part of our lives; a human sexuality that is unchained both from unwanted pregnancies and from violence.

But that is a hope, not a reality. At the moment, fear of change is increasing both the indiscriminate repression of all nonprocreative sex in the religious and "conservative" male world, and the pornographic vengeance against women's sexuality in the secular world of "liberal" and "radical" men. It's almost futuristic to debate what is and is not truly erotic, when many women are again being forced into compulsory motherhood, and the number of pornographic murders, tortures, and woman-hating images are on the increase in both popular culture and real life.

It's a familiar division: Wife or whore, "good" woman who is constantly vulnerable to pregnancy or "bad" woman who is unprotected from violence. Both roles would be upset if we were to control our own sexuality. And that's exactly what we must do.

In spite of all our atavistic suspicions and training for the "natural" role of motherhood, we took up the complicated battle for reproductive freedom. Our bodies had borne the health burden of endless births and poor abortions, and we had a greater motive for separating sexuality and conception.

Now we have to take up the equally complex burden of explaining that all non-procreative sex is not alike. We have a motive: Our right to a uniquely human sexuality, and sometimes even to survival. As it is, our bodies have too rarely been enough our own to develop erotica in our own lives, much less in art and literature. And our bodies have too often been the objects of pornography and the woman-hating, violent practice that it preaches. Consider also our spirits that break a little each time we see ourselves in chains or full labial display for the conquering male viewer, bruised or on our knees, screaming a real or pretended pain to delight the sadist, pretending to enjoy what we don't enjoy, to be blind to the images of our sisters that really haunt us—humiliated often enough ourselves by the truly obscene idea that sex and the domination of women must be combined.

Sexuality is human, free, separate—and so are we.

But until we untangle the lethal confusion of sex with violence, there will be more pornography and less erotica. There will be little murders in our beds—and very little love.

QUESTIONS FOR CONSIDERATION

1. When you read the title of this article, did you expect it to be one that was originally published in 1978? Explain your answer.
2. There are many claims in this essay. Which of them do you think is Steinem's main claim? Support your answer.
3. Not everyone agrees with Steinem's ideas in this essay. What are some of the counterarguments that might be made to challenge Steinem's ideas?
4. The internet has changed many things about our lives, including the proliferation and delivery of pornography. How do you think Steinem would feel about this today?
5. Steinem points out that forty years ago there was a war, as she describes it, over women's reproductive rights. Has the fight over reproductive rights changed? If so, how? If not, explain how the "war" has remained the same.

IDEAS FOR WRITING

A. **A Summary and Response Assignment.** Reread the final two sentences of Steinem's article. What do these lines mean? Summarize the parts of the article that help you to understand these final lines. Next, provide a personal response to the final two lines. Do you agree with Steinem? Why or why not?

B. **An Evaluative Assignment.** Steinem wrote this article in 1978 with the hope that social changes would result in greater respect for women. Evaluate the progress that has been made since Steinem wrote this article. Has the social change Steinem hoped for been realized? Support your answer with evidence.

C. **A Researched Argument.** Does pornography harm people? To answer this very broad question, you will need to narrow the topic and complete research. Write an argument in which you provide support for a claim on the topic you develop.

Love It or Hate It: Native Advertising on the Internet
George H. Pike

George H. Pike is the director of the Pritzker Legal Research Center at Northwestern University School of Law. He teaches legal research and copyright law and is especially interested in internet law for library professionals. This article was published in 2014 in Information Today, *a journal for which Pike has published a monthly column.*

Teaching Suggestion
Native advertising is ubiquitous and keeps evolving. Challenge students to find examples of hidden advertising in social media and websites.

> Most people, myself included, have a love-hate relationship with advertising in general and internet advertising in particular. More often than not, we hate the interruption presented by the advertising, whether it is the commercial break in our TV

1

show, the pages that we need to skip through to get to the magazine article, the popup we have to click out of on a webpage, or the video ad that's shown before our YouTube selection. Alternately, we love (or at least acknowledge and tolerate) that advertising supports the content being provided by the TV show, magazine article, webpage, or YouTube video.

Advertisers are, of course, aware of this consumer ambivalence and take steps to encourage consumers to be more welcoming of their advertising. Obviously, if the advertising is clever and engaging, it can go a long way toward being appreciated—as witnessed every year during the Super Bowl. If the advertising is relevant to the consumer, it can be more welcomed than irrelevant advertising. A more controversial technique is to make the advertising seem less like an advertisement and more like content that blends in with other content provided by the medium. On television, this type of advertising takes on the form of an "infomercial," while in print media, it is called an "advertorial." Now this form of advertising is gaining ground on the internet, and it's known as "native advertising."

Native within Its Surroundings

Native advertising is advertising that is intended to appear identical to other content presented by the content host. As described by Bloomberg BNA, it "appears native within its surroundings." In researching this column, one of the sources I used was an article from Forbes. In the article, which dealt with native advertising battlegrounds, Forbes acknowledged its own native advertising practices.

Forbes presents native advertising through what it calls "BrandVoice." After I viewed a recent Forbes webpage, a BrandVoice article titled "How Miami Is Solving Big Problems With Big Data" (onforb.es/liwdOOz) appeared after a series of "Top Stories," current news by staff and contributors, then "Most Popular" articles with a sidebar of links to social media content.

Forbes BrandVoice

The BrandVoice article looks identical to other Forbes articles with only a few exceptions: One is that part of the article link on the Forbes main page is a clear reference to IBM with IBM's logo and the phrase "IBM Smarter Planet Voice." The article itself is bylined by a manager at IBM, identified by name and job title. Several of the links within the article (but not all of them) are to pages within the IBM website. Interestingly, IBM is not specifically mentioned at all in the text of the article.

News article or advertising? When it becomes difficult to tell the difference, there is a possibility that the advertising could be seen as deceptive. Title 15, Section 1125 of the federal Lanham Act says that anyone who "misrepresents the nature, characteristics, qualities, or geographic origins of . . . goods, services, or commercial activities" in commercial advertising shall be held liable in a civil action (law.cornell.edu/uscode). An increasing number of stakeholders in the content, advertising, and consumer protection arenas are raising concerns and struggling to find a balance between effective native advertising and the law.

FTC Workshop

Recently, the Federal Trade Commission (FTC), which investigates deceptive advertising claims, held a workshop on native advertising at its headquarters in Washington, D.C. The speakers and panelists included representatives from consumer groups, the advertising and public relations industries, news outlets, and government agencies; journalists; and legal and journalism scholars.

Speakers at the workshop noted that native advertising is not necessarily a new phenomenon, nor is it inherently illegal. FTC investigations of native advertising date from nearly 100 years ago (to a case involving a then-newfangled electric vacuum cleaner) and include cases involving door-to-door sales (disguised as surveys), television infomercials (disguised as investigative reports), and web search engines (paid or natural search results).

Endorsement Guidelines

The key to the legal issues underlying native advertising rests with the FTC's endorsement guidelines, last updated in 2009. These guidelines, which have the force of law as federal regulations, define an endorsement as any advertising message that consumers are likely to believe reflects the opinion of a party other than the advertiser. (Forbes would be the endorser and IBM the advertiser in the previous example.) The guidelines go on to say that where there is a connection between the endorser and the seller that is "not reasonably expected by the audience," the connection must be disclosed. The guidelines are available at 1.usa.gov/QYwhql. But whether the disclosure is adequate can be difficult to determine. Was Forbes' disclosure adequate?

At least one advertising trade group has attempted to set out a list of best practices for handling disclosures of native advertising on the internet. The

Interactive Advertising Bureau (IAB; iab.net) identified several types of native internet advertising, including in-feed advertising (such as the Forbes example), paid search results, recommendation widgets (mini-ads), and promoted listings. For each of the types, the IAB recommends that the disclosure be large and visible enough for the consumer to notice, be in clear language that conveys that it is paid advertising, and be set apart so that a reasonable consumer can distinguish between paid advertising and published editorial content.

Self-Regulation, for Now

At this point, there seems to be a willingness among the stakeholders, including the FTC, to let the advertising and content industry self-regulate and identify a set of market-driven practices that comply with the FTC's guidelines. The practices must address the different types of native advertising on the internet, be functional in both traditional and mobile platforms, and, most critically, be in compliance with both the letter and the spirit of the FTC guidelines and the Lanham Act. When closing the FTC's native advertising workshop, Jessica Rich, director of the FTC's Bureau of Consumer Protection, indicated that native advertising is "stronger than ever," and is projected to bring in billions of dollars in advertising revenue. With this kind of money at stake, it is critical for the industry to remain on the "love" (or "tolerate") side of the consumer, rather than the "hate" side.

11

QUESTIONS FOR CONSIDERATION

1. Does Pike have a central claim in this article, and if so, what is it?
2. One of Pike's purposes is to define "native advertising" so that he can discuss it. What strategies does Pike use to define the concept? Do you think Pike's attempt to define the concept will be effective for general readers? Why or why not?
3. Are you familiar with the kind of native advertising that Pike is referring to? How does it differ from other kinds of ads that you have encountered?
4. Do you have confidence in the "advertising and content industry" that they can do the kind of self-regulating that Pike says is the status quo at this time? Why or why not?
5. Pike claims that most people understand and appreciate the relationship between advertising and the content that it supports. Have you ever thought about this relationship, and if so, what do you think?

IDEAS FOR WRITING

A. **An Informative Assignment.** Write an essay in which you explain the concept of native advertising, using examples you find from print or online as support.

B. **An Analytical Assignment.** Find at least three examples of native advertising online or in print. Write a compare-and-contrast analysis of their effectiveness, both generally and in relation to each other. You might find more traditional ads for the same products and use them in your analysis, as well.

C. **A Persuasive Assignment.** Search for recent cases in which advertisers were accused of violating the FCC regulations that Pike describes. Find the ads in question and write an essay that either defends the advertiser or supports the accusation of wrongdoing.

Teaching Suggestion
Public service advertisements are meant to be persuasive, but to effect persuasion, the ad creators must be in tune with their audience's values and motivations. Consider analyzing additional public service ads and discussing who the intended audience is and why the ad creators believed the ad would be effective. See https://www.adcouncil.org/ for additional examples.

It Shouldn't Be This Dangerous (Public Service Advertisement)

Government of Alberta, Canada

The image that follows is an example of a public service ad. Public service advertisements generally seek to convey messages that increase the safety or well-being of individuals or communities. The public service advertisement that follows was produced by the Canadian Government of Alberta.

Government of Alberta. "It shouldn't be this dangerous. Stop for flashing red lights" (advertisement). All rights reserved. Used with permission.

QUESTIONS FOR CONSIDERATION

1. What is the ad's message?
2. What impressions is the ad designed to create? How do these impressions support the text in the ad?
3. How effective would the ad be without the image? Explain your answer.
4. What details in the image contribute to the ad's power?
5. If you were an ad writer and hoped to communicate the message of this ad, what is another method you might use to do so?

IDEAS FOR WRITING

A. **An Informative Assignment.** One purpose of the ad is to increase public safety for school children. Select an issue related to public safety, and write an informative essay with the purpose of educating the public about the issue.

B. **An Evaluative Assignment.** Evaluate the effectiveness of this advertisement to achieve its purpose for a general audience. To evaluate the ad, figure out criteria that should be met for an ad to be effective. For instance, to be effective, an advertisement must be visually interesting enough to capture readers' attention. Once you have selected criteria, use them to evaluate the potential effectiveness of this ad.

C. **A Rhetorical Analysis Assignment.** Advertisements are examples of visual rhetoric. Write a rhetorical analysis of the advertisement, focusing on the methods the ad creators use to convince people to follow the laws about stopping for school buses.

Save a Life: Don't Drive Home Buzzed (Public Service Advertisement)

U.S. Department of Transportation and the Ad Council

This public service advertisement was created by the Ad Council in conjunction with the U.S. Department of Transportation. The Ad Council, whose full name is the Advertising Council, is a nonprofit organization that creates and makes available advertisements for good causes, such as public service announcements. In the ad that follows, the Ad Council partnered with the U.S. Department of Transportation, whose mission is "to ensure our nation has the safest, most efficient and modern transportation system in the world; that improves the quality of life for all American people and communities, from rural to urban, and increases the productivity and competitiveness of American workers and businesses."

Ad Council/US Department of Transportation

QUESTIONS FOR CONSIDERATION

1. What is the message conveyed by the image in the ad?
2. Was it difficult for you to figure out what the ad meant? Explain.
3. What details in the image contributes to the ad's power?
4. If you were an ad writer and hoped to communicate the message of this ad, what is another method you might use to do so?

IDEAS FOR WRITING

A. **An Analysis Assignment.** Do an internet search using the keywords "ad" and "buzzed driving." You will find other ads that attempt to convey the same message as this ad. Select one or two of the ads you find, and then write a comparative analysis in which you analyze the strength and weaknesses of each ad you have selected, including the advertisement printed here.

B. **A Rhetorical Analysis Assignment.** Advertisements are examples of visual rhetoric. Write a rhetorical analysis of the advertisement, focusing on the methods the ad creators use to convince people not to drive after any amount of drinking.

6 Personal Growth

How I Overcame My Stuttering
Justin Huang

Teaching Suggestion
Readers need not have personally struggled with stuttering to find Huang's essay interesting and instructive. Ask students to explain how Huang makes his struggle relevant to all readers.

When he wrote this article, Justin Huang was a senior in high school. Huang is from Ottawa, the capital of Canada. He writes, "I have had a noticeable stutter since middle school. . . . I worked with a speech therapist to correct the stutter. While [the work was] somewhat effective, I eventually decided to stop, as other developments in my life made me realize that my stutter was completely tied to my confidence." Huang's article appeared on the International Stuttering Association's website.

1 Beads of sweat began to collect on my forehead, as snickers of laughter echoed throughout the classroom. I opened my mouth to speak and a staccato of 'buh's' shot out. 'Buh-buh, buh-buh, b-bonjour'. Any confidence I had, disintegrated. And I trudged through my three-minute French presentation, facing for countless times my worst enemy—my stutter.

2 As I spoke, I could the feel the eyes of my classmates cutting to pieces any remains of my confidence. Even those who usually dozed off during presentations looked my direction, as if waiting to see when I would stutter next. Midway through, I hazarded a glance toward my French teacher. Usually kind and supportive, his face was draped with the initial stages of a frown. *This is going terribly*, I thought. My thoughts turned into anguish, and helplessly, I stumbled onward.

3 When the presentation was over, my mind tried to block out what had just happened, but the damage to my confidence had been done. I wondered why this

experience felt so awful. After all, stuttering was nothing new to me. Any time I was forced to speak in front of others, I would have to do battle with it. In French class, my worst class, I almost always lost. But even then, this was a new low. After talking to my parents about it, I realized I was disturbed by the fact that this was the worst my stuttering had ever been, and the worse it became, the more non-existent my confidence became. I was caught in a relentless downward spiral.

During that time, my brother was volunteering with the Red Cross and overheard that the organization was looking to reach out to schools in the Ottawa area, hoping to re-expand its Christmas season Poinsettia Campaign through school-wide fundraisers. Suddenly, here was an opportunity to make a positive difference in my community. For as long as I could remember, Christmas had been my favorite holiday. I always loved going with the family to pick up a poinsettia and Christmas tree from the local store. And going around with friends selling poinsettias to students and teachers sounded awesome.

Moreover, after asking around, it turned out that the Poinsettia Campaign was an old school tradition that had died out a few years earlier. There were plenty of good reasons to take on this opportunity, and yet I was caught in a mental tug-of-war. *It'll be fun to do with friends—but you're going to have to speak at school assembly—but you've always loved Christmas—but you're going to have to speak at school assembly—but you enjoy fundraising—you're still going to have to speak at school assembly.* While in the midst of my contemplation, my brother entered my room, surprised to find me sitting on my bed with a blank expression on my face. After I told him about the opportunity and my speaking-related concerns, he argued to me that I would ultimately enjoy the experience very much. I still wasn't convinced, but I reluctantly decided to move forward with the initiative.

The night before the first school assembly announcement, I rehearsed my speech at least a hundred times. Every time I stuttered on a word, I changed it to an easier one. By the time I had finished, my voice was nearly hoarse from practicing. But I had precisely crafted a stutter-friendly speech that would last a grand total of twenty-five seconds.

Then came presentation day. The chaotic sounds of hundreds of students and faculty filled the hall where school assembly was held each week. The first portion of school assembly is still a blur in my memory. All I remember is nervously fumbling around with my cue card, looking up at the projector screen every now and then to see how many presentations were left until mine. All the while, feelings of doubt filled my mind: *They're going to laugh. You don't have what it takes. You're just not "that person."* When my turn finally came, I shimmied through crowds of students onto the stage and walked to the podium accompanied by the two friends I had recruited to organize the campaign. My hands were ice cold and probably a little purple from lack of blood flow, and my stutter felt ready to ruthlessly embarrass me in front of the entire school. I was the last to present of the three of us. I walked up to the podium, took a deep breath, and got ready for the word staccatos to shoot out like they had in French class. But the weirdest thing happened: I spoke fluently. Word after word flowed off my tongue without a problem, and a moment later, the audience's applause rang in the air.

Over the following four weeks, I presented three more times, opting to do so alone each time. The night before the final presentation, my brother once again walked into my room. This time, he was rather confused. He expected that I would be furiously reciting and re-writing my speech, but instead the lights were off and I was sound asleep, brimming with confidence. 8

After this experience, life around me continued as normal, but the change I had undergone was unmistakable. Rather than avoiding anything that remotely involved public speaking, I began to embrace these opportunities. I started to actively search for ways in which I could take initiative. I had always been passionate in several school activities, ranging from cross-country and badminton to molecular modelling and the school musical. I gradually took on more leadership positions in each of these activities, and each time, my confidence soared. 9

At the end of this past year, I decided to apply for the school's ultimate position of social responsibility and leadership—student prefect. The decision held enormous personal significance, as it epitomized the marked change I had undergone since that time in French class a year earlier. Not only do prefects have to speak in front of the school frequently, they are expected to be leaders of the student body and ambassadors for the school. None of these things I would have dared to do a year ago. Not only did I have the stutter, but I simply didn't see myself as having what it took to be "that person." The only difference now? Confidence. I believe others at my school had noticed the change as well, since ultimately with their support, I was selected as a prefect. 10

In hindsight, I am in awe at the amount of change a year can entail. I had been caught up in a terrible cycle in which my stutter sucked my confidence, and the Poinsettia Campaign was the exact opportunity I needed to break out of it. Speaking in front of the school and coordinating the sale of poinsettias showed me I could 11 excel in positions of leadership. That crucial boost in confidence enabled me to pursue other leadership opportunities, to realize I could make a positive difference, and to once and for all, do away with the notion that I couldn't be "that person." In the meantime, I noticed that the more confident I became, the less I stuttered. And while my stutter still lingers to this day, I have chosen not to allow it to affect me. What happens now if I stutter? I have a split-second of embarrassment, but that's it.

Now, with school resuming in a week, I look forward to that first French class presentation. I am eager to see what a whole year of growth in confidence can do. Ultimately with or without this stutter, I feel the sky is the limit.

QUESTIONS FOR CONSIDERATION

1. How did Huang overcome his fear of stuttering?
2. What was Huang's purpose in writing this article?
3. What rhetorical strategies does Huang use to help make the article relevant to readers who do not have a problem with stuttering?
4. Are there any parts of Huang's essay that he should eliminate to make the essay more cohesive? Explain your answer.
5. Which part of Huang's essay did you find most interesting or compelling? What can you learn as a writer about how to make your own writing interesting or compelling by thinking about how Huang's essay affected you as a reader?

IDEAS FOR WRITING

A. **A Summary and Response Assignment.** Write a complete summary of Huang's essay. Respond to the summary by reflecting on what Huang has written. How are the ideas in Huang's essay relevant to you? What ideas were stimulated when you read Huang's text?

B. **A Reflective Assignment.** Most people have overcome something in their lives. From addiction, obesity, and abusive relationships to self-esteem or financial adversity, overcoming the problems we face is part of human growth and development. Share something you have overcome by writing a reflective essay.

C. **A Persuasive Assignment.** We all struggle to overcome personal obstacles and challenges. Sometimes our struggles seem impossible and we are tempted to give up. Select a challenge that many people face. For instance, staying in college and finishing a degree might be such a challenge. Write an essay designed to persuade readers that struggling to overcome the obstacle or win the challenge is worth the effort.

Find Your Fight (Advertisement)
U.S. Marine Corps

The advertisement that follows appeared on the Marines website. (The appearance of U.S. Department of Defense (DOD) visual information does not imply or constitute DOD endorsement.)

FIND YOUR FIGHT

Ours is a noble path and a demanding journey, reserved for those with the willingness to engage and determination to defeat all mental, moral and physical requirements to join the Marines.

Over fear and doubt, through fatigue and scrutiny—Marines win. Those few who comprise our enlisted and officer ranks possess the fight in them to win for us all and have earned the benefits and responsibilities of our title.

Teaching Suggestion
Consider having students analyze recruitment ads from other branches of the U.S. military, as well as from other countries. For instance, here is a recruitment for Russia's armed forces: https://www.youtube.com/watch?v=1idTSSc_7Ts

Even though the ad is in Russian, the visual rhetorical strategies are obvious and interesting as a comparison with American ads.

QUESTIONS FOR CONSIDERATION

1. What details in the image catch your attention? Why?
2. The image shows a Black man and a man who appears to be Caucasian. Why do you think the ad writers chose these individuals? What message is sent by the gender choices?
3. What is the ad's message? How effective would the ad be without the image?
4. What part of the ad's text is directly supported by the photo?
5. What is the most persuasive element of the ad, in your opinion?

IDEAS FOR WRITING

A. **An Informative Essay.** To ensure that the U.S. military is always well-staffed, the United States uses a Selective Service system. Before the creation of the Selective Service system in 1973, a mandatory draft system was in place. Write an informative essay in which you discuss how the mandatory draft worked and how the Selective Service works. In your essay, address the reasons the mandatory draft was eliminated, and discuss any current controversies or issues surrounding the Selective Service system.

B. **A Rhetorical Analysis.** Read the text of the advertisement, and write an essay in which you provide a rhetorical analysis of the text. Focus on appeals to ethos, pathos, and logos in your analysis.

C. **A Researched Argument Assignment.** Imagine the United States Marine Corps employed you to create an advertisement that would be effective for you and your friends, one that might convince you to enlist in the Marines. Create the advertisement, using any media you choose. For instance, you might create a video, a podcast, a visual advertisement, and so on.

Peace Corps' Influence Changed My Fate
Bishnu Maya Pariyar

Bishnu Maya Pariyar works as an outreach coordinator and counselor for victims of domestic and sexual violence. She is the founder of ADWAN.ORG, an organization focused on enhancing the lives of Dalit people and marginalized women. The organization has supported more than 14,900 children and more than 34,600 women and their family members in Nepal since 1998. She holds a master's degree in social work and was awarded an honorary doctorate from Pine Manor College.

Teaching Suggestion
The Peace Corps website offers many first-person narratives. Consider using this article and others on the site to introduce a first-person narrative assignment.

1   I was brought into the world destined for disadvantage and lifelong discrimination.

2   In Nepal, to be born *Dalit*, the lowest of societal castes, means to be born with the hand of fate rested squarely on your shoulders. It means that advancing economically and socially is nearly impossible. This fate is compounded with further difficulties if you are a woman.

3   In some of my earliest memories, I can recall the pain and anguish of being labeled "untouchable." For a child, beginning life defined as the lowest of low gives oneself an achingly powerful sense of worthlessness. Imagine yourself at eight years old playing with friends, but constantly made aware you are less than. Not able to go where the others went and not offered the same comforts as higher-caste children. Even in my own community, many places were off limits, including temples.

4   I consider myself lucky, however, because I had a father who understood my only path to overcome my fate was education. My father was a hardworking man who tailored clothes for high-caste people. Though this sounds as if it were his profession, in reality it was a form of slavery. The adversity he faced was a catalyst for working toward a different way of life for his daughter.

5   Eventually I did make it to primary school. This was no safe haven from ridicule, as my caste was in essence a scarlet letter. I faced torment and bullying not just from

other students, but from my teachers as well. Despite this, I made a goal for myself to excel. I was consistently ranked first in my courses, but because of my status I could only reach grade three. I thought this would be the end of my education, but the setback was only for a short while and eventually I was permitted to attend middle school.

By the time I was ready for the next step, I had continued to top my academic classes. So much so, in fact, that Manakamana Higher Secondary School in Gorkha approached my family and allowed me to attend their program. This was very fortunate, as my family could not have afforded to send me. Luckily my grades were considered beneficial to the school's image and they arranged for me to attend tuition-free. Secondly, and perhaps more importantly, it was here that I would meet the man who would make a profound difference on the arc of my life.

On my second day at Manakamana, I was approached by John. He was the school's science teacher and a Peace Corps Volunteer. Up to this point, I had not seen many foreigners. I was so afraid that he would not like me because of the perceived class difference ingrained in my self-concept. This makes it hard to trust others; it makes you scared they will humiliate you if given the opportunity.

Bishnu Maya Pariyar in 1989 in a photo taken by the Peace Corps volunteer who worked with her in Nepal. *Bishnu Maya Pariyar*

John, though, was so different. He didn't care what caste I was. He treated me equally and with respect and we grew very close during our work together. He made me feel so comfortable simply to exist as a worthy person in my own right. And it wasn't only me, there were so many other students he motivated during his Peace Corps service in Nepal.

He finished his service in 1990, but his relationship with me continued. Before he left, he encouraged me to finish and pass my "School Living Certificate." This is what would allow me to go to university. He told me if I passed, he would find a way to help me pay for further schooling, which was still completely out of reach for me.

In 1992, I passed my SLC exam. Soon after, I reached out to John to let him know about my achievement. He put me in contact with a friend of his, Pam, who was in Kathmandu teaching through a distance learning program for the University of Wisconsin. Working through the two of them and my high school's foundation, I was given a scholarship of $700.00. This was more money than I had seen in all of my years. It was absolutely life-changing.

This gracious act of support allowed me to pursue not only higher education, but my life's work and richness of purpose. Having Peace Corps and John in my life gave me positive reinforcement, allowing me to believe in myself. It also gave me the right tools to advance myself.

I used this motivation to found the Association of Dalit Women's Advancement of Nepal (ADWAN) in 1998. This organization has two central goals: empowering women through financial independence and empowering children through education. We work tirelessly to end oppression based on caste, gender and class. To date, ADWAN has helped approximately 50,000 Nepali people. This assistance comes in many forms, but notably the organization teaches women about business, aiming to equip them to thrive in the modern economy.

When we empower women, it empowers their family and the entire community. My example is proof that one can overcome adversity when both informal and formal structures exist to create a framework of support. In this regard, the Peace Corps is so important because it enacts a mission that positively impacts individuals and communities across the globe.

I was the first girl from my community to graduate high school. Now, through my organization and the efforts of others, this has become a reality for many other girls. The Peace Corps and a very special Volunteer helped me actualize my dreams and define my own fate. I now believe that nothing is impossible.

QUESTIONS FOR CONSIDERATION

1. What is the main idea of Pariyar's essay?
2. How does Pariyar feel about the caste system in Nepal? Provide evidence for your answer.
3. What function does the photograph serve? Is it necessary for Pariyar to make her point? Explain your answer.
4. Part of Pariyar's message concerns the importance of the Peace Corps. Could she have as effectively conveyed this message without using a first-person narrative? Explain your answer.
5. What is the dominant tone Pariyar uses in her essay? What is the purpose of this tone?

IDEAS FOR WRITING

A. **A Reflection Assignment.** Pariyar's essay concerns, in part, the caste system in Nepal, which is similar to that in India. Reflect on your observations of social class in the United States. Is there a similar, albeit informal, system in the United States? Write a reflective essay to share your insights on social class and how it affects the opportunities of Americans.

B. **An Informative Assignment.** Pariyar alludes to a strict caste system but does not fully explain this system. Moreover, she implies that some people are able to triumph over the system, as she herself did. What is the caste system in Nepal and India? Is it changing? How possible is it for a person to move from one caste to another? Conduct research to learn about this topic, and then write an informative essay.

C. **A Persuasive Assignment.** The Peace Corps describes its mission as threefold:

- To help the people of interested countries in meeting their need for trained men and women.
- To help promote a better understanding of Americans on the part of the peoples served.
- To help promote a better understanding of other peoples on the part of Americans.

Examine the Peace Corps website (peacecorps.gov) and then do an internet search using this question: "Is the Peace Corps ethical?" You will find a variety of viewpoints in response to this question. Write an essay in which you argue whether or not the Peace Corps—as it operates today—is an ethical agency.

Men Explain Toxic Masculinity to Me, A Man Writing About Toxic Masculinity

Timothy J. Hillegonds

Teaching Suggestion
Consider having students read Steinem's essay in tandem with Hillegonds's essay.

This article, written by Timothy J. Hillegonds, appeared in Salon. Hillegonds is a contributing editor for Slag Glass City, "creative nonfiction and multidisciplinary

media journal engaged with sustainability, identity, and art in urban environments."
He has written articles for a variety of journals and magazines, including in The Los
Angeles Review of Books, The Rumpus, *and other publications. He is the author of*
The Distance Between: A Memoir *(October 1, 2019; University of Nebraska Press).*

1.

At a coffee shop in Chicago not long ago, while quietly reading through printed galleys of the memoir I had spent the previous five years writing, I was interrupted by a man with long grey hair pulled back into a ponytail. He looked to be in his mid-50s and had the sun-weathered face of a man who'd probably spent a good deal of time working outdoors. "Are those galleys?" he asked, leaning over the table to eyeball the pages spread out before me.

I looked up at him, surprised and somewhat taken aback by the intrusion, but I forced a smile and said they were indeed galleys.

He moved in closer and asked what the book was about.

"It's a reckoning with toxic masculinity," I answered.

His eyes narrowed. "I hate that term," he said, using his hands to emphasize his disdain. "You shouldn't write about toxic masculinity because it doesn't exist. You should write about nourishing masculinity. You should write about..."

The man's instructions came emphatically and rapid fire, one after the other, about all the things I should write about instead of toxic masculinity, a thing he seemed to be insisting didn't exist while simultaneously proving that it did.

2.

According to the American Psychological Association, "masculinity ideology" is a certain set of descriptive, prescriptive, and small-minded perceptions about boys and men. There are, of course, differences in masculinity ideologies—some that are less small-minded, less restrictive than others—but there is also a particular constellation of standards that have held sway over large segments of the population for quite some time. Often, this particular ideology idealizes anti-femininity, achievement, eschewal of the appearance of weakness, and adventure, risk, and violence. Collectively, these are now referred to as "traditional masculinity ideology."

3.

I didn't set out to write a book about masculinity.

4.

    I certainly didn't set out to write a book about toxic masculinity.

5.

    I set out to write a story that I had been trying to tell for 20 years, a story that felt like it defined me in near-countless ways, a story about losing a father and becoming a father, about violence and rebellion, about work and friendship and loss, about trying to disappear myself—over and over again—with cocaine and vodka and pills.

    What I didn't understand when I began writing my story was that all of it was connected to my understanding of masculinity in ways I'm still trying to unpack. In the early writing process, as I began to rigorously interrogate the boy I was and the rageful, sometimes-violent young man I grew into, whose male role models included an abusive grandfather, an absent construction-worker father, and a loving, gentle, yet faithfully patriarchal stepfather, I began to see that it was all connected, that I had been conditioned—sometimes intentionally, sometimes unintentionally—to operate within a gender framework that valued work and power and maleness over everything else.

    What I discovered during the writing process is that masculinity is, at its core, a story—a story told to me by my family, my church, and society about who I'm supposed to be. That story—which I've come to understand is deeply influenced by race, class, culture, and sexuality—became one that I absorbed and believed, and one that I ultimately began to live out with reckless abandon. The messages I absorbed instructed me to never show fear, to dominate, to reject anything feminine that didn't directly benefit my position at the top of the gender hierarchy. Be a man, Tim, the instruction said. Be a man, Tim, no matter what the cost.

6.

    For a time, I engaged in a debate with the man in the coffee shop, indulging his opinions, listening to him give me all sorts of way to fix the book I had written that he had never read. A few minutes into our conversation, his friend came over, and then it was both of them explaining to me how I should change what I had written, how my book was going to harm men, how men like me are making it harder for men like them. "And there's toxic femininity too, you know," the second man said, quoting a line I'd heard before and completely missing the point. "It's not just men. There's toxic people everywhere."

At first the conversation felt like an opportunity to do some impromptu field research, a way for me to hear from men who were in different spots than I was, men who believed that everything was fine and the so-called masculinity crisis was nothing more than "fake news perpetuated by the liberal media." But as the conversation stretched past five minutes, and then past ten, I began to feel my frustration mounting to a level I know is dangerous for me in certain situations, a point where the rage and anger I've spent decades working through and getting a handle on began to make its way back to the surface. I could feel myself wanting to physically shut both of them up, to dominate them, to fire off a quick right hand/left hook combo that would drop each man where he stood.

But the second I recognized what I was feeling, and the second I recognized that my first instinctual response to what I was feeling was violence, I became acutely aware of how deeply problematic my masculine conditioning is, and how in so many ways I wasn't very different from the mansplaining men I was talking to.

7.

The pushback against the term "toxic masculinity" is often virulent and immediate. Bring it up among certain groups of men and you'll elicit an eye roll, a lecture, or even a confrontation, because a large portion of the male population believes that by putting the adjective in front of the noun it's somehow a damnation of all masculinity. (It's not.) Most people wouldn't assume that someone who says folding chairs make uncomfortable seats is implying all the world's chairs are uncomfortable, yet here we are with a whole segment of men who are essentially doing just that.

Part of the problem may stem from the fact that it's difficult to pin down an exact definition of toxic masculinity. Michael Salter, a board member for the International Society for the Study of Trauma and Dissociation, writes that the term "distinguishes 'toxic' traits such as aggression and self-entitlement from 'healthy' masculinity." *New York Times* Gender Initiative writer Maya Salam writes that toxic masculinity "is what can come of teaching boys that they can't express emotion openly; that they have to be 'tough all the time'; that anything other than that makes them 'feminine' or weak." In a piece written for The Good Men Project, popular blogger and dating coach Harris O'Malley defines it as a "term from social sciences that describes norms of accepted behaviors among men that are portrayed as good and natural but are, in reality, physically, socially and psychologically damaging."

While all these definitions are generally touching on some of the same ideas, they're not doing so as succinctly as this, which I found in an online dictionary of all places: "Toxic masculinity is a cultural concept of manliness that glorifies stoicism, strength, virility, and dominance, and that is socially maladaptive or harmful to mental health."

Socially maladaptive or harmful to mental health. The phrase sticks out to me as I consider my encounter in the coffee shop in Chicago with those two men. A right hand/left hook combo is a socially maladaptive response to a fairly standard disagreement, and not "an adequate or appropriate adjustment to the environment or situation."

In short, it's toxic masculinity.

8.

I can't pinpoint exactly when I began realizing that the book I was writing had as much to do with masculinity as it did young fatherhood and addiction and adolescent rage, but I know I began to suspect it was all connected at some point during the years-long revision process. My suspicions led me to think more intentionally about my personal experience as a boy and young man, which then prompted me to reflect much more deeply on how I performed masculinity. All of this reflecting sent me on a journey of discovery—one that I'm still very much on—that began with a conversation I had with my younger brother, who's a progressive pastor, in a coffee shop in Michigan.

"I just think the man has to be the leader," I said to him as we sipped our coffees and talked about marriage, something we were both fairly new to. "When it comes down to it, as the man, I'm the one who has to make the decisions and figure shit out."

He looked at me from across the table, one hand gently resting on the handle of his coffee cup, and smiled in a way that meant he lovingly disagreed. His challenge, which would ultimately change everything for me, was one simple word.

"Why?"

Perhaps it seems too easy, or too simplistic, but his question, to which I legitimately had no answer, was the first crack in the foundation I'd unknowingly built my entire worldview on. My brother was the first person who directly challenged my inherited patriarchal ideology, and in the days and weeks and months and years after that, as the question pulsed persistently inside my brain, I found myself on shaky footing, suddenly unsure about nearly everything I thought.

That initial conversation led to other conversations, first with my wife, who had so much to teach and show me about masculinity that I wondered why I'd waited so long to ask her about it. My conversations with her led to other ones—with my feminist mentor; with the women in my writing group; with my 21-year-old daughter, who's experiences with men (myself included) and masculinity had already, despite how young she is, made me want to weep.

The construct of masculinity was suddenly visible in nearly everything I focused my attention on—relationships, news, church structures, sports, products—and so was the fallout from a country built on that construct. I could no longer simply "respect women" (which I now know is decidedly different than treating women as equals) and "just try to be a good man" (which is so ambiguous it means next to nothing), because I began to see the problems within masculinity as the problems within myself, and I needed to dig in, to do some real work in understanding the part I played in all of it. If I wanted to be a different kind of man, I needed to first understand the man I was.

The conversations I had with my wife and mentor and daughter led me to some reading—books and essays by Lacy M. Johnson, Roxane Gay, Rebecca Solnit, Leslie Jamison, Melissa Febos, Thomas Page McBee, and Jared Yates Sexton. That reading led to still more conversations, this time with other men who were on similar journeys, men who were feeling some of the same things I was—mainly, that something was inherently flawed about the definitions of masculinity we were assigned and living into, and that we might be able to do something about it. I talked to straight men and gay men and men of color. I talked to men who inhabited masculinities far different than mine. I attended masculinity panels and masculinity groups and masculinity events where we engaged in uncomfortable exercises and felt all the shame and fear and anger we kept inside in front of one another. We talked about patriarchy and equity and consent and what it might look like to change, to transform, to inhabit healthier masculinities.

In the book "The Man They Wanted Me to Be: Toxic Masculinity and a Crisis of Our Own Making," Jared Yates Sexton likens toxic masculinity to a chronic illness: once a man is infected, he will always carry it with him. He also suggests thinking about toxic masculinity in the same way we think about people with substance use disorders. "Like an addict who gets their addiction under control," he writes, "I learned to view masculinity as a chronic problem I could never be totally cured of. Every day was a new struggle, as there was no such thing as conquering it."

As a man who's 14 years sober, this reframing makes sense to me. Not drinking is no longer the struggle it was in my first year of sobriety, but I still have to be vigilant. There are places I don't go, and people I don't hang out with, and at some point every day I think about the fact that I'm an addict and an alcoholic. With addiction, with masculinity, I've found freedom in naming the thing that once imprisoned me. I've found control in admitting just how out of control I was.

9.

I didn't set out to write a book about masculinity, but I now think: How could I not?

10.

At about the 15-minute mark in the coffee shop with those two men, as the anger inside me began to warm its way up my calves, through my pelvis, and into my chest, I began packing up my belongings. When I finished, I stood up, now eye level with the man who had first approached me. "Look," he said, as I pulled my backpack over my shoulders. "For me, it all starts with language. This is all a nonstarter for me because I can't get past the term 'toxic masculinity'."

"So because you don't like the term you're not willing to look at the issues the term is trying to shed light on?" I asked.

"Yep," he said. "For me, it's all about the language."

I pressed my lips together and shook my head, semi-politely told them to have a good day, walked outside and merged into the stream of people moving down the busy Chicago sidewalk. Taxis honked and train brakes squealed, and as I walked toward the El, it occurred to me that maybe that man was right in at least one way, that rethinking masculinity does indeed start with language, just not in the way he imagined.

Rethinking masculinity is a lot like learning a new language. It's difficult at first, and words can be hard to pronounce. It takes time and dedication and repetition and practice. It also takes conversations, especially uncomfortable ones, where we say the words we're learning to say, even if we don't quite know how to say them.

QUESTIONS FOR CONSIDERATION

1. What is toxic masculinity?
2. Why do you think Hillegonds uses numbers in his essay? What purpose do those numbers serve?
3. Hillegonds relates an experience he had in a coffee shop, an experience that provoked an emotional response. What is Hillegonds' tone in this essay? Is it emotional? Neutral? Cite evidence for your answer.
4. Hillegonds describes having a "loving, gentle, yet faithfully patriarchal stepfather." Why does Hillegonds associate his stepfather with toxic masculinity?
5. What purpose does Hillegonds hope to fulfill by writing this essay?

IDEAS FOR WRITING

A. **An Analysis Assignment.** Hillegonds cites The Good Men Project. Go to the project's website (https://goodmenproject.com/) and analyze the content. What is this project? What is its purpose? How does it try to accomplish its purpose? Write an analysis in which you present your findings.

B. **An Evaluative Assignment.** Elaborate on the ideas Hillegonds presents by evaluating a habit, practice, or tradition that you believe reinforces toxic masculinity. You will need to define toxic masculinity and to create criteria to measure the habit, practice, or tradition.

C. **A Persuasive Assignment.** What does it mean to be masculine? What does it mean to be feminine? Do these terms have any significance? Who gets to define these terms? Should we rethink the opposition between masculine and feminine? Write an essay in which you argue your point of view on this topic.

CREDITS

Page 489. "The Fracking of Rachel Carson," by Sandra Steingraber, which appeared in the Sept./Oct. 2012 edition of *Orion Magazine*. Used by permission.

Page 500. Calma, Justine. "Big Oil Touts Offshore Drilling Jobs to Communities Most Harmed by Oil." *Grist Magazine*, June 26, 2018. Used with permission.

Page 502. Sen, Basav. "Want to Create More Jobs? Reduce Fossil Fuel Use," *CounterPunch*, August 10, 2018. https://www.counterpunch.org/2018/08/10/want-to-create-more-jobs-reduce-fossil-fuel-use/. Copyright © CounterPunch. All rights reserved.

Page 506. Pedersen, April, "The Dog Delusion," *TheHumanist.com*, October 13, 2009. https://thehumanist.com/magazine/november-december-2009/features/the-dog-delusion. Used with permission.

Page 513. Heinlein, Sabine. "The Cruelty of Kindness," *Aeon*, https://aeon.co/essays/no-kill-animal-rescue-is-a-disaster-for-animal-welfare, ©Aeon Media Group Ltd. 2012–2019. Used with permission.

Page 523. Sanchez, Liz. "How Zoos Help Preserve the World's Species for the Future." *The Mercury News*, June 23, 2019. Used with permission.

Page 527, article and illustration. Moore, Darnell. "Urban Spaces and the Mattering of Black Lives—The Nature of Cities." *The Nature of Cities*. October 22, 2015. Accessed March 04, 2019. https://www.thenatureofcities.com/2015/10/23/urban-spaces-and-the-mattering-of-black-lives/. Used with permission.

Page 532. Ham, Andrew S., "I Am an Asian-American Who Benefits from Affirmative Action," The Harvard Crimson, Inc., February 15, 2019. https://www.thecrimson.com/article/2019/2/15/ham-asian-american-affirmative-action/. Copyright ©2019 The Harvard Crimson, Inc. Used with permission.

Page 535. Collins, Laura. "Pervasive Myths About Immigrants." *The Catalyst*. George W. Bush Institute. Accessed March 04, 2019. https://www.bushcenter.org/catalyst/immigration/collins-immigration-myths.html. Used with permission.

Page 540. Hogan, Linda, "Black Walnut: A Sweet Blood History," *Cold Mountain Review*, 2016. https://www.coldmountainreview.org/issues/fall-2016-special-issue-on-forests/black-walnut-a-sweet-blood-history-by-linda-hogan. Used with permission.

Page 546. Betts, Reginald Dwayne. "Only Once I Thought About Suicide." *The Yale Law Journal*. Accessed March 04, 2019. http://www.yalelawjournal.org/forum/only-once-i-thought-about-suicide. Used with permission.

Page 554. Hannah-Jones, Nikole. "Yes, Black America Fears the Police. Here's Why." *ProPublica*, March 4, 2015. Accessed March 05, 2019. https://www.propublica.org/article/yes-black-america-fears-the-police-heres-why. Used with permission.

Page 562. Wagner, Peter, and Wendy Sawyer. "Mass Incarceration: The Whole Pie 2019." *Prison Policy Initiative*, March 19, 2019. https://www.prisonpolicy.org/reports/pie2019.html. Used with permission.

Page 571. Alter, Rachel, and Tonay Flattum-Riemers. Earth Institute, Columbia University. Used with permission.

Page 574. Steinem, Gloria, "Erotica and Pornography," *Ms.*, 1986. Copyright © Gloria Steinem. With permission from the author.

Page 579. Pike, George H., "Love It or Hate It: Native Advertising on the Internet", SSRN, June 1, 2014. https://papers.ssrn.com/sol3/papers.cfm?abstract_id=2963142. Used with permission.

Page 586. Huang, Justin, "How I Overcame My Stuttering," International Stuttering Association, 2015. http://isad.isastutter.org/isad-2015/papers-presented-by-2015/stories-and-experiences-with-stuttering-by-pws/how-i-overcame-my-stuttering-and-why-thats-made-all-the-difference/. Copyright ©2015 by Justin Huang. All rights reserved. Used with permission.

Page 591. Pariyar, Bishnu Maya. Peace Corps' Influence Changed My Fate. Peace Corps, October 29, 2019. Used by permission of the author.

Page 595. Hillegonds, Timothy J. "Men Explain Toxic Masculinity to Me, a Man Writing about Toxic Masculinity." *Salon*, October 1, 2019. Used by permission.

PART 7 Handbook of Reading and Writing Skills

Improving Your Reading Skills

CHAPTER OBJECTIVES

You will learn to:
- Use an effective reading process.
- Identify main ideas and thesis statements.
- Make accurate inferences.

Connect Adaptive Learning Assignment Consider assigning Connect's Adaptive Learning Assignments to provide students with additional practice.

Teaching Resources See the Instructor's Manual (IM) for suggestions about how to teach this chapter.

The texts you will encounter in college require a diverse and effective set of reading skills. If you sometimes have difficulty understanding college reading assignments, you are not alone. The good news is that by using a new set of reading strategies, you can become a more critical, more effective reader. In this chapter we focus on methods you can start using immediately—and in all your classes—to bolster your ability to comprehend difficult texts.

1A. USING AN EFFECTIVE READING PROCESS

The process you use to read has a tremendous effect on your ability to understand and remember a text. In the pages that follow, you learn how to use a reading process that breaks down the task of reading into three stages: before reading, during reading, and after reading. You can use these steps whether you read in digital or paper format. Many digital platforms enable you to annotate and make notes, so as you examine the steps that follow, think about how you can adapt them for any digital texts you may have for your classes. The steps you can use during these stages are shown in Figure H1.1.

1A1. Before Reading

Instead of immediately reading the text, use these four activities to increase your comprehension.

Previewing the Text. Previewing means looking over a text without reading it word for word. If you can correctly anticipate what the text is about—the topic

Teaching Resources
Students may hesitate to take seriously these suggestions for improving reading comprehension. To demonstrate their value, use the exercise "How You Read *Matters*." It starts with a reading and comprehension questions; it then reminds students to use the suggestions in this chapter. Finally, it ends with a second reading and comprehension question set so that students can see the value in using a solid reading process.

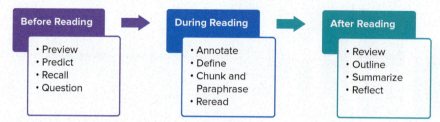

FIGURE H1.1 The stages of effective reading.

and the writer's point—understanding the finer points of the text will be much easier. Ask yourself these previewing questions:

Title
- What does the title suggest this text is about?
- Does the title present the text's main idea?

Headings
- What is the subject of the headings?
- Do the headings suggest the text's topic or main idea?

Formatted Words
- Are there any words underlined, italicized, boldfaced, or printed in a different color? If so, why are these words special? What can they tell you about the topic or main idea?

Repeated Words and Phrases
- Which words and phrases are often repeated?
- For which ideas does the writer use synonyms?
- What do these repetitions and synonyms tell you about the topic or the main idea?

Graphics
- What do the illustrations, tables, charts, or other graphics tell you about the topic?
- Do the graphics convey the main idea?

Introduction and Conclusion
- After reading the introduction paragraph, can you figure out the topic or the writer's main idea?
- Does the conclusion paragraph restate the writer's main idea or confirm any idea about the topic?

Making Predictions. After you have previewed the text carefully, the next step is to make some predictions. Thinking about what you have seen and read, ask yourself these questions:

- What do you predict the topic of the reading will be?
- What do you predict the writer will say about the topic?
- Do you think the writer will be merely providing information, or will the writer be supporting an opinion?

Jot down your answers before you read. After reading, go back and see if your predictions were correct. The better you get at previewing, the better you will become at making good predictions about what the writer will say.

Recalling by Thinking about What You Already Know. One strategy for understanding and remembering what you read is to tie the new information (what you are reading) to old information (what you already know). For example, if you are reading a chapter about the use of DNA evidence in criminal investigations, make a list of what you already know about the topic. Your knowledge may come from movies or television shows, but that is okay! By recalling what you already know about the topic, your brain can simply add the new information to the existing information. When you try to remember what you have read, your brain has a "file" it can refer to.

After you read the article, go back and add information you did not previously know. Here is an example of a student's recalling activity before and after reading a textbook passage on DNA in forensic science.

> **Lennon, on what he already knows:** "I watch *Forensic Files*, and I've learned from that show that DNA evidence is crucial. To get it, you need bodily fluids or cells. Victims even try to leave their own DNA at crime scenes. One way to get DNA is to swab someone's mouth or to use hair pulled out with the roots attached."
>
> **Lennon, on what he learned:** "When I read the text, I learned new info. There are DNA databases that help police match a DNA sample with a known criminal. These days, DNA is being used to prove innocence, as well as guilt. The demand for DNA testing is so high that it can take a long time for results to come back."

Asking Questions. Before you read, think of some questions you would like the text to answer. By finding the answers to these questions, you will be more likely to understand and remember what you read. If no questions come to mind, create some using *who*, *what*, *where*, *when*, *why*, and *how*. By formulating questions such as these, you can look for answers as you read the text.

> **Lennon, on asking questions:** "I came up with seven questions. They were not all answered in the text, but I did find answers to most."
>
> - What exactly is DNA?
> - Who uses DNA? Do all police departments gather it?
> - When is DNA most useful? Are there times when it's not useful?

> - How much does a DNA test cost?
> - How accurate are the tests?
> - Where are the tests done?
> - Why does it take so long to get back results?

1A2. During Reading

Once you have spent some time on prereading strategies, you should be ready to read the chapter or article. Use these four strategies to read effectively.

Annotating Effectively. One of the best ways to understand a text is to mark the text while reading it. By "voicing" your questions in annotations, you become more aware of needing answers to those questions; consequently, you will be more likely to look for possible answers as you continue reading. Marking significant features or content in a text will also help you remember those items.

> **Teaching Resources**
> Consider using the exercise "Annotating Effectively."

- **Mark new information.** If you already know something, there is no need to mark it.
- **Use highlighters sparingly.** Highlight no more than 20% of a page.
- **Focus on vocabulary.** Write a one- to two-word definition for any word that is unfamiliar.
- **Talk to the text.** Ask the writer questions: *"Why true?" "Always the case?"* Make connections between different parts of a text: "See p. 50." Connect the text to your experiences: *"Reminds me of . . . ."*
- **Make comparisons.** Make notes in the margins about others' views: "Smith disagrees. Says air pollution is only getting worse."
- **Develop a system of codes.** Use a question mark for confusing passages, exclamation points for important points, and a star for the main idea.
- **Use sticky notes or comments.** Use a sticky note or comment feature when you find information you will likely need to return to, and mark it with the content on the page, such as "stats on pollution."
- **Paraphrase.** Put ideas into your own words.

Defining Unfamiliar Words. An unfamiliar word can pose a challenge to your understanding of a text. Three ways to learn a new word are to consult a dictionary, use word parts to determine the word's meaning, and use context clues to speculate on what the unfamiliar word means.

- **Using a dictionary—correctly.** Dictionaries are helpful only if you can find the appropriate meaning for the word in context. In Figure H1.2, notice that the word *cache* has multiple meanings. Be sure to read the various meanings and consider the context of the word when determining which meaning applies.

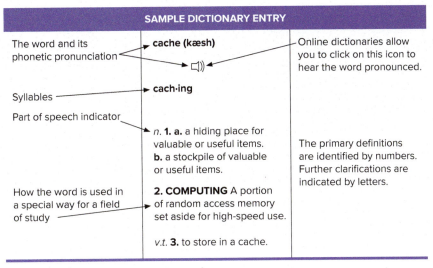

FIGURE H1.2 Dictionary entry for *cache*.

- **Learning and using common word parts.** One way to increase your vocabulary is to learn the meanings of individual word parts. If you memorize the word parts in Table H1.1, you will be well equipped to figure out the meanings of many of the new words you encounter.

TABLE H1.1 Common Prefixes, Suffixes, and Roots

COMMON PREFIXES		
Prefix	Meaning	Example
anti-	against, opposite	antisocial
auto-	self	autobiography
bi-	two	bicycle
com-, con-	with, together	communicate, context
dis-	not, opposite of	dislike
em-, en-	to cause to be, to put into or onto, to go into or onto	embattle, enable
ex-, exo-	out of, from	exoskeleton
fore-	earlier	foreshadow
hom-, homo-	same	homogeneous
hype-	over, too much	hperactive
im-	not	impatient

(Continued on next page)

TABLE H1.1 Common Prefixes, Suffixes, and Roots *(Continued from previous page)*

COMMON PREFIXES		
Prefix	Meaning	Example
in-, il-, im-	not	insufficient, illiterate, immature
inter-	between	interstate
micro-	small, tiny	microchip
mid-	middle	midline
mis-	bad, wrong	misbehave
neo-	new, recent, revived	neonatal
poly-	many, much	polygon
pre-	before	premarital
pro-	forward	proceed
quad-	four	quadrilateral
re-	again, back	rejoin
retro-	back, backward	retroactive
se-	apart	separate
semi-	half	semisolid
sub-	under, beneath, secondary	subterranean
super-	above, on top of, beyond	superimpose, superintendent
tele-	far, distant	telephone
trans-	across, change, through	transfer, transmit
tri-	three	tricycle
un-	not, opposite of	unhappy
uni-	one, single	unicycle
-able, -ible	can be done	laughable, edible,
-age	result of an action/collection	manage
-al, -ial	related to, characterized by	parental, trivial
-an, -ian	one having a certain skill, relating to, belonging to	artisan, Haitian
-ation, ion, ition, -tion	act of, state of	graduation, isolation
-en	made of, to make	brighten, wooden
-ence, -ance	act or condition of	governance
-ent, -ant	an action or condition, causing a specific action	obedient, inhabitant
-er, -or	person connected with, comparative degree	competitor, greater

COMMON PREFIXES		
Prefix	Meaning	Example
-fy	to make, to form into	liquefy
-hood	state, quality, condition of	adulthood
-ic	relating to, characterized by	historic
-ice	state or quality of	cowardice
-ide	chemical	peroxide
-ish	like, having the characteristics of, inclined or trending to	childish
-ity, -ty	state of, quality of	beauty, prosperity
-ive, -ative, -tive	inclined or tending toward an action	active, inquisitive
-ize	to make, to cause to become	energize
-less	without	homeless
-logy, -ology, -ologist	science of, one who studies	psychology, ecologist
-ment	act, process	torment, replacement
-ness	condition, state of	happiness
-ous, -eous, -ious	full of or characterized by	joyous, rambunctious
-ward	characterized by a thing, quality, state, or action	backward, inward
-ways	in what manner	sideways
amo, amatum	love	amorous
aqua	water	aquatics
aud, audi, aus	to hear, listen	audiophile
bene, boun, bon	good, well	benefit
biblio	book	bibliography
bio	life	biological
chrom, chron	time	synchronous
dico, dictum, dict	to say, tell, speak	dictation
fact	make, do	manufacture
geo	earth, ground, soil	geological
graph	writing	biography
inter	between	interrelated
junct	join	junction
log, logos	word or study	dialogue

(Continued on next page)

TABLE H1.1 Common Prefixes, Suffixes, and Roots *(Continued from previous page)*

COMMON PREFIXES

Prefix	Meaning	Example
magnus	large	magnificent
meter, metron	measure	thermometer
path, pathos	feeling, suffering	sympathy
phone	sound	phonetics
populous	people	population
pro	for	proponent
scribe, script	to write	transcribe
sol	sun	solar
sonus	sound	sonogram
spectro, spect, spec	to see, watch, observe	prospect
struct	to build	destruction
syn, sym	the same, alike	sync, synonym
terra	land	subterranean
trans	across	translate
visum, video	to see	videographer
vivo	live	vibrant

Teaching Resources
Consider using the exercise "Working with Vocabulary."

- **Using context clues.** The immediate context of a word is the sentence in which it appears and sometimes the sentences nearby. By analyzing the context in which a word appears, you can often get a rough sense of its meaning. The four steps shown in Figure H1.3 will help you use context clues effectively.

  1. **Determine the word type.** First, identify the word's part of speech. Consider the word *concurred* in the example that follows. *Concurred* functions as a verb in the sentence.

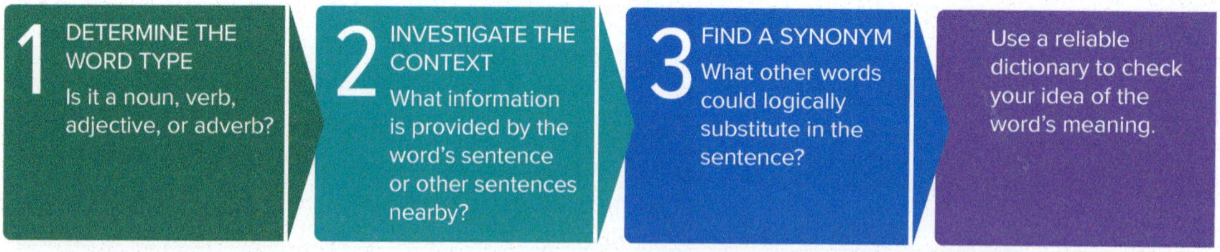

1 DETERMINE THE WORD TYPE Is it a noun, verb, adjective, or adverb?

2 INVESTIGATE THE CONTEXT What information is provided by the word's sentence or other sentences nearby?

3 FIND A SYNONYM What other words could logically substitute in the sentence?

Use a reliable dictionary to check your idea of the word's meaning.

FIGURE H1.3 Using context clues to determine a word's meaning.

> **Example:** Ray's stubbornness often leads him to make mistakes. Last year, he told his friends and family that he had decided to buy a new car. Not a single friend or family member **concurred** with his idea, but Ray bought the car anyway. He soon realized that to pay for the car, he would have to drop out of college and work full-time. Ray insists on learning the hard way.

2. **Examine the context.** Investigate the context—the sentences around the word—to get clues that can help you figure out the word's meaning.
3. **Find synonyms.** Once you have used the context to understand the writer's point, you can find a synonym to help you define the new word. A synonym is a word that means the same thing as another word. Take the unfamiliar word out of the sentence and plug in other words that might make sense. Think through each potential synonym in this way.

> **Example:** Not a single friend or family member _____ with his idea, but Ray bought the car anyway.
>
> **Try this:** Not a single friend or family member **agreed** with his idea, but Ray bought the car anyway.
>
> If the synonym makes sense and if it fits in the context of the sentence and paragraph, you may have found the word's meaning. The only way to be sure is to use a dictionary to check.

Chunking and paraphrasing. Dense texts contain multiple complex ideas. Reading such texts quickly is difficult unless you are an expert in the subject area. To understand dense texts, use chunking, a method of reading slowly and figuring out meanings, bit by bit, followed by paraphrasing—putting the chunk of information into your own words. Do this until you comprehend the whole. Here is an example of a dense text that has been chunked into smaller parts.

Teaching Suggestion
Even students with strong reading skills sometimes struggle with dense college texts. Consider having students read a difficult essay early in the semester and use chunking and paraphrasing as an intentional method for comprehension. The IM for this chapter presents additional ideas to reinforce reading comprehension in the composition classroom.

Difficult Text	Chunked Text	Paraphrased Chunks
Exposure to the social ecology of poor urban neighborhoods significantly increases the incidence of traumatic stress disorders, placing children growing up in such neighborhoods at disproportionate risk. Although the risk factors for and effects of childhood complex traumatic stress disorders are well documented, there is little intervention research to guide the delivery of services to this population.	Exposure to the social ecology of poor urban neighborhoods / significantly increases the incidence of traumatic stress disorders, / placing children growing up in such neighborhoods at disproportionate risk. / Although the risk factors for and effects of childhood complex traumatic stress disorders are well documented, / there is little intervention research to guide the delivery of services to this population.	Poor neighborhoods in cities have a certain "social ecology"—the way that people in the community relate to the environment, including those around them, the events in the environment, and the physical environment itself. / In poor urban neighborhoods, the conditions increase the incidences (numbers) of traumatic stress disorders (mental illness caused by exposure to stress). / Children in poor neighborhoods are more likely to experience traumatic stress disorder than other children. / Researchers have proven that these children have more chance of experiencing traumatic stress disorder, but / few researchers have figured out how to intervene—how to make the situation better by delivering mental health services.

Kiser, Laurel. "Protecting children from the dangers of urban poverty." *Clinical Psychology Review* 27, no. 2 (2007): 211–25.

Rereading Parts or the Whole. When a text is difficult, you may need to reread parts over and over, and rereading the entire text is reasonable. You will probably find that as you reread the text, your understanding begins to clear up.

1A3. After Reading

As crucial as the first two stages of reading are, the final stage has real effects on your long-term memory of the content you have read. By using the following four after-reading strategies, you can increase your memory and your understanding of the text.

Reviewing. When you finish reading, go back through the text. Reread your annotations, and reread any passages you found confusing. Review each concept in the text until you feel confident that you understand it. Review new vocabulary words and make a list of them.

Outlining. Outlining gives you a way to understand how the ideas in the text relate to each other. One way to misunderstand is to fail to grasp the relationship of the ideas in a text. Which ideas are most important? Which ideas support those important ones? Being able to see the structure of a text by outlining it is crucial for understanding. Outlining is also a way to take notes in an organized way. By putting your notes in outline form, you can see how the text coheres and how ideas relate to each other.

To write an outline for a text you are reading, you need to find the writer's main idea and determine the major supporting points. Sometimes the writer provides clues, such as headings and subheadings. In a text that does not contain headings and subheadings, you can still distinguish the elements of importance and determine their relationship to one another. The annotations in the following essay identify the elements a reader would use to construct an outline.

How Delaying Gratification Predicts Future Success
Kari Gardner

"I want what I want, and I want it now." We live in a world in which instant gratification is not merely desired: it's expected. If Internet access is delayed for even a few seconds, we are frustrated. If our fast food is not fast enough, we are miffed, and so it goes.

Introduction: examples of how people have trouble delaying gratification

What is required in these circumstances is delayed gratification, the ability to postpone the fulfillment of an immediate desire in order to obtain a more substantial reward in the future. To put it more informally, <u>delayed gratification means putting off having something now so you can get something better later on</u>.

Definition

Educators and psychologists alike say that being able to tolerate delayed gratification is an extremely valuable skill. People who can put off immediate gratification are more likely to have what it takes to be successful in the important things in life. And there is research to support that opinion.

Thesis statement

In the late 1960s and early 1970s, psychologists at Stanford University (led by Walter Mischel) performed a series of studies that came to be known as the Marshmallow Experiment. Young children (from four to six years old) were given a large, fluffy marshmallow and were told they could eat the marshmallow now, or they could wait fifteen minutes and get a second marshmallow.

Major supporting point 1 (implied): The Marshmallow Experiment shows that delayed gratification skills lead to more success in life.

Details: focus on how the experiment was set up

Details: focus on what happened in the experiment	Many of the kids who were able to delay gratification distracted themselves from the marshmallow by covering their eyes with their hands, turning their backs to the treat, kicking the table, and so forth. Other children who successfully delayed eating the marshmallow used their imaginations to reframe the treat as something else. For example, by thinking about the marshmallow as a cloud or by thinking the marshmallow was just a picture of a marshmallow, children were able to resist eating it immediately.
Details: the conclusion drawn from the experiment	Of course, a significant number of children simply could not wait. Some nibbled on the marshmallow and eventually popped the whole thing into their mouths, and some ate it almost immediately.
	In follow-up studies years later, the psychologists determined that the children who were able to wait longer—to postpone their gratification—tended to do substantially better as adults than those children who were less patient. The psychologists based their assessment on the analysis of the test subjects' levels of behavioral problems, drug and alcohol addiction, educational achievement, SAT scores, and other measures. Although recent studies have suggested that the fundamental issue is more complex than simple self-control, the basic point still stands: it is important to learn to tolerate delayed gratification.
Major supporting point 2	Psychological tests are not the only way to demonstrate the importance of delayed gratification. Proof that it pays to put off pleasure is all around us.
Details: people who delay gratification to pursue success	People who have the patience and willpower to regularly invest even small amounts of money can easily become very wealthy—if they are willing to wait long enough for their money to multiply. Students who seek college degrees earn them by putting off pleasure today for the reward of a degree tomorrow. And athletes who make it to the top know very well the importance of working hard today so that they can perform well tomorrow.
	It will always be easier to eat the marshmallow right away, but doing so may not always be the best choice.

To outline a text, write the main idea (whether stated in a thesis statement, as in this case, or implied), the major supporting points, and the supporting details that follow the major supporting points. When writing an outline, always use quotation marks if you use actual phrases and sentences from the text, as shown in the outline that follows. Doing so enables you to remember which words are yours and which came from the source.

Outline of "How Delaying Gratification Predicts Future Success" by Kari Gardner

Introduction: Provides examples of how people have trouble tolerating delayed gratification. **Definition of delayed gratification:** "the ability to postpone the fulfillment of an immediate desire in order to obtain a more substantial reward in the future."

Thesis statement: "People who can put off immediate gratification are more likely to have what it takes to be successful in the important things in life."

Major supporting point 1 (implied): The Marshmallow Experiment shows that delayed gratification skills lead to more success in life.

Supporting details:

- How the experiment was set up: Children were given the option of one marshmallow now or two later.
- What happened in the experiment: Some children waited to eat the marshmallow, and some did not.
- The conclusion drawn from the experiment: Children who waited had more success as adults.
  - Assessment based on behavioral problems, drug and alcohol addiction, educational achievement, SAT scores

Major supporting point 2: "Proof that it pays to put off pleasure is all around us."

Supporting details:

- People who invest (end up wealthy if they wait)
- Students who graduate (put off pleasure today for reward tomorrow)
- Athletes who train (practice today for performance rewards tomorrow)

Summarizing. By putting what you have read into your own words, you are forced to condense a vast amount of information into only the most important elements of that information. A summary consists of the writer's thesis statement and the major supporting ideas that develop the thesis statement. Summarizing helps you to be sure you can walk away from the text with an understanding of at least these most important elements, but it also can help you see the relationship among the ideas in a text. Be sure to write an outline *before* you summarize. Your outline will give you the most important ideas, and you can then put those ideas into your own words in a summary. For more on summarizing, see Chapter 2.

> **Summary of "How Delaying Gratification Predicts Future Success" by Kari Gardner**
>
> Gardner's essay concerns the issue of delayed gratification. Gardner defines delayed gratification as "the ability to postpone the fulfillment of an immediate desire in order to obtain a more substantial reward in the future."
>
> The essay's thesis statement is that if you are able to delay gratification (by putting off pleasurable activities), you will have more success in life.
>
> Gardner proves the thesis by discussing the Marshmallow Experiment in which children were given the option of eating one marshmallow immediately or waiting fifteen minutes and getting a second marshmallow. The children who waited for the second marshmallow ended up becoming more successful adults. They had fewer behavioral problems, less drug and alcohol addiction, greater educational success, and higher SAT scores.
>
> Another point Gardner makes about delaying gratification is that people who are able to wait sometimes end up getting benefits. For example, people who invest and are patient can become wealthy. Students who work hard in college can graduate, and athletes who train hard can succeed in their sports.

Reflecting. When you reflect on a text, you relate what you have learned to your own thinking, experience, and learning. Reflection goes a step beyond understanding what the text says; it prompts you to consider *how the text relates to you*. Learning theorists have shown that reflection may be one of most important learning activities we engage in. Imagine, for example, studying to be a nurse and reading about compassionate care. Without reflection, the reader may not apply the information to their practice as a nurse; and this failure to reflect can result in very little change or growth, both of which are the purpose of understanding compassionate care.

1B. IDENTIFYING MAIN IDEAS

Using an effective reading process is important, but it will be ineffective if you are unable to identify main ideas. A stated main idea for a text longer than one paragraph is a **thesis statement**; the stated main idea of a paragraph is a **topic sentence**. In both cases—paragraphs and longer texts—main ideas may be present but may be unstated. In such cases, these main ideas are implied, and you will need to put the main idea into your own words.

1B1. Finding the Main Idea of a Paragraph

The main idea of a paragraph is expressed in a topic sentence, and additional sentences in the paragraph are called supporting sentences. These additional sentences provide explanations, examples, and other kinds of support to help readers understand the topic sentence. Mark the topic sentence in each paragraph.

A topic sentence . . .

- **Expresses the main point in a paragraph.** It provides the exact point the writer hopes the reader will remember or believe.
- **Expresses the broadest idea in the paragraph.** It is broad enough to cover all the ideas in the paragraph.
- **Presents an idea that requires support**. It makes a point that must be explained further or backed up with evidence.
- **Is a statement, not a question.** Because it makes a point, a topic sentence cannot be a question.

Let's look at a paragraph and try to figure out the topic sentence. *Note*: While a topic sentence is often placed first, it does not have to be.

> [1]What is the most important consideration when choosing a career? [2]It is not salary, and it is not status. [3]For many people, the most important factor in finding a career is what the job will require on a daily basis. [4]For example, Leah Reem worked hard in college and law school to become an attorney. [5]After six months on the job, she realized that she hated sitting in an office every day. [6]She often felt too tired to exercise when she got home, and she found herself gaining weight and simply feeling depressed. [7]She began to realize that the daily requirements of legal work were not making her happy, so she quit her job and found a job working with horses. [8]While the new job paid much less, Leah found it very satisfying. [9]If she had known how the daily tasks involved in being a lawyer would affect her, Leah would have chosen a different career field.

First, we will eliminate some of the sentences.

- *Eliminate Sentence 1:* This sentence is not the topic sentence because it's a question. Topic sentences are always statements.
- *Eliminate Sentence 2:* This sentence does not tell us what the rest of the paragraph discusses, so it is not the topic sentence.
- *Eliminate Sentences 4-9:* This long example is being used to support an idea (the topic sentence), so none of these sentences is the topic sentence.

Now, we are left with one sentence—sentence 3. Does it meet the requirements for topic sentences?

> For many people, the most important factor in finding a career is what the job will require on a daily basis.

We can check that sentence 3 is the topic sentence by asking ourselves whether the sentence has the four characteristics of a topic sentence. This one does, so it is the topic sentence.

1B2. Finding the Implied Main Idea of a Paragraph

Some paragraphs present an implied main idea, an idea that is suggested by the ideas in the paragraph but not stated directly. Readers must figure out the implied main idea and put it into their own words. Use the modified four-step process in Figure H1.4 to identify the implied main idea, put it into your own words, and create an implied topic sentence.

What follows is a paragraph with an implied main idea, so the paragraph does not have a directly stated topic sentence. As you read the paragraph, pay attention to the terms in bold type. These terms give clues to the topic.

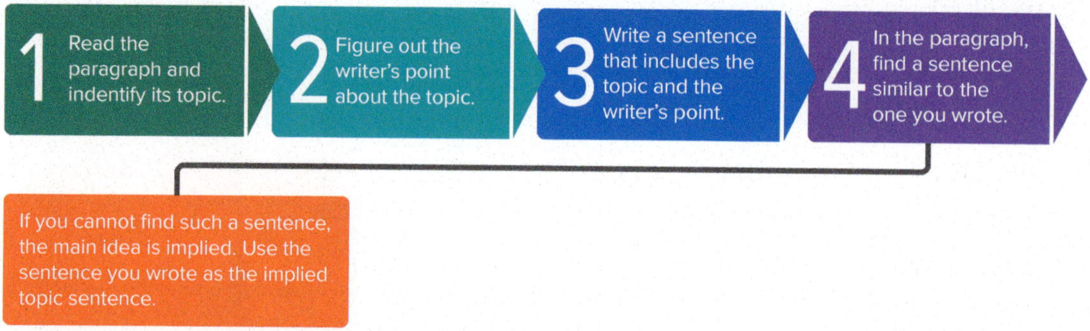

1 Read the paragraph and indentify its topic. → **2** Figure out the writer's point about the topic. → **3** Write a sentence that includes the topic and the writer's point. → **4** In the paragraph, find a sentence similar to the one you wrote.

If you cannot find such a sentence, the main idea is implied. Use the sentence you wrote as the implied topic sentence.

FIGURE H1.4 Identifying an implied main idea.

> For many years, **smoking on airplanes** was a **social norm**, an **accepted behavior in our society**. Although travelers could choose to sit in a nonsmoking area of the plane, they could not expect to breathe clean air since smoke permeated the plane. By the year 2000, however, smoking had been banned on all commercial flights. Many younger travelers have never flown on a plane where smoking was allowed. **Another changing social norm** we can examine is that of **body art**. Getting a tattoo used to be a behavior associated with rebelliousness—and often lawlessness. Tattoos were for people in gangs, for bikers, for inmates, and for some people in the armed services. Today, tattoos are as common as pierced ears. People from all walks of life choose to get tattoos, and slowly, people are becoming less judgmental about those who have tattoos.

Notice how we can use the process for identifying an implied main idea.

- Read the paragraph and identify its topic.

  Topic: The paragraph gives us two examples of social norms (accepted behaviors), so the topic is "social norms."

- Figure out the writer's point about the topic.

  Writer's point: The writer uses examples of social norms that have changed over time—smoking on airplanes and getting tattoos. So the point is that social norms can change.

- Write a sentence that includes the topic and the writer's point.

  Our sentence: Social norms can change over time.

- In the paragraph, find a sentence similar to the one you wrote. If you cannot find such a sentence, the main idea is implied. Use the sentence you wrote as the implied topic sentence.

1B3. Finding the Thesis Statement of an Essay

The main idea of an essay is its thesis statement. The thesis statement provides the writer's topic and the point the writer wishes to make about the topic. Often, a thesis statement is expressed in a single sentence, but sometimes it spans two or three sentences. Like a topic sentence, a thesis statement has particular characteristics. A thesis statement:

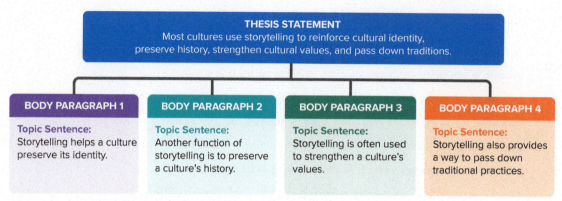

FIGURE H1.5 How thesis statements relate to topic sentences.

- **Expresses the most important point in an essay.** The thesis statement tells readers the exact point the writer hopes readers will remember or believe.
- **Presents an idea that requires support.** The thesis statement makes a point that needs to be explained further or backed up with evidence.
- **Expresses the broadest idea in the essay.** The thesis statement is broad enough to forecast or imply the ideas presented in the essay's other paragraphs.
- **Is not a question.** The idea or opinion is a statement.

You may have noticed that the characteristics of thesis statements are similar to those of topic sentences. In fact, thesis statements and topic sentences are similar in that they both communicate main ideas. The difference between them lies in their functions within an essay. If you have only a single paragraph, you have only one single main idea, expressed either in an explicit topic sentence or in an implied topic sentence. You already know the purpose of the topic sentence: it tells you the most important point of the paragraph.

What happens when paragraphs are put together in an essay? These paragraphs still have topic sentences, and each topic sentence still tells the reader the most important point of its paragraph. However, the paragraphs in an essay serve to support the thesis statement. You can see an example of this in Figure H1.5. The thesis statement ("Most cultures use storytelling to reinforce cultural identity, preserve history, strengthen cultural values, and pass down traditions") presents all the reasons the writer will discuss in the paper. The thesis statement, clearly, is broader than any of the topic sentences. In other words, because the topic sentences each present just a single reason, they are narrower than the thesis statement.

1B4. Using Topic Sentences to Identify the Thesis Statement

You can use a process for finding thesis statements that is similar to the one you used for finding topic sentences. Figure H1.6 will help you. The example that

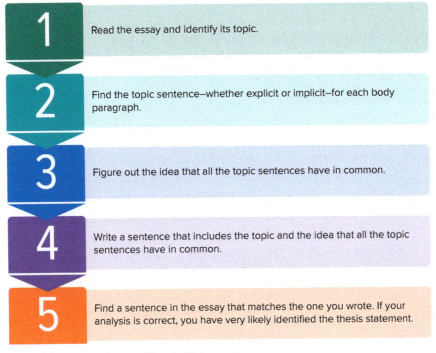

FIGURE H1.6 Identifying a Thesis Statement

follows shows how one student, Sarit, annotated topic sentences and the other important elements in a text to identify the thesis statement.

> Why Emotional Intelligence Matters—At Work
>
> Do you know anyone who is not necessarily the smartest member of a work group but who is a great team player and always seems to contribute significantly? On the other hand, do you know someone who is "book smart" but seems to have a difficult time getting along with coworkers? The first person has high "emotional intelligence." The second person does not. Emotional intelligence (EI) refers to how well people understand their own feelings as well as the emotions of others. Surprisingly, perhaps, being "book

Step 1—Identify topic. Emotional intelligence?

Definition. Maybe the entire essay's main idea is to define emotional intelligence.

Topic—EI and career success?	smart" is not sufficient for career success. We have learned in recent years that successful employees—those who move the most quickly up the ladder—possess greater emotional intelligence skills than their coworkers.
Step 2—Find the topic sentences.	
Topic sentence	**Awareness of your emotions is one way EI makes you a better employee.** Intentionally thinking about how you are feeling is a crucial skill. For example, if you are irritable, you may have a harder time with a planning session at the office than you otherwise would. Realizing that you are grumpy does not instantly make you happy, but it does give you a heads-up that you need to be especially careful as you relate to your coworkers or customers or supervisors. Sometimes people with low emotional intelligence will think their moods justify bad behavior. You may even have heard comments like "Don't mind Jessica; she's always moody." The truth is, Jessica won't be the one getting the promotion.
Topic—being a better employee?	
Emotional intelligence again—topic?	
	Empathy means putting yourself in another person's shoes emotionally. **Beyond being self-aware, employees who interpret the emotions of others by being empathetic are assets in the workplace.** Can you imagine how the other person feels in a given situation? If one of your colleagues has just come from an evaluation with his supervisor and snaps at you when you say "Hello," he might be feeling upset because of what his boss had to say. Recognizing your coworker's emotional situation would help smooth over hurt feelings. Similarly, a salesperson who can empathize with customers will have more pleasant interactions with them; as a consequence, she might even make more sales!
Topic sentence	
A benefit of emotional intelligence	
Topic sentence	**Stress management is another EI skill that makes employees more valuable.** A person who has methods for relieving her stress is much less likely to blow up at a coworker or a customer. One who can control her stress is also a more efficient employee because she is not distracted by the tension that has built up inside her psyche. Controlling stress is not always an easy thing to do; people who are successful at keeping their stress level down can rise above their colleagues and become more valued employees.
Topic—how emotional intelligence benefits you?	

Unpleasant or difficult situations inevitably occur in the workplace. Workers who are able to adapt fairly quickly when frustrations or disappointments occur will be able to proceed with occupational tasks. Employers can trust employees who are adaptable; such employees will make the adjustments needed to get the work done. Workers who are prone to "drama" over frustrations or disappointments will be labeled "difficult" and will not be the ones on the promotion list. Employees who have emotional flexibility are considered more dependable than those who do not.

> Topic—emotional intelligence at work?
>
> Topic sentence at end of paragraph

Teamwork is crucial in almost every vocation, and EI makes employees better team players. Working well with clients or customers is also critically important in many occupational settings. Being able to recognize and relate to the feelings of others and being aware of your own feelings will increase your ability to work well with others. That is why people with high EI are more successful in their careers than people with low EI.

> Topic sentence
>
> EI is tied to career success.

Here is how Sarit used the five-step process to figure out the thesis statement of this essay.

1. Identify the topic.

   Topic: emotional intelligence at work

2. Find the topic sentence—whether explicit or implicit—for each body paragraph.

   Sarit listed the topic sentences:

   Awareness of your emotions is one way EI makes you a better employee.

   Beyond being self-aware, employees who interpret the emotions of others by being empathetic are assets in the workplace.

   Stress management is another EI skill that makes employees more valuable.

   Teamwork is crucial in almost every vocation, and EI makes employees better team players.

3. Figure out the idea that all the topic sentences have in common.

> Shared idea: Sarit realized that these sentences all tell us that emotional intelligence skills can make people better employees.

4. Write a sentence that includes the topic and the idea that all the topic sentences have in common.

> Sarit's sentence combining the topic and the shared idea: "People who have emotional intelligence skills make better employees" or "Emotionally intelligent workers make good employees because they are aware of their own emotions, empathetic of others' feelings, capable of managing stress, and good at working in teams."

5. Find a sentence in the essay that matches the one you wrote. If your analysis is correct, you have very likely identified the thesis statement.

> Essay's thesis statement: Sarit looked through the essay and underlined this sentence as the thesis statement: "We have learned in recent years that successful employees—those who move the most quickly up the ladder—possess greater emotional intelligence skills than their coworkers."

Sarit notices that two sentences could be the thesis statement. She decides that the first statement, which more fully expresses the main idea, is the thesis statement and that the sentence in the conclusion simply reiterates the main idea. Not all essays include repeated thesis statements as this example does. As a flexible reader, you need to be aware that essays do not follow a strict formula. Some writers place the thesis statement in the middle of an essay, and sometimes the thesis statement occurs only at the very end.

1B5. Figuring Out an Implied Thesis Statement in an Essay

Just as some paragraphs do not have explicit topic sentences, some essays do not contain explicit thesis statements. The main idea—and thesis statement—in such essays is implied. Readers must figure out the main idea through the essay's content. We can use steps from the same process to find implied thesis statements as we use to find explicit ones. Lucas needs to analyze an essay to determine its main idea for an assignment in his sociology class. He determines that the essay is on the topic of learning disorders in children. To identify the writer's point about the topic, he first annotates the function of each topic sentence.

> **Topic sentence for paragraph 1:** Parents often notice physical difficulties with fine motor skills first.
>
> **Topic sentence for paragraph 2:** Trouble in particular classes—such as math or reading—is a symptom that may indicate particular learning disabilities.
>
> **Topic sentence for paragraph 3:** Some learning disabilities are identified by a child's social behaviors.
>
> **Topic sentence for paragraph 4:** Language difficulties can also signal learning disorders.

By looking for a common point that unites all four paragraphs, Lucas can see that they all concern symptoms of learning disorders. Now he is ready to write a sentence combining the writer's topic and main point. Here is Lucas's statement of the essay's implied main idea:

> Four types of symptoms are associated with learning disorders in children.
> Writers's point about the topic   Topic

Lucas's sentence expresses the implied main idea of the essay. When the thesis statement is implied, write out the thesis statement yourself, as Lucas did. You will have an easier time remembering the essay's main idea if you write it down in your own words.

1C. MAKING ACCURATE INFERENCES

An **inference** is a conclusion a person draws based on evidence. When we read, we infer by examining the information the writer provides. On the other hand, when we speak or write, we can imply meanings without stating them outright. For instance, when we need to finish a conversation, we might say something such as "It's getting late." Our words imply a deeper meaning—"We need to end this conversation"—and we hope our listeners will infer this meaning from what they hear us say.

One way to make accurate inferences is to consider details. To be sound, an inference must be based on the actual information in a text. Read the following passage, and notice the details that are highlighted.

inference: A conclusion based on evidence.

Teaching Resources
Consider using the exercise "Making Accurate Inferences."

As I walked to my trigonometry class on the first day of the semester, I felt full of hope. Math had never been an easy subject for me, but I knew that with determination, I could do anything. I really believed that.

I found a seat in the middle of the classroom and glanced at the people around me. Most looked nonchalant, as if taking a class in trig were not a big deal. No one spoke.

Five minutes after the class was supposed to begin, a man who looked too young to be a professor walked into the class, slung his gray, worn backpack on the professor's table, and started writing an equation on the board. He muttered something about page 33, so I fumbled through my textbook to find the page. Nothing on the page looked remotely like what the professor had written on the board.

He kept explaining. Something.

"You understand?" he asked the class, turning back to the board before anyone could answer.

I felt that sinking feeling in my stomach that I have felt in so many math classes before. It would be a long semester after all.

To make a sound inference, read the text and pay attention to details. Think about the ideas that the details suggest. Write a sentence that expresses an inference. Figure H1.7 shows the process for drawing sound inferences and a few examples. For a conclusion to be considered a sound inference, you must always be able to support the inference with details from the text.

1C1. Avoiding Inaccurate Inferences

When you read a text, all kinds of ideas come to mind. For example, if you once experienced a math class that was similar to the one described in the text, your personal experience might pop into your mind. If it did, you might be tempted to take some of the details from your experience and apply them to what you are reading. Doing so could lead you to create unsupported inferences. Figure H1.8 gives some examples.

Be careful about using your personal experiences and ideas to draw inferences. Stick to the details in the text, and you will be able to draw inferences that are sound and reasonable.

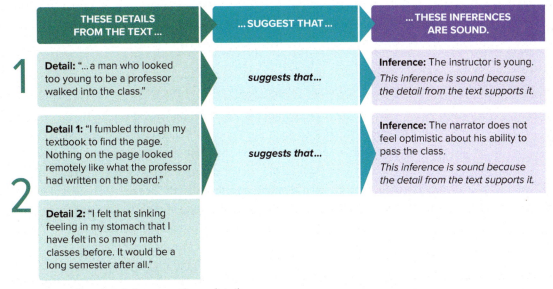

FIGURE H1.7 Drawing inferences from details.

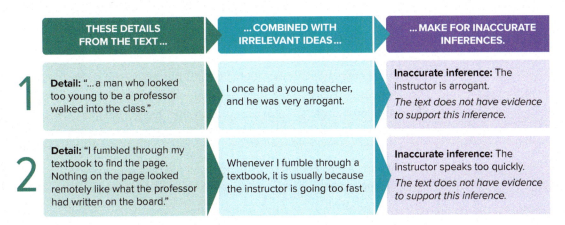

FIGURE H1.8 Making inaccurate inferences.

1C2. Using Common Knowledge

Common knowledge refers to information that most people have or ideas that most people would easily and readily believe or accept. For instance, it is common knowledge that Barack Obama was the first African American president of the United States, that lightning and thunder signal rain, and that children need supervision. You can use common knowledge to help make inferences.

Now let's look at a text that is a bit more complex and use it to judge inferences. Some of the inferences rely on details as well as common knowledge. Read and carefully annotate the following selection from *A First Look at Communication Theory* by Em Griffin. Pay special attention to the details it offers.

What We Can Learn from the *Challenger* Disaster
Em Griffin

[1]On the morning of January 28, 1986, the space shuttle *Challenger* blasted off from the Kennedy Space Center in Florida. [2]Seventy-three seconds later, millions of adults and school children watched on television as the rocket disintegrated in a fiery explosion, and the capsule plunged into the Atlantic Ocean.

[3]The death of all seven crew members, and particularly teacher Christa McAuliffe, shocked the nation. [4]For many Americans, the *Challenger* disaster marked the end of a love affair with space. [5]As they learned in the months that followed, the tragedy could have been—should have been—avoided.

[6]President Reagan immediately appointed a select commission to determine the probable cause(s) of the accident. [7]The panel heard four months of testimony from NASA officials, rocket engineers, astronauts, and anyone else who might have knowledge about the failed mission. [8]In a five-volume published report, the presidential commission identified the primary cause of the accident as a failure in the joint between two stages of the rocket that allowed hot gases to escape during the "burn." [9]Volatile rocket fuel spewed out when a rubber O-ring failed to seal the joint.

[10]The average citizen could understand the mechanics of the commission's finding. [11]After all, everyone knows what happens when you pour gasoline on an open flame. [12]What people found difficult to fathom was why NASA had launched the *Challenger* when there was good reason to believe the conditions weren't safe. [13]In addition to the defective seal, the commission also concluded that a highly flawed decision process was an important contributing cause of the disaster. [14]Communication, as well as combustion, was responsible for the tragedy.

After you read the passage, notice in Figure H1.9 how we can use the details to draw a sound inference when we apply some common knowledge to the details.

FIGURE H1.9 Making inferences supported by details and common knowledge.

1C3. Avoiding Unsupported Inferences

Now let's consider some unsupported inferences. The example in Figure H1.10 is not based on details from the text. Notice how easy it is to make conclusions, especially judgments, that are not supported by the information in the text.

As you look for inferences in texts, make sure you use the actual details that the text supplies, not ideas you bring to the text. Be sure you can point to the details that make your inferences sound.

1C4. Analyzing Tone

Tone is the attitude with which a message is conveyed. We might use a tone of respect when we speak, or we might use a tone that reveals frustration, anger, or impatience. Both voice and body language help us discern tone in face-to-face communication. In texts, however, we depend on textual clues to help us identify

THIS DETAIL FROM THE TEXT…	…IS NOT ENOUGH FOR…	…THIS UNSUPPORTED INFERENCE.
Detail: "Volatile rocket fuel spewed out when a rubber O-ring failed to seal the joint."	*…is not enough for…*	**Unsupported inference:** NASA engineers did not know how to design flawless O-rings. *This inference is not sound because there are no details to support it. The O-ring failed, and communication contributed to this failure. But the text does not say the engineers lacked knowledge. Sentence 5 says that "the tragedy could have been–should have been–avoided." This line suggests the engineers could make flawless O-rings.*

FIGURE H1.10 Unsupported inferences.

tone. Identifying the tone of a text can help you both make inferences and understand the writer's purpose.

Have you ever noticed how difficult it is to determine the tone of a text message or an email? Read the email message that follows. What is its tone?

> Sherrie,
>
> You asked for some help in choosing a major. How can I possibly help you with that?
>
> —Dr. Zimmerman

As you read the email message, did you hear a helpful tone in the last sentence, or did you hear a sarcastic tone? Readers might hear a sarcastic tone, and if they do, they might make the inference that the professor is being rude. Because readers could infer a sarcastic tone, it would be better to write a reply that leaves no room to wonder about the writer's attitude.

Compare the following message. Notice how adding a few extra details and making intentional choices about wording help the writer convey a tone that is decidedly positive. Writers must carefully select their words to help readers understand the tone they hope to establish.

> Sherrie,
>
> You asked for some help in choosing a major. I'd be glad to help you if you think I can be of assistance.
>
> I will be in my office tomorrow from 1:00 to 5:00. Feel free to drop by, or schedule a different time by contacting Ms. Dulane, my secretary.
>
> —Dr. Zimmerman

Objective Tone. One way to understand tone is to consider two types: objective and subjective. When a writer attempts to write a text without tone or with a neutral tone, we say that the writer uses an objective tone. Imagine a news anchor reading the evening news. The anchor's job is to minimize the tone in their voice so that they present the news in a nonbiased, or objective, manner. The anchor is speaking as a reader, not as an individual. Thus, we are not supposed to focus on the anchor and their particular views. Read the following text for an example of objective tone.

> People who are regularly late for meetings or other appointments can eventually develop a reputation for being less dependable than others. Coworkers and acquaintances rarely know or understand the situations that cause a person to be habitually late, and even if they are aware of such circumstances, they may still come to view the late person as unreliable. In turn, having a reputation as an unreliable person makes it more difficult to receive promotions or be entrusted with high-level tasks.

To identify objective tone, look for these characteristics. An objective tone:

- **Avoids emotionally charged terms.** In the example of objective tone, the term "unreliable person" is far less emotionally charged than the term "loser" or "slacker" would be.
- **Uses impartial, unbiased language.** The example above does not present language that is judgmental about people who are habitually late. The writer simply explains a possible effect of being consistently late.
- **Is used in formal (professional and academic) writing.** Not only does slang (such as the word "loser") convey an emotional and biased tone, but it also makes a text informal.

When a writer uses an objective tone, readers are more likely to infer that the information is reliable. They may not be correct, of course, but readers expect reliable information to be delivered in an impersonal, objective way. Thus, when we see the use of an objective tone, we can use it as a clue for making inferences. For example, in the paragraph about people who are habitually late, it would be wrong to make the inference that the writer has disdain for such people. The writer does not reveal his or her own attitude toward the subject.

We would also be wrong to infer that the writer is never late for her own appointments. The writer reveals nothing about his or her behaviors and attitudes. For all we know, the writer is a habitually late person! Thus, when you identify an objective tone, you cannot make inferences about the writer's attitude toward the topic.

Subjective Tone. A subjective tone is used when a writer is not trying to present information in a neutral way. We have shown how news anchors attempt to use an objective tone so that they do not reveal their personal biases about issues. Political commentators, on the other hand, discuss news events but do so in a subjective, biased way. They are paid to offer their opinions on current events, so using a subjective tone is appropriate.

The use of a subjective tone is often intentional: writers hope readers will come to share the same emotions or opinions as they do. Read the following example to become familiar with subjective tone:

> I work with a poor colleague who is always late. He's not only late to meetings, but he's late to work every single day. The variety of excuses he uses when he stumbles through the door each morning is always amusing. He cannot help but utter some lame excuse. "I was caught in traffic. Darn freeway!" or "I can't believe my alarm clock failed me again!" It would be so much better—and so much more appropriate—for him to creep over to his office and slink into his chair like the clueless buffoon he is.

When a text is written in a subjective tone, readers are more likely to see the text as biased. Bias is not necessarily a bad thing: an opinion is a bias. It is a point of view that one holds, and there are probably reasons one holds that point of view. When a writer presents information that reveals their bias, the writer often uses a subjective tone. Because bias reveals a point of view, a text that reveals a writer's bias is probably a text that has as its goal persuasion. Thus, by figuring out the tone of a text, you will have a better understanding of the writer's purpose.

In addition, recognizing tone can help you to draw accurate inferences. In the example above, the writer's tone provides clues that help readers make these accurate inferences:

The writer has disrespect for the colleague.

The writer does not think the colleague's reasons for being late are legitimate.

The writer feels superior to the colleague.

Analyzing the details and tone of a text helps you as a reader to more critically comprehend what you read and to make inferences that are accurate.

CHAPTER PROJECT Reading Skills

In this chapter, you have read about strategies you can use to become a better reader. The assignment that follows provides you with an opportunity to put those strategies to work. Follow these instructions.

1. In Part 6, find the article by George Pike, "Love It or Hate It: Native Advertising on the Internet."
2. Use the prereading strategies in this chapter to prepare to read the article.
3. Use the during-reading strategies to read and annotate the article. Prepare an outline, and then write a summary based on your outline.
4. Use the after-reading strategies to write a paragraph about how you would teach the ideas in this article to someone who had not read it. Next, write a paragraph in which you reflect on how the information in the article is pertinent and relevant to you personally.

H2 Improving Your Writing Skills

Connect Adaptive Learning Assignment
Consider assigning Connect's Adaptive Learning Assignments to provide students with additional practice.

CHAPTER OBJECTIVES

You will learn to:
- Write clear and correct sentences.
- Write well-developed paragraphs.
- Use transitions appropriately.
- Avoid pronoun reference errors.
- Avoid verb tense errors.
- Use capitalization properly.
- Use commas and apostrophes correctly.
- Use the correct word for your meaning.

Teaching Resources
See the Instructor's Manual (IM) for suggestions about how to use this chapter.

If you have ever struggled with writing, you are not alone. The chapters in this book focus primarily on how to think rhetorically so that you become a better writer and critical thinker. But to be effective, thinking must be expressed grammatically and clearly. In this chapter, you will have the opportunity to review some of the most common errors in sentence structure, grammar, and mechanics so that your writing is clear, correct, and effective.

2A SENTENCE BASICS

Good writing begins with well-written sentences. The suggestions that follow will give you ideas for writing clear and well-structured sentences. We will first review basic sentence grammar.

2A.1 Subjects

subject: The main noun or pronoun in a sentence.

A complete sentence must contain a subject (the main noun or pronoun in a sentence) and a predicate (the part of the sentence that contains the verb).

The **subject** tells the reader who or what the sentence is about.

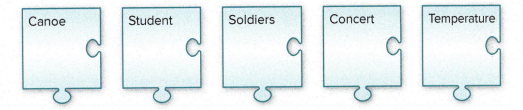

The *complete subject* may include additional information.

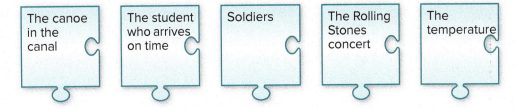

The subject may be simple (one noun or pronoun) or compound (more than one noun or pronoun).

Simple subject: canoe

Compound subject: canoe and oar

Identifying Subjects in Longer Sentences. Some sentences contain several nouns, as the following example shows. Not all of the underlined words (all nouns) are the subject.

> Manny's Taco Truck on Grand Street sells many more tacos in one year than all the Mexican restaurants near the college.

To find the simple subject, ask, "What is the main noun in the sentence?" In other words, ask, "Which noun is the main focus of the other ideas in the sentence?" In the example, *Manny's Taco Truck* is the main noun. Thus, *Manny's Taco Truck* is the subject.

Sometimes a subject is placed in the middle of a sentence or even at the end. Another way to identify the subject is to examine the verbs in the sentence. Which verb seems the most important? Figuring out the most important verb can help you figure out the subject.

> From the bridge over the Mississippi River, Tina could see for miles.

Verb: could see

Who could see? Tina

Tina is the subject.

Unspoken You as the Subject. Sometimes the subject of a sentence is *you,* even though the pronoun is left out.

Complete sentence: Take out the trash.

Unspoken subject: <u>You</u> take out the trash.

predicate: The part of a sentence containing the main verb that tells what the subject is or does.

2A.2 Predicates

The **predicate** is the part of a sentence containing the verb. Each subject needs a verb. The verb helps the writer make a point about the subject. Here are examples of verbs:

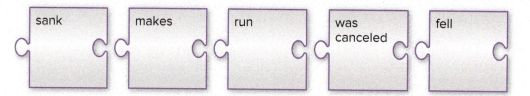

Sometimes verbs contain additional information. The verb, plus any information added to it, is the predicate of the sentence.

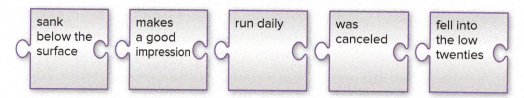

When a subject and predicate are combined, a sentence is formed:

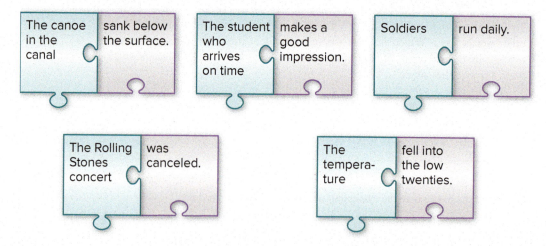

To avoid sentence grammar errors, make sure all the sentences you write include both a subject and a predicate.

Simple Predicates. The simple predicate is the main verb of a sentence.

> The cracks in the ceiling <u>are</u> ugly.
>
> Deanna <u>cooked</u> breakfast.

The simple predicate can also be compound. A compound predicate includes two or more verbs joined by a conjunction.

> Deanna <u>cooked and cleaned</u> all day.

Complete Predicates. The complete predicate includes the main verb plus any additional information in the sentence about the verb.

> Renato <u>slept well past noon on the day of the exam.</u>
>
> *(Complete predicate tells more about how Renato slept.)*
>
> The laughing child <u>was rolling on the floor with the cat</u>.
>
> *(Complete predicate tells more about how the child was rolling.)*

Placement of Predicates. In some sentences, the predicate comes before the subject.

> <u>Sitting on the steps were</u> three white rabbits.

▶ **ACTIVITY 1 Identifying Subjects and Predicates**

Identify the complete subject and complete predicate in the following sentences:

A. Max decided to enroll in summer class and find a part-time job.

B. Aschelle and her friends were the first to arrive.

2B SENTENCE TYPES

Learning to write four different types of complete sentences can help you add richness and variety to your writing. These four types are simple sentences, compound sentences, complex sentences, and compound-complex sentences.

2B.1 Simple Sentences

simple sentence: A single independent clause.

A clause is a group of words containing a subject and a verb. A **simple sentence** consists of one independent clause.

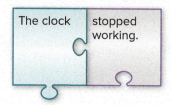

Subject + Predicate = Independent clause

independent clause: A group of words that can stand alone, forming a complete sentence.

An **independent clause** is a group of words that can stand alone. It is a complete sentence.

2B.2 Compound Sentences

compound sentence: Two or more independent clauses joined correctly to form a sentence.

A **compound sentence** consists of two or more independent clauses. A compound sentence is two sentences joined correctly.

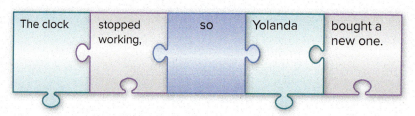

Independent clause + Independent clause = Compound sentence

coordinating conjunction: A word that joins two elements, for example, *and*, *but*, and *or*.

Using a Coordinating Conjunction. To join two sentences together, you can use a **coordinating conjunction**. Only seven coordinating conjunctions exist, and you can remember them with the acronym, FANBOYS: *For, And, Nor, But, Or, Yet, So.*

To make a compound sentence, simply use a comma plus an appropriate coordinating conjunction between the two independent clauses.

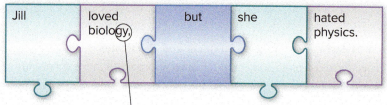

Independent clause + Comma + Coordinating conjunction + Independent clause = Compound sentence

TABLE H2.1 Coordinating Conjunctions (FANBOYS) for Compound Sentences

Conjunction	When to Use	Example
for	Use before a sentence that offers an explanation.	We did not stay, for our daughter was not feeling well.
and	Use to add information.	The wedding was beautiful, and the bride was vibrant.
nor	Use to add a negative point.	I do not like cloudy days, nor does my sister.
but	Use to indicate a change in direction or to show contrast.	Jill wanted to dance, but she was too tired.
or	Use to present an alternative.	Kim will find a ride home, or she will call a taxi.
yet	Use to say "in spite of," "still," or "even though."	It was cold outside, yet Bill did not want to put on his jacket.
so	Use to show a result or consequence.	The movie was scary, so Tina decided not to watch it.

Each coordinating conjunction has a particular use, as shown in Table H2.1.

When you use a coordinating conjunction to join two independent clauses to create a compound sentence, use a comma before the coordinating conjunction:

> We found ten rattlesnakes on the ranch, and they were all babies.
>
> *(comma + coordinating conjunction)*

Do not use a comma before a coordinating conjunction if the part of the sentence after the conjunction is not an independent clause:

> We found ten rattlesnakes on the ranch and five copperheads.
>
> *(no comma because "five copperheads" is not an independent clause)*

Using a Semicolon and Transitional Word. Another way to join two independent clauses is to use a semicolon with a transitional word or expression. The following list contains some common transitional words:

also	furthermore	nevertheless	still
besides	however	next	then
consequently	instead	otherwise	therefore
finally	meanwhile	similarly	thus

A semicolon plus a transitional word works just like a coordinating conjunction does to join two independent clauses. Add a comma after the transitional word.

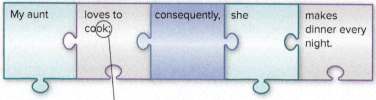

Independent clause + Semicolon + Transitional word + Comma + Independent clause = Compound sentence

Transitional words and expressions help readers understand a sentence's meaning. Table H2.2 shows the function of some of these words in compound sentences.

A transitional word can also be used to add information to a single independent clause. In such a case, the sentence is usually punctuated with commas, as these examples demonstrate:

> I thought I was smart. However, I learned that I was ignorant about a few things.
>
> Jim was late. We had dinner, therefore, at 9:00.
>
> Sean wanted to buy my car. He wanted to buy my trailer also.

TABLE H2.2 Transitional Words for Compound Sentences

Transitional Word	What It Does	Example
also, besides, furthermore, moreover	Adds information	No employee will be excused from training; furthermore, no credit will be granted if an employee is late.
conversely, however, instead, nevertheless	Shows a contrast or difference	The employees were not happy about training; however, they ended up enjoying the sessions.
also, likewise, similarly	Shows a similarity	Janice is a good manager; also, she happens to be my sister.
consequently, therefore, thus	Shows a result	Janice attended the training; therefore, she was certified the next day.
finally, next, subsequently, then	Indicates a time relationship	Training was the first step; next, the employees will work in groups.

2B.3 Complex Sentences

A **complex sentence** includes an independent clause (simple sentence) and at least one dependent clause. A **dependent clause** cannot stand alone. To make a dependent clause, a dependent word is added to an independent clause:

complex sentence: A dependent clause and an independent clause, joined correctly to form a sentence.

dependent clause: A clause (a group of words with a subject and verb) that cannot stand alone.

> **Independent clause:** The class was canceled.
>
> **Dependent clause:** <u>Although</u> the class was canceled

In the example above, by adding "although," the writer has made the clause dependent. If a clause becomes dependent, it cannot stand alone as a complete sentence.

To write a grammatically correct complete sentence with a dependent clause, the dependent clause must be added to an independent clause:

> <u>Although the class was canceled,</u> <u>I stayed in the room and studied.</u>
>
> Dependent clause + independent clause

Here are some common dependent words:

after	even though	than	when	which
although	if	that	whenever	while
as	once	though	where	who
because	rather than	unless	wherever	whom
before	since	until	whether	why
even if	so that	what		

When a dependent word comes first in the sentence, use a comma after its clause.

> Because she had enjoyed math in high <u>school, Janice</u> looked forward to her college math class.

When a dependent word comes after an independent clause, do not use a comma before it.

> Janice looked forward to her college math <u>class because</u> she had enjoyed math in high school.

2B.4 Complex Sentences with More than One Dependent Clause

A complex sentence may include more than one dependent clause. Notice that the decision to use a comma depends on where the dependent clause is placed.

> <u>Although classes had ended</u>, the bookstore remained open <u>because shipments were still arriving.</u>
>
> Dependent clause + independent clause + dependent clause

2B.5 Compound-Complex Sentences

compound-complex sentence: Two or more independent clauses plus one or more dependent clauses correctly joined together to form a sentence.

A **compound-complex sentence** contains two or more independent clauses plus one or more dependent clauses.

> <u>Since Jennifer excels in art</u>, she is happy the project requires illustrations, and she is hoping to impress her instructor with her skills.
>
> dependent clause + two independent clauses = compound-complex sentence

▶ **ACTIVITY 2 Writing Varied Sentence Types**

Using the simple sentence that follows, add clauses to create a compound sentence, a complex sentence, and a compound-complex sentence.

> **Simple sentence:** Psychology would be a difficult class.

2C AVOIDING SENTENCE FRAGMENTS

Fragments are sets of words that look like sentences but are actually not complete sentences.

fragment: A set of words that looks like a sentence but is actually not a complete sentence.

> **Complete sentence:** I liked working outside today.
>
> **Fragment:** Even though the unending rain had turned the yard into a swamp, and the mosquitoes were constantly biting.

The second set of words is not a complete sentence, although it is quite long. Good writing should be free of sentence fragments, and in this section, we focus on how to identify them and avoid them.

2C.1 Missing Subject or Verb Fragments

A complete sentence must have both a subject and a verb.

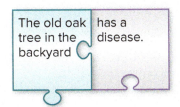

If the set of words presents only a subject, a sentence fragment results.

To make this fragment into a sentence, we need a verb.

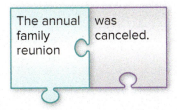

The set of words can now function as a sentence, an independent clause.

A set of words that includes only a verb is also a sentence fragment.

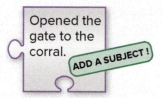

To make this fragment into a sentence, we need the subject.

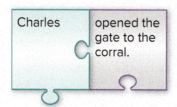

Sometimes spotting fragments is difficult when you read sentences in a paragraph. Look at the underlined word group in the paragraph that follows:

> Charles woke up at five o'clock. The sun had not even peeped over the horizon yet. He walked across the wet grass. <u>Opened the gate to the corral</u>. Pumpkin, the new foal, was standing by her mother.

"Opened the gate to the corral" is a fragment. However, because the fragment is within a paragraph, it is easy to overlook. Here are some tips:

- Analyze each sentence individually, thinking about the sentence only and not the thoughts around it.
- Start with the last sentence in the paragraph, and work backward. This way, you will not be influenced by the sentences before (or after) the sentence you are analyzing.
- Circle the subject and underline the predicate to make sure the sentence contains both.

2C.2 Phrase Fragments

Phrases are sets of words that convey information but are not complete sentences. A phrase by itself is a fragment. Many phrase fragments start with a preposition: *from, in, of, out, through,* and so on.

> **Fragment:** From the upper deck of the cruise liner.
>
> **Corrected:** From the upper deck of the cruise liner, we could see the entire coastline.

When you use a word that begins with -ing, a fragment can occur.

> **Fragment:** Standing in the hallway with her head hanging down.
>
> **Corrected:** Standing in the hallway with her head hanging down, the little girl looked sad.

A set of words that begins with *to* and contains a verb can be a sentence fragment, as the following example shows:

> **Fragment:** To spend three weeks on vacation without a phone or computer.
>
> **Corrected:** To spend three weeks on vacation without a phone or computer would be amazing.

2C.3 Dependent-Clause Fragments

Word groups that begin with dependent words are fragments unless they are joined to a complete sentence.

> **Fragment:** Shanna was late to class again. Because the train was late.
>
> **Corrected:** Shanna was late to class again because the train was late.

Question words make up an especially important group of dependent words.

| who | what | where | why | how much |
| whom | whose | when | which | how many |

A question is a complete sentence, but it is easy to create a fragment when using one of these words in a sentence that is not a question.

Question: Which restaurant is the best for dieters?

Fragment: I like Fred's Diner. Which is the best restaurant for dieters.

Corrected: I like Fred's Diner, which is the best restaurant for dieters.

2C.4 Extra Information Fragments

Sometimes writers provide added details in word groups that can look like complete sentences but actually are not. These are extra-information fragments.

Fragment: The little girl loved her old doll. The one her grandmother had given her.

Corrected: The little girl loved her old doll, the one her grandmother had given her.

Fragment: For students who are not mathematically inclined, some college classes require more study. Such as algebra, physics, and chemistry.

Corrected: For students who are not mathematically inclined, some college classes require more study, such as algebra, physics, and chemistry.

▶ **ACTIVITY 3 Correcting Fragments**

Read the following paragraph. Identify and correct any fragments.

The class will meet in Room 116. The one with the open door. Professor Gonzalez will be talking about the midterm exam. Since

> the exam is next week. She will cover grammar, especially fragments. She will also talk about how to complete the final course project. A collection of poems. Although students will be allowed to select poems for their collections. The poems must come from the textbook. Students will also have to write a poem in iambic pentameter. Which might be a challenge for some students.

2D AVOIDING RUN-ONS AND COMMA SPLICES

When two independent clauses are joined improperly, the result is a run-on sentence or a comma splice. A run-on sentence is two (or more) independent clauses joined without any punctuation or conjunction. Run-on sentences are also called fused sentences.

> <u>I knew I would be late</u> <u>my alarm didn't go off again!</u>
>
> Independent clause + independent clause = run-on sentence

A common misperception is to think a run-on sentence can be fixed by inserting a comma, like this:

> <u>I knew I would be late,</u> <u>my alarm didn't go off again!</u>
>
> independent clause + independent clause = comma splice

A comma alone cannot join two independent clauses. Using just a comma to join two independent clauses without including a coordinating conjunction results in a comma splice.

To correct run-on sentences or comma splices, you can either join the two independent clauses using a proper method, or you can separate them, creating two sentences.

2D.1 Joining the Clauses of a Run-on or Comma Splice

You can use a coordinating conjunction and a comma.

> **Comma splice:** I knew I would be <u>late, my</u> alarm didn't go off again!
>
> **Corrected:** I knew I would <u>be late, for my</u> alarm didn't go off again!

If the content of the two sentences is closely connected, you can use a semicolon.

> **Run-on:** I knew I would be late my alarm didn't go off again!
>
> **Corrected:** I knew I would be late; my alarm didn't go off again!

You can also make one of the clauses into a dependent clause.

> **Comma splice:** I knew I would be late, my alarm didn't go off again!
>
> **Corrected:** I knew I would be <u>late because my</u> alarm didn't go off again!

2D.2 Separating the Clauses of a Run-on or Comma Splice

If you decide to separate the two clauses rather than join them, use a period after the first sentence, and start the second sentence with a capital letter.

> **Run-on:** I knew I would be late my alarm didn't go off again!
>
> **Corrected:** I knew I would be late. My alarm didn't go off again!

▶ **ACTIVITY 4** Correcting Run-Ons and Comma Splices

Read the paragraph that follows. First, identify any run-ons or comma splices. Then rewrite the paragraph, correcting the run-ons and comma splices.

> Knowing the amount of calories, fat, and salt in fast foods can help you eat more healthfully. Many restaurants now offer information about their food, this information should be posted in the restaurant. If you cannot find nutritional information, ask an employee for it. You can easily eat more healthful fast food. Choose places that offer salads, find restaurants that have soups and vegetables on their menus. Even salads, however, can be unhealthy so avoid high-fat items such as creamy dressing, bacon bits, and shredded cheese. These all add fat and calories. Healthier sandwiches may be available these include regular-size or junior-size sandwiches with lean meats. Adding bacon, cheese, or mayo will increase the fat and calories. Filling your sandwich with vegetables is a much healthier choice.

2E WRITING CLEAR SENTENCES

More important than using impressive words or complex sentence structures is communicating clearly. Use the tips that follow to improve the clarity of the sentences you compose.

- **Present only one idea in a sentence.** A common error is to try to cram too many ideas into a single sentence. Doing so can result in confusion for the reader as well as incorrectly formed sentences.

  Needs improvement: The various fees associated with making a parking mistake and subsequently getting a fine can add up to exorbitant amounts, amounts that many people end up not paying because the fees are simply too high.

  Improved: Fees for parking violations can be very high. These overly high fees often remain unpaid.

- **Avoid making a sentence overly wordy.** Deleting unnecessary words keeps sentences focused.

  Needs improvement: Most children who bring home homework and work on their own without adult help to complete it often lack the kind of direction and supervision they need in order to get the work done efficiently and successfully.

  Improved: Most children need direct supervision to complete their homework successfully.

- **Use words that are specific instead of abstract.** When you use words that are more concrete and specific, readers can more quickly understand your point.

Needs improvement: Certain illnesses can greatly interfere with a student's attendance.

Improved: Illnesses such as chronic fatigue syndrome and cancer can interfere with a student's attendance.

- **Use natural language.** Avoid the temptation to use words that are not in your normal vocabulary (unless you are writing in an academic discipline and need to use words from that discipline).

  Needs improvement: My sister was inebriated in a public venue, so she was incarcerated the evening before.

  Improved: My sister was drunk in public, so she was jailed last night.

- **Avoid clichés and fillers.** Do not express your thoughts in clichés or use words and phrases that do not serve much function.

  Needs improvement: In my opinion, when you are in a new relationship, you are on an emotional rollercoaster.

  Improved: When you are in a new relationship, your emotions may be unpredictable.

▶ **ACTIVITY 5 Revising Unclear Sentences**

Revise each of the sentences that follows:

1. In this day and age, some young people choose not to pay for cable television or satellite television because they know they can get their television programs in another way which might be streaming from the internet or using a streaming device.
2. Taking a class online, a class on the internet, can be harder than a person thinks because the student has to stay motivated and be in charge of time management making sure to do the work on time and ask questions when necessary.
3. After breaking his mother's decorative ceramic piece, the juvenile attempted to eradicate any remaining evidence.
4. From the dawn of time, people have debated whether polygamy is moral or not.
5. A group of angry individuals gathered in front of the dining establishment and yelled epithets that called into question the establishment's discrimination policies.

2F WRITING SENTENCES WITH PARALLEL STRUCTURE

Parallelism is the use of consistent structure for all elements in a series of two or more elements. (Hint: Look for a conjunction such as *and* that links the items.)

> **Parallel:** Bullying in schools is a serious problem because it can cause extreme anguish and result in serious physical harm.
>
> *(The two reasons for the seriousness of bullying are presented in parallel form.)*
>
> **Parallel:** Knowledge of geography is necessary for jobs in commerce, important for careers in sales, and essential for careers in international business.
>
> *(The three items in the series are presented in parallel form; each contains an adjective followed by a prepositional phrase.)*

Because thesis statements often present series of elements, always check to ensure that your thesis statement is in parallel form. While parallelism is especially important in thesis statements, every sentence that presents a series of elements should reflect parallel form.

To use parallelism in sentences, follow these guidelines:

- Identify items in the sentence that could be put in parallel form, usually a series of two or more similar elements joined by a coordinating conjunction (for, and, nor, but, or, yet, so).
- Make sure the items in the series are alike in their parts of speech. Make changes in wording, if necessary, to achieve parallelism.

> **Not Parallel:** Micah liked skiing, jogging, and to skateboard.
>
> **Parallel:** Micah liked skiing, jogging, and skateboarding.

▶ **ACTIVITY 6 Creating Parallelism**

Combine each set of sentences below into a thesis statement that demonstrates parallelism.

1. Ideas to combine:
   - Climate change affects sea levels.
   - Climate change creates changes in precipitation patterns.
   - Ecosystems are also affected by climate change.

2. Ideas to combine:
   - The use of drones reduces military casualties.
   - The cost of military engagement is decreased when drones are used.
   - Drones do less damage to cities than traditional warfare does.

2G WRITING GOOD PARAGRAPHS

A paragraph is a cohesive set of sentences that, together, make a point. The number of sentences in a paragraph varies widely. For instance, professional writers sometimes use one-sentence paragraphs for emphasis. In college, most assignments require paragraphs that are well-developed; that is, you need to write paragraphs that include a main idea (topic sentence) and support for that idea. By keeping your audience in mind as you write, you can figure out how much information readers need to fully understand or accept the main idea you are writing about.

2G.1 Topic Sentences

The main idea of a paragraph is expressed in a topic sentence, and additional sentences in the paragraph are called supporting sentences. These additional sentences provide explanations, examples, and other kinds of support to help readers understand the topic sentence. A topic sentence:

- **Expresses the main point in a paragraph.** It provides the exact point the writer hopes the reader will remember or believe.
- **Expresses the broadest idea in the paragraph.** It is broad enough to cover all the ideas in the paragraph.
- **Presents an idea that requires support.** It makes a point that must be explained further or backed up with evidence.
- **Is a statement, not a question.** Because it makes a point, a topic sentence cannot be a question.

2G.2 Paragraph Support

Within each paragraph, additional details help readers understand the major supporting point. These additional sentences provide supporting details that relate directly to the topic sentence.

The supporting details offer further information (examples, explanations, statistics, quotations, anecdotes, and facts) for the topic sentence. Read the example that follows, showing how supporting details work to develop a topic sentence.

Topic sentence → Storytelling is used to communicate a culture's values.

Support:
Stories explain
Example from Aesop

Often, stories are used to explain to young people the meanings and reasons for certain values. For example, the story known as "The Boy Who

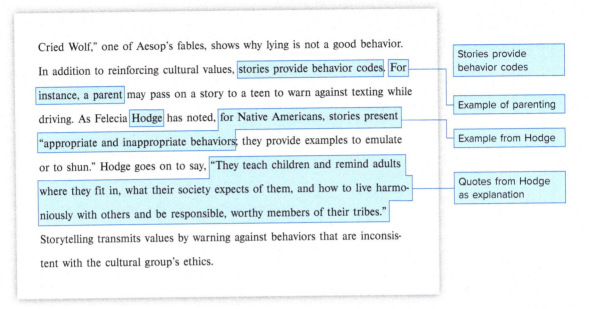

Cried Wolf," one of Aesop's fables, shows why lying is not a good behavior. In addition to reinforcing cultural values, stories provide behavior codes. For instance, a parent may pass on a story to a teen to warn against texting while driving. As Felecia Hodge has noted, for Native Americans, stories present "appropriate and inappropriate behaviors; they provide examples to emulate or to shun." Hodge goes on to say, "They teach children and remind adults where they fit in, what their society expects of them, and how to live harmoniously with others and be responsible, worthy members of their tribes." Storytelling transmits values by warning against behaviors that are inconsistent with the cultural group's ethics.

A well-developed paragraph presents enough support so that the most important questions readers might have will be answered.

Additionally, the support in a well-written paragraph is cohesive; that is, each sentence adds to or in some other way relates to the sentences around it. Any ideas that do not pertain to the topic sentence should be placed in a different paragraph. A paragraph is a chunk of meaning; by reading a single paragraph, a reader should be able to articulate the main idea and the basis (support) for that idea.

One way to help readers see how the ideas in a paragraph relate to each other is to use transitions (see Table H2.3). Notice how transitions show the logical relationships among ideas in the following paragraph:

> Good reasons exist on both sides of the debate about whether it is wise to take out student loans. <u>On the one hand</u>, taking out student loans seems logical. College graduates, <u>after all</u>, statistically earn much more than those who do not have degrees. <u>Thus</u>, it seems likely that college graduates will be able to pay off their loans. <u>On the other hand</u>, taking out student loans is fraught with risk. <u>Clearly</u>, college students cannot be certain they will find good jobs after graduation. <u>Additionally</u>, even if they do find good jobs, their entry-level salaries may not be high enough for both a comfortable life and the repayment of student debt.

TABLE H2.3 Common Transition Words and Phrases

Clarification			
for example	in other words	specifically	to demonstrate
for instance	in reality	that is	to explain further
indeed	put another way	to clarify	to illustrate
in fact	simply stated		

Sequences or Time Order			
about	final	next	soon
after	first, second, ... last	now	to begin
as	immediately	often	until
as soon as	in the future	one, another	when
at the same time	later	previously	while
during	meanwhile	simultaneously	

Similarity or Addition			
additionally	as well	for instance	moreover
again	besides	furthermore	next
along with	equally important	in addition	plus
also	for another thing	in the same way	similarly
another	for example	likewise	

Contrast			
although	even though	on the contrary	otherwise
conversely	however	on the one hand, on the other hand	still
counter to	in spite of this		yet
despite	nevertheless		

Conclusion or Summary			
accordingly	in summary	lastly	the final point
in closing	in the end	the bottom line	to conclude
in short			

Cause and Effect			
as a consequence	because	resulting in	therefore
as a result	consequently	so then	thus
at last			

Direction			
above	below	next to	there
across	beyond	opposite	to the left
against	here	over	to the right
behind	nearby	overhead	

▶ **ACTIVITY 7 Improving the Development of a Paragraph**

The following paragraph's main idea needs better development. List questions readers might ask, and use the answers to rewrite the paragraph.

> Some people opt to purchase smartphones instead of laptop computers because the apps on smartphones can do almost everything one expects from a computer. While reading the screen may be a bit more difficult with a smartphone, the computing capabilities are quite amazing.

2H AVOIDING PRONOUN REFERENCE AND VERB TENSE ERRORS

Study the pages that follow to improve in these common problem areas: using pronouns and staying consistent in verb tense.

2H.1 Pronoun Reference Errors

Of all the pronoun errors, pronoun reference errors are the worst in terms of making one's writing difficult to understand. Sometimes a pronoun reference is vague or unclear. If the pronoun can refer to more than one noun, or antecedent, readers will be confused.

> **Unclear antecedent:** The drought and water shortage caught citizens by surprise, but the city was prepared for <u>it</u>.

Is *drought* the antecedent of *it*, or is *water shortage* the antecedent? What happens if we change *it* to *them*?

> **Unclear antecedent:** The drought and water shortage caught citizens by surprise, but the city was prepared for <u>them</u>.

This sentence is also confusing! What does the word *them* refer to—the drought and water shortage or the citizens? Notice how the corrected version of the sentence clears up any potential confusion.

> **Corrected:** The drought and water shortage caught citizens by surprise, but the city was prepared for <u>both events</u>.

In the final version, the writer chooses to use a synonym (both events) rather than a pronoun because using a pronoun would cause confusion.

There are two main ways to correct unclear pronoun reference: place pronouns near their antecedents and supply a missing antecedent.

- **Place antecedents appropriately.** Sometimes in paragraphs, the pronoun gets separated too far from the antecedent, and the separation can result in confusion. The reader may forget what antecedent the pronoun is referring to.

> **Faulty:** Citizens had hoped <u>the water shortage</u> in July would last only briefly. They began to water their lawns less frequently than usual, conserve water in their homes, and comply with the city's additional conservation guidelines. But <u>it</u> did not.
>
> **Corrected:** Citizens had hoped <u>the water shortage</u> in July would last only briefly. They began to water their lawns less frequently than usual, conserve water in their homes, and comply with the city's additional conservation guidelines. But <u>the water shortage</u> did not last briefly. <u>It</u> continued for another six weeks.

Use a pronoun only if the antecedent is nearby. Notice that the last sentence uses *it*, but because *the water shortage* is nearby, the reference for *it* is easily identified.

- **Supply missing antecedents.** Sometimes an antecedent is missing altogether. In some cases, the writer may believe he has provided an antecedent but actually has not.

> **Faulty:** The citizens conserved water in a number of ways. They saw <u>it</u> as a serious responsibility.

What noun or noun phrase is the antecedent for the pronoun *it*? The writer may mean to say that "conserving water" was seen as a serious responsibility. Notice, however, that the phrase *conserving water* does not appear in the first sentence. Thus, there is no antecedent for the pronoun.

> **Corrected:** The citizens conserved water in a number of ways. They saw <u>conserving water</u> as a serious responsibility.

▶ **ACTIVITY 8 Making Clear Antecedents for Pronouns**

Combine the following ideas into a paragraph. Use at least two pronouns, and make sure the antecedents for the pronouns are clearly identifiable.

- One highly contagious disease is chicken pox (varicella).
- The most common symptoms are rash, fever, headache, sore throat, and cough.
- Chicken pox can also lead to very serious complications for vulnerable people.
- The best protection against chicken pox is the chicken pox vaccine.
- The chicken pox vaccine has been used widely in the United States since 1995.

2H.2 Verb Tense Consistency

As a writer, you must choose the verb tense you will use to convey information. Verbs express more than the action that happens in a sentence. Verb tenses tell when the action takes place—past, present, or future. For example, in each of the following sentences the tense of the underlined verb expresses the timing of the nurse's action.

> **Past:** Earlier this morning, the nurse <u>examined</u> the patients' charts.
>
> **Present:** The nurse always <u>examines</u> the patients' charts at 10 a.m.
>
> **Future:** Tomorrow morning the nurse <u>will examine</u> the patients' charts.

Even without the phrases *Earlier this morning* and *Tomorrow morning*, readers would know which action already happened (past) and which action will happen (future) because of the verb tense.

For the most part, verbs in a text should remain consistent in tense, although there are places where tenses can change. Follow these guidelines to select the best tense for the information you are conveying:

Use past tense for narrative. Most narratives recount events that have happened. So when writers tell a story, they most commonly use past tense. Present tense is less useful for narratives and is best avoided.

Use present tense for most academic writing. For almost all academic writing, present tense is the correct tense, even when you are writing about the views of a person who died hundreds of years ago.

> Anorexia nervosa is an eating disorder that is notoriously difficult to treat because patients often deny they have the disorder.

When the goal is to compare historical events or historical ideas, use past tense, as the following example illustrates:

> In the 1950s, women were expected to take care of most of the domestic chores involved in raising a family, such as cooking and cleaning. In the 1960s and 1970s, women increasingly joined the workforce, and attitudes about domestic responsibilities began to change.

Another exception is the use of past tense to describe research processes or studies. Notice the verb tenses in the example that follows:

> The "Play to Learn Program" <u>was</u> a three-year study conducted by the Arcadian Research Group. The focus of the study <u>was</u> to figure out whether children could more easily master a foreign language by using play strategies instead of traditional learning strategies.

Avoid unnecessary shifts in tense. Generally, verbs should remain in the same tense throughout a passage. Notice how the shifts in tense in this example are unnecessary and even confusing. In the first sentence, the verbs are in the present tense (claims, change, processes), while the verbs in the second sentence are in both the past tense (wrote) and the present tense (act).

> **Faulty shift in tense:** Margaret Trent claims that social media change the way the brain processes information. She wrote that social media act as "catalysts of neural development."
>
> **Corrected:** Margaret Trent claims that social media change the way the brain processes information. She writes that social media act as "catalysts of neural development."

Sometimes shifts in tense are acceptable or even necessary, such as when a writer changes from a narrative to another type of writing. Consider the following example. It incorporates the initial sentence we quoted earlier as an example of present tense in academic writing.

> Anorexia nervosa is an eating disorder that is notoriously difficult to treat because patients often deny they have the disorder. Recall that Jennifer, one of the women contacted by researchers, claimed that she did not have anorexia, even though her BMI was only 17.

Notice that the writer uses present tense but switches, appropriately, to past tense to explain a historical event.

▶ **ACTIVITY 9 Choosing Appropriate Tenses**

Use the sentences that follow to create a paragraph. Select appropriate verb tenses.

- Benjamin Franklin is a scientist and a writer.
- He wrote *Poor Richard's Almanac*.
- He is known for his autobiography.
- Franklin signs the three most important documents of the revolutionary era: the Declaration of Independence, the peace treaty with Britain that ended the Revolutionary War, and the Constitution.
- He is the only person to sign all three.

21 AVOIDING COMMON PUNCTUATION ERRORS

Of all the many punctuation errors, three of the most common are errors in using apostrophes, commas, and quotation marks. Use these guidelines to master the usage of these punctuation marks.

21.1 Commas

Commas are primarily used to separate or to join elements within a sentence. The following rules concern some of the more ordinary uses of commas.

Using Commas after Introductory Elements. A comma should follow several types of words, phrases, and clauses that are used to begin a sentence.

Use	Example
After a prepositional phrase of three or more words	After the St. Patrick's Day parade, we had lunch at a pub.
After an introductory verbal phrase	Talking rapidly, the agent described every detail about the house.
After some single words to clarify meaning or insert a useful phrase	Yes, I did think her apology was sincere.
After a dependent clause that begins a sentence	Although my family was out of town, I still enjoyed the holidays.

Note that when a dependent clause is placed at the end of a sentence, no comma is needed.

> Children need time to relax when they get home from school.
>
> No one realized how much of a pest he had been until he left.

Using Commas with Conjunctions. If two sentences are joined together with a FANBOYS conjunction (for, and, nor, but, or, yet, so), a comma is needed before the conjunction.

> The parrot chattered incessantly, for it hoped someone would give it a cracker.
>
> Meteorology is not the same subject as climatology, but they are related.

Using Commas in a Series. Use commas to separate elements in a series.

> The cake is moist, sweet, and delicious.
>
> The mayor ran for reelection, won the race, and continued his political career.

Note that omitting the comma before the word *and* or *or* in a series is grammatically acceptable in journalism and other types of writing. However, because leaving out the comma can sometimes cause confusion, many writers include it. In academic writing, a comma is always used before *and* or *or*.

Using Commas between Adjectives. Sometimes a noun is preceded by two adjectives that modify the noun separately. A comma between such dual adjectives is required.

> The grand, glorious staircase makes the home seem regal.
>
> Sweet, sticky cakes were served with the tea.
>
> She freely offered advice to the sincere, curious girl.

Using Commas with Nonessential Elements. Sometimes we add information to sentences that is not essential. When information is not essential to the meaning of the sentence, use commas around the nonessential information.

> Skydivers, who risk their lives because of their hobby, have a hard time getting life insurance.
>
> The marriage license, although tattered and torn, was still intact.
>
> The state of Alaska, which is known for its extreme weather, enacted a new law.

In all three examples, the information surrounded by commas can be left out of the sentences, and the meaning of the sentences will still be clear.

If the information is essential to the meaning of the sentence, do not use commas.

> Helicopter pilots in the Coast Guard are highly trained.
>
> *(This information identifies the particular pilots who are highly trained, so the information is essential and setting the phrase off with commas would be incorrect.)*
>
> The marriage license of Jimmy and JoAnn Walton was still intact.
>
> *(This information tells which marriage license, so it is essential information and setting the phrase off with commas would be incorrect.)*
>
> The city that lies to the south of Wichita was undamaged by the tornado.
>
> *(Since the sentence's purpose is to communicate that a particular city was undamaged, the highlighted information is essential and setting it off with commas would be incorrect.)*

Other Uses of Commas. Some commas are required simply as technical punctuation details based on rules developed by printers, who desire consistency in producing published works.

Function	Example
To separate elements in addresses	811 Martin Drive, Richmond, VA
To separate the day of the month from the year and year from whatever follows (when needed)	Wynn was born on May 16, 1887, and he died on May 17, 1989.
To separate the day of the week from the month	I arrived on Tuesday, April 18.
To introduce a quotation	In the words of Enrique Marquez, "An epidemic is a disease gone rogue."
To separate a person's name from a title that follows it	Soo Kim, mayor of Yuma, is the host for the week.

Several situations involving comma usage require special attention, as the chart below illustrates.

Typical Usage	Trouble Spot
To separate the day of the month from the year	Do *not* use a comma to separate the month from the year.
Example: Wynn was born on May 15, 1887.	Example: He died in May 1989.
To set off dialogue	Do *not* use a comma when dialogue is described but not quoted directly.
Example: Jayne said, "I wish I knew how to skate."	Example: Jayne said that she wished she knew how to skate.
To introduce a quote from a written source	Do *not* use a comma when the word *that* is used to transition into a quotation.
Example: The CDC report stated, "No significant outbreak of the virus has occurred."	Example: The CDC report stated that no significant outbreak of the virus had occurred.

▶ **ACTIVITY 10** **Using Commas Correctly**

Add commas where necessary to the paragraph that follows:

> I needed to take three science courses in college so I chose to take anatomy physiology and microbiology. The intriguing stimulating courses provided me with information I use to this day. I learned about the bones in the human body the major body systems and the principal types of diseases. My professor a retired cardiologist had years of surgical experience from which to draw wonderful stories so he made the classes very entertaining. His classes convinced me that I would love to become a certified nursing assistant a licensed vocational nurse or a registered nurse and so I am very glad that I took those courses.

21.2 Apostrophes

Apostrophes are used for two principal reasons: to create contractions and to show possession by a noun.

Apostrophe Use in Contractions. A contraction is a word formed by the merging of two other words. When the words are merged, one or more letters are dropped. An apostrophe's role is to stand in for the dropped letters. The key to forming contractions correctly is to use the apostrophe in the very place that the omitted letters once stood. Generally speaking, contractions should be used sparingly in academic or formal writing.

Original Words	Letters Omitted	Contraction
do + not	*o* in *not*	don't
should + have	*ha*	should've
he + will	*wi*	he'll

Apostrophe Use to Show Possession. For a singular noun, simply add –'s to the noun in order to show possession. Names are treated in the same manner as other nouns.

Singular Noun	Possessive
the coach	the coach's cap
a truck	a truck's tires
a New York Yankee	a New York Yankee's hits
the scientist	the scientist's graph
a city	a city's schools

For a plural noun, follow these rules to show possession:

1. If the plural noun ends in –s, add only an apostrophe.
2. If the plural noun does not end in –s, add –'s.

Plural Noun	Possessive
the coaches	the coaches' caps
the trucks	the trucks' tires
New York Yankees	the New York Yankees' hits
scientists	the scientists' graphs
ten cities	ten cities' schools
children (no -s)	children's toys
women (no -s)	women's vote

▶ **ACTIVITY 11** **Using Apostrophes**

Add apostrophes where needed in the following paragraph:

> Decia had made very good grades in high school, so she was quite surprised when her first semesters grades in college were so poor. Decias surprise turned to disappointment. She began to doubt whether college was for her. Her mothers advice was to work with a tutor the next semester. Both parents counseled Decia not to give

up. Her parents ideas also included advising Decia to give up her part-time job, to spend more time studying, and to practice patience. Decia wondered what patience had to do with success. Her parents pointed out that many students want instant gratification. They dont like waiting for success. College successes, however, require students ways of thinking to change. Students must spend time (and have patience) to learn how to learn in college. Once Decia accepted the fact that she wasnt a failure and that she just had to work harder and stick with her college plan, her grades began to improve. Decias last three semesters grades mostly been very good, with only one C. Decia is determined to finish her degree.

2J USING APPROPRIATE CAPITALIZATION

Capital letters help readers more clearly understand a text in many ways. In this section, we look at several of the most important functions of capital letters.

2J.1 Using Capital Letters to Begin Sentences

Always start a sentence with a capital letter. Doing so helps readers clearly see where a new sentence begins.

> An old key dangled from the rusty lock. Jill wondered if the key worked.

2J.2 Using Capital Letters for Proper Nouns

A common noun is a word for a person, place, thing, or idea. A proper noun is the name of a specific person, place, thing, or idea.

Common Noun	Proper Noun
a high school	Roosevelt High School
a city	New Orleans

You can determine whether a noun is common or proper with this test:

- Ask yourself, "Did someone give this noun a specific name?"
- If the answer is yes, the noun is more likely a proper noun than a common noun.

Noun	Test	Conclusion
Public library	*Did someone give this noun a specific name?* No.	This is not a proper noun. It is a common noun and should not be capitalized.
Facebook	*Did someone give this noun a specific name?* Yes. It is the name of a specific social media site.	This is a proper noun. It should be capitalized.

Table A2.4 presents examples of common and proper nouns. Review each noun in the chart so that you are familiar with the types of nouns to capitalize.

TABLE A2.4 Common and Proper Nouns

Category	Common Noun	Proper Noun
Names	daughter	Sarah
	senator	Senator Mary Hampton
Nicknames		John "Chops" Harris
Places	city	Philadelphia
	state	Florida
	country	Turkey
Specific sites or places	mountain	Mount Rushmore
	river	Ohio River
	beach	Stinson Beach
	planet	Venus
Buildings, institutions, companies	courthouse	Clemson County Courthouse
	college	Jackson Community College
	school	Trinity Middle School
	insurance company	Plimpton Insurance Group
Events, days, months	war	the Civil War
	holiday	the Fourth of July
	day	Sunday
	month	March
Brand names	games	Monopoly, Minecraft
	soda	Coke, Pepsi
	jeans	Levi's
Races and nationalities		Asian
		African American
		French
Languages		English
		Spanish
		American Sign Language
Governmental institutions, agencies, programs, laws	agency	the Food and Drug Administration
	health-care law	the Affordable Care Act

A Few Tricky Proper Nouns. Some common nouns become proper nouns depending on their uses. Use these guidelines for such nouns.

Common Noun	Proper Noun
earth *Mixing earth with peat moss results in rich soil for plants.*	Capitalize *Earth* when talking about it as a planet. *Compared with Mars, Earth is a much cooler planet.*
mother (and other family names) *Would your mother like a ride on the motorcycle?*	Capitalize a family name when you are using it as the person's actual name. *I think Mother would like a ride on the motorcycle.*
bible *Jim is so knowledgeable about bikes that he could write the bible of bike ownership.*	Capitalize *Bible* and any words that refer to specific books of sacred writings such as *Torah, Book of Mormon, Quran,* and *Bhagavad Gita.* *The Hebrew Bible and the Christian Scriptures are best-sellers at many bookstores.* Note: Do not capitalize the adjective form, *biblical*.

Using a Capital Letter for the Pronoun *I*. Although it is acceptable to use a lowercase *i* when texting, do not do so when you are writing for college or work. When using I as a pronoun, always capitalize it.

▶ **ACTIVITY 12 Using Correct Capitalization**

Capitalize any letters that should be capitalized in the sentences that follow.

  A. When i was in middle school, we did not have smart phones.
  B. My first phone was a motorola flip phone.
  C. When I turned thirteen, in june of 2003, i got my first phone.

2K MASTERING COMMONLY CONFUSED WORDS

Sometimes writing mistakes occur because a writer confuses one word for another. Become familiar with the words you often confuse, and take the time to learn how to use them properly. The list that follows presents some of the more commonly confused words.

accept/except

accept = (verb) to receive; to take in

except = (preposition) other than

advice/advise

advice = (noun) a recommendation as a guide to action; words of counsel

advise = (verb) to give advice; to counsel; to offer a suggestion

affect/effect

affect = (verb) to influence or change

effect = (noun) result

allot/a lot

allot = (verb) to provide

a lot = (noun) a group of items; many

Note: Alot is an incorrect spelling of *a lot* and is not a word.

ready/already

all ready = (adverbial phrase) entirely prepared; set to proceed

already = (adverb) has occurred previously

bare/bear

bare = (verb) to reveal

(adjective) to be in a revealed state

bear = (verb) to support or carry (both literally and figuratively)

(noun) a very large mammal with stocky legs, a long snout, and shaggy fur

brake/break

brake = (noun) the part of a vehicle that causes slowing and stopping

(verb) to slow or stop something, such as a vehicle

break = (noun) a recess period; a fracture (as in a bone)

(verb) to split into pieces; to interrupt; to take a recess

breath/breathe

breath = (noun) a single inhalation and exhalation of air

breathe = (verb) to inhale and exhale air

cite/sight/site

cite = (verb) to make reference to; to create a citation

sight = (noun) the faculty of vision; something seen

(verb) to see something; to adjust the aiming apparatus (as of a gun)

site = (noun) a location; a piece of land

clothes/cloths

clothes = (plural noun) attire, apparel, garments

cloths = (noun, plural of cloth) pieces of fabric, such as those used for cleaning

coarse/course

coarse = (adjective) rough; vulgar; unsophisticated (as in coarse humor)

course = (noun) route; sequence; an academic class

(verb) to run through (as in blood coursing through a person's veins)

complement/compliment

complement = (noun) something that completes or makes perfect

(verb) to provide an addition that fits well or is appropriate

compliment = (noun) an expression of approval, esteem, or acknowledgment

(verb) to offer praise, admiration, or respect

conscience/conscious

conscience = (noun) a person's intuitive sense of right and wrong

conscious = (adjective) awake; intentional

desert/dessert

desert = (noun) a dry, arid area, typically with a very warm climate

dessert = (noun) a sweet treat, usually the last course in a meal

forth/fourth

forth = (adverb) onward; forward

fourth = (adjective) something that is number

hear/here

hear = (verb) to perceive sound

here = (adverb) in or at this place

hole/whole

hole = (noun) gap; opening

whole = (adjective) entire; complete

its/it's

its = (adjective) possessive form of it

it's = (contraction) it is

lead/led

The usage of these words is especially complicated, so we will lay out the variations in a chart.

Word	Part of Speech	Rhymes with	Definition
lead	verb, present tense	bead, deed, feed	to guide, especially by going in advance
lead	noun	head, dead, red	a type of metal; a pencil's marking substance
led	verb, past tense	head, dead, red	past tense of the verb lead

loose/lose

loose = (adjective) not tight

lose = (verb) to not retain; to fail to win

passed/past

passed = (verb, past tense) proceeded; happened; exceeded

past = (adjective) a time ago

(noun) a time before the present

peace/piece

peace = (noun) tranquility; a sense of calm

piece = (noun) a part of something

quiet/quit/quite

quiet = (adjective) noiseless

quit = (verb) to stop

quite = (adverb) completely; wholly

sale/sell

sale = (noun) an event where items are offered for purchase

sell = (verb) to offer for purchase

set/sit

set = (verb) to place something down; to fix or arrange something

sit = (verb) to rest the body on the buttocks

their/there/they're

their = (adjectival pronoun) possessive form of they

there = (adverb) in or at that place (as opposed to here)

they're = (contraction) they are

threw/through

threw = (verb) past tense of throw

through = (preposition) in one side and out the other side of something

to/too/two

to = (preposition) indicates movement toward something

too = (adverb) also; in addition to

two = (noun, adjective) the number 2

weather/whether

weather = (noun) the condition of the atmosphere during some period of time

(verb) to endure (as in to weather a storm)

whether = (conjunction) function word that introduces two alternatives

we're/were

we're = (contraction) we are

were = (verb) a past tense form of the verb to be

who's/whose

who's = (contraction) who is

whose = (adjective) indicates possession (Whose can also be used as an interrogative, a word used to ask a question, in the same manner as who, what, and why.)

your/you're

your = (adjective) indicates possession

you're = (contraction) you are

▶ **ACTIVITY 13 Using Commonly Confused Words**

Select three words that you commonly confuse. Write a sentence demonstrating you can use the word appropriately.

Glossary

A

ad hominem A fallacy in which a speaker or writer is attacked personally rather than his or her argument. The Latin means "to the person."

appeal An attempt to gain support for a claim by using logic, emotions, or credibility.

appeal to ethos A rhetorical strategy that uses the writer's authority, good character, and good intentions or the authority of others to attempt to persuade.

appeal to logos A rhetorical strategy that uses logical reasoning to attempt to persuade.

appeal to pathos A rhetorical strategy that taps into readers' emotions to attempt to persuade.

argument A claim supported by reasons.

argument to ignorance A fallacy in which a claim is made on the basis that there is no evidence to prove the claim untrue.

B

backing Support for a warrant in an argument.

bandwagon A fallacy in which a claim is supported by the idea that "everyone does it" rather than by sound reasons or evidence.

begging the question A fallacy wherein an unproven or questionable premise is used as support for a claim. Also called circular reasoning.

bias In argument, a point of view or opinion.

Boolean operators Words that limit or expand the scope of a keyword search: primarily AND, OR, and NOT.

C

cause and effect A rhetorical pattern in which the factors that contributed to an event or resulted from an event are presented.

cherry picking A fallacy in which only the evidence that supports a claim is considered; other evidence is ignored.

claim The thesis statement of a persuasively oriented text; a statement of the writer's opinion or assertion of an arguable point.

classical argument A form of persuasive argument with a five-part structure that originated with the ancient Greeks.

classification A rhetorical pattern in which things are separated into types, classes, or kinds according to their characteristics.

comparison and contrast A rhetorical pattern in which the similarities (comparing) and differences (contrasting) of two or more things are discussed.

complex sentence A dependent clause and an independent clause joined correctly to form a sentence.

compound sentence Two or more independent clauses joined correctly to form a sentence.

compound-complex sentence Two or more independent clauses plus one or more dependent clauses joined correctly to form a sentence.

concession An acknowledgment that part of an opposing argument is correct; it is part of a rebuttal.

confirmation In classical argument, the presentation of the claim and its support.

coordinating conjunction A word that joins two elements; for example, *and, but,* and *or.*

correlation error A fallacy in which it is claimed that two events are related causally, but in fact the two events are simply correlated or take place at the same time.

counterargument An argument that opposes the writer's claim or one of the writer's reasons.

D

definition A rhetorical pattern in which the meaning of a word or phrase is discussed.

dependent clause A clause (a group of words with a subject and verb) that cannot stand alone.

description A rhetorical pattern in which language is used to help readers understand the physical attributes of something or to understand what something is like.

E

editing Correcting errors in grammar and mechanics.

either/or fallacy A fallacy in which two options are presented as the only options when there are others; also called the *false dilemma.*

ethos See *appeal to ethos.*

F

fallacy An error in reasoning.
false authority A fallacy in which someone is represented as an authority on an issue when in fact he or she is not qualified to be an authority.
false dilemma See *either/or fallacy*.
field research Data collection through first-hand observation, surveys, interviews, and so on.
fragment A set of words that looks like a sentence but is actually not a complete sentence.

G

genre A type or form of writing, for example, an email, a short story, or a research paper.
grounds Support for a reason in an argument.
guilt by association A fallacy in which a person is discredited because of his or her affiliations with others rather than on the merits of his or her argument.

H

hasty generalization A fallacy in which a conclusion is drawn on insufficient evidence.

I

illustration A rhetorical pattern in which an example or a graphic helps readers understand a concept.
independent clause A group of words that can stand alone, forming a complete sentence.
inference A conclusion based on evidence.

L

loaded language Words with powerful negative or positive connotations.
logos See *appeal to logos*.

M

mechanics Rules about written language, including capitalization, punctuation, use of numerals, and spelling.

N

narration A rhetorical pattern that tells a story, whether fiction or nonfiction; in classical argument, a presentation of the background or back story that provides information necessary for the audience to understand the claim and its support.
non sequitur A fallacy in which a conclusion is drawn that does not follow from the evidence. The Latin means "it does not follow."

P

pathos See *appeal to pathos*.
peer review A process for receiving suggestions for revision by exchanging papers with classmates or others and answering a set of specific review questions.
plagiarism Using another person's ideas, words, or works without giving proper credit.
post hoc, ergo propter hoc A fallacy in which it is argued that X caused Y because X occurred before Y without a proof of a causal connection. The Latin means "after this, therefore because of this."
predicate The part of a sentence containing the main verb that tells what the subject is or does.
primary source A source consisting of first-hand information or direct evidence; for example, a work of art, the text of a law, or an eyewitness report.
process analysis A rhetorical pattern in which the stages, phases, or steps that are used to accomplish a purpose are identified.

Q

qualifier A word or phrase that limits a claim.

R

reading rhetorically A type of reading that reveals the *how* (the strategies) of a text and not merely the *what* (the message).
reason A main point that helps make a claim true or believable.
rebuttal A response to a counterargument that refutes it but may also concede to any part of it that is correct.
red herring A fallacy in which distraction or a change of subject is used to shift attention away from the issue at hand.
refutation A writer's attempt to show the flaws in the counterargument; it is part of a rebuttal.
revising Improving the content, organization, and language of a draft by adding, deleting, moving, and replacing copy.
rhetoric The use of tools and strategies to convey a message or persuade.
rhetorical analysis An examination of the strategies a writer uses to create an effective message.
rhetorical patterns Thinking patterns—description, narration, definition, illustration, classification, comparison and contrast, cause and effect, and process analysis—that are used as ways to support main ideas. Sometimes called *rhetorical modes*.
rhetorical situation A situation consisting of the writer or speaker, the message, and the audience.
Rogerian argument A form of argument that seeks to establish common ground rather than to persuade.
rubric A set of criteria used to evaluate an assignment.

S

sampling bias A fallacy in which data is collected on a nonrepresentative selection of subjects.

secondary source A source consisting of second-hand information about a topic or a primary source, for example, a journal article.

simple sentence A single independent clause.

slippery slope A fallacy in which it is predicted that something undesirable will happen as a result of an action (or inaction) yet there is not enough evidence to make the prediction. Can be used as a scare tactic or appeal to fear.

strawman A fallacy in which the argument of the opposition is falsely represented.

subject The main noun or pronoun in a sentence.

summary A shortened version of a text that presents basic source information, the writer's thesis, and the major lines of support for the thesis.

support Explanations, examples, or evidence that provide proof for a reason.

sweeping generalization A fallacy in which a statement is made about a group when the evidence applies to only some of its members.

T

thesis The main idea of a text. When stated directly in a sentence, it is called a *thesis statement*.

Toulmin analysis A system of analyzing the parts of an argument and how they work together; developed by British philosher Stephen Toulmin.

tu quoque A fallacy in which an opponent is criticized to divert attention from one's own actions. The Latin means "you too."

V

visual argument A form of argument that uses images or graphics to persuade.

W

warrant The assumption, belief, or value that ties a reason to the claim of an argument.

working bibliography A list of citations for sources one may use in a research project.

writer's mindset An awareness of the rhetorical means by which language can be used to communicate, influence, and persuade.

Index

A

Abrams, Reese, 159-170
Abstract vs. concrete language, 57, 649
Academic rhetoric, 7-8
Academic Search Complete (EBSCO), 231
Acceda Noticias database, 231
Accuracy
   appeal to ethos and, 352
   of cause and effect, 77
   of classifications, 71
   of inferences, 324-325, 625-627
   of outlines, 32
   of source representations, 251
   of summaries, 16
Ad hominem fallacy, 369, 376, 390, 451
Adjectives, comma use with, 661
Advertisements
   appeals in, 203, 351, 353-354
   cigarette, 306-308
   in newspapers, 238
   public service, 583-586
   on social media, 7
   during Super Bowl, 14
   as visual arguments, 406, 416, 417, 419
Agricola database, 231
AHFS Consumer Medication Information, 231
Alter, Rachel, 571-574
Alt HealthWatch, 231
American Fact Finder, 234
American Psychological Association (APA) style
   annotated bibliography in, 242
   formatting papers in, 296-303
   informative writing in, 136-140
   in-text citations in, 286-289
   references list in, 289-295, 301-303
   student writing samples, 296-303
America's News Magazines, 232
Analysis. *See also* Process analysis; Rhetorical analysis; Toulmin analysis
   of appeals, 356-361, 389
   of cause and effect, 76
   of claims, 204, 206, 388, 389
   of classification, 71
   of comparison and contrast, 73
   cost/benefit, 147, 162, 165-170
   of definition, 69
   descriptive, 62, 147
   in evaluative writing, 176
   of fallacies, 376-381, 390-391, 451
   of grading rubrics, 39
   of illustration, 66
   literary, 147
   method of, 144-146
   of narration, 64
   objective, 146, 162
   of persuasive writing, 10
   predictive, 147
   product, 147, 158-159
   of reasons, 204, 207, 388, 389
   of research, 429-432
   of rhetorical situation, 4-6, 10, 14, 25, 387-388
   of rhetorical strategies, 25-27
   of speaker's purpose, 312-313
   subjective, 146, 162
   of text from writer's mindset, 24, 28, 29
   types of, 146, 147
   of visual arguments, 418-419
   of writer's purpose, 24, 312-313
   of writing assignments, 36-39
Analytical reading, 15, 24-28, 30
Analytical writing, 143-171
   audience for, 144-146, 148, 153, 160
   creating analytical texts, 146
   drafting, 161-162
   editing and formatting, 165
   message in, 160
   model examples of, 148-157, 165-170
   organization of, 161, 162, 164
   outlines for, 160-161
   planning for, 159-161
   point of view in, 146, 162
   projects involving, 157-159
   purpose of, 144, 145, 147, 153
   recursive writing in, 162, 163

Analytical writing (*continued*)
  revising, 163–165
  rhetorical strategies in, 148, 153, 157, 170
  rhetorical thinking in, 147–148
  speaker in, 159
  terms and phrases for, 163
  thesis statements in, 160
  topics for, 157, 159
  types of, 143
  from writer's mindset, 144–147
AND, in search strategies, 232
Anecdotes, 63, 64
Animal welfare, anthology of readings on, 506–526
Annotated bibliographies, 241–243
Annotation
  of analytical writing, 149–152
  of arguments, 316–319
  of assignments, 38
  of descriptive words, 62
  of evaluative writing, 178–179
  of informative writing, 116–119
  of persuasive writing, 205–206
  in reading process, 606
  of reflective writing, 86–91
  for rhetorical analysis, 385–387
  of sources, 17, 249, 250
  of thesis statements, 17
  of topic sentences, 625
Antecedents for pronouns, 57, 655–657
Anthology of readings, 489–601
  animal welfare, 506–526
  crime and punishment, 546–571
  diversity, 526–546
  environmental issues, 489–506
  media and culture, 571–586
  personal growth, 586–601
APA style. *See* American Psychological Association style
Apostrophes, guidelines for use of, 663–665
Appeals, 349–364
  in advertisements, 203, 351, 353–354
  analysis of, 356–361, 389
  in classical arguments, 409
  in conclusions, 464
  defined, 349
  to ethos (*See* Ethos)
  in introductions, 461–462
  to logos (*See* Logos)
  misidentifying and overlooking, 362–364
  to pathos (*See* Pathos)
  reasons and, 355, 444
Argument-from-ignorance fallacy, 372, 377, 390, 451
Arguments. *See also* Persuasive writing
  analysis of (*See* Rhetorical analysis; Toulmin analysis)

  appeals and (*See* Appeals)
  claims and (*See* Claims)
  clarity of, 471, 474
  classical, 405–412
  counterarguments (*See* Counterarguments)
  critiquing, 307–308
  definitions of, 306, 308
  editing, 478
  fallacies in (*See* Fallacies)
  formatting, 479
  genre and, 313–315
  identification of, 308–315
  issue questions and, 426–427
  length issues and, 486–488
  model examples of, 316–320, 479–486
  one-sided, 454–455
  organization of, 470–471, 473
  outlines for, 440–441, 452
  projects involving, 424–425
  purpose of, 305, 313
  reasons and (*See* Reasons)
  research and sources for, 230, 428–432
  revising, 467–478
  rhetorical situation and, 311–315
  Rogerian, 406, 412–416
  speaker in, 306
  strategies for, 366–376
  topics for, 220–221, 425–427
  visual, 406, 416–422
Aristotle, 407
ArticleFirst database, 232
Articles. *See also* Journals; Magazines; Newspapers
  on references list, 290–291
  summaries of, 16, 22
  on works-cited page, 273–274
Artistic evaluations, 176
Attributions for quotations, 226–227
Attributive tags, 112, 251–252, 254–255, 450
Audience
  for analytical writing, 144–146, 148, 153, 160
  classification and, 71
  comparison and contrast and, 71
  counterarguments and, 454–455, 459
  critical, 476–478
  definition and, 69
  description and, 63
  evaluation of, 236, 240
  for evaluative writing, 177, 188
  general, 454, 455, 459, 469–475
  hostile, 454, 455, 459
  illustration and, 67
  for informative writing, 116, 119–120, 128
  narration and, 65

for persuasive writing, 204, 206–207, 212
process analysis and, 80
reasons based on, 434–436, 444
for reflective writing, 84–85, 96
for research, 230
in rhetorical situation, 4, 6, 25, 311, 387
sympathetic, 454, 455, 459
for writing assignments, 39
Authors, evaluation of, 235–236, 240

B

Background information
  in arguments, 306, 441
  in evaluative writing, 189, 190, 192
  in informative writing, 132
  in introductions, 141, 461
  in reflective writing, 91–92, 100
  source use for, 246, 248
Backing, 331–332, 336–337, 388, 436
Bandwagon fallacy, 373, 377, 390, 451
Baracos, Jose, 17, 19–24
Baran, Stanley, 17–28, 30–32
Begging the question fallacy, 371, 376, 390, 451
Bentley, Guy, 384–387
Betts, Reginald Dwayne, 546–553
Biases
  defined, 312
  sampling bias fallacy, 375, 377, 390, 451
  in sources, 235–240
  of writer/speaker, 311–312, 632
Bibliographies. *See also* Sources
  annotated, 241–243
  opposing viewpoints in, 439
  on websites, 238, 239, 264
  working, 223–224, 226
"Big Oil Touts Offshore Drilling Jobs to Communities Most Harmed by Oil" (Calma), 499–502
Black Lives Matter (BLM) movement, 157, 530, 532, 555, 560–561
"Black Walnut: A Sweet Blood History" (Hogan), 62, 540–546
Block arrangements, 74, 191, 198–199
Block (indented) quotations, 487
Blog posts, 3, 84–86, 95–96
Bookmarking sources, 224
Books
  bibliographic information for, 264–265
  on references list, 292
  on works-cited page, 274–275
Boolean operators, 232–233
"Breaking Down the Anti-Vaccine Echo Chamber" (Alter & Flattum-Riemers), 571–574
Brevity of summaries, 16

Brief definitions, 69
Broader context, in rhetorical situation, 5, 311
Bulleted lists, 24
Bureau of Justice Statistics, 234

C

Calma, Justine, 499–502
Capitalization guidelines, 665–667
Causal analysis, 147
Causal chains, 77
Cause and effect
  analysis of, 76
  appeal to logos and, 355
  claims of, 433, 435
  defined, 75
  key words and phrases for, 82
  in persuasive writing, 75
  purpose for using, 76
  as rhetorical pattern, 75–77, 82
  rhetorical thinking and, 77
  sample writing with, 75–76
  as writing tool, 77
"The CDC Botched Its Vaping Investigation and Helped Spark a National Panic" (Bentley), 384–387
CDC Wonder database, 234
Census Bureau, U.S., 234
Charts
  as arguments, 418, 421, 422
  for sources, 249–250, 259
  Viewpoints Charts, 430–432
Checklists for writing assignments, 49, 53
Cherry picking fallacy, 375–377, 390, 425, 429, 451
Chestek, Ken, 350
Chicago Manual of Style, 262
Chunking, 611–612
Citation generators, 271, 303–304
Citations. *See* In-text citations
City-Data database, 234
Claims. *See also* Arguments; Reasons
  analysis of, 204, 206, 388, 389
  clarity of, 471, 474
  in classical arguments, 408
  defined, 201, 308, 309
  drafting, 212, 432–434
  examples of, 308–309, 328
  explicit, 309
  exploring merits of, 313
  facts vs., 309
  identification of, 310–311, 315
  implicit, 309
  inference of unstated claims, 325
  in outlines, 213
  personal preferences vs., 309

Claims. (*continued*)
    qualifiers for, 329, 336, 337, 388, 432-433
    revising, 469, 473
    in Toulmin model, 328-329, 335-337, 388
    types of, 433
    on Viewpoints Charts, 430
Clarity
    in analytical writing, 162, 164
    of arguments, 471, 474
    of expression, 471-472, 474
    illustration for, 67
    in informative writing, 130, 132
    in persuasive writing, 214, 215
    in reflective writing, 98
    revising for, 471-472, 474
    of sentences, 45, 57-58, 164, 215, 471-472, 649-650
Classical arguments, 405-412
    conclusion in, 410-411
    confirmation in, 409
    defined, 405
    history of, 406-407
    introduction in, 407-408
    model example of, 411-412
    narration in, 408-409
    purpose of, 405-406
    refutation in, 409-411
Classification
    analysis of, 71
    appeal to logos and, 355
    defined, 69
    key words and phrases for, 82
    purpose for using, 70
    as rhetorical pattern, 69-72, 82
    rhetorical thinking and, 71
    sample writing with, 70-71
    as writing tool, 71-72
Clauses
    dependent, 641-642, 645-646, 648, 660
    independent, 638-643, 647
Clichés, 650
Cloud-based file systems, 225
Coding systems, 606
Cohesion, 43
Collins, Laura, 535-540
Commas, guidelines for use of, 660-663
Comma splices, 647-649
Comment feature, for annotating, 606
Common knowledge, 247, 248, 259-260, 627-629
Commonly confused words, 667-671
Common nouns, 665-667
Communication
    elements of, 4

    email, 8, 630
    importance of, 1-2
    interpersonal, 9
    rhetorical patterns in, 59
Communication Matters (Floyd), 67-68
Comparative analysis, 147
Comparative evaluations, 187, 198-199
Comparison and contrast
    analysis of, 73
    classification and, 71
    criteria for, 74
    defined, 72
    key words and phrases for, 82
    purpose for using, 73
    as rhetorical pattern, 71-75, 82
    rhetorical thinking and, 73
    sample writing with, 72
    as writing tool, 74-75
Complex sentences, 641-642
Compound-complex sentences, 642
Compound predicates, 637
Compound sentences, 638-640
Compound subjects, 635
Concessions
    avoiding confusion in, 336, 465-466
    defined, 202, 332-333, 454, 455
    identification of, 334
    refutations and, 410, 457-458
    in Rogerian arguments, 413, 414
Conclusions
    in analytical writing, 162-164
    appeals in, 464
    in classical arguments, 410-411
    drafting, 463-465
    in evaluative writing, 192
    evidence for, 162
    in informative writing, 132
    model example of, 464-465
    in persuasive writing, 215
    in previewing texts, 604
    in reflective writing, 102
    revising, 45-46, 488
    in rhetorical analysis, 392
    strategies for writing, 141-142
Concrete language
    abstract language vs., 57, 649
    in descriptive writing, 62
    in reflective writing, 91, 92, 98
Confirmation, in classical arguments, 409
Conjunctions, 638-639, 647, 648, 651, 660
Context
    historical context of sources, 236
    narration and, 65, 408

for quotations, 470
in rhetorical situation, 5, 311
Context clues, 610–611
Contractions, apostrophe use in, 663–664
Contrast. *See* Comparison and contrast
Coordinating conjunctions, 638–639, 647, 648, 651, 660
Coronavirus. *See* COVID-19 pandemic
Correlation errors, 368
Cost/benefit analysis, 147, 162, 165–170
Counterarguments. *See also* Rebuttals
  analysis of, 204, 207, 388
  defined, 202, 453
  fallacies in, 457
  identification of, 334, 453
  methods for addressing, 454–455, 459
  in outlines, 213
  revising, 476
  source types for, 230
  in Toulmin model, 332–334, 337, 388
COVID-19 pandemic (2020)
  as arguable issue, 220
  basic facts regarding, 309
  in broader context, 5
  informative essay on, 141, 142
  practice exercises involving, 83
  researched argument involving, 424, 426, 429, 435–436
  rhetorical analysis project on, 399–401
  in writing samples, 455, 460, 462, 464, 477–484, 519
Cover letters, 16
Credibility
  ethos and, 203, 215, 350
  of sources, 230, 233, 235–241, 443
  of websites, 238–241
  of writer, 246, 442
Crime and punishment, anthology of readings on, 546–571
Critical annotated bibliographies, 241–242
Critical audiences, 476–478
Critical reading, 15, 28, 30, 44
"The Cruelty of Kindness" (Heinlein), 512–522

D

Databases. *See also specific databases*
  advantages of using multiple databases, 438
  library, 223, 231–233, 263, 428
  online, 223–225, 231–234, 263, 428
Data.gov database, 234
Date of sources, 236, 240
DeCicca, Lauren, 505–506
Décor, messages conveyed through, 10
Definition
  analysis of, 69
  appeal to logos and, 355
  claims of, 433, 435
  classification and, 71
  defined, 67
  extended vs. brief, 69
  key words and phrases for, 82
  purpose for using, 68
  as rhetorical pattern, 67–69, 71, 82
  rhetorical thinking and, 69
  sample writing with, 67–68
  of unfamiliar words, 606–611
  as writing tool, 69
Deleting sources, 226
Delgado, Tierra, 187–198
Democracies, public rhetoric in, 7
Dependent clauses, 641–642, 645–646, 648, 660
Description
  analysis of, 62, 147
  defined, 61
  key words and phrases for, 81
  purpose for using, 61, 63
  in reflective writing, 62, 91–92, 98, 100
  as rhetorical pattern, 61–63, 81
  rhetorical thinking and, 62
  sample writing with, 62
  as writing tool, 62, 63
Descriptive annotated bibliographies, 241
Details
  analytical, 147
  descriptive, 63
  emotional response to, 354
  inferences and, 625–629
  in outlines, 32
  for paragraph support, 652
  purpose of, 63
  in reflective writing, 85, 91–92
  sensory, 63
  in summaries, 17
  in visual arguments, 419, 420
Dialogue
  quotations for, 111–112
  in reflective writing, 98, 100, 101
  in Rogerian arguments, 413
  rules for writing, 112
Dictionaries, 606–607
Digest of Education Statistics, 234
Digital object identifiers (DOIs), 273, 290–291
Direct quotations, 112, 247, 252–256, 445–446, 449–450
Diversity, anthology of readings on, 526–546
"The Dog Delusion" (Pedersen), 72, 506–512
Downloading sources, 225
Drafting
  analytical writing, 161–162

Drafting (*continued*)
  claims, 212, 432-434
  conclusions, 463-465
  content for reasons, 445-446, 448-450
  evaluative writing, 190-191
  informative writing, 130-131
  introductions, 461-463
  persuasive writing, 214
  reflective writing, 100
  rhetorical analysis, 393-394
  thesis statements, 41-42
  in writing process, 43, 55

E

"Easter Rock 1983" (González), 86-92
EasyBib citation generator, 304
EBSCO (Academic Search Complete), 231
Editing
  analytical writing, 165
  arguments, 478
  evaluative writing, 194
  informative writing, 136
  persuasive writing, 217
  reflective writing, 104
  in writing process, 49, 56
Effect. *See* Cause and effect
Effectiveness evaluations, 176
Ehrenberg, Rachel, 120-125
Either/or fallacy, 366, 370, 376, 381, 390, 451
Ellipsis, 255-256
Email communication, 8, 630
Emotional appeals. *See* Pathos
Emotional connotation of words, 24
Environment, messages conveyed through, 10
Environmental issues, anthology of readings on, 489-506
Epstein, Alex, 321-324
"Equal When Separate" (Owens), 360-361
"Erotica and Pornography" (Steinem), 574-579
Errors
  in analytical writing, 165
  in evaluative writing, 194
  identification of, 49
  in informative writing, 136
  in persuasive writing, 217
  in punctuation, 660-665
  in reflective writing, 104
  in source analysis, 429
Essays
  argument, 202, 310
  comparative, 60
  evaluative, 28, 174
  informative, 114, 141, 142

  narrative, 63, 84
  persuasive, 236
  reflective, 62, 85, 86
  research-based, 246
  rhetorical analysis, 384, 391, 392
  thesis statements in, 619-625
Ethos
  analysis of, 207, 215, 389
  in classical arguments, 407, 408
  credibility and, 203, 215, 350
  defined, 203, 351
  demonstration of, 352-353
  identifying appeals to, 353
  introductions and, 461
  overview, 203, 350
  purpose of appeals to, 362-363
  reasons and, 444
"Evaluating Information: The Cornerstone of Civic Online Reasoning" (Stanford History Education Group), 180-186
Evaluation
  artistic, 176
  of audience, 236, 240
  of authors, 235-236, 240
  comparative, 187, 198-199
  of effectiveness, 176
  external, 235, 237
  internal, 235
  literary, 176, 178-180
  predictive, 176
  of process, 176
  of products, 176
  of reasons, 436-437
  rhetorical, 176
  of sources, 176, 177, 187, 235-241
  of websites, 177, 187, 235, 237-241
  of writer's purpose, 240
Evaluative writing, 174-199
  analysis section of, 176
  audience for, 177, 188
  criteria in, 176-177, 180, 188-190
  drafting, 190-191
  editing and formatting, 194
  judgment section of, 176, 189, 192
  message in, 188
  model examples of, 178-186, 194-198
  organization of, 189, 191, 198-199
  outlines for, 189-190
  planning for, 175-176, 188-190
  projects involving, 186-187
  purpose of, 174, 176, 177, 180
  recursive writing in, 191
  revising, 191-194

rhetorical situation in, 175
rhetorical strategies in, 180, 186, 198
rhetorical thinking in, 175, 177
speaker in, 188
terms and phrases for, 191
thesis statements in, 188
topics for, 186-188
types of, 176
from writer's mindset, 175-177
Evidence
amount and type of, 449
for conclusions, 162
criteria for, 442-443
introduction of, 448, 449-450
situations requiring use of, 248
to support reasons, 441-444
Examples
in informative writing, 130
in persuasive writing, 201-202
as rhetorical tools, 65, 69
Executive summaries, 16, 180-186
Experts, 246-248, 428, 442, 443
Explicit claims, 309
Expression, clarity of, 471-472, 474
Extended definitions, 69
External evaluations, 235, 237
Extra-information fragments, 646
Extroverts, 53

F

Fact, claims of, 433, 435
Factual information databases, 233, 234
Fairness
appeal to ethos and, 352
of comparison and contrast, 73
of source representations, 251
Fallacies, 365-381
ad hominem, 369, 376, 390, 451
analysis of, 376-381, 390-391, 451
argument-from-ignorance, 372, 377, 390, 451
avoidance of, 450
bandwagon, 373, 377, 390, 451
begging the question, 371, 376, 390, 451
cherry picking, 375-377, 390, 425, 429, 451
common errors in analysis of, 380-381
confusion among, 381
correlation errors, 368
in counterarguments, 457
defined, 365
either/or, 366, 370, 376, 381, 390, 451
false authority, 368-369, 376, 390, 451
guilt-by-association, 369, 376, 390, 451
hasty generalization, 371, 377, 381, 390, 451

identification of, 369-370, 372, 375, 376, 451
loaded language, 370-371, 376, 390, 451
manipulative-appeal-to-emotion, 374, 377, 390, 451
non sequitur, 373, 377, 390, 451
post hoc, ergo propter hoc, 367-368, 376, 381, 390, 451
red herring, 372-373, 377, 390, 451
sampling bias, 375, 377, 390, 451
slippery slope, 366-367, 376, 381, 390, 451
strawman, 370
sweeping generalization, 371-372, 377, 381, 390, 451
tu quoque, 373, 377, 390, 451
weak analogy, 374
False authority fallacy, 368-369, 376, 390, 451
False dilemmas. *See* Either/or fallacy
Field research, 229, 230
Figurative language, 354
Filters, in database searches, 233
Final drafts, 50-53
"Finding a Treatment for Anorexia" (Manning), 279-285, 296-303
"Find Your Fight" (advertisement), 590-591
First person point of view, 24, 171-172, 312
First person pronouns, 171, 312
Fisher, Sarit, 340-343
Flattum-Riemers, Tonay, 571-574
Flowcharts, 80
Floyd, Kory, 68
Focus of summaries, 16
Folstein, Maddy, 178-180
"A Food Pantry Worth Admiring" (Delgado), 194-198
Formatting
analytical writing, 165
in APA style, 296-303
arguments, 479
evaluative writing, 194
informative writing, 136
in MLA style, 278-285
persuasive writing, 217
quotations, 253-254
reflective writing, 104
of words in texts, 604
in writing process, 50, 56
"The Fracking of Rachel Carson: Silent Spring's Lost Legacy, Told in Fifty Parts" (Steingraber), 489-499
Fragments, 643-647
correcting, 646-647
defined, 643
dependent clause, 645-646
extra information, 646
missing subject or verb, 643-644
phrases, 644-645
Fused (run-on) sentences, 647-649
Future tense, 657

G

Gallup Poll database, 234
Gardner, Kari, 613-615
General audiences, 454, 455, 459, 469-475
Genre
    arguments and, 313-315
    defined, 6
    in reflective writing, 84
    in rhetorical situation, 6, 311
    of writing assignments, 39
GoFundMe campaigns, 60-61, 81, 187
González, Rigoberto, 86-92
Grading rubrics, 39-40, 43
Grammar checkers, 49, 104, 165, 194, 217
Graphs, as arguments, 418, 422
"Greater good" concept, 456
Greene, Mark, 316-320
Greenstone, Michael, 148-153
Griffin, Em, 628
Grounds, 329, 336-337, 388, 436, 456
Guidance rubrics, 39-40, 43, 427-428, 467-469
Guilt-by-association fallacy, 369, 376, 390, 451

H

Ham, Andrew, 532-535
Hannah-Jones, Nikole, 553-561
Hasty generalization fallacy, 371, 377, 381, 390, 451
Headers, 50
Headings, 50, 604
Heinlein, Sabine, 512-522
Hillegonds, Timothy J., 594-601
Historical context of sources, 236
Hogan, Linda, 62, 540-546
Hostile audiences, 454, 455, 459
"'Hostiles' Tries to Revise History and Western Film Traditions" (Folstein), 178-180
"How Delaying Gratification Predicts Future Success" (Gardner), 613-615
"How Football Can Wreck a University" (Zaretsky), 343-346
"How I Overcame My Stuttering" (Huang), 64, 586-589
"How Zoos Help Preserve the World's Species for the Future" (Sanchez), 523-525
Huang, Justin, 64, 586-589

I

"I Am an Asian-American Who Benefits from Affirmative Action" (Ham), 532-535
Illustration
    analysis of, 66
    defined, 65
    key words and phrases for, 82
    process analysis and, 80
    purpose for using, 66
    as rhetorical pattern, 65-67, 82
    rhetorical thinking and, 67
    sample writing with, 65
    as writing tool, 67
Immediate situation, in rhetorical situation, 5, 311
Implicit claims, 309
Implied main ideas, 618-619, 625
Indentations, 50
Indented (block) quotations, 487
Independent clauses, 638-643, 647
Indirect quotations, 111-112, 247, 256, 270-271, 289
Inferences, 625-632
    accuracy of, 324-325, 625-627
    common knowledge and, 627-629
    defined, 625
    details and, 625-629
    tone of, 629-632
    unsupported, 629
Infographics, 79, 80, 418, 420, 422
Informal research, 12-13
Informative writing, 114-140
    audience for, 116, 119-120, 128
    drafting, 130-131
    editing and formatting, 136
    message in, 116, 120, 128
    model examples of, 116-125, 136-140
    organization of, 132
    outlines for, 128-130
    planning for, 128-130
    projects involving, 126-127
    purpose of, 115
    recursive writing in, 131-132
    revising, 132-135
    rhetorical strategies in, 115-116, 119-120, 125, 140
    rhetorical thinking in, 115-116, 130-131
    speaker in, 128
    terms and phrases for, 131
    thesis statements in, 128
    topics for, 126-127
    types of, 114
    from writer's mindset, 115
Internal evaluations, 235
Internet. *See* Websites
Interpersonal communication, 9
"Interpreting Intentional Imprecision" (Baran), 17-28, 30-32
In-text citations. *See also* Sources
    APA style for, 286-289
    formatting, 50
    MLA style for, 267-271
    multiple works by same author, 269-270, 288

one author, 268, 287
for quotations, 226-227, 270-271, 289
three or more authors, 269, 288
two authors, 268-269, 287
without author, 270, 289
Introductions
in analytical writing, 164
appeals in, 461-462
background information in, 141, 461
in classical arguments, 407-408
drafting, 461-463
in evaluative writing, 192
of evidence, 448, 449-450
in informative writing, 132
model example of, 462-463
in persuasive writing, 213, 215
points of view in, 461
in previewing texts, 604
in reflective writing, 102
revising, 45-47, 488
in rhetorical analysis, 320-321, 392
strategies for writing, 141
Introductory elements, comma use with, 660
Introverts, 53
"Is Starting College and Not Finishing Really That Bad?" (Greenstone & Looney), 148-153
Issue questions, 426-427
"It Shouldn't Be This Dangerous" (public service advertisement), 583-584
"It's Time to Decriminalize Sex Work" (Rosen), 205-207

J

Johansen, Steve, 350
Johnson, Nathanael, 153-157
Journalistic questions, 40, 487
Journals
bibliographic information for, 266-267
peer-reviewed, 228, 231, 237, 443
on references list, 291
on works-cited page, 273
Journal writing, 84
"'Juvenile Lifers' Deserve Second Chance" (Lavy), 357-358

K

Keyword searches, 232, 233, 438

L

Language
abstract, 57, 649
concrete, 57, 62, 91, 92, 98, 649
figurative, 354

loaded, 370-371, 376, 390, 451
natural, 650
Lavy, Jody Kent, 357-358
Learning management systems, 304
Lee, Janilyn, 96-110
Length requirements, 486-488
Library databases, 223, 231-233, 263, 428
Line spacing, 50
Literary analysis, 147
Literary evaluations, 176, 178-180
Loaded language, 370-371, 376, 390, 451
Logos
analysis of, 207, 389
defined, 203, 355
identifying appeals to, 356, 363-364
overview, 203, 350
reasons and, 355, 444
Looney, Adam, 148-153
"Love It or Hate It: Native Advertising on the Internet" (Pike), 579-583

M

Magazines
biases within, 237
informative writing in, 114
introductions in, 461
as public rhetoric, 7
on references list, 291
on works-cited page, 273
Main ideas, 616-625. *See also* Thesis statements
Manipulative-appeal-to-emotion fallacy, 374, 377, 390, 451
Manning, Tori
annotated bibliographies by, 241-242
APA style paper, 296-303
in-text citations by, 226-227
MLA style paper, 279-285
on organization, 225
outline by, 250-251
on plagiarism avoidance, 259
quotation use by, 252-256
on rhetorical use of sources, 248
on searching effectively, 233
on selecting sources, 227
source chart by, 249-250
summary by, 257
Margins, 50
Martinez, Jesse, 211-220
"Mass Incarceration: The Whole Pie" (Sawyer & Wagner), 65-66, 561-571
Mechanics, defined, 49
Media and culture, anthology of readings on, 571-586
Meeting minutes, 16

Memes, as arguments, 417, 418
Memoirs, 84, 92
"Men Explain Toxic Masculinity to Me, A Man Writing About Toxic Masculinity" (Hillegonds), 594–601
Message
    in analytical writing, 160
    counterarguments and, 459
    in evaluative writing, 188
    in informative writing, 116, 120, 128
    in persuasive writing, 212
    in reflective writing, 85, 92, 96
    in response papers, 23
    in rhetorical situation, 4, 6, 25, 311, 387
Microrevising, 162
Microsoft Word, 49
Migliore, Lauren, 75–76, 116–120
Mindset, defined, 3. *See also* Writer's mindset
MLA Handbook, 255, 261, 262, 271–272, 278
Modern Language Association (MLA) style
    analytical writing in, 165–170
    annotated bibliography in, 241
    checking for, 285
    evaluative writing in, 194–198
    formatting papers in, 278–285
    in-text citations in, 267–271
    persuasive writing in, 217–220
    reflective writing in, 104–111
    student writing samples, 279–285
    works-cited page in, 271–278, 283–285
Moore, Darnell L., 526–532
"The Moral Case for the Fossil Fuel Industry" (Epstein), 321–324

N

Narration
    analysis of, 64
    in classical arguments, 408–409
    defined, 63
    key words and phrases for, 82
    past tense for, 658
    purpose for using, 63
    in reflective writing, 98, 101–102
    as rhetorical pattern, 63–65, 82
    rhetorical thinking and, 64
    sample writing with, 64
    as writing tool, 65
National Center for Health Statistics, 234
National Institute of Mental Health, 70–71
Natural language, 650
Newspapers
    advertisements in, 238
    arguments in, 306
    informative writing in, 114
    as public rhetoric, 7
    on references list, 291
    on works-cited page, 273
Nonessential elements, comma use with, 661
Non sequitur fallacy, 373, 377, 390, 451
NOT, in search strategies, 233
Nouns, common vs. proper, 665–667

O

Objective analysis, 146, 162
Objective tone, 312, 352, 630–631
Objectivity of summaries, 16
Off-the-page prewriting, 40, 128, 160
One-sided arguments, 454–455
Online databases, 223–225, 231–234, 263, 428
"Only Once I Thought about Suicide" (Betts), 546–553
On Rhetoric (Aristotle), 407
On-the-page prewriting, 40, 97, 128, 160
Opening arguments, 306, 407–408
Opposing viewpoints, 432, 439
OR, in search strategies, 232
Organization
    of analytical writing, 161, 162, 164
    appeal to logos and, 355
    of arguments, 470–471, 473
    assistance with, 54
    of cause and effect, 77
    of comparison and contrast, 74
    of evaluative writing, 189, 191, 198–199
    of informative writing, 132
    of persuasive writing, 213–215
    of reasons, 444–445, 449, 450
    of reflective writing, 102
    in research, 222–223, 225–227
    revising for, 45, 470–471, 473
    of rhetorical analysis, 391–393, 402–403
Outlines
    accuracy of, 32
    for analytical writing, 160–161
    for arguments, 440–441, 452
    for evaluative writing, 189–190
    for informative writing, 128–130
    for persuasive writing, 213, 214
    in reading process, 613–615
    for reflective writing, 98–100
    reverse, 191–192, 470
    for rhetorical analysis, 392–393
    sources in, 19–20, 30–32, 250–251
    supporting points in, 19–20, 31–32
    templates for, 452
    thesis statements in, 19, 30–31, 42
Owens, Ernest, 360–361

P

Pandemic. *See* COVID-19 pandemic
Paragraph development, 652–655
Parallelism, 650–652
Paraphrasing, 247, 257, 445, 606, 611–612
Pariyar, Bishnu Maya, 591–594
Past tense, 657–659
Pathos
    analysis of, 207, 215, 389
    conclusions and, 464
    defined, 203, 354
    identifying appeals to, 354–355
    introductions and, 462
    overview, 203, 350
    reasons and, 444
    words used in appeals to, 362
"Peace Corps' Influence Changed My Fate" (Pariyar), 591–594
Pedersen, April, 72, 506–512
Peer review
    of analytical writing, 164
    defined, 43
    of evaluative writing, 192
    guidelines for, 44–45
    of informative writing, 133
    of persuasive writing, 215
    of reflective writing, 102
    revisions resulting from, 46
Peer-reviewed journals, 228, 231, 237, 443
Personal growth, anthology of readings on, 586–601
Personality considerations, 53–54
Personalized writing process, 53–56
Personal rhetoric, 8–10
Persuasive writing, 200–221. *See also* Arguments
    analysis of, 10
    appeals for, 203–204
    audience for, 204, 206–207, 212
    cause and effect in, 75
    drafting, 214
    editing and formatting, 217
    elements of, 201–203
    message in, 212
    model examples of, 205–210, 217–220
    outlines for, 213, 214
    planning for, 203, 212–213
    projects involving, 210–211
    purpose of, 200
    recursive writing in, 214
    revising, 215–217
    rhetorical strategies in, 206–207, 210, 219–220
    rhetorical thinking in, 204
    social change through, 7
    speaker in, 212
    terms and phrases for, 214
    thesis statements in, 201
    topics for, 210–212, 220–221
    from writer's mindset, 200–204
"Pervasive Myths about Immigrants" (Collins), 535–540
Pew Research Center, 234
Photographs, as arguments, 416–417, 422
Phrase fragments, 644–645
Pike, George H., 579–583
Plagiarism
    avoidance of, 222, 223, 226–227, 258–259
    checking for, 304, 479
    defined, 258
    quotations and, 32
    unintentional, 250, 258, 427
Planning
    analytical writing, 159–161
    evaluative writing, 175–176, 188–190
    informative writing, 128–130
    persuasive writing, 203, 212–213
    reflective writing, 97–99
    rhetorical analysis, 391–392
    source use, 249
    in writing process, 38–42, 55
Point-by-point arrangements, 74, 198–199
Point of view
    in analytical writing, 146, 162
    in arguments, 306, 428
    first person, 24, 171–172, 312
    in introductions, 461
    for response papers, 23, 24
    second person, 172–173
    third person, 146, 162, 171–173, 312
Policy, claims of, 433, 435
Possession, apostrophe use for, 664
Post hoc, ergo propter hoc fallacy, 367–368, 376, 381, 390, 451
Postreading strategies, 612–616
"The Power of Crowds" (Wilson), 136–140
Predicates, 636–637, 644
Predictive analysis, 147
Predictive evaluations, 176
Prefixes, 607–608
Prereading strategies, 603–606
Present tense, 657–659
Previewing texts, 603–604
Prewriting
    in analytical writing, 160
    in informative writing, 128
    off-the-page, 40, 128, 160
    on-the-page, 40, 97, 128, 160
    in persuasive writing, 212
    in planning stage of writing process, 40–41
    in reflective writing, 97

Primary sources, 227, 230
Process analysis
  analysis of, 79
  defined, 78
  key words and phrases for, 82
  purpose for using, 78, 147
  as rhetorical pattern, 78–80, 82
  rhetorical thinking and, 79
  sample of, 78–79
  as writing tool, 80
Process evaluations, 176
Procrastination, 54
Product analysis, 147, 158–159
Product evaluations, 176
Professional rhetoric, 7–8
Pronouns
  antecedents for, 57, 655–657
  capitalization of "I," 667
  first person, 171, 312
  reference errors, 655–657
  second person, 171
  third person, 171, 312
Proper nouns, 665–667
Publication Manual of the American Psychological Association, 255, 261, 262, 289, 296. *See also* American Psychological Association (APA) style
Publications, analyzing reputation of, 314
"Public Health First" (Reich), 399–401
Public rhetoric, 7
Public service advertisements, 583–586
Punctuation errors, 660–665
Purpose. *See also* Writer's purpose
  of analytical writing, 144, 145, 147, 153
  for cause and effect, 77
  of classical arguments, 405–406
  for comparison and contrast, 74
  conclusions and, 141
  for definition, 68
  for description, 61, 63
  of evaluative writing, 174, 176, 177, 180
  for illustration, 66
  of informative writing, 115
  introductions and, 141
  for narration, 63
  narration and, 65
  of organization decisions, 471, 473
  of persuasive writing, 200
  for process analysis, 80
  of reading, 15–16
  of reflective writing, 85
  in revising for unity, 470, 473
  of rhetorical analysis, 147, 383–384
  of sources, 240
  of speaker, 312–313
  of topic sentences, 652
  of Toulmin analysis, 334
  of writing assignments, 39

Q

Qualifiers, 77, 329, 336, 337, 388, 432–433
Quotations
  appeal to ethos and, 352
  attributions for, 226–227
  context for, 470
  copying, 226
  for dialogue, 111–112
  direct, 112, 247, 252–256, 445–446, 449–450
  ellipsis and, 255–256
  explanation of, 247, 248
  formatting, 253–254
  indented (block), 487
  indirect, 111–112, 247, 256, 270–271, 289
  integration of, 252–256
  in-text citations for, 226–227, 270–271, 289
  plagiarism and, 32
  purpose of, 24
  when and how to use, 247, 248

R

Readability of sources, 236
Reading process, 603–632. *See also* Rhetorical reading
  annotating in, 606
  asking questions in, 605–606
  chunking in, 611–612
  defining unfamiliar words in, 606–611
  inferences in, 625–632
  main idea identification in, 616–625
  outlining in, 613–615
  overview of stages, 603, 604
  paraphrasing in, 611–612
  postreading strategies, 612–616
  predictions regarding text, 604–605
  prereading strategies, 603–606
  previewing text, 603–604
  recalling activity in, 605
  reflecting in, 616
  reviewing and rereading text, 612
  summaries in, 615–616
Reasons. *See also* Arguments; Claims
  analysis of, 204, 207, 388, 389
  appeals and, 355, 444
  audience-based, 434–436, 444
  clarity of, 471, 474
  in classical arguments, 409, 410
  defined, 201, 329

drafting content for, 445-446, 448-450
evaluation of, 436-437
identification of, 310-311, 315
in inference of unstated claims, 325
organization of, 444-445, 449, 450
in outlines, 213
revising, 215, 469, 473, 476
selection of, 434-436
summaries of, 463-464
support for, 310, 441-444, 446-448, 469, 473
in Toulmin model, 329, 335-337, 388
on Viewpoints Charts, 430

Rebuttals. *See also* Counterarguments
analysis of, 204, 207, 337, 388
clarity of, 471, 474
defined, 202, 332
elements of, 454, 455
model example of, 459-460
in outlines, 213
rhetorically effective, 455-458
in Toulmin model, 332-333, 337, 388

Recall of information, 605

Recursive writing
in analytical writing, 162, 163
in evaluative writing, 191
in informative writing, 131-132
in persuasive writing, 214
in reflective writing, 101
steps and use of, 34-36, 38

Red flags for sources, 240

Red herring fallacy, 372-373, 377, 390, 451

"Reducing Food Waste Takes More Than Finishing Your Plate" (Johnson), 153-157

References list
articles on, 290-291
books on, 292
Internet sources on, 293-294
miscellaneous sources on, 294-295
model example of, 301-303
for multiple authors, 289-290

Reflection on texts, 616

Reflective writing, 84-111
audience for, 84-85, 96
blog posts as, 3, 84-86, 95-96
description in, 62, 91-92, 98, 100
drafting, 100
editing and formatting, 104
genres associated with, 84
message in, 85, 92, 96
model examples of, 86-94, 104-111
narration in, 98, 101-102
organization of, 102
outlines for, 98-100

planning for, 97-99
projects involving, 95-96
purpose of, 85
recursive writing in, 101
revising, 101-104
rhetorical strategies in, 91-92, 94, 111
rhetorical thinking in, 85
speaker in, 91, 96
terms and phrases for, 100
thesis statements in, 92, 97, 98
topics for, 85, 86, 91, 95-97
from writer's mindset, 84-85

Refutations, 202, 333-334, 409-411, 454-458

Reich, Robert, 399-401

Repeated sources, 257

Repeated words and phrases, 604

Rereading texts, 612

Research. *See also* Sources
analysis of, 429-432
for arguments, 230, 428-432
audience for, 230
field research, 229, 230
informal, 12-13
from multiple viewpoints, 437-439
organization in, 222-223, 225-227
process for, 222-227
summaries in, 16
time management for, 243-244
topic questions in, 227

Response papers, 22-24

Reverse outlines, 191-192, 470

Revising
analytical writing, 163-165
arguments, 467-478
claims, 469, 473
for clarity, 471-472, 474
conclusions, 45-46, 488
for critical audiences, 476-478
for development, 469, 473
evaluative writing, 191-194
for general audiences, 469-475
informative writing, 132-135
introductions, 45-47, 488
microrevising, 162
for organization, 45, 470-471, 473
persuasive writing, 215-217
reasons, 215, 469, 473, 476
reflective writing, 101-104
rhetorical analysis, 394-395
rubrics for, 467-469
sentences, 130, 488, 650
for unity, 470, 473
in writing process, 43, 45-48, 56

Reynolds, Joel Michael, 338-340
Rhetoric
    academic, 7-8
    defined, 2, 9
    Greek, 203, 406-407
    personal, 8-10
    professional, 7-8
    public, 7
    visual elements of, 416
Rhetorical analysis, 383-403
    annotations for, 385-387
    of appeals, 389
    conclusion in, 392
    defined, 24, 308
    drafting, 393-394
    of fallacies, 390-391
    introduction in, 320-321, 392
    model example of, 395-399
    organization of, 391-393, 402-403
    outlines for, 392-393
    overview, 315-316
    planning for, 391-392
    as process and product, 384
    projects involving, 399-401
    purpose of, 147, 383-384
    revising, 394-395
    of rhetorical situation, 25, 387-388
    of rhetorical strategies, 25-28
    thesis statement in, 392-393, 403
    of Toulmin elements, 388-389
    of writer's purpose, 24
"A Rhetorical Analysis: 'The CDC Botched Its Vaping Investigation and Helped Spark a National Panic'" (Trinh), 395-399
Rhetorical domains, 7-9
Rhetorical evaluations, 176
Rhetorical modes. *See* Rhetorical patterns
Rhetorical patterns, 59-83
    cause and effect, 75-77, 82
    classification, 69-72, 82
    comparison and contrast, 71-75, 82
    defined, 59
    definition, 67-69, 71, 82
    description, 61-63, 81
    illustration, 65-67, 82
    key words and phrases for, 81-82
    narration, 63-65, 82
    process analysis, 78-80, 82
    projects involving, 80-81, 84
    as writing tools, 59-61
Rhetorical reading, 14-30
    analysis of, 15, 24-28, 30
    for critiquing, 15, 28, 30, 44
    defined, 14
    improvement of writing through, 29
    purpose of, 15-16
    summary of, 29
    for understanding, 15-24, 30
Rhetorical situation
    analysis of, 4-6, 10, 14, 25, 387-388
    arguments and, 311-315, 406, 419, 420
    audience in, 4, 6, 25, 311, 387
    classification and, 71
    comparison and contrast and, 74
    in evaluative writing, 175
    genre in, 6, 311
    illustration and, 67
    message in, 4, 6, 25, 311, 387
    source types and, 230
    speaker in, 4, 6, 25, 311, 387
    writer in, 4-6, 25, 311, 387
Rhetorical strategies
    analysis of, 25-27
    in analytical writing, 148, 153, 157, 170
    in evaluative writing, 180, 186, 198
    examples of, 24
    in informative writing, 115-116, 119-120, 125, 140
    narration and, 65
    in persuasive writing, 206-207, 210, 219-220
    in reflective writing, 91-92, 94, 111
    use of sources as, 246
Rhetorical thinking
    in analytical writing, 147-148
    cause and effect and, 77
    classical arguments and, 408-411
    classification and, 71
    comparison and contrast and, 73
    definition and, 69
    description and, 62
    domains of, 7-9
    in evaluative writing, 175, 177
    examples of, 2-3
    illustration and, 67
    in informative writing, 115-116, 130-131
    narration and, 64
    in persuasive writing, 204
    process analysis and, 79
    projects involving, 11-12
    in reflective writing, 85
    Rogerian arguments and, 414
    social media and, 2-4, 7
    on source use, 246, 258
    strategies for development of, 9-10
    visual arguments and, 419-420
    in writing process, 34, 36-38, 40, 42, 55
Robbins, Ruth Anne, 350

Rogerian arguments, 406, 412-416
Rogers, Carl, 412, 413
Root words, 609-610
Rosen, David, 205-207
Rubrics, 39-40, 43, 427-428, 467-469
Run-on sentences, 647-649

S

Sampling bias fallacy, 375, 377, 390, 451
Sanchez, Liz, 523-525
"Save a Life: Don't Drive Home Buzzed" (public service advertisement), 584-586
Saving sources, 225
Sawyer, Wendy, 65-66, 561-571
Search strategies for sources, 230-235
Search terms, 232, 233, 438
Secondary sources, 228-230
Second person point of view, 172-173
Second person pronouns, 171
Semicolons, guidelines for use of, 639-640, 648
Sen, Basav, 502-504
Sensory details, 63
Sentences, 634-652. *See also* Topic sentences
   capitalization of, 665
   clarity of, 45, 57-58, 164, 215, 471-472, 649-650
   complex, 641-642
   compound, 638-640
   compound-complex, 642
   fragments, 643-647
   with parallel structure, 650-652
   predicates in, 636-637, 644
   revising, 130, 488, 650
   run-on, 647-649
   simple, 638
   subjects in, 634-636, 643-644
Series, comma use in, 661
Sheehy, Kyle, 207-210
"Should College Athletes Be Paid?" (Martinez), 217-220
"Should College Students Adopt Dogs? A Cost/Benefit Analysis" (Abrams), 165-170
Simple predicates, 637
Simple sentences, 638
Simple subjects, 635
Slang words, 69
Slippery slope fallacy, 366-367, 376, 381, 390, 451
Social media
   advertisements on, 7
   misinformation on, 442
   as public rhetoric, 7
   rhetorical thinking and, 2-4, 7
   as source for research, 235
"Social Media in the Classroom" (Williams), 51-53
Socrates, 84

Sources, 222-259. *See also* Bibliographies; In-text citations; Plagiarism; Research; Works-cited page
   in analytical writing, 160
   annotation of, 17, 249, 250
   for arguments, 230, 428-432
   biases in, 235-240
   bibliographic information on, 263-267
   bookmarking, 224
   charts for, 249-250, 259
   citation generators for, 271, 303-304
   credibility of, 230, 233, 235-241, 443
   date and historical context of, 236, 240
   deleting, 226
   downloading and saving, 225
   evaluation of, 176, 177, 187, 235-241
   fair and accurate representation of, 251
   information on, 20
   integration of, 251-258, 449
   on Internet, 233-235
   from online databases, 223-225, 231-234, 263, 428
   outlining, 19-20, 30-32, 250-251
   paraphrasing, 247, 257, 445
   practical strategies for working with, 249-251
   primary, 227, 230
   readability of, 236
   red flags for, 240
   references list of, 289-295, 301-303
   repeated, 257
   in revising for unity, 470, 473
   search strategies for, 230-235
   secondary, 228-230
   on statistical and factual information, 233, 234
   summaries of, 247, 256-257, 445
   types of, 227-230
   Viewpoints Charts for, 430-432
   when and how to use, 246-248
"South Africans Protest against Rhino Poaching" (photograph), 525-526
Spalding, Jada
   on checking for fallacies, 450
   conclusion by, 464-465
   on conducting research, 429
   on counterarguments, 455, 458
   on drafting content for reasons, 448
   on evaluating reasons, 437
   on evidence selection, 443
   final draft of argument, 479-486
   guidance rubric by, 427, 468-469
   introduction by, 462-463
   outline by, 440-441
   on reason selection, 434-436
   rebuttal by, 459-460
   revisions by, 474-478

Spalding, Jada (*continued*)
   on support for reasons, 446–448
   on topic selection, 426
   Viewpoints Chart by, 431
   on writing claims, 434
Speaker
   in analytical writing, 159
   in arguments, 306
   biases of, 311–312, 632
   credentials of, 311
   in evaluative writing, 188
   identification of, 315
   in informative writing, 128
   in persuasive writing, 212
   in reflective writing, 91, 96
   in rhetorical situation, 4, 6, 25, 311, 387
   tone and voice of, 312, 352, 353
Spelling checkers, 49, 104, 136, 165, 194, 217
"Standardized Test Requirement Should Be Removed from College Admissions" (Sheehy), 207–210
Stanford History Education Group, 180–186
Statistical Abstract of the United States, 234
Statistical databases, 233, 234
"Stay Wild" (Lee), 104–111
Steinem, Gloria, 574–579
Steingraber, Sandra, 489–499
Stereotypes, 71
Sticky notes, for annotating, 606
Strawman fallacy, 370
Student writing samples
   analytical writing, 165–170
   in APA style, 296–303
   arguments, 479–486
   conclusions, 464–465
   evaluative writing, 194–198
   final drafts, 50–53
   informative writing, 136–140
   introductions, 462–463
   in MLA style, 279–285
   rebuttals, 459–460
   reflective writing, 104–111
   response papers, 23–24
   revisions, 474–475, 477–478
   rhetorical analysis, 395–399
   summaries, 21–22
   Toulmin analysis, 338–343
Style guides
   APA (*See* American Psychological Association style)
   Chicago Manual of Style, 262
   importance of, 261–262
   MLA (*See* Modern Language Association style)
   online resources for, 262
Subject-by-subject arrangements. *See* Block arrangements

Subjective analysis, 146, 162
Subjective tone, 312, 631–632
Subjects of sentences, 634–636, 643–644
Suffixes, 608–609
Summaries
   characteristics of, 16
   creation and integration of, 256–257
   defined, 16
   executive, 16, 180–186
   model example of, 21–22
   in reading process, 615–616
   of reasons in support of claims, 463–464
   response papers and, 22–24
   of sources, 247, 256–257, 445
   templates for, 449
   types of, 16
   writing process for, 17–21
"A Summary of 'Interpreting Intentional Imprecision'" (Baracos), 21–22
Super Bowl advertisements, 14
Support
   in analytical writing, 161
   for outlines, 19–20, 31–32
   in paragraphs, 652–655
   in persuasive writing, 201–202, 213
   for reasons, 310, 441–444, 446–448, 469, 473
   for thesis statements, 20–21, 31–32, 45, 201
Sweeping generalization fallacy, 371–372, 377, 381, 390, 451
Syllabus, messages conveyed through, 10
Symbols, as arguments, 416
Sympathetic audiences, 454, 455, 459
Synonyms, 232, 611

T

Task calendars, 244
Templates
   for introducing evidence, 449–450
   for outlines, 452
   for works-cited page, 271
Tenses, verb, 100, 657–659
Testimonials, 67
Textbooks, 114
"Thais Rally in Bangkok for Global Climate Strike" (DeCicca), 505–506
Thesis, defined, 16
Thesis statements
   in analytical writing, 160
   annotation of, 17
   defined, 616
   drafting, 41–42
   in evaluative writing, 188
   identification of, 619–625
   implied, 625
   in informative writing, 128

introductions and, 141
in outlines, 19, 30-31, 42
with parallel structure, 651
in persuasive writing, 201
presentation in summaries, 20
in reflective writing, 92, 97, 98
revising, 45
in rhetorical analysis, 392-393, 403
supporting points for, 20-21, 31-32, 45, 201
"Thinking of Getting a Tattoo? Think Again" (Velez), 377-379
Third person point of view, 146, 162, 171-173, 312
Third person pronouns, 171, 312
"Thoughts after an Owl" (Tonino), 92-94
Time management, 54, 243-244
Tone
   of inferences, 629-632
   objective, 312, 352, 630-631
   subjective, 312, 631-632
   of writer/speaker, 312, 352, 353
Tonino, Leath, 92-94
Topic questions, 227
Topics
   for analytical writing, 157, 159
   for arguments, 220-221, 425-427
   for evaluative writing, 186-188
   for informative writing, 126-127
   for persuasive writing, 210-212, 220-221
   for reflective writing, 85, 86, 91, 95-97
Topic sentences, 616-625
   annotation of, 625
   defined, 616-617
   identification of, 617-619
   implied, 618-619
   purpose of, 652
   in thesis statement identification, 620-624
Toulmin, Stephen, 327
Toulmin analysis, 327-348
   areas of confusion in, 334-337
   backing in, 331-332, 336-337, 388
   claims in, 328-329, 335-337, 388
   concessions in, 202, 332-334, 336
   counterarguments in, 332-334, 337, 388
   defined, 327
   familiarity with, 346-348
   grounds in, 329, 336-337, 388
   implied elements in, 334
   model example of, 338-343
   "out of order" elements in, 335
   overview, 327-328
   projects involving, 343-346
   purpose of, 334
   qualifiers in, 329, 336, 337, 388
   reasons in, 329, 335-337, 388
   rebuttals in, 332-333, 337, 388
   refutations in, 333-334
   similar elements in, 335-337
   warrants in, 329-331, 337, 388
"A Toulmin Analysis of an Argument" (Fisher), 340-343
Transitions
   in analytical writing, 164
   in compound sentences, 639-640
   in informative writing, 131, 132
   organization and, 45
   for paragraph support, 653-654
   in process analysis, 80
   in reflective writing, 100
Trinh, Jacob, 387-389, 391-399
Tu quoque fallacy, 373, 377, 390, 451
Turnitin plagiarism checking service, 304

U

Understanding
   in informative writing, 120
   revising for, 45
   in rhetorical reading, 15-24, 30
   source use for, 246
Uniform Crime Reports, 234
Unity, revising for, 470, 473
Unspoken subjects, 636
Unsupported inferences, 629
"Urban Spaces and the Mattering of Black Lives" (Moore), 526-532

V

Vague terminology, 472, 474
Value, claims of, 433, 435
Velez, Martina, 377-379
Verbs
   missing verb fragments, 643-644
   predicates and, 636-637, 644
   tense of, 100, 657-659
Viewpoints Charts, 430-432
"The Violent Brain: Ingredients of a Mass Murderer" (Migliore), 75-76, 116-120
Visual arguments, 416-422
   advertisements, 406, 416, 417, 419
   analysis of, 418-419
   charts, 418, 421, 422
   creation of, 418, 420-422
   defined, 406
   graphs, 418, 422
   infographics, 418, 420, 422
   memes, 417, 418
   photographs, 416-417, 422
   symbols, 416
Voice, in writing assignments, 39, 245-246, 248

W

Wagner, Peter, 65–66, 561–571
"Want to Create More Jobs? Reduce Fossil Fuel Use" (Sen), 502–504
Warrants, 329–331, 337, 388, 436, 476
Weak analogy fallacy, 374
Websites
　biases of, 237–240
　bibliographic information for, 238, 239, 264
　credibility of, 238–241
　evaluation of, 177, 187, 235, 237–241
　informative, 126–127
　on references list, 291, 293–294
　as sources for research, 233–235
　on works-cited page, 274–276
"What We Can Learn from the Challenger Disaster" (Griffin), 628
"What We Do and Don't Know about How to Prevent Gun Violence" (Ehrenberg), 120–125
"Why Employers Should Adopt Telecommuting Policies" (Spalding), 479–486
"Why Manning Up Is the Worst Thing to Do" (Greene), 316–320
"Why Parents Should Think Twice About Tracking Apps for Their Kids" (Reynolds), 338–340
Williams, Alexis, 36–42, 46–48, 50–53
Wilson, Liam, 127–140
Working bibliographies, 223–224, 226
Workplace rhetoric, 7–8
Works-cited page
　articles on, 273–274
　books on, 274–275
　creation of, 223–224
　formatting, 50
　Internet sources on, 275–276
　miscellaneous sources on, 276–278
　MLA style for, 271–278, 283–285
　for multiple authors, 272
　organization and, 222–223
　primary sources on, 227
　templates for, 271
Writer
　in analytical writing, 159
　biases of, 311–312, 632
　credentials of, 311
　credibility of, 246, 442
　in evaluative writing, 188
　in informative writing, 115, 119, 128
　mindset of (*See* Writer's mindset)
　in persuasive writing, 212
　purpose of (*See* Writer's purpose)
　in reflective writing, 96
　in rhetorical situation, 4–6, 25, 311, 387
　tone and voice of, 312, 352, 353
Writer's mindset
　analysis of texts with, 24, 28, 29
　analytical writing from, 144–147
　composing with (*See* Writing process)
　critiquing texts with, 28, 29
　defined, 3
　development of, 9–10
　evaluative writing from, 175–177
　informative writing from, 115
　persuasive writing from, 200–204
　reading with (*See* Rhetorical reading)
　reflective writing from, 84–85
　using sources from, 245–248
Writer's purpose
　analysis of, 24, 312–313
　evaluation of, 240
　identification of, 315
　in informative writing, 119
　in reflective writing, 91
　rhetorical patterns and, 59–61
　in rhetorical situation, 5–6, 311
Writing process, 34–56
　analytical (*See* Analytical writing)
　drafting stage of, 43, 55
　editing stage of, 49, 56
　evaluative (*See* Evaluative writing)
　final drafts in, 50–53
　formatting stage of, 50, 56
　informative (*See* Informative writing)
　peer review in, 43–46
　personalizing, 53–56
　persuasive (*See* Persuasive writing)
　planning stage of, 38–42, 55
　recursive (*See* Recursive writing)
　reflective (*See* Reflective writing)
　revising stage of, 43, 45–48, 56
　rhetorical reading and, 29
　rhetorical thinking in, 34, 36–38, 40, 42, 55
　for summaries, 17–21

Y

"Yes, Black America Fears the Police. Here's Why." (Hannah-Jones), 553–561

Z

Zaretsky, Robert, 343–346